Praise for John Ghazvinian's

America and Iran

"Beautifully laid out and at times reading like a thriller you don't want to put down."
　　　　—Hooman Majd, author of *The Ayatollah Begs to Differ*

"A magnificent, bold, wide-reaching and potentially significant book on the thorny subject of Iranian-American relations. . . . History as history should be written: accessible, humane, thoughtful, insightful and in places extremely funny."
　　　　　　　　　　　　　　　　　　　—*Catholic Herald*

"History in the hands of a master. Ghazvinian leads us far beyond the mindless shouting of recent decades to tell a story of friendship, sacrifice, and discovery. Should be required reading in both Tehran and Washington."
　　　　　　　　　　　—Ambassador John Limbert,
　　U.S. Deputy Assistant Secretary of State for Iran (2009–10);
　　　former hostage in the U.S. embassy in Tehran (1979–81)

"Extensively researched and very well-written. . . . Anyone who reads the book will come away with a deeper understanding of the policy decisions and political upheavals that have shaped this relationship."　　　　　　　—*The American Conservative*

"Timely and vividly engaging. . . . [Ghazvinian] captures the details of this complex relationship and clearly explains how both countries have been forced to respond to each other positively and harshly based on historical circumstances and conditions."　　　　　　　　　　　　　　　—*Library Journal*

JOHN GHAZVINIAN

America and Iran

John Ghazvinian was born in Iran and raised in London and Los Angeles. He has a doctorate in history from Oxford University and was the recipient of a Public Scholars fellowship from the National Endowment for the Humanities in 2016–2017, as well as a fellowship from the Carnegie Corporation's special initiative on Islam in 2009–2010. Ghazvinian's writing has appeared in *Newsweek*, *The Sunday Times* (London), *New Statesman*, *Slate*, and *The Nation*. He directs the Middle East Center at the University of Pennsylvania and lives in Philadelphia.

ALSO BY JOHN GHAZVINIAN

Untapped: The Scramble for Africa's Oil

America and Iran

A HISTORY,
1720 TO THE PRESENT

JOHN GHAZVINIAN

VINTAGE BOOKS
A DIVISION OF PENGUIN RANDOM HOUSE LLC
NEW YORK

The Library of Congress has cataloged the Knopf edition as follows:
Names: Ghazvinian, John H. (John Hossein), author.
Title: America and Iran : a history, 1720 to the present /
John Ghazvinian.
Description: First edition. | New York : Alfred A. Knopf, 2021. |
Includes bibliographical references and index.
Identifiers: LCCN 2019057328 (print) | LCCN 2019057329 (ebook)
Subjects: LCSH: Iran—Foreign relations—United States. |
United States—Foreign relations—Iran. | Iran—History.
Classification: LCC E183.8.I55 G45 2020 (print) | LCC E183.8.I55 (ebook) |
DDC 327.55073—dc23
LC record available at http://lccn.loc.gov/2019057328
LC ebook record available at https://lccn.loc.gov/2019057329

Vintage Books Trade Paperback ISBN: 978-0-307-47238-0
eBook ISBN: 978-0-525-65932-7

Author photograph © Helena Raju
Book design by Soonyoung Kwon

www.vintagebooks.com

Printed in the United States of America
10 9 8 7 6 5 4 3 2 1

To my parents, of course,
who lived too much of this history

When the lingering sorrow of separation lifts,
The nightingale will tear back into the rose garden
Its throat filled with song

این تطاول که کشید از غم هجران بلبل
تا سراپرده گل نعره زنان خواهد شد

—HAFEZ, FOURTEENTH-CENTURY PERSIAN POET

The Iranian revolution is a fact of history, but between American and Iranian basic national interests there need be no permanent conflict.

—RONALD REAGAN,
PRESIDENT OF THE UNITED STATES, NOVEMBER 1986

Contents

PART III

Autumn

PART IV

Winter

Introduction

For a historian—for any storyteller, really—the challenge is always where to begin.

Does the story begin on the day the star-crossed lovers meet? Does it begin, as it does in the immortal poetry of Omar Khayyam, on the secluded riverbank, with a jug of wine and a loaf of bread, and that moment of blossoming, freshly emergent romance? For those telling the story of Iran and America, alas, it does not. This is a story that always seems to begin at the very *end*, at the moment when swords are drawn and voices are raised—when tempers are flaring and the lovers have gone their separate ways.

In the United States, so often, the story begins in 1979, with those famous grainy television pictures—the bearded revolutionaries climbing the wall of the U.S. embassy in Tehran and taking sixty-six Americans hostage, leading them blindfolded and bewildered into the street for all the world to see. It begins with a radical, hateful, anti-American revolution, and all the menacing symbolism and fanatical Middle Eastern blood-thirst that image conjures up. The very moment that America and Iran broke off ties—the moment that ended more than a century of warm and friendly relations—has become Day One, Chapter One, Verse One. The Book of Genesis.

It is an odd way to write history, this—beginning at the end. But this is the way the story is told in the United States. A catalog of Iran's sins—ranging from "support for terrorism" to "pursuit of nuclear weapons"—generally follows in the 1980s, 1990s, and 2000s, with the accusation that all these activities stem ultimately from the radicalism of the Islamic Republic that was created forty years ago, and the ideology of hatred and hostility it has cultivated ever since. The Iran hostage crisis of 1979 has become a kind of original sin—the moment the serpent slipped into the Garden of Eden and brought an end to the comfortable illusion of American global invincibility. The unforgivable has become the unforgiven. And nothing has been the same since.

In Iran, meanwhile, the story usually begins in 1953, with an original sin of a different kind. It begins with Mohammad Mosaddeq—a name largely forgotten by Americans, but a national hero to many Iranians. It begins with that hot afternoon in August 1953, when the CIA engineered a coup against Mosaddeq, the elected—and wildly popular—prime minister of Iran. It begins with the thugs and newspaper editors who were hired by the CIA to create trouble on the streets and give the army the cover it needed to remove the prime minister. Mosaddeq—a great admirer of democracy and human rights—had represented the hope of a generation. It was a generation that had adored America—a generation raised on years of John Wayne movies and big, stylish Chevrolets—but that quickly grew to hate it. Another ending, treated as a beginning.

This is the way the story is told in Iran. After the 1953 coup, Iran's young king—the shah*—returned from a brief exile and spent the next twenty-five years increasing his dictatorial grip on the country, bolstered by billions of dollars in weapons and training from the United States. His feared secret police jailed and tortured thousands, the royal family pilfered spectacular sums from the Iranian treasury, corrupt courtiers engaged in a lavish and opulent lifestyle, as one American president after another toasted the shah for his "steadfast" friendship. And then—only *then*—in 1979, did the hated and hollow regime finally collapse, brought down by millions of revolutionaries streaming through the streets, a handful of them so angry that they seized the U.S. embassy and took its employees hostage.

So it has remained, for forty years. History—like almost everything else—has become a casualty in the long-running war of words between Iran and the United States. For more than forty years, those who like to look for someone to blame, or something to defend, have stood in their respective corners, trading accusations about the relative criminality of the CIA coup and the embassy hostage crisis, taking very little interest in the idea that there might be a richer, more sophisticated way to look at the history that has transpired between these two nations. For more than forty years, history has been treated as a competitive sport—just another arena of contestation in the seemingly endless array of disagreements and accusations that have been hurled back and forth between Iran and the United States. And for more than forty years, endings, ruptures, and angry disagreements—rather

---

* *Shah* is the Persian word for "king."

than beginnings, attractions, and initial infatuations—have become the starting point for every conversation about Iran and America.

We are all much poorer for it.

∞

The history of U.S.-Iranian relations did not begin in 1979, and it did not begin in 1953. It began hundreds of years ago—when the United States was still a handful of British colonies and Iran was still known to the outside world as the Persian Empire.* And it began with something much more interesting than hostile acts and mutual accusations about "original sins."

When we choose to take this long-term approach to history, we discover something surprising. For hundreds of years, it turns out, well before their governments had any serious high-level interaction, the peoples of Iran and America looked at each other with a remarkable degree of fascination, admiration, warmth, and benevolence. In the 1720s colonial American newspapers wrote at length, and with great sympathy, about the political affairs of the Persian Empire. In the 1790s, Thomas Jefferson and John Quincy Adams studied Persian history as they looked for inspiration and guidance on how to run their new nation. From the 1850s to the 1920s, Persian newspapers constantly urged their readers to learn from America's example and develop their country into a progressive, prosperous constitutional republic. In 1919 there were reports of *pro-American* riots on the streets of Tehran.

This is where the story of Iran and America really begins. And this is what has been missing most acutely from all our discussions of the subject. Well before governments in Tehran and Washington began to step on each other's toes in our own lifetimes—well before the "Great Satan" and "Axis of Evil" speeches, well before Mosaddeq and the hostage crisis and Ayatollah Khomeini—relations between these two countries were animated by a spirit of common respect and mutual understanding.

---

* Iranians have always called their country "Iran," but for centuries Europeans (and later, Americans) erroneously referred to it as "Persia"—a reflection of the facts that the Persians were historically the most dominant of Iran's many ethnic groups, and that it was the Persians who had created the first Iranian empire, in the days of Cyrus and Alexander. This confusion is understandable, but it is somewhat akin to referring to France as "Gaul" or to Italians as "Romans." In 1935, Iran formally declared its desire to be known as Iran, not Persia. In order to avoid confusion and awkwardness when quoting from contemporary Western sources, or discussing institutions with names like the "Anglo-Persian Oil Company" or the "Persia Mission" of the American Presbyterian Church, I have mostly chosen to use *Persia* and *Persians* when discussing events before 1935, and *Iran* and *Iranians* for events after 1935.

It is this spirit—far more than any supposed original sins—that should mark the beginning of their interaction in the pages of history. And it is out of a desire to bring this history to light that this book has been written.

ɷ

For the past forty years, Iran and the United States—once the closest of allies—have had almost no relationship at all. There have been no meetings between heads of state, no exchange of diplomats, no official channels for the two governments to express their concerns and views to each other. There have been no embassies, no trade missions, virtually no tourists, no student exchange programs, no military coordination or communication. Only very recently has there even been any contact between officials of the two countries.

This has created a gulf of understanding of epic proportions. Today decision-makers in neither country know, with any real depth or conviction, what their counterparts are thinking. Today an enormous chasm exists between Iran and the United States—the kind of chasm that, even in the darkest days of the Cold War, never existed between the United States and the Soviet Union.

To the uninitiated observer, the most obvious risk from this prolonged estrangement appears to be that of all-out war. But this is not the most pressing reason to study the history of U.S.-Iranian relations today. Certainly, tensions between the two countries do periodically flare up, to the point that a military confrontation appears imminent. But it would be a mistake to let these be the only moments that capture our attention. Understanding Iran—and the history of U.S. relations with Iran—is important not just because Iran is "the next country we might be bombing." Iran is not just another crisis. It is not just another bushfire in the seemingly endless series of conflagrations and catastrophes that have engulfed the Middle East in recent years.

Iran is a nation of 80 million people. It is the second-largest country in the Middle East, both by population and by area. And it is an immeasurably important part of the region's politics. For centuries, Iran has been at the crossroads of civilizations—a meeting place of cultures along the ancient Silk Road, and the key power along both the north-south axis between Russia and the Persian Gulf and the east-west axis between Asia and the Middle East. It is one of the world's most important petroleum producers—sitting atop the world's second-largest reserves of conventional crude oil and its single-largest reserves of natural gas. Iran controls maritime access to the Strait of Hormuz, gateway to one-fifth of the world's oil supply. And Iran has one of the most dynamic, educated, and cosmopolitan populations in the Middle East—a population that, however it might sometimes appear, is far more modern, outward-looking, and comfortable with Western cultural norms than many of its neighbors. To be estranged from a nation like this— at any point in history, much less at a time when the Middle East presents such enormous challenges—would be senseless and self-defeating.

Iran is also, of course, the world's only Shia nation. Although it is not the only nation with a Shia majority (neighboring Iraq is 60 percent Shia, and several other countries have sizable Shia minorities), Iran is the undisputed *political leader* of the Shia Muslim world. Its population is more than 90 percent Shia, and if you look at a map of the region broken down by religious allegiances, Iran emerges very clearly as the center of gravity of Shiism. Iran is to Shia Islam roughly what the Vatican is to the Catholic Church, or what Moscow once was for the Communist bloc. For the United States to close itself off to a country that exercises immense political leadership over one of the two major sects of Islam makes little sense under the current circumstances.

Finally, it is worth remembering that Iran is one of the world's oldest, proudest, and most enduring civilizations. Unlike other countries in the region, Iran was not created by British or French colonial elites drawing lines in the sand or handing over power to native political elites. Rather, Iran has had three thousand years of (mostly) continuous nationhood, interrupted only by a period of foreign domination in the Middle Ages. Along with China, Egypt, Greece, and Ethiopia, Iran is one of the very few nation-states that can legitimately claim to have existed more or less continuously since antiquity. It is also one of only seven or eight nations that were never colonized by European powers.* Culturally, historically, and politically, Iran has an extraordinarily strong sense of its identity and its regional significance. It is an unavoidable presence in any discussion of the Middle East.

For all these reasons, Iran merits close attention. And for all these reasons, none of us can afford to be overly complacent about the antagonism that exists between Iran and the United States today. Though it may not be obvious on a day-to-day basis, the poisonous atmosphere that has accumulated over the years between these countries has caused tremendous damage—to the United States, to Iran, to the Middle East, and to the world as a whole. It has become, in the words of the fourteenth-century Persian poet Hafez, a kind of "lingering sorrow of separation."

---

* Though these things can be debated endlessly, by my estimation, Japan, China, Thailand, Korea, Afghanistan, Ethiopia, and Mongolia are the only other major nations that can justifiably claim never to have been colonies, protectorates, or mandates of European powers at any point in their modern history.

It should now be blisteringly clear that America's foreign policy in the Middle East is stuck—and that it is stuck in ways that could benefit enormously from an improved relationship with Iran. In Afghanistan, Iran's eastern neighbor, U.S. troops have struggled for nearly two decades trying to defeat Taliban, al-Qaeda, and other Sunni radical groups—unable to capitalize on Iran's deep, long-standing ties with local tribal forces (or its hatred of the Taliban, which dates back to the 1990s). In Iraq, Iran's western neighbor, America has expended prodigious amounts of money and manpower since 2003 but has not been able to capitalize on Iran's great influence with the Shia population there (or its same basic desire to see stability and order prevail). In Syria, Lebanon, and the Palestinian territories—where America's most important ally, Israel, feels surrounded by enemies—Iran has built up a formidable array of alliances and could play a decisive role in either advancing or undermining any potential peace agreements. Even in unexpected places, like Yemen, Bahrain, and Egypt, Iran has relationships with local actors that could be leveraged in a very different direction if circumstances ever allowed for it.

In short, there is not a single problem the United States is dealing with in the Middle East that cannot be traced, in one way or another, to its dysfunctional relationship with Iran. And there is not a single problem that would not, to some degree, benefit from an improvement in that relationship. For forty years, America's attempts to advance its interests in the Middle East have suffered immeasurably because of this relationship of bile and hostility that exists with the Islamic Republic. Yet that same relationship, paradoxically, could prove to be the key that unlocks so much—if only it were allowed to turn in the opposite direction.

☙

When I set out, in 2007, to tell the story of Iran and America, I felt it was important that each country have a chance to be heard—properly, on its own terms, without the filter of a political agenda. I felt it was important not to apportion blame, or to look for culprits and victims, or to take sides. What was missing from most discussions, I thought, was a fair, dispassionate record of the many events that have led up to the present-day impasse. I wanted this to be the first book that was written neither "from Tehran" nor "from Washington" but rather was unencumbered by the reflexive assumptions and ideological baggage that so frequently characterize writings on this subject.

Part of this, for me, meant doing something many Americans writing on this subject never do, which was to actually *go* to Iran. I was born in that country, in 1974, but left at the age of one, and had never been back. In a way, this meant that Iran was as alien to me as it is to most Americans. But it also meant I had the ability to travel there without much difficulty—a privilege that I felt it was important to make use of.

By traveling around the country—talking to Iranians from all walks of life but also, crucially, scouring through archives not easily accessible to Western scholars—I hoped to create a richer, more sophisticated version of this story. And I hoped to take the information I found in Iranian archives and place it alongside similar evidence from the United States—allowing each country's sources to speak for themselves. I knew this was not the first book ever written on the history of U.S.-Iranian relations, and that it would not be the last. I did, however, want it to be the first that used both American *and* Iranian archives. For ten years, from 2007 to 2017, I engaged in what I believe is the most exhaustive and wide-ranging study ever undertaken on the history of U.S.-Iranian relations.[*] And the result, I hope, is the first really comprehensive attempt to understand how these two countries have ended up in the confrontational position they are in today.

But my aim has not been just to be comprehensive for its own sake—or to laboriously hash out every tedious detail of U.S.-Iranian relations. My aim has been to make the case for a more enlightened principle: that history can be a force for peace. If this book accomplishes only one thing, it should be to help readers in both Iran and the United States understand that there is nothing inherently grotesque or untrustworthy about the "enemy" on the other side. If one thing should quickly become obvious, it is that both countries have occasionally made decisions that seem beastly and reprehensible to the other, but that they have done so as a result of peculiar historical circumstances, conditions, and considerations—not because they are inexplicably evil.

Informing my narrative throughout this book has been a conviction—unspoken for the most part and perhaps even naïve at times—that the current state of antagonism between Iran and America is wholly unnecessary. What I hope emerges from these pages is a portrait of two countries with far more in common than they ever will have to drive them apart—and far more in common than either cares to admit. And what I hope every reasonable reader will conclude from this narrative is that the time is long overdue for a mending of fences. Though there are people in both countries—and indeed in other countries—who believe their interests are best served by perpetual antagonism between Iran and America, I believe most people reading these words will not share this cynical perspective. The

---

[*] For more details, please see the Acknowledgments.

security and prosperity of the United States, the security and prosperity of Iran, the cause of world peace, and even—if I may be so bold—the nobler instincts of humanity will be better served in a world where America and Iran learn to set aside their differences. And it is my earnest hope that this book, by telling the story of how it all came to be, might play some small role in hastening that possibility.

PART I

Spring

East of Eden

Once upon a time in Iran, there was a city that gave men butterflies. Centuries before the ayatollah, before the shah—before even Muhammad and Jesus Christ shook up their respective corners of the Middle East—the emperors of Persia had built one of the most magnificent capital cities the world had ever known. It was called Persepolis—literally, the "city of Persians." And such was its reputation that even the mightiest of princes, as they saw it coming slowly into view after days and weeks of trekking across the desert, could feel themselves reduced to nervous wrecks.

Once a year, in ancient times—on the first day of spring—rulers of the twenty-eight great kingdoms that Persia had conquered were expected to journey to Persepolis to pay tribute to their lord and master, the "King of Kings." And they never failed to carry out this duty. From the Mediterranean city of Sardis would come the obscenely wealthy kings of Lydia, carrying all the riches of Croesus to lay at the feet of the shah. From Memphis and Alexandria came Egyptian nobles, their Nubian slaves in tow. From the hills of Bactria, the "emperor of a thousand cities" brought his camels laden with gold. Timidly they would all climb the enormous staircase to the Apadana Palace and walk through the fabled Gate of All Nations, hoping what they had brought would prove worthy of their overlord, the Persian emperor. Hoping he would have mercy this year and not reduce their meager satrapies to weeping hillocks of rubble.

At its height in the fifth century B.C., the Persian Empire ruled over 60 million of the world's 100 million people—making Persepolis, for all intents and purposes, the capital city of all humanity. And anyone who laid eyes on this fabled city could not fail to come away in awe of its power and opulence. Great stone columns, capped by winged bulls, soared into the sky at the entrance to every ceremonial building. Palaces and throne rooms, overflowing with jewels and sumptuous furnishings, shimmered in the midday sun. Tombs of ancient emperors, chiseled into the surrounding cliffs, loomed dramatically over the landscape below. It was the kind of place one had to see to believe—a city designed to strike reverence into the hearts of visitors and remind them of their own insignificance before the mightiest empire the world had ever known.

Like so many other imperial projects, the famous "city of Persians" long ago went the way of all souls. Burned and pillaged by Alexander the Great and his army of conquering Greeks in 330 B.C. (legend has it they required three thousand camels to cart away all its gold and jewels), its columns still reach proudly into the cloudless blue sky, in one of the most remote and unpopulated corners of Iran. Today, though, it is not Sogdian princes but busloads of tourists—Japanese, Germans, occasionally even Americans— who are driven across the vast, hot, and flat Morqab Plain to pay their tribute. As they approach the ruins of Persepolis, they marvel, just as the Elamites and the Babylonians once did, at a city that seems to rise out of nowhere—the final punctuation mark at the end of a merciless expanse of dust.

And as modern visitors scramble among ancient tombs and statues, snapping pictures and admiring what is left of the palaces of Darius and Xerxes, they often notice, just off to the side, a rusting metal grandstand— rows of empty spectator seating rising like bleachers at a high school football field. These are the ruins of a much more recent emperor.

ॐ

In October 1971 the Shah of Iran—Mohammad Reza Pahlavi, King of Kings, Light of the Aryans, Imperial Majesty and Commander-in-Chief of four hundred thousand fearsome (if somewhat modernized) Persian warriors— chose Persepolis as the backdrop for one of the most audacious, expensive, and self-indulgent spectacles of the modern era: celebrations marking the 2,500-year anniversary of the Iranian monarchy. Attempting to replicate the rituals of Persian emperors from centuries past, he summoned the world's most powerful leaders before the Apadana Palace and asked them to marvel at the greatness of his "empire." Only this time Iran was picking up the tab. Ten kings, twenty-one princes and princesses, nine sheikhs, two sultans, a grand duke, a cardinal, sixteen presidents, three prime ministers, and four vice presidents were flown into Shiraz and transported—some by helicopter and some in red Mercedes limousines—across the desert to Persepolis, where four full days of feasting awaited them. Princess Grace of Monaco, King Hussein of Jordan, President Nikolai Podgorny of the USSR, Vice

President Spiro Agnew of the United States—all mingled among balls and banquets, parades and performances, and a light and sound show described by observers as the "world's greatest fireworks display." At least six hundred journalists were also flown in, together with their satellite trucks and cameras, so that no corner of the globe would be deprived of its chance to witness the historic occasion.

The shah did not cut corners. The legendary French hotelier Max Blouet was persuaded to come out of retirement to coordinate the event. Catering was provided by Maxim's of Paris, which closed its doors two weeks early to prepare for the feast. Thirty cooks, 150 waiters, twenty-two tons of provisions—including such precious cargo as freshly picked raspberries—were all flown in from Paris on a fleet of jumbo jets. Five thousand bottles of wine and champagne were sent to Iran a month early, to give them time to settle and adjust to the climate. At the gala banquet, the menu, Maxim's finest, included quail eggs stuffed with caviar, crayfish mousse, and rack of lamb with truffles—all washed down with a 1945 Château Lafitte Rothschild. The main course, "imperial peacock," was roasted and stuffed with foie gras and served "surrounded by its court" of jellied quail. Ninety-two of the regal birds were arranged along the banquet table, their tail feathers fully spread, to symbolize the magnificence of the Peacock Throne (the traditional seat of Iranian monarchs since 1739). The five-and-a-half-hour feast went down in the *Guinness Book of Records* as the longest and most lavish in modern history.

And this wasn't the half of it. To ensure the comfort of the shah's guests, they were housed in what were modestly described as "tents"—luxury air-conditioned apartments covered in blue and gold cloth, designed by Jansen of Paris (famous for its renovations of Buckingham Palace and the White House). Each "tent" boasted two bedrooms, two marble bathrooms, servants' quarters, a kitchenette, and three telephone lines. The main banquet tent, meanwhile, was stuffed with Louis XV furniture, crystal chandeliers, and a 235-foot mahogany dining table. Special tents with casino and gaming tables were set up, along with sixteen hair salons staffed by beauticians from Elizabeth Arden and other leading Paris houses—all flown in to help guests look their best for each night's festivities.

No one ever found out how much all this feasting and festoonery ended up costing Iran. The shah's defenders suggested impossibly low figures around $4 million and claimed most of it came from "private business contributions," while his detractors threw around equally outlandish figures in the hundreds of millions (close to $2 billion in today's money). But whatever the exact figure, it did not look good. As French waiters poured liters of claret into the goblets of kings, in the eastern province of Sistan-Baluchistan, severe food shortages were driving villagers to the brink of famine. Even in Fars Province, where Persepolis was located, there had been reports of malnutrition, and the shah found himself facing awkward questions from the international press corps. At a Tehran news conference, a Swedish journalist asked him pointedly if he knew how much all the festivities were going to cost. "Do you know how much a kilo of meat and a kilo of bread cost?" the shah replied, just as pointedly. The journalist shook his head. "So why are you asking me?" the shah sniffed.

American journalists were a little gentler with the shah. In the United States, where the appetite for imperial pomp and pageantry was limitless, the Persepolis celebrations were met with squeals of delight. The *Los Angeles Times* reported that "there isn't likely to be [a celebration] to match it for another 25 centuries." The normally sedate *New York Times* marveled that "some of the emeralds in [Empress Farah's] crown were the size of golf balls. Her diamonds were only slightly smaller." The entire event was broadcast via satellite, and hosted by a young Barbara Walters on NBC, to an estimated audience of 10 million Americans. Orson Welles narrated the official documentary, *Flames of Persia*. And the U.S. *chargé d'affaires* in Tehran

"The most expensive party in history": Persepolis, 1971. Festivities marking the twenty-five-hundredth anniversary of the Persian monarchy were estimated to cost in the tens of millions of dollars.

In the banquet tent at Persepolis, seated left to right: Prince Rainier of Monaco, Prince Philip of Great Britain, Crown Prince Carl Gustaf of Sweden, and Vice President Spiro Agnew of the United States.

congratulated the event's organizer, telling him it was "the best exercise in public relations" he had ever seen.

The shah lapped it all up. Prideful, insecure, plagued by demons few around him fully understood, and constantly concerned with demonstrating the prestige of his ancient throne, the fifty-two-year-old monarch was never more at home than when he was basking in the praise of his American friends. And at Persepolis in 1971, he was in his element. Surveying the grounds majestically, like a schoolmaster peering through his spectacles with his famously stern and piercing eyes, puffed up with pride like the peacocks on the banquet tables as he welcomed one king after another to his desert encampment, the shah glowed with satisfaction. This was his roost. He ruled it—with a degree of absolute, unquestioned power that few of his predecessors had ever managed to summon. And he was happy to let the world know it.

☙

Ten years later he was dead. And so was the 2,500-year-old empire that he had gone to such lengths to celebrate. Gone was the Peacock Throne. Gone was the King of Kings. Gone were the armies of fawning courtiers lined up dutifully in their gold-threaded uniforms. In the place of the shah was a man of God—an "ayatollah" in a black turban and a gray barbed-wire beard, whose eyebrows seemed permanently knitted in anger and whose open palm seemed permanently spread out over oceans of seething crowds, their fists rising and falling in unison as they rhythmically chanted *Death to America! Death to America!* In place of the imperial nation of Iran, the modern incarnation of the Persian Empire of centuries past, there was now something calling itself the "Islamic Republic"—severe, austere, a vast landscape of rage, painted only in shades of black, and mercilessly unforgiving of anything it deemed to be "Western arrogance." In place of a cooing Barbara Walters, American television carried wall-to-wall programming about fifty-two hostages and their hellish ordeal at the hands of sweating Iranian revolutionaries.

Those ten fateful years—from 1971 to 1981—were perhaps the most decisive, transformative, and unforgettable decade in the history of America's long and tortured relationship with Iran. For ten years, give or take, American military equipment had landed like snowflakes on the lap of a grateful shah. Chinook helicopters, F-14 Tomcats, Patton tanks, Sidewinder missiles—nothing was off-limits if the shah desired it. In Washington in 1972, Secretary of State Henry Kissinger gave him carte blanche, instructing the Pentagon that decisions about Iranian arms sales "should be left primarily to the government of Iran." And over the next few years, Iran quickly became the world's largest single purchaser of U.S. weapons, accounting for more than one-third of Washington's international arms sales. By 1978, Iran was spending $10 billion a year on U.S. arms (around $50 billion in today's money) and had amassed the most powerful military in the Middle East. If ever there was occasion for some lamentatious Roman poet to sing of "arms and the man," this was it.

But it was not just arms. By 1978 some fifty thousand Americans were living in Iran. "Technical advisers," military contractors, schoolteachers, oil executives, development "experts," tour guides, archaeologists, hippies waylaid on the trail from Goa to Zanzibar—all of them, in one way or another, buying into the idea that Iran was a progressive, dynamic nation of the future that was benefiting handsomely from the hand of American friendship. And for the U.S. government, this was just about the best piece of news coming out of the Middle East. In Washington, the shah was seen as a much-needed alternative to the radical, troublesome, evil Arabs—less Muslim somehow, less threatening, more benign. The Arab world in the 1970s, seen from Washington, was a hopeless, never-ending psychodrama of airplane hijackings, bomb plots, socialist revolutions, interminable wars with

Israel. Just to the east, though, lay a more peaceful kingdom—a "natural ally" whose romantic Persian past, secular institutions, Western-educated elites, stable politics, and anti-Communist ruler made it a more reliable partner for the United States. This was the most durable, dependable, reassuring alliance America enjoyed in the Middle East. And it had felt like it would never end. As late as December 1977—just one week before the revolution broke out—President Jimmy Carter stood at a banquet in Tehran, raised his glass to the shah, and, repeating a phrase used by countless American officials since the 1950s, toasted Iran as an "island of stability in one of the more troubled regions of the world."

The equation worked just as powerfully in the other direction. For despite the ugsome spectacle of Vietnam in the 1960s, most Iranians still viewed America as a basically virtuous nation, in stark contrast to the European powers that had been divvying up the Middle East for decades. When the shah had come to power in 1941, Iran was still feeling the effects of nearly two centuries as a pawn in the imperial ambitions of Britain, Russia, and, to a lesser extent, France. Thus, whenever Iranians thought of "the West," their minds turned instinctively to the image of greedy, self-interested Europeans. But when they looked just a little *further* west, they saw a more benevolent power—a nation born out of opposition to empire and colonialism, infused with noble idealism, with a foreign policy that seemed largely selfless and respectful of the concerns of weaker nations. Though this image of America had begun to fray by the 1970s, it still held sway with bourgeois elites in Iran and especially with the shah himself. Just as Americans looked past the radicalism of the Arab world and found a "nicer Middle East" on its periphery—one with a friendlier face and a reliable ally at its helm— Iranians looked past Europe and found a "nicer West"—one that seemed to live and breathe its liberal ideals and was ready to extend the hand of genuine partnership.

This idea—that both Iran and the United States could reach beyond the countries that frustrated them and find a "natural ally"—had a long pedigree, one that has not always been fully appreciated by historians. Decade after decade, dating back at least to the 1850s, successive Iranian governments had looked to the United States as a potential "third force" that could counteract the pressures from Britain and Russia. Decade after decade, Americans had looked to Iran as a mystical, benevolent, faraway Persian kingdom that seemed more appealing than the radical, hostile Arab world. This belief in an "alternative" force, lying just over the horizon, proved powerful and durable in both the American psyche and the Iranian—and arguably really fully disappeared only after 1979. When examined in its full historical dimensions, it goes a long way toward explaining how these two countries became such friends in the first place—and why it might not be so hard for them to see each other this way again. This fundamental attraction, this narrative of two countries on opposite sides of the world that were able to look beyond their own immediate trouble spots and find common ground—this is the core of our story.

☙

So the obvious first questions are: How exactly did all this come about? And when? At what point in history, exactly, did the peoples of these two countries begin to see each other as "natural allies"? And for what reasons? These questions are almost never asked by historians—who typically seem more concerned with explaining how everything went *wrong* for Iran and America than with understanding how so many things initially went *right*. And the answers, perhaps, will come as a surprise, even to those who believe they know the story of Iran and America well.

The very first newspapers published in North America, it turns out, were absolutely enchanted by Iran. In the 1720s, at a time when "the United States" had yet to come into existence, and Britain's North American colonies were largely a land of yeoman farmers, tobacco plantations, and quiet settler villagers, newspapers in Boston and Philadelphia reported regularly on events in the Persian Empire—with a breathless, even hysterical energy. Week in and week out, publications like the *Boston News-Letter,* the *Boston Gazette,* and Philadelphia's *American Weekly Mercury* fell over one another to feed (and stoke) the public appetite for information about Persia. At one point, the *Mercury* was regularly devoting 25 to 30 percent of its column-inches to Persian affairs. In July 1724 the newspaper even led with a regretful note: "We have at present no News concerning" the situation, "neither do we hear anything from Persia." In the American colonies in the 1720s, the mere absence of news from Iran was a front-page story.

Though this might seem odd or surprising, the reason was fairly straightforward. In the summer of 1722, in the lawless Pashtun tribal regions of Kandahar, a revolt had broken out against the authority of the shah. The Afghan rebel Mahmud Hotaki, angered by Persian attempts to force his people to convert from Sunni to Shia Islam, had led an attack on Persian garrisons, then swept across the eastern provinces of the empire and laid siege to the capital, Isfahan, for six months. The brutal siege had starved eighty thousand people to death and brought chaos to the Persian Empire. So it was merely the big news story of the day when Americans first started publishing newspapers. What was perhaps most extraordinary about the American press coverage though (at least from a twenty-first-century perspective) was how overtly one-sided it all was—or, rather, which side it took. The American media in the 1720s were uniformly, passionately, and unapologetically pro-Iranian.

As news trickled in from Persia during these years, colonial American newspapers went into overdrive, openly cheering for the Persian king to defeat "the usurper" Mahmud. In October 1723 the *Boston Gazette* reported with horror that "the Usurper . . . having possess'd himself of all the Riches of Persia, [now] puts all to Fire and Sword to establish his ill got Power." In July 1724 the *Boston News-Letter* was even more puffed up with outrage. Mahmud, it claimed, "was not satisfied with the barbarous Death & cruel Murder of [the shah], nor with the inhuman Cruelties committed upon all his affectionate Adherents, but has farther extended his Tyranny." It hoped someone would soon "extirpate the flagitious Tyrant, and cut his Adherents off the Face of the Earth."

Why would news of civil war in imperial Persia have aroused such passions in Massachusetts and Pennsylvania in 1722? And why would Americans have been so quick to take the side of the Persians? The answer, in part, has to do with the peculiar understanding that North Americans had of Middle East politics in this period. Because Mahmud had rebelled explicitly in the name of Sunni Islam against his Shia overlords, Americans believed he must have received encouragement, and even diplomatic recognition, from the hated Ottoman Empire. To colonial Americans, this could mean only one thing: the rebellion was part of a larger proxy war between Sunni Ottoman Turks and their Shia Persian rivals—the region's two great superpowers. It was another sign of the creeping expansionism of Ottoman Turkey, an evil empire that they had been told was a danger to Christendom—and to their very way of life.

In article after article, American newspapers blasted what they believed was a pattern of collusion between the Ottomans and the Afghan rebels.* In May 1723 the *Boston News-Letter* reported angrily that the Ottoman sultan had sent "all kinds of Provisions & Ammunition" to support the uprising.

---

* The reality, not surprisingly, was more complicated. Initially, the Ottomans seemed to maintain neutrality or even tacitly support the Persian monarchy. But as the conflict dragged on, and the Russians began taking advantage of the situation to make territorial gains at the expense of Persia, the Ottomans felt compelled to get involved. This latter stage of the conflict, roughly 1723 and early 1724, coincided with Mahmud's consolidation of power over Persia. The Ottomans' main priority was to deter Russia from advancing into Persia, and the best way to do so was to recognize Mahmud and offer him assistance against Russia (while also possibly strengthening the Sublime Porte's own position in Persia). If anything, the later stages of the conflict were more like a proxy war between Russia and Turkey, contested on the field of a weak Persian state. Still, Americans clearly felt alarmed by the possibility of Ottoman expansion, as around this time the newspaper coverage began to take a more urgent tone.

In February 1724 the same newspaper told readers the whole rebellion had taken place "by the Instigation of the Ottoman Porte, which maintains an underhand Correspondence with" Mahmud. And in May 1724, when Isfahan finally fell, the *New England Courant* claimed "the Turks very much rejoyced at" hearing the news.

In the early eighteenth century, most white residents of North America still considered themselves loyal British subjects—as well as active participants in the broader world of European Christendom. And there was a history there. In 1683 the Ottoman Empire had laid siege to Vienna. One hundred and fifty years before that, the Ottomans had taken Hungary and the Balkans, and they now seemed to be threatening all of Christian Europe with their mighty armies. Worst of all, since the year 634, there had generally been some form of Turkish or Arab rule in Jerusalem, provoking Europeans to go on Crusades against the "infidel" Turks and their "occupation" of the Holy Land. Given this long history of confrontation between Christian Europe and its eastern periphery, Americans naturally felt hostile toward anything Turkish or Arab. It was also easy to romanticize and idealize Persia simply because it was an avowed enemy of the Ottoman Empire. For decades, in fact, European monarchs had explored the possibility of a Persian-European alliance against the Turks. It was the oldest political principle in the book: the enemy of my enemy is my friend.

Politics, though, was only part of the story; there was also the complex matter of religion. For generations of New England Puritans, especially, raised on years of Sunday school and Bible study, Persia was forever the land of the Three Magi*—the "wise men from the East" who had come to Bethlehem bearing gold, frankincense, and myrrh for the baby Jesus. Persia was also the land of Cyrus the Great, the famous king who, in Ezra 1:1, is praised for liberating the Jews from the Babylonian captivity. By contrast, the Ottoman Empire was heir to the ancient kingdom of Babylon†— the hated empire whose name the Book of Revelation equates with every imaginable kind of evil. Even more important, because virtually every place described in the Bible was now under the control of the hated Ottomans, pious Christians felt the Turks had "defiled" all their holy sites—and their writings vividly reflected this. But just to the east of the sultan's dominions lay Persia—a fairytale land, home to hardly a single location of biblical significance. By what must have seemed an extraordinary coincidence, the Persian Empire began just to the east of where Christians believed the

---

* *Magus* (pl. *magi*), comes from the Old Persian word for "Zoroastrian." Our word *magic* derives from the same root.

† The fact that the Turks were not actually Babylonian was beside the point; what mattered was that one race of infidels had inherited the kingdom of Babylon from another.

Garden of Eden had been—just past the last of the major sites of biblical interest.

This kind of biblical interpretation of the Middle East, with all its skewed comparisons of Ottomans and Persians, both reflected and reinforced the political prejudices of the day. Books published in Britain at this time, widely consumed in colonial America, were full of lopsided sympathy for Persia in its rivalry with the Ottomans. British writers generally described Persians as a noble, courageous, civilized race, while they condemned Turks as tyrannical, savage, incurably evil infidels. Travel books, scholarly accounts, religious manuals, and newspapers always referred to the "inhuman Turke" or the "terrible Turke"—while the Persians rarely received anything but praise.* Almost on cue, whenever British travelers crossed from the Ottoman Empire into the shah's dominions, their tone brightened. Instead of condemnation and hatred, they expressed admiration and awe. The "*Turkes* be not comparable to the *Persian* for magnanimity and nobleness of mind," wrote one traveler. Another contrasted "the treachery, the covetousnesse, the wrath, the cruelties, the impietie, the wickednesse of these triumphing Turkes" with the "peace & tranquilitie" of the Persian villages. As for the shah, he was "verie absolute both in perfection of his bodies, and his minde," and a Christian-Persian alliance could easily defeat the Turks. Most impressive of all to British travelers was the legendary city of Isfahan—the grand new capital of the Persian Empire, with its broad, double-laned boulevards, reflecting pools, and magnificent palaces and mosques, all covered in turquoise. Home to six hundred thousand people at its height, Isfahan rivaled London for the distinction of the world's largest city in the seventeenth century. But London couldn't hope to compete with its beauty. European visitors were regularly rendered speechless when they arrived, struggling to describe what they saw.

Thus, when the Afghan revolt broke out in 1722, Americans were transfixed. After decades of hearing about the glories of the shahs—the heirs of Cyrus the Great and the wise Magi—Americans had developed an affinity both for Persia and for the Persian monarch. And they were incensed to find that he was now under assault from east and west by a crude axis of evil formed between the Turkish sultan and the Afghan rebels. For the first time in history, and without fully understanding the conflict, Americans were becoming absorbed into a complicated world of Sunnis and Shias, Pashtuns and Persians. And they had no hesitation about taking sides.

---

* Shakespeare's plays are replete with references to the "barbarous" Turk but describe the Safavid (Persian) emperor as "the great Sophy" and allude to his legendary wealth and power with an awestruck tone.

Newspapers made heroic, if somewhat crude, attempts to help Americans understand the difference between Shia and Sunni Islam, and how this sectarian split had contributed to the conflict. Because the Persians were Shia—a minority sect viewed by most Muslims as heretical—some in America optimistically assumed that perhaps Persians were a little *less* Muslim or even not Muslim at all. (The conflict was sometimes described as a holy war between "Muslims and Persians.") One newspaper explained that Sunnis were followers of Muhammad and therefore were true Muslims, while the Shia were only "followers of Hali" or Ali. Another claimed the Persians worshipped Ali "as equal to Mahomet himself"—suggesting that this made them altogether different from the evil Muslims of the Ottoman Empire. It was a spectacular misreading of the difference between Sunni and Shia, but a revealing insight into just how badly some Christians wanted to believe in the existence of a lesser of two evils in the Middle East.

As the 1720s progressed, some colonial Americans displayed a budding "Persophilia"—a romantic idealization of Persian culture and Persian themes. Newspapers began carrying advertisements for Persian rugs. In 1724, *The Persian Cromwell,* a disparaging book about the life of Mahmud Hotaki, quickly made its way into libraries in the America colonies. In 1729, Benjamin Franklin praised the ancient Persians for the value they placed on education and virtue and suggested Americans follow the example. Perhaps most tellingly, the writings of Cotton Mather—one of the most influential religious leaders in colonial America—were rich with pro-Persian sentiment. Though his writings were virulently anti-Islamic, he often went out of his way to point out examples of virtuous behavior by Persians—even suggesting that such stories should shame his fellow Christians into behaving more piously.

By 1727, a full five years after the Afghan rebellion, American interest in Persia showed no signs of abating. That year the *Weekly Mercury* ran a special nine-part series—a first for an American newspaper—explaining the background and chronology of recent events. In grueling, grisly detail, the *Mercury* reported on the extraordinary siege of Isfahan, depicting the Persians as victims of Sunni Afghan aggression. It described starving citizens examining human carcasses in the hope of finding bits of flesh to chew on, and mothers driven to feasting on their newborns. The shah himself was reduced to eating the flesh of his horses, it was written, just before he succumbed to the Afghans and ran weeping through the streets dressed in black. American readers learned that when the evil Mahmud was finally crowned, his victory parade required vast quantities of perfume to cover the stench of rotting corpses. "So many carcasses were thrown into the river," reported the *Mercury,* that for a full year afterward "no Body could without Horror think of eating any Fish."

Never before had an American newspaper offered its readers this kind of sensationalistic, in-depth coverage of an international event, and the format proved a runaway success. Just twenty years earlier American newspapers had barely existed. The few that had appeared regularly were dry, dusty affairs, reprinting tired stories about European diplomacy culled from the London papers. Now, though, thanks to the Persian conflict, colonial newspapers began to find their voice.

And that was not all. For the first time in history, Americans were demonstrating that very basic instinct that would become so vividly apparent by the 1970s—their willingness to believe that if they just reached over and beyond the infidel empire of the Middle East, they would find an idyllic civilization waiting in the periphery. A civilization that was somehow a little less Muslim, a little less Arab, a little less evil. For the first time, Americans had looked over at Persia and convinced themselves they were looking at a land ruled by a wise and enlightened shah whose interests overlapped considerably with their own.

There would be so much more where that came from.

ᎤᏗ

For the remainder of the eighteenth century, Americans continued to display signs of this budding Persophilia, though not always with the same level of energy and visibility as in the 1720s. In 1761, "rich Persia carpets" were being advertised in Boston, and in 1774 a "very large Persian carpet" was auctioned in New York. In 1765, Harvard began offering its first lessons in the Persian language. And after the turmoil of the American Revolution subsided, leaders of the new republic proved no less interested in learning about Persia than they had been in earlier decades. If anything, the elites seemed to have a *greater* appetite for information—an appetite fueled perhaps by the realization that an independent United States could no longer rely on Britain to keep it informed about world affairs. In the 1790s and early 1800s, the influential Salem preacher William Bentley taught himself Persian and collected dozens of volumes of Persian literature—several of which he carefully annotated—including narratives of travels in Persia, discourses on Persian science and astronomy, Zoroastrian religious texts, and three Persian dictionaries.

The most obvious association Americans had with the name *Persia,* though, was still its ancient history. In the eighteenth and nineteenth cen-

"*Xerxes* the Great did die, and so must you and I":
Generations of American schoolchildren, from the 1690s
until well past 1800, associated the letter *X* not with
xylophones but with the name of an ancient Persian
emperor. (Two million copies of *The New England Primer,* a
textbook for teaching children to read and spell, are believed
to have been sold during this time.)

turies, ordinary Americans had an easy intimacy with the glories of the
ancient Persian Empire—a form of cultural literacy that has entirely van-
ished in recent generations. Cyrus the Great was a household name, widely
celebrated as the magnanimous ruler who had freed the Jews from Babylon
(an act for which Protestants, full of millennial fixations, were eternally
grateful). The names Xerxes and Darius tripped comfortably off the tongues
of small children, in a way that would be hard to imagine today. Americans with even the most basic schooling had an awareness of the legend-

ary empire of ancient Persia. Almost every schoolchild during these years learned the ABCs by memorizing the rhyming couplets of *The New England Primer*—meaning that five-year-olds across America associated the letter *X* not with xylophones but with the rhyme "*Xerxes* the Great did die, and so must you and I." *Abbott's Histories,* a series of biographical sketches of great leaders—and a staple of American education for generations*—consisted of twenty-two biographies, of which only four were devoted to non-Western leaders. One was Genghis Khan. The other three were Xerxes, Cyrus, and Darius.

This appreciation for ancient Persia was particularly pronounced among America's Founding Fathers. Like other Enlightenment thinkers of the time, Benjamin Franklin, Thomas Jefferson, and James Madison—indeed, almost every person whose face appears on American currency today—were all intimately familiar with ancient Persian history. And they were particularly impressed by the legendary emperors Cyrus, Darius, and Xerxes, whose exemplary leadership abilities they saw as a potential model for the new republic. They drew much of their information from the *Cyropaedia,* a biography of Cyrus written by the ancient Greeks around 370 B.C., which describes Cyrus as a wise, just, and benevolent despot who relied on humanity and decency rather than brutality to secure the loyalty of his subjects. It is easy to see why this model would have appealed to early American leaders. The *Cyropaedia* was like a kinder, gentler version of Machiavelli—a prescription for leadership that emphasized the consent of citizens rather than the raw power of tyranny. Jefferson liked the book enough to own two copies, and evidence suggests he read them with enough care that he was able to point out inconsistencies between them. John Adams owned several, too, and wrote notes to himself in the margins. In 1783 his son, John Quincy Adams, was even advised by his mother to emulate Cyrus and avoid the temptations of excessive power.

As the nineteenth century wore on and the United States began to think of itself as a rapidly expanding continental empire, references to ancient Persia became commonplace in American culture. In 1854, during a Senate debate about the so-called "Nebraska question," Sen. Edward Everett argued that the Midwest would one day play a decisive role in American history, suggesting that "these infant territories . . . stand where Persia, Media† and Assyria [once] stood in the continent of Asia, destined to hold the balance

---

* Abraham Lincoln once admitted he was "indebted" to Abbott's biographies "for all the historical knowledge I have." The series eventually became known as Makers of History and is still popular in the home-schooling movement.

† Media, like Persia, was one of the ancient kingdoms of Iran. (The Persians defeated and eventually absorbed the Medes.)

of power—to be the centers of influence to the East and to the West." Everett had taught Persian at Harvard forty years earlier, so perhaps the comparison came naturally to him. But he was not alone. Several American towns during this period changed their names to Media or Persia or even Cyrus. In 1834, Sylvanus Cobb, a prominent Universalist preacher from Maine, saw nothing strange in naming his twin sons Darius and Cyrus.[*] And in 1858, David Dorr, a freed slave famous for his global travels, declared that American liberty was such an inspiration to the world that "the American people are to be the Medes and Persians of the nineteenth century."

It would be a huge exaggeration to say that Americans somehow "modeled" their new republic on Persian ideals. But if one browses through catalogs of early American libraries, it is striking to consistently see Persian tales and biographies of Cyrus side by side with the Christian prayer books and Greco-Roman histories one might expect to find. As they settled down to the hard work of building a new republic, this first generation of Americans—citizens of an independent United States—was prepared to cast its net far and wide in search of lessons and examples. And that even, occasionally, meant looking to Iran.

☙

The Persians, meanwhile, had a similar fascination with and idealization of the United States—but it came about much later, and for much more practical, urgent reasons. For most of the eighteenth century, Persia was consumed by domestic political turmoil, and for most of the nineteenth century, with fending off the machinations and exploitative practices of the European powers. For Persia, these were difficult years. And the United States was not initially of great interest.

The legendary empire of the Persians never fully recovered from the Afghan raids of the 1720s. In the half-century that followed, the country was steadily reduced to chaos, anarchy, and seemingly endless tribal warfare. Not until 1794 was the pain of these years finally brought to an end by a new ruling dynasty, the Qajars—who would remain in power until 1925. The first two Qajar shahs quickly reconquered Georgia, which had intermittently slipped in and out of Persian control over the previous 250 years, and they solidified Persian sovereignty over the volatile eastern provinces around Khorasan and Afghanistan. And to cement their rule, they built a

---

* The third son, Sylvanus Jr., obviously felt left out, as he went on to write a novel called *The King and Cobbler: A Romance of Ancient Persia*.

new imperial capital at the foothills of the Alborz Mountains—in a small village by the name of Tehran.

In their early days, the Qajars brought a measure of desperately needed political stability after nearly a century of turmoil. The second Qajar ruler, Fath Ali Shah, governed Persia from 1797 to 1834—a thirty-seven-year period notable for no major internal conflicts, steady growth in economic prosperity, and the return of prestige to the imperial court. Under Fath Ali Shah, a culture of grandeur and elaborate court ceremony—missing for nearly a century—reasserted itself in Persia. The new king presided over a renaissance in Persian arts and painting and endowed numerous new titles, thrones, and palaces, famously bedecking them with jewels larger than any-one had ever seen. And for the first time in history, Persia began to have seri-ous, sustained political relations with the Western powers. In the years from 1801 to 1809, important treaties were signed with Britain, France, and Rus-sia, and one of Napoleon's generals was invited to Persia to help modernize the army. Relations with the newly established United States, however, were not immediately on the agenda.

America, as far as anyone in Persia was concerned, was terra incognita—a savage continent full of wild, half-naked cannibals. Despite the turmoil of the eighteenth century, Persia still saw itself as one of the world's great empires, a proud and ancient civilization ruled by the Shahen Shah, the King of Kings, who sat on the famous Peacock Throne—studded with enough diamonds to buy North America several times over. In fact, for Persians, there was no such place as America, much less the United States. The name they used on the rare occasions when they discussed American affairs was *yengi donya*—a Turkish phrase meaning "new world." In the imagination of Persians, *yengi donya* held a kind of mystical, almost fairytale allure—like a place that existed only in stories. In 1807, when the South Carolina gentle-man Joel Roberts Poinsett* briefly crossed the border from Russia into Per-sia, he found the local tribal chief "knew something of France and England and more of Russia. . . . But of America, of the nation beyond the great

---

* Poinsett (the man who would later give his name to the poinsettia plant) was the first U.S. citizen recorded as setting foot on Persian soil. However, it is impossible to say with any certainty who the *very* first Americans and Persians to interact were. To some extent, it depends on how one defines Americans. From 1687 to 1692, for example, Boston-born Elihu Yale (benefactor of the college that today bears his name) served as governor of the Madras Colony in India—where he was heavily exposed to the Persianate culture of the Mughal court, conducted business in Persian, and received a special envoy sent by the shah of Persia. But these were, for the most part, the experiences of British colonial officials—men who had deep, genuine roots in New England but who also belonged to a global elite for whom interest in Persia was a natural extension of colonial administration.

waters he had merely heard and believed in its existence with the [scanty] faith with which he listened to an Arabian or Persian tale."

This is not to say that educated Persians were totally unaware of America. Visiting British diplomats frequently reported that America was "a subject upon which all Persians are very curious and inquisitive." In the early 1800s, Persian-language books chronicled American history from the arrival of Columbus in Hispaniola to the War of Independence. Persian readers were even given a flavor of slavery and race relations in the United States, as one book explained how in America "people born with fair hair" were treated with respect while "darker people" were not. In 1809 the shah himself took an interest in America, asking the visiting British diplomat Harford Jones to tell him more about this "new world" he kept hearing about. "What sort of a place is it?" Fath Ali Shah asked Jones. "How do you get at it? Is it underground?"

Possibly the shah was being playful, or possibly he was ignorant. Either way, stories like this reflect the kind of atmosphere in which the subject of America was treated at the Qajar court in its early days. In the early 1800s, by and large, Persia thought it stood on top of the world and had little interest in a distant land of tobacco farms and small wooden churches.

It was only when living, breathing Americans began arriving in Persia in the 1830s—populating the mountain villages of the country's northwestern frontier—that this outlook would slowly change.

Tashrifat

Almost certainly the first Americans and Persians to interact in person were rum traders. In the first half of 1830 alone, some 12 million gallons of "Boston Particular" (rum laced with whiskey) sailed across the Black Sea and into Persia. ("Scarcely an American vessel," the U.S. legation in Constantinople reported, "arrives at Smyrna from the United States that does not bring from 50 to 100 casks, much of which finds its way into Persia and the neighboring countries.") However, this insalubrious trade left few records and probably fewer enduring bonds. In the end, it was less New England rum than New England religion that produced the first sustained, meaningful, documented U.S.-Persian relationship.

Decade after decade, from the 1830s to the 1930s, American Presbyterian missionaries came to Persia to build schools and hospitals and churches. They spent years learning their way around unfamiliar customs. They became fluent in Persian and other local languages, translating the Bible and bringing literacy into far-flung villages. Many Americans spent their whole lives in Persia. Generations were born, generations were married, and generations were buried on Persian soil. Some had no idea what the United States even looked like. They were sent to Persia by the American Board of Commissioners for Foreign Missions (ABCFM)—the main oversight body for American missionaries overseas. And their presence there amounted to the first exercise of American "soft power" in the Middle East.

Though we might assume, from our present-day vantage point, that these American missionaries were seeking to convert Muslims to Christianity, in fact, they were focused on a very different quarry. In northwestern Persia, in the mountains of the Caucasus, lived thousands of Armenians, Assyrians, and Chaldeans who for centuries had recognized Jesus Christ as their lord and savior—the Christians of the Middle East. For American

Presbyterians, this was a much more exciting opportunity than the conversion of mere heathens. Here they had a chance to convert Persians who were already Christians to what they believed was a *better* form of Christianity.

Persia's native Christian population was (and remains) one of the most ancient Christian communities on earth. The Armenians were many in number and well organized, and they had historically proven to be hostile to missionaries. The Chaldeans were almost too small of a community to merit attention. But the community of thirty thousand Assyrians seemed promising as candidates for proselytizing. Their presence in Persia dated to the fifth century, when the followers of Nestorius, the patriarch of Constantinople, had been excommunicated after a dispute about the nature of Christ and given refuge by the Persian king. Over the past fourteen hundred years, they had lived in poverty and isolation, cut off from Western Christendom and presided over by clergy with little access to European Christian teachings. Forgotten both by mainstream Christianity and by their Persian hosts, the Assyrians had gradually crafted their own version of Christianity—one based largely on rituals passed down through generations of their tight-knit community.

To the American missionaries, this made them perfect candidates for "re-education." Although Persia's Assyrians were a unique and fragile Christian sect, Americans of the 1820s saw in them a twisted and degenerate form of Christianity in desperate need of reform—and this gave them a great sense of excitement about the work that lay ahead. In one of its first reports on the subject, the ABCFM proclaimed breathlessly that in Persia, as throughout the Middle East, "the whole mingled population is in a state of deplorable ignorance and degradation, destitute of the means of divine knowledge." Like their neighbors across the region, the people of Persia were "bewildered with vain imaginations and strong delusions" and were practically begging for a bit of spiritual enlightenment from America.

And so it began. In 1829 the ABCFM selected two upstanding young men—twenty-nine-year-old Yale graduate Eli Smith and twenty-seven-year-old Harrison Dwight from upstate New York—to undertake an exploratory mission into Armenia, Georgia, and Persia and report on the possibilities. And in November 1830, after a lengthy ocean crossing from Boston to Malta, nine days across the Mediterranean to Smyrna, a week on Tartar post-horses, a stay in Constantinople to obtain travel documents, and a two-hundred-mile journey across Anatolia by oxcart, the pair finally arrived—dressed in flowing Turkish robes, with turbans wrapped around their heads—in the mountains of northwestern Persia. Freezing temperatures followed by a hot, dry wind and swarms of mosquitoes sent both men into repeated bouts of fever. But their enthusiasm for the Lord's work was not diminished. After several weeks recovering and exploring the area around the city of Urmia—where the Assyrian community was concentrated—Smith and Dwight relayed their findings back to Boston, giddy with excitement.

The Assyrians, they said, were a noble but ignorant people—carrying on Christian rituals they barely understood and practically begging for American salvation. They had kept an ancient manuscript of the New Testament in a locked box for centuries, but no one could read it. They had no complete Bibles in their possession, and their priests seemed excited about the idea of having fresh texts to study. The two young Americans spent only a few days in Urmia but came away sure of their conclusions. "In all my journeys I have seen no people as willing to accept the gospel as the Assyrians of Persia," Smith wrote back to Boston. "This field is white and ready for the harvest."

Mission accomplished, the pair returned to Boston in 1831. And two years later, on their recommendation, the ABCFM sent two more Americans—Justin Perkins, a twenty-nine-year-old tutor from Amherst College in Massachusetts, and his heavily pregnant young bride, Charlotte—to establish a permanent mission in Urmia. The following year the Perkinses were joined by another young couple, the physician Asahel Grant and his wife Judith. And in November 1835, the two couples set up a primary school in Urmia and began translating the New Testament into Syriac. The school opened its doors in January 1836, offering seven pupils the chance to learn the Syriac alphabet and memorize the Lord's Prayer. Two years later Judith Grant opened a girls' school nearby.

In 1837 a few more missionaries arrived, and over the next several years, Americans set up a thriving community of earnest young Presbyterians, all eager to "run their hoes through the fields of the Lord," "sow the seeds of holy salvation," and generally indulge their fascination with agricultural metaphors. In 1840 they recruited the Illinois printer Edwin Breath to drag a high-volume, custom-built printing press across the mountains into Urmia, and began cranking out schoolbooks and religious tracts—sometimes at the astonishing rate of a half-million pages a year. As European Jesuits were also doing work in the area, the competition for souls quickly became fierce. One of the first publications the Americans handed out was called *Twenty-two Plain Reasons for not Being a Roman Catholic*. Other pamphlets dealt with everything from food hygiene to home economics. In 1852 came a full Syriac translation of the Bible that Perkins had worked on for seventeen years (the version still used by Assyrian Protestants). By the time Breath's press succumbed to old age in 1892, the missionaries could boast they had printed some 30 million pages of American know-how for the benighted residents of northwestern Persia.

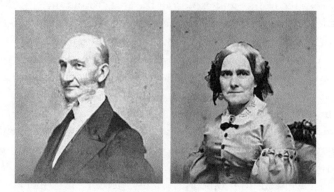

The first Americans: Presbyterian missionaries Justin and Charlotte Perkins arrived in Persia in 1833, with Charlotte heavily pregnant. They established a boys' school in Urmia and produced the first Syriac translation of the New Testament, still widely used by Assyrian Protestants. Their arrival ushered in a century of American missionary activity in Persia.

Though American missionaries in Persia did achieve a number of conversions among the local Christian population, their most enduring successes were in more prosaic areas, such as the establishment of schools and clinics. In 1843 the energetic Fidelia Fiske took control of the girls' school that Judith Grant had founded five years earlier and steadily increased attendance to forty pupils. The boys' school started by Perkins, meanwhile, moved to a site outside Urmia and by 1879 had been reestablished as Urmia College, offering medical, theological, and "preparatory" schooling. By 1895, 117 American schools, with over 2,400 pupils, were operating in Persia. And medical work thrived just as much. Dr. Grant was renowned for his operations on cataracts—literally removing the fog of blindness from the eyes of heathens. Several later doctors also achieved legendary status. The most successful was Joseph Cochran, whose name became synonymous with medical work in Persia. In 1878, together with his wife Katherine, Cochran acquired a fifteen-hectare garden in Urmia and built a modern hospital with capacity for one hundred patients, along with a small college for training physicians—the first Western-style medical school in Persia. Cochran quickly became a local hero for his medical work, and when he died in 1905, ten thousand mourners were said to have poured onto the streets of Urmia for his funeral.

All this missionary activity did not come cheaply, and the ABCFM relied heavily on churchgoer donations. And this, in turn, meant that the

Board plowed considerable time and resources into domestic outreach efforts, holding informational presentations after Sunday-morning church services, educating Americans about Persian history, geography, languages, culture, politics, and religion, and recruiting young Americans to consider careers as missionaries. Without ever intending to, the Board was becoming an early version of *National Geographic*. In 1841 the ABCFM even sponsored a visit to the United States by Mar Yohannan, the Assyrian bishop of Urmia. Probably the first Persian whom ordinary Americans had ever seen in the flesh, Yohannan arrived in New York to a rapturous crowd and was immediately packed off on a year-long speaking tour across the United States. Thousands of curious spectators turned out to see the Persian cleric with his exotic robes, long beard, and sumptuous silk turban.

The American missionaries genuinely believed they were on the verge of converting thousands of Persians to Presbyterian Christianity. In that respect, they failed spectacularly. Despite one hundred years of proselytizing and a certain amount of natural population growth, today no more than a few hundred Protestant Christians live in Iran. In another important respect, however, the American missionaries succeeded beyond their wildest dreams. For a full century, their work transcended the schools and

First American Protestant church established in Iran (1853). A small congregation of Protestants—descendants of people converted by American missionaries—continues to worship here.

Mar Yohannan, Bishop of Urmia: The first Iranian
known to have visited the United States. In 1841,
Mar Yohannan arrived to a rapturous crowd in
New York and then went on a year-long publicity
tour sponsored by the Presbyterian Church.
Enjoying his newfound celebrity, he often walked
into country taverns to lecture the bewildered
patrons in his broken English on the evils of drink.

clinics they built, and the language textbooks they wrote: it dominated and
defined the relationship between the United States and Persia. In countless subtle ways, American missionaries acted as informal intermediaries
between American policy makers in Washington, American diplomats in
Tehran, and Persian officialdom. Generation after generation—until well
into the 1950s—many a high-level American official assigned by the State
Department to deal with Iranian affairs was himself a former missionary
or the child of missionaries or was in some other way deeply influenced by
the work of Protestant missionaries. For decades, American diplomats in
Tehran, if they did not already have a strong understanding of the country
(and they often didn't), were forced to rely on the experience and expertise
of resident American missionaries. And for generations, much of Iran's own
political elite—cabinet ministers, technocrats, even prime ministers—was
drawn from the ranks of men who had been educated in American mission
schools. Even as late as the 1970s, meetings between Iranian and American

officials often resembled informal reunions of alumni of the American Presbyterian mission schools established more than a century earlier.

☙

What was perhaps most remarkable about the American missionaries' century-long enterprise was that for the first fifty years, they operated in Persia almost entirely by themselves. Until 1883 the United States sent no official diplomatic legation to Tehran—no embassy or ambassador to represent their interests or provide them with legal protection if they needed it. On the rare occasion Americans in Persia ran into trouble, they relied quietly on British diplomats for help. Even from 1838 to 1841, when Britain and Persia broke off ties during a dispute over Afghanistan, it was the shah—not the U.S. government—who quickly stepped in to protect the American missionaries, issuing a royal *farman* (decree) in support of their work and demanding they come to no harm.

The U.S. government during this period was wedded to a policy of strict—almost extreme—isolationism. Following Thomas Jefferson's warning against "entangling alliances" in distant lands, successive U.S. administrations in the nineteenth century refused even to engage with countries as far away as Persia, believing no essential U.S. interests to be at stake. This policy of strict isolationism would remain in place until the early 1940s. As a result, most historians who have studied the U.S.-Iranian relationship (using only U.S. sources) have begun their narratives around 1940, on the casual assumption that U.S.-Iranian relations barely existed before the United States became interested. This reflects a limited, skewed, and one-sided approach to history.

Though Washington maintained a posture of aloof neutrality toward Persia before 1940, Tehran's attitude could not have been more different. The Persian government in the nineteenth and early twentieth centuries saw cultivating an official relationship with the United States as a critical foreign-policy priority, almost a matter of life and death. In fact, some of the very first disagreements between Washington and Tehran came about because Persia wanted the United States to become *more* involved in its affairs, and the United States refused—a fact that might come as a surprise to twenty-first-century observers of U.S.-Iranian relations. This critical part of the story is precisely the aspect most consistently missed by historians who approach this subject only from the perspective of U.S. sources, U.S. priorities, and U.S. foreign policy.

☙

In 1849 the Persian government turned to the United States for a simple reason: it was sick of dealing with Europe. In the early nineteenth century, Britain, Russia, and France had all jockeyed for position in Persia, each attempting to use the shah's territory as a defensive bulwark against the other two powers' Asian ambitions. In Europe, they called it the "Great Game"—a fierce struggle for supremacy in Central Asia, fought mainly between Britain and Russia, each of which hoped to block the other from gaining access to strategic assets. Russia's goal was to gain access to warm-water ports in the Persian Gulf; Britain's was to create an unbroken chain of influence from the Mediterranean to its colony in India. At various points, Britain and Russia both took advantage of Persia's military weakness to launch invasions and to force the shah to make political and economic concessions that were increasingly crippling—forging treaties, then reneging on them with bewildering speed when circumstances changed. Though this behavior made sense in the context of European power politics, from the Persian vantage point, it was rascally and duplicitous behavior.

The tone for these years was set by the infamous Treaty of Turkmenchai of 1828, a crucial turning point in modern Iranian history. After the Russian army inflicted a particularly crushing defeat on the Persians at Turkmenchai, the concluding treaty forced Persia to pay Russia an indemnity of 20 million rubles—an unheard-of sum in its day. Even more remarkable, the treaty gave Russia the right to sell goods virtually tax-free in Persia, and it afforded Russian subjects legal immunity for crimes they committed on Persian soil. The Russians thus deftly used their military victory to establish a permanent sphere of influence over their southern neighbor. They called these heavy-handed measures, which went far beyond the typical provisions of a peace treaty, "extraterritorial privileges." The Persians called them "capitulations." But whatever they were called, their effects were devastating, cruel, and immediate. The Persian economy went into a tailspin as cheap Russian products flooded the market. Ancient handicrafts, like textiles and woven silk, were decimated. The 20-million-ruble indemnity bankrupted the Persian treasury, forcing Tehran to sign up for crippling loans from Russian banks—loans that ushered in a cycle of indebtedness, bankruptcy, and dependency.

But the most devastating impact of the treaty was the precedent it established. In 1841, after Britain defeated Persia in a three-year war over Afghanistan, it demanded (and got) peace terms identical to those the Russians got at Turkmenchai. Once Britain and Russia were enjoying such privileges, other European powers asked for similar perks, in exchange for loans or other emoluments—money Persia desperately needed to pay off its debts. A vicious cycle thus took effect: extraterritorial privileges given to one country bankrupted the Persian treasury, forcing it to give privileges to another country to pay off its loans. From 1855 to 1900, no fewer than fifteen Western nations invoked the precedent of Turkmenchai as they negotiated treaties with Persia. The empire's carcass was slowly being picked clean.

For Persia, the Treaty of Turkmenchai was far more than a peace agreement—it was a humiliation of epic proportions. For the first time since Alexander the Great marched out of Persepolis with his three thousand camels laden with gold, Western powers had gained the right to plunder the Persian treasury and to dictate from distant capitals the country's internal affairs. But unlike the imperialist projects under way in other parts of the world, this was not a straightforward conquest or colonization. Rather, it was something subtler and ultimately more toxic—a form of indirect political interference. For the remainder of the nineteenth century, Britain and Russia would more or less run Persia from behind the scenes, using bribes, economic leverage, and political intrigue to stage-manage the decisions of the Persian government. It left Persians with a lingering feeling of resentment and suspicion toward the European powers.

It was in this atmosphere that the United States first began to look attractive. In the 1830s and '40s, the Persians noticed that a few dozen people from the "new world" had turned up in the mountains around Urmia with nothing more than a printing press and some medical supplies and begun building schools and clinics. These missionaries (*mobalaqin-e mashabi,* the Persians called them, or "spiritual messengers") looked like Europeans, spoke like Europeans, and dressed like Europeans, but their attitudes and their behavior toward Persia could not have been less European. They appeared, bizarrely, to have no connection with their government and no interest in making demands on the Persian government. Their own government hadn't even bothered to send an ambassador to Tehran or to initiate negotiations for a treaty. For whatever inexplicable reason, these Americans appeared to have come to Persia just to help.

For a while the Persian government was too busy fighting wars with Russia and Britain to pay much attention to the United States. But then in 1848, a young and energetic new shah named Naser al-Din came to power, determined to save the bankrupt Persian treasury from the crippling capitulations. The seventeen-year-old shah appointed as his prime minister the highly promising and capable young modernizer Amir Kabir, who immediately saw the potential of a U.S. friendship. After years of losing battles against Britain and Russia, Amir Kabir felt keenly Persia's military and technological inferiority and was convinced his country could learn a lot from the West. But it must no longer learn such lessons, he felt, from the losing end of a gun barrel. The United States had declared its independence from

Britain, fought a war for it, and won. Surely, he reasoned, this was a country that would instinctively understand Persia's desire for a little respect from Europe. A friendship with America, perhaps, could bring the advantages and know-how of Western civilization without the duplicity, greed, and self-interest that usually accompanied it.

Like dozens of Persian politicians who would follow in his footsteps, Amir Kabir was deeply impressed by the accomplishments of the West but was adamant that Western technological and political advances should be incorporated into Persia without putting the country in a servile position. More important, he was the first to recognize that to balance the pressures from Russia and Britain, Persia would need a "third force" of some sort to use as leverage against them. The United States, as a rising power, was an ideal candidate.

ᴄ𝐬

In the 1840s, as luck would have it, American disputes with Britain over the Oregon Territory had created a flare-up of anti-British feeling in the United States, leaving many in Washington on the lookout for opportunities to encroach on the interests of their former colonial power. So in 1849, Amir Kabir instructed a Persian envoy heading for Constantinople to approach the American minister there and initiate a dialogue. The meeting took place in an atmosphere of such secrecy that virtually nothing is known about it. But the following year a similar effort was made—this time between the Persian minister in Constantinople, Davud Khan, and his American counterpart, George Perkins Marsh. Again, the first priority for both men was to make sure the British didn't find out.

For a year and a half, Davud and Marsh met in total secrecy with the knowledge and support of their respective governments. And in October 1851, in Constantinople, they signed the Treaty of Friendship, Commerce, and Navigation between Persia and the United States. It was a remarkably fair and respectful document compared with other treaties being foisted on Tehran in this period, and it was guaranteed to put a knot in the tail of the British Lion. Among its provisions was a clause allowing the United States to set up a consulate in Bushehr, an important southern trading port where the British had all but declared squatter's rights. Marsh felt he had achieved an impressive victory.

Unfortunately, the U.S. Senate didn't see it that way. When news of the treaty reached Washington, senators complained that Marsh had failed to secure a clause giving American citizens the same privileges and immunities that other Western nations enjoyed in Persia, and they refused to ratify it. Marsh went back to Davud, who promised to see what he could do, but before Marsh heard back, the situation in Tehran changed dramatically. Amir Kabir was murdered by his enemies and replaced with a prime minister seen as more loyal to British interests. The window for negotiations with the United States closed firmly, and the treaty expired before it could be ratified. Marsh was convinced that a British hand was lurking in the background.

In 1854 the two countries tried again—this time in an atmosphere of secrecy bordering on paranoia. On the U.S. end, Marsh had been replaced as minister by Carroll Spence, a tough-minded diplomat with a long history of anti-British sentiment, for whom a U.S.-Persian treaty was both a patriotic duty and a chance to deliver a black eye to London. Unfortunately, however, positions had hardened since the previous attempt. Both sides had developed such an obsession with Britain that they came to the table with demands that seemed utterly outrageous to the other. Persian relations with Britain had taken a nosedive over Afghanistan, and the shah was now fixated on obtaining an American security umbrella in the Gulf. His list of demands was audacious: the purchase of American warships, manned by American officers, and full U.S. naval protection of Persian merchant shipping, complete with the Stars and Stripes flying from every Persian commercial vessel in the Gulf. For the Americans, always wary of "entangling alliances," these demands were unacceptable.

The United States had its own set of requirements that the Persians found equally objectionable. Spence had been instructed to demand a clause guaranteeing U.S. citizens the same "extraterritorial privileges" that the Russians had extracted at Turkmenchai. For the Persians, this tiresomely familiar request came as a tremendous disappointment. The whole point of pursuing an alliance with the United States, they felt, was that it would *not* be like all those other Western nations. American negotiators insisted they simply wanted to be treated on an equal footing with Europe. But the Persians dug in their heels, telling their American counterparts that the humiliating conditions they had agreed to with other nations had been the result of military defeats or emergency loan agreements. Giving Americans the same privileges would create an even more damaging precedent than Turkmenchai: it would mean, in effect, that any nation with diplomatic ties with Persia would be *automatically* entitled to extraterritorial privileges.

It took nearly two years—and a twist of fate—for the deadlock to break. At the end of 1856, Persia was once again at war with Britain, and the shah now desperately wanted an American alliance he could wave in front of British eyeballs. With little further discussion, he agreed to give the Americans all the privileges they had asked for—including immunity from

Persian law for U.S. citizens, and exemptions from Persian taxes for U.S. businesses. The treaty was quickly concluded and signed on December 13, then was ratified by both countries in early 1857. The shah never got the American security guarantees he had hoped for, but there was no going back—the United States and Persia had become friends.

ભ

The opening words of the treaty told Americans everything they would ever need to know about Persia. "The President of the United States," it began:

> and His Majesty as exalted as the Planet Saturn; the Sovereign to whom the Sun serves as a standard; whose splendour and magnificence are equal to that of the Skies; the Sublime Sovereign, the Monarch whose armies are as numerous as the Stars; whose greatness calls to mind that of Jeinshid; whose magnificence equals that of Darius; the Heir of the Crown and Throne of the Kayanians; the Sublime Emperor of all Persia . . .

And so on and so on. The Persians were great sticklers for ceremony, it turned out, and now that the treaty was ratified, they expected an exchange of gifts to mark the important occasion. At Spence's insistence, the United States spent $10,000 (close to $1 million in today's money) on diamond-studded snuffboxes and weapons for the shah. The State Department protested bitterly, as it was not in the habit of spending such outrageous sums, but Spence put his foot down, knowing that these gifts paled in comparison with what Persia had received from Napoleon and others. Spence's brother Charles was dispatched to Tehran to deliver the gifts in person—a gesture the shah appreciated so much that he decorated the young man with the Order of the Lion and Sun, the country's highest honor.

These demonstrations of protocol seemed a trivial and tedious distraction to the United States, which liked to think of itself as a humble, pragmatic power, removed from the blandishments of the old world. But to Persians, courtesy, respect, and ceremony were as fundamental to political relations as any practical matter of policy. They even had a word for it, one virtually impossible to translate into any Western tongue. Ritual, respect, protocol, form, ceremony, courtesy—the Persians called it all *tashrifat,* and you ignored it at your peril. This was a lesson the United States would learn again and again in its dealings with Iran—often the hard way.

ભ

With a treaty in place, the next challenge was to translate it into an exchange of living, breathing diplomats. Initially, there was every reason to believe the matter would be straightforward. The U.S. president, James Buchanan, gave firm support to the idea of establishing a permanent legation in Tehran and sending over an ambassador (or "resident minister," as ambassadors were then known),* and he urged Congress to approve the necessary funds. "The Shah has manifested an earnest disposition to cultivate friendly relations with our country," Buchanan argued in his first State of the Union message in December 1857. From the Persian side, meanwhile, the prime minister, Mirza Agha Khan Nuri, tried to nudge things along by writing a personal letter to Carroll Spence—who was back in Washington and had become Persia's biggest cheerleader in America.

Spence, who was now on something of an anti-British crusade, advocated forcefully for a Tehran embassy as a way to weaken British influence in Asia. Persia's long border with British India, he wrote to the State Department, as well as the "national feeling of hatred" its people had for Britain, had the potential to make the country a "most serviceable ally" for the United States. Setting up a legation in Tehran could "at some future date . . . [help] us in annoying a nation [Britain], which has never ceased to interfere with our foreign policy." The U.S. House of Representatives, however, was not convinced by this naked Brit-baiting. In January 1859, citing budgetary constraints, it rejected the request for funding.

In Tehran, where the finer points of American politics were not always appreciated, this decision was utterly mystifying. Why, the Persians wondered, had the United States spent all this effort to negotiate a treaty, only to turn around and refuse to fund a legation? Why spend $10,000 on snuffboxes, then balk at $5,000 for a minister's salary? Once again the occidental mind was proving an irrational and mercurial thing. But the Persians were also left feeling that the dignity of the shah had been insulted. For them, the whole point of concluding a treaty with the United States had been to send a message to Britain and Russia; the unexpected snub from Congress had left them looking foolish. At the very least, they now suggested, the United States should offer some symbolic gesture to make clear that it was serious about its Persian friendship. Anything less would be a breach of *tashrifat*.

As it happened, the navy frigate USS *Minnesota* was on its way to China at the time. It was ordered to make a stop in the Gulf and fire off a few cer-

---

* Traditionally, the terms *embassy* and *ambassador* were reserved for diplomatic exchanges conducted among the great royal heads of state in Europe. The United States thus referred to its ambassadors as "resident ministers" and its embassies as "legations"—technically lower in rank. After World War II, the idea that some nations' sovereignty was more prestigious than others' fell out of favor, and *ambassador* and *embassy* became the standard usage throughout the world.

emonial cannons in honor of U.S.-Persian friendship. The Persians appreciated the gesture, but from the American side there was no further talk about establishing a legation. The round of volleys that the good ship *Minnesota* fired into the empty starlit sky turned out to be the last official interaction between the United States and Persia for more than twenty years.

In 1861, just two years after Congress rejected funding for a Tehran legation, the United States slid into a catastrophic civil war. Six hundred thousand Americans lost their lives in the conflict, at the end of which the U.S. government was left with the challenge of reintegrating several southern states, with devastated economies, into the national union. In the midst of this long and painful process, in 1873, the United States, along with most of the industrialized world, fell into economic depression. Given these circumstances, foreign affairs slipped down the list of priorities in Washington. Setting up a U.S. legation in Persia seemed almost obscenely frivolous.

But the more distant the Americans became, the more interested Persians seemed to be in all things American. In 1873 and 1878, during his state visits to Europe, Naser al-Din Shah observed with admiration the wealthy Americans congregating on London's Regent Street and the bales of American cotton being unloaded at Liverpool docks. In the 1870s, Persian newspapers ran frequent stories about American prowess and ingenuity, inviting readers to marvel at how quickly the United States had advanced in the few short decades since it had gained independence. In New York, readers were told, awesome hotels were being built—one with room for seven hundred guests. A San Francisco man had reached the North Pole, and a train had run from Jersey City to Trenton—a distance of fifty miles—in just fifty-nine minutes. America was praised for its culture of integrity, hard work, and sobriety. And Persian editorialists were particularly impressed by the temperance movement, marveling that people whose religion did not forbid drink were taking a firmer stand against drunkenness than Muslims did. Most controversially, the official government newspaper, *Iran,* edited by the wily Itimad os-Saltaneh, suggested obliquely that the key to America's rapid advancement had been its free press and the atmosphere of open debate in Congress. Never before had such an obvious challenge to the shah's authority appeared in print in Tehran.

By the 1870s, Persians had grown utterly disgusted with the endless capitulations and commercial privileges that European powers were demanding of them, and they were hoping a more meaningful relationship might soon be possible with the United States—a rising power they saw as pleasingly anti-imperialist in its ideology. Persian reformists frequently noted the contrast between America—a nation born out of revolutionary opposition to tyranny and colonialism—and the Great Powers of Europe. The United States, to their great admiration, minded its own business and seemed to respect the sovereignty and dignity of powerless nations. The Europeans did nothing of the kind. Indeed, in 1872, as Persia's desperation for cash grew, the British aristocrat Baron Julius de Reuter swooped in and acquired, for the mere sum of $200,000, control over Persia's future mineral exploration rights, factories, road-building projects, irrigation, and agriculture—along with the rights to build a railway from the Caspian Sea to the Gulf coast. The Reuter concession was unparalleled: for the first time in history, a sovereign state had surrendered, during peacetime, the right to develop its own infrastructure to a foreign private citizen. Worse, it had

Naser al-Din Shah (1848–96): The first Persian monarch to travel to the West, Naser al-Din admired the United States and presided over the tentative early years of relations between the two countries.

been agreed to at the apex of the Industrial Revolution—at precisely the moment when Persia most needed to take command of its economic development in order to have a prayer of competing with the West.

In the late 1870s, when the United States finally began to emerge from its long trauma of Civil War and Reconstruction, a booming economy and the demands of new millionaires pushed American traders into ever more exotic corners of the world. Persian carpets were all the rage in the drawing rooms of New York and Philadelphia. Persian dates and nuts increasingly found appreciative consumers. In Tehran, meanwhile, the dernier cri was to be seen smoking Virginia tobacco and wearing clothes made of Mississippi cotton. In just the few short years since the Civil War, U.S.-Persian trade had quietly reached into the tens of millions—still small in comparison with other countries but far too large to be ignored.

From many corners now, the message being sent to Washington was the same: it was time to open a legation in Tehran. In 1879 the USS *Ticonderoga* called in the Gulf, where its captain, Commodore Robert Shufeldt, informed the secretary of the navy that the trading possibilities with Persia were excellent. A U.S. legation, he said, was long overdue. The American minister in Vienna, John Kasson, urged the secretary of state to make the establishment of a Tehran legation a top priority. Persia was not just an eager market for American cotton, he noted. Lately, American petroleum was also making its way into the country.

What finally tipped the balance in favor of a U.S. legation in Tehran, though, was not commercial considerations but an immediate concern about the safety of American missionaries. In October 1880 a major Kurdish rebellion broke out in northwestern Persia, where Americans were heavily concentrated. In Washington, concern for the fate of Americans trapped in Urmia grew quickly. Rep. Rufus R. Dawes (R-Ohio)—a devout Presbyterian whose sister and brother-in-law happened to live in Urmia—appealed to Secretary of State William Evarts to take action to protect Americans from becoming "the victims of Mohammedan fury." Months dragged on without a response. In March 1882, Dawes tried to tack an amendment onto a House appropriations bill, extending the accreditation of the U.S. minister in Constantinople to include Persia (thus giving the United States an official channel to the Persian government). Dawes made his case passionately and in explicitly Christian terms. "Persia is one of the oldest, and was, at one time, the most powerful nationality on earth," he argued. But it "has become effete, superannuated, and insignificant . . . because of the blighting influence of Mohammedanism. The young and vigorous Christian civilization of America has stretched out an arm to lift that nation from its moral degradation."

Supporters of the appropriations bill angrily interrupted Dawes—they were in a rush to pass it and were in no mood to entertain frivolous amendments proposed by men full of Bible talk. But Dawes did not give up. A month later, along with a few sympathetic colleagues, he pushed another resolution, this time authorizing the secretary of state to set up a legation in Tehran and appropriating funds for the purpose. When the bill reached the House floor, Dawes was once again met with jeers and mockery. But this time he looked his adversary, Rep. William S. Holman (R-IN), in the eye and said quietly, "Remember that my sister is there in peril, and let this go for me." Holman went quiet and took his seat.

"By such slender threads hang important things," Dawes later recalled. And indeed they did. Holman yielded the floor to Dawes's friend, fellow Presbyterian and former Pennsylvania governor Andrew Curtin, a legendary orator, who rose to his feet and delivered a powerful, emotional appeal for the establishment of a U.S. embassy in Tehran. Persia's was the "oldest government in the world," he began, "and a country now growing to great consequence commercially." It was a strategic makeweight between Britain and Russia, and the shah seemed eager to build a relationship with the United States. "Persia can probably never again rule the world as under Cyrus," Curtin argued. "But the wheel of history will soon bring round the day when its commercial and religious influences will again reach over a hundred millions of people."

The old man's eloquence did the trick. The bill squeaked through under a suspension of the rules before Congress adjourned for the summer. On August 7, 1882, President Chester Arthur signed HR 6743 into law, and the following year America's first official envoy to Persia was on his way to Tehran.

The Amateurs

At first blush, Samuel Greene Wheeler Benjamin seemed like just the right man to serve as America's first-ever ambassador to Tehran. Born in Greece to missionary parents and deeply familiar with Eastern cultures, he was energetic and outgoing, spoke several languages, and loved to travel. Described as a "cosmopolitan adventurer who became sickly only when he stayed in one place too long," Benjamin had dabbled in everything from painting to amateur sailing to freelance journalism but never settled on anything in particular. He was every inch the gentleman-dilettante the State Department favored in those days when it hired diplomats.

But alas, Benjamin's bombastic personality was something of an acquired taste. Short, loud, and opinionated—sometimes irascibly single-minded—he was inclined to swell up with indignation over a minor matter of punctilio. What he lacked in height (and tact), he tried to make up for by standing as straight as a plank and blustering from behind what one biographer called an "imposing mustache." At times he was his own worst enemy.

On paper, Benjamin was eminently qualified for the job. But opening a new legation in a land as far away and unfamiliar as Persia would take a lot more than an impressive CV. The court of the Peacock Throne in 1883 was a place where centuries of tradition, wealth, and imperial grandeur intersected with the strategic interests and cloak-and-dagger intrigues of Europe's greatest powers. For an American to step into this atmosphere and survive, much less succeed, would require bottomless reserves of patience, a natural aptitude for subtlety, and—perhaps most important—enough money to project an aura of personal dignity. On all three measures, Benjamin fell far short.

As early as 1856, Carroll Spence had recommended a salary of at least $12,000 for the new U.S. minister in Tehran, arguing that anything less would bring disgrace on the United States. The journey from Constantinople was long and arduous and likely to deplete funds quickly, he said. And once the minister was in Tehran, he would need to live "in a becoming manner," employing a respectable number of servants and keeping a summer residence in the northern suburbs like all the other diplomats. The Europeans would sneer at an American minister running a shoestring operation, and the Persians would be baffled. But in 1882 the Senate approved only $5,000, with an additional $3,000 for expenses. To his credit, Benjamin did not put up much of a protest. But it was a serious error of judgment on the part of Washington.

From the moment Benjamin arrived in Persia, the contrast between his low-budget American amateurism and the rich and elaborate ceremony of the Qajar court became blindingly, and embarrassingly, obvious. Arriving by boat near the city of Rasht, Benjamin received a welcome he described as "almost unique for hospitality." Cannons were fired in his honor, trumpets blared, and for several days, the disheveled American and his family stayed at the palace of the provincial governor while they were presented with elegant banquets and showered with gifts. An urgent message arrived from Tehran, informing Benjamin that the shah was about to leave town for the summer, and that Persian custom did not allow foreign envoys entry into Tehran unless the monarch was present. Leaving his wife and luggage in Rasht, Benjamin rode to Tehran at a "hard gallop"—frequently changing horses and, incredibly, covering two hundred miles of rough, mostly mountainous terrain in just two days. When he arrived, filthy and sweaty, his groin recalling every inch of the unfamiliar saddle (he hadn't ridden a horse in years), Benjamin was amazed to see the welcome prepared for him by the King of Kings.

From Qazvin, some one hundred miles to the west, Benjamin's entry into Tehran was escorted by a thousand royal guards magnificently attired in ceremonial uniforms. The report of his arrival took up the first three pages of Tehran's four-page newspaper. Spectators thronged the streets, and as Benjamin's procession entered the palace, a blast of cannon in honor of the United States echoed across the entire city. The heavily perspiring American was then led before the shah, where he read out a speech prepared by President Chester Arthur. The monarch inquired politely after Arthur's health and then expressed, "in the most emphatic manner," his hope that

Samuel Greene Wheeler Benjamin, the
first U.S. minister (ambassador) to Persia
(1883–85): Blustering, pompous, and prone
to conflict, Benjamin was a passionate
believer in U.S.-Persian friendship and
wrote the first American best seller about
the country, *Persia and the Persians*.

there would be an American legation in Tehran for the rest of eternity. As
Benjamin stood there in his plain black suit,[*] his eyes were drawn to the
buttons on the shah's frock coat. They were diamonds, "fully the size of
pigeon's eggs."

Awestruck by his new surroundings, Benjamin slumped off to his first
night's accommodation—a living-room sofa at the home of American missionaries. The State Department had refused funding for the purchase of a
legation compound, so Benjamin's first task the next morning was to scope
out the city's rental market. America's first representative to the court of the
Peacock Throne had arrived looking, and probably smelling, like a student
backpacker who had missed his last connection. It was an embarrassing way
to begin.

⊂⊗

But money problems were quickly eclipsed by the unbreakable beast that
was Benjamin's ego. As a child in Greece, Benjamin had watched his father
serve briefly as honorary U.S. consul, only to be treated with sneering dis-
dain by European diplomats who had no time for American "amateurs."

---

[*] Traditionally, European countries issued special ceremonial costumes for their ministers and
ambassadors to use on formal occasions such as this. But the United States insisted that all its
diplomats wear simple black suits.

The experience had left him resentful, and his two years in Tehran were often overshadowed by a neurotic fixation on the opinions of European diplomats.

Within hours of his arrival in Tehran, Benjamin became obsessed with demonstrating the prestige of the United States—purchasing, with his own money, a hundred-foot flagpole so the Stars and Stripes would be visible from every corner of Tehran. Soon afterward he became convinced that the Russian minister was sabotaging his efforts to promote U.S.-Persian trade and demanded a special top-secret courier to carry his messages—a request the State Department found preposterous. Undeterred, Benjamin began harrying the Russians directly, writing the Russian minister an angry note, in English, telling him to cease and desist. As French was the international language of diplomacy then, the note was returned unread. "There is no question that the Russian minister speaks sufficient English to understand the notes," Benjamin fumed, but Washington was unimpressed. Benjamin was told that, in the future, he should take his concerns directly to the Persian government rather than to the Russians—and keep all his correspondence in French.

But it was no use. Benjamin would happily walk a hundred miles to receive an insult from a European. When the German minister, Ernst von Braunschweig, failed to call on Benjamin's wife on her appointed day for receiving visitors, Benjamin dashed off a blistering note to the German legation, full of indignation, and demanding an apology. The kaiser's envoy wrote back that "neither his position nor his personal dignity allow him to accept such insulting expression." The nasty feud between the two men continued for months. Benjamin initially tried to hide the dispute from the State Department, but this only made his superiors lose more patience with him.

When he wasn't picking fights with the Great Powers of Europe, Benjamin did an excellent job of antagonizing his Persian hosts. On one occasion, his servants got into a fistfight with the shah's royal cavalry escort, and Benjamin demanded redress, insisting that the shah's servants be beaten, to restore the dignity and prestige of the United States. As a courtesy, the shah complied, assuming Benjamin would do the same with his own servants. But when the American failed to take the hint, the shah's dignity was severely bruised. (History doesn't record how the servants felt.)

Historians have frequently described Benjamin's tenure in Tehran as a series of needless and unprovoked conflicts, constant embarrassment, and a general climate of clownish amateurism. But this is not entirely fair. Far more than almost any U.S. minister who succeeded him, Benjamin loved and respected the cultures of the Muslim world and went out of his way to understand the Persian perspective. If anything, in fact, it was his passion for Persia—his driving commitment to the importance of the U.S.-Persian relationship, and his single-minded, almost maniacal desire to do his job well—that often got him in trouble. In their first few meetings, the shah informed Benjamin that he desired better trading links with the United States as a counterbalance to the European powers, and Benjamin never let go of this idea. In dispatch after dispatch, he pestered the State Department to make Persian trade a priority and to encourage American businesses to come to Tehran and begin exploiting the country's oil and mineral wealth. As ever, though, Washington was staunchly isolationist, reluctant to offer even basic support for commercial relations overseas. Benjamin, like U.S. ministers in many parts of the world, bitterly resented watching European investors gain lucrative contracts with the support of their governments while American businesses were left to fend for themselves on the open market.

In early 1885, there was a new administration in Washington. Though Benjamin liked and respected Grover Cleveland, he was a lifelong Republican and not about to change parties to stay in Persia. He left reluctantly, convinced that with a few more years he could have created important new commercial and political alliances. When he returned to America, he gave an impassioned lecture about his experiences to an audience of fifteen hundred people who had packed into Chickering Hall in New York, telling them about the beauty of Persia and the progress it was making. The following year Benjamin's book—*Persia and the Persians*—appeared in print and quickly became a best seller, introducing more Americans to Persia than probably any publication in the nineteenth century.[*]

But for the forty-eight-year-old Benjamin, it was the end of that magical chapter of his life. For the rest of his days, he settled into obscurity, living in Vermont and writing occasional travel articles for *Harper's* magazine. He never tried his hand at diplomacy again.

◌◎

Benjamin was the first but certainly not the last of a long line of "gentlemen-amateurs" to represent the United States in Persia in the late nineteenth century. His appointment, and those that followed, reflected the general approach to diplomacy and foreign relations that the United States took in this era of limited engagement. Men with a smattering of knowledge,

---

[*] The book would remain, for decades, the standard American work on Iran. As late as the 1970s, it was still being handed out as a party favor at official functions celebrating U.S.-Iranian friendship.

worldliness, and education, often without any experience in politics, were sent to far-flung locales and expected to do little more than behave "honorably" and stay out of trouble. The job of U.S. minister to Persia in the 1880s, if performed successfully, was to relay information, attend social events, go on hunting trips in the mountains, and spend lazy afternoons wandering through exotic bazaars. This remained the established pattern until well into the 1940s. The result was sometimes shocking levels of incompetence, amateurism, and freelance adventurism.

Benjamin's replacement in Tehran, for example, was Frederick Winston, a cantankerous sixty-year-old lawyer with no diplomatic experience who resigned after only a month at his post. Winston, in turn, was replaced by E. Spencer Pratt—a thrity-five-year-old from Mobile, Alabama. And so it went on. In 1891, Washington sent Truxtun Beale, a young Californian who was heir to the largest private landholding fortune in the United States, only to have him respond with adolescent humor to his new surroundings. And for the rest of the 1890s, America was represented in Tehran by a series of rank amateurs whose lack of preparation for the job of U.S. minister communicated a powerful message of benign neglect to the shah. There was, in 1893, Watson Sperry, a journalist from Delaware who lasted just six months. Then there was sixty-six-year-old Alexander McDonald, an obscure Virginia Presbyterian who served out the last four years of his life in Persia. He was replaced, in 1897, by Arthur Hardy, whose last full-time job had been as editor of *Cosmopolitan*.

Though the overall trajectory from 1885 to 1900 was one of amateurism and neglect from the American side, there was one noteworthy exception. In 1886, Winston, who had initially claimed "there is no American trade worth mentioning and no prospect for any" on his arrival in Tehran, quit his post and secretly attempted to negotiate a harebrained $100 million railway contract with the shah on behalf of a consortium of U.S. investors. The idea went nowhere, but his successor, Pratt, plotted behind the State Department's back to bring another millionaire rail magnate, Francis Clergue, from Maine to Persia to revive the idea. It was a fascinating window into just how little oversight Washington exercised over this early generation of amateur diplomats (U.S. National Archives, for example, contain no record of Pratt's adventures; they exist only in Iranian government collections). But it was an even more fascinating window into the strength of British and Russian influence in Tehran.

The shah, who had struck up a warm friendship with Pratt, was initially thrilled at the thought of Americans building a railway across Persia. A national rail network was a critical part of his vision for modernizing the country, and something he had long dreamed of, but his plans had always been thwarted by Britain and Russia—each of which feared that a rail line across Persia would make it easier for the other power to threaten its commercial sphere of influence. Pratt came breathtakingly close to overcoming all this—engineering a commercial agreement that would have represented an extraordinary coup for American influence in Persia. Working secretly with an American missionary, W. W. Torrence, he secured a contract for the latter to dig artesian wells and drill for oil throughout the country (the first American petroleum contract in the Middle East), and then tacked onto this the right to build a railway from Tehran to Mohammareh on the Persian Gulf. Clergue then arrived from Maine and bribed the Russian minister into silence, while reassuring the British minister that he had no "political objectives" in Persia.

But still, it was never to be. The Russian government got wind of what was happening and forcefully intervened. The shah was quickly pressured into signing an agreement that gave Russia the right of first refusal over all railway construction in Persia for the next forty years. And Britain was pacified with a contract to oversee the new Imperial Bank of Persia. As for the railway network the country so badly needed, Britain and Russia colluded to ensure it would not get built until the 1930s.

CB

If American diplomatic forays into Persia in these early years were marked by disregard, neglect, and unscripted adventurism, the attitude on the Persian side could not have been more different.

In the summer of 1888, the shah sent his first envoy to Washington to set up a legation. Hossein Qoli Khan Nuri—one of the most distinguished public officials in Tehran, son of a former prime minister,[*] and a high-ranking official in the Foreign Ministry—had previously served as Persia's consul-general in British India. Unlike the American ministers in Tehran at this time, he was no gentleman-amateur. He was a serious diplomat, and his appointment reflected the mood of optimism and possibility that was in the air at the time. For Persia, it was a historic moment.

When Nuri arrived in America in October 1888, though, his appointment was treated as little more than a curiosity. *The New York Times* described him as "a small man and spare of flesh," with features "of a distinctly Eastern cast, the nose being large and curved, the complexion swarthy, and the eyes small and beadlike in their jetty brightness." The tabloids were much

---

[*] And not just any prime minister. Mirza Aqa Khan Nuri, Etemad ol-Dowleh, was one of the most prominent and long-serving prime ministers of nineteenth-century Persia (1851–58).

harsher. There were howls of mockery about Nuri's long and unusual name, rendering Qoli as "Mr. Ghooly." (Some papers joked it sounded rather Irish.) Other stories sneered about how it had taken him two months to arrive in New York—and were laced with pungent allusions to the lengthy stopover he had made to enjoy the "fascinations of Paris." In fact, Nuri had never been to Paris, and two months was a reasonable journey time from Tehran to New York. (With the wind at his back, Benjamin had taken sixty-five days.) It was Nuri's first experience with the rough-and-tumble of American democracy, and it was a striking contrast to what he was accustomed to back home.

Five years earlier, when Samuel Benjamin had arrived in Persia, the Persian press had dutifully glowed and fawned over the important occasion, and the young man's triumphal entry into Tehran had been accompanied by blaring trumpets, roaring cannons, and the thundering hooves of a thousand liveried horsemen. When Nuri's ship pulled up to the 22nd Street Pier on Manhattan's west side, however, he was met by a junior official who helped check him into a local hotel for the night. The contrast in reception only became more apparent when Nuri arrived in Washington the next day to present his credentials to President Grover Cleveland—an awkward encounter if ever there was one. Assuming Nuri would have the luxury of an extended private meeting with the president, the shah had written a lengthy, passionate address to Cleveland, pleading for his help against Britain and Russia—and Nuri had been instructed to read it aloud. But when the moment came, he was surprised to find himself ushered into the White House for a quick exchange of formalities—an inappropriate moment for a speech.

But Nuri had no choice. "The old established and independent kingdom" of Persia, he began, had "a special message to Her Young and prosperous and powerful sister." Persia was desperate to modernize, "but we have two great neighbours which instead of assisting us . . . are always . . . repulsing us from our progress." The shah did not want America to "lose anything for our sake" but hoped that Cleveland would see fit to "help us with your sciences and industries and send your companies and [merchants] and manufactures to our country." In conclusion, the shah hoped that "our request . . . will be strictly secret from any person besides your Highness." This last line must have sounded odd with Secretary of State Thomas Bayard standing in the room.

Embarrassed by this initial encounter with Cleveland, Nuri wrote informally to Bayard, asking when he might expect a proper opportunity for an audience with the president. In his letter, Nuri reminded Bayard that the shah's birthday was just two days away and that, on this "happy and auspi-

cious occasion for our most Holy and All-Powerful Lord His August Imperial Majesty," a congratulatory telegram from Cleveland would do wonders
for U.S.-Persian relations. This suggestion was in line with diplomatic practice, but then Nuri suggested the State Department also send a "person of
high standing" to the Persian legation to deliver birthday greetings in person. Nuri's letter spoke volumes about the gulf between Persian *tashrifat* and
the businesslike pragmatism of American government. It is unclear whether
the shah ever got his birthday telegram, but Nuri was gently informed that
protocol in Washington was that foreign envoys conducted all discussions
with the secretary of state and met the president only on ceremonial occasions. He would not be speaking to Cleveland again.

ᘓ

A more pompous figure might have puffed up with indignation at these
initial encounters, or perceived them as snubs to the dignity of Persia. But
Nuri found the experience eye-opening. In his early reports back to Tehran,
he buzzed with excitement over the American way of life. This was a hardworking, ambitious, efficient nation, he wrote, and its political system was
marked by an impressive culture of integrity and accountability. That he
was not allowed to be alone with the president showed how even the loftiest
figure in America was not exempt from public scrutiny. Nuri was also struck
by the rigors of representative democracy. An election was coming up, he
said, and it was unclear whether Cleveland would even still be president in
a few months—his fate was entirely in the hands of the American people.
It was a novel system, Nuri admitted, but he thought it worked brilliantly.
America had "the greatest government in the world," he raved. "A far cry
from Berlin or Istanbul or London or Paris or Vienna."

Nuri was playing with fire. Persia in the nineteenth century was an
absolute monarchy. The shah, like many monarchs of the age, was regarded
as above the law, exempt from criticism and accountable only to God. The
Qajar court, moreover, was a crucible of intrigue and cronyism, where the
purchase and sale of offices was routine and the most important decisions
were made in an atmosphere of secrecy. So Nuri's chirpy enthusiasm about
American democracy was bound to ruffle feathers. But he didn't let that stop
him. Nuri felt America was a country that was going places, and that Persia's
relationship with the United States would soon prove far more important
than its relations with European nations. "Close the legations in Berlin,
Vienna, London and Istanbul if you like, but don't close the legation in the
yengi donya," he urged his bosses. "Treat our friendship with this nation as
important."

It was not merely American politics that left Nuri besotted. He wrote with enthusiasm about the cultural life and economic vibrancy he saw in New York. Broadway theaters put on satirical plays mocking the English and the Russians, he noted, and "everyone laughs"—surely a promising sign for Persian-American relations. Americans were "orderly" and "peace-loving," interested in education and material advancement. They had built "steamless railways" that crossed suspension bridges and climbed up mountainsides. Electric lighting was everywhere, and the streets were free of mud. ("Bismarck should be ashamed," he snorted.) In short, Nuri believed, in America "the world that Allah and the Prophet Muhammad had intended had finally come to fruition."

Alas, the shine eventually wore off. In June 1889, as Naser al-Din Shah prepared to embark on his third trip to Europe, American newspapers used the occasion to remind readers of some rather unflattering stories about the condition in which he had left Buckingham Palace on his last trip. Whether there was any truth to these rumors is unclear, but by the time the American press got hold of them, they were transformed into a tawdry parody of journalism. The *Los Angeles Times* called the shah a "dirty despot" and a "filthy boor" and claimed Buckingham Palace had to be "disinfected" after he left. Nuri was deeply distressed and insulted by what he was reading. In an interview with a Washington reporter, he drew a pointed comparison between the kindness the shah had shown to the American minister in Tehran and to American missionaries living in Persia, adding that if anyone in Persia wrote such insulting things about the president of the United States, he would be locked up in prison. And then came the coup de grâce. He was so outraged by the coverage, Nuri added, that he was resigning his post in protest.

Nuri seemed genuinely crestfallen that his beloved America had let him down so badly. "When I arrived in this country," he said, "I saw the statue of Liberty Enlightening the World. I was glad, and I thought, 'Here one can live always without trouble or annoyance.' Now, after being here nine months, I go away as fast as I can, and like a prisoner escaping from his prison."

☙

History has not been kind to Hossein Qoli Khan Nuri. In the United States, newspapers long remembered his indignation at their coverage, and for much of the 1890s, they were rarely able to mention Persia without some sneering reference to the incident. In his native Persia, meanwhile, Nuri quickly acquired the nickname "Hajji Washington"—a mocking refer-

ence to the pilgrimage, or *hajj,* he had made to the American capital.* He
was ridiculed by his political enemies, who spread the rumor that he was a
"lunatic" who had been "thrown out" of the United States in disgrace. The
reputation stuck, and he was mocked again in the 1980s by a popular Iranian film based on his life, *Hajji Washington* (not released until 1991). The
movie portrayed him savagely—depicting a self-important, bloviating ass
who made a fool of himself and his country.

None of this was true, and none of it was fair. A close look at Iranian
government archives reveals that Nuri was in fact on a one-year contract,
and that he left Washington exactly when he was supposed to. By the time
the unpleasant stories about the shah began to appear in American newspapers, Nuri was already packing his bags. And when the reporter called on
him a week before his departure, Nuri perhaps sensed an opportunity to
lend weight to his outrage and depict it as the cause of his recall. Or he may
have done no such thing—and the newspapers might simply have created a
story out of nothing. After all, in his final interview, Nuri never said he was
leaving *because* of the poor press coverage—merely that he was leaving *and*
was disappointed by the press coverage.

Whatever the case, his departure appeared to mark the end of an era,
and the beginning of a more uncertain time, for U.S.-Persian relations. In
Persia, the 1890s would turn out to be a turbulent decade—full of rebellion,
hardship, and political turmoil—leaving little time for the cultivation of
closer ties with the United States. It would be nearly ten years before Persia
sent a new minister to Washington. And the American side, during these
same years, offered little more than bumptious amateurism.

U.S. relations with Persia during this period were sometimes characterized by moments of catastrophic failure and embarrassment. In May
1893, for example, the Persian government sent twenty-two delegates on
a two-month trip from Tehran to Chicago—the longest journey of any
nation—to represent the country at the Chicago World's Fair, only to find
their goodwill mission overshadowed by a tawdry scandal. The Persians had
pulled out all the stops, renting out eighteen hundred square feet of exhibition space to display priceless antiques, ornamental tiles, brasswork, miniature paintings, Kerman shawls, and rare rugs from the Imperial Museum in
Tehran. But some enterprising soul (we may never know who) had the idea
to introduce a troupe of belly dancers to the pavilion as a gimmick to draw

---

* The feeling of the joke can be hard to convey in English. The term *hajji* before a man's name is
traditionally a term of respect, reflecting the fact that he has been to Mecca. But it can also have a
jocular quality if said in a certain way. A loose English translation might be "Little Lord Washington" or "Grandpa Washington."

Hossein Qoli Khan Nuri, "Hajji Washington." The first Persian minister (ambassador) to the United States (1888–89), Nuri has long been an object of ridicule in his native Iran. However, archives reveal him to be a great admirer of the United States who performed his duty with dedication and passion. In one of his first dispatches back to Tehran, he described the United States as a land in which everything "that Allah and the Prophet Mohammad intended had finally come to fruition."

more visitors.* Before long, the crowds who had gathered to admire Persian rugs were being swamped by long lines of men who stood outside the Persian Palace eagerly awaiting a chance to watch "Belle Baya" and her friends perform the "hoochie koochie." Word quickly spread of the "suggestively lascivious contorting of the abdominal muscles" on offer, and the Midway Plaisance turned into a circus. "Extremely ungraceful and almost shockingly disgusting," one observer complained of the dancing. "It is the coarse animal passion of the East, not the chaste sentiment of Christian lands," snorted another. And yet the men kept coming. Every day from ten a.m. to ten p.m., the Persian Palace was packed, with the dancers performing in shifts so there was never a break in the action. The Persian government was incensed.

The lowest point in U.S.-Persian relations, though, came in March 1896, when the U.S. consul in Bushehr complained that a rowdy mob had prevented him from erecting a flagpole at the consulate. The American minister in Tehran complained to the Persian government about the "direct insult" to the United States. But then it emerged that the consul—a Persian-Armenian with British and American passports—had been using the U.S. consulate as a cover for a grain- and arms-smuggling operation. The British considered him "untrustworthy" and poured scorn on his version of events.

---

* Belly dancing is an Arab, not a Persian, art form, and the women were entertainers hired from the demimonde of Paris. But this ethnographic detail mattered little to anyone in Chicago.

Persian Palace, Chicago World's Fair (1893): Americans had their first chance to view hundreds of priceless objects from Persia, but the display was quickly upstaged by a scandal involving belly dancers. Tehran's anger and embarrassment overshadowed U.S.-Persian relations for years thereafter.

Matters quickly escalated, and the Persian government convened a special commission to discuss the incident. At the commission's first meeting, the U.S. *chargé* in Tehran, John Tyler, became so angry that he kicked over the table and began screaming in rage. "All the *farmans* [decrees] and stamps and signatures of the Shah and the prime minister aren't worth a cent!" he shouted, as piles of legal documents went flying into the air.

It would be hard to imagine a more diplomatically indelicate turn of events, and in a quiet year, the flagpole incident would unquestionably have turned into a festering source of friction between the Persian and American governments. But perhaps fortunately for both countries, within a matter of weeks, it would be overshadowed by something even more dramatic.

4

The Professionals

ℭℬ ℬ℧

The spring of 1896 should have been a season of celebration for the people of Persia. According to the lunar calendar, May 17 marked the beginning of the fiftieth year of Naser al-Din Shah's reign—the first golden jubilee in Persian history.[*] To celebrate, a full slate of ostentatious festivities had been prepared for the public. There were going to be triumphal processions, symbolic reenactments of the bonds of eternal love between the shah and his loyal subjects. Thousands of people were expected to line the parade route, looking dutifully jubilant in the hot sun, as they cheered and ululated. It was just the kind of boost the shah's ailing kingship needed.

But it was never to be. Naser al-Din's popularity had slipped in recent years, perhaps more than he realized. After half a century of his rule, the vast majority of Persians were still poor, still illiterate, and still at the mercy of wealthy feudal landowners. Persia still lacked a railway network. It lacked its own telegraph lines. It lacked a functioning modern bureaucracy. Worst of all, perhaps, it seemed to lack backbone. The perception was growing that the country's most important assets had been sold off to foreigners, leaving bazaar merchants—Persia's traditional middle class and the engine of its economy—struggling to survive. On the appointed day in May 1896, therefore, the crowds turned out in the streets of Tehran, as instructed, but it was not to celebrate Naser al-Din Shah's golden jubilee. It was to attend his funeral. They came not to praise Caesar but to bury him.

On May 1, just two weeks before the scheduled festivities, the shah had paid a visit to the holy shrine of Abd-el-Azim, a few miles south of Tehran.

---

[*] The last shah to have spent fifty years or more on the throne was Shah Tahmasp (1524–76). But the concept of a jubilee celebration was a newer, Western invention. Naser al-Din Shah almost certainly got the idea from Queen Victoria's golden jubilee in 1887.

As he was walking out of the mosque, a scruffy-looking man approached. In one hand, he held a petition, rolled up and tied with a ribbon. In the other, concealed from view, he held a rusty revolver. As the shah put out his hand to receive the petition, a hail of bullets tore into his ribcage.

The assassination of a head of state always has a destabilizing effect on a nation. But if that head of state happens to be an absolute monarch who has held power for half a century, and who has made no serious attempts to prepare his country for what might happen after his death, then the potential for turmoil is especially high. And so it was in Persia in 1896. The shah's prime minister, Amin os-Soltan, standing near the shah when he was shot, wasted no time. Within seconds, he instructed the military brass to fan out across Tehran with troop reinforcements. Then he bustled the shah's body, still warm and sticky with blood, into the royal carriage and instructed the driver to ride slowly and calmly back to the Golestan Palace as if nothing had happened. As the imperial procession made its way through the streets, Amin os-Soltan propped the shah's lifeless body against his own and maneuvered the arms and head so the shah appeared to be waving and nodding to cheering onlookers. "Long live the shah!" the prime minister could hear people shouting from rooftops and balconies, as he sweated and strained under the weight of the royal corpse.

By the time the shah, or what was left of him, reached Tehran, his assassin had been apprehended and was being closely interrogated. Mirza Reza Kermani, it quickly became clear, was not simply a deranged gunman acting on his own. He was a devout follower of the influential religious scholar Jamal al-Din Afghani, who had been exiled in 1890 after preaching against the shah's inability to stand up to European powers. When asked why he had killed the shah, he replied by quoting a verse from the poet Rumi: "The fish begins to stink at the head, not the tail." He continued: "I have rendered a service to all creatures and to the nation and the state alike. I have watered this seed, and it is beginning to sprout. All men were asleep, and they are now awakening."

Nothing like this had been heard before. For centuries—millennia, in fact—Persian kings had been slaughtered by foreign invaders, fallen victim to rival claimants to the throne, or simply succumbed to old age and infirmity. Never had an ordinary Persian subject decided to express his frustrations with the direction the country was going in by walking up to the shah and pumping him full of bullets.

But Persia in the 1890s was a very different country from the one it had been even a generation earlier. In 1891 thousands had rebelled publicly against the shah's awarding of a tobacco monopoly to a British company. And since then something had shifted. Mosques and bazaars had become

Funeral of Naser al-Din Shah (May 1896): The assassination of the shah ushered in a volatile three decades in Persian politics but also gradually strengthened and professionalized U.S.-Persian relations.

corridors of opposition, full of aromatic talk about the shah's shortcomings. Between the prattle of merchants and the lamentations of ayatollahs could be heard sly allusions to his greed and debauchery, his failure to protect Persian sovereignty against European encroachments, and the climate of corruption and avarice at the imperial court. Over bubbling hookahs and steaming trays of tea, a new generation of Persian intellectuals were buzzing with ideas—ideas with big, European-sounding names: *Nasionalizm. Liberalizm. Sosializm.* Some even talked of imposing constitutional limits on the powers of the Peacock Throne. Perhaps most important, religious leaders, long quiescent, now filled their Friday sermons with words like *tyranny, autocracy,* and *corruption* and made pointed comparisons to the government of justice and humanity that the Prophet Muhammad had established in Medina. And why, the preachers frequently asked, were Persia's greatest assets in the hands of infidels?

Idealists and intellectuals, merchants and mullahs, romantics and radicals—it was an intoxicating combination of forces. All were slowly coming together to call for a new Persia: a Persia strong and sovereign, standing on its own feet without foreign interference. This unlikely alliance of religious leaders, merchants, and reformist intellectuals proved to be a powerful force that would rear its head many times over the next several generations. In the 1890s it resulted in a nationwide tobacco rebellion and the shah's assassination. A decade later it would produce a constitutional revolution.

In the 1950s, an international standoff over oil. And in 1979, it would bring the entire rotting edifice of Persian monarchy crashing to the ground.

☙

But that was far in the future. In 1896, Mirza Reza Kermani's assassination of the shah accomplished precisely nothing. Naser al-Din was succeeded by his son Muzaffar al-Din, who simply turned out to be a weaker and sicklier version of his father. And the walking carcass of the Persian Empire simply staggered on, feebler and more susceptible to the machinations of foreign powers than ever.

Already forty-three years old and suffering from failing kidneys and a bad heart when he ascended to the Peacock Throne, Muzaffar al-Din had spent his entire life waiting for the chance to be shah, and it showed. In his thirty-four years as crown prince, he had gradually grown to resent his father, and in later years the two men had barely spoken. As a result, Muzaffar al-Din was in the dark about what to expect when he became king. During his time as governor-general of the northwestern city of Tabriz, he had accumulated a retinue of useless, self-serving hangers-on who knew nothing of political life in Tehran and were focused entirely on padding their own purses. Muzaffar al-Din was also deeply superstitious and terrified of thunderstorms. As he rotted in splendid isolation, he surrounded himself with an ever-growing number of astrologers and mystics who helped him interpret "prophetic" weather patterns. Childlike, fascinated by newfangled gadgets, he loved nothing more than playing with guns. Of politics he knew less than nothing. So when the sudden news of his father's assassination reached him in Tabriz, he picked up and moved to Tehran with his bottom-feeders and his yes-men, his stargazers and his soothsayers, in tow. It was not an auspicious beginning.

In 1900, four years into his reign, the new shah's health was deteriorating, and his doctors recommended a visit to the mineral spas of Europe. He was happy to comply, turning his spa treatment into one of the most outlandish spending sprees the world had ever seen. Before he left for Europe, he borrowed $12 million—roughly $1 billion in today's money—from Russia to finance his trip. As security for the loan, he pledged all of Persia's customs revenue. The following year he made another European trip, and in 1902 a third. By the time he was finished with his travels, Persia owed Russia $20 million, a debt that would balloon in the years after his death.[*]

---

[*] By 1914, Persia's national debt would reach $34 million, and by 1919, $53 million.

Muzaffar al-Din Shah (1896–1907). Presiding over the deterioration of royal authority and absolutism, this shah racked up astronomical debts and left Persia deeply exposed to foreign financial control. His reign culminated in a constitutional revolution and the creation of a national parliament.

Eventually, the Persian government was forced to pledge almost its *entire revenue stream* to Russian banks. When that wasn't enough, the shah was compelled to recruit the Belgian customs official Joseph Naus to bring order to the chaos that was the bureau of customs and excise. Before long Naus and the Belgians were, in effect, running Persia's finance ministry. But even this was not the worst of it. In 1901 the shah became so desperate for cash that for a mere £20,000, he gave a British entrepreneur the right to drill for oil almost anywhere in Persia for the next sixty years—a decision that would haunt Iran for generations. Muzaffar al-Din Shah was in power for only ten years, from 1896 to January 1907. But in this short time, he left Persia with debt almost mathematically impossible for his successors to repay. It was an act of naked transgression against the Persian treasury— the kind of greedy self-gratification that can only be described as fiscal rape.

Yet despite these indiscretions, despite this monstrous irresponsibility, Muzaffar al-Din's reign had another side, one that is not always fully appreciated. For much of his time in power, he was served by remarkably competent, reform-minded ministers, who ushered in important bureaucratic and administrative advances and introduced a measure of efficiency and

professionalism into the Persian civil service. This atmosphere extended to
the Foreign Ministry, run by the talented Moshir od-Dowleh. And this, in
turn, meant that, for the first time in years, Persia was able to devote serious,
sustained attention to its relationship with the United States.

☙

In December 1900, after a hiatus of more than eleven years, a new Persian minister arrived in Washington—General Izhaq Khan Moffakham
od-Dowleh—with clear instructions to promote and regulate U.S.-Persian
trade. His appointment was long overdue. Within a few weeks of his arrival,
he received more than two hundred expressions of interest from American
businesses eager to trade with Persia. In response to this surge in interest, Tehran instructed Izhaq to establish consulates in every American city
where there appeared to be a demand for Persian merchandise or an interest
in Persian markets among the business community.

In 1901 the Persian community in the United States was virtually nonexistent, so Izhaq turned mostly to Armenian Ottoman émigrés to staff these
new consulates. In 1902 Dikran Kelekian, an antiques trader from Turkey
who had been living in New York for nine years and had supplied many
of the wares displayed at the 1893 Chicago World's Fair, turned his Fifth
Avenue art gallery into the "Imperial Consulate of Persia in New York."
The following year another Armenian, Haig Herant Pakradooni, was made
Persian consul in Philadelphia. And Alfonso Rutis, a Brazilian rug trader
based in New Jersey, became consul-general for New Jersey and Pennsylvania. The year after that, yet another Armenian rug trader from Istanbul,
Milton Seropyan, was made Persian consul in St. Louis. None of these men
had ever set foot in Persia, and it is unlikely they spoke a word of Persian.
But they all had a clear commercial interest in improving U.S.-Persian ties,
and they represented the first serious expansion of Persian commercial activity in the United States.

Not by coincidence, the rug trade played a central role in all this. At
the turn of the century, the United States had become the world's undisputed economic powerhouse, and the volume of merchandise passing back
and forth between the United States and Persia was growing—much of
it related to the trade in antique carpets. By the 1890s, Persian rugs had
become a must-have accessory in the Gilded Age mansions sprouting along
Fifth Avenue in Manhattan and in Newport, Rhode Island. The wealthiest
Americans, eager to emulate the houses of European aristocrats, deemed
an antique Persian rug in the home essential—and a growing industry of
experts were dedicated to helping them purchase such rugs.

Under Izhaq, Persia's diplomatic representation in the United States began to resemble an international business network of rug traders, art dealers, and industrialists with big ideas. Izhaq's cousin, Morteza Khan, director of the newly established Bureau of American Affairs at the Foreign Ministry in Tehran, supported this vision for expanding and professionalizing the Persian presence in America. Together Izhaq and Morteza presided over a sweeping expansion of diplomatic activity not just in the United States but throughout the Americas, including Argentina, Colombia, Haiti, and Uruguay. In 1904, when Izhaq returned to Tehran, Morteza—the logical choice—replaced him as minister to Washington.

Between them, Izhaq and Morteza achieved great success in their efforts to increase Persia's profile in America, to the point where they frequently featured in the gossip pages of American newspapers. Suave, sophisticated characters who charmed much of official Washington and the American public with their cosmopolitan manners and lavish embassy soirees, they were portrayed as exotic, eligible, and fabulously wealthy Persian playboys. "A Multi-Millionaire from the Land of Omar Khayyam," *The New York Times* called Morteza, six foot four and one of the wealthiest men in all Persia. Izhaq, meanwhile, was "a man of imposing presence, tall, athletic and of rather handsome features. He is unmarried and travels alone."

Away from the media spotlight, one of Izhaq's most concrete achievements was securing his country's participation in the St. Louis World's Fair of 1904. In Tehran, memories of the 1893 Chicago belly-dancing scandal were still fresh, and Muzaffar al-Din Shah was said to be reluctant to participate in the St. Louis fair at all. But Izhaq reported to the shah (probably with great exaggeration) that he had struck up a friendship with Theodore Roosevelt, and that the president was considering personally inviting the shah to St. Louis. Fearing that it might be rude to refuse to participate at all, the Persian government quickly agreed to have a pavilion constructed in St. Louis, with Dikran Kelekian acting as commissioner. To demonstrate his goodwill, the shah even sent his prime minister, Amin os-Soltan, to St. Louis—the highest-ranking Persian official to have visited the United States until that point.

For Persia, the event was a tremendous success, drowning out any lingering embarrassment about Chicago. Visitors widely admired an enormous hand-woven Persian rug, valued at $17,500. Newspapers cooed over the Persian "fire-dancers" and "snake-charmers" on offer at the Persian pavilion. And a merchant selling Persian *zulbia* (a sort of sweet latticed pastry) made a historic contribution to American popular culture when he wrapped one of his concoctions around a scoop of ice cream, thus introducing Americans to the concept of the waffle cone.

Despite the infantilism and ignorance of Muzaffar al-Din Shah, a climate of professionalism and competence was creeping into the management of U.S.-Persian relations. New consulates were opening, trade relations were improving, and perhaps most important, legations were being staffed by people who seemed to have some idea what they were doing. But diplomacy was about a lot more than carpets and waffle cones. These were volatile times in Persia, and officials in both capitals would soon find themselves forced to deal with serious issues of international relations—occasionally even matters of life and death. No one knew it at the time—not the missionaries, not the diplomats, not even the shah (perhaps least of all the shah)—but Persia in 1905 was on the verge of a revolution. It was a revolution that had been brewing for years, since at least the accession of Muzaffar al-Din Shah to the throne a decade earlier, and it was being driven in large part by reformist newspapers that were feeling more and more emboldened about making direct criticisms of the government. An extraordinary transformation had taken place in the ten years of Muzaffar al-Din Shah's reign. In 1896, Persia had been an absolute monarchy, in which dissent was heard only in whispers. In 1905, it was still an absolute monarchy, but now the sound of dissent was deafening.

Over the next five years, Persia—the land of Cyrus and Darius, the ancient empire that had known only centuries of kingship, autocracy, and aristocracy—experienced its first truly popular uprising. Known in Persian as the Mashruteh, and in English as the Constitutional Revolution, the years from 1906 to 1911 were a period of great ferment and turmoil. There would be coups and confrontations, sieges and surrenders, riots and running battles, all fought in the name of bringing the king down to size and subjecting him to the legal framework of a written constitution.

The trouble began in December 1905, when the governor of Tehran accused sugar merchants of profiteering and had two of them publicly whipped to set an example. For the bazaar community, long a bastion of conservatism and respect for the traditional order, this was an outrageous provocation. Pouring into the square in front of the city's main mosque to demonstrate support for the merchants, they were joined within hours by several hundred respected clerics. The country's economy quickly ground to a standstill.

The shah's government forcibly dispersed the protesters, but within hours the crowd recongregated—larger and angrier—five miles south of

Tehran, at the more spacious shrine of Abd-el-Azim. The sit-in (a traditional form of protest known as a *bast*) lasted a month, during which time the bazaar remained closed, and basic staples such as rice and sugar began to run in seriously short supply. Desperate to end what amounted to a national strike, the shah finally relented and agreed to the protesters' demands—which included, unusually, a representative assembly to air their grievances. The protesters dispersed, but in the first months of 1906, it gradually became obvious the shah was in no rush to implement his promise. His health was deteriorating, and he was rarely seen in public anymore.

In the summer of 1906, the grumbling grew loud again. Prominent clerics angrily denounced the government from their pulpits. Newspapers—now less inhibited about criticizing the country's rulers—sprouted on street corners faster than they could be shut down. Then one day the unthinkable happened. During a protest over the government's handling of religious affairs, the shah's troops opened fire and killed twenty-two demonstrators. The first of these victims was wearing a black turban, meaning he was a *seyyed*—a direct descendant of the Prophet Muhammad. And as he lay bleeding on the ground, he clutched a Quran in his hand.

Tehran erupted. Crowds of mourners, beside themselves with grief, carried the young man's body through the streets, venting their anger at the callousness of the government. Thousands of clerics marched fifty miles south to Qom—then as now, the center of Islamic learning in Persia—and staged another *bast*. Meanwhile, in the well-heeled northern suburbs, an even more dramatic demonstration took place at the British legation's summer residence in Qolhak. The British, sympathetic to the demonstrators' concerns, allowed the protest to go ahead, and within hours word spread through Tehran. First hundreds, then thousands walked up the hill to Qolhak, and before long, merchants, clerics and people from all walks of life were congregating on the premises. Within a few days, fourteen thousand people were crowded into the legation gardens, all sitting cross-legged and refusing to move. Protesters repeated earlier calls for a representative assembly but now broadened this demand to include more than just the interests of clerical and merchant classes. At Qolhak in July 1906, fourteen thousand people demanded something that had never been demanded in Persia: a Majles, or national parliament.

This time the shah had no choice but to give in. On August 5 he issued a royal proclamation promising a parliament, and by October elections for the first Majles, consisting of 156 deputies, had been duly initiated. A complicated system of electors and delegates was set up—one that unfolded over several weeks and ultimately resulted in a mix of clerics and guild representatives.

It was a scruffy and demotic bunch. Virtually absent were the wealthy landowners who for centuries had dominated Persia's quasi-feudal political culture. The Majles was, by any standard, a house of commons rather than a house of lords. One wealthy Boston blueblood living in Tehran recoiled in horror at the shameless mingling of classes. "Persia is in a very trying phase," she wrote to her family. "At the Assembly a Prince of the highest family sits next a Mahometan soap-boiler, for example—one, cultivated, the other absolutely ignorant. . . . Oh! The contrast is complete, the two sets of brains at exact antipodes."

Persia had managed to put together a legislative assembly so rudely representative, so shamelessly democratic, that it made even Americans queasy. This was a genuine revolution: popular, vernacular, and raw, with all the messiness and unpredictability that the ruling classes abhorred. And perhaps most important, it had taken place with very little bloodshed. Nothing like this had ever been seen anywhere in Asia.

But there was a larger accomplishment as well—one that might come

Protesters demanding limitations in royal powers and the
introduction of a representative assembly, 1906.

as a surprise to modern-day readers accustomed to hearing about benighted and backward religious thinking in the Middle East. In Persia, it was the clerics—the ayatollahs, the *mujtahids,* the seminary scholars, and the everyday village preachers—who were at the forefront of the movement for constitutional rights and liberties. This, again, was a phenomenon with almost no precedent in history. In Western revolutions—the French and Russian ones, most famously—the priesthood had been on the side of the king and the forces of conservatism. Here, however, they had risen up and demanded—in the name of Allah, the Quran, and the martyrdom of Hussein—that the rights of the people be respected. They made it clear that as men of God, they stood on the side of progress, democracy, and national independence—joining with merchants, students, intellectuals, and modernizers to lend the Constitutional Revolution an air of godly legitimacy that no one could argue with.

In Persia, in other words, the world's first Muslim democracy had been born.

☙

The first order of business for the new Majles was to write and approve a constitution. Over the course of several weeks in the autumn of 1906, the deputies hammered out a document that was remarkably progressive for its day. It enshrined concepts of equality, personal rights, and freedom of the press—even universal public education. It described the shah as "under the rule of law" and his crown as a "gift given to him by the people." At the same time, though, in a nod to tradition, it created a council of five clerics, to be convened from among the country's most respected ayatollahs, with the power to determine whether laws passed by the Majles were in accordance with Islamic precepts.* The constitution also required the shah to seek the approval of the Majles before applying for foreign loans or signing treaties with foreign powers. For the constitutionalists, these points were all critical. What has so often been described by scholars as a "constitutional revolution" was also a religious revolution and a nationalist revolution.

In October 1906 the shah, now barely able to move without help, was presented with the draft constitution. He delayed and ducked, hoping the issue would somehow disappear. But he was badly out of step with the

---

* The Guardian Council of legal and religious scholars, created by the Islamic Republic in 1979, is often depicted as an alien and theocratic invention, but it was in fact a long-overdue implementation of this constitutional clause.

times, and eventually he saw that he had no choice. On December 31, 1906, he ran his pudgy and gangrenous fingers over the document and placed his signature in the margin, giving Persia its first constitution.

Five days later he was dead.

⚬⚭

There was something bitterly poetic about the image of Muzaffar al-Din Shah's bloated carcass being propped up in bed just long enough to sign the death warrant on a century of Qajar despotism. But the poetry was quickly displaced by the prosaic realities of Persian politics. The shah's successor, his son Mohammad Ali, was an unreconstructed tyrant who hated everything the Constitutional Revolution stood for. He was also closely allied to Russia, which was implacably opposed to the revolution and preferred to nudge Mohammad Ali Shah back in the direction of a clientist relationship. In the first year of his reign, Mohammad Ali Shah reluctantly tolerated the Majles. But in early 1907, after the Majles rejected, much to everyone's surprise, a new British-Russian loan of £400,000, tensions rose. In February it went one step further: it gave the hated Belgian customs officials their marching orders and passed a law establishing an independent National Bank of Persia. In all these actions, the Majles was reflecting the popular mood on the street—a mood sick to death of watching Persian officials take their orders from foreign powers. The new shah, by contrast, continued to defend the old order, doing everything he could to weaken the power of parliament so he could continue to enjoy loans from Russia. The battle lines were being drawn.

On August 31, 1907, a political bombshell exploded across Tehran. Britain and Russia announced an agreement to cooperate against the influence of German power encroaching in Europe—and in the process, to end their century-old rivalry over Persia.* In southern Persia, including the Gulf coast and the border with India, Russia agreed not to pursue commercial or other concessions, giving Britain free rein to consolidate its interests. In northern Persia, including Tehran and most of the important cities, Britain agreed to give Russia a free hand. Incredibly, neither Britain nor Russia felt it necessary to inform the Persian government that its country was being, in effect, partitioned into zones of foreign domination. Not even the shah was told.

When news of the Anglo-Russian agreement leaked out in Tehran, it caused an enormous uproar. Reformist newspapers condemned it, calling

---

* The agreement is commonly taught to Western students of history as the third leg of the Triple Entente.

it "the end of Persia's independence and autonomy." On the floor of the Majles, elected representatives, instantly radicalized, used their new roles to give voice to the anger of the Persian public. The shah and his government, by contrast, seemed more interested in preserving their relations with Russia.

A serious rift was clearly opening between king and parliament. Over the course of the next several months, the shah's patience with the rambunctious Majles wore thin, and the dispute escalated into a full-scale standoff. In September the Majles accused several cabinet ministers of being British agents and demanded their resignation. In October and November clerics denounced the shah openly from their pulpits, and newspapers blasted him as "the King of tyrants and the Chief of traitors"—a man whose government was selling Persia "piecemeal to foreigners." In December the shah attempted to instigate a coup against the Majles, hiring bands of street thugs to stir up disorder outside the parliament building. In February 1908 the conflict took on a more dangerous dimension after a bomb was thrown at the shah's car. In June the shah launched a full-scale crackdown, arresting political activists, declaring martial law, and—the ultimate insult—putting all of Tehran under the authority of the hated Cossack brigade, an elite military unit led by the Russian colonel Vladimir Liakhov.

Tensions continued to rise until, on June 23, the shah ordered the Cossacks to firebomb the parliament building. This act precipitated an eight-hour gun battle, during which several prominent constitutionalists were killed.

Persia was now in a state of civil war.

❧

On one side of the conflict were the constitutionalists, who quickly established a stronghold in the northwestern city of Tabriz—a long-standing bastion of leftist radicalism. On the other were the shah and his defenders, supported heavily by Russia. For the remainder of 1908, Tabriz was the scene of bloody battles as the dashing Sattar Khan, a sort of Persian precursor to Che Guevara, rallied the city into volunteer militias and fought off thousands of royalist troops with only a few hundred motivated recruits. The government responded by surrounding and blockading the city, setting in motion one of the most gruesome sieges in Persia's modern history. For a full year, the shah's army starved the city of supplies. Children were seen walking through the streets like living carcasses, their eyes bulging as they fed on grass and leaves.

Eventually, in July 1909, Tabriz relented, and Russian Cossacks came

No. 311 Tauris en révolution — Les volontaires

Civil war: Revolutionaries in Tabriz fight for the new constitution against the return of royal autocracy in 1908–9.

pouring into the city. But the revolutionaries soon regrouped in Gilan, 150 miles to the east, as well as Isfahan, and marched to Tehran. There they overwhelmed the shah who, fearing for his life, took refuge in the Russian legation and later fled to Russia, leaving his eleven-year-old son Ahmad to take over as shah. This, in effect, was a victory for the constitutionalists. A regency government was set up to "guide" the new shah in his decisions, and elections were held for a new Majles. Persia now had only a figurehead monarch.

It was also in Tabriz, on the morning of April 19, 1909, that a twenty-four-year-old American missionary, Howard Baskerville, gave his life for the cause of the Persian revolution. A couple of hours before sunrise that day, Baskerville—who had been working as a schoolteacher in Tabriz—gathered his class of 150 high school students and led them on a slow, muddy crawl to the Qaramelik gardens on the western outskirts of the city. By the time they arrived, all but a handful had abandoned him. But Baskerville, smitten with the cause, was determined to make a stand. Hearing the sound of royalist snipers, he opened fire. For a moment, there was no response, and he stood up—a fateful mistake. The bullet tore through his chest and came out the other side. Within fifteen minutes he was dead.

The official U.S. response to Baskerville's death was tepid: the young man had been warned against getting involved in political activity and was therefore acting alone. Newspapers in the United States dismissed him, cruelly, as a soldier of fortune. But in Tabriz, Baskerville became a hero. Merchants wove a special memorial carpet with a giant portrait of Baskerville in the middle. No less a figure than Sattar Khan sent a telegram to Baskerville's mother in Minnesota, expressing condolence and gratitude and telling her that her son had become, for the Persian freedom movement, "like Lafayette."

Baskerville's funeral was an unforgettable affair. Thousands of grisly fighters turned up to pay their respects, crowding the streets and courtyard around the American Protestant church. Fiery speeches were made, including one that contrasted the heroic Baskerville, who had "freely mingled his blood with our blood for the cause of freedom," with foreign diplomats and missionaries, who were always "sucking the blood of Persia" and "never deigning to help the poor who were dying all round them." One mourner stood and pointed at the U.S. consul, William Doty, shouting that he "could do nothing but stand and hold his hat at the grave."*

In the final analysis, Baskerville's tender young life was lost in vain. His sacrifice made no material difference to the success of the constitutionalist struggle. And in his native country, his story slipped quickly into obscurity. But among the Persian people, the name Baskerville has never been forgotten. In 2004 the Cultural Heritage Organization of Iran chose to honor Baskerville by erecting a large bronze bust in his honor at the Museum of the Constitutional Revolution in Tabriz. A whole room of the museum is dedicated to him, stuffed with mementoes from his time in Persia. And to this day, the label by his bust describes Baskerville as a *shahid* (martyr)—the noblest term that Islam has for a person who gives up their life in the name of a just cause.

---

* Fifty years later, in April 1959, many of these same fighters gathered again to mark the anniversary of Baskerville's death. They were old men now, and many wept openly as they sang old revolutionary songs. But this time, ironically, the memorial service was organized by the U.S. consulate in Tabriz. (David McDowell, note appended to Sarah McDowell, childhood diary.)

The Man from Manila

On March 4, 1909, when the new U.S. president, William Howard Taft, took the oath of office, his inaugural address made no mention of the chaotic situation unfolding in Persia. He made no condemnation of the way the shah had firebombed the parliament building, shut down the constitutional process, and reduced the uncooperative citizens of Tabriz to famine. He expressed no concern for the fact that Persia was sliding into civil war. Even six weeks later, when Baskerville died in battle, Washington issued no official statement, no expression of sympathy, not even condolences to the young man's family.

Many of Persia's constitutionalist revolutionaries regarded the United States as the ultimate embodiment of representative government—a country founded, more than a century earlier, on the principle of opposition to absolute monarchy. So the American refusal to express even vague rhetorical support for their cause came as a disappointment. At the same time, however, America's aloof and neutral posture gave it an irresistible allure. During the last four years of their struggle, Persia's revolutionaries had noticed, the conduct of the United States had been strikingly different from that of the European powers. In 1907 Britain and Russia had taken advantage of Persia's weakness to carve out spheres of influence in its north and south. The United States, by contrast, had maintained its ironclad refusal to become enmeshed in Persia's affairs.

The Anglo-Russian agreement of 1907 had made the need for a "third force" in Persian affairs pressing. In the past, Britain and Russia had always acted as natural counterweights, each power constantly frustrating the ambitions of the other and preventing it from exerting excessive influence. But now, unexpectedly, Britain and Russia were on the same side of the coin—a potential disaster for Persia. With its sphere of influence in the north, Russia in effect controlled 60 percent of Persia's wealth and two-thirds of its population. In the south, Britain controlled access to the Gulf and to India. Even worse, from the perspective of the constitutionalists, Britain—initially sympathetic to the revolution—had abandoned its principled support, in favor of its own concerns. The constitutionalists felt entirely on their own—and in desperate need of allies.

This feeling of desperation led Tehran to make, for the first time in history, a formal request for help from the United States. The second Majles debated the request—its members had been elected in November 1909 following a surge in support for reformist and constitutionalist politicians. And the request met with little opposition. Inside and outside parliament, constitutionalists argued that the United States was a hardworking, efficient country, guided by a strong sense of integrity—and that if Persia wanted to get its house in order, it should employ the independent advice of some good, honest Americans.* "It is well-known," wrote an influential newspaper, that "Americans conduct official business in a straightforward way—free of red tape and obstructionism." The Majles agreed. In September 1910, with the political situation stabilizing and Mohammad Ali Shah safely out of the country, its members voted overwhelmingly to authorize an official request to Washington for an American financial adviser.

But the request went even further. It offered to give sweeping executive and administrative power over the country's finances to a team of American financial experts—in effect, making them high-level employees of the Persian government. Nothing like this had ever been suggested before. The United States had sent financial advisory missions overseas, most notably to China and Mexico. But what the Persians were asking for was different. The Persian *chargé* in Washington, unabashed in his language, even used the word "treasurer-general" during discussions with American officials.

In late December, as the State Department considered the request, President Taft stepped in and recommended a friend of his, thirty-four-year-old W. Morgan Shuster, as a possible candidate: he was a lawyer and a rising star in the Washington political world. Given this personal endorsement by the president, the State Department felt it had little choice but to approve the mission. On February 24, 1911, the assistant secretary of state offered Shuster the job of a lifetime: treasurer-general of Persia.

---

* The second Majles was perhaps the most pro-American in Iranian history. The tone was set on its first day, when the member for Azerbaijan, Taqizadeh, stood up to make an emotional speech in honor of Baskerville.

The State Department made one important proviso, however: Shuster and his team were to see themselves not as representatives of the U.S. government but as private citizens employed by Persia. Shuster and his team were free to go to Tehran, the State Department said, but—short of an immediate danger to their lives—they had to understand they would be entirely on their own once they got there.

❧

That fine-toothed distinction was of little interest to Persia's constitutionalists, who erupted with joy when they heard the news. "The American government is sending us their best people," crowed the reformist papers, "and they are coming with the full support of their government." This, they said, would send a powerful message to Britain and Russia. "They will understand that the United States has influence in our country," wrote one newspaper, "and Iran can begin to feel more secure."

When the new treasurer-general of Persia, along with his four assistants and their families, arrived in Tehran in May 1911, he was mobbed by well-wishers and supporters. Even "before we could unpack a trunk," wrote Shuster in his memoirs, "callers of all kinds began to pour in upon us, and . . . the stream, from early morning till late at night, never seemed to diminish." So highly was the United States regarded in Persia now, and so thoroughly loathed were Britain and Russia, that a thirty-four-year-old American lawyer and his assistants were treated like an army of liberators. "Looking back to that time," wrote Shuster in his memoirs, "I am still unable to imagine what the name 'American' conveyed, or what any American could have previously done, to have excited the interests of the Persian people to the extent which we apparently did."

Many a man his age would have blanched at all the attention. Many would have imploded with self-doubt under the weight of such high expectations. But if anyone had proved, again and again, that he could step into a situation like this and thrive, it was Morgan Shuster. Over six feet tall, with broad shoulders and a serious, intense face, he was every inch the can-do American trailblazer, with a résumé to match. A former cadet corps leader, class president, and captain of the football team, he had graduated at the top of his class at George Washington University before going on to an impressive career as a colonial administrator in America's newly acquired overseas territories. After just two years in Cuba working as a customs collector, he had been transferred to Manila and put in charge of the Philippine customs service—at the age of twenty-four. Six years later he was secretary of public

Treasurer-general of Persia: W. Morgan Shuster. The thirty-four-year-old Washington lawyer was hired by Tehran in 1911 to bring order to the country's finances following the revolution. In the process, he became passionate about the Persian nationalist cause and brazenly resisted Russian interference in the country's affairs. Though he lasted only seven months in the job, he became a hero to Persians as well as a celebrity in the United States. His best-selling book, *The Strangling of Persia,* placed the blame for Persia's problems squarely at the door of British and Russian imperialism.

instruction—overseeing the bureau of education, the prison system, the bureau of printing, the medical college, and eventually the organization of the government university.[*]

Shuster did not disappoint. In his first two weeks in Tehran, he won the respect of his hosts by refusing to pay courtesy calls at the British and Russian legations. He was not a diplomat, he argued, and had not been sent by the U.S. government. He was an employee of the Persian government, and it was up to the British and Russian ministers to come to *his* office if they wished to see him. It was a dangerous way to start, but as a matter of protocol, Shuster was precisely right. More important, he was sending a powerful symbolic message to the country that had just hired him. This kind of muscular rebuff to the imperial powers was something Persians had waited years to see from the United States.

Two weeks later Shuster urged the Majles to give him "full and complete powers in the handling of Persia's finances," and the legislative body, bursting with pro-American sentiment, complied. It was an extraordinary vote of confidence, and Shuster immediately got to work. As it was late June and Tehran's suffocating heat was moving in, the Europeans had all retired to their cool, breezy summer residences in the hills of Shemiran. But Shuster stayed anchored to his desk at the Atabak Palace in central Tehran's

---

[*] In Manila Shuster made the acquaintance of Taft, who at the time was governor-general of the Philippines. The future president was impressed by the young man's energy and competence and largely responsible for his meteoric rise.

sweltering dust bowl. By August, the air was hot and thick with pale yellow dust, so Shuster moved his office to the basement—determined that nothing should distract him from the task of sorting out Persia's finances.

What he found astonished him. "I might say that the Persian finances were tangled," he wrote, "had there been any to tangle." The "so-called Ministry of Finance," he discovered, was "presided over by a succession of Persian gentlemen whose sole claims to financial genius lay in their having run through their own money and thus become in need of pecuniary recuperation." There appeared to be nothing resembling a national budget in written form. Important positions were simply "doled out . . . to those having sufficient family or political influence to obtain them," and since no one knew how long they would keep their jobs, bureaucrats lined their pockets with alacrity. "The general atmosphere of the department," he said, "might be summed up in the time-honored adage, *carpe diem.*"

Worst of all, Shuster said, Persia—which he considered "the oriental center of civilization"—had been reduced to an undignified free-for-all for the worst kinds of parasitic Europeans. "Imagine if you will," he wrote:

> a fast decaying government amid whose tottering ruins a heterogeneous collection of Belgian customs officers, Italian gendarmes, German artillery sergeants, French savants, . . . Austrian military instructors, English bank clerks, Turkish and Armenian courtiers, and last, but not least, a goodly sprinkling of Russian Cossack officers . . . all go through the daily task of giving the Imperial Persian Government a strong shot toward bankruptcy, with a sly side push in the direction of their own particular political or personal interests.

For Shuster, his appointment as treasurer-general was already something much more than just a matter of collecting taxes and centralizing fiscal structures. By introducing a measure of financial stability and integrity to Persia, he increasingly believed, he could protect the country's very independence.

Soon after his arrival, Shuster put together a "treasury gendarmerie"—a police force dedicated to enforcing tax collection—and naïvely decided that a British army major, C. B. Stokes, should be put in charge because he was the best qualified. But the British objected, concerned about upsetting the balance of power with Russia. Since the new gendarmerie's jurisdiction would extend over the entire country—including northern Persia, where the Russians claimed a sphere of influence—Russia might see this as a violation of the 1907 Agreement. To avoid disturbing the equilibrium, Shuster would have to choose a commander from a neutral country. This was how the game was played.

Shuster had put himself in a far more complicated and far more overtly political situation than his job as treasurer-general required, but he was not about to shrink from the fight. Frustrated by the heavy-handed tactics of Britain and Russia, as the summer went on he showed more overt sympathy with the constitutionalist movement. This only made the British and Russian legations more suspicious and more inclined to obstruct his progress. In late July the former shah, Mohammed Ali, sneaked from Russia back into Persia, apparently encountering little resistance from the Russians. The British and Russian legations both declared, ominously, that they would not interfere—in effect, giving the former shah a green light to overturn the victory the constitutionalists had won with such difficulty in 1909. But it was also a subtle hint to Shuster. After all, it was the Majles that had hired him. And if Mohammed Ali could marshal his forces, depose his son Ahmad Shah from the throne, and abolish the Majles again, as he had done in 1908, the first person to be out of a job would be Morgan Shuster.

Shuster's response, characteristically, was to begin organizing a national resistance movement. He persuaded the government to declare Mohammed Ali and his brothers outlaws and place a bounty on their heads. He wired funds to Bakhtiari tribal chiefs in the south and enlisted them in the resistance. He did much the same with Armenian militias in the northwest. He even stashed fifteen hundred rifles and six hundred thousand cartridges in his office at the Atabak Palace. "Firearms," he explained, "have a strange and mysterious way of evaporating in Persia."

Somewhere along the way, Shuster had become much more than treasurer-general. To many in Persia, he was now a leader of the constitutionalist revolution—even, arguably, the last, best hope for Persia's independence in the face of British and Russian aggression. On October 10 he sent his treasury gendarmes to seize property belonging to the former shah's brothers—an unmistakable shot across the bow of the Russian Empire. Thrilled by what they were seeing, lawmakers in the Majles, in a show of solidarity, bravely rallied around Shuster, authorizing him to bring ten more American advisers to Tehran at his earliest convenience.

Russia was stunned by this act of defiance. For decades, the Persian government had behaved as a malleable collection of puppets, easily intimidated or coerced into acting in Russia's interests. But now the script was changing. Persia's elected representatives were rallying behind an idealistic young American and defiantly declaring their independence. Incensed,

St. Petersburg felt it was left with no choice but to respond with a tumescent show of force. In late November, thousands of Russian troops poured into northern Persia, and the Russian minister in Tehran demanded that Majles remove Shuster from his position.

It was an extraordinary response from Russia, demonstrating barefaced disregard for the will of the Persian people.* But even more extraordinary was the show of defiance the Majles put up in response. Rather than crumpling, it asked Russia for a forty-eight-hour window before the ultimatum was enforced. This brief hiatus, the deputies reasoned, would allow them to make an appeal to the court of international public opinion. The Russians agreed to the forty-eight-hour window, and the Majles dashed off a passionate letter to the one institution it thought would be most sympathetic to its plight—the U.S. Congress—asking for its support as a fellow parliamentary body. "You who have tasted the benefits of liberty," the letter asked, "would you witness the fall of any people whose only fault was to sympathize with your system to save its future?"

The document was written in French—a language few in Congress understood—and was received on the floor of the U.S. Capitol with laughter and shrugs. Unfazed, the Persian legation in Washington made several urgent appeals to the State Department, and Shuster himself cabled a hasty op-ed to the *Los Angeles Times*. It was all in vain. The State Department had earlier made clear it could not come to Shuster's aid in any explicitly political matter. And more generally, Washington was not about to lose sleep over the dying breaths of constitutional government in a faraway land like Persia. At its most crucial hour, Persia's plucky little democracy movement reached out to the United States hoping for some expression of solidarity— and received no response.

As the forty-eight-hour grace period ticked away, Russia repeated its ultimatum. And with just one hour to go, Majles deputies piled hurriedly into the parliament building to cast their votes. With the galleries packed and the atmosphere inside and outside the building extremely tense, no one wanted to be the first to speak. What, after all, could be said? The deputies were being asked to ratify their own surrender as a sovereign, constitutional, independent body in the face of a foreign military invasion. Eventually, an elderly cleric stood and made a simple statement: "It may be the will of Allah that our liberty and our sovereignty shall be taken from us by force, but let us not sign them away with our own hands!"

This did the trick. One by one, Majles members stood and made defiant

---

* As part of its ultimatum, Russia even demanded Persia pay an indemnity to cover the cost of the troop movement.

speeches against Russia and in support of Shuster. And by the time it was over, they had unanimously rejected Russia's ultimatum.

In the streets, there was jubilation—along with loud calls for a boycott of Russian goods. For an entire day, the steam locomotive that carried pilgrims to Abd-el-Azim was empty of passengers as rumors spread that it was Russian-owned. (It was actually Belgian.) In the south of Persia, a similar boycott went into effect against British goods. Persian history was entering uncharted waters. As eighteen thousand Russian troops polished their rifles in Gilan and Tabriz, an American citizen stood in naked defiance of the old imperial powers, and the country was rallying behind him.

In mid-December the second wave of American advisers (the ones the Majles had authorized in an act of spite against Russia) began arriving in Tehran—slightly bewildered by what they were walking into. They found Shuster holed up at the Atabak Palace, the mirror behind his desk strafed with bullet holes. The treasurer-general hadn't left the building in thirty days. There had been numerous threats against his life, and when he did eventually leave the palace, it was in the company of 150 bodyguards. This was hardly a salubrious working environment for a group of accountants and pencil-sharpening bookkeepers. Clearly, something would have to give. And that something was not likely to be the Russian Army.

On December 24 the old order reasserted itself. Persian politicians closely allied with Russia staged a violent coup d'état against the Majles. The doors to the parliament building were blocked, Shuster's contract was terminated, and martial law was declared. In northern towns, Russian soldiers campaigning to reassert control went on an orgy of destruction, killing hundreds of women and children. In Tehran, a pliant, pro-Russian government was put in place to guide the thirteen-year-old Ahmad Shah. And it was three more years before another Majles was permitted to sit (by which point it was stacked with deputies in the pay of Britain and Russia). Shuster had come to Persia on a three-year contract but lasted only seven months. His daredevil efforts to protect Persia's integrity and independence had gone down in crashing defeat. So too, it seemed, had the Constitutional Revolution itself.

೦೩

To the thousands of ordinary Persians who had supported the struggle for democracy, Morgan Shuster became a national hero—a resolute defender of Persia's independence against the arrogance of foreign imperialism. When he and his wife left Tehran in January 1912, crowds of cheering supporters surrounded their motorcar, following them all the way to the edge of the city—some even waving American flags. The famed poet Aref Qazvini composed a verse mourning Shuster's departure. There were even reports— hard to confirm—that the chief ayatollah of Isfahan was encouraging his followers to wage jihad on behalf of Shuster. Never before had an American commanded such admiration in Iran, and never would it happen again.

Americans, too, were besotted. Even before Shuster and his team arrived in Tehran, American newspapers had cheered the heroism of the "Five Young Yankees" sailing to the aid of the "ancient but . . . newly awakened monarchy." As the months wore on, magazine after magazine had run feature stories about Shuster's desperate struggles against the European powers and his defiant campaign for Persian independence. Persia, an exotic kingdom that few Americans could locate on a map, was cast as a heroic underdog, fighting the Great Powers with the support of an athletic and unflappable young American. The storyline was irresistible. Americans rallied to the cause of Persia in a way that would have been hard to imagine a few years earlier. In December 1911, as he was trapped in the Atabak Palace, listening to bullets whizzing past the windows, telegrams were pouring in from ordinary Americans, Shuster reported, urging him on to victory. When news of the Russian ultimatum was pasted across American newspapers, the State Department, too, was flooded with letters and petitions—all appealing to President Taft to help poor Persia in its struggle with Russia.

By the time Shuster returned to the United States in February 1912, he had become a national celebrity. In Philadelphia, a stampede broke out as five thousand people surged down Walnut Street toward Witherspoon Hall to hear his first speech on American soil. Police had to be called out to maintain order. The next day, in New York, he spoke at three separate functions in one night at the Waldorf-Astoria. Two days later he packed Carnegie Hall. Within a few months, the speaking tour was followed with a book, *The Strangling of Persia,* in which Shuster shared with Americans "the rapidly shifting scenes attending the downfall of this ancient nation— scenes in which two powerful and presumably enlightened Christian countries played fast and loose with truth, honor, decency and law."

At every appearance along his speaking tour, Shuster attempted to vindicate the decisions he had made as treasurer-general. The young man wowed audiences with breathless narratives about the savage game Britain and Russia were playing. He spoke in long and aromatic phrases about constitutions and capitulations, tsarist armies and bloodcurdling ultimatums. Everyone nodded and tut-tutted and stroked their chins with concern. But let it not be forgotten that Shuster was also thirty-five years old and a former college football-player. As he spoke, no doubt, many in his audiences were at least as captivated by his stage presence as they were by anything he had to say about the Persian treasury or the Russian sphere of influence. He was smooth and convincing, patient and winsome—and not too taxing on the eye. America had found its first celebrity pundit on the Middle East.

What Shuster had done for Persian-American relations was about much more than tax codes and fiscal discipline. He had turned his financial mission into an act of international solidarity. And in the process, he had achieved something more intangible. When he arrived in Tehran in May 1911, Persians and Americans barely knew one another. By the time he left in January 1912, they were full of mutual admiration. Ordinary Persians—though disappointed by the failure of the United States to come to their aid—saw ordinary Americans as people passionately committed to independence, fair play, and democratic principles. Ordinary Americans perceived Persia as a proud and ancient nation struggling to create a democracy in the teeth of European greed and imperialism. For the first time in history, the people of Persia and the United States looked at each other with the mutual respect that so badly eluded later generations.

෮

Over the next several years, in the cultural imagination of Americans, Persia would gradually become something more than a heroic and downtrodden nation in the throes of a constitutional crisis. It would also become sexy. A romantic, poetic energy increasingly surrounded discussions of the country. Every daring young blade who wanted to impress the object of his attentions now would give her a copy of the *Rubaiyat* of Omar Khayyam, with its lusty quatrains about jugs of wine and lovers on secluded riverbanks. At high society functions in 1912 and 1913, "Persian dress" was often the prescribed theme for the evening. For one debutante ball in November 1913, the Waldorf-Astoria in New York was transformed into an elaborate "Persian Garden," as society girls swanned about in "harem skirts" and jeweled tunics, many with "gauzy veils" draped seductively across their adolescent faces.

It would be far too much to give Shuster all the credit for this. American newspapers and magazines had covered Persia's Constitutional Revolution with excitement since its outbreak in early 1906 and generally shown great sympathy for Persia's struggle. In 1908 the influential Philadelphia industrialist W. P. Cresson had published a widely read book, *Persia: The Awakening East,* which provided Americans with a vivid, first-hand account of the dramatic changes he had seen taking place in that far-off land. Cresson's

Persia Season in New York: The Shuster episode ushered in a period of
fascination with Persian fashion, culture, history, and politics before
the First World War. This society ball at the Waldorf-Astoria featured
debutantes in "Persian dress."

writing was heavily excerpted in *National Geographic* and paired with striking photographs depicting thousands of turbaned protesters at the British
legation demanding an elected parliament. In 1908 such arresting images
began percolating into American drawing rooms, and Persian politics was
inching its way into the American psyche.

And it was not just Persian politics. In 1912, when the new General Post
Office Building in New York was searching for a motto to adorn its grandi-

ose columns above Eighth Avenue, it turned to the ancient Greek historian Herodotus, who had written admiringly of the Persian Empire's efficient postal system. "Neither snow nor rain nor heat nor gloom of night stays these couriers from the swift completion of their appointed rounds," reads the inscription that was chiseled above the columns. The empire of Cyrus merged easily with the struggles of the constitutionalists in 1912, making Persia something of a model nation in the minds of Americans.

Between the poetry of Omar Khayyam and the politics of Morgan Shuster, between the romance and sensuality of the Persia brand and the gritty determination of the Constitutional Revolutionaries, Americans had more reasons to love Persia than ever before. But they also, increasingly, were influenced by more than just distant press reports and florid fairy tales. For the first time, they found themselves in the presence of living, breathing Persians. The number of Persians in America was still very small in the early twentieth century, but the streets of Chicago's Near North Side were beginning to fill with people chattering away in a language no one around them

"Neither snow nor rain nor heat nor gloom of night stays these couriers from the swift completion of their appointed rounds": Chiseled on the General Post Office Building in New York in 1912 (the year of Shuster's celebrity tour of the United States), the unofficial motto of the U.S. Postal Service is a reference to the vast, efficient postal service of the ancient Persian Empire.

The first Iranian-Americans: Assyrian immigrants in Chicago, 1903.

had heard before. Persian carpenters, Persian bricklayers, Persian factory workers—people who knew nothing of the splendors of the Qajar court or the intrigues of great powers—were coming to call the United States home.

It is impossible to identify the *very* first Persian-Americans.[*] But in the 1880s and 1890s a trickle of Assyrian Christians from Persia, probably inspired by American missionaries in their midst, had begun arriving. Initially, most were young men pursuing theological studies in American seminaries. In 1905 thirty Assyrian families were living around the intersection of Clark and Huron streets in Chicago. By 1910, Chicago's Assyrian-Persian population numbered over a thousand. It was an active and close-knit Christian community—construction workers, tailors, shopkeepers—with a Persian church and a Persian Sunday school. By 1912, Chicago was even

[*] In the 1860s the Persian globe-trotter Mirza Mohammad Ali Mahallati—better known as Hajj Sayyah—had spent ten years roaming the United States, living for a time in San Francisco. He claimed to have met President Ulysses Grant on several occasions. Hajj Sayyah was so impressed with the American system of government and way of life that he became a naturalized citizen in 1875. He can therefore claim to have been the first recorded Iranian-American in history, but he was a bit of an outlier. Hajj Sayyah returned to Persia in 1877 and got involved with radical antimonarchist activities in the 1890s. He went on to play a significant role in the constitutional revolution. (Ali Ferdowsi, "Hajj Sayyah," *Encyclopaedia Iranica*.)

home to a Persian consulate, run by the manufacturing mogul Richard Crane (great-grandfather of the actor Chevy Chase).*

At a different time and under different circumstances, these budding Persian-American interactions might have acted as a bridge between the two countries, laying the foundations for cultural exchange and understanding. But in the early 1910s a great calamity was about to befall not just Persia and America but virtually every member of the human race—a calamity that would leave little room for friendship and goodwill between nations.

* During the First World War, massacres of Assyrians would force many more families to flee Persia, and by the 1920s Chicago's Assyrian community would be three thousand strong. Some Chicago Assyrians migrated a second time, to the central valley of California, where the climate and geography reminded them of northwestern Persia. By the 1920s, hundreds of Assyrians were living in and around the town of Turlock, California, whose southern suburbs became known as "Little Urmia." Today Turlock is home to some fifteen thousand people of Iranian-Assyrian descent.

War and Peace

⌘

In 1914 war turned Europe into the darkest shade of hell. The world's wealthiest, most powerful continent—the repository of centuries of sophistication and civilization—was engulfed in a conflict of obscene proportions. Nations that had once claimed to have all the answers—sending stiff-collared bureaucrats into deepest Africa to rid the natives of their savagery and barbarism—now stuffed their own teenagers into freezing trenches and told them to throw canisters of phosgene gas at each other. From every corner of their privileged and beautiful palaces, kaisers and kings, prime ministers and emperors, declared they were fighting in the name of something noble and glorious—a "war to end all wars," they called it. They sent 15 million people to their deaths.

Looking at a map of the world, there seems no reason why World War I should have had anything to do with Persia. This was nothing if not a European conflict, born on the streets of Sarajevo and fought in the trenches of Ypres and Flanders Fields. And certainly the Persian government did everything it could to keep it that way. Within the war's first few weeks, Persia officially declared its neutrality, for the benefit of anyone who happened to be listening. But no one was. From the outbreak of European hostilities in 1914 until even after the war ended in 1918, Persia played host to military campaigns and heated clashes between the marauding armies of the Great Powers—all of which seemed oblivious to the idea that there was still such a thing as a Persian government. As the adolescent shah sat on his throne in Tehran, helpless to enforce his own neutrality declaration, Russian, German, British, Ottoman, and French soldiers crisscrossed the open expanses of his dying empire. Persia was the great undeclared battlefield of the Great War.

The Russians were the first to make their presence felt. With several thousand soldiers already fanned out across northern Persia following the Morgan Shuster standoff, Russia saw no reason to withdraw its forces. After the war broke out, these troops clashed with those of the nearby Ottoman Empire, which had joined the conflict on the side of Germany and Austria (against Britain and Russia). The initial Ottoman-Russian battles took place on Ottoman soil, but in the winter of 1914, trouble spilled over the border when the Ottomans invaded Persia and snatched Urmia and Tabriz from Russian hands.

Though the Persian government remained neutral, most Persians sympathized strongly with the Ottomans, largely because they loathed Russia and her new ally Britain and hoped that the Ottoman-German alliance could deliver a decisive defeat to these two long-standing foes. Many Persians also saw the Russian-Ottoman conflict in religious terms, a perception that stemmed from several provocatively anti-Muslim actions Russia had taken during the three years it had occupied northern Persia. In Mashhad, Russian troops had shelled one of the holiest shrines in Shia Islam. In Tabriz and Urmia, Russians had hanged several respected clerics suspected of Ottoman sympathies. Russia had even armed and trained Assyrian Christians, provoking them to go on bloody rampages against Muslim villages, where they massacred hundreds.

The Ottoman occupation of Urmia and Tabriz lasted only five months, but these were months American missionaries would never forget. For their first eighty years in Persia, the missionaries had avoided taking sides in political clashes that did not directly affect them. Now, though, they sided explicitly with the local Christian population—and by extension Russia—against the Ottomans. For many, it was a simple matter of religious loyalty. Just as local Muslims perceived Russia as perpetrating assaults on Islam, Christian missionaries saw the Ottomans and their Kurdish militias as an infidel army that could be stopped only with a righteous "crusade"—a word that increasingly crept into their writings.

Since the United States was officially neutral, the missionaries handed out American flags to local Christians to fly from their houses, as a symbol of neutrality to ward off Ottoman-Kurdish attacks. (The head of the Protestant mission in Urmia, William Shedd, so liberally festooned his street with the Stars and Stripes that his wife thought "the sight was like a Fourth of July.") One Illinois physician, Harry Packard, described by contemporaries as a "big man with a big voice, [who] on horseback . . . looked like a general," rode through local villages waving an enormous American flag, looking for Christians to rescue. For many missionaries, the flag became a symbol of their battle against the forces of Islam—uniting, as one pamphlet put it, "the cause of Christ and the cause of America."

But it did not end there. The Americans also opened the doors of their mission to local Christians who needed to escape the violence—a spontaneous act of religious solidarity that had consequences far wilder than anyone could have predicted. Before the Americans knew it, fifteen thousand Assyrians and Armenians poured into the mission compound, squeezing into whatever nooks and crannies they could find. Hallways, closets, even bathrooms were stuffed with people, "not lying-down but sitting-up." Living in these cramped, unsanitary conditions for several months, three thousand (including several Americans) died of cholera, dysentery, or typhus and were buried in mass graves dug through the snow. But the missionaries did their best to provide food and shelter. It was daring work, but their actions created in the wider community the unpleasant impression that the missionaries were interested in saving only Christian lives. Local Muslims, the majority, deeply resented the special treatment that their Christian neighbors were receiving during a time of hardship.

By mid-1915, Russia was back in control of Persia's north, and for the next two years it carried out brutal campaigns against Muslims, both in Turkey and in Persia. In the eastern Ottoman Empire, overzealous Russian soldiers slaughtered as much as 80 percent of the Kurdish population. Similar atrocities took place in Persia. The months wore on, the seasons changed, the bodies piled up. And over time the cycles of ethnic cleansing seemed never to end. But in the spring of 1917, two events changed the situation dramatically. In March an earth-shattering revolution in Russia brought an end to five hundred years of tsarist rule and would lead, in October, to a seizure of power by the Bolsheviks, a Communist faction dedicated to ending Russia's participation in the Great War.

And in April the United States entered the conflict.

As the Russian revolution unfolded over the course of 1917, Russia's presence in northern Persia disintegrated, leaving a yawning power vacuum and relieving the pressure on the Ottoman Empire. The British, naturally, were eager to fill this vacuum, but since they had no real influence or experience in northern Persia, they approached American missionaries and urged them to arm and organize Assyrian and Armenian militias to fight the Ottomans—picking up where Russia had left off. The United States and Britain were now wartime allies, so it would have been unseemly for the missionaries to refuse. But in reality, they needed little arm-twisting. For Americans in Persia, joining the war effort against the Muslim Ottomans was not just a patriotic duty. It was also a holy war, and one they took up with relish.

In January 1918, William Shedd accepted the position of U.S. consul in Urmia, an unprecedented appointment of an American missionary to an explicitly political role. The star-spangled bullhorn Harry Packard became commander of the armed Assyrian police force—just as religious violence was beginning to spiral out of control. In February, the Kurdish leader Ismail Semitqu assassinated a prominent Assyrian bishop, after which Christian militias went wild, butchering as many as ten thousand Muslims. Few of their friends in the American missionary community protested.

The Americans' complicity in this massacre earned them the lasting hatred of communities where they had lived peacefully for eighty years. The American mission established by Justin Perkins and Asahel Grant in 1834—known to generations of Urmians as a harmless collective of reedy schoolteachers and soft-spoken doctors—was now seen by the region's Muslim majority as a sanctimonious cudgel at the disposal of a Russian-British-Christian axis of evil. Local authorities, concerned that American missionaries were becoming a threat to intercommunal relations, longed to see them gone. They got their wish. In the summer of 1918 the Ottomans pushed into Urmia, rounded up American missionaries, and packed them off to solitary confinement on a garden estate in Tabriz.

About a year after the war ended, Packard would return to Urmia and gingerly attempt to reestablish the American mission, but the results would be disastrous. A severe famine broke out, with hunger so widespread that people were seen eating "dogs, dead animals, grass, and even human beings." Tensions between communities were as high as ever, but Packard appeared to have learned nothing from previous years. One of his first acts upon returning to Urmia was to round up nine hundred Christians and provide them food and water at the mission compound. For the starving residents of Urmia, this was the final straw—a riot broke out. Locals looted the American mission for desperately needed supplies and killed 270 of the Christian refugees inside. The Persian army rescued Packard himself from the mayhem, but not until 1923 would any American dare set foot in Urmia again.

ᙈ

For the Persian government, the real problem during all these years was not war, it was weakness. After Morgan Shuster and the Majles succumbed to the Russian ultimatum in 1911, Persia entered a ten-year period of severe decline—a decade marked by the lowest and most despicable state of subservience to foreign powers in its modern history. The Russian and British spheres of influence solidified, while the central government in Tehran was reduced to irrelevance. A third Majles was elected in 1915, but Russian Cossacks rapidly pressured it out of existence. A defiant rump reconvened in

Qom, fifty miles south of Tehran, and for a while Persia found itself with two governments—neither of which exercised power over anything much at all. The shah and his cabinet became a collection of British marionettes, growing rich on "stipends" that London paid into their personal bank accounts in exchange for political favors. When the money wasn't enough, the British handed out titles and honorary knighthoods—all happily lapped up by politicians. It was a squalid, sordid way to run a country.

Though Americans took far less advantage of Persia than anyone else during the war years, the absence of a strong central authority in Tehran offered them no shortage of opportunities. The U.S. minister in Tehran, John Caldwell—described by contemporaries as a "tactless, untrained blunderer" who would have made "a good grocer but never a diplomat"—quietly supplemented his income by illegally exporting Persian carpets. Another adventurous American, John Merrill, found himself training hundreds of soldiers in the Persian gendarmerie despite the fact that he had flunked out of West Point. This was Persia in the 1910s: a semilawless free-for-all where acres of pelf were available to anyone with the stomach to seek it out.

And the suffering was almost biblical. Urmia—and northwestern Persia generally—saw the worst of the fighting during the war, but hardship and misery were felt nationwide. The presence of foreign troops in Persia meant many more mouths to feed, and when the Russian revolution broke out in 1917, the crisis became a catastrophe. Food imports from the north fell dramatically. Across Persia, bellies distended and rib cages grew more visible. In 1918 and 1919 one hundred thousand people starved to death. Ten thousand villages were deserted as their inhabitants succumbed to famine. In Hamedan and Kermanshah, people were reduced to living in caves, and the traditional carpet-weaving industry of western Persia collapsed entirely. For a country that had asked to play no part in the war, it was quite a punishment. "Persia," said the British minister Harold Nicolson at the close of the conflict, "has been exposed to violations and suffering not endured by any other neutral country."

In the United States, there was genuine concern for the suffering of Persia—but that concern was reserved only for Christian minorities. From 1915 Americans were urged to donate to the American Committee for Relief in the Near East,* an umbrella organization that provided food and humanitarian aid to Christian communities in the region. It raised more than $2 million, but how much went toward relieving suffering is

---

* The name of this organization was originally the American Committee for Armenian and Syrian Relief, but after 1918 it was known as the American Committee for Relief in the Near East, or more commonly, as Near East Relief. The Persian part of the operation was the Persian Relief Committee, under whose auspices the American-Persian Relief Commission was sent to Persia in 1918.

The Great Persian Famine (1917–19): Though Persia was officially
neutral during the First World War, virtually every belligerent
ignored its neutrality declaration, resulting in widespread
suffering. At least 2 million Iranians are believed to have died
of famine and disease as a result of disruptions to supply lines.
Persia attempted to seek reparations at Versailles after the war,
but it was denied a seat at the Peace Conference.

unclear. In 1917 missionaries in Urmia diverted relief money to buy weapons for Assyrian-Armenian militias, and that same year the relief committee fell into a protracted dispute with an Armenian landlord over unpaid
rent. In 1918 the committee sent a high-profile Persian Commission—led
by the president of Columbia University—to Persia. The visit was billed as
a historic event, but the commission sashayed into Persia in a caravan of
brand-new Ford motorcars, and its participants dined at elegant banquets
held in European legations under electric lighting. Such details were kept
well hidden from the American public.

The Persian government, meanwhile, turned repeatedly to the United
States for help, each request more desperate-sounding than the last. Every
time it came up empty-handed. In 1917, the Persian minister in Washington traveled to New York hoping to talk Morgan Shuster into returning
as treasurer-general. But the State Department, which now hated Shuster, torpedoed the idea. The Persians then made several secret requests
to Washington for loans. At one point, the shah even offered to sell the
United States his country's crown jewels, valued at $35 million. Finally

in 1916, fearing for his life, the shah secretly asked the U.S. minister in Tehran if he could take asylum in the American legation. The request—highly unusual from a sitting head of state—was refused. Two months later the shah made an even more outlandish suggestion: Would it be possible, he asked, to fly the Stars and Stripes from the Imperial Palace?

It had come to this. The ShahenShah—the King of Kings and the Shadow of God on Earth; His Majesty as Exalted as the Planet Saturn; the Sovereign to Whom the Sun Serves as a Standard; the Sublime Emperor of all Persia—was now little more than a cowering pubescent wretch, desperate to put himself at the mercy of anyone who might listen. And really, no one was. The request for an American flag was refused, leaving Ahmad Shah to ponder his fate in splendid isolation, surrounded by the dusty chandeliers of his Imperial Palace. The rabble of leeches that made up his government were unable to help. Britain and Russia had licked the country's carcass clean. The American government, as always, was indifferent. Even the saintly American missionaries were now arming Persian Christians for a holy war against Islam. In little over a century, the Qajars had turned Persia into a country on life support.

❧

As the 1910s drew to a close, the mood in all quarters was one of crisis and desperation. Persia was suffering through its worst national emergency since the eighteenth century. The revolutionaries had achieved a written constitution and an elected parliament, but the dream of ridding Persia of foreign interference was further from realization than ever. Across the political spectrum, Persians believed that if their country did not reassert control over its own affairs, it could very well cease to exist as an independent nation. Persia's constitutionalists—who for years had argued that limitations on the shah's powers would inevitably lead to a more robust and independent foreign policy—now realized that the second part of this promise was unfulfilled. Increasingly, therefore, many activists of this generation began referring to themselves not just as constitutionalists but also "nationalists."

Nationalism was hardly a new concept in Persia—its roots went back well into the nineteenth century. But by the late 1910s, nationalism was becoming mainstream—increasingly the defining credo of nearly every segment of Persian political opinion. There were liberal nationalists, conservative nationalists, religious nationalists, socialist nationalists, and many others besides. Persians now saw in grim detail how badly foreign powers had taken advantage of their weakness over the past century, and they were determined to map out a different future. Territorial integrity, an end to capitulations, and a measure of economic independence were all now seen as basic foundations for building a modern state.

During these years Persians heard encouraging noises coming out of the United States. The U.S. president, Woodrow Wilson, appeared to be cut from cloth very different from that of his predecessors. An intellectual, an idealist, and an internationalist, Wilson had in 1916 proclaimed that the era of U.S. isolationism was over, saying America could "no longer indulge [its] traditional provincialism" and should instead "play a leading part in the world drama." He stressed his belief that "the people of small and weak states have the right to be dealt with exactly as the people of big and powerful states." In his Fourteen Points address of January 1918, he outlined a postwar world in which Great Powers would no longer be allowed "private understandings" that divided up weaker states, and imperialism would be a thing of the past. Wilson, many in Persia felt, was speaking directly to them.

The first concern of Persian nationalists was to ensure that their country's interests were adequately represented at the Paris Peace Conference, scheduled to take place in early 1919. Wilson had promised that Paris would lay the foundations for a new, more enlightened global order, in which the rights of all states and peoples were respected—and Persia was eager to make sure it was not left on the sidelines. After all the violations of Persia's boundaries and all the painful effects of war-induced famine and disease, the government believed it was entitled to reparations. It also sought the abolition of capitulations and other unfair treaties that for decades had compromised Persia's economic freedom. Most important of all, though, the Persian government just wanted a seat at the table—a chance to air its grievances publicly before the international community. For a country that had spent the previous century being treated like an oversize doormat, this symbolic recognition was an important first step. If Wilson was serious about self-determination for "the little along with the great and powerful," Persians reasoned, then surely this was their moment.

Not surprisingly perhaps, Britain had other ideas.

⊗

At the end of the First World War, Britain faced an opportunity in Persia that was almost too good to be true. Its great Russian rival, following the Bolshevik Revolution, pledged to become a respectful neighbor to Persia—canceling, in a fit of revolutionary idealism, all treaties, concessions, and unfair trading privileges. Gone, almost overnight, were the decades of capitulations enshrined at Turkmenchai in 1828. Gone were the Russian soldiers in the north and the Russian sphere of influence agreed with Britain in 1907. Russia even canceled, unilaterally, all of Persia's debts. For Persia, this was a welcome breather after decades of tsarist interference. For Britain, however, it was the opportunity of a century: the chance to consolidate its position in Persia once and for all.

As fate would have it, Britain's foreign secretary in 1919 was a man virtually obsessed with Persia. George Curzon, Earl of Keddleston, formerly viceroy of India, had spent a lifetime immersed in Asian affairs, dreaming of the day when British dominance of the continent would be complete. In 1892 he had written *Persia and the Persian Question,* a thirteen-hundred-page collection of observations gleaned during his travels, and he could justifiably claim to know Persia better than any British foreign secretary before him. For Curzon, the importance of Persia was clear: it was nothing less than the key to the security of British India. With the Ottoman Empire defeated in the Great War, Britain was carving out "mandates" for itself in Iraq, Transjordan, and Palestine. Hegemony over Persia could be the final link in an unbroken chain of British influence running from the Mediterranean all the way to India. Curzon's lifelong dream was achingly close to reality.

Curzon was a throwback to a bygone age, a colonial adventurist who had cut his teeth in the days of the Reuter concession and the British tobacco monopoly. To him, the idea of Persia sitting at the table in Paris, publicly airing its grievances like a full-fledged member of the world community, was utter anathema. He instructed the British Foreign Office to do everything possible to prevent it from happening. In Tehran, through the winter of 1918–19, the British legation exerted heavy pressure on the shah and his government, telling them Persia had no reason to seek representation at the conference—Britain could speak on its behalf. In January 1919, just as the conference was about to begin, the British minister in Tehran was even given the green light to "bribe persons whom he thinks worth bribing."

It didn't work this time. In a surprisingly bold act of defiance, Persia sent a team of senior politicians to Paris to press what it believed were legitimate demands. Exasperated, Britain tried to bar the delegation from the conference—a move that provoked irritation from Washington. In April 1919, during a meeting of leaders, Wilson argued that Persia deserved a seat at the table, owing to the unusual amount of devastation it had suffered during the war. Britain's prime minister, David Lloyd George, replied bluntly that his foreign minister "was opposed to the admission of Persia"—without giving a reason. Privately, Wilson felt Britain had failed to absorb the spirit of Paris and was behaving like a schoolyard bully. The world was changing, he believed, and haughty imperialist arrogance no longer had a place. Though Wilson was not about to get into a public disagreement with an ally, behind the scenes, tensions rapidly rose between the United States and Britain over the issue of Persian representation.

In the end, all the maneuvering turned out to be irrelevant. Away from the conference table, unknown to the Americans—and even to much of the Persian government—Britain had opened discussions with the shah and a few of his cronies on a secret parallel track. As early as August 1918, even before the war ended, Britain had pushed the shah to replace his left-leaning prime minister with Vusuq od-Dowleh, a politician seen as more pliable to British interests. The shah had been reluctant, but Britain had offered the king a monthly personal "stipend" of $20,000—payable "for as long as he retains Vusuq-od-dowleh loyally." Desperate for cash, the shah had done as he was asked—then looked the other way as Vusuq proceeded to negotiate a secret agreement with the British. The ensuing document—the Anglo-Persian Agreement of 1919—stipulated that the British government would address all the concerns the Persians had wanted to raise in Paris, but without involving the international community. Britain would help Persia pursue its postwar claims and settle its boundaries. It would also give Persia a $10 million loan to help with its dire cash shortage. In return, Britain would gain the right to send "advisers" to Tehran to run government ministries and control Persia's military and financial affairs. In theory, Persia would get everything it had asked for, but it would give up the lion's share of its sovereignty—becoming, in effect, another piece of Britain's property portfolio in the Middle East.[*]

When the Anglo-Persian Agreement was announced to the public on August 10, 1919, all of Persia exploded in anger. From every *minbar* of every mosque, clerics denounced the historic surrender of Persian sovereignty to infidels. Left-wing democrats and nationalists cranked out furious newspaper editorials blasting the treachery of the government and the craftiness of its British paymasters. Emotional demonstrations broke out across the country. The British protested plaintively that the public misunderstood the agreement, and that Britain was motivated only by a desire to assist Persia back onto its feet. But no one in Persia was buying it. If Britain's intentions were really so altruistic, nationalists asked, why had they felt the need to

---

[*] The British carefully avoided using the word *mandate* during the negotiations, knowing this imperial vocabulary would raise the sanctimonious hackles of the Wilson administration. But in effect, they were offering Persia precisely the same mandate status as that given to the former territories of the Ottoman Empire.

negotiate the Agreement in secret? Why had they had to bribe a handful of aristocrats in order to obtain the shah's signature?*

In the United States as well, the announcement of the agreement was greeted with outrage. The Wilson administration, caught off-guard, felt betrayed—even humiliated—by Britain's barefaced disregard for the principles the president had outlined. Worse, Wilson's Republican opponents seized on the agreement in their attempts to block Senate approval for his proposed League of Nations. The Anglo-Persian Agreement, they said, was proof that the Great Powers could never be trusted and that Wilson had been naïve to think the United States could change the world by introducing a global debating chamber.

Not only had Britain made a mockery of the Fourteen Points—in the middle of the Paris Peace Conference—but it had also added to the president's domestic woes. The Wilson administration was livid. Publicly, the White House was reluctant to criticize Britain—a stance that frustrated Persian nationalists—but privately the Americans were fuming. The U.S. minister in Tehran, John Caldwell, wrote angrily back to Washington about "the manner in which the Anglo-Persian Treaty was consummated, against the wishes of the entire Persian public, and forced on the nation by the most unpopular cabinet, which . . . was placed in power by the British authorities." The secretary of state, Robert Lansing, agreed and began looking for some subtle way for Washington to distance itself from London. Eventually, Lansing asked Caldwell to publish an open letter in the Persian press, making it clear that the United States had done its best to include Persia at the peace conference and had been "surprised" to hear of Britain's secret agreement with Tehran.

It was an extraordinary statement—one of the few times in history that Washington has so publicly criticized its British allies. But what happened next was even more unprecedented. Caldwell—who was even angrier about the Anglo-Persian Agreement than Secretary Lansing—walked through the streets of Tehran with his staff, handing out thousands of typed copies of the State Department's communiqué.

The reaction was beyond anything Caldwell could have expected. Jubilant crowds poured into the streets, celebrating the news that the United States had opposed the Anglo-Persian Agreement. Hundreds flocked to the U.S. legation, seeking "asylum" from their own government—a government they claimed had sold its people into British slavery. Across the

---

* Rumors of a "British bribe" had started percolating through Tehran within hours of the agreement being announced.

country, bazaars closed for days in a show of solidarity with the United States. Tehran, for the first and last time in its history, was the scene of a pro-American riot.

♋

One small detail remained to be worked out before the Anglo-Persian Agreement could go into effect, however. According to the 1906 constitution, Persia could not enter into any foreign treaty without the consent of the Majles. But there had been no sitting Majles since 1915, so ratification had to await a fresh round of elections. And parliamentary elections in Persia were always a lengthy, complicated process, involving a system of electoral colleges, guild meetings, and rural and provincial balloting. They could sometimes take months. And this is where Britain's plans began to unravel.

The British viewed parliamentary ratification as a tedious formality and set about manipulating the election process, distributing bribes and activating secret agents in various parts of the country. By August 1919, when the Anglo-Persian Agreement was announced, half the members of parliament had already been elected, and most were dutiful British surrogates. Britain confidently assumed the remaining deputies could also be easily fixed and took to acting as though the agreement were already in force. A team of British advisers was selected in the autumn of 1919, and in December a British military contingent arrived to reorganize the Persian armed forces, in accordance with the agreement's terms. In the spring of 1920, the British treasury official Sydney Armitage-Smith arrived with a financial team, impatient to take over the Persian treasury.

These high-handed tactics played right into the hands of Persian nationalists. In the remaining weeks of the election campaign, nationalist candidates—benefiting from unprecedented levels of animosity toward Britain—picked up a large number of seats. Minister Caldwell reported to Washington that "not a single Persian who is honest and uninstigated by a hope of reward is found in favor of the treaty." The British minister reported much the same to London, urging Foreign Secretary Curzon to consider a change in tactics. At the very least, he argued, Britain should *appear* to respect the parliamentary process—perhaps by refraining from sending more advisers or by waiting patiently for Majles to make its deliberations. Curzon ordered his underling to keep quiet.

The Anglo-Persian Agreement now faced opposition from Persian popular opinion, from the United States, and even from a vocal group of critics

"These people have got to be taught at whatever cost to them that they cannot get on without us. I don't mind at all their noses being rubbed in the dust." Lord Curzon, British foreign secretary (1919–24). An ardent imperialist, Curzon hoped Persia could be the final link in an unbroken chain of British influence from the Mediterranean to India. Visible U.S. opposition to Britain's plans resulted, in Tehran, in a surge of goodwill toward the United States.

in the British parliament and press. The only ally the British government seemed to have was the docile Persian government it had bought and paid for. But even that proved illusory. In June 1920 the government of Vusuq od-Dowleh collapsed under the weight of its own unpopularity. It was replaced by a more nationalistic government that insisted the Anglo-Persian Agreement could not go into effect until the entire Majles had been elected and had had a chance to debate the issue.

It was now obvious to everyone, except perhaps Curzon, that Britain's attempt to establish hegemony over Persia was on the verge of failure. Astute British officials recognized that their country had badly overplayed its hand—that Britain was now swimming upstream in a momentous current of Persian nationalism, and that its best move would be to work out a hasty exit strategy. Curzon continued to insist it was a simple matter of standing firm. ("These people have got to be taught at whatever cost to them that they cannot get on without us," he later wrote. "I don't at all mind their noses being rubbed in the dust.") But all around him—whether at the Foreign Office in London or the British legation in Tehran—his underlings were telling him that the game was over, that it was time to cut and run.

One such official was Gen. Edmund Ironside—who, since late 1920, had been in charge of Persia's elite Cossack Brigade. Reading the writing on the wall, Ironside argued that the least of all evils, from Britain's perspective, was to get British troops out of Persia and leave behind a strong, centralized Persian state that might prove friendly in the future. He identified a Persian soldier who he felt was especially tough and disciplined—a man by the name of Reza Khan—and placed him in command of the Cossack Brigade. Ironside then informed Reza that if he wished to overthrow the government, Britain would not stand in his way.

Functionally illiterate and bathed in the logic of strength and power, Reza was not about to let this opportunity pass him by. On February 21, 1921, he marched twenty-five hundred Cossack cavalry from their base in Qazvin to Tehran and staged a decisive coup d'état—overthrowing a Persian government that had fallen to such depths of decrepitude that it could probably have been pushed aside with much less. Reza's friend and ally Seyyed Zia Tabatabai became prime minister, and within a few weeks Reza became minister of war.

One of the new government's first actions was to reject the Anglo-Persian Agreement that had been signed by the shah eighteen months earlier. Instead it signed a new Treaty of Friendship with Russia, in which the latter promised to respect Persia's territorial integrity except in cases of immediate threat to Russian security. With these two actions, the new government made the clearest, most powerful statement any Persian government had ever made about the status of the two Great Powers on its territory. It also, in the process, rendered all the machinations and suspense over the parliamentary elections irrelevant. When the fourth Majles finally convened in June, it wasted no time condemning the Anglo-Persian Agreement and praising the new government's decision. But after all the buildup, there was nothing actually left for the Majles to ratify. Reza had already seen to it that the agreement was dead on arrival.

ся

The collapse of tsarist Russia in 1917 had dealt Britain an extraordinary hand. Never before had it found itself in a position to consolidate control over Persia so comprehensively and so unambiguously. Never before had it come so close to fulfilling its ambition to create an unbroken chain of influence from the edges of Europe to the Indian Raj. But by 1921 this historic opportunity had unraveled into an unmitigated foreign policy catastrophe.

Partly, this dismal failure came about because Britain's ambitions ran headfirst into a swelling tide of Persian nationalism. Partly, it was due to the sheer arrogance with which Britain handled the situation. And partly, it was due to the fact that the Russians had set a powerful example—voluntarily renouncing their interests in Persia and demonstrating to the Persian public that a more respectful relationship with the Great Powers was possible. But to a great extent, Britain's failure was also the result of a new tone of respect for the integrity of weaker nations that was emerging from the United States. In Paris, at a crucial moment in history, America had stood up for Persia, in a way that emboldened Persian nationalists to reject the Anglo-Persian Agreement.

Historians will debate which of these several factors ultimately proved decisive, but one thing is clear: in 1921, Persia defiantly pressed the reset button on its relations with the European powers. Though it took Britain and Russia many years to appreciate this fully, the days when an unhealthy, overweight shah could sit languidly on his jewel-encrusted throne and take orders from London and St. Petersburg were over. The new appetite in Persia was for strength, resolve, and backbone. And Reza Khan—with his boxer's jaw, his ramrod posture, his soldier's physique, and his military fatigues— seemed the embodiment of this new attitude. Ordinary Persians saw his meteoric rise to power—from a mid-ranking Cossack officer to minister of war in just a few months—as a potent indication of the kind of leadership he offered.

In a country in which cabinet positions had traditionally been the exclusive preserve of old-line aristocrats with powerful family connections, Reza Khan's achievement was remarkable and unprecedented. But it was nothing compared to what lay ahead for this hard-nosed soldier in the next few years.

PART II

Summer

"The Sordid Side"

In Persia, the long wait appeared to be over. After half a century of coaxing and cajoling from Persian leaders, the United States finally appeared ready to take a greater interest in the country's problems. In Washington, the administration of Woodrow Wilson had made a genuine effort to distance itself from Britain and had demonstrated its solidarity with the Persian people. Even more remarkably, it appeared to have done so out of principled, even altruistic, sympathy for the predicament of weak nations and concern for international peace and justice. But there was a little more to the story than that.

In October 1919, when relations between the United States and Britain were at their tensest, the American minister in London, John Davis, paid a visit to Lord Curzon to discuss the situation in Persia. In calm and sober tones, the two men exchanged their respective views on what had taken place. The American minister claimed that Britain appeared to be seeking hegemony over Persia. Curzon countered that this represented an essential misunderstanding of the situation—that Britain's goals were merely to help Persia stand on its feet. The discussion unfolded along much the same lines as those along which it had unfolded publicly in recent months. But then, unexpectedly, Davis broke from the script and addressed what he believed was the elephant in the room. He suggested that perhaps Britain's true goal was to obtain mastery over the region's considerable petroleum deposits, and even to "discriminate against" American oil companies operating there. To his surprise, Curzon did not dismiss this florid accusation but instead admitted, with typical aristocratic understatement, that perhaps that was "the sordid side of the situation."

It would be easy to read too much into this exchange. When the United States came to the defense of Persia's sovereignty in 1919, it had been motivated by a sincere commitment to Wilsonian principles. The very public spat with Britain was primarily a result of competing visions for how the world should be managed, not a fig-leaf covering some sinister scramble for Persia's oil. At the same time, however, it would be naïve to imagine that the United States, any more than any other country, was oblivious to Persia's potential as a producer of petroleum. These were changing times, after all—a world in which oil would soon be king.

☙

In 1910 the United States had more oil than it knew what to do with. From the foothills of western Pennsylvania to the swampy rivers of East Texas, great rumbling geysers had splattered out oil at the rate of half a million barrels a day, faster than Americans could consume it.[*] But by 1920, that had changed. The war had depleted the world's oil supplies, and America found itself consuming two-thirds of the world's oil but producing only one-seventh. Britain, meanwhile, faced a similar predicament. Traditionally reliant on domestic coal supplies, prewar Britain had found itself in a rapidly accelerating arms race with Germany, both countries pushing to build bigger, bolder, and more modern warships. In 1906 the Royal Navy had unveiled the HMS *Dreadnought,* an eighteen-thousand-ton battleship that revolutionized gunboat design and sent the Germans scrambling to keep up. The drive for speed and power was unrelenting, and Britain would soon have to find a new fuel to power its fleet.

For several years, as luck would have it, an eccentric British-Australian millionaire, William Knox D'Arcy, and his team of mineral geologists had been drilling in southwestern Persia. On May 26, 1908, D'Arcy announced that his men had struck oil. It was a prodigious, spectacular, and unprecedented find, the largest discovery of petroleum the world had ever seen. It was also the first in the history of the Middle East. News that the region might contain enormous reservoirs of petroleum fundamentally altered the way London made decisions. In 1912 the Royal Navy quickly converted its entire fleet from coal to oil. Two years later, when war broke out, the British government purchased a 51 percent stake in D'Arcy's company, now known

---

[*] When it came to controlling global oil supply, America was the Saudi Arabia of the 1910s. Up until the First World War, the United States had sold oil in large quantities to Europe, Asia, and even the Middle East. In 1909 alone, some one thousand cases of American kerosene were sent, of all places, to Persia. During the war, when oil was desperately needed along the front lines, the United States had become an unofficial filling station for the Allies, supplying 80 percent of British, French, and Russian needs.

as the Anglo-Persian Oil Company (APOC). Within just a few years, oil from Persia had become a strategic national asset for the British Empire.

As the war came to a close in 1918, American oil companies began to eye Britain's Persian prize. The British sphere of influence in the south of the country, where D'Arcy had drilling rights, was clearly off limits, but might the north prove lucrative? Britain was busy negotiating the Anglo-Persian Agreement, hoping to gain dominance over *all* of Persia, and it was not about to make room for a bunch of opportunistic American oilmen. In 1920, at the height of the crisis, Lord Curzon warned the government in Tehran that "any attempt to introduce" the American oil industry into Persia "would mean a competition which would be a source of certain trouble in the future and which the British Government could not be expected to regard with any favour." It was no idle threat. Over the next few years, Britain would find a way to block every attempt by American companies to pick up concessions in Persia.

Thus began one of the great unspoken rivalries of the twentieth century: the competition between the United States and Great Britain for Iran's vast petroleum bounty. It was a gentlemanly rivalry, one rarely acknowledged by officials of either power. But it would serve as a backdrop to many of the most important and transformative events in modern Iranian history.

☙

In December 1920, as the streets of Tehran fizzed with anger over the proposed Anglo-Persian Agreement, Arthur Millspaugh, an official at the State Department's office of the foreign trade adviser, received an unexpected visit from the Persian minister to Washington. The minister told Millspaugh that the British held "a whip-hand over the Persian government," but that a generous American loan could quickly change all that. U.S. financial support to Persia would obviate the country's need for money from Britain and place the Majles in a much stronger position to reject the Anglo-Persian Agreement. The Persian minister went even further. Once the British were out of the picture, he said, the path would be wide open for Americans seeking oil concessions in the north of Persia. Millspaugh was intrigued.

Six months later, with a vigorous new government in power in Tehran and the Anglo-Persian Agreement forcefully rejected, the Persians finally seemed in a position to call the shots in their own country. Not surprisingly, an immediate clamor went up to bring back Morgan Shuster. Persian newspapers demanded that the newly assembled fourth Majles make the recall of Shuster one of its first priorities, and there was also talk of employing a dozen American agricultural advisers. For the United States, it was a historic opportunity, its first real chance to gain a foothold in Persian affairs. The U.S. *chargé* in Tehran, Cornelius Engert, communicated the urgency of the situation to his bosses at the State Department. "The present would . . . seem to be a particularly favorable moment for some American company to apply for oil concession in North Persia," he wrote to Washington. "No time should be lost if we intend to participate in Persia's economic development."

To indicate just how serious it was about cementing a new relationship with the United States, the Persian government in July 1921 appointed an energetic new minister to Washington, Hossein Ala. Forty-three years old, dynamic, experienced, and educated in England—comfortable in the company of Westerners—Ala represented a notable break from the three decades of amateurs who preceded him.[*] And when he arrived in Washington, Ala brought with him a clearly worded set of instructions: (1) get a large-scale loan from the U.S. government; (2) arrange for a new treasurer-general (preferably Morgan Shuster), along with several agricultural advisers; and (3) offer an exploration concession to an American oil company.

It might seem curious that Persia, having fought so hard against the Anglo-Persian Agreement, would be so eager to rush headlong into a similar arrangement with the United States. But it is a testament to how strongly Persian nationalists idealized America that very few in Persia thought to see it that way. In 1921 most Persians took it as a given that the United States was an instinctively anti-imperial power and would never dream of taking advantage of Persia the way the British had. The more important big difference, perhaps, was that Persia was now in control of the process. It would decide when, where, and how foreign advisers would be deployed.[†]

CS

When Ala arrived in Washington in the summer of 1921 to take up his post, he was pleasantly surprised by the warmth of his welcome. American newspapers were gleefully describing Persia as a country that had "miraculously come back to life" under the leadership of Reza Khan. American oil executives and railway magnates were dropping off their business cards at

---

[*] Ala's father had been Persian minister in London, and the young man had spent twelve years at the Foreign Ministry in Tehran before becoming Persia's minister to Spain in 1918.

[†] In nationalist circles in Tehran, a few lonely voices raised concerns about the advisability of a hasty American embrace. One of the loudest belonged to the new finance minister, Mohammad Mosaddeq, who argued that Persia's path to true independence did not lie in hiring yet another team of foreign advisers. Thirty years later history would hear much more from this man, and very much along the same lines. But for the moment, he was overruled.

the Persian legation, hoping for a few minutes of Ala's time. Even middle America, it seemed, was smitten. The big Hollywood film for Christmas 1922 was *Omar the Tentmaker*, a Boris Karloff picture based on the life of Omar Khayyam.

The first Persian minister to be fluent in English, the energetic Ala embarked on an ambitious speaking tour of the United States. In unlikely places like Flint, Michigan, and Fort Wayne, Indiana, curious locals packed into lecture halls to hear about the commercial and cultural opportunities opening up in Persia. At every appearance, Ala, speaking in his cut-glass Oxbridge accent and standing in his crisply tailored suit and neatly trimmed mustache, joked winsomely with his audience that it was time to start thinking of Persia as "much more than just cats and carpets." The catchy line encapsulated perfectly the state of relations between the two countries at that moment. Forty years had passed since the United States and Persia began exchanging diplomats—years marked by a conspicuous absence of serious, sustained engagement. In another forty years, the story would be very different. But for Iran and America, this was a unique moment of curiosity, of budding friendship, and of exploring early opportunities—before the songs of innocence turned into songs of experience. These were the days when everything still seemed possible, and no one yet seemed angry.

The Persian government, for its part, wasted no time in embracing the United States. In November 1921, following a few promising discussions between Ala, Millspaugh, and American oil executives in New York and Washington, the Majles in Tehran voted to offer a northern oil concession to the Standard Oil Company of New Jersey. In the same bill the Majles also made a request for an American financial adviser and a $10 million loan. The clear implication was that if America wanted the oil, it would have to send advisers and cash.

Given the principled moral stand the United States had taken on behalf of Persia in 1919, the Persians hoped that, using oil concessions as bait, they might lure Washington into becoming a more robust, reliable protector of Persian interests against British encroachments. But they misjudged the situation. When push came to shove, Washington's desire to avoid upsetting London far outweighed its commercial or moral inclinations. Just a few weeks after its last meeting with Ala, the State Department informed him rather curtly that the United States was not interested in being a "make-weight" against Britain, and that Persia should consider "some well-thought-out plan of cooperation" for the northern oil concession—the implication being that Britain should be involved. To make matters worse, news leaked that Standard had begun negotiating a fifty-fifty joint venture with the Anglo-Persian Oil Company. Ala was furious. As desperate as

Persia was for the loan, the slightest whiff of British involvement was bound to destroy the deal.

When news reached Tehran that Standard Oil had formed a partnership with APOC, the reaction was swift and furious. The Persian press condemned Standard as a Trojan horse for British influence, and an infuriated Majles passed a resolution making clear that *any* kind of British participation was unacceptable. At this point the Americans began making life unnecessarily complicated for themselves. In March 1922 one of Standard's competitors in the United States, the Sinclair Consolidated Oil Corporation, swooped in with a rival bid. The Persians were bewildered by this turn of events. Still hoping for some kind of American oil deal, the Majles hastily amended its original bill so that every mention of "Standard Oil" now read "Standard Oil *or any other independent American company*"— then waited for a clear signal from the U.S. government about which company had its backing.

The American attachment to principles of free market competition proved fatal. Washington refused to take sides between Sinclair and Standard, and as the squabbling between the two companies intensified and grew more public, the Persians lost patience. The deal was left hanging by a thread.

⅓

In November 1922, hoping to fulfill at least one of Persia's requests, the State Department sent Millspaugh to Tehran to act as financial adviser to the Persian government.[*] Attempting to pick up where Shuster had left off eleven years earlier, Millspaugh began putting the books in order and restructuring Persia's dysfunctional taxation system. But Arthur Millspaugh was no Morgan Shuster. He was every bit as abrasive and headstrong, but he lacked Shuster's burning moral commitment to Persian nationalism. He introduced taxes that hit the poor hard and simultaneously infuriated vested interests and landed aristocrats with his dogged insistence that they pay their share like everybody else. To make matters worse, Millspaugh got into an embarrassing turf battle with the American minister in Tehran, Joseph Kornfeld (who held the distinction of being the first rabbi in history to serve as a U.S. diplomat). Tehran's political circles soon got the impression that

---

[*] The Persians had hoped for Shuster, but the State Department believed Shuster was a troublemaker and ruled out sending him. The assistant secretary of state cautioned in a memo that "it would not help matters to send over a cocky American whose apparent ambition might be to run the whole Persian Government and defy the rest of the world." On the strong anti-Shuster sentiment in the State Department, see Yeselson, *Diplomatic Relations,* pp. 182–83.

Kornfeld favored giving the oil concession to Sinclair, while Millspaugh supported Standard. Since Kornfeld was the official U.S. representative, Persians believed he reflected America's true intentions and assumed Millspaugh was under British influence. Enraged, Millspaugh complained to the State Department that this lack of unity was damaging America's image in Persia. Much to his surprise, the department agreed. Its new director of Near East Affairs, Allen Dulles, took Millspaugh's side against his own employee,[*] saying that Kornfeld "has unfortunately come under the influence of the rabid anti-British element among the Persians."

Divided, dyspeptic, and lacking the clear backing of their own government, American oil companies and U.S. officials in Persia now looked like a sinking boatload of bickering fools. Their weakness was in stark contrast to the strength and decisiveness displayed by the Persian government— specifically, by Reza Khan. Already, in his two short years since becoming minister of war, Reza had developed a reputation as an effective, powerful man of action—a human knuckle-duster, unafraid to crack a few skulls in his drive to deliver results. In October 1923 he had become prime minister. Wasting no time bringing the Standard-Sinclair dispute to a decisive resolution, in December he unilaterally decided in favor of Sinclair.

But Reza's muscular intervention was foiled by bad timing. In January 1924, as the Majles debated ratification of the Sinclair deal, the spectacular Teapot Dome scandal erupted in the United States. Harry Sinclair, the company's founder and chief executive, found himself at the center of a Senate investigation of historic proportions, charged with paying $100,000 in bribes for a Wyoming oil field. Tehran assumed that with its chief executive now disgraced, Sinclair was unlikely to secure the promised $10 million loan from the U.S. government—an essential part of the deal for the Persians. Already irritated with Standard for its secret dealings with the British, the Tehran press now grew hostile to Sinclair as well—and, increasingly, to the United States in general. It was hard, in 1924, to see how things could get much worse for Americans in Persia. But they did.

On July 18, a mob of frenzied religious pilgrims beat to death Robert Imbrie, a midcareer U.S. consul on temporary assignment in Tehran. They had mistaken his identity. The Persian government "expressed its profound sorrow" and convened a special military tribunal to prosecute three teenagers who had incited the mob. It agreed to a U.S. government demand for a $60,000 indemnity for Imbrie's widow and $110,000 to cover the cost of sending a U.S. Navy warship to Bushehr to bring back the consul's body,

---

[*] Millspaugh, technically, was an employee not of the State Department but of the Persian government.

along with a full military salute for the ship. In November 1924, all three boys were shot to death in front of the U.S. *chargé*, Wallace Murray. The government initially had tried to commute the sentences of the two youngest—a seventeen-year-old *seyyed* and a fourteen-year-old camel driver—to life in prison, but the Americans protested in the strongest terms. (An internal State Department memo argued that it did not matter how young the boys were because "human life as such is not greatly valued by orientals.")

In the United States, Harry Sinclair quickly used the Imbrie incident to claim that Persia was a dangerous place to do business and backed out of the oil concession. But in reality, this was a face-saving measure. Sinclair had enough troubles to deal with at home, and besides, over the course of 1924, vast new oil fields had been discovered in Texas and California, and the price of oil had plummeted. For American oil companies, foreign exploration was no longer as urgent a priority, or as lucrative a proposition, as it had been three years earlier. The window had closed.

In 1921 the United States—vastly popular in Persia—had had an extraordinary opportunity to break Britain's burgeoning monopoly on Middle Eastern oil and to gain permanent influence in a country that would one day prove vitally important to American interests. Instead, its first serious attempt to secure a foothold in Persia fizzled out in a messy ganglion of competing interests, petty personality squabbles, lack of clear leadership, and British intrigue. At the end of it all, in 1924, Persia's oil was still entirely in British hands, and it would remain that way for another thirty years. America had bungled its moment, every bit as badly as Britain had a few years earlier.

The Warrior-King

As American business struggled to establish a foothold in Persia, Reza continued to consolidate his power. Already prime minister, he now set his sights on an even more ambitious target: total control of Persia. In November 1923 he persuaded the overweight Ahmad Shah to take an extended trip to Europe—ostensibly to recover his health—then assumed day-to-day control over almost all matters of government. Over the next several months, as the twenty-five-year-old shah experimented with crash diets in distant European spa towns, it became obvious to everyone who was really running the country. Toward the end of 1925, Ahmad Shah—perhaps aware that to his subjects he was becoming little more than a face on a postage stamp—sent word of his plans to return to Tehran. But it was not going to be so simple. In his absence, Reza had bullied every newspaper editor into running articles advocating the abolition of the monarchy and the creation of a modern republic.

This idea proved a little too radical for most Persians, who were still mostly attached to the traditional symbolism of the ancient kingship. Many also worried that a republic might pave the way for a secular dictatorship. However, it was also clear that the Qajar dynasty had outlived its usefulness. After firebombing parliament, besieging Tabriz, running up debts, and generally allowing Persia to become a playground for foreign powers, the royal family had forfeited any right to expect love and obedience from their subjects. Throughout 1924 and 1925 there were loud, open condemnations of Ahmad Shah on the streets of Tehran, as well as in pulpits and the pages of newspapers.

In October 1925 the Majles voted overwhelmingly in favor of a bill to abolish the Qajar dynasty and "entrust the provisional government to the person of Reza Khan." And in early December they went one step further. A constituent assembly was hastily arranged to amend the constitution and bestow the title of "Shah" on Reza and his heirs. The Qajar dynasty was officially declared defunct and replaced with the house of Pahlavi—the new surname chosen by Reza. Ahmad Shah took the hint and remained in France, where he would die a few years later of kidney failure at the age of thirty-two.

There was perhaps no finer metaphor in the course of modern Persian history. For more than a century, the Qajar dynasty had allowed Persia to become the sick man of Asia, a bloated corpse permanently hooked up to a steady intravenous drip of loans and cash infusions from European capitals. Now the dynasty itself finally expired, fittingly enough, on a hospital bed in Paris.

☙

You don't have to be a professional historian to appreciate how profoundly Persia changed when Reza Khan became Reza Shah Pahlavi. All you have to do is look at newsreels from the early 1900s. The last three Qajar shahs all move slowly, regally, ceremoniously, like men who have been bred for kingship (and suffered a lifetime of gout in the process). Reza, by contrast, has a brisk, no-nonsense gait. Slim and stern, he strides around in military khakis, jackboots pulled up to his knees. You can almost hear him shouting "left-right-left" in his head as he walks. In a particularly striking film, on his coronation day in February 1926, Reza marches up to the Peacock Throne and plonks himself down, leaning forward, legs spread. His forearms rest on his thighs, like those of a victorious boxer who can't wait for the post-fight press conference to be over. The man looks out of place, as if he would rather be doing push-ups.

Reza had joined the Cossack Brigade at the age of sixteen and remained a soldier until the day he became shah. For thirty years his life had been dictated by the rhythms of military life, and he never abandoned the belief that discipline and order were the keys to the regeneration of Persia. As shah, he was always up before first light, typically receiving visitors from six a.m. Like a ruthless PE teacher, he scolded his countrymen for allowing laziness to impede their progress. He set up institutions like Boy and Girl Scouts to instill physical fitness, self-sufficiency, and patriotism, and a national conscription law to expand and professionalize the armed forces. By the end of Reza's reign in 1941, Persia's troop numbers would grow from 40,000 to an extraordinary 127,000 (making it one of the world's largest armies on the eve of the Second World War). In the 1920s some 40 percent of the state's budget was spent on defense.

Part drill sergeant, part action figure, Reza hated everything the Qajars had stood for—their idleness, their complacency, their corruption, their cosmopolitan manners, their love of luxury. Most of all, he hated their sense of entitlement. Aloof and intimidating, Reza spoke a crude, rustic form of Persian that embarrassed his cabinet ministers, and he was suspicious of anything that suggested aristocratic privilege—or even comfort. The Imperial Palace was equipped with a magnificent four-poster bed, but he never went near it. For the fifteen years of his rule, His Imperial Majesty slept on the floor.

If there was one thing the new shah was consumed with more than discipline and order, it was modernity. He was determined to drag Persia, kicking and screaming, into the twentieth century. This meant railways. It meant factories. It meant all the chugging, belching machinery of the industrial age. Under Reza Shah, Persia would get its first air force—complete with 154 aircraft by 1936. It got its first Western-style university. A north-south railway was finally completed in 1938. Ten thousand miles of roads were laid out, and motorcars were eagerly shipped in from the United States. The country switched to the metric system. Aristocratic titles were abolished. Foreign visitors were instructed not to take photographs of camels. This was a modern country now, they were told, not some picturesque old ruin.

Strength, modernity, progress: all these, Reza felt, were now within reach—but only if Persia learned to stand on its own feet and stopped begging for scraps at the table of the Great Powers. From the very start of his reign, therefore, he made an effort to purge the nation of foreign influences. In stark contrast to the Qajars who had preceded him, he refused to travel abroad.* He was not interested in junkets to European capitals, and he loathed the pomp and ceremony of state visits. Unusually for a Persian king, he never learned a foreign language, not even a few words of Russian. But far and away the biggest step he took to rid Persia of foreign interference was the abolition, in 1927, of the humiliating gravy train of capitulations that had been set in motion by the Treaty of Turkmenchai in 1828. Soviet Russia had already given up its "extraterritorial privileges." But now Britain, France, Belgium, the United States, and a dozen other nations found themselves stripped of rights they had enjoyed for decades. No longer would cheap foreign goods be allowed to flood into Persia tax free. No longer

---

* The lone exception was a trip he made to Turkey in 1934, to meet his hero, President Mustafa Kemal (known popularly as Atatürk). Following the collapse of the Ottoman Empire, Kemal had revolutionized his country—undertaking massive industrialization, separating religion from government, requiring Turks to wear Western clothes, and "purifying" the Turkish language. Reza was awestruck by Atatürk's transformation of a decadent oriental kingdom into a dynamic new republic and hoped to learn from his example.

The warrior-king: Reza Shah Pahlavi (1926–41) inspecting the ancient ruins of Persepolis. A former Cossack soldier, Reza combined a belief in military order and modernity with a renewed emphasis on Iran's pre-Islamic past. On the right is his eldest son, Mohammad Reza, the future and final shah of Iran.

would foreign nationals enjoy exemptions from Persian law. If a foreigner committed a crime on Persian soil, he would be tried in a Persian court. After ninety-nine years of Persia's cowering servitude, Reza—suddenly, unilaterally, and without discussion or debate—informed the world that the party was over.

Perhaps nothing symbolized Reza's nationalistic political philosophy more than the country's change of name. Iranians had always, in their own language, called their country "Iran." But Europeans had called it "Persia." And while speaking English or French or other languages, Iranians had generally defaulted to this more traditional (if slightly inaccurate) term, either out of a desire to be respectful or simply to be understood. Beginning in 1935, Reza Shah declared that Iran was Iran. This was not just a nationalistic move; it was also a way of emphasizing the nation's Aryan (and thus pre-Islamic) heritage. The decision was enforced in classic Reza style. Foreign capitals were informed that Iran's central post office would begin returning all overseas mail unopened if it was addressed to "Persia."

This obsession with purging foreign influences has often led historians to describe Reza Shah as a brass-knuckled patriot, a nationalist. But *nationalism* is a word that can mean different things to different people. For Reza Shah—unlike for others of his generation—nationalism was not merely an ideology aimed at creating a bit of breathing room from the encroachments of foreign powers. Many Persian politicians had tried to do that before him, and many would try again after him. For Reza, nationalism was about redefining what it meant to be Persian.

Broadly speaking, two distinct forms of nationalism were competing for primacy in Persia in the 1920s. The first, which historians often refer to as "liberal nationalism," was inspired by the principles of the Constitutional Revolution. It upheld democracy, progressive social reforms, and freedom of the press as the best paths to national strength and independence. The other, a more conservative, backward-looking form sometimes described as "revivalist nationalism," had a more fascist, racialist, atavistic quality. It was dedicated to resurrecting Persia's ancient glories, instilling military strength, and making the trains run on time. It focused on discipline and order and on the existence of a glorious, mystical past, before people became lazy and immoral. Reza Shah very much belonged to the second camp.

Under Reza Shah, liberal nationalists would eventually go into hibernation—or, rather, submission. Their newspapers would be shut down, their leaders imprisoned, their rare protests fired on by unflinching Cossacks. Reza Shah's version of Persian nationalism would allow no room for dissenting voices. For all that he accomplished in Iran, he would never make an attempt to be anything other than a tyrant. He was a brute, a bully, and a dictator—a man built of steel and thunder who was most in his element surveying columns of goose-stepping soldiers.

☙

There is perhaps no better way to understand the psychological impact Reza Shah had on his country than to stand, today, on Ferdowsi Avenue in central Tehran, a few yards from the German embassy, and gaze across the street at the headquarters of the National Bank of Iran. An almost perfect replica of the U.S. Federal Reserve Bank building in Washington, this heavy concrete box, with its neoclassical columns and hard modernist angles, is a typical example of 1930s civic architecture. But look more closely, and you begin to understand what modernity really meant to Reza. The four soaring columns that hold up the portico are capped with winged bulls, replicas of the giant capitals at Persepolis. All along the flat roof are stair-step crenellations that, similarly, echo the grand staircase at Persepolis. On either side of the entrance is a huge bas-relief of an ancient imperial soldier. And the most

striking exterior feature is a pair of spreading eagle wings with a human figure in the middle, hovering over the portico. This is a *faravahar,* the ancient
symbol of Zoroastrianism, the religion practiced by Persians before the Arab
invasion of A.D. 633.

For Reza Shah, the National Bank was much more than a building.
It was a message. Since 1889, the British-run Imperial Bank of Persia had
held a monopoly over all aspects of the country's banking. It had printed
money, controlled foreign exchange, and safeguarded government revenues.
But in 1928 Reza Shah declared an end to all that: Persia would have its own
national bank. And to symbolize this change, he commissioned a building that would be a temple of high modernism, all square edges and jack-
hammer attitude. In a country accustomed to turquoise-tiled domes, wispy
minarets, and sublime arches, this severe, blocklike architecture signified
not just strength and progress but also a conclusive break with the lavish
and limp-wristed venality of the Qajar era. And by slapping references to
ancient Persepolis all over the building, Reza turned it into something even
more powerful—a reminder of the age when the Persian Empire ruled over
half the civilized world. For Reza Shah, modernity and progress went hand
in hand with the nation's ancient soul, which he felt had been ignored for
too long. The *faravahar* spreading its wings over the treasure vaults was an
unofficial symbol of the new Persia—potent and proud, ancient and modern, all at the same time.

In contrast, Islam was nowhere to be seen. There were no Quranic
inscriptions on the building, no intricate tilework, no Arabic calligraphy.
Reza was certainly no secularist. Publicly, he projected an image of himself
as a pious Muslim. But he was always a touch embarrassed by Islam—self-
conscious about how the West perceived its traditions and convinced it was
to blame for much of Persia's "backwardness." Islam, Reza felt, was an alien
religion that had been brought to Persia by Arabs thirteen hundred years
earlier and that had held the country back every bit as much as the more
recent European interference. Persia could never achieve true progress until
all foreign influences were removed. And that meant *all* foreign influences.

It was an unprecedented position for a shah to take. For centuries, Persian kings had been known ceremonially as Zilollah—the Shadow of God—
a title that carried with it an expectation that they would respect Islamic
teachings and acknowledge the authority of the clergy. In turn, the clerics
were expected to render unto Caesar and to not get overly involved with
politics, content in the knowledge that they held enormous influence over
people's souls. There had always been tensions, as there have been between
church and state in almost every country on earth. But since the sixteenth
century, when the Safavids made Shia Islam the state religion, Persia's mon-

National Bank of Iran (c. 1930) and Federal Reserve Bank of the United States (1935–37). Built around the same time, the Iranian version adds ancient Persian soldiers to the columns and substitutes the Zoroastrian *faravahar* for the American eagle. The building epitomizes Reza Shah's political philosophy of associating ancient Persian history with modernity and playing down the centuries of Islamic history that had traditionally defined the country. This tendency of the Pahlavi dynasty would contribute in 1979 to the spectacular backlash of the Islamic Revolution.

archs had understood that they were ruling over a country with the Islamic faith at the center of its identity. In 1926 that changed.

With uncompromising, breathtaking, almost manic energy, Reza Shah set about removing all signs of what he called *vahshigari-e Arab*—Arab barbarity—in Persian culture. School textbooks were rewritten to emphasize the nation's ancient history. Money and stamps were printed showing the *faravahar*. Street signs were rewritten to remove all traces of the Arabic language. In 1925 even the Islamic calendar, based on lunar months, was abruptly abolished and replaced with the Zoroastrian solar calendar.*

Reza saw Persia's religious leaders as a rival power base and was determined to reduce them in stature. In 1928 he virtually abolished sharia, reforming the legal code so that clerics could preside only over matters of marriage and divorce. Schools were put under state control, leaving clerics only a handful of religious seminaries to run. Religious leaders who objected were arrested, imprisoned, tortured—sometimes even hanged. One clergyman dared to suggest that the shah's wife was immodestly dressed during her visit to a holy shrine. Reza personally drove to the mosque, marched in without removing his boots (a major sacrilege), and in front of all the congregants, whipped the cleric with his cane. Hell had no fury like a parvenu scorned.

Reza's assault on traditional religious values extended to sumptuary laws as well. In 1928, as part of an effort to encourage Persians to wear more "modern" (i.e., Western) clothing, he rammed a law through the Majles requiring adult males to shave their beards and to replace their traditional *kolah-jobbeh* with European-style suits and front-brimmed caps. From 1936 women were required to remove their traditional Islamic headcoverings and wear European-style hats instead—or simply go bareheaded. A woman who failed to comply would be stopped in the streets by gendarmes and aggressively stripped of her hijab. If she put up resistance, she was beaten or imprisoned. The shah declared January 7 (the anniversary of the new law) a national holiday—"women's emancipation day." But few women felt emancipated.†

In the 1920s and 1930s, resentment of laws of this kind built steadily. But there was little anyone could do. On one occasion in 1935, thousands

---

* Reza enforced this latter change so thoroughly that within a couple of generations, the Muslim calendar was largely forgotten, used only in mosques and religious records. Even after 1979, the newly empowered Islamic revolutionaries did not attempt to return to the Islamic calendar. Iran today continues to use a Zoroastrian calendar.

† Embarrassed at being seen in public unveiled, many women abandoned their studies or gave up their jobs. A law intended to advance women's "progress" thus achieved the opposite effect. The law was repealed in 1941, but by then, a generation of Iranian women had lost the opportunity to become educated or enter the workforce.

took refuge in the holy shrine of Emam Reza in Mashhad to protest the hated intrusions into their personal lives. But when the shah heard what was happening, he ordered troops to storm the sanctuary and open fire on the protesters. Seven hundred people were machine-gunned to death inside the mosque—one of the most gruesome acts of state repression in modern Iranian history.

Reza's assault on Islam and his elevation of ancient Persian history created a deep fracture at the heart of Iranian society—a national schizophrenia that has never fully healed. For centuries, Persians had seen no contradiction between the glorious legacy of Cyrus the Great and the spiritual certainty of Islam. Like modern-day Greeks who embrace Christianity but still take pride in stories about Zeus and Odysseus, Persians had identified happily with both the Islamic and the pre-Islamic facets of their heritage. But Reza was the first shah to tell Persians explicitly that they had to choose one over the other. By equating Islam with backwardness and ancient Persia with modernity and progress, he set in motion an unfortunate polarization that would eventually culminate in a historic backlash. For the sizable minority of European-educated intellectuals who had begun flirting with secularism and blood-and-soil nationalism, Reza's ideology contained an intoxicating message. But for a larger number of Persians, his assault on their beloved religion was a national trauma.

03

For a handful of American archaeologists, meanwhile, it was a career opportunity. Here was a king utterly absorbed with the idea that his nation's ancient soul lay hidden in the mists of time, obscured by centuries of Arabic junk. But Reza was an ignoramus, an unschooled and barely literate man who had only the most tenuous understanding of his nation's past. Before Persia could be made to relive its ancient glories, he would need to find out what exactly those ancient glories were.

In 1922 a group of nationalist intellectuals came together to form the Society for National Heritage, with the goal of laying the groundwork for a National Museum. Reza supported this homegrown effort, but what really piqued his interest was a speech he heard in 1925 by a visiting American art historian, Arthur Upham Pope. "Despite the admixture of other blood," Pope said in his speech, Persians were "still a gifted people." Persia's problem, he explained, was that it had suffered a "disastrous break" in its artistic traditions. The Qajars, especially, had been "an unqualified calamity" for Persian art—monarchs with "no taste." The true spirit and genius of the

Persian people lay in its ancient empire. The ears of the old Cossack pricked up at every word.

Pope had no formal training in archaeology—only a master's degree in philosophy—and a reputation for being self-dramatizing, sanctimonious, and generally impossible to deal with. But he had a way with words and was full of genuine, highly infectious enthusiasm for Persian history. Reza was transfixed by Pope's speech. Within hours of hearing it, he ordered it translated, published, and distributed to schoolteachers all across the country. Pope quickly reinvented himself as an international promoter of Persian heritage. Convincing the Persian government that the upcoming 1926 World's Fair in Philadelphia could become a major showcase, Pope was duly named commissioner of the Persian delegation. He went into overdrive, working for months with a group of big-name international experts—including Laurence Binyon of the British Museum and Gaston Migeon of the Louvre—to put together an exhibit that could give Americans the greatest exposure to Persian history and culture they had ever received.

The experience was full of setbacks and frustrations, and Pope melodramatically complained of frequent attacks of "angina," but his efforts paid off in spectacular style. On the banks of Edgewater Lake in South Philadelphia, a large-scale replica of the great seventeenth-century mosque of Isfahan was erected, complete with a pair of fifteenth-century wooden doors shipped over for the occasion. Pope stuffed it with rugs, tapestries, brasswork, miniatures, ancient manuscripts, and pottery. When space ran out, he arranged for a large exhibition of Persian art at the Pennsylvania Museum in nearby Fairmount Park. The pavilion became one of the highlights of the Fair—winning the gold medal for architecture—and the museum exhibit proved so popular, it was held over into the new year. In barely a year, Arthur Upham Pope had gone from near obscurity to become an unofficial brand ambassador for Persia in the United States. He had given Persia blockbuster appeal among everyday Americans and curated an exhibition that was covered on the front pages of American newspapers.

This was exactly the kind of success-driven attitude Persians had grown to love about Americans. The United States had emerged from the Great War, it seemed, with a sense of can-do enthusiasm and naked ambition, a vertiginous upward ascent that was as exciting for the world to watch as the stock market rallies of the Roaring Twenties. With their newfound fortunes, American millionaires were building museums the size of aircraft hangars and setting up lavish endowments. Those museums needed to be filled, however, and cash alone was not going to do the trick. Just as Persia needed the expertise of American art historians and archaeologists, America's new metropolitan elite needed little chunks of ancient Persia to stroll past and

Helen Keller with Arthur Upham Pope. A tireless promoter of Persian art and archaeology (and himself), Pope played a critical role in developing the visual iconography of the Pahlavi state. In 1927, in part because of Pope's efforts, Iran abruptly abolished a French archaeology monopoly and offered the country's key sites to teams of Americans—ushering in an age of U.S. domination of the Iranian heritage industry.

admire during a Sunday afternoon at the museum. It was a match made in heaven.

In 1927 the Majles abruptly abolished an earlier French archaeology monopoly and offered the country's most promising sites to teams of Americans—ushering in an extraordinary age of American involvement in Persia's budding heritage industry. From 1931 to 1936 the University of Pennsylvania sponsored three digs—at Turang Tappeh, Tappeh Hessar, and Rayy, and New York's Metropolitan Museum undertook excavations at Qasr-e Abu Nasr. Probably the most important work, though, was done by the University of Chicago, which undertook the first-ever aerial reconnaissance of Persia and, from 1931 to 1939, performed the first exhaustive excavation of Persepolis. From a purely political point of view, this was huge. Thanks to the Chicago team, the great city of Persepolis—which had gathered dust for thousands of years—was brought back to life, to be placed at the vanguard of Reza Shah's revitalization of the Persian nation. Americans, intentionally or not, were becoming explicitly associated with the Pahlavi ideology.

☙

In the 1920s, as American archaeologists dug through the ruins of Persepolis, and as American oil companies fantasized about what other riches might lie beneath Persian soil, one group of Americans grew distinctly uneasy about the direction the U.S.-Persian relationship was going in: the Protestant mis-

Robert Dyson of the University of Pennsylvania Museum
with a golden bowl discovered at Hasanlu, 1958. Penn,
along with the University of Chicago and New York's
Metropolitan Museum, would play a leading role in
Iranian archaeology.

sionaries. After nearly a century as America's unofficial ambassadors in Persia, the missionaries were keenly aware that commerce, culture, and industry
were rapidly emerging as the new drivers of the bilateral relationship—and
that their own influence was on the decline. "British and American syndi-
cates are reported to be negotiating with [Persia] for commercial and other
concessions," the ABCFM wrote nervously in its annual report for 1922—
the year Standard Oil and Sinclair were duking it out over access to Persia's oil: "Christian forces must not be less eager to influence her spiritual
life. Until the present, America has been known in . . . Persia as interested
chiefly in philanthropic and religious work. She must not yield leadership
to those whose objective is exploitation and financial gain."

Like all foreigners in Persia, though, American missionaries found
themselves having to adapt rapidly to the nationalistic, authoritarian rule of

Reza Shah. It was not always an easy transition to make. Forced to abandon overt proselytizing, American missionaries shifted their emphasis to education and schooling, hoping to demonstrate to the authorities that they could play a useful role in the modernization of Persia. Mission schools made Christianity a far smaller part of their curricula, stressing instead such practical, "modern" subjects as economics, agriculture, and physiology. The missionary community had great anxiety about moving away from the core biblical curriculum, but missionaries reassured themselves (and their donors back home) that if they could help Reza Shah shape Persia into a modern Western society, its future generations would naturally see the appeal of Christianity and seek it out on their own. It was a much subtler approach to missionary work than Americans had used in the past, emphasizing modernity as a path to Christianity, rather than Christianity as a path to modernity.

This new phase of American missionary activity was epitomized by the Alborz School of Tehran, a legendary private boarding school that flourished in the 1920s and early 1930s under the energetic direction of Samuel Jordan, a six-foot-tall Presbyterian minister from the backwoods of Pennsylvania who has often been described as the "father of modern education in Iran." Alborz was a unique institution. Jordan's educational philosophy stressed hard work, discipline, self-sufficiency, and piety. Dormitories were simple and spare, and students were required to make their own beds and take turns clearing up at the cafeteria—a dash of American egalitarianism that came as a complete shock to the sons of noblemen and princes. Alborz permitted no smoking, no drinking, no swearing, and no breaking of the (Christian) Sabbath.

For much of the 1920s, Reza welcomed the American mission schools, which he felt could play an important role in his modernizing agenda. He saw schools like Alborz as fertile breeding grounds for future leaders who would be able to run government ministries without the assistance of European advisers. And they turned out to do exactly that. For generations, Jordan's school would function as a production line for the bureaucrats and technocrats who steered Iran's transition from a traditional Middle Eastern kingdom to a dynamic modern state. Though it was not often publicized, right up to the time of the 1979 Islamic Revolution, many of Iran's government ministries were stuffed with graduates of Alborz.

The love affair between Reza and the American schools went in both directions. American missionaries were quietly appreciative of the shah's attacks on Islamic clergy and his glorification of pre-Islamic themes—which they hoped would make it easier for Persians to convert to Christianity. Many missionaries even took refuge in an explicitly racialist philosophy

Samuel Jordan, legendary American missionary in Iran. Founder of the Alborz School, later Alborz College of Tehran, the lanky Pennsylvanian presided over the institution from 1898 to 1940, transforming it into a critical breeding ground for generations of Iranian politicians and technocrats. A major thoroughfare named for him in Tehran is still largely (though unofficially) referred to as "Jordan Street."

to justify their approval for Reza's agenda, arguing that, as an Aryan race, Persians needed to rid themselves of the Semitic (i.e., Arab) degeneracy of Islam in order to fulfill their true potential. Islam "is not suited to the Persian character and never was," wrote one American missionary in 1927. "The Persians did not accept Islam of their own choice; it was forced on them at the point of a sword. And they have been trying ever since to get rid of some of its teachings, against which the Aryan mind rebels."

For the first few years of Reza's rule, American missionaries and the new shah seemed to be ideological soulmates, fellow travelers in a campaign to "purify" and modernize the Persian soul. But it would not be long before it became obvious that the marriage was one of convenience. The very idea of foreign-run schools, after all, was logically incompatible with a nationalizing agenda. And American curricula—filled with lessons on civics, democracy, and the history of constitutional government—seemed geared toward creating a generation of future revolutionaries. Never a democrat—neither in rhetoric nor by instinct—Reza feared that Persians who graduated from American schools would eventually demand more rights and liberties and perhaps even form a dangerous fifth column in the heart of the Pahlavi state. From 1927, therefore, the Education Ministry demanded that all foreign-run schools in Persia teach a government curriculum and administer only government-approved proficiency exams. The missionaries vigorously resisted, as it meant they would no longer be able to teach the Bible. But after a little tense wrangling, a compromise was reached, allowing mission schools to teach "ethics," with lesson plans based largely on the Bible. This bought the missionaries a little time, but more such problems would come up over the next few years, and creative solutions could be dreamed up only so many times.

As the Persian government moved toward a complete nationalization of the education system, the very existence of American schools was inevitably called into question. In August 1932, just thirty days before the start of the school year—and just as a fresh crop of American teachers were on their way to Persia—the government announced that all foreign-run primary schools would be shut down and transferred to government administration. There was to be a new national system of public schools, free and open to both sexes. From there, things only went downhill for the missionaries. In 1934, in response to an Assyrian uprising in neighboring Iraq,[*] the Persian government declared that Urmia was "unsafe" for foreigners and ordered the missionaries to sell their properties to the state and disperse to Tehran and other cities. The following year it declared martial law in Urmia and banned

---

[*] With the breakup of the Ottoman Empire, its three easternmost provinces, Baghdad, Basra, and Mosul, had been cobbled together as the semi-independent kingdom of Iraq, under British mandate.

Alborz College in 1930.

all foreigners from entering the city. And there was even more bad news to come. In August 1939 the Iranian government, which had already abolished foreign-run primary schools, announced it was nationalizing all secondary schools as well, including even Alborz. This made it official. A hundred years after it began—one hundred years after the arrival of Justin Perkins and Asahel Grant in the snow-covered foothills of the Zagros Mountains—the American missionary enterprise in Iran came to an end.[*]

⚬

The missionaries were not the only Americans in Persia to feel the winds of change blowing against them. In 1927 the American financial adviser, Arthur Millspaugh, was given his marching orders, following a series of disputes with the Persian government. ("There can't be two shahs in this country," Reza Shah declared as he terminated Millspaugh's contract.) And in January 1930 an American railway construction project ended in disaster after Reza Shah's royal carriage was jolted violently off its tracks on opening day, forcing him to evacuate in the middle of a driving rainstorm. The Persian government ultimately refused to pay the American construction firm, Henry Ulen & Company of Chicago, its last payment of $160,000, and the dispute dragged on for months, as a German company was brought in to finish the work.

By far the worst moment in U.S.-Persian relations, though, came in November 1935, when the Persian minister to Washington, Ghaffar Jalal, was pulled over for speeding in the small town of Elkton, Maryland—precipitating a bizarre sequence of events that culminated in a three-year break in diplomatic relations between the two countries. The routine traffic stop had quickly escalated into a shouting match, with Jalal led away in handcuffs as he tried, in vain, to explain the concept of diplomatic immunity. American newspapers had a field day, and Reza Shah became so infuriated at the tone of the press coverage (one tabloid erroneously described him as a former "stable boy" in the British legation) that he ordered the closure of the Iranian legation in Washington and demanded a formal apology from the United States. The dispute was resolved in 1939 with a little skillful

---

[*] Reza's nationalization drive was not the only factor adversely affecting the fortunes of American missionaries. During the Great Depression, donations from churchgoing Americans to the ABCFM dried up, forcing the board to slash its funding for overseas missions. Among the rank-and-file membership of the church, meanwhile, a significant cultural shift was taking place. A younger generation, known as "Presbyterian modernists," argued that in the twentieth century the conversion of heathens was outdated. The church, they said, should focus its efforts on alleviating poverty instead.

Ghaffar Jalal, Iranian minister (ambassador) to the
United States (1933–36), and his British wife, Agnes.
In November 1935 the Jalals and their chauffeur were
arrested for speeding in Elkton, Maryland. The dispute
escalated into a full-scale standoff between Iran and the
United States, resulting in a three-year downgrade in
diplomatic relations.

diplomacy, but the damage was done. Jalal, who had been in such a rush to
get from Washington to New York on that fateful November morning, had
been on his way to conclude a deal with the American Banknote Company
for the printing of Iranian paper currency. Instead, the contract went to a
German company.

For Reza Shah, all these experiences added up to a striking lesson in
the differences between Americans and Germans—and inevitably, between
democracy and fascism. Reza had never been a great believer in democracy,
but as the 1930s wore on, he would have more opportunities to watch the
United States and Germany in action, and more reasons to conclude that

only one was destined for greatness. By the end of the decade, Reza was intoxicated by the discipline, efficiency, and military precision of Germany— and disillusioned by the open, anarchic, and unwieldy United States. When it came time to replace Millspaugh with a new financial adviser, he chose to bring in a team from Germany. He awarded exclusive rights to develop Persia's air transport services to a German company, the Junkers Corporation of Dessau. These decisions were emblematic of Reza's grow- ing fascination with the efficient, orderly, and disciplined state emerging in Germany in the 1930s. Reza admired the way Paul von Hindenburg and his National People's Party had employed the vocabulary of modernity and militarism to drag Germany up by the bootstraps after the hyperin- flation and cultural permissiveness of the 1920s. After decades of decline under the Qajars, he felt, this was the kind of thing Persia could learn from.

Reza Shah was nothing if not a pragmatist, and as long as Americans performed a function within his modernizing and nationalizing agenda, he still warmly welcomed them. He left the archaeologists from Chicago and Pennsylvania alone to dig through the ruins of Persepolis. In 1933, when Reza Shah gave his first interview to a foreign journalist, he chose an Ameri- can for the occasion. And he always encouraged American businessmen. In the early 1930s, Persia imported fifteen hundred cars and trucks a year— almost all from General Motors. In 1932, fully 90 percent of the nation's cars were American. Underwood typewriters and Singer sewing machines flooded into Persia, along with all manner of agricultural machinery. In the other direction, Persian carpets continued to sell well in the United States, and by the mid-1930s pistachios and dates were wildly fashionable among American tastemakers. With very little fanfare, the United States had become Persia's third-largest trading partner.

Nevertheless, by the late 1930s, it was hard not to notice that, at least informally, Iran had taken something of a German turn. Hundreds of Ger- man engineers, German businessmen, and German technical advisers had been brought in to help build and run Iran's new textile mills, mines, rail- ways, and air transport. And trading links between the two countries were closer than ever. In 1933, Germany had been Iran's fourth-largest trading partner, behind the Soviet Union, Britain, and the United States. By 1937 it was in second place, and by 1941, first place. Between 1939 and 1941, nearly half of Iran's trade was conducted with Germany.

When the Second World War broke out in 1939, therefore, it came as no great surprise that Iran immediately declared its neutrality, just as it had at the onset of the First World War.

This is not to say, as historians sometimes lazily imply, that Reza Shah was some sort of Nazi sympathizer. Iran was a neutral country. It had been a neutral country throughout its modern history,* and that was not about to change. Moreover, many Iranians nursed a soft spot for Germany dating back to the First World War, when the kaiser's army had fought the hated British and Russians. Naturally, then, in 1939, as Britain and the USSR lined up under the Allied banner against the Axis powers of Germany and Italy, in the Iranian imagination this situation appeared about to repeat itself. And the Nazis were quick to look for ways to tap into this reservoir of goodwill. Convinced that Iran's traditional animosity toward Britain and Russia could be manipulated to their favor, the Germans went out of their way to court Reza Shah into joining their cause—even renaming one of Berlin's streets Persische Strasse (Persian Street), as the city's mayor performed three *sieg heils* in honor of Reza at the ribbon-cutting ceremony. Hours of German radio propaganda broadcast into Iran, moreover, informed the Iranian people that Germany officially considered Iran an Aryan nation—an honorary member of the master race, superior to the Semitic Arabs.

The word *Aryan* is derived from the Latin word *Arianus*, meaning "Iranian." So if anyone should have been handing out certificates of racial purity, it was Iran. But the Germans were making a clever political move. The image of strength, discipline, and unity projected by the Nazis was a natural fit with Reza's stiff-shouldered ideology. And some Iranian nationalists—particularly those of an authoritarian persuasion—were intoxicated by the message of militarism and racial purity they heard coming out of Germany. Nevertheless, Germany's crude appeal to Persian pride revealed a fundamental misreading of Iranian nationalism. Neither Reza Shah nor the Iranian people had spent decades trying to free themselves from the pressures of Britain and Russia only to go running into the arms of Germany. Nor did Iranians have any special excitement about marching off to war on behalf of a distant European nation. Iran's increase in commercial and advisory links with Germany in the 1930s was a reflection of economic and political priorities. Iran, as always, was eager to reduce the influence of Britain and Russia, and the break in relations with Washington in 1936 had made the United States less attractive as a "third force." Germany just happened to be in the right place at the right time.

---

* The last time Iran had actively participated in a war was the 1850s. The last time it invaded another nation was 1816.

Still, the Allies were worried. By July 1941 more than two thousand Germans were living in Iran or passing through the country as "tourists." Some of these private citizens were conducting espionage on behalf of the Nazis, and the Allies feared they could easily be marshaled into a dangerous fifth column—or perhaps even engineer a coup and turn Iran into a full-fledged member of the Axis. For the Allies, that would be a doomsday scenario. In 1941, Britain's Abadan oil refinery, in southwestern Iran, was producing 8 million tons of fuel a year for the Allied war effort. If Iran fell into German hands, the loss of this key strategic asset would cripple the Royal Navy. Just as it had been during the First World War, Iran was the engine room for the fight against Germany—and could not be allowed to fall.

For the first two years of the war, the Allies reluctantly tolerated Iran's declaration of neutrality. But in 1941 their strategic calculus was changing. As Germany racked up victories in Europe, and as Hitler launched Operation Barbarossa—the massive, four-million-man air-and-land invasion of the USSR that brought him several hundred miles closer to Moscow— the Allies knew their only chance of defeating him was to get supplies and matériel into Russia to help it resist the German advance. And the only practical way to do that was through Iran. Reza Shah had just completed the 866-mile Trans-Iranian Railway, linking the southern port cities of the Gulf (where British ships dominated) with the Caspian Sea in the north (on the other side of which was Russia). This modern marvel now beckoned as an obvious corridor for transporting American Lend-Lease aid to the Soviet Union.[*]

In July 1941 Britain and Russia gave Reza Shah an ultimatum: Join the Allies, declare war on Germany, and expel all German citizens from Iran, or face the consequences. Reza refused. So on August 25, 1941, British and Soviet forces launched a full-scale invasion of Iran and demanded Reza Shah's abdication. Royal Navy gunboats landed in surprise attacks along the Persian Gulf coast and dispatched troops to occupy Iran's ports, oil fields, and southern cities, as the Royal Air Force bombed targets. The Soviets did much the same in the north. Tanks rolled through the streets of Tehran, as the shah's government scrambled to put together a response. The Imperial Iranian Army—now numbering 125,000 men—put up a semblance of resistance, but it was no match for the combined might of Britain and the USSR.

For the second time in history, Britain and Russia had put their rivalry

---

[*] In June 1941 the United States, which had not yet entered the war, dropped its policy of neutrality and committed to providing material support, known as Lend-Lease, to Britain and the USSR.

Allied invasion of Iran, September 1941: Iran had declared its neutrality in the
Second World War, but the presence of German agents on Iranian soil, and
the strategic importance of the transport corridor from British positions in the
Persian Gulf to the Soviet Union in the north, meant the Allies were unable
to tolerate Iranian neutrality for long. A swift invasion of Iran by British and
Soviet forces ended in Iran's surrender, the country's accession to the Allied
cause, and the abdication of Reza Shah.

aside in the face of a common threat from Germany. And for the second
time in history, Iran's world had been turned upside down. In 1907, when
the Anglo-Russian agreement carved Persia into British and Russian spheres
of influence, it had provoked a groundswell of anger from the constitutionalist movement and provoked a civil war. This time, though, there
was no such grassroots resistance. Over the past fifteen years, Reza Shah
had squelched every power base that was not directly loyal to him—every
mosque, every bazaar guild, every political party, every civic organization.
The warrior-king had ruled entirely with the support of his beloved national
army. Now that the army was crumbling, he was on his own.

In his final desperate hour, Reza Shah reached out to the United
States. Appealing to the spirit of the Atlantic Charter, which Roosevelt and
Churchill had signed just ten days earlier, promising "a peace which will
afford to all nations the means of dwelling in safety within their own boundaries," Reza sent—directly to the White House—an urgent cable begging

Soviet tankmen of the Sixth Armored Division drive through the streets of
Tabriz on a T-26 tank, August 1941.

for condemnation of Britain and Russia's unprovoked aggression. But he
was whistling past the graveyard. In 1941 the United States was on the verge
of joining the war on the side of the Allies and was not about to abandon
Britain and Russia over some lofty principle involving Iranian independence. FDR took nearly a week to reply to Reza's telegram, and when he
did, it was with all the canned sincerity of a college admissions rejection
letter. The United States, said the president, had nothing but respect for the
principle of Iranian independence, but he urged the shah to "view the situation in its full perspective."

Three weeks later it was all over for Reza Shah. The Imperial Iranian
Army surrendered to the Allies, and Reza was forced to abdicate. Within
hours he fled south to Isfahan, and ten days later he was escorted onto a
British vessel on the Persian Gulf and packed off to the East African island
of Mauritius.* Iran—for the first time since 1452—was entirely under foreign military occupation.

CB

* In February, Reza was moved again—this time to South Africa, where he became gravely ill. He
spent his final two years on a sprawling colonial estate, eating only rice and boiled chicken. He
died in Johannesburg on July 26, 1944.

With Reza Shah out of the way, the immediate question for the British and Soviet occupiers was who the new shah should be. Reza's unpopularity was an obvious argument for bringing back the Qajar dynasty, which also had a strong constitutional claim against the coup d'état of 1925. But there was a big problem with reverting to the Qajars: Ahmad Shah had died eleven years earlier, and the next in line, his nephew Hamid, had lived in England since he was five years old and spoke no Persian. Thoroughly English as he was in his education and social connections, the Iranian public could not conceivably welcome him as their king. The preservation of the Pahlavi dynasty was the only option available.[*]

On September 16, 1941, therefore, Reza's son, Mohammad Reza Pahlavi, took over from his father as the new Shah of Iran. He would be the last man in history to hold that ancient title.

---

[*] It is tempting to imagine what might have happened if the Qajars had been allowed to return to power in 1941. Hamid Qajar died in 1988, and his son, heir presumptive to the Qajar crown, today lives a quiet life of exile in the suburbs of Dallas. His daughter, Sarah Shahi, is a former cheerleader for the Dallas Cowboys and is best known for playing a Mexican-American character on the Showtime lesbian drama *The L-Word*. Unlike some of her ancestors, she is fluent in Persian.

Hello Johnny

Mohammad Reza Pahlavi was not quite twenty-two when he became shah, and there was still a lot that Iranians didn't know about him. But one thing was already clear: he was not going to be a chip off the old block.

The crown prince had spent his formative years at the prestigious Le Rosey boarding school in Switzerland, where he had developed a keen interest in alpine skiing and tennis and cultivated friendships with the children of the world's wealthiest and most important people. Unlike his father, who could barely read or write his *own* language, Mohammad Reza was fluent in French and English and well versed in Western history and literature—the kind of dashing, cultivated Europhile who knew the difference between a chateaubriand and a glass of Chablis. Unlike his father, who had left Iran only once in his life, Mohammad Reza was a globe-trotter, with a passion for Italian sports cars and glamorous women—a handsome, stylish cosmopolitan whose picture often appeared in European gossip magazines. Seen next to the graying old Cossack who had given him life, it was sometimes hard to believe the two men were even related—let alone father and son.

When Mohammad Reza returned to Tehran at the end of his studies in 1936, his father—no doubt horrified by the crisply tailored dandelion that stood before him—had swiftly enrolled him in the national military academy. This final, desperate effort to stiffen the boy's spine seemed to do some good. The crown prince learned to fly airplanes and shoot off a Maxim gun, and he worked hard to overcome his reputation as an urbane and vacuous playboy. In preparation for his future role as king, he spent hours memorizing the technical specifications of tanks and aircraft. He developed the quixotic fascination with military hardware that would later become a hallmark of his regime. Although he had less than twenty hours of flight training and terrified anyone who sat in the cockpit with him, he enthusias-

In the Name of the Father: Iran's new young shah, Mohammad Reza Pahlavi (1941–79) (right), shortly before acceding to the throne, September 1941. The last man in history to hold that ancient title, the shah lived largely in the shadow of his formidable father (left) for the first decade of his reign.

tically reinvented himself as a daredevil fighter pilot. But Mohammad Reza never seemed cut out to play the part of a soldier. As a child, he had nearly died from bouts of typhoid and malaria, leaving him with weak muscle tissue and perpetual digestion problems. He was shy and awkward and never seemed comfortable in the company of men. Those close to him said that some part of him always knew he was not the man of steel and thunder his father had been.

In fact, Mohammad Reza had never really known his father. Packed away to Switzerland when he was only eleven, he returned to Iran at seventeen—just five years before Reza's overthrow. During that brief window of time together, the two men's relationship had resembled that of a drill sergeant and his prize cadet. The crown prince would spend his days at the military academy, seeing his father only for troop inspections or awkward man-to-man lunches, during which he would be quizzed on what he was learning. In his memoirs, Mohammad Reza later admitted his love for his father had been one of "respectful awe" rather than real affection. "Those eyes could make a man shrivel up inside," he wrote of Reza's penetrating stare. "He was a powerful and formidable man and the good heart that beat beneath his rough cavalryman's exterior was not easily reached."

Once he was in power, Mohammad Reza Shah discovered that things only got harder. The second-generation ruler of a dynasty established by a Cossack peasant under questionable circumstances, he always found it difficult to project authority. In the political arena, the aging Qajar-era aristocrats resented having to bow and scrape before a kid half their age and offered him only sneering obstructionism. At home, his fiercely intimidating mother, Taj ol-Moluk, never grew tired of reminding him that he was a weakling who fell short of his father's legacy. Mohammad Reza's twin sister, the fiery princess Ashraf, constantly egged him on to be tougher and more unforgiving with political enemies—in short, to be more like their father. But this was easier said than done. In May 1941, in one of his last cabinet meetings, Reza Shah had taken out his riding crop and savagely whipped his finance minister after the poor man failed to produce some papers he had been asked for. Those would have been tough boots for anyone to step into. Besides, a new era seemed to call for a new formula.

Aware that the Iranian people were desperate for greater personal freedom after years of tyranny, Mohammad Reza Shah nursed a vague aspiration to go down in history as a liberalizing monarch. But the temptation to play the benevolent king often conflicted with a nagging worry that he would be perceived as weak. Never sure whether he would rather be loved for being a democrat or feared for being a dictator, Mohammad Reza would, at different times during his thirty-seven years in power, try out both roles—and succeed at neither. Every time he tried to play the tough guy, he looked unconvincing. Every time he tried too hard to be liked, his mother and sister came down on him like a ton of bricks.

Aloof and childlike, the new shah often came across as an overgrown boy playing at being emperor. He seemed lost amid the complexities of court politics, struggling to balance the various factions and power bases that were reemerging after years in hibernation. When a crucial decision had to be made, he would vacillate, deliberate, and ask everybody around him what they thought. Then he would vacillate again. At one point, during a crucial standoff with one of his prime ministers, an exasperated Princess Ashraf asked him "whether he was man or mouse." It was a question Mohammad Reza Shah never fully managed to answer.

ಚಿ

In 1941 the first order of business for the new shah was to learn how to navigate the treacherous shoals of international power politics. Aware that he would not even be in power had it not been for the Allied invasion of his country, he knew he had to play his cards carefully, or he too could easily be disposed of. But he also felt strongly that if Iran was going to be a respected, powerful nation, it had to rid itself once and for all of its tiresome dependence on the whims of London and Moscow.

Like generations of Iranian leaders before him, Mohammad Reza believed the best way to preserve Iran's independence was to find a third power to serve as its "protector" against Britain and Russia. His father had turned to Germany to fill this role, but that had backfired spectacularly. The shah understood that what the country needed now was a strategic partner powerful enough to keep Britain and Russia in check—but one that was fighting on the same side in the war, and thus unlikely to be perceived as a threat. In 1941 only one country fitted this description, and that was the United States of America.

From the day he became shah, Mohammad Reza Pahlavi made Iran's relations with Washington into a cornerstone of his foreign policy—and this, perhaps more than anything else, distinguished his reign from those of previous shahs. Iranian leaders had always hoped to develop closer relations with the United States, but only this last shah really succeeded in doing so. By the end of his reign, in the 1970s, the bilateral relationship would become so close that it would turn into a political liability for the shah—a source of anger among his people and a powerful spark for the Islamic Revolution of 1979. But at the beginning of the 1940s, it seemed like a prudent, sensible step. America was a rising power—probably the world's next great superpower—and it would be foolish for Iran not to cultivate its friendship.

In January 1942, Iran, Britain, and the Soviet Union signed the so-called Tripartite Treaty—yet another lopsided arrangement allowing the Great Powers to divvy up Iran between them. The word *Tripartite* was deceptive—Iran had no choice but to sign the agreement, as British and Russian troops had already invaded. Signing it created the fiction that the occupation of Iran was some sort of cooperative agreement among three countries. Unlike past such arrangements, in fact, this one contained no pussyfooting talk of "spheres of influence" or a "neutral zone" in the middle of the country. The northern tier of Iran became a Russian-controlled zone, and the rest a British-controlled zone. In effect, the Allies turned Iran into a giant transport corridor connecting the USSR to the British-controlled waters of the Persian Gulf.

The Tripartite Treaty stipulated that all Allied forces would leave Iranian soil within six months of the end of the war. But given past history, the shah's advisers did not trust the British or the Soviets to hold up their end of this bargain. The only solution, they felt, was to invite in the United States to act as a counterbalance. With a large, high-profile American presence on Iranian soil, they reasoned, Britain and Russia would not dare overstay their welcome. After all, America had reaffirmed its Wilsonian commitment to support the territorial integrity of small and vulnerable nations six months earlier by signing the Atlantic Charter. In early 1942, therefore, the Iranian government communicated to Washington that it would welcome any kind of assistance the United States was able to provide.

In early 1942, as it happened, America was experiencing a major realignment in its own thinking. In December 1941 the Japanese had launched a devastating surprise attack on the U.S. naval base at Pearl Harbor, which propelled the United States into joining the Allied war effort. It had also shaken Americans out of their traditional unwillingness to engage with foreign affairs. In the months that followed Pearl Harbor, decision makers in Washington recognized that volatility and aggression in remote parts of the world could easily land on America's doorstep, and that isolationism had outlived its usefulness. In order to safeguard the country's security, it was obviously necessary to join the war—but after the war was over, it would also be necessary to play a major role in defining how the world would look. This, in turn, would require the projection of American power and influence to all corners of the globe, in a way that had never before been contemplated in American history.

Washington regarded Iran, in particular, as a country that required American engagement. The thinking was that when the war ended, Iran could easily become the scene of a destabilizing, even devastating, British-Soviet conflict. With thousands of British and Russian troops occupying various corners of the country, a clash seemed inevitable. But if the United States stepped in and helped build Iran into a strong, durable nation, Britain and Russia would be far less likely to go at each other's throats there. Not only would Iran be able to stand on its feet, but the chance of a fresh cycle of superpower conflict and global instability following the war would be reduced. America, and the world, would be safer.

A remarkable strain of idealism lay behind this kind of thinking. In 1942 the U.S. government genuinely believed it could send large numbers of advisers and technical consultants to Iran and somehow remain above the fray—immune to the complexities and moral compromises that had dogged the Great Powers in the past. The United States was a purely benevolent power, Washington believed, and the honesty of its intentions would protect it from the temptations of imperialism. "The United States alone," read an influential State Department memorandum in January 1943, "is in a position to build up Iran to the point at which it will stand in need of neither British nor Russian assistance to maintain order in its own house." The memo, which recommended a robust, comprehensive American advisory program for Iran, received enthusiastic endorsements at every level of the

U.S. government—including the White House. President Roosevelt wrote to his secretary of state, Cordell Hull, that he was "rather thrilled with the idea of using Iran as an example of what we could do by an unselfish American policy. We could not take on a more difficult nation than Iran. I should like, however, to have a try at it."

Over the next six months, the U.S. government authorized three major advisory missions to Iran—and in November 1942 Americans began arriving by the planeload. First on the scene was the Gendarmerie Mission, directed by Col. H. Norman Schwarzkopf (a former New Jersey police commissioner),* whose job was to reorganize Iran's rural police force. Second was the U.S. Army Mission (later known as ARMISH), headed by Maj. Gen. Clarence Ridley, intended to strengthen and modernize the Imperial Iranian Army. And the third leg of the triangle was yet another civilian financial advisory mission, headed once again by the irascible Arthur Millspaugh.

These three well-meaning advisory missions were dwarfed by a much larger and more visible American presence in Iran, one with a very different agenda. From December 1942 the United States sent thirty thousand non-

---

* Schwarzkopf's son, Norman Jr.—the 1990s Gulf War commander known as "Stormin' Norman"—lived in Tehran as a teenager and attended the American School.

Persian corridor: From 1942 to 1945, some 5.5 million tons of U.S. matériel was transported from British positions in the Persian Gulf to the Soviet Union along the Trans-Iranian Railway and specially built roads—making a critical difference in the Allied war effort. Here, U.S. fighter planes, destined for Russia, are assembled in Iran.

combatant troops to oversee the transport of wartime supplies to the Soviet Union. The so-called Persian Gulf Command (PGC) was responsible for expanding port and rail facilities, running the Trans-Iranian Railway, assembling trucks, and building roads to convey war matériel from British forces in the Gulf up to the Russian border. From 1942 to 1945, some 5.5 million tons of supplies—everything from canned food to Studebaker trucks to B-24 bombers (a "special surprise to Hitler," as the American troops described it)—made their way to Russia along the so-called Persian Corridor, with the help of American personnel. By 1943, one-third of all Lend-Lease aid from the United States to the Soviet Union was going through Iran.

For three full years, American GIs (and their Iranian laborers) toiled in the sweltering heat of southern Iran—enduring sandstorms and temperatures that sometime rose to 130 degrees in the shade and pitching tents in foot-deep mud—as they bundled crates and palettes off ships and onto trucks and railway carriages bound northward for the snowy-white Russian steppe. At all times their mission was top secret; the soldiers were never told where they were going, only that they would be away from home for nine months. Not even their families knew where they were until the day they returned. (Letters to and from Iran had so many holes cut into them by military censors that the soldiers nicknamed them "lace curtains.") Yet despite all the secrecy and anonymity, they understood that something utterly essential was taking place. "You are undertaking the most important job of your life," the soldiers were told just before they arrived. "There is no other war theater where military success by the United States and her fighting allies will contribute more to final victory over the Axis."

ໝ

In November 1943 the leaders of the "Big Three" wartime powers—Franklin Roosevelt, Winston Churchill, and Josef Stalin—gathered in Tehran for a critical summit to discuss the progress of the war. It was the first time the three men met face to face, and for nearly a week, the Iranian capital was plunged into what a contemporary report described as "the greatest security measures in the history of the middle east." Lest the Nazis find out about the meeting and try to assassinate any of the leaders, the conference took place in an atmosphere of extreme secrecy. Entire sections of Tehran were cordoned off; radio stations were taken off the air; and no one, not even residents, was told what was happening. To divert attention, the international media were given a wild goose to chase—they were instructed to gather at the King David Hotel in Jerusalem for a "major event."

Tehran Conference, December 1943. At this historic first meeting of the
"Big Three," the Allied powers made preparations for the D-Day invasion of
Normandy. They also discussed the special situation of Iran and pledged to
remove their forces from the country within six months of the end of the war.

The main purpose of the Tehran Conference was to discuss modalities for opening the long-desired western front against Germany, and over the course of three days, it laid the groundwork for what would eventually become the D-Day invasion of Normandy. But Roosevelt, Churchill, and Stalin also found time to discuss Iran, which they agreed had suffered "special economic difficulties" as a result of disruptions to its food supply and demands made on its transport infrastructure. Following the conference, the United States, Britain, and the USSR issued a joint declaration pledging to respect the "independence, sovereignty and territorial integrity of Iran." Ten months earlier the Tripartite Treaty had made the same promise, but that document had lacked American political muscle. Now, with thirty thousand soldiers spread across the country, the United States had an obligation to clarify its position in Iran—and reassure Iranians that the occupation of their country was temporary.

The declaration was an important victory for the shah, but the Tehran Conference also left the twenty-four-year-old king looking foolish and weak. His capital city had been turned into an enormous armed camp by foreign forces—hardly the image a new ruler would want to project to his people. To add insult to injury, on the second day of the conference, the delegates celebrated Churchill's sixty-ninth birthday at a lavish dinner to which not a single Iranian official—not even the shah—was invited. As Roosevelt, Stalin, and Churchill drank toasts to one another late into the night, a thirteenth-century blue and white Persian bowl sat on the table in front of them—a birthday gift from Roosevelt to Churchill. It was the only thing Iranian about the evening and a powerful metaphor for the attitude of the Allies toward their surroundings. Over the next few days, meetings of the Big Three took place almost entirely on the grounds of the Soviet legation. In effect, the Tehran Conference was hosted not by the shah but by Josef Stalin.

What particularly crawled up the shah's nose, however, was the failure of Roosevelt to pay him a courtesy visit during his three-day stay in Tehran. Even Stalin went to the Imperial Palace during his first few hours in Tehran and then graciously received the shah's return visit. Roosevelt, by contrast, seemed oblivious to this point of protocol, and the shah fumed for days before breaking down and taking the humiliating step of calling on Roosevelt at the Russian legation. The two men spoke for nearly two hours, but Roosevelt never returned the visit, instead spending his free time visiting

The king and the president. The twenty-four-year-old shah bitterly resented Roosevelt's failure to pay him a courtesy visit during his stay in Tehran. Eventually the shah gave up and went to the Soviet legation to call on FDR. The body language at that meeting—the first between U.S. and Iranian leaders—speaks volumes about the direction that Iranian foreign policy was about to take under the new shah.

U.S. troops at the Amirabad army barracks. The experience left the shah feeling badly snubbed. In almost every conceivable way, he had been treated as an afterthought in his own country.

Roosevelt salvaged the situation somewhat when, on his way out of Tehran, he sent the shah a typewritten note thanking him for his hospitality. At the bottom, the president added in his own hand a casual postscript: "I greatly hope that we shall have the pleasure of a visit from you to Washington." For the next five years, the shah would cling to these words like a besotted schoolgirl. At every opportunity, in almost every conversation with American officials, he would subtly remind them of this exchange— constantly angling and hinting, looking forward to the day when the handwritten note would magically transform itself into an official invitation to visit the United States.

⟨⟩

FDR was not the only American to offend Iranian sensibilities during these years. From 1943 to 1945, thirty thousand American soldiers continued to live and work in cities and villages across Iran as part of the Persian Gulf Command—and their behavior often left the locals feeling bitterly resentful. Many American GIs were scrupulously polite and respectful and formed genuine bonds of friendship with the Iranians they interacted with. But inevitably, some did not. Traffic accidents were a particular source of friction. In small towns—where Iranian pedestrians were accustomed only to donkey carts and bicycles and had not yet developed the habit of jumping out of the way of speeding jeeps—injuries and fatalities were reported at an alarming rate.

In Tehran, meanwhile, at all hours of the day and night, American soldiers could be found passed out in gutters or staggering about in groups, starting fights and greeting young women with loud wolf whistles. These were lean years in Iran, and inevitably, some local girls sold their services to the comparatively wealthy Americans. But many GIs didn't understand the difference between prostitutes and ordinary women walking down the street, grabbing and groping at whoever made her way past their bloodshot eyes. Within a few months, the elegant cafés and theaters along the Avenue Lalezar—Tehran's upmarket shopping street—looked like a sleazy nickelodeon of hustlers and whores, all pitching their services. "Hello Johnny" was the phrase on the lips of every hungry Iranian—the generic greeting called out by locals as American GIs walked by. Boys stood round ready to give Johnny a shoeshine. Girls winked and puckered at Johnny and offered him a little more.

In 1943 and 1944 complaints against American GIs reached a climax. Scarcely a day went by without the Iranian Interior Ministry passing an embarrassing report of some kind to the U.S. legation. "The conduct of American forces in Tehran leaves something to be desired," the U.S. minister, Louis Dreyfus, cabled back to Washington sheepishly as the reports piled up. With no official treaty governing the presence of American troops, the GIs were in effect immune from Iranian law. If a soldier ran over and killed an Iranian pedestrian, the worst he could expect was a note of reprimand from his commanding officer. When it came to brawling, boozing, and fornicating, Johnny was able to act with impunity—and he knew it.

What made the behavior of American soldiers particularly galling in the eyes of Iranians was the fact that their country was going hungry again. The Allied occupation had brought severe food shortages to virtually every part of the country as the Russians diverted precious wheat supplies to feed their own forces, and the presence of wealthy British and American personnel drove up prices and encouraged hoarding. By 1944 buying bread on the open market was almost impossible, and even Tehran's wealthiest residents were forced to rely on government-subsidized *nan-e-silu* (silo bread) for their survival. (Iranians regularly found pests and vermin baked into the bread—even, occasionally, whole mice or strips of shoe leather.) Against this backdrop, thousands of American soldiers were seen lurching from café to café with rolls of cash, irrigating themselves with gallons of prized Russian vodka and slaking their sexual appetites on the daughters of Persia. For most Iranians, the GIs were the first Americans they had ever met, and the introduction was disappointing.

This was a shame, because of the three wartime Allies, the United States probably came closest to showing genuine, altruistic concern for Iran's deteriorating food situation. In the north, the Russians were profiteering, buying up scarce food supplies and selling them for export. And at various times, both Britain and Russia withheld grain deliveries as a way to bully the Iranian government into offering more favorable trade concessions. During the harsh winter of 1942—a season preceded by dismal harvest failures and marked by extreme cold and hunger—the American minister in Tehran fumed over these actions by Britain and Russia, complaining that it was unconscionable to use food as a political weapon.

It also escaped the attention of most Iranians that their own royal family was largely oblivious to their suffering. "Need a dozen very large and very beautiful diamonds," the shah's sister Princess Shams cabled to her ailing father, the exiled Reza Shah, in Johannesburg in October 1942. "Some very white, others pink, bluish, and downright yellow. Pay no attention to price tag." As the princess awaited her reply, the streets of Tehran were filling with rioters demanding bread.

℞

When the war came to an end in August 1945, Iran found itself facing a familiar problem: Russian soldiers who were in no hurry to leave. At the Tehran Conference two years earlier, all three Allied powers had promised to remove their troops from Iranian soil within six months of the end of hostilities, so Iran had expected a full withdrawal by March 2, 1946. Britain and the United States publicly stated their intentions to be gone well before March, but the Soviet Union refused to commit to a firm deadline. In late 1945, far from beginning a troop pullout, the Russians stepped up their activities in Iran and even supported the creation of an autonomous People's Government of Azerbaijan in the northwest. From the American perspective, these were worrying developments.

For Iran, this blatant act of Soviet brinkmanship marked the first true test of its newly invigorated relationship with the United States. Would the Americans, many in Tehran now wondered, follow through on their commitments and *insist* that the Soviets withdraw their forces? Perhaps the better question was: Who else could? The war had crippled the British economy, leaving London in no position to confront Moscow. And anyway, the Iranians would have seen a British démarche against Russia as cynical and self-interested. In December 1945, during a high-level background discussion, British and American officials acknowledged that, at this juncture, "American leadership on the basis of principle would be more effective than British leadership." It was a watershed moment. At any point in the past hundred years, Britain would have dropped everything to block Russia from making inroads into Iran. But now, for the first time in history, London recognized that its authority was waning, and that it was too exhausted and bankrupted by war to play a major role in Iran. The only reasonable option was to stand back and allow the United States to lead, while providing tactical and logistical assistance where required.

In the event, American leadership turned out to be less than what the Iranians had hoped for. Rather than confronting Russia directly, in January 1946, just weeks before the troop withdrawal deadline, the United States recommended that Iran take its case before the newly formed United Nations. In early March, Secretary of State James Byrnes sent a strongly worded note to Moscow reminding the Soviets of their treaty obligation. But this was as far as it went. Concluding that a public showdown with the USSR during the UN's opening session would have a corrosive effect on the fragile new institution, the United States chose to maintain a neutral silence. And in the end, Soviet forces sauntered out of Iran on their own terms, and very much at their own pace, in May 1946, two months after the agreed deadline. They withdrew largely as a result of deft maneuvering by the Iranian prime minister, Ahmad Qavam, who had offered the Soviets a vague promise of oil concessions (which he ultimately failed to deliver). But for many years thereafter, American cold warriors portrayed the withdrawal as a powerful lesson in what the United States could achieve when it had the courage to "stand up" to the menace of Communism. For the first time in history, they said, America had "faced down" the USSR and scored an important early victory in the Cold War. President Harry Truman even claimed in his memoirs that he had given Stalin an "ultimatum," threatening to send warships to defend Iran.

In fact, there is no record of such an ultimatum. Most historians now believe it was a combination of Qavam's tactical sagacity and Moscow's internal political calculations that brought about the Soviet withdrawal. Nevertheless, the United States did make a principled stand for Iranian independence in 1946, however mild that stand might have been. At one point, the U.S. ambassador, George Allen, made an unusually strong speech in Tehran reminding "patriotic Iranians" that "the American people will support fully their freedom to make their own choice."

This heightened U.S. interest in Iran marked a new phase in the relationship between Washington and Tehran—and a new phase in the shah's leadership. As his thirtieth birthday approached, a far more robust political presence by the U.S. embassy in Tehran was already becoming a defining hallmark of his reign. Another question, however, remained unresolved: What kind of relationship was the shah going to have with his own people?

Tehran Spring

By the late 1940s, Tehran had been Iran's national capital for 150 years, but it could sometimes feel like an overgrown village with a handful of palaces and embassies. In dusty alleys, old men still pushed donkey carts slowly from house to house, delivering the day's water and swapping stories. Behind high-walled courtyards, traditional families still lived traditional lives, gathering for lunch around pots of stew and radishes. Barefoot dervishes still spent their days in prayer, and parts of town could still be eerily quiet at midday. In many quarters and for many of its residents, Tehran was less of an imperial capital than a collection of private lives, held together by walls and doors and muffled conversations.

But increasingly, along some of the broader boulevards and avenues that Reza Shah had built in the 1930s, a very different world was emerging— a world of anonymity, and chance encounters. There were men in three- piece suits and fedoras hopping on and off buses, women in hats and pencil dresses looking into shop windows and chatting energetically about the merchandise. There were traffic lights and barber shops and cafés where a young man could sit and while away a few hours with the friends he had met at university. There was bustle, and there was clamor. And, for the first time since the constitutional revolution, there was something resembling a "public sphere." Life for the average Tehrani was no longer defined only by extended families and kinship networks. Hopes and frustrations were beginning to seep out from behind closed doors and onto the street—and politics was no exception.

One street in particular served as a conduit for the restlessness and pent- up energy of young, middle-class Tehranis in the late 1940s: a long, straight avenue called Shah Abad, then Eslambul, then Naderi (the name changed every mile or two). At one end of the avenue was the Majles building, where

Communists and nationalists would gather, handing out newspapers and holding up banners in the middle of traffic. A few blocks west was the girls' school, Shahdokht, where teenage boys with greased-up pompadours congregated in the early afternoons, nudging and grinning and egging one another on. A little further along, where Shah Abad became Eslambul, one could get a tailored suit or a European-style *coiffure* in the shadows of the British and Russian embassies (which sat, appropriately enough, with their backs to each other). Still further, there was the Hotel Naderi, an elegant new establishment with a garden café that served up generous scoops of ice cream and put on live music in the summers. Every few yards was a spot where a young man might bump into a group of friends, exchange ciga-rettes, and end up talking politics with people he barely knew. It was not exactly the Boulevard du Montparnasse, but after sixteen years of dictator-ship, it felt a little like springtime in Tehran.

None of this would last. In 1953, Iran would swing violently back down the path of dictatorship, and over the next twenty-five years, the energetic political culture of the 1940s would gradually disappear as activists struggled under the constant surveillance of the shah's secret police. But for a few brief years, from 1945 to 1953, Tehran had its Left Bank moment—a moment that, to this day, a certain generation of Iranians remember fondly as a time when anything seemed possible.

ભ

The Tehran Spring, if we can be permitted to call it that, began with a bungled attempt at repression. In the winter of 1943–44 the young shah made the mistake of thinking he was his father and tried, in an amateurish way, to rig the first Majles election to be held under his watch. It backfired spectacularly. His vote-rigging measures were half-hearted and obvious. The result was a badly divided parliament, with a slim majority of conservative loyalists and many deputies ready to settle scores and do battle with the Pahlavi king. Into the long-quiescent parliament chamber marched dozens of indignant new deputies representing virtually every imaginable interest group that had been beaten into submission over the previous twenty years: leftists aligned with the pro-Soviet Tudeh Party; restive tribal nomads from the central plain; reactionary politicians from the old feudal elite; liberal social democrats; and religious conservatives preaching a return to Islamic values and greater power for the clergy. The only thing all these wildly diver-gent groups had in common was a pent-up hatred of the Pahlavi dynasty and a desire to limit the shah's powers.

What Mohammad Reza Shah had failed to understand was that if you were going to be a tyrant, you actually had to *be* a tyrant. You had to send in the army to supervise polls and leave your opponents fearing for their lives. Instead, in his typically indecisive way, he had tried to be a liberalizer as well, relaxing censorship laws, issuing a blanket amnesty for political prisoners of his father's regime, and allowing political parties to operate freely. In the run-up to the 1944 election, Iran had begun to look like a genuinely pluralistic democracy, with a flurry of new publications and manifestos reaching the country's eager readers every day. "There are 47 newspapers in Tehran," noted the British ambassador with amazement, "a city of only 750,000 inhabitants." It was a genie that could not be easily put back into its bottle. After sixteen years of repressive dictatorship, people were being allowed to read and write what they wanted. They were not about to be told their votes didn't count.

But the shah didn't learn. In 1947 he rigged another round of parliamentary elections. This time he was more successful, and the new Majles was packed with conservatives loyal to the shah and his prime minister. With nowhere else to go, opposition poured onto the streets—angrier than ever and baying for free elections. With so many interest groups pursuing radically divergent agendas, the shah found himself overwhelmed, with little idea how to respond. By this point, the last of the Allied forces had withdrawn, and his father was dead and buried. He was therefore left to manage the country largely on his own—or more likely, to mismanage it. Every day something else seemed to spiral out of his control. Between 1945 and 1951, there would be eleven changes of prime minister. Where forty-seven newspapers had circulated in 1944, by 1951 more than seven hundred appeared in Tehran *alone*—many of them overtly hostile to the shah.

Broadly speaking, in the late 1940s, opposition to the young shah came from three sources. First was the Tudeh, a doctrinaire Marxist party loyal to Moscow with by far the best organization, discipline, and membership numbers of any political party in Iran, but without widespread public support. The second source of opposition was the religious establishment, which still resented Reza Shah's relentless assault on the place of Islam in Iranian society.* But the third, and increasingly potent, source of opposition was a lively, eclectic coalition of secular liberals, democrats, and progressive nationalists.

---

* The majority of Iran's ayatollahs during these years were moderates or conservatives, men who were prepared to work within the system solely to ensure that the country did not completely forget its Muslim roots. A very tiny minority articulated a more radical ideology, but in the 1940s few Iranians had any sympathy with extremism. Hard as it might be to believe in the context of later events, at this point in Iran's history, Islamic fundamentalism was a considerably longer shot than Communism.

In the late 1940s, Iran had a small but growing middle class of skilled professionals, bankers, lawyers, student idealists, and intellectuals—a modern bourgeoisie impatient to move ahead with the democratic reforms that had been interrupted in the 1910s. This large and varied group increasingly found itself intoxicated by a blend of nationalism and Western-style liberalism. It also, uniquely, had the ability to hold the middle ground between the Communists and the religious conservatives, peeling off moderate elements from both camps and accommodating everybody under a big tent. Liberal nationalists had a simple message: increase democracy, end royal dictatorship, and free Iran from foreign interference. Put another way, they saw themselves as the natural heirs to the Constitutional Revolution.

Initially, Iranian liberals suffered from a lack of organization and unity, perhaps the inevitable result of their diversity and their respect for differences of opinion. But between 1947 and 1953, they united behind a rather unlikely leader: an aging Qajar-era aristocrat by the name of Mohammad Mosaddeq. Mosaddeq was already pushing seventy when he emerged as the de facto leader of the liberal opposition. He was as bald as a melon, walked with a cane, and suffered from a nervous condition that often manifested itself in the form of fainting spells. But he was also one of the most charismatic, free-spirited, and uncompromising figures of the twentieth century. Iranian politics was in for the ride of its life.

cs

Born around 1882 into a world of extraordinary privilege and pedigree—his father a prominent government official and his mother a respected Qajar princess—Mohammad Mosaddeq had already spent decades as a sort of oddball superstar in Tehran politics. A brilliant legal scholar who studied finance at the Sorbonne and earned a law doctorate in Switzerland in the 1910s, he had a reputation for an unusual, even extreme, dedication to integrity. In 1918, as deputy finance minister, he had exposed an embezzlement operation run by the ministry's top directors. He even had his own mother fined for falling behind in her taxes. But what Mosaddeq was most known for was his lifelong belief that Iran needed to take responsibility for its own problems and stop looking to outside powers for assistance. In 1921, following the demise of the hated Anglo-Persian Agreement, Mosaddeq— although he admired Morgan Shuster as much as anyone—had been one of very few nationalist politicians to oppose the idea of bringing him back. "A nation that cannot administer its own house without the aid of others," he had said, "is unworthy of living."

Elected to the Majles in 1924, Mosaddeq had led the seething opposition to Millspaugh and spoken out against what he described as creeping tyranny, condemning Reza Shah for rigging elections and wasting money on improvements to royal palaces. In the 1928 elections, to no one's surprise, he was prevented from running as a candidate. And for the next thirteen years, he retired to his family estate in Ahmadabad, ninety miles west of Tehran, where he passed his time cultivating seeds and learning about herbal medicine. But he was not forgotten. By maintaining a dignified silence, Mosaddeq gradually built up an extraordinary level of prestige and respect among the new generation of educated middle-class Iranians. And in 1944, with Reza Shah gone, he was elected overwhelmingly to represent the city of Tehran in the fourteenth Majles.

At sixty-two, Mosaddeq was back in his natural habitat. From the floor of the parliament chamber, he made impassioned speeches in favor of democracy and transparent government. He argued that the shah's powers should be made "ceremonial," if only to protect him from himself and thus preserve the institution of monarchy (a position that now appears tragically prophetic). When a justice committee investigation into allegations of corruption and vote-rigging refused to make its files public, Mosaddeq stormed out of the Majles building, calling it a "den of thieves." Within hours, a crowd of excited law students had gathered in front of Mosaddeq's house, begging him to come outside. When he emerged, they carried him on their shoulders back to the Majles—where an even larger crowd of demonstrators had gathered to voice their support.

As thousands of eager young idealists began looking to him for leadership, Mosaddeq used his platform in the fourteenth Majles to condemn his old nemesis, Arthur Millspaugh—now in Iran for a second time and more unpopular than ever. And yet every time he criticized Millspaugh, Mosaddeq took pains to emphasize his admiration and respect for Americans in general—most of whom, he was "sure," would "not want one of their citizens . . . to treat us the way [Millspaugh] does." He contrasted the financial adviser with generations of benevolent Americans, whose popularity in Iran was "an indicator of the warm feeling Iranians have for Americans." "Iranians will never forget that America defended Iran in 1919," he said, "and they will always appreciate that help."

During the fourteenth Majles, Mosaddeq articulated what he called the principle of "negative equilibrium." Traditionally, Iranian foreign policy had involved balancing Britain and Russia by giving each country some special favor in order to offset the excessive influence of the other. But every time Iran granted a concession to one power, the other had complained, and Iran had felt compelled to offer it the same, or a similar, privilege—resulting in a gradual erosion of independence. Negative equilibrium, Mosaddeq said, would turn that process on its head. He suggested giving *less* to one of the two Great Powers as a way of reducing its influence, then giving less to the other to even the balance. That way, over time, Iranians would gain control over their own country and their own destiny.

By the time the fourteenth Majles came to an end in March 1946, Mosaddeq had become a hero to a generation of democracy activists, nationalists, and progressive intellectuals. It was obvious that the shah's regime would have to come to terms with him in some way. The way it chose was vote rigging, during the elections to the fifteenth Majles in January 1947. At polling stations throughout the country, intimidation and fraud were widely reported. Voters turned up to find their paper ballots already filled in for them by polling officers. "The methods of ballot-box stuffing," wrote an American journalist, "were as intricate as a Persian carpet but as effective as Jersey City's best." Outraged, Mosaddeq wrote open letters to the shah and the prime minister, but to no avail. Then he led a large-scale sit-in on the grounds of the Imperial Palace. None of it made any difference, and he was prevented from winning a seat in the fifteenth Majles.

As Iran's pro-democracy movement gained momentum, one group of protesters approached the U.S. embassy to ask if they could sit *bast* on its grounds. The symbolism of this request was hard to miss. In 1906, during the Constitutional Revolution, thousands of demonstrators had congregated on the grounds of the British legation, believing that, of all the Great Powers, Britain, as a constitutional monarchy, was least likely to be hostile to their cause. Now in 1947, a new generation of activists saw the United States as their natural ally in the struggle against tyranny. Mosaddeq—consistent with his lifelong belief that Iranians should not look to foreign powers for help—chose to take his *bast* directly to the shah's palace. But many of his followers explicitly saw their struggle for democracy and independence as synonymous with American values, which spoke volumes about the level of prestige that the United States enjoyed in Iran in the 1940s.

In the event, the American ambassador, George Allen, refused their request. Understandably, he was reluctant to implicate the United States in a domestic Iranian political movement. But his decision also reflected a more general discomfort that American officialdom had with the Iranian democracy movement. Allen, like most Americans involved in Iran policy, tended to accept at face value the shah's claim that Iran was "not ready" for democracy. U.S. support for Iran in these years was very much focused on strengthening the shah's position and helping him meet internal security challenges. As early as 1944, Allen's predecessor, Leland Morris, had suggested to his bosses in Washington that U.S. policy should focus on "strengthening the hand" of the shah and that what Iran most needed was "the rise of a strong individual." Later that year a visiting American envoy, Averell Harriman, accepted the shah's claim that Iran "could not be truly democratic . . . until the people had acquired sufficient education to understand the principle of democratic government." Harriman never asked the shah how such education was going to come about, when Iran spent 30 to 40 percent of its budget on the police and military and less than 6 percent on education.

The shah very much appreciated the confidence the Americans seemed to have in his personal leadership and quickly maneuvered to expand his constitutional powers. At the beginning of 1948, with a cooperative Majles at his disposal and the troublesome Mosaddeq in "retirement" following the loss of his seat, the shah proposed a raft of extraconstitutional powers—including, most controversially, the power to dissolve the Majles when he deemed it necessary. The State Department expressed some (mild) concern about this suggestion. But the shah warned his American friends that a failure to solidify his power over the Majles opened the risk of Soviet infiltration. What might be considered "dictatorial measures" in America, he reassured them, were entirely appropriate in the Iranian context.

Initially, Washington reacted with skepticism. But in February 1948 a much more sympathetic U.S. ambassador, John Wiley, arrived in Tehran. A colorful career diplomat who had previously served in Estonia, Latvia, and Colombia, Wiley was competent but had never set foot in the Middle East, and his understanding of Iran was based mostly on what he had gleaned from the *Hajji Baba** books he had read in his youth. "Iran is a country of opaque mist," he wrote to Washington when he first arrived in Tehran. Dealing with the irrational natives was "like eating soup with a fork." And what Iran needed most was a strongman monarch, backed by an army "capable primarily of maintaining order within the country."

Not surprisingly, Wiley got along famously with the shah, and the two men frequently indulged in two- or three-hour lunches to discuss policy. But Wiley rarely found time to gauge the mood outside the walls of the Imperial Palace, and he took very little interest in Mosaddeq or the rising democracy movement lapping against the edges of the shah's marble redoubt. Even

---

* An instant best seller in 1824, *The Adventures of Hajji Baba of Ispahan,* by the British diplomat James Morier, went through dozens of editions and was consistently hailed for its supposedly perspicacious insights into the infuriating nature of the "Persian character." Morier hated his time in Persia, and made no attempt to hide it. The novel stresses the deceitfulness and duplicity of Persians, who are depicted cheating, cozening, and confusing one another at every opportunity. His unflattering caricature of Iran remained popular well into the twentieth century, and was adapted into a popular motion picture in 1954. Though the book has slipped into obscurity, for generations, virtually every American was familiar with the adventures of Hajji Baba—which also meant virtually every American had a ready reservoir of easy stereotypes to associate with Persia.

after two years in Tehran, he remained convinced that Iranians could not be trusted with democracy—or indeed with anything else. "The chance of salvaging anything substantial out of the careening lunacy of the Persian," he warned his successor in 1951, "is most astronomically remote."

In February 1949, during a visit to Tehran University, the shah narrowly survived an assassination attempt at the hands of two radical Communists with very bad aim. Despite standing just yards from the shah, the sharp-shooting Bolsheviks managed to miss their target—but one of the bullets grazed the shah's right cheek, and the next day's papers were full of heroic pictures of the young monarch wearing bandages across his face and vow-ing to stamp out the menace of Communism. A wave of public sympathy followed, and the shah wasted no time milking the situation for his own ends. He banned the Tudeh Party, and given the sudden spike in public support for the monarchy, the Majles found it hard to say no to the shah's requests for greater executive authority. An upper chamber, or Senate, was created—and the shah was given the power to appoint half its members. Then within days, a bill was pushed through the Majles that gave the shah all the expanded royal prerogatives he had so badly wanted—including, finally, the right to dissolve the Majles.

Six months later the country prepared for elections to the sixteenth Majles, and given the shah's drift toward dictatorship, this set of polls was clearly going to be even more contentious than the previous two. Mosaddeq had been coaxed out of retirement by his legions of supporters, and the shah appeared more determined than ever to ensure the elections were rigged. But the mood was shifting against him. Dozens of newspapers were now calling attention to the problem of electoral fraud, and thousands of young activists were filling the streets, demanding a fair election. In October 1949, Mosaddeq led another sit-in in the gardens of the Imperial Palace and pre-sented the shah with a list of demands, but he received no answer. Then on October 23, 1949, in a historic development, a diverse coalition of parties and interest groups announced they would begin working together as a political bloc dedicated to preserving Iran's independence and to promoting democracy and the rule of law. The coalition would be led by Mosaddeq and would be known as the Jebhe-ye Melli, the National Front.

At the American embassy, there were shrugs and yawns. Deputy mission chief Arthur Richards dismissed the front as an "election time hodgepodge" with "no true permanent organization nor . . . any perceivable program." Ambassador Wiley, too, seemed uninterested, dismissing Mosaddeq's popu-lar movement as one that "seems to have no program and appears to be based largely on emotions and futile gestures." But the Americans badly misunderstood the National Front. Mosaddeq deliberately kept its organi-

U.S. ambassador John Wiley (1948–51). A colorful figure with no prior experience in the Middle East, the diplomat was the first to give unconditional backing to the idea that the shah should rule as a strongman, backed by an army "capable of maintaining order." Convinced that Iranians could not be trusted with democracy, he complained that "Iran is a country of opaque mist" and that dealing with the irrational natives was "like eating soup with a fork." He got along well with the shah.

zation loose and decentralized so that the widest possible cross-section of Iranian public opinion could be accommodated in the grassroots coalition— with everyone from left-wing socialists to religious conservatives welcome to join. Although liberal nationalism was an explicit part of its ideology, at this early stage, the front functioned mostly as a pro-democracy movement— and this was the key to its immense popularity. After years of rigged elections, Iranians wanted to see an honest process, and they were thrilled to have the front fighting in their corner.

As elections unfolded during October and November 1949, the vote-rigging became so blatant that even the semiofficial government newspaper *Ettela'at* began demanding explanations. Wiley, Richards, and much of the embassy's political staff, however, continued to pay little attention to what was taking place around them. Besotted by their admiration for the shah, they seemed unable, or unwilling, to understand just how badly the king was losing his grip on the political situation. At one point, the shah's own brother, Prince Abdul Reza, privately told Wiley that the "elections could not have been worse." But still the message did not get through.

On November 2—just two weeks before the shah was scheduled to fly to the United States for a historic visit (the first ever by an Iranian king)— one of his senior cabinet ministers, Abdul Hossein Hazhir, was assassinated in front of a polling station. The shah was quick to play down the incident, reassuring Ambassador Wiley that it was the work of Communist troublemakers—and Wiley seemed to accept this explanation. But the Majles elections were now turning into an ugly distraction from the shah's upcoming trip. British diplomats strongly advised the shah against leaving the country during such a volatile time. But Wiley disagreed. "I think in spite of insistence British Ambassador . . . we must let Shah make trip as planned—take it as a 'calculated risk,'" he cabled to the State Department on November 8. Just one hour later, without any trace of irony, Wiley cabled Washington again, this time to request that the U.S. Army send a supply of teargas canisters to Tehran—"as there is real possibility of need for them."

Mohammad Reza Shah had been itching to visit the United States since the end of 1943, when FDR had scribbled that hasty thank-you note on his way out of Tehran. But pressing issues of one kind or another—the war, the 1946 Soviet withdrawal crisis, Truman's 1948 reelection campaign, the attempt on the shah's life—had always made it hard to find the right time for a visit. Finally, a date was selected for late November 1949, and the shah was determined not to let anything derail it.

Less than two weeks after the Hazhir assassination—as newspapers fizzed with anger, as Mosaddeq commandeered public opinion in the streets of Tehran, and as senior politicians were loudly accused of coordinating the theft of ballot boxes—the shah was on a plane to New York, no doubt relieved to be leaving behind the chaos of Iranian politics for a month.

◌

In true Persian style, the shah came bearing gifts for the White House—an eleven-piece *khatam* (wooden inlay) desk set; a portrait of the American president carved in ivory; and priceless rugs for Truman's wife and daughter. The shah reportedly had "stripped the Palace of the Queen Mother in order to find suitable gifts for the eminent Americans whom he will meet." He and his entourage stuffed their plane so full of heavy Persian antiquities that it proved unable to carry the load. A second four-engine aircraft had to be called into service just to transport the shah's luggage.

Once the entourage arrived in New York, the royal visit kicked off with a banquet at the legendary Persian Room at the Plaza Hotel. Then the shah embarked on a whirlwind tour of eight American states. In Washington, he was made honorary captain of the George Washington University foot-

The first of many visits: The shah arrives in Washington, November 1949. The royal visit to the United States—the first by an Iranian head of state—took place against a backdrop of growing political protests and opposition back home.

ball team during a match against Georgetown. In New York, he opened a landmark exhibit of Iranian art at the Metropolitan Museum. He visited a General Motors plant in Detroit, took tea with Eleanor Roosevelt at Hyde Park, and even found time to visit the Grand Canyon, Las Vegas, the Hoover Dam, Phoenix, San Diego, and Los Angeles—topping it all off with a week of skiing in Sun Valley, Idaho. If at any point the shah worried about the unraveling political situation back in Iran, he did an excellent job of hiding it.

What the shah did seem concerned about, during his trip to the United States, was building up his war chest. Fixated as ever on military hardware, he asked his hosts to include a visit to an aircraft carrier, and he pressed Washington relentlessly for a military aid package. U.S. officials offered Iran modest financial aid in line with the so-called Seven-Year Plan, a joint U.S.-Iranian effort to restructure Iran's economic productivity and promote development. But to the shah, that was a depressing distraction. What he wanted was military hardware and cash: concrete, high-prestige demonstrations of America's commitment to his regime. Anything less, he feared, might make his big, expensive trip to the United States look like a waste of time.

The philosophical differences between the American and Iranian positions were stark. During bilateral meetings in Washington, Secretary of State Dean Acheson suggested the shah focus on internal stability rather than militarization. If Iran developed its economy via the Seven-Year Plan, he said, it could become a stable, prosperous nation and therefore less susceptible to pro-Soviet agitation. But the shah was bored senseless by such tedious sermonizing. He insisted it was unrealistic to work on the Seven-Year Plan before he was sure Iran was safe from external attack—and that could be achieved only by means of a military buildup. These fundamentally different priorities led to considerable frustration during his visit. Again and again American officials found that when discussions turned to military matters, the shah got prickly and defensive, insisting he knew more than anyone else about his country's needs. Background memoranda warned State Department officials that the shah "considers himself the foremost professional soldier in Iran" and that he "would be mortally offended if he were to be bluntly contradicted in a matter of opinion on military matters." Although "his knowledge of the military profession is far less than he thinks," the shah "is convinced he is a completely competent military strategist and as a strategist is convinced Iran needs, and should have, much more aid than this Government is in a position to grant. He is extremely touchy on this subject and should be handled with great care."

While the shah was in Washington, the Americans did their best to raise their concerns about the deteriorating political situation in Iran. The State Department urged him to consider allowing Majles elections to reflect at least some vague respect for the democratic process. To show his good faith, the shah reluctantly agreed to put a stop to the most egregious incidents of vote-rigging. But this was a decision he would quickly come to regret. By the time he returned from his trip at the end of 1949, the election process was completed, and the National Front had won eight seats in the new Majles. In a body of 102 deputies, it did not exactly represent a revolution. But it did mean that Mosaddeq and his allies now had an important platform. Newspapers would cover their speeches on the floor of the Majles, and people in towns and villages far from Tehran would read them.

Life for the shah was about to get difficult.

"One Penny More"

If Mohammad Mosaddeq had been only a democrat, he would probably not have had a fraction of the impact he has had on the history of U.S.-Iranian relations. If he had limited himself to advocating the rule of law and parliamentary democracy, his name might not still be drifting, like a stubborn wisp, through every obituary and epitaph that has ever been written on the death of U.S.-Iranian relations. A certain generation of Iranians would have remembered him as a vigorous campaigner and an honorable politician—a "liberal," a "reformist," and a "constitutionalist." And that would have been the end of the story.

But Mosaddeq was not just a democrat; he was also a nationalist. Because as far as he was concerned, there was no meaningful way to separate the two. How could a country be a democracy if it did not have genuine control over its own affairs? Why let people have a parliament and a free press and a regular election cycle if foreign players in distant capitals made all the really important decisions? To Mosaddeq, democracy did not just mean holding an election every couple of years. It also meant listening to what the people wanted. And in Iran what the people wanted was an end to the merry-go-round of concessions and capitulations and advisory missions that had turned the country into a free-for-all for foreign powers for nearly a century. Decade after decade, this was the one thing almost everyone had agreed on, be they radical Communists, radical Islamists, or something in between. On the rare occasions when the Iranian people had been consulted, they had always made it clear their chief political concern was the sovereignty and integrity of the nation. To Mosaddeq, these were the true sinews of democracy.

The equation worked just as powerfully in the other direction. For Mosaddeq, blind nationalism was worth very little in the absence of democracy and popular participation. One had only to look at the 1920s and 1930s for proof of that. Reza Shah had thundered into town on his white horse, promising to lance the boil of spineless servility left behind by the Qajars. In the process, he had evinced a kind of *cultural* nationalism—banning all traces of Arab-Islamic influence and promoting a militaristic modernism intended to reinvigorate the nation's soul. But in the end, he had turned out to be a dictator—telling Iranians what they could and couldn't wear, assaulting their beloved religious traditions, and shutting down newspapers that disagreed with him.

Mosaddeq's idea of nationalism was a little more relaxed than this. It was nationalism and not xenophobia. Mosaddeq was never hostile to foreign cultures, and he never argued that Iran had to "purge" or "purify" itself of the "backwardness" of Islam. He remained, throughout his life, a secular politician and a great admirer of Western constitutional traditions, but he did not worship blindly at the altar of pseudomodernity the way Reza Shah had—hoping neurotically that if Iran could just build enough railways and factories, or rip enough veils from the heads of women, the West would finally take it seriously. Mosaddeq was no more embarrassed by the ordinary man's attachment to Islamic traditions than he was by his own Swiss doctorate. (When his wife chose to remove her hijab and his mother chose to retain hers, he judged neither woman for her decision.) For Mosaddeq, nationalism was not a question of cheap symbolic gestures or uniform dress codes. It was about a simple principle that anyone could understand: Iran's assets should be controlled by Iranians, for the benefit of the Iranian people.

At other points in history, this belief would have had Mosaddeq battling the British tobacco monopoly or fulminating against Russian control over the Cossack Brigade. In an earlier era, he might have raised his banner against foreign encroachments on Iran's railways or foreign management of its customs revenue. But in 1950 such battles, once epic, now seemed quaint. By the mid-twentieth century, Iran had emerged as one of the world's largest producers of oil, and Mosaddeq stepped into a situation in which the stakes were exponentially higher than any earlier generation of nationalists could have possibly imagined. Iranian oil was fast becoming a precious commodity, fetching hundreds of millions of dollars in markets around the world. But virtually none of this spectacular wealth was making its way back into the country that produced it. In 1950, Iran's oil was—as it always had been—entirely in the hands of the British Empire.

Mosaddeq was in for the fight of his life.

CB

We cannot fully understand how the United States became involved in the British-dominated world of Iranian oil unless we first take a closer look at Britain's own entry into that world. And this, in turn, takes us back to the days of Muzaffar al-Din Shah, the weak and sickly Qajar king who, in 1901, bankrupt and desperate for cash, awarded an exclusive sixty-year petroleum exploration contract to the British entrepreneur William Knox D'Arcy.

For a mere £20,000 signing bonus, D'Arcy had been handed what later turned out to be one of the most lucrative contracts in human history: the right to drill for oil almost anywhere in Iran. In 1908, D'Arcy's men struck oil—the biggest discovery the world had ever seen—and the British government had quickly bought a 51 percent stake in D'Arcy's company, renamed the Anglo-Persian Oil Company (APOC). The Royal Navy's battleships were speedily converted from coal to oil, a process completed in the spring of 1914, just weeks before the First World War broke out. Thanks to this unexpected boost from the oil fields of Persia, Britain found itself in possession of all the fuel it needed to score a decisive victory in its fight against Germany—and then spent the next thirty years transforming itself into a modern, prosperous twentieth-century economy, driven by the power of the internal combustion engine. "Fortune," recalled Winston Churchill a few years later, "brought us a prize from fairyland far beyond our brightest dreams."

For the people of Iran, however, Fortune brought something else entirely. On the saltwater marshes of Abadan, the British built a vast network of flow stations, pipelines, and gas flares that gradually made life a living hell for the desert tribes and traditional communities in the area. A giant refinery was built,* followed quickly by a power station, a water filtration facility, tract housing, and even a small railway. Within a few years, Abadan was transformed from a sleepy community of camel-herding nomads into a teeming city of one hundred thousand people—almost all of them in some way connected to the Anglo-Persian Oil Company.

For the British managers and petroleum engineers in Abadan, there were shops, cinemas, and residential developments complete with English-style terraced houses and luscious green lawns—but for the native population, there was nothing. Iranian laborers were housed in filthy slums and dormitories with primitive sanitation facilities, and they were strictly forbidden to mix with the company's British employees. In the searing desert heat, which often exceeded 120 degrees in summer, water fountains were labeled "Not for Iranians." In the luxurious Persian Club, uniformed waiters served

---

* The Abadan refinery was the largest in the world until Iraqi forces destroyed it in 1980.

cocktails against a backdrop conspicuously free of actual Persians. Many of APOC's employees had previously worked as colonial administrators in British India and seemed unable (or unwilling) to adjust to the fact that they were now guests in a sovereign nation. They drove their cars on the left side of the street, received the *Times* by air mail, and operated separate buses for British and Persian employees. As the years wore on, inevitably, a cloud of frustration rose from the pestilential slums of Abadan, and Churchill's "brightest dreams" began to look more like an Anglo-Persian nightmare.

It was not only working conditions. According to the terms of its contract, APOC was required to give Iran 16 percent of its profits—but in practice, the company paid much less. A series of sophisticated accounting techniques moved the bulk of APOC's profits away from its Iranian balance sheet and onto downstream activities such as overseas distribution and marketing, and allocated losses and operating expenses to exploration work in Iran. To make matters worse, the Royal Navy was allowed to buy Iran's oil at a deep discount. APOC paid little in the way of taxes or import duties to Iran, claiming it was subject only to the British exchequer. APOC also refused to appoint Iranians to its board of directors and did not allow the Iranian government to inspect its books.

In 1933, Reza Shah had demanded a fresh contract with APOC. But the company agreed only to token adjustments, such as vague promises to improve conditions at Abadan, a modest increase in royalty payments, and a reduction in the area of its drilling concession.[*] In a nod to Reza's nationalist sensibilities, APOC changed its name to the Anglo-Iranian Oil Company (AIOC). But in practice, little changed. Throughout the 1930s, workers at Abadan continued to live in a sprawling shantytown of tin-roofed huts nicknamed Kaqazabad, or the "City Built of Paper." There was still no electricity or running water. Laborers were paid fifty cents a day and given no vacation, sick pay, or disability compensation. The company still engaged in slippery accounting practices and shared only a meager percentage of its profits with Iran. And Britain's armed forces were still permitted to buy huge quantities of oil at a deep discount. In the late 1940s, therefore, the Iranian government sat down once again with the AIOC and hammered out a fresh compromise—the so-called Supplemental Agreement of July 1949.[†]

---

[*] APOC agreed to pay a minimum of $5 million a year in royalties. But this figure was expressed in absolute terms rather than as a percentage of profits, so as APOC's profits soared into the hundreds of millions over the course of the 1930s and 1940s, it became irrelevant. The reduction in the concession, from 500,000 square miles to 100,000, was also not painful, as Iran's big oil fields were concentrated along the Persian Gulf coast.

[†] It is also known as the Gass-Golshayan Agreement, after the respective signatories, AIOC managing director Sir Neville Gass and Iranian finance minister Abbas-Qoli Golshayan.

Once again the AIOC made a vague promise to improve working conditions in Abadan, and once again the size of the concession was reduced slightly. But the company still refused to allow Iran to inspect its accounts, and it still refused to meaningfully increase Iran's share of the profits.* When the Supplemental Agreement was announced, therefore, the reaction in Tehran was overwhelmingly negative. Public opinion had shifted definitively against the AIOC, and there was great resistance—much of it led by Mosaddeq—to the idea of a minor tweak of this kind. In the pages of newspapers and in street demonstrations, a great cry went up, urging the Majles not to ratify the Supplemental Agreement.

What the AIOC had failed to understand was that Iran in 1949 was a very different place from the one-man banana republic it had been under Reza Shah. Where once it had had a blustering tin-pot dictator and a rubber-stamp parliament to deal with, now the streets were full of passionate young nationalists, and scores of daily newspapers were ready to condemn any Iranian government that allowed itself to be played for a fool by foreign powers. Mosaddeq and the eight lawmakers from the National Front, especially, represented something never before seen in Iranian politics. Beholden to no interest group and regarded as something like the authentic voice of the Iranian public, the front deputies enjoyed a level of influence far beyond their limited numbers. Mosaddeq himself approached stratospheric levels of popularity: he was regarded almost universally as the only politician in Iran who would stand up for his country and not be bought or compromised behind the scenes by the British. Not surprisingly, then, when the sixteenth Majles convened in 1950 and was presented with a request to ratify the Supplemental Agreement, it formed a Petroleum Affairs Committee and handed Mosaddeq the chairmanship.

The shah and his prime minister, Mohammad Sa'ed, were suddenly in a difficult position. Accustomed to prioritizing the concerns of the British, they now recognized they could not risk acting recklessly against the mood on the streets. And they had little appetite for a public showdown with Mosaddeq. Sa'ed initially refused to present the Supplemental Agreement for a vote and tendered his resignation. His replacement, Ali Mansur, lasted just two months before he, too, lost his nerve. Sensing the gathering storm clouds of nationalism, the British urged the shah to appoint a strongman—Gen. Ali Razmara, chief of staff of the armed forces—as prime minister, in order to drive the agreement through parliament. The shah was uncomfort-

---

* The AIOC promised that Iran's royalties would not be allowed to fall below $20 million annually, but given that the company was now pulling in close to $500 million a year from Iranian oil, this figure was preposterously low.

able with Razmara, suspecting him of harboring ambitions to overthrow the monarchy. But the United States seconded Britain's opinion, arguing he was probably the best option available.* "Surveying the heads of political life in Iran, one detects more dandruff than hair," Wiley wrote to Washington in May 1950. "And by a process of elimination, there is an inclination to revert to . . . General Razmara as the potential strongman."

When it became clear that the army chief of staff was being considered as a potential prime minister, Mosaddeq reacted with one of his classic parliamentary performances. "As long as we have life in our bodies, the National Front will be opposed to a Razmara-led government," he thundered from the floor of the Majles in June 1950. Putting a uniformed general in charge of the country, he warned, would "usher in a half-century of militarism." Behind the scenes, however, the decision had already been made. Both the United States and Britain were urging the shah to choose Razmara, and the Soviets had been quietly promised that Razmara would free Tudeh political prisoners once he was in power. With all three powers singing from the same hymnal, the thirty-year-old shah felt he had little choice in the matter. On June 26, 1950, he bit the bullet and invited General Razmara to exchange his military fatigues for the jewel-encrusted tunic of the Imperial Court.

In an earlier era, perhaps, powerful nations had been able to work behind the scenes like this, manipulating the shah's choice of prime minister without eliciting much reaction from the general public. But in 1950, Iran—like much of the developing world—was changing. As rumors spread through Tehran that the United States had cooperated with Britain to install Razmara, people reacted with anger and disbelief. "The Americans should be careful not to mistake this country for the Philippines or Hawaii," the nationalist newspaper *Bakhtar* fumed. The new U.S. ambassador, Henry Grady, who had the misfortune to arrive in Tehran just four days after Razmara's appointment, was welcomed by angry demonstrations that quickly escalated into a riot and left several people dead. A few days later, when Grady presided over the U.S. embassy's annual Fourth of July party, the leaders of the National Front chose not to attend.

The summer of 1950 was the first time Americans found themselves on the receiving end of an overt demonstration of resentment from the Iranian public. What was striking, however, was just how oddly *pro*-American the resentment sounded at this stage. In 1950 even the harshest criticisms

---

* Razmara had risen through the ranks of General Schwarzkopf's gendarmerie—a force with a reputation as a right-wing anti-Communist brigade—and was close to several officials at the U.S. embassy.

of America were expressed in a language of surprise and disappointment rather than hostility. They often suggested that Americans should "know better"; that they had "strayed from their principles" or been "tricked" by the crafty British. Even at the height of a splenetic assault on American policy, *Bakhtar* appealed to the principles of the Monroe Doctrine, quoted Mark Twain warning his countrymen against imperialism, and it praised the long tradition of neutrality the United States had adopted before World War I. "America's mistakes in foreign countries may not be intentional," the paper argued, suggesting that they might be typical of "young peoples and new countries that have not tasted the unpleasant events of the ages or experienced the vicissitudes of history." Britain had never had it so good in the pages of *Bakhtar*.

In a way, Iran's nationalist newspapers were right in thinking that the United States was not fully complicit in the British agenda. Behind the scenes, many officials in Washington were deeply uncomfortable with London's behavior and believed the AIOC's stubbornness was putting it on a fast track to disaster. Though he never said so in public, President Truman believed that oil-rich nations like Iran were "right" to want to control their own resources and had a "good case against some groups of foreign capital." Privately, American officials, from Secretary of State Dean Acheson to Ambassador Grady, regularly blasted the British approach as arrogant, imperialistic, and likely to drive Iran in the direction of Soviet socialism. The British, meanwhile, felt that Grady and his friends at the State Department were inexperienced and pitifully naïve—"unsuited," as the British ambassador put it, "to dealing with Persian deviousness and intrigue." British officials resented the enormous popularity Americans had built up in Iran and were increasingly nervous about the possibility of American oil companies intruding on their patch. Very little of this intense British-American rivalry, however, was aired in public, so in June 1950, when the United States appeared to give its backing to Razmara, the Iranian public was left with the impression that Washington had taken orders from London.

CB

Once he was actually in power, Razmara made a genuine attempt to work out a compromise. He urged the AIOC to understand that the Supplemental Agreement stood a much better chance of being ratified if the company made a few token concessions as a demonstration of its sensitivity to public opinion. The British response was dismissive and facetious. Razmara was told that the Supplemental Agreement represented the company's "final offer" and that the only gesture of goodwill it might consider "was perhaps free medical treatment of certain hysterical deputies who continued to denounce the Supplemental Agreement" (a reference to Mosaddeq). It was the opening salvo in what turned out to be an extraordinary year in British-Iranian relations. Over the next twelve months, the British would demonstrate an uncanny ability to misjudge the mood in Iran, missing opportunity after opportunity to achieve a workable compromise and avoid a public showdown with Mosaddeq. It was a textbook example of how not to handle a budding nationalist movement in a faraway fairyland.

The first signs of trouble came in September 1950, when the Americans sent Assistant Secretary of State George McGhee to London to persuade the AIOC to do a deal with Razmara. A former Rhodes scholar with a doctorate from Oxford, a self-professed anglophile, and a Texan who had made a fortune in the oil industry, the assistant secretary seemed just the man to speak truth to the AIOC. But from the moment he walked into the AIOC boardroom, the conversation was frosty. McGhee told the AIOC that he had shared the substance of Razmara's demands with some of his buddies in the American oil industry, and they had been "amazed" by how little the Iranians were asking. The heart of the matter, he said, was their simple request to inspect the company's books and the appointment of a few token Iranians to management positions. The only truly "financial" concession Razmara was requesting was that Iran be allowed to buy oil from AIOC at the same low price that the British armed forces did—hardly an unreasonable demand considering that it was Iran's oil in the first place. When McGhee finished speaking, the board of directors met his gaze with a stony silence. "One penny more and the company goes broke," sniffed Sir William Fraser, the chairman.

In 1950 alone the Anglo-Iranian Oil Company had made around $1 billion in profits from Iran and paid only $80 million to the Iranian government. The idea that it was about to go broke was preposterous. And yet Fraser's attitude was typical of AIOC executives: a generally unimaginative lot who rarely left London, they took the view that Iran's ungrateful natives were best seen and not heard. Fraser himself was an accountant by training, a gray and cautious Scotsman who had never set foot in Iran. Under his direction, the AIOC's managers in Abadan operated what economists call an "enclave industry"—a concentrated island of economic activity, managed entirely from overseas, making no effort to become integrated into the economy of the host nation. A special American envoy sent to Iran was shocked to discover that by the end of his three-week visit, he had spent more time in Tehran than all of the AIOC's board of directors combined. "Never in [my] entire experience," he reported, "had [I] known a company where absentee management was so malignant."

Within the British government, too, many officials were concerned about the behavior of the company, feeling it was trapped in an outdated colonial mentality. The British ambassador in Washington, Sir Oliver Franks, complained that "the real trouble with AIOC is that they have not got enough past the stage of western paternalism [which is] a bit out of fashion in this decade." His counterpart in Moscow agreed, telling the Foreign Office that AIOC managers were "still living in the world of 1910" and had failed to absorb the news that the British Empire was no longer in a position to dictate terms to faraway corners of the globe. One government minister singled out Fraser for blame, describing him as a "second-rate intellect" who had "all the contempt of a Glasgow accountant for anything which cannot be shown on a balance sheet." Indeed, many AIOC personnel would later admit that under Fraser, the company had waited far too long to wake up to the realities of the 1950s and made the mistake of regarding Iran's nationalization drive as a cheap populist stunt that would blow over as soon as the insolent natives realized what they had got themselves into. "At no time before [1950] did anyone contemplate that we would not stay [in Iran] forever," recalled the AIOC's general manager Eric Drake in a later interview. "There was no reason why it should ever come to an end as far as we could see."

When push came to shove, though, the British government demanded little accountability from the AIOC. Although the UK taxpayer was the majority shareholder in the company, the postwar Labour government of Clement Attlee always seemed intimidated and slightly in awe of the AIOC. Fraser and his men, in turn, went out of their way not to consult with Attlee's government, whose left-wing politics they instinctively distrusted. The result, in the words of John Wiley, was an *imperium in imperio*—a state-within-a-state whose actions were never subjected to serious government oversight. "I know of no instance when the Government exercised its power of veto over the Board," Wiley wrote after his retirement, and "no instance where the Company . . . seriously consulted the British Embassy in formulating its policies." On the ground in Iran, it was much the same story. The AIOC's managers "acted like pro-consuls," recalled one American official. "In most of the cities in Iran, the residence of the [AIOC] representative . . . far outshone the residence of the British consul." Over time the AIOC came to exist in an impregnable cocoon, never having to answer to external authorities, either British or Iranian. Complacency and arrogance became endemic to the company's culture.

The reason for this was simple: the British government desperately needed the AIOC's cash. World War II had left Britain virtually bankrupt, and in the following years, the Labour government had launched an ambitious plan to create a cradle-to-grave welfare state in the United Kingdom. It had nationalized the coal mines, the railways, and the steel industry; provided workers with pensions, sickness, and unemployment benefits; and in 1948 created the National Health Service to provide free, universal medical care to every British subject. All this, in turn, was dependent on the cash that flowed into government coffers from the Anglo-Iranian Oil Company. In 1951 the British ambassador in Washington, Sir Oliver Franks, told the State Department his government was pulling in $500 million per year from Iranian oil. Without this money, Franks said, Britain would not be able to pay for its rearmament program, and there would be a serious blow to "our cost of living." Franks asked his American friends to understand that when it came to maintaining the prosperity of postwar Britain, maintaining control of Iranian oil was nothing less than "a prime strategic necessity."

At the beginning of 1951, one of the AIOC's senior managers, Sir Frederick Leggett, tried to sound a warning, arguing the company desperately needed to make a "fresh start" with Iran, "on the basis of equal partnership," or risk outright nationalization. But he was swiftly overruled. Leggett even complained to the government that his AIOC colleagues were "helpless, niggling, without an idea between them, confused, hide-bound, smallminded, blind" and "generally ineffective." Again he got nowhere. The Foreign Office admitted that Leggett's assessments "coincide in general . . . with our own impression," but it did nothing to force a change in the company's behavior. Socialism, decent working conditions, access to health care, housing, and sanitation—the lofty ideals that the Labour Party had spent a century championing at home—were, it seemed, not appropriate for the Iranian employees of a British company overseas. What was good for the goose in Aberdeen was never offered to the gander in Abadan.

Cʒ

In September 1950 the British were blessed with an Iranian prime minister who—despite extreme public antipathy to the AIOC—was prepared to give his full backing to the Supplemental Agreement and probably had the votes to secure its ratification. All he needed were a few symbolic concessions to give the public the impression he had "wrestled" a good deal out of Britain. Instead, he was abandoned to the wolves. As ferocious press attacks against Razmara mounted, the British ambassador, Sir Francis Shepherd, sent the prime minister a letter remarkable for its tone-deafness—advising him to take a "strong line of conduct" against those Iranians who were not appreciative of "the immense service to mankind of the British people in recent times." Clearly, Razmara was going to be on his own. In October, when he argued for ratification of the Supplemental Agreement from the floor of the Majles, he was, in effect, asking deputies to approve a British ultimatum—a document unilaterally handed down from London, with zero modifications. Not surprisingly, he was shouted down—mocked and pilloried as a British patsy. On the streets of Tehran, the reaction was even more ferocious, loudly condemning Razmara as a traitor. By the time the matter came before the Petroleum Committee on November 25, there was little question which way the vote was going to go. The Supplemental Agreement was unanimously rejected.

Four weeks later, in nearby Saudi Arabia, the American oil consortium Aramco announced that it had concluded a deal to share its profits on a fifty-fifty basis with the Saudi royal family. If ever there was a stark reminder of just how differently the Americans and British behaved in the Middle East, this was it. The fifty-fifty principle had, in the words of George McGhee, "an aura of fairness understandable to the ordinary man," and he urged his British counterparts to consider something similar in Iran. The British were furious at the timing of the Aramco announcement, but they could also see that times were changing. Behind the scenes, the AIOC scrambled to talk with Razmara about a fifty-fifty arrangement—a radical climb down from their position just a few weeks earlier. By now, however, the situation had developed a momentum of its own. As Razmara negotiated in secret with the British, in January 1951 thousands poured onto the streets of Tehran to protest the AIOC. Expressing years—if not generations—of frustration with the company and the British generally, they had a single, simple demand they now shouted at the tops of their voices: *Nationalize Anglo-Iranian.*

All this could have been avoided. Just two months earlier the Majles had rejected nationalization as too radical, preferring to tweak the terms of the Supplemental Agreement rather than buy out the AIOC's assets and throw it out of the country. A fifty-fifty arrangement would have sailed through parliament with little opposition, and both sides could have claimed victory. The AIOC would have had a new operating agreement in its hands. The pro-British Razmara would have remained in power. And the National Front's influence would have been significantly diminished. Now, instead, the AIOC, an immovable object, faced an unstoppable force. The Iranian people had decided a basic principle was at stake—the one Mosaddeq had been talking about for years—and that was their right to control their own resources.

For reasons that will only ever be known to him, Razmara kept this new round of negotiations with the British a secret. Perhaps he hoped to take credit for persuading the AIOC to sign a fifty-fifty agreement, or perhaps he thought he could secure something even better. In any event, it all came to an end for Razmara on March 7, 1951, when he walked into Tehran's central mosque for a memorial service and was greeted in the courtyard by three bullets from a Colt revolver. He died instantly. The shah blamed religious extremists, but the suspicion that the shah himself—who still saw the general as a threat—might have been behind the assassination has never been put to rest. Whatever the case, the British had lost one of their last dependable allies on the Iranian political scene.

Sensing the volatility of the situation, Britain's ambassador publicly announced for the first time that his government was prepared to consider a fifty-fifty arrangement with Iran. But his statement only demonstrated how out of touch the British had become. In the high-voltage atmosphere of March 1951, no Iranian politician was going to contradict the public clamor for nationalization. Even the new prime minister, Hossein Ala, politely demurred. The same Hossein Ala who had grown up in London and attended the best British boarding schools; whose father had once served as Persian ambassador in London. It would have been hard to find a more pro-British politician in Iran—or a more powerful demonstration of how decisively the earth had shifted beneath the belly of the British lion. Ala broke the news gently to his friends in the British embassy. The idea of nationalization had "penetrated far and wide," he said. "A fifty-fifty arrangement might have been accepted a little while ago," he explained regretfully. "But now something more would be required."

On March 15, 1951, ninety-six deputies walked solemnly into the Majles chamber to consider a bill presented by the National Front calling for the nationalization of Iran's oil industry. All ninety-six deputies voted in favor. Even in the Senate, half of whose members were appointed by the shah, the vote was unanimous. The British had been dealt a defeat of historic proportions. But worse was still to come. A month later the Majles Petroleum Committee passed a draft nine-point law outlining how nationalization was going to proceed. Ala, unhappy that he had not been consulted about this step and unwilling to give it his support, resigned as prime minister—leaving a vacuum for the man of the hour to step into.

In the spring of 1951, Mohammad Mosaddeq was, in the words of one biographer, so popular he was "unable even to step onto the streets without being mobbed by admirers." The job of prime minister was his for the asking. But the shah found himself under heavy British pressure not to give the job to Mosaddeq.* Following the "advice" of the British embassy,

---

* Two years earlier, the shah had had the constitution amended to give himself the power to appoint prime ministers directly. However, the Majles still had the power to approve or reject his choice.

Mohammad Mosaddeq, prime minister (1951–53). An ardent nationalist and democrat, Mosaddeq reached soaring heights of popularity with Iran's growing population of young, modern, and educated middle classes. After nationalizing the Anglo-Iranian Oil Company, he fought an epic feud with the British government. He was eventually brought down in a military coup funded and heavily choreographed by the U.S. Central Intelligence Agency.

he nominated instead Seyyed Zia Tabatabai—the man who had helped his father to power in 1921 and subsequently built up a thirty-year reputation as an unscrupulous wheeler-dealer and unflinching servant of British interests. But the Majles rebelled lustily against his choice, voting 79 to 12 to recommend Mosaddeq instead. In the face of overwhelming popular sentiment, there was little more the shah could do for his friends in London.

Before accepting the job of prime minister, Mosaddeq insisted that the Majles approve a step-by-step plan that he had drawn up for how nationalization was going to proceed. His plan called for a special committee to determine a reasonable compensation payment for the AIOC, the creation of a new National Iranian Oil Company (NIOC), and a fund to send Iranians abroad to learn how to manage their country's oil industry. This plan, too, passed unanimously.

Suddenly the mighty British Empire, powered to victory in two world wars by a seemingly infinite supply of Iranian oil, found itself staring over a precipice that everyone—most of all its American friends—had tried repeatedly to warn it about. Not only had its worst nemesis in Iran been elected prime minister, but the country's parliament had put Britain on notice by passing a bill nationalizing the once-invincible Anglo-Iranian Oil Company. For a country that had just won a decisive victory in the Second World War, this was an abrupt and unexpected reversal of fortune—and even Britain's closest allies shook their heads in disappointment. "Never," mused Secretary of State Dean Acheson, "had so few lost so much so stupidly and so fast."

The British government, incandescent with anger, refused to accept what had happened. It dispatched more Royal Navy gunboats to the Persian Gulf, protesting bitterly that Iran's action was of dubious legality. What followed next was a titanic struggle, one that would embroil Britain and Iran for two long years in one of the most public and damaging political disputes in the history of the modern Middle East. Eventually, that struggle would end, in 1953, with a victory of sorts for the British.

But it would also, in the process, push the United States into making a decision for which it is still paying the price.

The Liberty Bell and the Wool Pajamas

CR RO

You could hear it everywhere that spring. The sound of victory—sweet, naked, and uncomplicated. In remote and windswept corners of Iran, illiterate tribal nomads sang songs of praise to the new prime minister. In the city, Radio Tehran announced that "all of Iran's misery, wretchedness, lawlessness and corruption during the last fifty years" were finally coming to an end. In dusty bazaars, merchants who had once passed their days fiddling with worry beads began doing a brisk trade in commemorative plates and bowls with Mosaddeq's face on them. The influential Ayatollah Abolqasem Kashani even compared Mosaddeq to the ancient kings of Persia. Cyrus, he suggested, or perhaps Darius. A man for the ages—come to set his people free.

For Iranians, the election of Mosaddeq, and the nationalization of the oil industry, were only the first steps in what everyone knew was going to be a long and difficult battle with the Anglo-Iranian Oil Company. But they also represented something never before seen in Iranian politics. For the first time in history, the nation's parliament had acted truly independently and stood up for the wishes of the Iranian people. For the first time, it had elected a prime minister supported by the public rather than by the shah or the British. And for the first time, it had passed a law that was a direct and unmistakable challenge to the foreign powers that for decades had dominated Iran's internal affairs. "The British Empire had been slapped in the face," recalled a prominent Iranian who lived through it all. "And Iran felt a triumph it had been awaiting for fifty years."

Possibly the only person resisting the urge to get swept up in the euphoria was the new prime minister himself. If there was one thing Mosaddeq had learned to loathe during his long and unpredictable career, it was the culture of sycophancy and empty flattery that had traditionally marked Iranian politics, and as prime minister he did all he could to discourage it. On assuming power, he quietly asked Tehran's newspaper editors to avoid praising him too lavishly and to allow space for dissenting points of view. When he heard that a group of citizens was planning to erect a statue of him in a Tehran square, he quickly put a stop to it, making an impassioned statement about the dangers of "idolatry." In his first month as prime minister, he even wrote privately to the chief of police, asking him to make sure that people who criticized his government did not run into "difficulties" as a result of their views. "No nation gets anywhere under the shadow of dictatorship," Mosaddeq had said in 1944, from the floor of parliament. As prime minister, he was determined to live by those words.

There were other, smaller gestures as well, harbingers of a changing political vocabulary in Tehran. As prime minister, Mosaddeq refused to be called "Your Excellency" and refused to collect his salary, asking that the money instead be spent on scholarships for law students. He declined the official limousine put at his disposal and was often spotted driving through town in his own lime-green Pontiac Chieftain. When he was told that twenty-four soldiers would be placed on guard duty in front of his house, Mosaddeq insisted on providing them with food and lodging and paying their salaries himself. Believing that an Iranian—especially one born into a wealthy landowning family—should not need material inducements to do the work of his country, Mosaddeq had, throughout his fifty-year career in public life, gone out of his way not to accept money from the taxpayer, and he was not about to start now.

There is a famous picture of Mosaddeq in his old age, well-known to every Iranian. It shows him frail, sitting on the ground, wrapped in a simple dark cloak, and holding a wooden cane. Surrounded only by twigs and tree branches, he looks like a Franciscan friar, a humble man who has given away everything and been reduced to poverty. There are other pictures of him, though—equally famous—that reveal a more rambunctious personality. One shows Mosaddeq braying like a horse at one of his own jokes. Another shows him thrusting his hand into the air as he declares his defiance of a military tribunal. In these photographs, the prime minister comes across less as an impoverished martyr than as a scene-stealing ham—a puckish rebel gleefully mocking the phalanxes of stuffed shirts who stand in his way. Taken together, both sets of images reveal something about the man, the secret to his idiosyncratic appeal. Until Mosaddeq came along, Iranian politicians had been stern and self-important figures—aloof, expressionless, and thoroughly at home amid the pomp and circumstance of the Imperial Court. Mosaddeq was the antidote to all that. With his round and hairless head, his frail physique and his monkish asceticism, he was a little bit Gandhi—and with his fiery, uncompromising insistence that Iran's oil belonged to the Iranian people, a little bit Hugo Chavez.

For both these sins, the British hated him.

CB

As prime minister, Mosaddeq's first task was to reassure the world that nationalization would proceed in an orderly, responsible fashion—and that he was not some wild revolutionary bent on bringing the oil industry to a standstill. In a relatively friendly meeting with the British ambassador, he insisted his government harbored no ill will toward Britain and emphasized that Britain would have priority in the purchase of Iranian oil. The AIOC, meanwhile, would receive compensation for its losses and was welcome to participate in the nationalization process—even, if it wished, to appoint representatives to the committee overseeing the transition. The company, however, refused to cooperate. As far as the AIOC was concerned, nationalization was an illegal and intolerable breach of contract, and it was not about to give any portion of the process its seal of approval.

Following the AIOC's lead, the British government lodged an appeal against Iran at the International Court of Justice in The Hague—and hopes of compromise evaporated. Mosaddeq, ever the constitutional lawyer, reminded Britain that the World Court had no jurisdiction over a commercial contract and that every country had a right to nationalize its industries—a position with which the United States wholeheartedly (if quietly) agreed. Secretary Acheson gently informed Britain that State Department lawyers were having trouble seeing a legal case for the AIOC, beyond the general principle that "breach of contract involved payment of damages or compensation." Fundamentally, Acheson said, "no Government can deny itself the sovereign rights to nationalize an industry within its territory." Beyond the legal evaluation, Acheson also had a bit of advice for his British friends. Nationalization, he said, would go ahead in Iran with British cooperation or without. It was simply the direction the world was going now, and Britain would be foolish to stand on the wrong side of history. If the AIOC could just accept the basic *principle* of nationalization, Acheson suggested, it would be in a much stronger position to shape the terms of the final settlement.

America's advice was ignored. Britain continued to treat Iran's oil nationalization law as a flagrant act of criminality—and the result was a nasty standoff between Iran and the AIOC. In June 1951, following a thirty-day grace period, Mosaddeq sent gendarmes to seize offices and assets operated by the AIOC, which he now pointedly referred to as the "former company." The British responded with their own show of muscle, threatening to subject Iran's oil exports to a naval blockade and even raising the possibility of military action. Tensions quickly mounted, and by the end of June, Mehdi Bazargan, director of the newly formed National Iranian Oil Company (NIOC), was on his way to Abadan to make it clear who was in charge. British tankers, Bazargan announced, could not continue loading oil until they provided itemized receipts to the Iranian government. The AIOC laughed off the idea as preposterous. From London, the company chairman, Sir William Fraser, ordered all his ships to pump their oil back into the storage tanks of Abadan and return home empty—effectively bringing the export of Iranian oil to a halt. "When they need money," Fraser said publicly, "they will come crawling to us on their bellies."

This was exactly the kind of drama the United States had hoped to avoid. If the British followed through on their threat to starve and humiliate Iran into submission, the Truman administration now feared, the Iranian economy would go into free fall, precipitating chaos, unrest, and hunger—the ideal conditions for a Soviet-backed coup. If, on the other hand, Britain chose military action, the result would be even worse. The issue would get dragged before the United Nations, where the United States would have to choose between taking a principled stand for Iranian independence (as

Directors of the newly renamed Anglo-Iranian Oil Company announce to workers that the British company has been taken into national ownership.

it had done against the Soviets in 1946) or siding with its British ally—and inviting a chorus of condemnation from across the third world, possibly even driving millions of Iranians into overt sympathy with Moscow. Whichever way the British-Iranian standoff played out, it seemed, it had the makings of a catastrophe.

In Washington, President Truman gathered his National Security Council for urgent talks—and found the mood around the table decidedly pessimistic. Most of his deputies felt the United States had only one real option: to treat the nationalization of Iranian oil as a fait accompli. It had clearly become a matter of existential importance to the Iranian people, and the sooner the British could be persuaded to accept it, the sooner the crisis could be resolved. Many in the administration felt genuine sympathy for Iran's position and believed the root of the crisis lay with Britain's inability to adapt to the times. Mosaddeq, in the words of Dean Acheson, represented a "very deep revolution, nationalist in character, which was sweeping not only Iran but the whole Middle East"—and Britain needed to wake up to it. Throughout the spring of 1951, therefore, Washington took a strong and surprisingly public line against its British ally. In Tehran, the U.S. ambassador, Henry Grady, said that nationalization was an "accomplished fact" and "it would be wise for Britain to adopt a conciliatory attitude."

London was incensed. Britain's friendship with the United States, it assumed, was a little more durable than this—and Washington's failure to take a more forceful line against Iran seemed disgraceful. Nevertheless, the British recognized that they could ill afford to upset the Americans and that they would have to at least go through the motions of engaging Mosaddeq before calling out the gunboats. For the next several weeks, therefore, the British government spoke frequently and publicly about its desire to find a peaceful resolution to the dispute.

Mosaddeq, too, attempted conciliation. On June 28 he urged AIOC employees to remain in the country and continue their work under the authority of the newly created NIOC—with the same salaries, benefits, and legal rights. "Our country will welcome you warmly," he said. The response from the AIOC was swift and unequivocal. Fraser had no intention of allowing the AIOC's years of expertise to fall into the hands of Iranians, and he forbade his employees to accept Mosaddeq's offer. Then, for good measure, he ordered all but the most essential staff to return to Britain.

With the AIOC's operations in Iran now effectively abandoned, Iranians saw little reason to continue tiptoeing around the sensibilities of the "former company." At the end of June, the Iranian government told the AIOC that all its properties were now subject to search and seizure. AIOC officials scrambled to move sensitive files to the British embassy for safekeeping, even as Iranian authorities went to the home of the AIOC's Tehran chief, Sir Richard Seddon, and found mountains of documents—including a number still burning in the fireplace. Within hours, Seddon's home turned into a bustling crime scene. Photographers recorded the "evidence" and developed prints in the bathtub, while translators worked in the living room, scrambling to put together a dossier of records to release to the public.

The picture that emerged from the AIOC's secret documents proved enormously embarrassing to the British. Over the years, it turned out, the company had interfered relentlessly in Iranian politics, bribing cabinet ministers and Majles deputies and working to force out politicians who were unfriendly to its interests. It had paid newspaper editors to write unflattering stories about National Front leaders (often accusing them, ironically, of being British agents). It had even helped write speeches in support of the Supplemental Agreement for former prime minister Razmara. When these revelations hit the next morning's papers, they ignited a blaze of anger and recrimination. Politicians who had cooperated with the AIOC were condemned as traitors, and Mosaddeq blasted what he called the company's history of "sinister and inadmissible interventions" in Iranian affairs.

London began to go on a war footing. "We have only for one moment to stretch out a terrible right arm," growled the Tory peer Duff Cooper, "and we should hear no more from Persia but the scampering of timid feet." With a general election fast approaching and an economic crisis to deal with, Labour Party bosses privately urged more vigorous action from the government. "Persian oil is of vital importance to our economy," noted Foreign Secretary Herbert Morrison. "Parliamentary and public feeling . . . would not readily accept a position where we surrender effective control of an asset of such magnitude." The military chiefs agreed. In July 1951 the First Lord of the Admiralty argued that the British public was "tired of being pushed around by Persian pip-squeaks" and that a successful military operation would give "everyone a fillip and dispel the dumps and doldrums" brought about by economic recession. Detailed plans were drawn up for an air and sea operation, codenamed Plan Y, that would involve 70,000 troops in the invasion and occupation of Iran's oil fields.

When word reached Washington that London was considering a military option, President Truman communicated to Prime Minister Attlee, in the strongest possible terms, that he should think again. Truman made it clear the United States would support British military action in Iran, but only if it was in response to a clear act of aggression from the USSR. Otherwise, he said, Britain would be on its own.

Attlee's government got the message and shelved its military plans, but the matter was still far from resolved. In Tehran, Ambassador Grady reported with alarm that the British appeared to be looking for other, secretive ways to remove Mosaddeq from power, with little concern for the consequences. Grady was astonished to observe Britain operating with what he felt was a mindset belonging more to the 1910s than to the 1950s—apparently "determined to follow the old tactics of getting the government out with which it has difficulties." Mosaddeq, he noted with frustration, "has the backing of 95 to 98 percent of the people of this country. It is utter folly to try to push him out."

Increasingly, Truman found himself in an impossible position. London was adamant that the quickest way to resolve the crisis would be for the United States and Britain to present a united front against Mosaddeq. But Truman, convinced that a confrontational approach would only play into the hands of the Soviets, preferred to play the honest broker—to try to convince Britain to accept the principle of nationalization, while simultaneously pressing Iran to be flexible in its execution. The British were having none of it. Iranian oil, they explained, was "*the* major asset which we hold in the field of raw materials. Control of that asset is of supreme importance." Iran, meanwhile, was equally determined that there be no turning back from this historic moment of national liberation.

Truman thus found himself caught between two entrenched and thoroughly irreconcilable positions. Exasperated, running out of options, yet keenly aware that he was peering over the precipice into what was fast becoming his greatest foreign policy crisis since Korea, he did what American presidents always do when nothing else seems to be working. He assigned a special envoy.

⅓

W. Averell Harriman—multimillionaire banker, former cabinet secretary, ambassador, head of the Marshall Plan in Europe, thoroughbred racing tycoon, Yale and Groton graduate, Skull and Bones man, and heir to his father's immense Union Pacific Railroad fortune—arrived in Tehran in mid-July to find that no one particularly wanted him there. "What is the use of Harriman flying here?" asked the British ambassador at a press conference. "We are not inviting mediation in this matter." The streets of Tehran, for their part, were even less welcoming. On the day Harriman arrived, ten thousand demonstrators—convinced by Communist propaganda that he was there to back up the British position—gathered to chant "Down with Harriman."

As if all this weren't challenging enough, Harriman was informed on his arrival that Mosaddeq was gravely ill. Harriman and his team dutifully headed to Mosaddeq's house, were shown straight into the upstairs bedroom, and found the prime minister propped up in bed, looking pallid and sickly. His hands were crossed on his chest, and as the visitors walked into the room, he managed only to flutter the fingers slightly. Throughout his life, Mosaddeq had suffered from an unusual neurological disorder that brought about moments of extreme physical frailty—even bouts of bleeding from the mouth or stomach. The condition had never been properly diagnosed, but it sometimes had emotional as well as physical manifestations. Once or twice in his career—such as during a particularly passionate Majles speech—he had wept openly, just before fainting and collapsing to the floor. The Western media had been quick to latch on to all this—developing a stock image of the prime minister as a weeping, fainting hysteric. The "fabulous invalid," one American magazine had called him, a "tremulous, crotchety Premier." Journalists particularly delighted in the fact that Mosaddeq saw nothing unusual in conducting cabinet meetings from the comfort of his bed—the only world leader to be regularly photographed in his pajamas.

Like all caricatures, this one had a grain of truth in its hyperbole—Mosaddeq could be difficult, emotional, and downright eccentric. But the figure Harriman found in Tehran was far more complex than he had been led to expect—a well-mannered, savvy negotiator who was exasperating only in his deliberately roundabout and philosophical debating style and his dogged attachment to principle. Time and again Harriman sat by Mosaddeq's bed and tried to explain the dynamics of the petroleum industry to him, hoping to convince him that the realities of distribution networks and exploration technology would make it difficult for Iran to produce oil on its own and enjoy large profits. But none of it was of the slightest interest to Mosaddeq, who saw the whole thing as a matter of national independence. At one point, when Harriman asked Mosaddeq to show more flexibility, he responded by comparing Iran's struggles with the British to the Boston Tea Party of 1773. What, he asked, would America's Founding Fathers have thought if some Iranians had turned up on the wharf and tried to persuade them not to throw the tea overboard?

Unquestionably, discussing practicalities with Mosaddeq could sometimes be frustrating and wearying—even surreal. Nevertheless, despite their different negotiating styles, Mosaddeq and Harriman established a good rapport and, after seven days of talks, arrived at a proposal that appeared tantalizingly close to resolving the issue. A British negotiator sent from London, Sir Richard Stokes, was told that Iran was prepared to negotiate a compensation package for the AIOC if the British government would "recognize the principle of nationalization." But Britain recoiled at the suggestion. Stokes was instructed to make "no further concessions" and to return home immediately.

The next day Mosaddeq held a press conference to announce his disappointment that the talks had failed. "The result is nothing," he said. "It is no good. Everything is finished." Hours later Prime Minister Attlee cabled Truman, barely able to disguise his glee. "I think you'll agree breakdown in talks entirely due to Persian side," Attlee wrote. "Only course now is, we hope, for complete U.S. support of His Majesty's Government." Truman flatly disagreed, telling Attlee that the United States was not about to act in a way that "would appear to be in opposition to the legitimate aspirations of the Iranian people."

For London, this was the final straw. Obviously Washington was never going to share its sense of urgency. It would have to take matters into its own hands. At the end of August, London slapped a series of harsh economic sanctions on Tehran, blocking the import of crucial supplies such as sugar and steel, and freezing Iran's access to its hard-currency accounts at British banks. The British also went out of their way to make sure the Iranians couldn't run a successful oil industry in their absence. They sabotaged key parts and machinery at the Abadan refinery or left them inoperable. When Iran tried to recruit foreign petroleum experts, Britain persuaded several European countries not to allow exit visas to citizens traveling to Iran. Finally, Britain, whose ships were already patrolling the Gulf, threatened to intercept any foreign tanker caught transporting "stolen oil from Persia." Iran's oil revenue plummeted from $125,000 a day to less than $3,000. For all practical purposes, Iran was now under an international embargo.

Convinced the wagons had finally begun to circle around Mosaddeq, the British decided it was time to take their case to the United Nations. A successful resolution against Iran in the Security Council, Foreign Secretary Morrison felt, might finally demonstrate to the world that "we have been the saints and Mossadegh has been the naughty boy." Washington advised strongly against such action, afraid the Soviets would use the opportunity to pose as standard-bearers for the world's poorer nations by vetoing Britain's resolution. Britain, as ever, seemed deaf to American advice—convinced the Iranians would be so out of their depth at the UN that they would have a hard time persuading anyone to take their side.

It was quite possibly the worst political miscalculation of 1951. As soon as Mosaddeq heard Britain was going to the UN, he announced he would fly to New York personally and present Iran's case. A shrewd and eloquent constitutional lawyer with a flair for showmanship, Mosaddeq knew he had a compelling moral argument, one likely to win sympathy from much of the developing world. The chance to prosecute the British Empire before a jury of international opinion was simply too good to pass up.

☙

Mosaddeq's plane touched down at New York's Idlewild Airport on October 8, 1951, and he was met on the tarmac by a huddle of hyperactive reporters and sundry well-wishers, some of them waving Iranian and American flags and shouting "Long live the champion of Asia's people!" After all the buildup, America was finally getting to meet Mosaddeq in person, and curiosity was running high. "The Fainting Fanatic," as *Newsweek* had dubbed him, was fast becoming a media sensation in the United States—ridiculed as a clown and a buffoon but also (and often in the same breath) hailed as the Thomas Jefferson of the Middle East. As he shuffled slowly down the stairs and onto the runway, Mosaddeq appeared frail and exhausted by the journey, but he found the energy to read a short statement into the nest of microphones that had been prepared for him. "Great similarity," he said, "exists between the efforts and sacrifices of the Iranian people today [and] what your ancestors did two hundred years ago to release their homeland from the fetters of economic and political imperialism."

Mosaddeq was convinced that the American public would feel a natural kinship with Iran's struggle. But at the United Nations, he was up against a formidable opponent. Britain's ambassador, Sir Gladwyn Jebb, was a smooth and sophisticated diplomat, unafraid of a fight. And when the debate kicked off at the Security Council, Jebb opened with fireworks, accusing Iran of endangering the activities of "a great enterprise, the proper functioning of which is of immense benefit not only to the United Kingdom and Iran but to the whole free world." The Iranians, Jebb said, had made "wild accusations" and were guilty of "base ingratitude." Mosaddeq failed to appreciate the "prudent and far-sighted" actions of the AIOC and had taken an attitude that was "so entirely negative." The "distressing situation which has arisen," said Jebb, was "entirely owing to his own folly."

Mosaddeq presented a slightly different version of events. The UN, he reminded Jebb, was the "ultimate refuge of weak and oppressed nations, the last champion of their rights." For Britain to bring a resolution before the Security Council portraying itself as a victim, struggling to contend with the hostile and aggressive actions of the big, bad Iranians, was to make a mockery of the institution. Britain was cynically trying "to persuade world opinion that the lamb had devoured the wolf." The British government had rejected all attempts at negotiation and "instead used every illegitimate

"Champion of Asia's people": Mosaddeq shares a joke with Ernest Gross, U.S. delegate to the United Nations, during a break in the proceedings, October 1951. The prime minister was in the United States to face off with Britain at a special session of the UN Security Council, but he extended his visit for three weeks of talks with U.S. officials aimed at resolving the dispute. In the process, he became a celebrity in the United States.

means of economic, psychological and military pressure that it could lay its hands on to break our will." Mosaddeq found it ironic that Britain claimed Iran's actions were a threat to world peace. "Having first concentrated its warships along our coasts and paratroopers at nearby bases," Britain now "makes a great parade of its love for peace," he mused. "It required a deficient sense of humor, to suggest that a nation as weak as Iran can endanger world peace. . . . Iran has stationed no gunboats in the Thames."

By the time Mosaddeq finished, the British resolution reeked of death and defeat. The Security Council was, by definition, a forum for discussing imminent threats to international peace and security—not commercial disputes between private companies and sovereign nations. Britain's case was thin, and Mosaddeq's stirring oratory had only drawn attention to that fact. The United States did its best to throw its ally a lifeline by watering down the language of the resolution, but India and Yugoslavia quickly added amendments of their own in support of Iran, and hopes of a British victory dwindled. After a little more debate, the council decided the best course of action was to "postpone the discussion"—in effect, sparing Britain the humiliation of an actual vote. It was, in real-world political terms, a catastrophic defeat for the British.

From his triumphant performance in New York, Mosaddeq headed straight to Philadelphia for a specially arranged visit to Independence Hall. The symbolism was lost on no one. In the very spot where, 175 years earlier, rebellious American colonists had gathered to put their signatures to a declaration of independence from the British Empire, Mosaddeq now sat with a pen in his hand, signing the guest book, as the mayor and local dignitaries looked on. "The hardy men who first settled this continent more than three centuries ago would have understood our action," he told a crowd of cheering Americans, "and I do not doubt that their descendants will understand it." Before leaving Philadelphia, Mosaddeq paused to examine the Liberty Bell. He appeared utterly captivated—running his finger down the crack, carefully studying the inscription, and generally giving the impression of a man in the presence of something sacred. "In my country, liberty is still to be won," he said with emotion. "In yours it is already an immortal tradition." The next morning the photograph of the prime minister and the Liberty Bell was on the front page of every American newspaper.

From Philadelphia, it was on to Washington, where the man of the hour changed back into his pajamas. Following a meeting with Truman at the White House, Mosaddeq was escorted to the presidential suite at Walter Reed Army Medical Center. Assistant Secretary McGhee was dispatched to Mosaddeq's hospital bed. He persuaded Mosaddeq to postpone his return to Tehran, and for the next three weeks, Mosaddeq and McGhee sat together, day after day, one man in a suit and the other in pajamas—spending, by McGhee's estimate, some eighty hours in private discussions.

During the discussions, McGhee came up with a creative proposal for a joint partnership between the NIOC and the AIOC that he felt both parties could be persuaded to accept. It established the ironclad principle of nationalization and put Iran in charge of exploration and production, but it gave Britain responsibility for the marketing, shipping, and sale of Iranian oil internationally. The contract would be in effect for fifteen years, and the price of Iran's oil would be determined by negotiations between Britain and Iran—with the proviso that it would not exceed $1.10 per barrel. Mosaddeq indicated he was prepared to open discussions with the British along these general principles, and McGhee was thrilled. He seemed on the cusp of a historic agreement.

While McGhee and Mosaddeq hammered out the details of the compromise package, however, British domestic politics intervened. On October 25 the Conservative Party, led by former prime minister Winston

Prime Minister Mosaddeq with President Truman at the White House.

Churchill, squeaked through with a narrow victory at the polls—bringing to power a government even less sympathetic to compromise than its predecessor had been. For Churchill, who had personally supervised the Royal Navy's conversion to oil in 1914 and had come of age at a time when the sun would seemingly never set on the British Empire, Iranian oil was more than a strategic interest—it was a national birthright. His new foreign secretary, Anthony Eden, was equally immovable. In late October, Acheson met five times with Eden, hoping to convince him that the McGhee-Mosaddeq proposal deserved to be taken seriously. But it was no use. The sticking point was the principle of nationalization, which Eden refused even to consider.

When McGhee heard from Acheson that the British had rejected his proposal, he was devastated. "To me it was almost the end of the world," he later recalled. "I attached so much importance to an agreement and honestly thought we had provided the British with a basis for one." Mosaddeq, by contrast, accepted the news with quiet resignation. "You have come to send me home," he predicted, as soon as he saw McGhee's long face that morning. Sagelike, Mosaddeq behaved as if he knew something McGhee didn't—and in a way he did. McGhee had assumed all along that if only the right language could be found or the right dollar amount established per barrel of oil, then the British might come to accept the principle of nation-alization in exchange for some continued role in the Iranian oil industry. The reality, however, was that he was dealing with two positions that had become existentially irreconcilable: one nation determined to exercise con-trol over its natural resources, and the other determined never to let that happen. There was no middle ground.

Mosaddeq, who had long ago recognized this fact, was not the least surprised to hear the British had rejected the McGhee formula. "You have never understood," he said gently to his friend. "This is basically a political issue."

03

If McGhee had any doubt about the wisdom of that statement, all he had to do was sit aboard Mosaddeq's plane for the journey back to Tehran. At every fuel stop along the way, jubilant crowds welcomed the prime minister, cheering and hurrahing for the man who had stood up for the impover-ished nations of the world. In Cairo, the airport shut down as thousands stampeded into the terminal building to catch a glimpse of the Middle East's hero. Within hours the entire city turned into a sea of demonstrators waving placards reading "Long live Mosaddeq!" and Egyptian newspapers hailed the arrival of the man who had "conquered history."

Tehran, meanwhile, welcomed Mosaddeq home as if he were a living, breathing messiah. It took over an hour for his lime-green Pontiac Chieftain to travel the four miles from Mehrabad Airport to his house on Kakh Street, inching forward through the tens of thousands crammed into the streets. Young men climbed over one another for a chance to touch it; thick layers of flowers piled up like snow on the windshield. One disheveled old man even tried to throw himself under its wheels as a human sacrifice and had to be pulled away by police before the procession could continue.

But it was not just the people of Iran and the Middle East who were intoxicated by Mosaddeq's burgeoning national liberation movement. In the United States, a Gallup poll taken shortly after Mosaddeq's UN appear-ance showed that only 2 percent of Americans felt the United States should take Britain's side against Iran. Only six years after American GIs fought side by side with British soldiers on the beaches of Normandy, this was a remarkable public relations victory for Mosaddeq. When the Iranian prime minister first arrived in New York, American newspapers had described him as "feeble, senile, and probably a lunatic," taking at face value what had been printed in the British press. After six weeks in the United States, however,

Mosaddeq had managed to win over the American public with a unique mix of eccentricity, charm, and rhetorical eloquence.

Mosaddeq's nationally televised performance at the UN, in particular, had left Americans deeply impressed. In 1951 the United Nations was still something of a brave experiment, in a world not used to seeing rich and poor nations sitting at the same table, speaking to each other as equals. Television too was a new phenomenon, and places like "Persia" were known to Americans mostly through the pages of *National Geographic* or Hollywood films that reduced the inhabitants to picturesque extras herding camels and grunting in monosyllables. In 1951 most Americans had never seen a real, live Persian, much less one who wore a three-piece suit, spoke in eloquent French, and could present a sophisticated legal argument over the course of several hours. By the time he left the United States, the Iranian prime minister had become something more than the man who gelded the British Empire. He was also a national celebrity, so much so that *Time* magazine named him its Man of the Year for 1951.

From all this, the newly elected British government could draw only one conclusion: Mosaddeq was a dangerous, reckless villain who had to be taken out of the picture. The Conservative thinking in the corridors of power was that under Labour, Britain had tried for too long to protest legally the violations of the AIOC's commercial contracts, and no one had listened. The blockade on Iranian oil and the crippling sanctions that Britain imposed on Iran's economy had only made the Iranian public— and much of the world—rally around Mosaddeq. After taking a number of steps that the Conservatives regarded as restrained and nonconfrontational, a mood of belligerence and impatience was growing, a consensus that legalistic measures were having no efficacy. The time had come, in the words of one British official, to stop being so "United Nationsy." The time had come for regime change in Tehran.

Britain spent the first months of 1952 looking for ways to undermine, embarrass, and generally discredit Mosaddeq in the eyes of the Iranian public. In January it made a heavy-handed attempt to influence the outcome of that season's Majles elections. As soon as the first round of voting began, the old British networks went into overdrive. Voting in Tehran proceeded smoothly, but then reports of rioting trickled in from the provinces—rioting that was almost certainly the work of British agents. Very quickly, the security situation surrounding ballot boxes deteriorated. Eventually Mosaddeq felt he had no choice but to suspend the election until it could take place in a nonviolent atmosphere. His political enemies and the British pounced on this decision, gleefully portraying him as a dictator and hypocrite.

Britain's ongoing embargo of Iranian oil, meanwhile, was taking a serious toll. With oil revenue shriveling from $45 million in 1950 to less than $1 million by 1952, government employees were going unpaid, basic services had trouble functioning, and Mosaddeq found it virtually impossible to implement his ambitious social program. To make matters worse, thirty thousand Iranians had lost their jobs when the Abadan refinery was shuttered, making demand for welfare and social services higher than ever. At one point, things got so bad that Iran's overseas diplomats had to be recalled for lack of funds—the British blockade on Iran's access to hard-currency accounts meant they could not be paid in foreign exchange.

Yet remarkably, the public was still largely behind Mosaddeq. Far from capitulating, the prime minister struck a Churchillian note, asking Iranians to pitch in and work together during this period of austerity, reminding them that future generations would thank them for their fighting spirit.[*] "If the Iranian nation," he said, "aspires to regain the status and position it deserves, it must not shrink from deprivation, self-sacrifice, and loyalty to its homeland." The public, almost uniformly, responded. Children turned up at school selling "deficit bonds" to raise money for the state; housewives accepted bread rationing with little grumbling. A spirit of camaraderie and collective sacrifice infused daily life now—something not previously seen in the conduct of Iranian foreign policy. Iranians, it seemed, were coming to the conclusion that the nationalization of oil was their fundamental right—and they were prepared to make considerable personal sacrifices to defend it. Had he not been on the other side of the fence, Churchill himself might well have said of the Iranians that this was their finest hour.

In June 1952, Britain turned up the pressure even more by filing a lawsuit at the International Court of Justice at The Hague. Once again Mosaddeq's rhetorical and argumentative skills were called upon, and once again he put in an unforgettable performance—arriving at the World Court to tell the judges in person that they had no jurisdiction over a commercial dispute between a private company and a host nation. Britain's lawyers tried to cast the AIOC's 1933 contract with Iran as a "convention" between the British and Iranian governments. But when the judges handed down their ruling, it was yet another embarrassment for Britain. They had been so easily convinced by Iran's argument that even the British representative on the fourteen-judge panel voted against his country—a first in the history of the

* Mosaddeq was right about this much. To this day, Iranian postage stamps and other official memorabilia celebrate the anniversary of the oil nationalization. March 20, the date on which Mosaddeq's nationalization bill went into law, is today Oil Nationalization Day, a national holiday in Iran.

court. Afterward the chief British lawyer sheepishly admitted that he probably would have done the same.

Mosaddeq returned to Tehran from The Hague to find a country almost beside itself with jubilation and pride. And yet Iran was also, paradoxically, becoming difficult to govern. Despite his enormous popularity, Mosaddeq still felt unable to allow Majles elections to resume without the threat of British sabotage, and riots and civil disturbances were becoming a regular feature of political life. Day by day, economic hardships multiplied, and day by day, the Communists grew louder and stronger—just as the Americans had predicted they would—accusing Mosaddeq of being a Western puppet and openly demanding his (and the shah's) overthrow and the establishment of a people's republic.

Mosaddeq also found himself in a standoff with the shah. Worried that Majles elections could not take place in an atmosphere of insecurity, Mosaddeq asked the shah for control of the armed forces—a power that was constitutionally his but that, under the Pahlavis, had traditionally been left to the shah. Mohammad Reza—the ersatz soldier-king, the boy cadet warned by his father never to loosen his grip on the country's military apparatus—was not about to give up this privilege. "Better that I pack my suitcase and leave the country," he told Mosaddeq during a tense three-hour meeting at the Imperial Palace. Mosaddeq responded by handing in his resignation.

The veteran politician Ahmad Qavam was quickly appointed to replace him, but his government lasted only five days, the shortest in Iranian history. Immediately condemned as a British stooge and facing thousands of angry nationalists protesting Mosaddeq's resignation, Qavam declared martial law and sent out riot police across Tehran. On the third day of his government, troops opened fire on demonstrators, killing dozens.[*] On day five, Mosaddeq was summoned to the Imperial Palace and offered his old job back.

It was now obvious to the shah, as it was to everyone else, that little remained to stop Mosaddeq from brushing aside the monarchy and establishing a republic with himself as president. Public opinion increasingly saw the shah as a British puppet, and Mosaddeq as the true patriot. And the shah—who had witnessed his own father's rise to power—understood better than anyone where this could lead. In reality, the shah had little reason to worry, as Mosaddeq was a committed royalist. To assuage the shah's anxiet-

---

[*] The events of that day became known as the Uprising of 30 Tir, after the corresponding date on the Persian calendar, and have since been memorialized by the Islamic Republic as the first great popular uprising against the shah's regime. Following the 1979 Revolution, the street that ran in front of Qavam's old house was pointedly renamed 30 Tir Street.

ies, Mosaddeq invited him to name three generals he personally trusted to act as advisers to the government, and he took steps to civilianize the War Ministry (renamed the Defense Ministry). To demonstrate his sincerity, he even sent the shah a copy of the Quran, writing on the flyleaf, "Consider me an enemy of this Holy Book if I ever betray His Majesty, or the constitution, or if I accept the presidency after others have changed the constitution."

Privately, Mosaddeq's message to the shah was simple: "Let the king reign, and let his prime ministers rule." He had repeatedly said as much during Majles debates of the 1940s, and he said it again now. If the shah's powers were made ceremonial, he argued, then the shah could sit back and allow himself to be adored by his people as a symbol of national pride. It was the model adopted by countless European monarchies, and history had shown that it was the only real way for the institution of kingship to survive in the modern age. "You could go down in history as an immensely popular monarch if you cooperated with democratic and nationalist forces," Mosaddeq told him. It was the best advice Mohammad Reza Shah never took.

○ʒ

By the time the long, hot summer of 1952 came to an end, the Iranian public appeared divided in its attitude toward the United States. On the one hand, the belief was growing that American policy in Iran was uncertain and confused, and that Washington's lack of experience in the region was making it too quick to follow London's lead. Many Iranians were convinced that Washington had engineered the installation of Qavam as prime minister and was now working hand in glove with London to undermine Mosaddeq. Their ire was raised more when the Truman administration cooperated with the British embargo of Iranian oil, and then again when Washington decided, under heavy pressure from London, to cancel millions of dollars in agricultural and technical assistance. Starved for cash and facing a severe budget crisis, Mosaddeq was now blasted from the left for having gone cap in hand to the United States in the first place—condemned by well-organized communist propaganda as an American "puppet." Words like that had an effect. The Tudeh Party was able to organize large anti-American demonstrations in major cities, and Iranian politicians, who had previously never been shy about praising the United States, increasingly discovered it was the kiss of death even to be seen socializing with Americans. At a weekend party given by the U.S. embassy in late July, one hundred elite Iranians were invited but only a handful turned up. A similar event the following week was quietly canceled.

And yet, in the hearts of many Iranians, there was still an enormous reservoir of affection for American values—especially for the selfless contributions made by previous generations of Americans in Iran. Mosaddeq himself was a child of the Constitutional Revolution—part of a generation that had come of age in the era of Baskerville and Shuster, Woodrow Wilson, and the Fourteen Points. It was hard for him—much harder than for some of his younger supporters—to think of America as anything other than an enlightened nation, whose democratic values always placed it on the right side of history. And he was not alone. In June 1952, as Communists and nationalists were busy staging demonstrations and tearing one another's posters off the walls, news arrived in Tehran that the old schoolmaster Samuel Jordan had died. For a brief moment, the city went quiet. Placards denouncing Western imperialism were set aside to make way for a more dignified procession. Mourners—thousands of them—filed through the streets of the capital, descending on what was once the American College of Tehran to pay their respects to the beloved old Presbyterian. It was, in a sense, a final requiem for a more innocent time.

Despite this brief moment of civility, Tehran that summer was a decidedly volatile place. Virtually every weekend, crowds of agitated young men swirled around the gates of the parliament building, engaging in demonstrations, counterdemonstrations, and fistfights. In late July all this turmoil prompted Secretary Acheson to write to London with new proposals—and an earnest plea to find some way out of the impasse. The British took two weeks to reply, and when they did, they half-heartedly proposed that perhaps managers from the AIOC could sit down with the Iranians and try to hammer something out. Acheson was incensed. Exploding in anger at the British ambassador, he accused Britain of refusing to take seriously the depth of Iranian frustration—and worse, of making a mockery of America's well-intentioned attempts to find a resolution. Britain's reply, he said, was "related and relevant to our proposal . . . only by being expressed on paper by means of a typewriter."

To Acheson, it was obvious the government of Winston Churchill was no longer interested in finding a diplomatic solution. "The whole tone of the correspondence on the British side," he later recalled, "suggested that it was edited by the Anglo-Iranian Oil Company." But Acheson had long since given up on the AIOC's ability to play a constructive role in the dispute. "Past history," he wrote, "made abundantly clear the unsuitability of the Company to the role of diplomatic agent."

Mosaddeq had much the same kind of experience with Churchill. Toward the end of the summer, he made one more attempt to bridge the gap, suggesting that Iran and Britain submit to arbitration at the World Court to determine a fair, final tally of compensation payments and lost revenues on both sides. On its face, Mosaddeq's offer appeared reasonable, and Truman strongly urged Churchill to accept it. But it was no use. As far as Churchill was concerned, the Anglo-Iranian dispute had moved past the point of discussions about barrels of oil and international arbitration. It had moved into a new phase—a final showdown, in which there could be only one victor.

Neither Truman nor Mosaddeq knew it at the time, but the British had gone to see a man about a coup.

1953

In 1952, if you had landed in Tehran and said you were in search of a man who looked nothing like Mosaddeq, sounded nothing like Mosaddeq, and acted nothing like Mosaddeq, you would have been quickly steered in the direction of Brig. Gen. Fazlollah Zahedi. If you said you were tired of listening to the bald, frail, and bedridden intellectual droning on about freedom of the press and constitutional government, and you just wanted a bit of red-blooded, brass-knuckled authoritarianism to quicken your pulse, then there was no question about it. Zahedi was your man.

With his full head of hair, his battering-ram physique, and a schoolboy smirk that always made him look like he was up to his eyebrows in sin, Zahedi was everything Mosaddeq was not. Fifty-four years old and a veteran of the old Cossack Brigade, he was a product of the law-and-order right wing of Iranian politics—a hang-'em-and-flog-'em, take-no-prisoners action hero baked in the timeless mold of Reza Shah. There was no Swiss doctorate here—only a high-school diploma and a couple of years at the national military academy, followed by a long career in the armed forces. There was no inclination for verbal sparring matches or eloquent repartee—no aristocrat's love for the bon mot or the well-chosen understatement. A notorious gambler and sexual athlete whose first marriage had ended in divorce before he was thirty, Zahedi's skills seemed to lie in the pursuit of less cerebral pleasures. He was, in the final analysis, a soldier, a fascist, and an unapologetic playboy.

Given how little Zahedi and Mosaddeq had in common, it is hard to believe the two men could ever have sustained a five-minute conversation, let alone worked together in politics. And yet in 1951, Zahedi briefly served as interior minister in Mosaddeq's first government. The experiment had lasted just two months. In August of that year, Zahedi had ordered police to shoot live rounds at a peaceful demonstration, and Mosaddeq had fired him on the spot.

The political disagreement between the two men might have ended there, but unfortunately for Mosaddeq, Zahedi was more than just a trigger-happy reactionary. He was also a first-class soldier. And he happened to know a thing or two about overthrowing a government. In 1921, when the future Reza Shah had come thundering into Tehran with his Cossack cavalry, it was Zahedi—then just a twenty-three-year-old officer in the Tehran police force—who had helped secure the streets of the capital and ensure the coup went off successfully. Impressed by the young commander's martial skills, Reza had taken Zahedi under his wing after that, and quickly allowed him to rise to the rank of brigadier-general—the youngest in Iranian history. The rapid promotion gave Zahedi his first real taste for the thrill of strong-man politics and authoritarian government—as well as a lifelong feeling of loyalty to the Pahlavi dynasty.

For Britain in 1952, Zahedi was the obvious man to lead a coup against Mosaddeq—and not only because he was a skilled military tactician. Zahedi was also, importantly, regarded with approval by the United States. In the 1940s, Zahedi had formed close ties with Gen. Norman Schwarzkopf and the Gendarmerie Mission—a force with a reputation for militant anti-Communism—and enjoyed friendly relations with the U.S. embassy. Since the Americans had proved to be reluctant allies in the fight against Mosad-deq, the British reasoned, anyone they chose to lead a coup would have to be someone who was not going to arouse U.S. antagonism.

In Washington, the Truman administration was still opposed to all talk of a coup, but its time was running out. Nineteen fifty-two was an election year, and Truman had made it clear he would not be seeking another term in office. With a lame-duck president in the White House, the British knew their latitude for maneuver was greater than it had been for some time. So in the late summer of 1952, Britain's spy networks in Tehran went into action. Quietly approaching Zahedi through intermediaries and secret channels, they began laying out plans for a coup d'état to remove Moham-mad Mosaddeq from power. Zahedi was all ears.

Zahedi's first task was to exploit existing tensions within the National Front and persuade Mosaddeq's most important allies to turn against him. He began with the biggest prize of all, Ayatollah Abolqasem Kashani—a fiery, influential cleric who had rallied religious conservatives and poorer Iranians behind Mosaddeq's nationalization program. Kashani, frustrated by Mosaddeq's secular approach to government, was already wavering, and the British believed he could easily be nudged into open opposition. So in the autumn of 1952, Zahedi went to work on twisting the ayatollah's arm. A similar effort was made to pry away Muzaffar Baqa'i, leader of the left-wing Toilers Party and another important Mosaddeq ally. By picking off the preacher Kashani and the socialist Baqa'i, the British hoped to chip away at the National Front from both its right and left wings and leave Mosaddeq's grand coalition looking vulnerable.

Inevitably, the flurry of closed-door meetings between Zahedi, the British, Kashani, Baqa'i, and others began to look suspicious, and before long rumors were swirling that the British embassy was laying the groundwork for a coup. Mosaddeq, incensed by such reports, reminded Britain that the purpose of an embassy was to promote friendship and cooperation, not to plot the overthrow of the host government. On October 22 he went a step further. Given the evidence that Britain was actively trying to destabilize his government, he said, Iran would be breaking off relations. The government closed the British embassy and ordered all British officials to leave the country.

In Washington, news of Britain's expulsion from Iran was received with dismay—but also a certain measure of quiet vindication. For years, Americans had had to listen to sneering British diplomats tell them they were naïve and inexperienced—that they were overly idealistic about Iranians—and that everything was under control. "We have had hundreds of years of experience on how to treat the natives," the British had insisted, when American officials had tried to nudge them to improve living conditions in Abadan. In just two years, however, the empire that claimed to have all the answers had lost control of its most important overseas asset. The AIOC had been nationalized. And now, all its diplomats were getting kicked out of the country as well.

Truman found it hard to muster sympathy for Britain. "We tried to get the block-headed British to have their oil company make a fair deal with Iran," he wrote to his old friend Henry Grady. But "no, no, they could not do that. They knew all about how to handle it [and] we didn't."

∞

Those words were Truman's last on the subject. On November 4, American voters went to the polls to choose his successor and delivered a verdict that would turn out to have a decisive impact on U.S. policy toward Iran. In a fiercely fought election, Gen. Dwight David Eisenhower, hero of the Second World War, supreme commander of NATO, and aging source of inspiration to centrist Republicans, won in a landslide over his Democratic rival, Gov. Adlai Stevenson of Illinois. Eisenhower's victory gave the Republicans control of the White House for the first time in twenty years—and brought to power an administration with a very different set of priorities.

Throughout the election campaign, Eisenhower had accused the Democrats of being "soft on Communism"—of allowing Soviet spies and Communist sympathizers to infiltrate the highest levels of the federal government. He had railed against "Korea, Communism and corruption." He had implied that the Democrats did not really want to win the Korean War and promised that, once in office, he would take vigorous steps against the creeping red menace—in Pyongyang, in Washington, or anywhere else it dared to rear its head. The British knew immediately that this single-minded determination was something they could work with.

On October 31, 1952, four days before the election, Mosaddeq recorded a special televised message addressed directly to the American people. Speaking in English for the first time in his career, he informed them that Iran was surprised that "the British Government would cause relations between the two countries to sink so low as to keep millions of bereaved Iranians in the gravest economic chaos," all for the sake of a "profit-loving oil company." Mosaddeq hoped "all honest peoples of the world, and particularly the noble and humanitarian people of the United States of America, [would] give us all moral support and material assistance for the realization of our national salvation." The message was set to be aired sometime after the election, as an olive branch to the new administration—but it never saw the light of day.

Instead, the British delivered their own message. On November 15 the intelligence operative Christopher "Monty" Woodhouse flew to Washington to present a secret proposal to the State Department and the newly formed Central Intelligence Agency for the overthrow of Mosaddeq. Code-named Operation Boot, the plan called for a massive campaign of scare-mongering propaganda, combined with violent street demonstrations, leading ultimately to the ouster of the prime minister in a climate of chaos that would leave the Iranian public grateful to have the whole episode behind them. But the British had just one problem. They had been expelled from Iran, and without officials on the ground, they were in no position to instigate a coup. This, they hoped, was where the CIA might come in.

Of course, the United States was not about to overthrow Iran's government simply to do Britain a favor. And it was even less likely to do so in order to restore the Anglo-Iranian Oil Company to its former monopoly. But if there was one thing that did motivate U.S. foreign policy in 1952, it was fear of Communism. Already, American forces had spent two years on the Korean peninsula, fighting and dying in a war intended to prevent Chinese and Soviet socialism from spreading into Southeast Asia, and they had no desire to repeat the experience in the Middle East. If the British expected to get anywhere with their American friends, therefore, they needed to speak their language. And Woodhouse understood this instinctively. "Not wishing to be accused of trying to use the Americans to pull British chestnuts out of the fire," he later recalled of his approach in those initial meetings, "I decided to emphasise the Communist threat."

Throughout November and December, the British shamelessly exploited the Republicans' preoccupation with Communism—feeding exaggerated and faulty intelligence to their less-experienced American counterparts. Mosaddeq, they claimed, was now relying heavily on the Tudeh Party for support and would soon have no choice but to start making significant concessions to Communists in order to keep the National Front in power. Yes, he might *seem* like a nice, cuddly democrat, but experience had shown that a nation like Iran was not really "ready" for democracy. Mosaddeq-style liberalism in a third-world country could easily lead to chaos, and chaos would lead to Soviet scheming, and before anyone knew it, we would all wake up and find that Iran had become a socialist republic at the heart of the strategically important Middle East.

At first, Britain encountered considerable resistance to its proposal. The CIA station chief in Tehran told his bosses in Washington that the scheme reeked of "putting U.S. support behind Anglo-French colonialism" and that it would be a mistake to get involved. But the British soon found a fast friend in Allen Dulles, the CIA's deputy director, who had been tipped to become director under the new administration. Dulles, like his brother John Foster Dulles, who was about to become secretary of state, was a fanatical anti-Communist, and as he listened to what the British were saying, his pulse began to quicken. Knowing that the outgoing Democratic administration would never agree to a covert operation against Mosaddeq, Dulles instructed CIA staff not to breathe a word of it to Truman and Acheson. "Let's not get this thing evolved," he said, "until the Republicans and my brother Foster take over."

The idea that Mosaddeq was about to deliver Iran into the hands of Soviet Communism was patently absurd. Privately, Britain's own assessment was that "there were no signs that Persia was nearer Communism" than it had been before he took office. And virtually every knowledgeable observer of Iran agreed that Mosaddeq was temperamentally and politically hostile to Communism. In 1944, while still a Majles deputy, he had famously blocked a Russian bid for an oil concession. As prime minister, he had purged the army of officers he considered sympathetic to Communism. Even when he nationalized the oil industry in 1951, he had made it clear he had no intention of replacing Britain with Russia—or even of selling oil to the USSR. "The Russians will receive nothing," he had said during his visit to the United States. "All of our oil output goes to our former customers. The West has priority." Again and again, Mosaddeq had proved himself to be, in the words of George McGhee, a Western-educated aristocrat with "no reason to be attracted to socialism or communism." In January 1953 a memorandum prepared by State Department experts for the incoming administration noted that Mosaddeq was "neither a communist nor a communist sympathizer." His nationalization agenda had "almost universal Iranian support," and he had a deeply antagonistic relationship with the Tudeh Party, which considered his overthrow a "high priority."

The Eisenhower administration ignored all these reports. Rather than listen to the advice of its own spies and bureaucrats, it got straight to work on the task of undermining Mosaddeq. Picking up where Britain had left off, the CIA initiated and funded a fierce campaign of propaganda in Iran's boisterous press. Day after day, newspapers were filled with creative insinuations about the prime minister, claiming one minute he was a Communist, the next a British agent, at other times a homosexual or an atheist or a Jew. Almost all these articles were written by the CIA. "Any article that I would write," Richard Cottam, an Iran specialist advising the CIA, later admitted, "would appear almost instantly, the next day, in the Iranian press." (Cottam estimated that in 1953 four-fifths of Tehran's newspapers were under CIA influence.) Mosaddeq, for whom freedom of the press was sacrosanct, refused to censor any of it.

But the press campaign against him was only the beginning. Early in 1953 the CIA hired the Rashidian brothers—a trio of wealthy Iranian businessmen who for several years had been receiving monthly stipends from London to run a network of undercover operatives—to push senior politicians, newspaper editors, preachers, merchants, and activists into active opposition to the government. Muzaffar Baqa'i, Hossein Makki, and Abolhassan Haerizadeh—all leaders of major political parties that belonged to the National Front—defected from the coalition, giving the impression that Mosaddeq's grand alliance was crumbling.* But the most devastating desertion was that of Ayatollah Kashani. In January 1953 the fiery old cleric declared himself in open opposition to Mosaddeq and described the prime

---

* Some of this bickering and fracturing in the front was organic, the natural fraying at the edges of a coalition that included diverse, and sometimes conflicting, interests. Religious conservatives, for example, had long pressed Mosaddeq to ban alcohol sales and enforce modest dress codes— ideas that were anathema to leftists, who had pushed him to enact socialist land reforms and give women the right to vote. Personality differences also played their part as several of Mosaddeq's deputies, impatient for power, criticized the prime minister's leadership style. In the final analysis, however, most evidence suggests the National Front would not have disintegrated as quickly or as dramatically as it did without the copious amounts of cash and arm-twisting supplied by British and American espionage networks.

minister as an infidel and a traitor. "Such men should be hanged by the people," Kashani thundered in one sermon.

On February 28 a mob of roughnecks from the poorer quarters of Tehran, incensed by false rumors that Mosaddeq had tried to nudge the shah from power, descended on Mosaddeq's house carrying knives and sticks and shouting "Long live the shah!" as they tried to break down the door. The prime minister, who was in bed working, climbed over the back wall of his garden and escaped, still wearing pajamas. Media reports described the riot as a spontaneous demonstration of popular support for the shah, but internal British documents suggest something far more orchestrated. The attack on Mosaddeq's house, the embassy reported, was "certainly organised by Kashani."

Abandoned by fair-weather friends like Kashani, actively opposed by the United States, Britain, Russia, and the shah, Mosaddeq in 1953 found it increasingly difficult to maintain tactical alliances among Iran's political elites and was forced to rely more and more on the support of the Tehran street. But street politics in Iran could be a fickle and unpredictable force. As winter turned to spring, Mosaddeq noticed that rallies held by his supporters were increasingly being overrun by Communists and turned into anti-American, anti-Western demonstrations. Although he didn't realize it, CIA agents were orchestrating this process, employing locals to pose as Communists and carry banners expressing their support for "Mosaddeq and Communism." Bit by bit, the thought was being planted in the mind of the average Iranian: What did it mean that Mosaddeq's premiership was being propped up by a groundswell of Communist support?

On cue, American newspapers and magazines began referring to Mosaddeq as a "fiery old demagogue" who was "allying himself with the Reds." An article in *Time* warned that "Tudeh infiltration of Mossadegh's government is now so deep that Communist agents can, in some cases, set government policy." The CIA, in turn, seized on these press reports and placed them in front of Eisenhower with a simple and urgent message: *Do something*.

Initially, the president was reluctant to approve a covert operation. Britain's entire approach to Iran had been "paternalistic," Eisenhower argued—Churchill was largely to blame for the situation, and it was a terrible idea for the United States to go galloping to his rescue. The British prime minister, Eisenhower confided in his diary, had an unhealthy obsession with "trying to relive the days of World War II," when the United States and Britain "were sitting on some rather Olympian platform with respect to the rest of the world and directing world affairs from that point of vantage." Those days were over, Eisenhower believed, and for America to follow Britain's lead would give Mosaddeq an opportunity to "accuse us of being a partner in browbeating a weak nation." When Britain's foreign secretary, Anthony Eden, visited Washington in March, Eisenhower told him bluntly that Mosaddeq was "the only hope for the West in Iran"—adding, for good measure: "I would like to give the guy ten million bucks."

Eventually, though, Eisenhower was brought around to the Dulles brothers' point of view. In a series of White House strategy meetings in the spring of 1953, the red-baiting brothers forcefully drove the agenda, and though some murmurings of concern were heard around the table, the atmosphere in the room made it clear that dissenting views were not welcome. By the end of May, the decision had been made.

Mosaddeq, unaware that any of this was taking place, still believed the United States was the one powerful country most likely to be sympathetic to Iran's plight. On May 28 he sent an urgent appeal to Eisenhower, telling him the economic situation in Iran was growing desperate and could be alleviated only with a $25 million loan—or, at the very least, permission to sell oil to the United States.

It took a month for Mosaddeq to receive a reply, and when he did, it was obvious America's attitude had changed. "The failure of Iran and the United Kingdom to reach an agreement," Eisenhower wrote, "has handicapped the Government of the United States in its efforts to help Iran. There is a strong feeling in the United States . . . that it would not be fair to the American taxpayers . . . to extend any considerable amount of economic aid to Iran so long as Iran could have access to funds derived from the sale of its oil."

The final decision to overthrow Mosaddeq had already been made by the time this letter was sent. The U.S. ambassador, Loy Henderson, had been recalled to Washington—officially for "consultations" with the State Department, but in reality to keep him out of harm's way. As far as Mosaddeq knew, he had written to the president and was awaiting his reply. But in Washington, the president had given his approval for covert action. Those few officials still opposed to the idea had been told to keep quiet or lose their jobs. Operational procedures were now being feverishly transmitted over the telephone lines at CIA headquarters.

And in June 1953, as Mosaddeq waited patiently for Eisenhower's response, a Quiet American was already on his way to Tehran.

⋄

Kermit Roosevelt, Jr., was the kind of young man every American mother would have wanted her daughter to marry in 1953. Polite and soft-spoken, a graduate of Harvard, the thirty-seven-year-old was the quintessential New England collegian, full of affable boathouse manners and always decked out

The Quiet American: Kermit Roosevelt, Jr.,
chief conspirator in the CIA's covert action
operation against Mosaddeq in August 1953.

in tortoiseshell spectacles and a worsted suit. Described by an acquaintance
as "well-educated rather than intellectual," Roosevelt, like many of the CIA's
early employees, was blessed with impeccable social connections: Teddy
Roosevelt was his grandfather, FDR was a distant cousin, and Winston
Churchill had been a good friend of his father's. When he arrived in Tehran, however, the Yankee blueblood identified himself to everyone as "James
Lochridge," a midlevel bureaucrat employed by the American embassy.

Roosevelt was joined in Tehran, on August 1, by General Schwarzkopf,
who came into town carrying two large sacks stuffed with cash. Schwarzkopf
renewed his old contacts in Iran's military and police, explaining to them
what was required. The secret mission, which the Americans code-named
Operation Ajax, had four principal elements. First, a vigorous propaganda
campaign conducted in the press would convince Iranians that Mosaddeq
was inclined toward Communism. Second, opposition politicians would
instigate riots and disturbances to give the impression Iran was teetering
on the verge of chaos and needed a steady hand at the wheel. Third, the
cooperation and support of military officers would be secured. And finally,
against this background, the shah would dismiss Mosaddeq and name General Zahedi as his replacement, bringing great relief to a frightened and
exhausted public.*

---

* A few years earlier, the CIA would not have needed to cook up such an elaborate plot—it would
merely have pressured the shah behind the scenes to fire his prime minister and name a more

To this end, Kermit Roosevelt began by paying the shah a series of confidence-building visits. Every night in early August at the stroke of midnight, the American spy—lying on the floorboards of a car with a blanket pulled over him—would be sneaked onto the grounds of the Imperial Palace, and every night the shah would meet him in the shadows near the palace entrance. What Roosevelt needed from the shah was his signature on two *farmans* (imperial decrees), one dismissing Mosaddeq and the other naming General Zahedi as prime minister. But the shah was anxious. Certainly, he had no objection to seeing Mosaddeq go. But he was apprehensive about putting his signature to the *farmans,* in case the plot failed and the public found out he had cooperated with it. That could spell the end of his reign and possibly even his life.

Finally, on the night of August 9, the shah agreed to sign the *farmans.* But he had one condition: once he signed the decrees, he and his wife would fly up to Ramsar on the Caspian Sea, where the royal family had a hunting lodge, so they would be out of harm's way during the coup. "If by any horrible chance things go wrong," he added, "the Empress and I will take our plane straight to Baghdad."

On August 15 ("coup day," as the Americans called it) things did, in fact, go wrong. A little after midnight, a military convoy snaked its way to Mosaddeq's house, the *farmans* in hand, ready to force the prime minister to resign and to arrest him if he resisted. But at the last minute, someone had tipped off Mosaddeq's chief of staff, and a contingent of troops was waiting at the house to arrest the plotters. For the next several hours, groups of coup plotters who had not heard the news continued with their individual missions—one contingent even dragging the foreign minister out of his bed, barefoot and shouting. Tehran was plunged into turmoil. Finally, at seven a.m., Mosaddeq came on the radio to announce that there had been an attempted coup, arranged by "foreign elements." On the Caspian coast, the shah heard Mosaddeq's voice on the radio and panicked. Piling himself and his wife onto a twin-engine Beechcraft, he flew directly to Baghdad. The royal couple arrived in the Iraqi capital—unannounced, ungroomed, and incognito—asking for the name of a "good hotel."

---

cooperative replacement. But the previous summer Mosaddeq's brief resignation and replacement by Qavam had resulted in widespread rioting and forced the shah to retract his decision. The British and Americans had taken away a powerful lesson, that Iran was now a nation in which public opinion mattered. No longer could foreign powers work behind the scenes, as they had done in the 1910s and '20s, to influence Iranian politics, however much the shah might be prepared to cooperate. They now had to bring the nation along with them—in the streets, in the newspapers, on the floor of the parliament. They had to convince the public that Mosaddeq was dangerous, reckless, and unpatriotic. And they had to reassure the shah that he would not be incurring the anger of his own people if he chose to get rid of him.

In Tehran, news of the failed coup and the shah's flight to Iraq was greeted with outrage and scorn. "O traitor!" roared Foreign Minister Hossein Fatemi in front of a frenzied crowd of supporters. "When you heard that your foreign plot had been defeated, you made your way to the nearest country where Britain has an embassy!" It was worse than Fatemi realized. In Baghdad, the shah quietly contacted the British and American ambassadors, requesting "urgent guidance" as to what his next move should be. He had even complained that he was a man of "very small means outside Iran" and begged the U.S. embassy to help him sell the aircraft he had arrived in. The royal couple then boarded the first commercial flight out of Iraq and ended up in Rome—where Italian press reports speculated wildly about what the "staffless, baggageless, moneyless" emperor was going to do so many miles from home. The newspapers in Tehran went even further. As far as most editors were concerned, the shah had "abdicated."

Given the angry atmosphere and fast-moving events in Tehran, the State Department reconciled itself to the idea that its grand design had failed. The United States, said a top official glumly, would now have to "make attempts to improve [its] relations with Mosaddeq." Urgent messages were sent to Roosevelt, telling him to come home immediately if he perceived his life was in danger. But the young spook was having none of it. Convinced there was an opportunity to strike again while the iron was still hot, Roosevelt decided to go rogue.

His first step was to contact General Zahedi and see if the latter was prepared to join him for a little freelance insurrection. The general eagerly agreed, and together the two men churned out thousands of photocopies of the shah's *farman* to distribute on the streets of Tehran. They persuaded several newspapers to publish it on their front pages the next morning. For the average Iranian, who still revered the ancient institution of monarchy, the sight of the *farman* had a powerful persuasive effect. Within twenty-four hours, large numbers of Iranians came to believe that Mosaddeq had disobeyed the shah's orders and tried to seize power for himself, then forced the monarch to leave the country. Yes, in other words, there had been a coup. But Mosaddeq was its perpetrator, and the shah its victim.

The press, both in Iran and around the world, readily accepted this version of events. Cinema newsreels in the West told moviegoers that the "dictator Mosaddeq" had tried to "seize power" and sent Iran's "beloved shah" into exile. The British newspaper *The Times* reported that Mosaddeq had "defeated both the Persian constitution and its most convinced upholder, the Shah himself . . . [and] is now in a position to gratify his long-standing dislike of the Imperial family." At that very moment, however, in one of the great ironies of history, Mosaddeq and his advisers were in fact looking for a way to preserve the shah's position. Had the shah abdicated? they wondered. Should they put together a regency council until he returned or some other arrangement was found? On the street, Communists were swarming like flies, plastering walls with leaflets calling for the abolition of the monarchy and the establishment of a "democratic republic." Mosaddeq ordered them torn down. He had taken an oath of loyalty to the shah and would not betray his word.

CB

As Mosaddeq agonized over the legal and moral implications of the shah's departure, Kermit Roosevelt continued work on his Plan B.

In the slums of south Tehran, there was (and still is) a centuries-old institution known as *zurkhaneh* (literally, "house of strength"), a highly ritualized network of athletic clubs where half-naked men, elaborately tattooed and clad only in colorful leggings, stand in octagonal pits and perform extraordinary feats of manliness, such as twirling heavy clubs and wrestling. In the 1950s many of Tehran's *zurkhaneh* champions functioned as local celebrities, heroes to the ragged neighborhood boys who packed into the houses of strength to watch what amounted to an early Iranian version of *American Gladiators.* Many also had informal links to Tehran's criminal underworld—to thugs and gangsters with names like Ali the Panther and Asqar the Cockroach. It was here, among the wrestlers and the roughnecks of south Tehran, that the CIA now went to work, giving the Rashidian brothers $50,000 (helpfully broken into small denominations) to distribute as they saw fit. In the course of a few hours, anyone in south Tehran who seemed hungry and muscular had been rounded up and told to report for duty the next morning.

At the center of the operation was a *zurkhaneh* giant by the name of Shaban the Brainless, a two-hundred-pound pachyderm of a man with a thick black beard and a torso that could block out the sun. Shaban and his men were given a simple set of instructions: The next morning they were to pretend they were Communist fanatics loyal to Mosaddeq and rampage through the streets behaving like hooligans. Then, once they had sufficiently outraged public opinion, they would be overwhelmed by much larger "patriotic" mobs proclaiming their loyalty to the shah. In reality, of course, both mobs would consist of paid agents of the CIA.

The next day the "pro-Mosaddeq" mob performed its assigned task magnificently. It streamed through the streets, beating people, smashing windows, looting, attacking mosques, and generally behaving like a pack of hyenas on the run from the zoo. A rhythmic chant of "We love Mosaddeq, and we love Communism!" was heard in the streets as rocks went crashing through the windows of local shops. At one point, the hired mob became so enthusiastic that it went off script and pulled down the statue of Reza Shah that stood in front of the Majles—an act of naked effrontery sure to outrage respectable Tehran society. When Kermit Roosevelt heard about the statue, he was thrilled. It was "the best thing we could have hoped for," he said. "The frosting on the cake."

The next morning was August 19, 1953—a date that an entire generation of Iranians will forever remember as the day the music died. From the winding lanes and intestine-like alleys of south Tehran came a thunderous column of demonstrators—waving, clapping, cheering, and shouting "Long live the shah!" as they marched into the city center. It was the same mob that twenty-four hours earlier had declared its undying love for Mosaddeq and Communism. Only now, instead of firebombing mosques and scaring little old ladies, they created a carnival atmosphere, complete with jugglers and tumblers and spinning *zurkhaneh* giants entertaining onlookers with their skills. At the edges of the crowd, ecstatic young men handed out

Operation Ajax: Gangs of wrestlers and bodybuilders from the slums of south Tehran, in the pay of the CIA, demonstrate in favor of the shah and against Mosaddeq, August 1953.

money and urged bystanders to join in the fun. It was a "mercenary mob," recalled the CIA's Richard Cottam. "It had no ideology. That mob was paid for by American dollars."

As morning turned to afternoon, the "pro-shah" demonstrators fanned out across the city, waving pictures of the monarch for the benefit of international news photographers. One group escorted General Zahedi, perched triumphantly atop a Sherman tank, to the radio station, where a bewildered newsreader was yanked out of his chair so the new prime minister could address the nation. Another group marched to Mosaddeq's house and attacked the property with tanks, bazookas, and artillery fire. For two hours, Mosaddeq refused to budge, telling an aide, "If it's going to be a *coup d'état*, I think it is better that I stay in this room and I die in this room." He was eventually overruled by his staff. For the second time in six months, the seventy-year-old Mosaddeq was forced to climb over his garden wall and disappear into hiding. This time, however, he would not be coming back. Hooligans spent the afternoon torching and looting his house, and an enormous melee ensued on the street. Several hours of pitched battle pitted young Mosaddeq supporters against gangs of south Tehran boys and security forces that the Rashidian network had bribed into a stupor that morning. By the time the sun finally set on that suffocatingly hot August

Coup day: Tanks in the streets of Tehran during the coup of August 1953.

afternoon, three hundred people had been killed—their clubbed and lacerated bodies lying motionless in the streets of central Tehran. Many of the dead "patriots" had 500-rial notes* in their pockets—the price of their loyalty, handed out that morning by the CIA.

If Roosevelt and his men felt any compunction about the death toll, they kept it close to their breasts. As darkness fell over Tehran that evening and General Zahedi's voice was heard on the radio, Roosevelt, Henderson, and Zahedi's son Ardeshir drained a bottle of champagne next to the swimming pool at the U.S. embassy. Back at CIA headquarters in Foggy Bottom, the mood was even more celebratory. Officials who just hours earlier had pleaded with Roosevelt to come home now ran up and down the corridors clutching streams of ticker tape with the latest cables from Tehran. The yelping and whooping carried on well into the evening, fueled by constant updates on the situation. "It was," in the words of one agency employee, a moment of unambiguous satisfaction—"a day that should never have ended."

❦

The corpses were still being counted when the shah returned to Tehran three days later, and there was no sign of champagne or streaming ticker tape. For his own safety, the monarch's arrival was not announced to the public in advance, and his route back to the palace was lined with tanks and soldiers to prevent unexpected disturbances. By any measure, this was hardly the triumphant return of a beloved king.

Still, to the victors go the spoils, and 1953 was no exception. On September 5, just two weeks after the shah's return, President Eisenhower announced $45 million in "emergency aid" for Iran—money the cash-starved government desperately needed to get back on its feet after two years of lost oil revenue. It was, perhaps intentionally, exactly twice the figure Mosaddeq had requested only a few weeks earlier. But it was barely a farthing compared with the largesse the shah would receive from the United States over the next twenty-five years. From 1953 to 1960 alone, $1 billion in cash and military aid would fall into the lap of America's new best friend. And by the 1970s, that figure would balloon into the tens of billions.

The CIA also did well out of Operation Ajax. Barely five years since its creation in 1948, the agency had never tried anything so daring as overthrowing a foreign government, but the Iranian coup was perceived as such a roaring success that it rapidly became a template for adventures

---

* In today's money, 500 rials is roughly equivalent to $100.

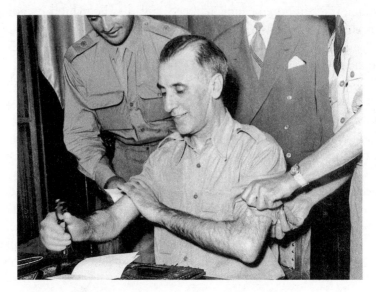

The strongman: Gen. Fazlollah Zahedi—playboy, adventurer, and military tactician with a long history of secret cooperation with British intelligence—writes a telegram to the shah in exile, informing him that Mosaddeq has been removed from power. Just before leaving the country, on Kermit Roosevelt's advice, the shah had signed an order naming Zahedi prime minister.

and experiments with regime change in far-flung corners of the globe— beginning with Guatemala in 1954. John Foster Dulles, in particular, was "so pleased . . . with the success of this thing that he decided that that was the way to deal with any difficult foreign situation," recalled Kermit Roosevelt in his retirement. Dulles was "licking his chops" after Iran and became such a proponent of foreign-policy-by-coup that he had to be told, ironically by Roosevelt, that "you just can't go around the world doing this kind of thing." Nevertheless, Dulles went down in American history as one of the heroes of the Cold War—his name still associated with every flight into and out of Washington's largest airport.

The biggest spoil of all, however, was reserved for the American oil industry. In 1954 control of Iran's oil would be divvied up between the AIOC and a consortium of American companies, each receiving a 40 percent stake and the remaining 20 percent divided between Royal Dutch Shell and France's national oil company. Officially, the international consortium would operate under the auspices of the National Iranian Oil Company, an entirely symbolic arrangement meant to perpetuate the illusion that Iran was in control of its oil industry. But whatever the affectations and technicalities of the new arrangement, there was no escaping the fact that, from 1953, the business of producing and selling Iranian oil took on a decidedly American accent.

As early as August 25, just six days after the coup, Churchill had warned of this—telling a cabinet meeting that now "it would be easy for the Americans, by the expenditure of a small amount of money, to keep all the benefits of many years of British work in Persia." And this is exactly what happened. Over the next twenty-five years, America's oil industry would make billions upon billions of dollars in Iran—money that could have remained in the hands of the AIOC and the British government had the company heeded the repeated warnings about its behavior. At the end of 1950, the AIOC had refused even to consider a fifty-fifty split in profits with Iran. Now, three years later, it was relieved just to be allowed back in—gratefully settling for a 40 percent stake in what had once been its own magnificent empire.[*]

The ultimate postscript to the coup of August 1953, though, was its transformative impact on the U.S.-Iranian relationship. For over a century, Iran had been the scene of an epic chess game between Britain and Russia, but from 1953 the United States began to supplant Britain as the dominant counterweight to Russian influence in the region. What had once been a rivalry between the imperial ambitions of expansionist European powers was now a Cold War battle between the dueling ideologies of Soviet Communism and Anglo-American capitalism—a drama in which Britain increasingly played only a supporting role. From the Iranian perspective, it was the worst of both worlds. Since the days of Amir Kabir in 1849, Iran's politicians had hoped the United States might one day act as a "third force" against the excesses of British and Russian imperialism. Instead, it seemed, the Americans had joined in the action, seizing on the decline of the British Empire as an opportunity to establish their own sphere of influence over Iran. Once upon a time, Iran had had two superpowers to worry about. Now it had three.

☙

As for Mosaddeq, there was to be no happy ending. Following the coup, the former prime minister was arrested on charges of treason (ostensibly for disobeying the *farman*) and hauled before a military tribunal. Courtrooms were the old man's natural habitat, and though the verdict was a foregone

---

[*] The company changed its name following the damaging dispute, in hopes of dispelling some of the old colonial associations. From 1954, the AIOC was known as British Petroleum, or BP. In the 1980s, the British government sold off its controlling stake in BP, and the company was gradually privatized. BP is today the third-largest private energy company in the world.

conclusion, he wasted no time running rhetorical circles around the prosecutors. Week in and week out, he exposed the moral and legal bankruptcy of the proceedings, helping to turn what was already a meretricious charade into a complete mockery. Week in and week out, as the proceedings were delayed, the shah worked desperately behind the scenes to pressure Mosaddeq to "settle out of court"—to admit guilt in exchange for a reduced or suspended sentence and an end to the embarrassing pantomime. At one point, the Imperial Palace even interrupted the trial to announce that the shah was prepared to "forgive" Mosaddeq and call an end to the proceedings. Mosaddeq, insulted by the suggestion, refused the king's pardon.

It was, in a way, appropriate that Mosaddeq—a brilliant orator and the first Iranian to earn a doctorate in law—spoke his final words to the nation from the familiar surroundings of a courtroom dock. "Throughout the course of my premiership," he said during his concluding defense, "I have had only one objective, and that was for the people of Iran to control their own destiny and for the fate of the nation to be determined by nothing other than the will of the people. . . . I did everything I could to achieve this."

And that was how it all ended. The prime minister who had kept the world on the edge of its seat for two years and four months—the contumacious sprite who had dared to tell the British Empire where to stick its oil monopoly and in the process became a hero to nationalists throughout the third world—was sentenced to three years in prison, to be followed by house arrest for the rest of his life.

Mossadeq served the jail term, from 1954 to 1956, in solitary confinement, and the house arrest at his country estate in Ahmad Abad, fifty miles west of Tehran. For the last decade of his life, he was not permitted to leave Ahmad Abad, and only immediate family members and a small circle of friends were allowed to visit, all closely monitored by the shah's secret police. Mosaddeq was finally laid to rest, in March 1967, under the floor of his small dining room. There was no funeral. In cities across Iran, it was made clear there were to be no public memorials or mourning ceremonies. Lengthy obituaries appeared in the international press, but newspapers in Iran gave Mosaddeq's death only scant coverage.

Until the very end, the shah lived in fear of Mosaddeq's popularity.

⋐ঽ

The events of 1953 had a transformative impact on history, yet they have always suffered from something of a silent epitaph. For years the U.S. role in the overthrow of Mosaddeq was an open secret, discussed at policy-wonk

Mosaddeq in exile. Following his overthrow, trial, and three years in prison, Mosaddeq spent the rest of his life under house arrest on his ancestral estate in Ahmad Abad. Newspapers were forbidden to mention his name. He was buried quietly under his dining-room floor in 1967, following a small family gathering.

dinners in Washington and in the occasional unauthorized memoir, but not widely aired in the media and not officially acknowledged. The largest chunk of missing information—the CIA's own internal history of Operation Ajax—was leaked to *The New York Times* in April 2000, but the document itself is still officially classified. Many of the United Kingdom's most sensitive documents on the episode will remain closed to the public until the year 2053.[*]

In Iran, it is much the same story. Today, even nearly 70 years after the fact, there is no "Mosaddeq Avenue" in Tehran, no "Mosaddeq International Airport," as there would be anywhere else in the world. The old man's face has never appeared on a postage stamp or a banknote. Both before and after the revolution, Mosaddeq's devotion to constitutionalism and liberal democracy was an awkward fit with the powers that be.[†] Even his grave at the estate in Ahmad Abad has become dusty and disheveled. It takes only

---

[*] Newsreels made by MovieTone and Pathé, many now available on the Internet, offer a fascinating glimpse into the way the 1953 coup was presented to American audiences at the time. Moviegoers were told that the "Iranian people" had staged a "countercoup" against Mosaddeq. Even *The New York Times*, on August 22, 1953, ran the front-page headline: SHAH, BACK IN IRAN, WILDLY ACCLAIMED; PRESTIGE AT PEAK.

[†] In the historiography of the Islamic Republic, Ayatollah Kashani is presented as the true hero, a national liberator who tried to bring Islamic government to Iran but was foiled by the pro-Western Mosaddeq.

an hour to get there from Tehran nowadays, thanks to a slick new six-lane expressway. But this tiny village is a place that history has been instructed to forget. There are no signs directing you to the site, no markers letting you know you've arrived. Access is granted only with prior permission from a board of trustees—a group of cantankerous old National Front activists, most now well into their eighties. Starved for funds, the board has been unable to pay for basic repairs, and the top floor of the house is now too fragile to receive visitors.

But it is all still there: The beloved 1950 lime-green Pontiac Chieftain, recovered by Mosaddeq's friends on the day his house in Tehran was ransacked. The simple stone slab in the dining room, where Mosaddeq lies buried. The black and white photograph of the prime minister running his hand down the crack of the Liberty Bell in Philadelphia.

And outside, leaning against a tree, rusting and surrounded by weeds, is the turquoise metal door that belonged to Mosaddeq's house in Tehran. It still bears every dent and bruise from the day Shaban the Brainless and his boys drove an army jeep against it like a battering ram.

PART III

Autumn

"Yes" and "Yes, Sir"

☙❧

Over the next twenty-five years, the shah of Iran would steadily sleepwalk his way out of the hearts of his people. Like a man bent on speeding the onset of his own political obituary, he would fall back on every shopworn cliché in the tyrant's playbook: brass bands and parading troops; secret police and secret prisons; egotistical building projects and pointless military buildups; bungled attempts at "modernization" that benefited only a handful of wealthy families. From the winter of 1953 to the winter of 1978, Iran was an unambiguous royal dictatorship—a place where sharply dressed goons knocked on people's doors at inconvenient hours and supine newspapers competed to write the most flattering headlines about the royal family. As the years slipped by and an entire generation lost the ability to participate in politics, the Tehran Spring came to feel like something that had never happened.

The forces of repression sprang into action almost immediately. Within hours of deposing Mosaddeq, the government of General Zahedi declared martial law and stationed soldiers on street corners. Bayonets and interrogations replaced the spirited cut-and-thrust of public debate, as dozens of newspapers were closed and public demonstrations were banned. One-third of the men appointed to Zahedi's cabinet in August 1953 were military generals, who wasted little time putting their stamp on the political scene. In the summer of 1954, to the delight of John Foster Dulles, the Iranian government launched a massive anti-Communist purge of the armed forces, rounding up nearly six hundred suspected Tudeh members and sentencing most to death or life imprisonment.

In the face of such overwhelming repression, the broken and dejected remnants of the National Front could muster little in the way of opposition. But they did not roll over and go to sleep. In the days following the coup, a handful of Mosaddeq's allies—still shell-shocked—gathered at the home of a prominent cleric, Ayatollah Reza Zanjani, to discuss forming a resistance movement. Someone suggested they choose a motto—something short and memorable that could be written on small scraps of paper, rolled up, and slipped into open windows without the police noticing. A three-word slogan was chosen, and in the days and weeks that followed, Zanjani and his friends furiously scribbled. For the rest of the summer, every time Tehran residents left their windows open, they found their homes littered with miniature scrolls bearing the message "The struggle continues."

It was wishful thinking. In November shopkeepers in the Tehran bazaar—long an incubator of Mosaddeq loyalism—went on strike to protest the government's decision to restore ties with Britain. On the twelfth tanks rolled in, and for hours soldiers stormed the market's narrow lanes and alleys, razing several sections of its old arcaded ceiling as punishment. A mysterious fire, suspected to be the work of the regime, later engulfed a section of the market. And at the end of 1953 the National Front was banned outright, its leaders and activists treated with only slightly more leniency than members of the Tudeh.

What was left of the front after this purge was a shell of its former self. Sincere, savvy, hardworking men—Allahyar Saleh, Ali Shaigan, Karim Sanjabi, Mehdi Bazargan—had all been mooted as potential leaders of the democratic-nationalist movement, but after 1953, the movement was badly divided. As ever, it lacked a centralized party machine, but now it also lacked a charismatic leader. Worse, the front was now illegal—an underground organization operating in a nation in which the mere mention of Mosaddeq's name could land a person in jail. In this atmosphere, there was little chance that an inspirational new savior would emerge, or that Iranians would get swept up in a popular movement against the shah and his foreign supporters. It would take another ten years, and an old man in a turban, before that could happen again.

☙

In December 1953 the American vice president, Richard Nixon, came to Tehran for a series of meetings with the shah and Iranian officials. It was the first time in history an American leader paid a dedicated visit to Iran. Nixon's visit provided the shah, now thirty-four and more firmly in control of his country, with a chance to demonstrate how far his relations with the United States had progressed. It also gave him a crucial stamp of legitimacy at a time when Iran, in the eyes of the international community, appeared consumed by instability. Most important, perhaps, it marked the beginning of a long and unusually close friendship between Nixon and the shah, a bond that would shape the course of U.S. Middle East policy for decades. The two men—both deeply insecure, both consumed by fears of plots and intrigues, and both haunted by demons that few around them fully understood—would remain friends for life, even years later, after both had been ousted from office.

As the vice president arrived in Tehran, the newly formed international oil consortium—composed 40 percent of BP and 40 percent of American oil companies—was busy negotiating an agreement for the production and sale of Iranian oil. Iran was told it should expect no more than a 50 percent share of profits, and the shah's government did not argue.* To the most fervent disciples of Mosaddeq, this craven capitulation to British-American interests was the final betrayal—and a powerful symbol of America's emerging role as "Britain's replacement" in Iranian politics. Nixon's presence in Tehran thus touched off a firestorm of angry protests. Two days before Nixon arrived at Tehran University to pick up an honorary law degree, students marched out of classes and shouted slogans against the Zahedi government. The regime responded by sending in soldiers to storm the campus. In the corridors of the engineering faculty, three students were shot dead.

For the rest of the 1950s, a client-patron relationship gradually emerged between Iran and the United States: every time Tehran did what Washington asked, it was rewarded with a swift and substantial injection of cash. In 1954, when the agreement with the international oil consortium was finalized, the shah received $127 million in fresh aid commitments. In 1955, when Iran joined the Baghdad Pact (a regional anti-Soviet alliance championed by Dulles), another lucrative aid package landed in his lap. In 1957 the shah endorsed the Eisenhower Doctrine, and the following year Iran joined the Central Treaty Organization, or CENTO (the successor to the Baghdad Pact). Both decisions resulted in fulsome financial rewards.

By the end of the decade, this merry-go-round of blandishments and favors would become a source of great resentment to Iran's modern, educated, and increasingly restless middle classes. The same people who had rallied round Mosaddeq now lapsed into disillusionment and cynicism as they watched their country turn into something resembling an American protectorate. For years, Iranians had believed they were about to embark

* Although details were not being released to the public, already it was obvious just how lopsided the arrangement was going to be. At this early stage, the negotiations were taking place in Washington and London between representatives of BP, the American companies, and the British and American governments. The Iranians would not be allowed to participate until April 1954, after the British and Americans had already agreed on terms among themselves. The idea behind this approach was to present Iran with a take-it-or-leave-it offer.

Consolidation: Vice President Richard Nixon goes to Tehran in the
immediate aftermath of the coup to bolster the shah's position and to meet
his new prime minister, Fazlollah Zahedi (right). His visit touched off days
of protests that culminated in the shah's forces shooting dead three students
at Tehran University.

on a free and independent future in which their country's actions would
not be constrained by lopsided arrangements with foreign powers. Instead,
it seemed, the shah had merely traded in the British lion for an American
eagle.

What Iran's middle classes resented even more than the shah's embrace of
Washington, though, was the shah himself. Reassured that he had the backing of the United States and Britain, the shah consolidated his position in
the 1950s—he expanded his constitutional powers, stifled dissenting voices,
and surrounded himself with men loyal to his personal rule. Voting in the
Majles elections of 1954 and 1956 was blatantly rigged—many of the same
south Tehran thugs who had helped overthrow Mosaddeq were wheeled
out again to intimidate voters. (Shaban the Brainless alone hospitalized fifty
people during the 1954 election.) The result was a parliament dominated by
old-guard aristocratic landowners and conservative politicians—all unshak-
ably loyal to the shah.

In 1955, the shah sacked General Zahedi. His government, like Mosaddeq's before it, had lasted only two years—a victim of the shah's traditional
lack of comfort with strong prime ministers. He replaced Zahedi first

with the now-aging Hossein Ala, then in 1957 with Manuchehr Eqbal, an obsequious politician who famously signed his letters to the shah, "Your Majesty's house-born slave." History has generally regarded Eqbal as the politician most responsible for introducing to the royal court a culture of extreme sycophancy, the bowing and scraping and empty obedience that would eventually hollow out the regime from within. It was Eqbal who, as prime minister, first declared that matters of foreign policy should be left entirely to the shah, and Eqbal who helped create a secret police force to monitor Iranians perceived as disloyal to the shah—the notorious SAVAK. Eqbal once confided to a friend that he would not so much as drink a glass of water "without the permission of His Imperial Majesty."

In 1957 the shah banned all existing political parties and announced that anyone wanting to participate in politics would have to do so through one of two newly created parties: the Melliyun (National Party) and the Mardom (People's Party). The idea was to form a two-party system based loosely on the American model of Democrats and Republicans. But when able, sincere politicians attempted to work within this system, they quickly discovered it was a vehicle for sycophancy, favoritism, and royal control of the political process. Melliyun and Mardom became laughingstocks among the Tehran intelligentsia—often jokingly referred to as the party of "Yes" and the party of "Yes, Sir."

⊗

It was not all doom and gloom and dreary dictatorship. The invigorated bilateral relationship between Iran and the United States also brought a wealth of opportunities for cultural, professional, and educational exchanges. From the mid-1950s many prominent Iranians went to the United States on so-called "leader grants" funded by the State Department, intended to help a rising generation of political elites become familiar with American expertise. Iran's best and brightest studied journalism at the University of Virginia, agriculture at Utah State, business administration at the University of Southern California. As these elites returned to Iran, they landed jobs in government and rose rapidly through the ranks to become valued members of the shah's apparatus. And as they did so, their personal connections to the United States proved critical. In subtle but important ways, this generation of technocrats helped ensure that Iran's modernization unfolded with a distinctly American flavor.

Educational reform was a particularly important area of bilateral cooperation. Traditionally, Iran's universities had been modeled on the French system, but in 1956, Eqbal, then chancellor of Tehran University, traveled to America on a leader grant and returned "bubbling over with enthusiasm for the United States." He was particularly struck by the American concept of the university "campus"—a centralized hub where all social, residential, and educational needs were met. Eqbal introduced the idea to the rapidly growing Tehran University, and the result was a university that, to this day, bears a striking resemblance to state university campuses throughout the United States. Before long, teams of American experts were brought over to advise Iran on how to create and run its newer universities as well. Amid the oil fields of the Persian Gulf, the Abadan Institute of Technology was set up with the help of a team from Lafayette College of Easton, Pennsylvania. And in 1960 the shah invited University of Pennsylvania president Gaylord Harnwell to Shiraz, determined that the city's new Pahlavi University would become the only institution in the Middle East to offer a fully American-style education.

As the 1950s progressed, an enormous amount of American aid money and technical advice made its way into Iran, most of it channeled through the Point Four agreement that Truman had signed into law in 1950. In 1953, Iran received $23 million; the following year that figure was increased to $85 million. Whereas in 1952 the U.S. embassy in Tehran had employed only ten "technical advisers," in 1956 that number ballooned to 207. American professional and educational organizations employed another hundred technicians, and between them, these Americans had a staff of some 3,800 Iranians. By the end of the decade, Iran hosted the largest and most intricate U.S. overseas aid mission in the world. And yet, perhaps inevitably given its size and complexity, the aid effort was badly managed. Americans in Iran often came across as brash and wealthy upstarts who were unwilling to listen or adapt their expertise to local needs. And on the Iranian side, dishonest actors took advantage of American inexperience to channel aid money into their own pockets. In 1956 a U.S. congressional investigation found that American assistance programs in Iran had been administered "in a loose, slipshod, and unbusinesslike manner" and that tracking exactly what happened to the funds was often impossible.

☙

The shah, meanwhile, spent nearly all his effort trying to convince the Eisenhower administration to increase its military support to Iran. Again and again in his conversations with U.S. officials, he harped on the theme of the Communist threat in Asia, warning that Washington was not fully appreciating Tehran's important role as a buffer against the Soviet Union—or its corresponding need for weaponry. Again and again Eisenhower resisted.

Disappointed, in 1956 and 1957 the shah began cultivating closer ties with the Soviets, making a state visit to Moscow and signing a number of treaties and trade agreements. The transparent bluff was designed to ensure that the United States did not take Iran's friendship for granted, but Eisenhower was unamused. In no uncertain terms, the president informed the shah that his "friends would be unhappy" if he signed a treaty with the USSR. "I am confident," Eisenhower wrote, "that you would not knowingly take a step which would imperil your country's security."

In the end, though, the shah got most of what he wanted from America—thanks to an unexpected turn of events in neighboring Iraq. On July 14, 1958, a bloody revolution broke out in Baghdad, replacing the pro-British monarchy with a socialist republic committed to a neutral position in the Cold War. Washington worried that something similar might happen in Iran, and quickly stepped up its financial and military commitments to the shah.* In March 1959 the shah showed his appreciation by signing a landmark defense agreement with the United States, cementing Iran's status as an American client state in the Middle East and ending its short-lived flirtation with Moscow. And in December, Eisenhower rewarded his newfound friend with an official visit to Tehran—the first by an American president.

For Eisenhower, Tehran was a five-hour stopover on a goodwill tour of eleven regional capitals from Karachi to Casablanca, but the shah milked his visit for everything it was worth. He declared a national holiday and ordered thousands of children to be at school at six a.m. so they could be on hand to cheer Eisenhower's arrival. As the president stepped off the plane, a squadron of fighter jets flew overhead and spelled out *Ike* in the sky. Nearly a million people lined the president's route into Tehran, dutifully cheering and waving as Eisenhower's motorcade passed under sixteen decorative arches hung with American flags and slogans like "We like Ike too—Welcome to Iran!" At the Marble Palace the president had twenty minutes to rest before beginning two hours of talks with the shah, followed by an address to a special session of the Majles. To ensure his maximum comfort during these twenty minutes, Eisenhower was given the bedroom once used by Reza Shah. Sixty typewriters and eight direct phone lines were put at the disposal of his staff.

---

* The same year Syria, led by the socialist Ba'ath party, entered into a formal union with Gamal Abdel Nasser's Egypt, creating the United Arab Republic (UAR), a left-leaning powerhouse that appeared poised to lead the Arab world in the direction of socialism and Cold War neutralism. Though the UAR would last only three years, the view from Washington in 1958 was that the Middle East was moving in the direction of third-world socialism, and that it was more urgent than ever to support a pro-American, conservative, anti-Communist ally like the shah.

"We like Ike too—Welcome to Iran!" The Eisenhower motorcade travels down a route lined with flowers and Persian carpets, March 1959.

One week before Eisenhower's arrival, the shah had declared triumphantly at a press conference that "our relations with the United States have never been so strong." And during his five-hour stay in Tehran, the president said nothing to contradict that, only praising the shah for his "wise leadership" and reaffirming America's commitment to future cooperation with Iran. In his address to the Majles, however, Eisenhower included a line that many interpreted as an indirect swipe at the shah and his obsession with military hardware. "In the long term," he stated, "military strength alone will not bring about just and permanent peace."

It was a gentle word of warning from an old friend who, six years earlier, had quietly intervened to secure Mohammad Reza Shah on his troublesome throne. But it was also a harbinger of things to come. Eisenhower was a realist, a hard-bitten man of war who was coming to accept the limitations of conventional military firepower in the atomic age. America's next president, however, would be a different kind of animal—a young and energetic idealist with a powerful vision for the projection of American leadership. And he would ask far more of the shah than had ever been asked of him before.

You Say You Want a Revolution?

From the moment John F. Kennedy bounded into the political spotlight, full of youthful idealism and talk of "moral leadership," the shah knew he had reason to worry. In his acceptance speech to the Democratic Convention in 1960, Kennedy had spoken of a "new frontier" and complained that one-third of the world "is the victim of cruel repression, and the other one-third is rocked by the pangs of poverty, hunger and envy." To the shah, Kennedy came across as pitifully naïve and possibly a little dangerous—an untested neophyte whose soaring speeches and big ideas revealed a poor understanding of the scabrous realities of international politics. As the campaign went on, the Iranian leader's nagging fears only got worse. In the weeks before election day, Kennedy repeatedly described the world as living in a "fantastically revolutionary era," marked by a "revolution in medicine," a "revolution in automation," a "revolution in space," and a "revolution for human rights." The shah, always paranoid about the designs of foreign powers, heard this talk of "revolution" as a cryptic message aimed directly at Iran. Kennedy, he feared, was planning to remove him from power.

Kennedy's opponent in the 1960 election was Vice President Richard Nixon—a man the shah felt would make for a far steadier hand at the wheel. To the shah, Nixon represented reassuring familiarity, a personification of the steadfast support he had enjoyed from the Eisenhower administration since the coup of 1953. As vice president, Nixon had proved a reliable friend, and the shah desperately hoped for the continuity that a Nixon presidency would bring. There were even allegations—never proven, but never fully investigated either—that the shah secretly funneled money to the Nixon campaign.

Unfortunately for the shah, it was Kennedy who emerged victorious.

And once he was in the White House, the energetic new president wasted little time telling the world what kind of leadership America was going to offer. In his inaugural address in January 1961, he spoke directly to "those peoples in the huts and villages across the globe struggling to break the bonds of mass misery," promising that America would join them in the fight against poverty and tyranny. Horrified, the shah immediately composed a long letter to Kennedy, describing Iran as a bastion of freedom in the region, whose citizens enjoyed a range of rights and liberties. To emphasize his concern, he asked the head of his secret police, Lt. Gen. Teimur Bakhtiar, to fly to Washington and deliver the letter in person.

The new occupants of the White House were still busy dusting off the bookshelves and getting the hang of the telephones when Bakhtiar arrived in Washington, but everyone soon realized that the shah and Kennedy were not going to see eye to eye. In its first few days, the new administration had already articulated a foreign policy vision that was a stark contrast to the fire-breathing anti-Communism of the Dulles brothers, and the shah didn't care for it one bit. Very quickly, conversations between the shah and American officials—whether in person or via telephone—took on a tense and uncooperative tone.

Starting from the premise that a well-fed, literate, healthy, and adequately housed population would have no reason to turn to Communism, the Kennedy administration argued that the best way to counteract the danger of Soviet infiltration in the developing world was to encourage foreign leaders to work toward eradicating poverty and inequality. The shah, by contrast, insisted that a leader's first job was to establish the strength and security of his country, in order to dissuade would-be Soviet invaders. What the shah wanted from America was fewer lectures about economic development and more of the latest military hardware—surface-to-air missiles, tactical weapons "with atomic delivery capability," Century-series aircraft, and destroyers. The National Security Council (NSC) balked at the shah's demands, describing them as "clearly beyond anything which the United States could reasonably furnish under current conditions." Perplexed by what seemed like an endless shopping list from Iran, the council concluded internally that "the Shah's demands for military assistance stem from an emotional attachment to military display."

The philosophical differences between the shah and the Kennedy administration might have faded into the background had it not been for an unexpected bit of provocation from Nikita Khrushchev. On April 10, 1961, during a retreat at his villa on the Black Sea, the Soviet premier boasted to an American journalist that Iran would soon be falling into the Soviet orbit—though, he hastened to add, entirely of its own volition. "You will assert that the Shah has been overthrown by the Communists," Khrushchev said, "and we shall be very glad to have it thought [that] we are the leaders of the progress of mankind." Twisting the knife, he added that while Kennedy meant well, no amount of liberal democratic reform could forestall the desire of the proletariat to free itself of feudalism and bourgeois capitalism. In Iran, he said, revolution was inevitable.

When Kennedy heard these comments, he became determined to prove Khrushchev wrong. Iran would serve as a test case, a powerful demonstration to the world that as long as free nations took care of their poorest citizens, no one should have any reason to turn to Communism. Within days of the Khrushchev comments, he asked the State Department and NSC to convene a special joint task force to discuss ways to ensure the success of administration strategy in Iran and to report its findings to him as soon as possible. The president's military aide, Gen. Ted Clifton, drew up a detailed military contingency plan that played out every possible scenario for Iran. Much to everyone's surprise, Iran was becoming a top priority for the new administration.

After nearly a month of discussions, the NSC's Iran Task Force reported that the United States had three basic options. It could encourage genuine democracy in Iran, but this would probably result in a weak, unpredictable government vulnerable to Soviet manipulation. It could back a right-wing dictatorship run by a military strongman, but this would be out of step with the tone Kennedy had set for American foreign policy. Or it could split the difference and find a politician who would make just enough reforms to win over the restless masses but still be relied on to maintain a pro-Western posture against the Soviet menace. This was clearly the preferred option.

The man Washington looked to as a potential engineer of the Iranian reformation was Ali Amini, a sensible, centrist politician with a doctorate in economics from the University of Paris, and a history of cordial relations with the American political establishment. Kennedy himself had befriended Amini in 1955, when the latter was Tehran's ambassador to Washington, and had been impressed by his sincerity and his awareness of the challenges his country faced. One of Iran's wealthiest landowners and grandson of a legendary prime minister,* Amini was an aristocrat from head to toe (a severe widow's peak and droopy eyelids even made him look a little like Count

---

* Amini's grandfather was Amin od-Dowleh, who served as Muzaffar al-Din Shah's energetic first prime minister from 1897 to 1898. Like his grandson, Amin od-Dowleh tried to reform the Qajar state after many years of stagnation and decline. Like his grandson, he lasted about a year, the victim of a system that did not want to reform itself.

Dracula). But Amini had also, briefly, been a member of the National Front and seemed genuinely committed to liberalization. To the United States, he appeared a competent, level-headed man who understood the needs of Iran's various political constituencies.

In Iran, however, Amini inspired only that timeless lack of enthusiasm that befalls a politician who tries to be all things to all people. His former allies in the National Front had never forgiven him for being one of the first to abandon Mosaddeq in 1952, or for the fact that in 1954, as finance minister in the Zahedi government, he had overseen the unpopular agreement with the international oil consortium. Amini's fellow aristocrats also distrusted him, feeling that his liberalizing tendencies and former membership in the front made him a traitor to his class. And as if this were not enough, Amini aroused deep suspicion in the shah. In 1958 the monarch had recalled Amini from his post in Washington, convinced that the ambassador was plotting with the Americans to stage a coup against him.

The United States was well aware of Amini's liabilities, in particular his difficult history with the Imperial Palace. "The most immediate threat to Amini will be from the Shah," concluded the task force in its preliminary report. It was "only a question of time before he starts to undercut [Amini] as he has all previous prime ministers." The alternatives, though, seemed bleak. The consensus in Washington was that backing an Amini government was a gamble, but that it was the "best, and perhaps last good, chance of forestalling Iran's slippery slide into chaos." Persuading the insecure shah to see things this way would be a challenge, but fortunately, the United States was not averse to greasing the royal palm. In April 1961 the shah was quietly informed that if he appointed Amini prime minister and gave him free rein to pursue a reform agenda, Iran would receive a loan of $33 million from the United States. This seemed to have the desired effect. On May 5, 1961, after a national teachers' strike and a period of crisis, Ali Amini was summoned to the Imperial Palace and asked to form a government.

At the White House, pulses quickened. Finally, it seemed, the United States had an opportunity to put in place a program of political and social reforms that would convince Iran that its future lay with the West. "Don't let today go by," cooed Walt Rostow, the president's deputy national security adviser, as he urged his colleagues to work with Amini and consolidate U.S. influence over the new government. "This could be a lucky break for us." The NSC encouraged President Kennedy to "take a strong line" and find "appropriate means of letting Shah know Amini is our boy (and ought to be his)."

CB

It didn't take Amini long to disappoint. During his first few months in office, he initiated ambitious changes, including an increase in teachers' salaries, an economic austerity program, and a high-profile campaign against corruption. Perhaps most important, the government embarked on far-reaching reform of land ownership—something first attempted by Mosaddeq in 1952 and now taken up with enthusiasm by Amini's leftist-populist agriculture minister, Hassan Arsanjani.

On paper, Amini's government was doing everything right, but politically, it succeeded only in making enemies. The aristocratic elite felt threatened by the speed and scale of land reform. The liberal middle classes were horrified when Amini asked the shah for a temporary dissolution of the Majles so he could enact his reform program by executive decree. Most damaging of all, however, Amini found himself locked in a constant battle with the shah, who resisted any effort to pay for social programs if it meant reducing the military budget. And almost universally, Iranians regarded Amini as someone who took his orders from Washington. Without a natural base of support within Iran, his government stood little chance of success.

No one enjoyed reminding Washington of this fact more than the shah himself. In all his discussions with the Kennedy administration, the shah insisted that Amini had his full support, but he was clearly only tolerating the prime minister as a favor to the United States. Amini was not very popular in Tehran, he explained. In August, as Amini came under severe criticism from all sides, the shah dryly remarked to U.S. officials that he "seemed to be Amini's only supporter" in Iran. The Americans had little to say in response, but such lukewarm backing from the monarch did not bode well for the government's chances.

At the end of 1961, violent clashes broke out at Tehran University as students protesting the shah were met with a heavy-handed response from government forces. The confrontation culminated, in January 1962, in the horrifying spectacle of a heavily armed parachute regiment storming the campus. The university's chancellor, Ahmad Farhad, resigned, calling the government raid a shameful demonstration of "cruelty, sadism, atrocity and vandalism."

At the White House, the atmosphere was one of brooding despair. The United States had put all its eggs in the Amini basket, only to see the prime minister move steadily to the right and lose the support of every important political constituency in Iran. There had been no Plan B. Participants at task force meetings described the mood as "extremely gloomy," and a memo sent to the president in August warned that "we are treading the thin edge of a potential disaster in Iran, for which Khrushchev sits patiently waiting."

Last of the reformists: Ali Amini, prime minister of Iran (1961–62). The Kennedy administration believed Amini, a liberal and former Mosaddeq supporter, had the "best, and perhaps last good, chance of forestalling Iran's slippery slide into chaos." Kennedy's advisers urged him to find "appropriate means of letting Shah know Amini is our boy, and ought to be his." But Amini enjoyed little support in Iran and was easily sidelined by the shah. It was the last time the United States put serious pressure on the shah to liberalize Iran's political process.

The task force urged Kennedy to take "crisis measures"—sending money to "keep Iran afloat financially," making it clear to the shah that "Amini is our man, and . . . needs all-out support." The shah should also be told, in the strongest terms, to "stop bleating to us about more military aid and instead make token cut in his own military outlays." The task force left no doubt how seriously it felt the situation should be taken: "Despite its much lower visibility, the continued slide towards chaos in Iran could result in as great a setback as Vietnam."

This pessimism was echoed on Capitol Hill, where several prominent lawmakers voiced fears for the long-term viability of the shah's regime. At an executive session of the Senate Foreign Relations Committee in June, Sen. Frank Church (D-ID) stated bluntly, "Khrushchev is right. I just think it is going to be a miracle if we save the Shah of Iran. All I know about history says he is not long for this world, nor his system. And when he goes down, boom, we go with him." Church's colleague, Sen. Hubert Humphrey (D-MN), agreed. "They are dead," he said of the shah and his cronies. "They just don't know it. I don't care what revolution it is. Somebody is going to get those fellows. They are out. It is just a matter of time."

In July 1962, Amini's government collapsed. As predicted, the trigger was not a failure to address the concerns of student activists or a lack of progress in implementing reforms. It was an old-fashioned political tug-of-war with the King of Kings. In the spring Amini had asked every government department to make cuts in its spending, but the shah had stepped in to insist there would be no reductions in the military budget. There was only one way for that story to end. Officially, Amini's reason for resigning was a lack of adequate funds from the United States, but there was no hiding the fact that he had crossed one of the biggest red lines in Iranian politics.

Amini was swiftly replaced by Asadollah Alam, a cardboard yes-man whose loyalty to the shah knew few limits. And it now looked increasingly obvious that Iran was on its way to an autocratic kingship. American diplomats in Tehran described Alam's appointment as the "closest thing to direct rule of Shah. Alam completely devoted servant . . . from outset there will be no question in anyone's mind of independence on part of PM." And indeed, for the next fifteen years, Iran's prime ministers would behave largely as if their job were to do what the shah told them to do.

What was much more troubling about the events of 1961 and 1962, however—at least from an American perspective—was the increasing tendency of young, educated, liberal, and middle-class Iranians to equate their frustrations with the shah with a more generalized frustration with the United States. An earlier generation of National Front activists, in the 1940s and 1950s, had given America the benefit of the doubt or assumed an inexperienced United States was being "duped" into doing the bidding of the British. But in the early 1960s, Iran's urban middle classes—younger, louder, and more numerous than ever before—were more likely to blame America directly for their problems. "This regime," warned a prominent American academic living in Iran in 1961, "is considered by most aware and articulate Iranians as reactionary, corrupt, and a tool of Western (and especially Anglo-American) imperialism." The State Department also worried, noting that "nowadays, with the US obviously in the Shah's graces, the term 'pro-American' is taking on the evil overtone which 'pro-British' [once] had."

None of these concerns seemed to affect American policy. In the spring of 1962 the White House received reports that the shah was "having a neurotic spell," consumed with fear that the United States no longer supported him. So the Kennedy administration, hoping to pick up his spirits, invited him to pay a state visit to the United States. The shah enthusiastically accepted the offer, and the result was the kind of telegenic display of Iranian-American friendship he delighted in. On the tarmac at Washington airport, Kennedy praised the Iranian king for leading a "historic fight" in the face of "great challenges." The shah was given a ticker-tape parade down Broadway, invited to address a joint session of Congress, and interviewed by CBS television—a broadcast that attracted 5 million viewers. TV cameras followed the shah's glamorous wife, twenty-three-year-old Empress Farah, as she relaxed on the White House lawn with Jacqueline Kennedy and played with the Kennedy children. At Cape Canaveral the shah watched NASA

Early concerns: Sen. Frank Church, right (D-ID), was one of the first to openly sound the alarm about the shah's regime on Capitol Hill. "I just think it is going to be a miracle if we save the Shah of Iran. All I know about history says he is not long for this world, nor his system. And when he goes down, boom, we go with him."

rockets being launched and quipped to reporters that Iran was "more interested in sinking deep wells than in going into outer space." The press lapped up every minute, and so did the shah. Even after the official portion of his visit was over, he found time to go to Philadelphia to pick up an honorary doctorate from the University of Pennsylvania—ostentatiously landing his helicopter in the middle of the university's football stadium.

In front of the cameras, the shah and JFK came across as natural allies. Both men were in their early forties, both were married to young and glamorous women whose faces were never far from the pages of *Life* magazine, and both had recently become fathers. John Jr. (a future president, so everyone thought) and Prince Reza (a future king, so everyone thought) had been born just three and a half weeks apart, and Kennedy congratulated the shah on this auspicious coincidence. But despite these superficial similarities, the shah and JFK had a tense relationship. Kennedy saw the shah as a tin-pot dictator and had little real respect for him. The shah, meanwhile, was acutely conscious that he lacked the charisma of his American counterpart, and he found it difficult to play the junior partner to someone his own age. Kennedy, to him, was still a parvenu, a young and inexperienced

The shah lands his helicopter in the University of Pennsylvania's football stadium, to receive an honorary doctorate, 1962.

upstart who had defeated his old friend Richard Nixon. Refusing to believe that anything like a genuine democracy existed in the United States, he grumbled to an aide that Kennedy must have won the 1960 election because Nixon had failed to buy enough votes.

Along with the lack of camaraderie between the two leaders came all the same issues that had dogged U.S.-Iranian relations during previous administrations. The shah was determined to convince Kennedy that, as a crucial anti-Soviet ally, Iran deserved a generous helping of money and military hardware, but the Americans were having none of it. The Kennedy White House thought it obvious Iran urgently needed to placate its urban middle classes and rural poor and to focus its efforts on education, health care, and rural development. Just as it did elsewhere in the world, the Kennedy administration argued that unless the shah put in place a controlled and orderly "revolution from above," he would soon be facing a violent revolution from below. An all-out Russian invasion of Iran seemed unlikely, but leftist politicians could easily play on Iran's restive population to bring about a pro-Soviet coup. What the shah needed was not a bigger army or expensive weapons to scare away the Russians. What he needed was to wake up to the dangers of internal unrest.

The shah receives an honorary doctorate from President
Gaylord Harnwell, University of Pennsylvania, 1962. Penn's
long legacy in Iranian archaeology allowed it to play a
critical role in the development of higher education in Iran.
Harnwell, together with Arthur Upham Pope, laid the
groundwork for Pahlavi University.

The message eventually got through. With great fanfare, in January
1963, the shah announced the launch of his White Revolution, a six-point
program that included a national literacy corps for rural communities, the
sale of government factories, voting rights for women, and comprehensive
land reform. In many ways, the measures he put forward were similar to
those proposed by Amini two years earlier, but the difference now was that
they were presented as coming directly from the shah rather than from his
government—a magnanimous gift from a king to his people.

The White Revolution, during the fifteen years it would remain in existence, was not without its successes. But these successes were often overshadowed by the climate of corruption and cynicism in which they took
place. In an effort to encourage aristocrats to cooperate with land redistribution, for example, the shah (the largest land owner in Iran) ostentatiously
sold off much of his own estate. But few saw this as an act of magnanimity,
since most of the Pahlavi estate consisted of properties the shah's father had
appropriated in the 1930s under dubious circumstances. Worse, it was later

Camelot: JFK and the shah had an uneasy relationship. The U.S.
president constantly pushed the Iranian leader to consider reform and
liberalization, but the shah felt Kennedy was naïve and idealistic and
insufficiently appreciative of Iran's need for military support against
Communism. In April 1962, Kennedy invited the insecure shah to
Washington to reassure him of U.S. support. At the state dinner, to help
ease tensions, the first lady pointedly wore a much smaller tiara than the
one worn by the empress.

discovered that one-third of land "redistributed" by the shah had gone to
his wealthy friends and political allies rather than to peasant farmers. Still,
despite the sometimes flagrant acts of corruption and the legendary ability
of the Iranian aristocracy to find and exploit loopholes, some genuine redistribution did take place, and the power of the "thousand families"—Persia's
traditional feudal elite—gradually declined over the course of the 1960s and
'70s.

The real trouble with the White Revolution, perhaps, was that it
was not accompanied by any serious political reform or expansion of the
democratic process. Iran in the 1960s had an electorate that was educated,
informed, and hungry to participate, but the White Revolution was simply imposed on them from above. There was no effort to relax press censorship so the Shah's ideas could be publicly debated; no effort to allow
political parties such as the National Front to form a loyal opposition. The
White Revolution—advertised as the greatest achievement in Iran's modern
history—was never even submitted to a vote in the Majles, because the

Majles had been dissolved two years earlier. Instead, a referendum was held in which 99.93 percent of voters supposedly gave their endorsement. After that point, anyone who dared criticize the extraordinary service the shah was doing for his people was labeled a "black" reactionary or a "red" radical.

Iranian newspapers and radio programs gushed dutifully about the "visionary" reforms introduced by the nation's great modernizing leader, but the public often felt excluded and insulted. In a country where elections were meaningless, giving women the vote struck most people as a cruel joke—a purely symbolic act intended to win praise for the shah in foreign capitals. And many religious leaders and rural conservatives saw women's suffrage as an affront to traditional values. What this meant in practice was that the shah alienated a large segment of the conservative population without giving liberals anything to cheer about. It was the same mistake his father had made: Focused obsessively on "modernizing" the country to impress the West, the shah left a generation—both liberals and conservatives—feeling that no one was listening to them.

Ultimately, many Iranians felt the White Revolution was a PR gimmick, a tawdry dog-and-pony show put on by the shah to convince the United States that he deserved more cash and military hardware. Iranians, acutely aware of their long history of shahs more interested in begging for scraps at the tables of foreign powers than in addressing the needs of their own people, found it a depressingly familiar spectacle. Iran, it seemed, had disentangled itself from a century of British and Russian domination but was fast becoming an American colony.

This anxiety about American influence could be felt at every level of Iranian society. By 1961, some five thousand Americans were living and working in Iran, where twenty years earlier there had been only a few hundred Presbyterian missionaries. Cinemas were opening at a rapid rate, with 150 Hollywood films a year shown to Iranian audiences. Flash Gordon and Annie Oakley were popular staples on Iranian television, and *Time* and *Newsweek* had a combined circulation of three thousand in Iran. The wealthiest Iranians, some forty thousand of whom were now traveling abroad every year, welcomed much of this as long-overdue "progress." But the seeds of resentment were gradually being sown among the country's poorer, more traditional communities. Increasingly, a Westernized elite, living in stately villas in the hills north of Tehran, looked down on anything Iranian or Islamic and spoke with condescension to residents of the poorer southern quarters. Even many who had never been abroad internalized the assumption that anything foreign was automatically better and came to regard the habits and attitudes of their parents' generation with frustration and shame. Hollywood movies taught Iranian men to believe that the way to impress a girl was to wolf-whistle loudly at her from across the street. With the benefit of hindsight, it is easy to see where all this was heading.

Iran was not the only country in the world to be struggling with social upheaval and rapid modernization in the 1960s. But in many other Asian, Latin American, and European nations, "Americanization" and techno-logical advancements were accompanied by tangible improvements in liv-ing standards. In Iran, this was much less the case. In 1963, when Iranians looked around, they saw a country awash in American money and Ameri-can advisers, but little in the way of genuine economic development. Only a small elite appeared able to enjoy the comforts of tail-finned Cadillacs and Maytag washing machines, leaving the rest to resent what seemed like an overly cozy relationship between Washington and the shah. A poll of young Iranians in 1963 revealed that 85 percent believed American aid to their country served only to "make the rich richer," and 50 percent felt the United States was "too much on the side of having things remain as they are."

In the first few months of 1963, frustration with the shah reached a boil-ing point. Students, teachers, intellectuals, professionals, bazaar merchants, and clerics all condemned what they felt was the government's drift toward autocracy and its inability to act independently of the United States. It was precisely the convergence of forces that had given birth to the Constitu-tional Revolution of 1906 and to the oil nationalization crisis of 1951—and by and large, the demands were much the same. But there was one crucial difference. After ten years of signing petitions and attending meetings, Ira-nian activists were disillusioned with liberalism. In the ten years since the United States stepped in to remove Mosaddeq from power, what was left of the National Front had failed to galvanize anything more than a talking-shop of intellectuals, students, and urban professionals. Democracy and liberty were charming ideas in the abstract, but the actions of the world's greatest democracy in 1953 had left many Iranians wondering if the time had come for something a little less accommodating and a little more forceful—or maybe something more rooted in their own traditions.

☙

In the spring of 1963, the bazaars of Tehran and other cities began to fill with posters depicting the face of a sixty-year-old ayatollah named Ruhollah Khomeini. At the Faezieh theological college in the holy city of Qom, Kho-meini was delivering lectures on ethics and Islamic philosophy that were harshly critical of the direction the country was going in, and his popularity was climbing rapidly. He was not yet well known among the middle-class intelligentsia in Tehran (city-slickers generally tended to dismiss clerics as "lice-ridden mullahs," superstitious simpletons with no understanding of the modern world), but in the poorer, shabbier precincts, it was a different story. Khomeini had a way about him when he spoke. He would furrow his brow, delivering lectures softly and succinctly, in a way that made even the most abstract religious concepts seem deeply applicable to the difficulties facing Iran in the modern era. He would talk with a quiet, brooding certainty about the dangers of becoming too Western—accusing the government of ignoring the needs of the poor and the pious in its rush to import whiz-bang American gadgetry. Though no one knew it at the time, this sixty-year-old cleric—this unassuming seminarian sitting cross-legged behind a microphone talking about tyranny and morality—would one day change the world.

In March 1963 thousands of Khomeini's students staged a protest against the shah and were met with a spray of bullets from the security forces. Dozens were killed. Over the next several weeks, tensions mounted as Khomeini's followers repeatedly attempted to hold demonstrations. Finally, on June 3, Khomeini delivered a particularly fiery sermon aimed directly at the shah himself. "You miserable wretch, isn't it time for you to think and reflect a little, to ponder where all this is leading you?" the ayatollah asked. "Do you know that when one day something changes, none of these people who surround you will be your friends?" Within twenty-four hours, Khomeini was led away in shackles and thrown into prison.

The shah couldn't have picked a worse day to arrest one of the country's leading clerical authorities. The third of June was Ashura, the anniversary of the murder and martyrdom of the emam Hussein in Karbala in A.D. 680 and the most important ceremony in Shia Islam. The symbolism of Ashura was enormous for Iran's majority-Shia population—an occasion when thousands dressed in black and marched through the streets weeping and pounding their chests, mourning Hussein's murder at the hands of the evil tyrant Yazid in the seventh century. Far more than a religious ritual, the Ashura mourning procession was a stirring piece of political theater, a chance to moan and weep at the injustice of the world and express solidarity with all innocent people killed by oppressive or illegitimate rulers.

On June 4, 1963, it meant more than ever. That afternoon, as temperatures climbed toward the hundred-degree mark in many parts of Iran, the religious processions turned into electrified rivers of public rage. Mourners—many of them not particularly religious, but recognizing a rare opportunity to voice their frustrations—poured into the streets, weeping and wailing, united in solidarity against the shah. Even the most casual observer could recognize that these dramatic scenes constituted a far greater

"You miserable wretch": The radical cleric Ayatollah Ruhollah Khomeini preached against the shah in June 1963 and was arrested. Washington worried about the spread of Communism into Iran but seemed unaware that disenfranchised, frustrated Iranians were beginning to coalesce around the ayatollah.

crisis than anything the monarch had faced in his twenty-two years on the throne. Determined not to allow Khomeini to gain the upper hand, the shah declared martial law and ordered tanks and troops into several of Iran's largest cities. Soldiers were told they should shoot to kill.

The result was a bloodbath. For two full days, the shah's forces clashed with mourners and demonstrators in scenes of horrifying violence. Several hundred people (some estimates suggested thousands) lost their lives, and in addition to Khomeini, some twenty-eight ayatollahs were arrested. In the process, something happened that could not be undone: millions of ordinary, God-fearing, mosque-going Iranians realized that the country's ruler resembled the tyrant Yazid, who had slaughtered the true believers at Karbala in A.D. 680. Khomeini, meanwhile, represented Hussein, a hero to the poor and downtrodden of the earth. For the shah, it was not a good position to be in.*

By unleashing his goons on something that was sacred, the shah had

* Today the Uprising of 15 Khordad (as that day's events are known) is commemorated in Iran as a national holiday.

foolishly relit the fuse on a phenomenon that had existed in Iran since December 1905, when a brutal act of government repression had first united modern liberals and religious traditionalists in common purpose against their tyrannical shah. In June 1963, the shah came away with the impression that he had the situation under control. But the image of air force fighter planes firing indiscriminately into streams of weeping, black-clad mourners was something the population would not soon forget.

cs

Five and a half months later, on November 22, 1963, an assassin's bullet tore through the skull of John Kennedy and brought one of the most ambitious, far-reaching presidencies of the twentieth century to an early and unexpected end. It also removed from the picture the last American president to make a serious attempt to push the shah of Iran in the direction of reform. History does not record the shah's reaction when he heard the news from Dallas, but in recent years, several courtiers who were present have described the shah as "not displeased." One even claims he asked for a drink to celebrate.

Such stories are almost certainly exaggerated, but one thing is certain. If the shah did raise a glass on that November evening in 1963, he would have been well advised to make it a double. The death of Kennedy might have felt like some kind of relief after a three-year political headache. But the Peacock Throne was about to have a much bigger problem on its hands.

This Turbulent Priest

In May 1964, after six months in prison, Ayatollah Khomeini emerged into the daylight to find his country even more saturated with cynicism about the shah's regime than it had been the previous year.[*] After nearly three years of autocratic rule, a new Majles had finally been elected, but as ever, it was stuffed with flimsy careerists and conservative elites—a collection of warm bodies whose sole purpose seemed to be to execute the shah's will. Worse, the lawmakers had been asked to approve a request from the United States for a status of forces agreement, a pact that would give American military personnel and advisers stationed in Iran, along with their staff and families, sweeping immunity from Iranian law. The smell of outrage was in the air.[†]

Even with a pro-American shah and a rubber-stamp Majles, the status of forces agreement struggled to win approval. The Iranian government, fearing a public backlash, repeatedly delayed presenting the bill, and even the most supine Majles deputies expressed concerns about the threat to Iranian sovereignty. But the Americans kept pressing, until eventually the government relented and submitted the matter to parliament. The final vote (70 to 62) was unusually close by Iranian standards, but the Americans

---

[*] Following his arrest in June 1963, Khomeini was detained for two months, then released in August—only to be rearrested in October, when he called for a boycott of Majles elections.

[†] The United States had negotiated similar pacts with NATO countries in the 1950s, but the agreement proposed for Iran went much further. In most European nations that hosted U.S. military bases, an American who committed a crime could be tried by either a U.S. tribunal or by the local authorities, depending on circumstances, and his staff and family were subject to the laws of the host country. What the Americans were asking for in Iran, by contrast, was total immunity from Iranian law for anyone remotely connected with the U.S. military—a degree of legal privilege that existed only in West Germany, where a virtual American raj had emerged from the ashes of Nazi surrender.

got what they wanted—an agreement that gave them blanket immunity to Iranian laws.

Twelve days later, as a token of thanks, the United States gave the shah a $200 million loan and told him he could spend it on all the American military technology he had had his eye on for the past few years. It was—until that point—the largest single foreign aid payment in Iranian history.

CB

Perhaps the Americans thought they were just showing appreciation for the gracious cooperation of a loyal ally. But they had forgotten—or failed to learn—a crucial lesson of Iranian history. To Iranians, the image of heaps of cash landing in the lap of a shah after he had granted special immunities to foreigners instantly brought to mind the shameful nineteenth-century Qajar shahs who had granted the Great Powers extraterritorial privileges in exchange for massive loans. The shah's father had abolished this hated practice in 1927, so why, many wondered, was it being revived in 1964? Secular liberals, religious conservatives, and other segments of the population again found themselves united in frustration over the shah's perceived spinelessness.* And as public irritation mounted, an old word—one not heard for decades—reentered the Iranian political lexicon: *capitulations.*

In his simple study in Qom, where he sat cross-legged on a dusty carpet surrounded by books, the Ayatollah Khomeini could sense that his moment had arrived. Angry, bewildered, betrayed, a nation of political orphans was looking for someone to provide the kind of leadership so sorely lacking in Tehran—a sermon, perhaps, or a piece of moral guidance for a shah with no backbone. And no one seemed better placed to deliver the critique than the holy man who had been rotting away under house arrest for most of a year. Within hours of the announcement of the $200 million loan, thousands of excited seminarians and curious citizens gathered at the Grand Mosque in Qom to hear what the old cleric was going to say. And Khomeini did not disappoint. As he slowly approached the microphone, he furrowed his famous brow and delivered what turned out to be the defining speech of his career.

"I can't express the pain in my heart," he began as the crowd fell silent. "My heart is under a heavy weight. For the past few days I have been unable to sleep as I hear the news of all these problems." Barely a minute into his

---

* Adding to the frustration was news that Pakistan, Indonesia, and Turkey had all received similar requests from the United States and had turned them down.

speech, grown men in the audience were weeping. Knowing he was talking not only to his following of Quranic scholars and theology students but also to a potentially national audience, Khomeini kept his speech short and simple and explained the issues in terms every Iranian could understand:

> They sold us. They sold our independence. . . . They passed a law in Majles. . . . All the American military advisers, with their families, their technical staff, their office staff, their domestic staff, and anyone who is attached to them—whatever crime these people commit in Iran they have immunity. If an American servant, an American cook shoots one of your [beloved religious leaders] in the middle of the bazaar, tramples him underfoot, Iran's police have no right to stop him. The courts of Iran have no right to try him! Or even question him! He has to go to America! There in America, the masters have to settle the matter. . . . They've given the people of Iran a status lower than that of American dogs. . . . Why have they done this? Because they needed a loan from America? . . . They have sold us to America.

By the time Khomeini was finished speaking, it was obvious that the earth had just moved. The next day's papers were banned from publishing the speech, but many Iranians saw a copy of it anyway. And in the days that followed, a generation of embittered cynics who had given up on politics found themselves re-electrified. Urban, middle-class professionals and secular intellectuals might have felt squeamish about allowing a conservative religious leader to set the political agenda. But there was also no denying that Khomeini had an uncanny ability to stir up mass sentiment against the shah—and as far as liberals were concerned, that could only be a good thing. Iran was alive again, in a way not seen since the days of Mosaddeq.

This time, however, the shah was taking no chances. Believing that, one way or another, the time had come to be rid of this turbulent priest, he arranged for Khomeini to be arrested—one last time—and packed off to exile in Turkey. On the face of it, this measure was extreme, but to the shah it felt like a necessary precaution. By sending the ayatollah to Turkey—a secular republic, with almost no Shia population, and strict laws separating religion from public life—the shah felt confident that Khomeini would be reduced in stature, and perhaps all the way into insignificance.

He would come to rue the day. Nearly a year later, Khomeini migrated from Turkey to Iraq, where he set up shop in Najaf—site of the most important shrine in Shia Islam—and began delivering sermons harshly critical of the shah's regime. Another fifteen years would pass before he was allowed to see his country again, but the old ayatollah would make good use of his time in exile. In Iraq, he would write, think, and preach extensively—and in the process formulate his most important ideas about the place of Islam in politics. Much of what he wrote and said would gradually be smuggled into Iran in grubby mimeographed pamphlets and bootleg cassette tapes—all feverishly copied and distributed by his followers at underground meetings and sold at market stalls under cover of secrecy.

At this early stage, when the shah's regime exercised ruthless control over all aspects of Iranian society, when his security apparatus numbered in the hundreds of thousands, and when his government enjoyed the fulsome backing of the United States and other powers, it was easy to dismiss Khomeini as a marginal figure—a gadfly whose appeal was limited to the poorer and more religious elements of society. It was hard to imagine, in 1964, that a cantankerous cleric delivering lectures in the dustbowl of Mesopotamia could ever cause a serious problem to the Shah of Shahs. But the ayatollah was a patient man. And he believed God was on his side.

 C3

Even with Khomeini out of the country, the shah struggled to exert control. In January 1965 a twenty-one-year-old son of a Tehran ironworker, disgruntled over the price of bread and the climate of corruption and moral decline in Iranian politics, walked up to the gates of the Majles building and shot to death the prime minister, Hassan Ali Mansur.[*] Three months later another young man, a promising member of the shah's Imperial Guard, unloaded the contents of a submachine gun in the direction of the King of Kings himself as the shah made his way into the Marble Palace. The shah survived the assassination attempt, just as he had in 1949. But this time there was no outpouring of public sympathy. In 1965 all but the most obtuse observer of Iranian politics could see that the shah had a problem on his hands—and that it was much bigger than Khomeini.

The shah's response to this wave of violence was to beef up his notorious secret police force, SAVAK.[†] Created in 1957 with help from the CIA, SAVAK had developed a reputation for thuggishness and brutality. But from 1965 it became the most feared instrument of repression and coercion Iran had ever known. Torture, widely used in the 1950s but nominally banned

[*] The shah blamed religious extremists for the assassination, and dozens of clerics were rounded up and tortured into making confessions—among them Akbar Hashemi Rafsanjani, who would go on to serve as Iran's president from 1989 to 1997.
[†] Persian acronym for Sazman-e Ettela'at va Amniat-e Keshvar, the State Information and Security Organization.

in 1961, once again became part of SAVAK's operating procedure. SAVAK received sweeping powers to "screen" candidates for jobs in government or education; to censor film, television, and newspapers; to manage the literacy corps and rural health corps (flagship programs of the White Revolution); and to control the issuance of passports, to ensure only loyal subjects could travel outside the country. Overseas, too, Iranian embassies were staffed with SAVAK agents tasked with monitoring the activities of Iranians living and studying abroad. By the late 1960s virtually every facet of Iranian public life was being closely monitored by SAVAK.

The climate of terror SAVAK created in the late 1960s only pushed larger numbers of otherwise moderate, apolitical Iranians into permanent disillusionment with their shah. Unable to channel their frustrations into constructive political activity, middle-class Iranians with means left the country or sent their children abroad to study. By the mid-1960s, the United States alone was home to tens of thousands of Iranian students, more than from any other country. And few were in any rush to return home. Virtually every American university had a large contingent of Iranian students on its campus—a population easily recognizable by its fierce and vociferous opposition to the shah.

From the late 1960s, the State Department, members of Congress, newspaper editors, and sundry American officials were routinely bombarded with letters from students and other Iranian-Americans attempting to raise awareness about the cruelty of the shah's regime. But such efforts rarely went anywhere. To American officialdom in the 1960s, the idea that the shah might be unpopular did not seem plausible. Policy makers continued to see the shah as the embodiment of progressive values, a courageous monarch leading his nation toward a prosperous, modern future. But in the late 1960s the shah made several official visits to the United States, and every time he arrived, his motorcade was accompanied by hundreds of protesters waving placards and shouting slogans. In 1967, SAVAK agents accompanying the shah on a visit to New York even noticed, for the first time, that several protesters outside the Waldorf-Astoria were holding up pictures of Khomeini.

C33

Back in Iran, the shah did what he could to quell the growing tide of opposition. In 1964 he created the New Iran Party (Hezb-e Iran Novin), designed to appeal to a generation of "new men"—technically skilled young Iranians who were prepared to engage in practical, constructive measures to modernize the country. Hoping to lure Iran's middle-class intelligentsia away from political opposition with the promise of prestigious job titles, ingratiating secretaries, chauffeured cars, and lucrative salaries, the shah rapidly expanded the state bureaucracy, creating nearly five hundred plum postings designed to entice highfliers with foreign Ph.D.'s. All this gave the shah a chance to answer his American critics—he could claim he was fostering multiparty democracy and attending to the liberal middle classes. But like the earlier Melliyun and Mardom parties, the New Iran Party was little more than a fast track into subservience. Anyone joining its ranks was subject to vigorous SAVAK screening, and the party did little to articulate genuinely independent policies. Nevertheless, many skilled professionals did join, out of genuine commitment to the shah or simply a desire for wealth, power, and prestige.

The embodiment of this new generation of technocrats was Amir Abbas Hoveida, who served as prime minister from 1965 to 1977 (the longest premiership in Iranian history). Bald, round, and short, Hoveida seemed almost physically designed to serve as a political football, and for most of his term he was exactly that. Caught between feuding factions, political intrigue, and his own policy priorities, Hoveida often functioned more as a glorified HR manager than a prime minister. But he was also emblematic of a new style taking hold in Iranian politics. A pipe-smoking, wise-cracking intellectual with a walking stick at hand and a flower poking through his lapel, Hoveida was fluent in six languages and well versed in French literature. And unlike the older generation of Iranian elites, who typically spoke only French and believed European models of development were best for Iran, Hoveida was fluent in English and stuffed his cabinet with figures who had studied or traveled in the United States.

Beneath Hoveida's cosmopolitan public persona lay a ruthless political operator—unafraid to crack a few skulls or ruin a few careers in the service of the Peacock Throne. And this ethos pervaded the ranks of the New Iran Party too. The Iranian ambassador to the United States, Hushang Ansary, appointed in 1967, was a lubricious liar and a charlatan, a man who never maintained eye contact and never missed an opportunity to line his own pocket. But Americans saw none of this. In the late 1960s, Ansary was one of the best-connected people in Washington, friendly with everyone from CIA chief Richard Helms to National Security Adviser Henry Kissinger to future secretary of state James Baker. They all found the New Iran crowd to be a breath of fresh air, a pioneering vanguard taking Iran into the modern age.

CS

No one felt this way more than President Lyndon Johnson, a tough-talking Texan pragmatist who quickly reaffirmed the close relationship that had existed between America and Iran in the 1950s. Unlike Kennedy, Johnson cared little what the shah did in his own country as long as he remained a stalwart American ally. Bogged down in a difficult, unpopular war in Vietnam, he was grateful for the shah's support—and for his ideological opposition to Communism globally. To Johnson, Iran was that rarest of birds—a third-world nation whose leader didn't reflexively sympathize with the North Vietnamese struggle against Yankee "imperialism." More important, Johnson appreciated the shah's opposition to the left-leaning Arab nationalism of Egypt's Gamal Abdel Nasser, as well as his quiet support for Israel.*

Washington in these years was still struggling to step into the global leadership vacuum created by the decline of the British Empire, especially in the Middle East. Johnson needed all the help he could get. In 1968, Britain unexpectedly announced that it would be withdrawing its troops from the Persian Gulf within three years, and Johnson was relieved when the shah volunteered to step in and act as America's policeman in the region. For the better part of a century, Britain had dominated Middle Eastern politics, but now the United States and Iran, working together, would defend what Washington increasingly believed were its three priorities in the region: fighting Communism, maintaining a steady supply of oil, and bolstering Israel.

For all his efforts, the shah hoped to be richly rewarded. At every opportunity, he lobbied the Johnson administration for massive increases in military support. When such increases were not forthcoming, he complained bitterly about the "indifference of his American friends." Reading defense industry journals, he helpfully pointed out when the latest American fighter jets were expected to roll off the assembly line. It was, in other words, the same basic message he had delivered to every American president for the previous twenty-five years. But the shah of the late 1960s differed from the shah of the 1940s and 1950s in one important way: he was not asking for a handout. In the mid-1960s, Iran's oil fields were producing more crude than ever, and in 1966 the shah had successfully negotiated a 75–25 split in profits with the international oil consortium—significantly increasing the amount of money Iran made from its oil. As a result, Iran's oil revenues, which had stood at $372 million a year in 1963, climbed to $908 million by

---

* Officially, Iran did not recognize Israel, but informal cooperation between the two nations was strong. (During the Arab-Israeli War of 1967, for example, Iran sent oil to Israel.) The shah saw Israel as a useful conduit to the U.S. political establishment, as well as an important buffer against Nasserite Arab nationalism. Israel, meanwhile, found in Iran a rare and much-welcome regional partner. For much of the 1960s and 1970s, relations between Iran and Israel were something of an open secret. Israel maintained an unofficial "embassy" in an unmarked building in Tehran. The Israeli "ambassador" enjoyed access to the shah, which was arranged via SAVAK—often without the knowledge of the Foreign Ministry.

1969. With this kind of money in the bank, Iran was no longer panhandling for freebies. It was now a customer of the American arms industry.

With this spike in oil revenue came a seismic shift in the nature and tone of the U.S.-Iranian relationship. In 1966 the United States declared that Iran was no longer a "developing" nation and therefore not eligible for technical or economic assistance. Within months, the American advisers, development experts, and agricultural consultants who had helped run the country since 1943—the largest U.S. aid mission in the world—packed up and went home. In their place came arms dealers, hotel and casino entre-preneurs, and snake-oil salesmen of every hue, who saw Iran not as a charity case but as a business opportunity. Iran was now told that if it wanted tanks or aircraft from the United States, it could put in a request and pay full market price—just as a European nation would.

The shah complained bitterly about the change in designation, arguing (with some justification) that full development was still a few years away.[*] But he did not let it distract him from the larger goal: getting more weapons out of America. Knowing that Johnson, perhaps more than any president before him, was acutely sensitive to Soviet encroachment on the Asian con-tinent, the shah fell back on his old tactic of warming up to Moscow as a way to remind Washington not to take his support for granted. In 1965 he made a state visit to Moscow and awarded the Soviets a contract to build steel mills and a gas pipeline in Iran. The following year he purchased $110 million in light armaments from Moscow. He reminded Washington that Iran shared an eleven-hundred-mile border with the Soviet Union. If the United States was serious about containing the spread of Communism, it would need to send weapons—without delay.

For the first time in years, the shah found the United States receptive to his entreaties. Distracted and demoralized by the never-ending nightmare of Vietnam, the Johnson White House had little energy to devote to the Middle East and was happy to allow the shah plenty of latitude as an Ameri-can proxy in the region. In 1969, Washington approved the sale to Iran of $289 million of military equipment—nearly three times the allocation for the previous year. From 1967 to 1970 the shah received forty Iroquois helicopters, two battleships, three gunboats, and nearly eight hundred Side-winder and Sparrow air-to-air missiles. But the real jaw-dropper was the sale of two squadrons of state-of-the-art F-4 fighter jets—the most advanced equipment then available. After the United Kingdom, Iran was the first country in the world to receive the new F-4s.

[*] Much of the Iranian public shared this irritation, believing that the change in designation was really an excuse for the U.S. defense industry to make money off Iran.

The boom before the bust: Rapid modernization, an overheated economy, deep inequality, rampant secularization. Iran's outward veneer to Western visitors was that of a success story. But trouble lay close to the surface.

The attitude of the shah's own people to this unprecedented military build-up—and indeed to the shah himself—was readily reflected in the Johnson administration's mailbag. From the late 1960s, the White House received a deluge of letters from Iranian-Americans desperate to warn America that the shah was unpopular at home—that he was torturing dissidents, locking up newspaper editors, and making a mockery of the democratic process. But little of this seemed to make an impact. U.S. officials with strong pro-Pahlavi leanings, such as National Security Advisers Walt Rostow and McGeorge Bundy, went out of their way to ensure that none

On May 15, Iran Air inaugurates faster, more direct service from New York to Tehran.

(Five flights weekly via London.)

The world's fastest growing airline.

For most of our thirty year history we have been serving our homeland. Air transportation is very important in Iran because of its enormous size. (It's larger than California, Texas and Montana combined.) And because of the terrain which is difficult to negotiate because it contains vast stretches of mountains.

But now that we have become an international carrier, we are going about it in a big way. Our route map includes most major European capitals, as well as Karachi, Bombay, Peking and Tokyo. And our transatlantic service will put us well on our way to becoming a worldwide airline.

In 1973, Iran Air passed the one million mark in passengers carried and our equipment is now all jet. We fly 707's, 727's and 737's. But 747 service will be available early in 1976. And in 1977, Iran Air will become a pioneer in supersonic flight when the majestic Concorde joins our fleet.

Along with our desire to expand our service is a desire to extend our service to all passengers. We have a 2,500 year old Persian tradition of hospitality to live up to and we're very proud of that heritage.

But as well as offering superb service, we offer a convenient schedule. There is only a London stopover on our New York to Tehran route, and there is no plane-change involved. So our guests needn't worry about baggage or connections on our flights.

They can just sit back and learn the Persian meaning of the word "welcome."

	MON.	WED.	THURS.	FRI.	SUN.
NEW YORK	LEAVE	2100	2100	2100	2100	2100
LONDON	ARRIVE	0835	0835	0835	0835	0835
	LEAVE	1030	1030	1025	1030	1030
TEHRAN	ARRIVE	1815	1815	1815	1815	1815

ALL TIMES LOCAL

Fly a new way to London.

London is a perfect stopover for passengers going to or coming from Iran. It lets you catch up with the time change and spend a few days exploring this exciting city.

But if London is your destination, Iran Air offers you fantastic onboard service. You can dine on American or Iranian specialities. And you can experience our distinctly Persian hospitality.

Welcome to Tehran.

Nothing illustrates the dynamic growth of Iran as does Tehran. In 1920 its population was a mere 200,000. But today, with more than 3,000,000 people, it is the largest city in western Asia, and is emerging as an important factor in world industry and economics. Tehran is becoming one of the more important and influential capitals on the globe.

The beauty of Tehran makes doing business a pleasure. Set against snow-capped mountains higher than the Alps, it is a city that spreads out in all directions. Everywhere you look you'll see modern buildings, monuments, museums, shops—all as new as today, but touched with the artistry of the Persian past.

The stunning Shahyad Tower exemplifies Tehran today. It was built four years ago to commemorate Iran's 2,500th anniversary and is the very symbol of a legendary civilization that has evolved into our vital, modern society.

Welcome to Isfahan.

As you descend on Isfahan your first impression is one of gazing down on a sparkling jewel in a tawny setting. And when you arrive, you'll see a different shade of blue everywhere you look. From a brilliant sapphire to a subtle aquamarine, all are shimmering against a Persian

blue sky. This is one of the world's most beautiful cities. Here you can see sights like the incredible Royal Square, seven times the size of the Piazza San Marco in Venice. And there is a plethora of beautiful buildings in Isfahan. It is a pleasant frustration to the visitor because you can't possibly see them all.

The bazaar is a delightful change of pace from the grandeur of the buildings. Beneath acres of multicolored cloth, idle in the joyful, lusty Persian tradition is on display. Craftsmen are creating Persian carpets, etching copper vessels and carving wooden blocks. They are a fascinating and engaging people.

And Isfahan's boasts of the Shah Abbas, voted for five consecutive years the most beautiful hotel in the world...it's certainly in the appropriate city.

Welcome to Persepolis.

Forty miles from the city of Shiraz is one of the wonders of the world. A marvel that lay dormant for nearly 2,500 years.

The ruins of Persepolis.

If you saw nothing else on your trip to Iran, you would think this one sight worth the journey. This is a treasure that rivals the Roman forum, the Acropolis and Stonehenge for drama, beauty and historical significance.

Many a visitor has, upon seeing this magnificent spectacle, been spellbound by its beauty.

Iran offers enough spectacles to keep you breathless for weeks. The elegance and opulence of the ancient kingdom and the excitement and vitality of a flourishing, modern nation.

Once you visit our land you'll understand what we mean when we say, "The fantasy that was Persia lives on in Fantastic Iran."

Call the travel expert... your travel agent. Or Iran Air.

IRAN AIR

We've been welcoming strangers for 2500 years.

Iran Air advertisements; Tehran's glamorous Chattanooga restaurant; Andy Warhol and Empress Farah.

of this criticism reached the eyes and ears of the president. And Johnson himself seemed uninclined to ask too many questions. As far as he was concerned, Iran was a rare example of a developing nation doing everything right. "What is going on in Iran," Johnson once remarked to a White House visitor, "is about the best thing going on anywhere in the world."

The U.S. media seemed to agree. American newspapers and television journalists portrayed the shah as an enlightened monarch who was dragging his nation into the twentieth century in the face of constant resistance from "entrenched interests" and "reactionary forces," such as landlords and religious leaders. "The Shah has been instrumental in leading the country into the modern era through land reform and other progressive programs," gushed *The New York Times* in 1967. "The Shah has worked hard to alleviate his country's poverty," wrote *Time* the same year. "While his Arab neighbors feuded, fussed and fought with each other, he was busy building, investing most of his oil earnings in development instead of armaments, plants instead of planes." An outlandish statement, perhaps, about a country where 43 percent of the state budget went to the military, but *Time* did not stop there. The shah "has allowed considerable freedom," concluded the magazine. "His once dreaded SAVAK . . . is now little more than an intelligence-gathering agency." He was a "pace-setting social reformer without whom Iran would long ago have turned to chaos."

In reality, however, the shah's "reforms" were failing badly. By the end of the 1960s, two-thirds of Iranians lacked access to medical facilities, unemployment was rising rapidly, and per capita income was stuck somewhere around $250 a year. With large numbers of skilled, educated Iranians living abroad, Iran had a severe shortage of engineers and technicians who could implement reforms, and the White Revolution had stalled. On paper, Iran's economy was "booming," with annual GDP growth of 12 percent in 1968 and 1969. However, those numbers were deceptive, the product of a massive oil bonanza that was not trickling down to meet the wider population. Like many developing nations that experience sudden resource wealth, Iran was spending its oil revenues on ostentatious building projects and imported luxuries, rather than investing in agricultural productivity or supporting traditional industries. In 1968, for the first time in its history, Iran was forced to import wheat to feed its people.

და

In 1967, against this backdrop of poverty, economic mismanagement, and underdevelopment, the shah felt the time had come to treat his people to a lavish coronation ceremony. Following the model established by Napoleon

Coronation of an emperor: In 1967 the shah treated the country to a lavish coronation
ceremony for himself and Empress Farah. That same year, for the first time in its
history, Iran was forced to import wheat to feed its people.

and Josephine in 1804, he arranged for an elaborate, weeklong spectacle that
culminated in him placing his father's crown on his own head and naming
himself *ShahenShah*—"King of Kings"—then turning to Queen Farah and
crowning her Empress of Iran. To make sure every detail of the coronation
was "correct," he sent courtiers to London to learn the ropes from Buckingham Palace (a slightly odd decision for a country with 2,500 years of its own
monarchical tradition). A gilded coronation carriage, costing $78,000, was
imported from Vienna* and drawn by eight white coach-horses from Hungary. The empress wore a green and white silk dress that twenty-two coutu-
riers from the House of Dior had worked on for four months, with a train
that required the effort of six handmaids to keep off the ground. Six million
colored light bulbs (all imported) lit up Tehran at night, and fireworks (also
imported) were set off every night for a week. In remote regions of the
country, where TV sets were still rare, the Imperial Iranian air force dropped
roses onto villages, along with pictures of the shah and the empress.

It had been twenty-six years since the shah ascended the throne, but
wartime occupation and political instability had always made an imperial

---

* The carriage, still intact today, sits outside the shah's former palace, a tourist attraction into which
people can climb and have their pictures taken.

coronation seem premature. By 1967, however, he was feeling firmly in control and believed the time had come to encourage a more robust cult of personality. Statues of the shah went up in public squares all over the country, and his book, *The White Revolution,* became required reading in schools. The final cost for the 1967 festivities ran into the millions—a bill met partly by the treasury and partly by the undignified spectacle of SAVAK agents snaking their way through the bazaars, pressuring merchants and others into making "contributions."

In Najaf, Ayatollah Khomeini said what so many were already thinking. "They bleed the hearts of the poor for money," he wrote in an open letter to Prime Minister Hoveida. "Sitting in your opulent palaces, which you change once every few years, you spend millions . . . with an extravagance our people cannot even imagine and steal it all from the purse of our wretched nation."

The words sound almost quaint in the context of what followed. Over the next decade, the Pahlavi regime would introduce to Iran a degree of decadence, opulent consumption, and corruption not seen since the last days of the Qajar Empire—nor, perhaps, since the last days of Rome. For a lucky few, there would be rivers of champagne, mountains of caviar, and a merry-go-round of favors, blandishments, and personal wealth. But for most, there would be only stagnation and spiraling poverty—together with political agitation, violent protests, and confrontations with a government that seemed to have lost touch with the needs of its people.

The 1970s would turn out to be an unforgettable decade in Iran. It would also be the last for the Pahlavi dynasty.

The Final Emperor

In October 1971 the shah of Iran invited the world to Persepolis. Choosing the ancient ruins of the capital of the Persian Empire as his backdrop, he played host to one of the most audacious, expensive, and self-indulgent spectacles of the modern era: celebrations marking the twenty-five-hundred-year anniversary of the Iranian monarchy. For four days, kings and presidents, princes and prime ministers, feasted and frolicked under luxurious air-conditioned tents in the middle of the desert, as the soaring, lit-up columns of the ruined capital loomed over them. A five-and-a-half-hour dinner featured roasted peacock, rack of lamb, jellied quail, caviar, and five thousand bottles of 1945 Château Lafitte. An army of international journalists, flown in at Iran's expense for the occasion, beamed the event by satellite to every corner of the globe—complete with military parades, a fireworks spectacular, balls, and pageants. Mohammad Reza Shah—son of a dirt-poor Cossack soldier from the mountains of Mazandaran—was letting the world know he had arrived.[*]

Amid all the pomp and circumstance, though, the shah forgot one important detail: this magnificent celebration of Iranian history was oddly lacking in anything authentically Iranian. Diners ate on plates of Limoges porcelain, drank Burgundy from Baccarat crystal glasses, and wiped their hands on linens from Porthault. The court livery worn by members of the shah's cabinet—$800 uniforms embroidered with two pounds of gold thread each—had been designed by Lanvin and flown back and forth to Paris several times for fittings. The fifteen hundred French cypress trees and

---

[*] Technically, the celebrations were ten years late. Cyrus had conquered Babylon and crowned himself "King of the four corners of the world" in 539 B.C., so the anniversary was actually 1961. But once the decision was made to mark the occasion, the celebrations took ten years to plan.

acres of petunias, carnations, and marigolds planted for the occasion were supplied by Truffaut, official horticulturalist of the Palace of Versailles. The souvenir book given to every guest—a collection of the shah's speeches— had been printed in England, bound in Belgium, and boxed in France. At the sumptuous banquet, prepared by Maxim's of Paris, only the caviar was Iranian.* Everything else—down to the last quail egg, the last fatted lamb, and the last supercilious waiter—was flown in from Paris. Little wonder that France's own president sent his regrets that he was unable to attend. "If I did go," he was said to have quipped, "they would probably make me head waiter."

Iranians felt snubbed. For months they had been told to expect a historic celebration that would bring immeasurable honor to Iran. But in the end, they were allowed nowhere near it. Fearing disruption by radicals, the organizers sealed off a ten-mile radius around Persepolis with barbed wire, uprooted tribal villagers, and stationed troops with submachine guns around the periphery. In the lead-up to the event, SAVAK agents went on an orgy of intimidation, arresting more than two thousand potential troublemakers. As a result, one of the most important milestones in Iranian history turned into a lavish party held in the middle of the desert for several hundred foreign dignitaries. Iranians who had hoped to take part in their nation's twenty-five-hundredth birthday party watched it on television like everyone else.

With all the princes and potentates assembled, the anniversary celebrations kicked off at the tomb of Cyrus the Great, where the shah turned and spoke directly to his ancient precursor:

> Cyrus! Great king! King of kings! Achaemenian king! King of the land of Iran! From me, King of kings of Iran and from my nation, I send greetings. . . . Cyrus, we have gathered here today at your eternal tomb to tell you: sleep in peace because we are awake. And we will always be awake to look after our proud inheritance.

The shah projected his voice slowly and theatrically, like a booming kettledrum, pausing frequently for effect. But cursed as he was with a thin, nasal, and watery voice, the overall impression was of a man straining to make himself heard. To his supporters, the shah's salute to Cyrus was a moment of devastating political theater. To his detractors, it was the beginning of the end—the unofficial start of his final, delusional decade in power.

Already the shah had declared 1971 would be the "Year of Cyrus the

---

* The shah, who was allergic to caviar, was served a French artichoke instead.

Great," and for twelve months, much of Iran's television and radio programming had been dedicated to Iran's ancient history. Now at Persepolis, the shah was behaving as if he had somehow *become* Cyrus, or the ancient emperor was speaking through him. In twelve years, he announced, Iranians would enter "the era of the Great Civilization," a time of spectacular national wealth and glory, equal to that of their ancient ancestors. To underline his point, he added a new title to his stable of imperial honorifics—one that emphasized Iran's pre-Islamic past. He would now be known officially not just as ShahenShah, "King of Kings," but also as Aryamehr—"Light of the Aryans."

From his exile in Iraq, Ayatollah Khomeini ridiculed the celebrations at Persepolis as the "devil's festival." He also declared, for the first time, his opposition to the very institution of monarchy—an important shift in his political position. "The title of King of Kings," he declared, "is the most hated of all titles in the sight of God." Islam had no place for kings—it was an egalitarian religion and should be concerned with the welfare of the poor and downtrodden. The obscene spectacle taking place at Persepolis, moreover, was fundamentally un-Islamic, an incubator of sin and decadence. "To participate in it," Khomeini said, was "to participate in the murder of the oppressed people of Iran."

Not all Iranians were so extreme in their criticism. But there is no question that something began to shift after Persepolis. Until 1971, overt opposition to the shah had been mostly limited to urban intellectuals, Com-

"Cyrus, sleep in peace because we are awake!": Persepolis 1971. At the tomb of Cyrus the Great (559–530 B.C.), founder of the Persian Empire, the shah declares Iran's strength and modernity in the twentieth century. Like his father, the shah associated modernity with Iran's ancient history and a rejection of Islamic traditionalism.

munists, and a tiny minority of religious radicals. After Persepolis, though, ordinary Iranians with emotional attachments and loyalty to the monarchy began to nurse doubts. Many considered the spectacle they saw on television to be far less dignified than the manifestation of national pride they had been led to expect. What they saw was a leader who was losing touch.

CB

If the shah was feeling on top of the world in the early 1970s, it was at least in part because his old friend Richard Nixon had become president of the United States at the beginning of 1969—and had shown unflinching support for Iran. For the shah, who had never stopped worrying about the possibility of his overthrow at the hands of foreign powers, Nixon's presence in the White House was deeply reassuring. And for Nixon, the friendship of the shah was equally critical.

Soon after assuming power, Nixon argued that, given the draining demands of Vietnam and the daunting complexity of the U.S.-Soviet rivalry, the United States could no longer afford to get bogged down in costly, unpopular wars in distant corners of the world. Instead, he believed, Washington needed to identify loyal regional allies, ask them to serve as guardians of U.S. interests, and where appropriate, arm them to the gills. This new strategy—known as the Nixon Doctrine— became a defining characteristic of American policy in the latter half of the Cold War, employed everywhere from Latin America to Southeast Asia. But it was in the Middle East that the Nixon Doctrine received its purest application.

The formula was simple: in exchange for providing Iran with massive quantities of American military hardware, the Nixon administration expected the country to become a "pillar" of U.S. policy in the Middle East.[*] In particular, it hoped the shah would provide a buffer for the United States against the twin dangers of Soviet Communism and Arab nationalism— the latter personified by Iraqi leader Saddam Hussein and Egypt's President Nasser. For years, Saddam and Nasser had both fostered ambitions of uniting the Arab world against U.S.-Israeli regional hegemony. To the Nixon administration, the shah seemed the ideal leader to stand in their way.

The shah jumped at the opportunity to serve as America's local sheriff. Like Persian leaders throughout history, he was deeply uncomfortable with the idea of a powerful Arab on his doorstep, and as a conservative monarch,

---

[*] The new posture was known as the "twin pillar policy," since it defined Iran and Saudi Arabia as America's most important surrogates in the region. In practice, however, the Saudis turned out to be less enthusiastic about the arrangement than the shah.

he nursed particular hostility to the socialist nationalism of Nasser and Saddam. In 1969, moreover, Saddam had seriously rattled the shah's cage by claiming that the oil-rich waterway along the Iran-Iraq border belonged to Iraq. But the shah's rivalry with Saddam became much more visible in April 1972, after Iraq signed a treaty of friendship with the Soviet Union. Suddenly, for the United States, the containment of Saddam became a strategic priority. The shah suggested that he could distract Saddam by supporting Kurdish rebels in Iraq, and Washington was quick to agree. For the next three years, the shah happily funneled $16 million from the CIA to Iraqi Kurds, along with the latest Soviet and Chinese weapons captured by the Americans in Vietnam.

But the shah's strategic value to the Nixon administration extended far beyond Iraq. As the last British troops left the region in 1971, the shah moved to fill the vacuum. In 1973 he sent troops into Oman to help the sultan put down a leftist rebellion, and he encouraged newly independent nations like Kuwait, Bahrain, and Qatar to develop a conservative, pro-Western posture. Farther afield, he helped the pro-American dictatorship of Pakistan's Zulfiqar Ali Bhutto suppress Baluchi rebels, and he sent arms to Somalia, to use in its war against Soviet-backed Ethiopia. Once upon a time Washington would have relied on the British to perform such services. Now it had the shah.

As Iran assumed a more prominent role in the neighborhood, the shah cultivated an image as an international statesman, doling out advice to superpowers and behaving as if he were the indispensable sage of global politics. He publicly told the United States it needed more "social discipline" and argued that Western nations had to be less wasteful in their use of oil. In an interview with British television, the shah took aim at Britain's welfare state, warning that "if you continue this way—a permissive, undisciplined society—you . . . will go bankrupt." Domestically, the shah projected an image of himself as one of history's greatest leaders. He promised his people they would soon enjoy a standard of living higher than Switzerland's and that Iran would become the "Japan of western Asia." In ten years, he said, Iran would be one of the five richest, most powerful nations in the world, and in twenty-five years it would surpass even Britain and France in its standard of living.

The Americans did nothing to discourage this megalomania. In private meetings in Washington, Nixon described the shah as a "revolutionary monarch" and called him "talented and hardworking, a man who produced progress with stability." As early as 1953, Nixon had decided he "sensed an inner strength" in the shah, and in 1969 he told him he hoped Iran would become the dominant power in the Persian Gulf when the British left. To

The blank check: During a landmark visit to Tehran in May
1972, President Nixon and his secretary of state, Henry Kissinger,
promised the shah unlimited American military sales, in exchange
for assurance that Iran would serve as a pillar of U.S. policy in the
region.

make this happen, however, Nixon believed the shah would need substantial military aid from the United States.

In May 1972, on the way back from a summit meeting in Moscow,
Nixon and Secretary of State Henry Kissinger stopped in Tehran for a
twenty-four-hour state visit that turned out to be a defining moment in the
history of U.S.-Iranian relations. Behind closed doors, the leaders agreed
that in return for the shah's unconditional support for American policy in
the region, Iran would be permitted to purchase as much military equipment as it wanted. There would be no more pesky oversight from the Pentagon, no more lectures about poverty reduction, no more questions asked.
Details of the pact were kept from the public, but in a follow-up memo
to the U.S. defense secretary, Kissinger made it clear that, effective immediately, "decisions on the acquisition of military equipment should be left
primarily to the government of Iran."

Never in American history had the United States reached such a wide-
ranging military understanding with a nonindustrialized nation. And never
had the shah felt so pleased with the treatment he had received from an
American president. After decades of being told by Washington that he

should focus on domestic challenges before embarking on an adventurous military buildup, he finally got what he had always wanted from America: a blank check. In return, the United States found itself a Middle Eastern ally whose loyalty was beyond dispute.

As he got up to leave at the end of his meeting with the shah, Nixon leaned across the table, looked his old friend in the eye, and summed up the new special relationship between Tehran and Washington in two simple words: "Protect me."

CB

What followed was the most gluttonous and unrestrained military buildup the world has ever known. Iran's annual arms purchases from the United States jumped from $113 million to nearly $400 million in 1971, then to $2.2 billion in 1973, and to $4.4 billion in 1974. From 1972 to 1977, Iran spent a total of $16 billion (roughly $70 billion in today's money) buying weapons from the United States. Most of this money was spent on aircraft, the shah's special fixation. The latest F-14s and F-15s (costing $17 million apiece, and until then available only to NATO allies) were now the shah's for the asking. Arms dealers joked that the shah "devoured [our] manuals in much the same way as other men read *Playboy*," and they were not wide of the mark. The shah was known to flip through *Jane's Defence Weekly*, point to the latest, most expensive fighter aircraft, then instruct his staff to order it. In 1974 the shah dropped $1.5 billion on eighty F-14 jets, single-handedly saving Long Island's struggling Grumman Aircraft Corporation from bankruptcy.

By 1976, Iran was spending as much on its military as China was, despite having an army a tenth the size and a population twenty times smaller. The annual defense budget, just $67 million in 1953, reached a dizzying $9.4 billion in 1977. Iran's armed forces also grew, from 161,000 troops in 1970 to 413,000 in 1978. Some of the shah's new toys came from other countries (Britain sold Iran fifteen hundred Chieftain tanks—more than its own armed forces used), but far and away his biggest arms supplier was the United States. In the mid-1970s, more than one-third of America's international arms sales went to Iran, which had become the largest single purchaser of U.S. weapons in the world. At one point orders from Tehran were coming in at such a rapid rate that the Pentagon warned that Iran was becoming a drain on its own resources.

Between the flood of arms purchases and a pair of civilian commercial agreements, the Iranian government in the 1970s spent well over $60 billion on American products and services—a sum that, just ten years earlier, would have been unfathomable to most Iranians. But for Iran, these were days of plenty: as America, and much of the Western world, found themselves rapidly running out of oil, Middle Eastern countries exercised far greater influence in world affairs. Sitting on one of the world's largest petroleum reserves, the shah turned the situation to his advantage. In 1970 he renegotiated Iran's agreement with the international oil consortium so that Iran would receive 55 percent of export revenues. The following year he hosted a meeting of OPEC, at which oil-producing nations agreed to exercise greater control over petroleum prices. In 1972 he even nationalized the Iranian oil industry, finally putting into effect—without any mention of the old man's name—the law passed by Mosaddeq twenty-one years earlier.

In control of its own resources for the first time, Iran began pumping oil at a much faster rate, and the country's oil income, an impressive $885 million in 1971, rose to $1.6 billion in 1972. But the biggest prize was yet to come. In 1973, Arab nations suspended oil sales to the West for its support of Israel in the October War. Iran shrewdly voiced moral support for the Arabs but did not take part in the embargo. Overnight the price of oil quadrupled, and Iran's oil revenue soared—from $4.4 billion in 1973 to $21.4 billion in 1974.[*]

In three short years, the shah had become utterly indispensable to the United States. As the single largest customer of the U.S. defense industry, he helped keep American arms manufacturers afloat at a time when the U.S. economy could ill afford large-scale job losses. As the world's largest non-Arab oil exporter, his country was also a pivotal part of Western energy security—arguably the final safety net protecting the United States from economic collapse. Iran also quietly supplied Israel with 50 percent of its oil during the Arab-Israeli war, making Washington more reluctant than ever to antagonize the shah.

Given all these factors, the Nixon administration was not about to impose limits on the shah's weapons purchases. And so the military buildup continued. In August 1975 the shah contracted for another $10 billion in hardware from the United States, including three hundred F-16s and two hundred F-18s—aircraft so advanced they were not yet in production. With 150 F-14s the shah had already ordered, Iran now had more fighter jets on the way than it could ever hope to absorb. State-of-the-art equipment, often worth hundreds of millions of dollars, sat in storage as Iranian airmen waited for American trainers to show them how to use it. Experts noted that Iran would need more than ten years to train its air force on all the new

---

[*] To put this in perspective, in 1954, just after the oil nationalization crisis, Iran's oil revenues had been a mere $34 million a year.

Arms and the shah: By the mid-1970s, Iran was the world's largest purchaser of
American military equipment, accounting for more than one-third of U.S. arms sales.

equipment (by which point it would be out of date). Pilots were trained on
the most advanced fighter jets, only to find themselves starting over on new
ones as soon as they arrived. The F-14s proved especially complicated. Even
the U.S. Navy had trouble operating them. To the Imperial Iranian Air
Force, they were little more than a $1.5 billion collection of trophies.

But the shah didn't care. With tens of billions of dollars sloshing through
the treasury and a never-ending supply of arms from Washington, he had
achieved his lifelong ambition: to become the kid with the biggest guns and
planes in the neighborhood. In November 1974 the cover of *Time* magazine
summed up the situation perfectly with a portrait of the shah and the cap-
tion "The Emperor of Oil."

The result, for the American defense industry, was El Dorado. Week in
and week out, the Pan Am flight from New York to Tehran was packed with
arms dealers and military contractors from America's major firms—Boeing,
Grumman, McDonnell Douglas, Northrup, Lockheed, Westinghouse—
all clutching the names and phone numbers of Iranian "agents" who had
promised to help them navigate the bureaucracy and gain access to the shah.
Gen. Ellis Williamson, chief of the U.S. military mission in Tehran, com-

plained that between 1971 and 1973, he was fielding thirty-five visits a week—an average of one every hour—from American arms contractors hoping for an introduction to the right people.

Iranians found this decentralized American approach baffling. Most nations wanting to sell weapons to Iran simply arranged a meeting with the Defense Ministry and made clear what kind of equipment was on offer. But the United States insisted on having its companies compete with one another in full view of the world. Meanwhile, the Americans had just as much trouble with the Iranian way of doing business—a maddening government bureaucracy that had to be circumvented by unctuous middlemen and unscrupulous agents who expected generous "gifts" for their trouble. Both in Washington and in Tehran, there was a lack of central oversight, leaving a multibillion-dollar business in the hands of people whose lack of moral hygiene could be detected a mile away.

The result was predictable. In 1976 it emerged that officials from Grumman had paid a $28 million "commission" to Iranian officials as part of a $2.2 billion contract for F-14s. And this was the tip of the iceberg. A congressional investigation revealed that Northrup and Textron had paid $700,000 and $2.9 million respectively to the shah's nephew, Prince Shahram, and to the chief of the Iranian air force, General Khatami. Four years earlier the U.S. embassy had compiled a list of American companies that it felt "certain" were involved in bribery, including such marquee names as Boeing, McDonnell Douglas, and RCA.

By 1976 the flow of U.S. military supplies into Iran had become so chaotic that the Senate Foreign Relations Committee warned of dire consequences ahead. The shah's unquenchable thirst for weapons, it said, had "created a bonanza for U.S. weapons manufacturers" but had the potential to become a threat to American security. Iran had become a regional superpower, and the shah's heavy reliance on U.S. military support meant the United States could easily find itself sucked into a major Middle East war to protect him. Even worse, if the shah's regime collapsed, billions of dollars of U.S. military equipment could fall into the hands of a government less friendly to the United States. American military experts stationed in Iran, contractually obliged to train Iranians, "could become, in a sense hostages" to a hostile power. Like all such warnings, the Senate report was ignored.

☙

As the shah turned himself into a military strongman on the international stage, he also beefed up instruments of coercion at home. In the 1970s his secret police force, the dreaded SAVAK, developed a more fearsome reputation than ever for torture, disappearances, extrajudicial killings, and intimidation. Reports filtering out of Iran were almost too horrific to believe. Political prisoners—thousands, possibly tens of thousands—had been taken to secret facilities and tortured into making confessions of antiregime activity. Human rights groups alleged "whipping and beating, electric shocks, the extraction of nails and teeth, boiling water pumped into the rectum, heavy weights hung on the testicles . . . inserting a broken bottle into the anus, and rape." A typical method was to tie the prisoner to a metal table covered in a wire mesh, which was gradually heated red hot like a toaster. Another—particularly favored for female prisoners—was to release live snakes onto the victim. The most notorious device was dubbed the Apollo, an electric chair with a metal mask designed to amplify the prisoner's screams and redirect the sounds into his own ears.

Whenever foreign journalists questioned the shah, he insisted that "Iran has no need to torture." Its people, he said, were just too enamored of their leader for such things to be necessary. But international human rights groups begged to differ. In 1975, Amnesty International reported that "no country in the world has a worse record in human rights than Iran." The widespread use of torture in Iran, it said, was "beyond belief."

Officially, SAVAK employed around three thousand full-time staff, but its network of paid informants and part-time spies, both at home and overseas, was estimated to number as many as fifty thousand people. Whatever the exact figure, domestic espionage was a fact of life for Iranians in the 1970s. No one ever quite knew who the spies in their midst might be, perhaps their closest friend, neighbor, driver, or colleague. In addition to SAVAK, the shah relied on several other secret intelligence divisions. The J2 department within the military, for one, complemented the work of SAVAK. The Imperial Iranian Inspectorate kept an eye on troublesome officers in the armed forces. The city police (*shahrbani*) retained its own espionage division. There was even something called Special Bureau (*daftar-e vizheh*)—an ultra-secretive force headed by the shah's childhood friend Hossein Fardoust. Its job was to spy on the political elite—and even on SAVAK itself.

What all this added up to was a toxic atmosphere. The classic tactic employed by SAVAK was to have its undercover operatives make disparaging comments about the shah, in the hopes of luring others into confiding their true feelings. Iranians soon learned that the shah's most vocal critics were likely to be SAVAK agents, and they began treading more carefully. To make matters more complicated, SAVAK planted rumors about *genuine* opposition activists, saying they were actually SAVAK agents and should be avoided. Before long, Iranians learned that no one could be trusted and that it was best never to discuss politics at all. "The walls have mice, and the mice have ears," went a traditional Iranian saying. Never had it been taken as literally as it was in the 1970s. Even in the privacy of their own homes, if someone made a political comment, people would cover the nearest electric outlet with their hands—only half-joking.

The precise extent to which the United States supported the shah's 1970s reign of terror is a matter of debate, but one thing is beyond dispute: Many of SAVAK's most senior officers received their training from the CIA, the FBI, and the Israeli secret police, Mossad. At a training site in McLean, Virginia, as many as four hundred SAVAK officers a year were taught surveillance techniques and the latest intelligence-gathering techniques. In 1973 the CIA relocated its Middle East headquarters from Cyprus to Tehran, and the outgoing director of the CIA, Richard Helms, was appointed U.S. ambassador to Iran. On the Iranian street, America's decision to send its top spy to run the Tehran embassy said everything that needed to be said about Washington's approach to the U.S.-Iranian relationship.

By the 1970s, the U.S. embassy in Tehran, once a modest neocolonial house surrounded by welcoming gardens, had become a sprawling, hyperfortified compound, home to hundreds of faceless officials—a foreboding bunker that Iranians sometimes referred to as the "nest of spies." Yet despite the heavy CIA presence, the U.S. government had a hard time finding out what was really going on. The shah didn't fully trust the CIA and restricted the movements of American spies in Iran. U.S. officials were prevented from speaking to opposition activists, and SAVAK agents followed them everywhere. Reluctant to antagonize the shah, successive U.S. administrations instructed their spies and diplomats in Tehran to cooperate with these restrictions, meaning that Washington learned less and less about Iran every week. At one point, the volume of CIA political reports coming out of Tehran dropped below that of the late 1940s.

Inevitably, over time, the U.S. government became dangerously dependent on Iranian government sources for its information about Iran. Its spies failed to pick up on even the most basic intelligence, such as the fact that by the mid-1970s the shah was suffering from cancer. Even as rumors of the shah's illness spread through Tehran, even as he looked thin and pallid, and even as he was seen popping pills during meetings, American officials reported to Washington the official Iranian line that the shah was in excellent health. Washington, in turn, took these reports at face value and described Iran as a Middle Eastern success story—a rapidly modernizing pro-Western country with only a few minor difficulties. It was, according to a line frequently repeated by U.S. officials, an "island of stability and prosperity" in an otherwise troubled region. But America was sleepwalking into a disaster.

⚃

At least part of the explanation for this institutional myopia lies in the Pahlavi elite's extraordinary web of social, financial, and personal connections with influential personalities in Washington. Throughout the 1970s, Henry Kissinger, Chase Manhattan Bank president David Rockefeller, old hands Kermit Roosevelt and Averill Harriman, and important senators from both parties—Jacob Javits, Barry Goldwater, Lloyd Bentsen, and Birch Bayh among them—acted almost as surrogates for the shah in Washington, making sure his regime was always presented in the most flattering light and was protected from excessive congressional scrutiny.

At the center of this Pahlavi-American lovefest was Ardeshir Zahedi, who from 1973 to 1978 served as Iran's ambassador to the United States—and turned the Iranian embassy into Washington's premier address for opulent parties and banquets. Son of the former prime minister and recently divorced from the shah's daughter, Zahedi arrived on Embassy Row, and the gossip columns lit up with stories about his love life. Models and movie stars flitted in and out of the embassy building. Zahedi's lavish soirées became a fixture on the Washington social circuit. Just in his first month, he hosted six epic dinner parties at the embassy, including one black-tie affair that ended with the ambassador climbing onto the marble dining table along with several female guests and undulating rhythmically to Persian pop music. By midnight, Zahedi's tie was off, his shirt was unbuttoned to his waist, and he was leading his guests in a conga line through the embassy, perspiring heavily.

Zahedi transformed the Iranian embassy into his personal bachelor pad, complete with sauna, massage room, and a ballroom decorated with floor-to-ceiling portraits of the shah and Empress Farah. Zahedi was driven around town in a Rolls-Royce Silver Shadow and employed an enormous staff of chauffeurs, maids, social secretaries, military attachés, and spies—in addition to a bevy of young women whose sole job appeared to be keeping important guests entertained. Stories coming out of the embassy increasingly involved drugs, sex, and political favors. American congressmen and journalists reportedly attended orgies at the embassy—parties where opium and hashish were smoked from hookahs as belly dancers cavorted on Washington's most influential laps. In 1978 *New York* magazine reported that one of the ambassador's parties ended with an "eastern senator" and a "midwest-

Toast of the Washington party circuit: Ardeshir Zahedi (left), Iran's last ambassador to the United States (1973–79), with Barbra Streisand. Zahedi's frequent parties at the embassy were lavish and legendary, drawing A-list celebrities, politicians, and journalists. Zahedi played a critical role in propagating a glamorous image of Iran among the American elite. American media largely went along with the narrative.

ern congressman" copulating with multiple prostitutes in full view of other guests. Both the senator and the congressman were known for their staunch pro-Iranian voting record on Capitol Hill.

Zahedi lubricated the friendship of America's political elite with a steady stream of gifts and social flattery. Every Christmas the embassy distributed more than a thousand presents around Washington, including 150 tins of caviar and ninety bottles of Dom Perignon champagne. Zahedi was especially attentive to the needs of the Washington press corps, making sure influential journalists were invited to embassy social events and treated like royalty. Barbara Walters was a favorite (in addition to caviar, she received Cartier silver and a diamond watch from the shah), but everyone from Tom Brokaw to *Time* magazine was wined and dined and flattered and fed with rosaceous stories about the shah's successes. Zahedi's lavish entertainment expenses broke budget after budget, and he constantly had to cable Tehran asking for more funds. But this was a trivial detail. Zahedi was focused on a larger mission: selling the American public on an image of Iran that was glamorous, urbane, and modern.

It seemed to work. Some American media outlets made an effort to resist the charm offensive, but most simply parroted what they were told. In 1974 *Time* declared that "Mohammad Reza Pahlavi has brought Iran to a threshold of grandeur that is at least analogous to what Cyrus the Great

achieved for ancient Persia." *The New York Times* was only slightly less effusive. "Iranians are responding to the Shah and his programs with new hope
and traditional awe," it gushed in June 1974. The opposition stimulated by
religious leaders in the 1960s "has been reduced, according to knowledgeable diplomats, to grumbling in the provinces." Apparently convinced that
the shah's leadership had turned Iran into such an exemplar of stability that
there was no longer much news to report, the *Times* even closed its Tehran
bureau in February 1977—just one year before the revolution broke out.

છ

At the beginning of 1975, the shah abolished all existing political parties and
replaced them with the Rastakhiz (Resurgence) Party. Unlike previous parties created by the shah, membership in Rastakhiz was not optional. Every
teacher, government employee, manager, company director, and journalist
was required to join. Voting in elections was made mandatory, and all collective organs—from women's groups to agricultural cooperatives to student
unions—were expected to function as part of the Rastakhiz machinery. Passive obedience and apathy were no longer acceptable. Iranians would now
have to demonstrate *active* loyalty to the shah through party membership.

To explain the philosophy behind Rastakhiz, the shah held a televised
press conference on March 4, during which he made a statement that
stunned almost everyone who heard it. "I have come to the conclusion,"
he said, "that we should separate the ranks of Iranians clearly, properly and
identifiably. . . . Those who believe in the constitution, the monarchy and
the [White] revolution will be on one side and those who do not believe in
these on the other." The latter group, he said,

> could be given passports tomorrow with the greatest of pleasure
> and without charging them any exit fees, so they can go, if they so
> wish, to any country they choose. This is because they cannot be
> regarded as Iranians. They have no home country and their activity
> is illegal. . . . Everyone must clarify his position in this country like
> a man.

If the shah was hoping to persuade educated, middle-class Iranians to
join Rastakhiz and take an active role in his modernization project, he could
not have come up with a more poorly judged way of doing it. Millions
of skilled professionals—precisely the people whose support he needed—
regarded the shah's love-it-or-leave-it, with-us-or-against-us rhetoric as
repugnant and insulting. But it only got worse. Giant billboards went up all

over Iran, some with pictures of the shah standing in the clouds, his arms extended like a guru. In interviews with foreign journalists, the shah said he was guided by "visions" and "messages" from the prophets. "I'm not entirely alone," he told one interviewer, "because I'm accompanied by a force that others can't see. My mystical force."

All this might have been tolerated had the shah delivered on a few of his economic promises. But after more than thirty years, many Iranian villages still lacked electricity, running water, paved roads, or medical facilities. Sixty percent of children did not finish primary school, and the overcrowded universities received ten times as many applicants than they could accept. The eradication of illiteracy and the land reform program—the shah's landmark initiatives—were stillborn. In 1976 the government surprised everyone by announcing that, for the first time in decades, the nation would face a budget deficit—$2.4 billion—despite bringing in a record $20 billion in oil revenues the previous year.

As rural communities struggled, hundreds of thousands flocked to the cities, causing a housing shortage and skyrocketing rents. From 1974 to 1978, the average monthly rent for a one-bedroom apartment in Tehran rose from $142 to $426. (The average monthly wage remained around $200.) Moreover, Iran's growing dependence on imported grain was causing severe inflation: in the 1970s prices went up an average of 20 percent every year, while salaries failed to keep pace. A generation earlier Tehran had been a sleepy collection of neighborhoods whose families looked out for one another; now it was a teeming metropolis the size of Shanghai or Bombay—home to 5 million people, many of them overwhelmed peasants living in ramshackle accommodations. No one had prepared for this. There had been no serious attempt to build public transport or develop an adequate electricity grid. Power shortages, pollution, traffic—problems in any modern city—took on epic proportions in Tehran. And compounding the problem was the lack of a political outlet. With nowhere to vent their frustrations, Iranians found that routine disagreements and traffic snarls frequently escalated to public shouting matches and worse. Drugs and alcohol became easy escapes for the alienated and the disaffected.

As tempers flared and the economy faltered, the streets of Tehran and other Iranian cities crawled with Americans. While the shah spent billions on the world's most advanced military equipment, the Pentagon sent hundreds of Americans to show his armed forces how to use it—and private military contractors hired thousands more. The number of Americans living in Iran climbed rapidly, from 8,000 at the beginning of the 1970s, to 24,000 in 1976, and finally to an estimated 50,000 or more on the eve of the revolution. Americans pouring into the country added to inflationary pressures on the housing market. Those who lived in private accommodations in town drove up local rents. Others lived in gated compounds, where everything from Wonder Bread to Oreo cookies was flown in from the United States, contributing nothing to the local economy. The American schools and American hospitals that had been built by Presbyterian missionaries generations earlier were turned into exclusive redoubts of American privilege. The American hospital in Tehran was open only to Americans, and the American schools, now converted into expensive private academies, taught a curriculum straight out of American suburbia. English was the sole language of instruction. There were no classes in Persian language or history, and extracurricular activities revolved around baseball, glee club, and yearbook.

Iranians who were struggling to make ends meet resented the fact that Americans in Iran were generally paid three or four times as much as locals with similar educations. And some Americans threw their money around like colonial viceroys, taking little interest in the host nation. The Vietnam War had just ended, and Americans who had made a killing in Southeast Asia—military contractors, shady businessmen, and fortune-seekers of all varieties—picked up and went to Iran, where a new bonanza seemed to be opening up. But Iranians did not take kindly to Americans who behaved as if they were still in Saigon. Public drunkenness and insults to women went down particularly poorly. Community relations hit a low point in 1976 after a number of Americans working in Isfahan were seen racing motorcycles into a local mosque.

The official U.S. presence in Iran was only slightly more edifying. At the U.S. embassy, fewer than 10 percent of officials were fluent in Persian (compared with 45 percent at the British embassy and 70 percent at the Soviet). Rare was the American official who ventured into rural communities or spent time in mosques, listening to the anger and frustration. Instead, life for American government employees centered on the U.S. commissary (the largest in the world), which sold $4 million worth of alcohol, cigarettes, pet food, and cola every year—all airlifted directly from the United States. In 1970 seventy-nine tons of pet food were flown in, leaving Iranians to grumble that "American dogs eat better than the average Iranian." Of course, many Americans came to Iran with good intentions and made a sincere effort to learn the language and live respectfully among their new neighbors. But those were not the ones who stood out.

⁂

As the 1970s wore on, the shah found himself contending with a shadowy network of guerrilla fighters, a motley collection of Marxists and Islamist radicals that grew larger and more violent every year. But he told anyone who would listen that it was nothing, just a few flea-infested troublemakers trying to derail the country's progress. "We want to catch up and do it quickly," he told *Time* in 1974. "In these very specific conditions, the blah-blahs of armchair critics are obviously ignored. If this is intolerance, I accept it." When a reporter asked how many political prisoners Iran had, he grew testy: "The number of political prisoners is exactly the same—no more and no less—than the number of traitors."

For the most part, the Americans believed him. Prevented from talking to anyone who might present an alternative viewpoint, locked away in an air-conditioned embassy compound that resembled a bunker, and instructed by Washington not to do anything that might upset the shah, they discovered the path of least resistance ran through the bar of the Tehran Hilton and the buffet tables of countless uptown dinner parties. Surrounded by Iranians who spoke good English, sent their children to Stanford, and seemed to embody all the "progress" and "modernity" of the 1970s, American officials marveled at the way the shah was transforming a feudal nation into a twentieth-century economic miracle. In a country with no opposition parties, no independent newspapers, and a climate of fear that prevented people from speaking their minds, it was all too easy to miss the magmatic resentment bubbling below the surface—easy to believe that a few bad apples would be dealt with by SAVAK and never heard from again.

Whenever the shah was asked about internal discontent, he exuded confidence, assuring his American friends that everything was under control. "I am in contact with my people," he told one television interviewer. "I go places and I talk to the people. I can claim to have the pulse of my people in my hand." In reality, however, the shah—who early in his reign had enjoyed racing sports cars through town—now crisscrossed Tehran almost exclusively by helicopter, to avoid the traffic. He had no idea how unpopular he had become.

Early in his reign, the shah had had to contend with tough, independent-minded politicians—many left over from the Qajar era—who made no attempt to hide their feelings. But in the mid-1970s he was surrounded by a parasitic, corrupt inner circle of advisers who competed with each other to tell him what he wanted to hear. Consumed by a lifelong fear of rival power centers, the shah had created a political culture that prized loyalty and obedience above all else, and discouraged dissent. The Imperial Court was a place where truth and objectivity went to die. Always a stickler for ceremony and prestige, the shah had turned the court into a circus of cringing, bowing, and insincere flattery, reminiscent of the court of Louis XVI.

The court of the Peacock Throne: By the end of the 1970s, the shah had
cultivated an atmosphere of obedience at the royal court. Courtiers and cabinet
ministers pay their respects during a formal audience with the monarch.

(Even the furniture was the same.) On formal occasions, cabinet ministers
lined up in ceremonial uniforms and kissed the shah's hand while reciting
lavish paeans to his greatness and glory. The court minister Asadollah Alam
once said publicly that "the Shah's only fault is that he is really too great for
his people—his ideas are too great for us."

To the shah, this atmosphere of total obedience was a sign of his strength,
his ability to strike terror into men's hearts. At long last, he thought, he was
doing justice to the fearsome legacy of his warrior father. But Tehran's more
seasoned observers were not impressed. Back in the 1930s, it was often said,
no one had dared tell Reza Shah a lie; now no one dared tell his son the
truth.

The Unthinkable

By the end of the 1970s, opposition to the shah was coming from three general directions. From his left, there were Communists—secular ideologues who looked at the grotesque inequalities of Iranian life, the decadence and bourgeois materialism that had infected society, and saw a powerful argument for Marxism. From his right, there were religious traditionalists who disliked many of the same phenomena but drew different conclusions, warning that the nation was slipping away from its Islamic moorings. And somewhere in the middle, there were liberal nationalists—the heirs of Mosaddeq—who were alarmed at the never-ending erosion of democracy and human rights.

Ten years earlier all three had been minor irritants, unlikely to pose a real threat to the shah's power. The Communists had been radical and implacable but few in number. Religious conservatives were by nature *conservative*, more interested in preserving the traditional rhythms of village life than launching a revolution. And the liberal nationalists had been too weak and divided to take seriously. A savvy and sagacious ruler could have found ways to accommodate, crush, or co-opt the demands of all three while simultaneously setting out his own unique vision for the future of the country. But Mohammad Reza Shah was not that man.

The most immediate threat to the shah, as ever, seemed to come from the left. Communism had a long, formidable history in Iran, and by the 1970s it was assuming ever more radical and menacing forms. The younger generation of Marxists had turned away from the old pro-Soviet Tudeh Party, which they saw as a vehicle for Russian imperialism. Like their counterparts in much of the world, they had little interest in serving as surrogates for the Soviet Union, which, in their eyes, had long ago lost its way. Rather than take their cues from the aging leaders of the Tudeh, these young radicals were inspired by the romantic jungle-fighters of the Cuban revolution and other third-world liberation movements. They began organizing themselves into secretive urban combat units dedicated to guerrilla tactics, political sabotage, and violent attacks on government targets.

In 1970 several of these leftist guerrilla groups formed a coalition called the Fadayin-e Khalq (FeK), or Devotees of the People. Around the same time, a rival group known as the Mojahedin-e Khalq (MeK)—Holy Warriors of the People—also emerged. The FeK was a classic "anti-imperialist" insurgency, a militant, secular movement similar in aims and methods to their contemporaries in the Baader-Meinhof gang in West Germany. The MeK, by contrast, were "Islamic leftists" and only vaguely Marxist in their thinking. They argued that Shia Islam—whose seventh-century martyrs, Hussein and Ali, had died fighting despotism—had pointed the way to a classless society.* Between them, the FeK and the MeK attracted large numbers of young, disaffected Iranians to the idea of armed struggle. They were particularly popular on university campuses, where gangs of leftist students commonly took to smashing lab equipment and intimidating professors. But they also proved effective at organizing rural commando units and attacking government installations in remote mountain villages.

In February 1971 thirteen young leftists launched an audacious raid on a gendarmerie post in the Caspian Sea village of Siahkal, killing three police officers. The government sent troops and helicopters into the mountains to find the culprits, who were captured and executed. But the national headlines generated by the incident inspired hundreds more like it, and before long the shah was facing a full-blown resistance movement. Between 1971 and 1975 there were an estimated four hundred bombings or attempted bombings in Iran, along with frequent violent scuffles between military commandos and university students. Increasingly, Americans living in Iran were also targeted. Between 1973 and 1976 leftists gunned down three U.S. Air Force colonels and three civilian contractors, and they made dozens of bomb threats against American organizations and installations.

While leftists were grabbing headlines in the 1970s, however, a deeper and far subtler threat to the shah's power was emerging, and it came from a completely different direction. Iran in the 1970s was still a largely poor and rural nation, with a reflexive attachment to traditional Islamic values—

---

* In 1975 the group would split over the question of just how far Islam could be reconciled with Marxism.

modesty, self-restraint, sobriety, respect for family and gender roles. There was a silent majority—a large segment of the population that was not interested in joining an underground militia or kidnapping politicians but still felt deeply troubled by the direction the country was going in. Runaway consumerism, materialist excess, the general climate of bourgeois decadence, and corruption among the Tehran elite—while these things drove some into the arms of Marx and Lenin, many more sought comfort in the reassuring certainties of their faith. And as they did, the shah found himself facing not just the violence of a secular left but also the condemnation of an ever-more-vocal religious right.

CS

In 1941, Mohammad Reza Shah had inherited from his father a country that was steadily modernizing, secularizing, and beginning to accept a separation of mosque and state. The clergy in the 1940s was dominated by "quietist" ayatollahs—conservative, pro-establishment clerics who had received their theological credentials from the state and preached loyalty to shah and country. Back then, it would have been almost unheard-of for anyone to argue that the clergy should have a commanding role over Iranian government.

But the shah, somewhat foolishly, escalated his father's assault on the *ulama* (Islamic clergy), depriving ayatollahs of ever more powers and privileges and helping to create a climate of open hostility between turban and crown. The big turning point in this conflict came in 1963, when the shah insisted that properties owned by the religious establishment should be included in the land reform initiatives of the White Revolution.* Ostensibly, he had intended land reform to address inequalities and allow peasant sharecroppers to become stakeholders in the nation's economy. But some of Iran's large estates were in the hands of the *ulama,* and the shah insisted these should also be fair game. The public, on the whole, did not agree. Clerical estates had functioned traditionally as charitable foundations, their profits distributed to the needy in an age-old system of poor relief. And even though some clerics pocketed proceeds and grew fat off the land, most Ira-

---

* Adding to this atmosphere of tension was the death, in 1961, of Grand Ayatollah Hossein Borujerdi, the most senior cleric in Iran and longtime ally of the monarchy. For nearly twenty years, he had dissuaded his fellow ayatollahs from taking activist positions in political matters. Borujerdi's death, however, cleared the path for a more radical generation of clerics to rise to prominence—among them Ayatollah Khomeini, who had always resented the anticlericalism of the Pahlavi regime and had little interest in keeping quiet about it. A former student of Borujerdi, Khomeini had, while Borujerdi was alive, refrained from political activity out of deference to the grand ayatollah. From 1962, though, Khomeini became more vocal.

nians did not view clerical estates as an obstacle to Iran's development. Nevertheless, the shah charged ahead—lumping the servants of God together with the feudal aristocracy and acidly describing them all as "reactionaries."

Deprived of their large landholdings, Iran's clerics became a poor and much-mistreated underclass. And their resentment escalated. In the 1940s, when the shah came to power, the stereotypical cleric had been a self-serving, entrenched member of the political establishment. But by the 1960s, he was a scrawny, lice-ridden wretch—treated with contempt by city slickers in Tehran but pitied by almost everyone else. Like a mendicant friar, he relied increasingly on donations from private citizens, receiving food and handouts from pious grandmothers. Increasingly, a feeling of humility pervaded clerical work, an aura of poverty and piety that made it easy for the *ulama* to elicit sympathy among other Iranians. The new style was typified by Khomeini, who famously abandoned the lofty heights of the *minbar* (the raised pulpit traditionally used to address congregants) and chose to sit on the floor while delivering his sermons.

The contrast between the monklike asceticism of the *ulama* and the sinful indulgence of the Tehran elite could not have been starker. While Khomeini sat on a dusty carpet and prayed, the shah and his cronies built multiplex cinemas that showed the latest Western movies—Italian soft erotica and racy Hollywood features like *The Spy Who Loved Me*. They sped around Tehran in designer sunglasses and danced in discothèques, wearing halter tops and platform heels. On the Persian Gulf island of Kish, the shah built an exclusive casino and luxury resort—a monument to all that was sinful under Islam. Twice a month a special Air France flight—a Concorde no less—arrived from Paris on the new runway at Kish, its supersonic cabin heaving with foie gras, magnums of champagne, and a fresh crop of girls procured for the shah and his friends by the legendary Madame Claude.

Though not all Iranians were aware of the sheer extent of pelf and perdition coursing through the veins of Tehran's body politic, enough stories circulated to create the impression of a political elite that was up to its ears in boozing, whoring, and gambling. And inevitably, as the government they despised sank into sinfulness and corruption, growing numbers of Iranians took refuge in their faith. In the decade from 1967 to 1977, the number of Iranians making pilgrimage to the holy city of Mashhad soared, from 332,000 to 3.5 million annually. During the same period, pilgrimages to Mecca increased from 12,000 a year to more than 100,000. The number of students enrolling in theological studies rose fourfold. And private donations to clerics rose from around $3 million a year to a whopping $250 million. From 1968 to 1978, more mosques were built in Iran than had been built in the previous two hundred years.

The shah did his best to contain this national mood of religious revivalism, or at least turn it to his own political benefit. Hoping to create a new generation of clerics obedient to his kingship, he established tight control over Tehran University's faculty of theology. He created a Religion Corps—modeled on the Literacy Corps—to go into villages and preach a version of Islam that put obedience to the shah at the center of its message. Tighter controls were placed on pilgrimages abroad, religious publishing houses were shut down, and clerics were bullied or bribed into becoming SAVAK informants.

But the shah's most cynical move was the government takeover of the Sazman-e Awqaf, the organization that administered the centuries-old tradition of charitable donations for the construction and maintenance of mosques and shrines. From the mid-1970s, control of these funds was put in the hands of secular figures with close ties to SAVAK, making ordinary Iranians much more reluctant to donate. Most egregiously, in 1974, Gen. Abdol Azim Valian, a deeply corrupt and unpopular figure, was appointed sacred guardian of the shrine of Emam Reza in Mashhad. That a man famed for his thieving and womanizing could be placed in charge of one of the holiest sites in Shia Islam struck many as a sacrilege. Even the shah's inner circle had trouble taking the appointment seriously. "I hear a rumor," quipped Prime Minister Hoveida to Valian at a cocktail party. "They say Emam Reza himself has descended from the heavens and has his arms wrapped round the golden domes of his shrine so you don't try to walk off with them."

The shah also cracked down on clerics critical of his regime. In June 1970, Mohammad Reza Saidi, a forty-one-year-old student of Khomeini, had criticized an investment seminar being held in Tehran by major American corporations like Westinghouse, PepsiCo, and American Express. He was tortured to death. "I swear to God," he is said to have hissed at his torturers, "if you kill me, in every drop of my blood you will see the holy name of Khomeini." And how right he was. Saidi was the first cleric to die at the hands of the shah's secret police in the 1970s, but he would not be the last. Over the next eight years, hundreds of religious leaders were tortured, jailed, and beaten for refusing to preach a message acceptable to the government.* Several more were killed. All this succeeded only in drawing more people into the mosques to hear what the shah found so objectionable.

In the late 1970s, as Islam became a growing channel for political oppo-

---

* The victims of this crackdown included many who would later go on to occupy positions of power in the Islamic Republic, including the current supreme leader of Iran, Ayatollah Ali Khamenei, and former president Akbar Hashemi Rafsanjani.

sition, the shah faced a peculiar political problem. It had been easy to crack down on Mosaddeq and the National Front, even on the Tudeh and other Marxist organizations. He had simply shut down their newspapers, banned their political parties, and co-opted their agenda. But shutting down God was a whole different story. Devout, sincere clerics could not easily be bought or bribed (though certainly some were). And there were no newspapers to shut down, because there was no need for newspapers. As he delivered his sermon on a Friday afternoon, the typical *imam-jomeh* told stories of heroes and villains drawn from the pages of the Holy Quran—simple stories that required him to do no more than pause dramatically at certain moments to let the parallels with the present day sink in.

In a nation where direct criticism of the government was dangerous, the metaphors and parables of religious teaching became the only opportunity for something resembling an open political discussion. Once a year, during the holy month of Moharram, illiterate, toothless peasants gathered in village squares across the country to watch *ta'ziyeh*, an emotionally charged Shia passion play in which the tragic deaths of Hussein, Ali, and other martyrs are acted out. But as they wept fulsome tears for their eighth-century martyrs—slaughtered by the evil tyrant Yazid on the battlefield of Karbala—in their hearts, villagers were weeping for their sons and brothers tortured by SAVAK. And there was nothing the shah could do to stop it. *Ta'ziyeh* was a thirteen-hundred-year-old tradition in Shia Islam. To ban it would have gone down as well as a Christian king canceling Christmas.

❧

Caught somewhere between the Marxist guerrillas blowing up buildings and the bearded clerics preaching hellfire and damnation was the third source of opposition to the Shah—the old liberal nationalists of the Mosaddeq era. A graying, balding generation of activists that came of age in 1953, few of Mosaddeq's educated, middle-class supporters had the temperament to join violent underground movements or radical mosque-based networks. Most had jobs and families to look after now. And ultimately they were democrats, committed to circulating petitions, drafting manifestos, and competing in elections. The shah's Iran no longer had room for such things. Those few who did try to keep the flame of liberal democracy alive, moreover, became badly divided over ideology and tactics. In the mid-1960s, the coalition's more secular members formed the Second National Front under the leadership of Karim Sanjabi, while a more religious wing joined Mehdi Bazargan to create the Freedom Movement of Iran. Sanjabi and the secularists pledged to work within the system to achieve modest reforms, while Bazargan and the Freedom Movement argued for abolishing the monarchy and establishing a democratic state guided by moderately Islamic values.*

After the overthrow of Mosaddeq, the shah had banned the National Front outright and arrested its most prominent leaders. In the face of torture and repression, deprived of the right to publish newspapers or put up candidates, many of the front's members had given up the fight. Opposition to the shah, they concluded, was for people with thicker skins—the young, the ragged, the radical, and the desperate. Worse, the front was now under fire from both left and right for being naïve and out of touch with the urgency of the times. Few Iranians disagreed with the desirability of free elections and an independent press. But a younger, more radical generation argued that the real lesson of 1953 was that liberal democracy was incapable of bringing about real change in Iran. Mosaddeq had played by the rules, and it had taken him nowhere.

In short, by the 1970s, all three ideological camps in Iran's opposition— the Communists, the religious conservatives, and the liberals—were suffering some sort of generational crisis. For the Communists, there were divisions between the old-guard Tudeh and the new cadres of guerrilla fighters and leftist paramilitaries. For the religious orders, there was a drift away from the quiet, establishment voices of conservatism toward the more rambunctious populism of Khomeini and his young followers. And among the old Mosaddeq liberals—with their salaried jobs and their comfortable middle-class lives—there was an almost total failure to connect with the anger of Tehran's youth. Left, right, and center, radicalism was the name of the game now, with youth and anger the only currencies that carried any weight. And in a way, this was the most tragic consequence of the coup of 1953. Because if anyone could have held the middle ground between the socialist left and the religious right—creating a meaningful, constructive opposition movement during the 1950s and 1960s and preventing the steady drift to extremism at both ends—it was probably the liberal nationalists. But they had never had a chance.

Finally, and perhaps most ominously, there was one other thing the three camps had in common by the mid-1970s: They were all angry with America. Each of them had arrived at this position for their own reasons, and in their own way, but they had all arrived there. For the Communists, hatred of capitalism and Western "imperialism" was already part of their DNA. For the religious conservatives, America—with its Hollywood mov-

---

* Both groups remained influential into the 1970s, but as the revolution approached, Bazargan and the Freedom Movement would play the more dominant role.

ies, consumerist ethos, and disco-fueled youth culture—increasingly represented all that was sinful in Iran, and the shah was a scoundrel for wanting to import Western values so slavishly. And for the liberal nationalists—the people who should have been most sympathetic to American values—anger over what the CIA had done in 1953 still seethed and festered.

For the United States—and for the shah who had attached his fortunes so vividly to his American allies—the prognosis was not good.

⬥

To most western observers, the idea that three such divergent ideologies—Communism, Islamism, and democratic nationalism—could unite behind a common purpose, much less overthrow one of the world's most ancient monarchies, remains one of the great mysteries of the Iranian Revolution. But the mystery becomes a little less mysterious if one understands the extraordinary intellectual atmosphere of Iran in the 1970s. Behind closed doors, away from the prying eyes of SAVAK, a wide assortment of thinkers and dreamers were fervently discussing their visions for a better Iran, and utopian ideas about socialism, God, and democracy were cross-pollinating in unexpected ways. These were young and idealistic days in Iran, a time when anything seemed possible.

Perhaps no one embodied this creative convergence of ideologies better than the legendary sociologist Ali Shariati. In the late 1960s the thirty-five-year-old Shariati had begun delivering lectures at the Hosseinieh Ershad in north Tehran, a scholarly center created by Bazargan for exploring progressive interpretations of Islam. A fierce, electrifying orator full of erudition and idealism, Shariati turned the Hosseinieh into the nerve center of Iranian intellectual life, a place where cutting-edge ideas about the synthesis of Islam, Marxism, and revolution were openly if nervously debated. Every time Shariati lectured, thousands of sweaty, wide-eyed students packed in like sardines to listen, their brows furrowed, their pulses racing, their pens poised to capture every word.

Shariati had earned his Ph.D. in Paris, where he had closely studied and translated the work of Jean-Paul Sartre, Che Guevara, and Frantz Fanon. Like almost every Paris-based intellectual of the time, he had been inspired by the student uprising of 1968 and heavily influenced by Marxist theory. But Shariati was also a devout Muslim, born into a family of provincial religious scholars, and felt Marxism, in its classical form, was a Western idea that could not be imported uncritically into an Iranian context. Iran, he said, had known only an "Asiatic mode of production." It had never experienced an industrial revolution or Western-style capitalism, and its people—

in stark contrast to Europeans—were still deeply attached to religion. The Tudeh, with its cold, soulless talk of atheism and "historical materialism," had failed to capture the popular mood. If Iranian intellectuals truly wanted to liberate their people, Shariati argued, they would first have to discover their own religious traditions, drawing strength from the stories of men like Abu Zarr, a seventh-century Muslim version of Robin Hood who had denounced the corruption of the caliphate and retired to the desert to fight on behalf of the poor. To Shariati, such figures were the world's first social-ists, part of a long and heroic tradition of "true" Islam that had been cor-rupted by a fossilized, institutionalized, state-sanctioned version. "It is not enough to say we must return to Islam," he once warned his audience:

We have to specify *which* Islam: that of Abu Zarr or that of Marwan the Ruler. Both are Islam, but there is a huge difference between the two. One is the Islam of the caliphate, of the palace, of the rulers. The other is the Islam of the people, of the exploited, and of the poor. Which Islam do you advocate? Moreover, it is not enough to say you advocate an Islam that is "concerned" with the poor. The caliphs said the same. True Islam is more than "concerned" with the poor. It struggles for justice, equality, and elimination of poverty.

With oratory like that, Shariati kept his audience spellbound. From 1967 to 1973, the young sociologist was a living legend at the Hosseinieh, cramming vast amounts of theory into his urgent lectures, never know-ing when SAVAK would shut the place down. Feverishly he spoke, and feverishly his audiences scribbled—comparing notes and secretly compiling transcripts and cassette tapes to study. Years later Shariati's Hosseinieh lec-tures were published in complete form. They ran to fifty volumes.

The key to Shariati's immense popularity among Tehran's young intel-lectuals was his ability to recast Shia Islam as a progressive, dynamic revolu-tionary force perfectly suited to the twentieth-century struggle against social injustice and the oppression of the poor. Rather than indulge in defeatist, fatalistic displays of weeping and mourning over the martyrdom of Hussein and Ali every year, he suggested, Shia Muslims should remember that their beloved martyrs died rebelling against tyranny, and follow suit. ("Every day is *ashura,* every place is Karbala," he famously declared.) Rather than fear or reject modernization, as some clerics did, Iranians should learn to respect themselves and their religion so they could adopt Western science and tech-nology without shame and inferiority complexes. Rather than focus on the lost privileges and lands of the *ulama,* they should turn their attention to the Algerian independence movement and the struggle of the Palestinians.

In Shariati's hands, Islam became a liberation theology, akin to the leftist philosophy influencing Catholic activists in Latin America around the same time.

Unsurprisingly, SAVAK shut down the Hosseinieh in 1973. Shariati went into hiding for a year, then he was arrested and subjected to eighteen months' imprisonment. In 1977, during a visit to England, he died of a mysterious heart attack at the age of forty-four—an event that naturally led many to speculate about the role of SAVAK. Whatever the case, Shariati's books continued to sell in the hundreds of thousands. More important, Shariati had helped create a climate in which philosophy was fashionable, and an older generation of Iranian intellectuals, like Bazargan—who had spent years exploring the progressive face of Islam but whose works had been largely ignored—now enjoyed a renaissance among the young.

To an increasingly frustrated generation of educated Iranians, these messages were seductive. More and more, it seemed, Islam was where all the cutting-edge thinking was taking place, and it was Islam that was going to set the people free. Across Tehran, earnest, sideburned students gathered in smoke-filled cafés to discuss the latest Shariati lectures with all the intensity of French intellectuals in Montmartre. At the universities, female students turned up at lectures wearing headscarves, sometimes out of religious devotion and sometimes just as a political statement. On every other street corner, booksellers set up tables stacked with books on Islamic philosophy, sometimes selling little more than the works of Shariati. By the end of the 1970s, posters bearing the faces of the old martyrs Hussein and Ali were omnipresent in Iran—iconic symbols of resistance, full of all the counter-cultural cachet of the Che Guevara posters going up in college dorm rooms throughout the Western world.

This was what the shah seemed incapable of understanding. To him, it was inconceivable that his people could turn their backs on the "Great Civilization" he was building and seek inspiration in a backward, obscurantist political philosophy that drew its inspiration from the Middle Ages. He constantly referred to his *ulama* critics as "reactionaries," superstitious religious fanatics irrationally threatened by the modern world. In his public statements, he tried to convince the modern middle classes—those who had benefited most from the White Revolution—that these cantankerous old clerics were no different from the selfish feudal aristocrats unwilling to relinquish their lands, and that all belonged to a crusty old order trying to keep Iran in the past.

But the shah was badly out of touch with the mood on the street. By the late 1970s in Iran, Islam was cool, in a way that the fifty-seven-year-old shah could never understand. It was becoming the new rock and roll.

A few intellectuals, however, do not a revolution make. Charismatic, uncompromising leadership is also required, and for Iran in the 1970s, it appeared in the charismatic, uncompromising form of Ayatollah Khomeini.

Khomeini was not the only, or even the most prominent, figure to oppose the shah in the last two decades of his reign. But he was the only one who seemed capable of leading a genuinely *revolutionary* movement. The desperate, impoverished masses who felt badly let down by the shah's unfulfilled promises remembered Khomeini fondly as the populist firebrand who had led a mass uprising in 1963 and very nearly precipitated a revolution. He was a fighter, at a time when the Iranian people desperately wanted someone to fight on their side.

The contrast between Khomeini and the more mainstream leaders of Iran's opposition was striking. The leader of the National Front, Karim Sanjabi, was a soft-spoken seventy-two-year-old law professor, a Kurdish aristocrat who had served as Mosaddeq's education minister and was known for his sophisticated presentation of Iran's legal case against AIOC at the World Court in 1952. But in the 1970s, that didn't thrill Iranians anymore. The battle had moved on, and with the smell of revolution in the air, all the talk in the marketplaces and mosques turned to the turbaned figure of the ayatollah. Certainly many secular liberals were uncomfortable with the idea that opposition to the shah should be led by a single-minded religious crusader. But they were also acutely aware that no one else had Khomeini's popular touch.

For more than a decade, Khomeini had been lecturing on philosophy and ethics in the Iraqi city of Najaf, where some of his more impassioned followers referred to him informally as "the Emam"—an extraordinarily lofty honor that placed him in the company of the original twelve descendants of Muhammad. From the mid-1970s, when improved Iran-Iraq relations made travel between the two countries easier, Iranians flocked to Najaf in larger numbers—thousands making the trip across the desert in shared motorcars or chartered buses heaving with luggage. Unlike Iranian intellectuals of the day, Khomeini had not studied in Europe and had little interest in creating a fusion between Islam and the Western philosophical tradition.* And for the most part, Khomeini's followers were not intellectuals either. They did not make the trek to Najaf in search of a theoretical reconciliation between

---

* Khomeini's writings and lectures reveal familiarity with Western thinkers, from Plato onward. But he always argued that Islam was a complete and perfect philosophy that made all others obsolete and unnecessary.

Islam and Jean-Paul Sartre. They were the Islamic equivalent of hippies—idealistic, cheerful seminary students and budding theologians who flocked to Najaf to bask in the company of kindred spirits. With their Volkswagen camper-vans and their big ideas about changing the world, the pilgrims on the Khomeini trail helped transform Najaf in the 1970s into something oddly reminiscent of what Woodstock had represented for a certain generation of Americans: a phenomenon of little interest to the elites of the day but one that, in retrospect, helped turn the world upside-down.

Unlike their Western counterparts, however, Iran's young idealists did not come home from Najaf reeking of free love and marijuana. Rather, their trunks were stuffed with bootleg tape recordings and hastily scribbled notes of Khomeini's teachings. They then distributed these illicit materials through Iran via an informal, rapidly growing "mosque network" that largely escaped the attention of the authorities. As ever, there was little the shah could do about it. Najaf, the resting place of Ali, was the most important pilgrimage destination in Shiism—and had been for twelve hundred years. The leader of the world's largest Shia nation could hardly tell his people not to go. Although the government imposed restrictions on travel to Iraq, it had no practical way to inspect the luggage of every pilgrim crossing the border. And it certainly had no way to inspect their hearts and minds. Thus, little by little, Iranians came back from Najaf with more than notes and cassette tapes. They came back with devotion to a man—a frenzied, almost cultlike reverence for the authority of "the Emam"—and a blueprint for a type of government never before seen in history.

From Najaf, Khomeini preached about *velayat-e-faqih*—a groundbreaking reinterpretation of a traditional Shia doctrine that can loosely be translated as "religious stewardship."* In its original, purest form, centuries earlier, *velayat-e-faqih* had meant that society required the guidance of religious scholars to answer difficult moral questions, resolve legal issues, distribute charity, and so on. But Khomeini extended this time-honored principle to its logical conclusion, arguing that religious philosophers should take stewardship of *all* earthly matters, including politics and government, to ensure a just, peaceful, and benevolent society. Monarchy, he said, was a pagan institution—corrupt, repressive, and premised on the

---

* The phrase is notoriously difficult to translate. *Velayat* means "guardianship" or "stewardship." *Faqih* derives from the Islamic concept of *fiqh*, or "religious jurisprudence." Thus, the *faqih* is one trained in *fiqh* and hence qualified to interpret Islamic law—in practice, the so-called *mujtaheds*, the most learned clerics in Shia Islam. Some scholars translate *velayat-e-faqih* as "guardianship of the jurist" or some equally awkward, unnatural-sounding phrase. A more appropriate translation might be "oversight by the most learned religious scholars"—a concept that, when applied to government the way Khomeini described, may be analogous to the Platonic idea of the "philosopher-king."

immoral assumption that one man was superior to another by virtue of his birth. No true Muslim could support such a system—and in fact all had a duty to resist it. This principled opposition to kingship set Khomeini apart from his fellow ayatollahs, most of whom demanded simply that the shah adhere to the 1906 constitution. Though no one knew it at the time, *velayat-e-faqih* would become the foundational philosophy of the Islamic Republic.

In the late 1970s, Khomeini achieved a level of stardom almost impossible to compete with. He was particularly popular in the slums of south Tehran, where thousands had recently arrived from the provinces and discovered to their bitter disappointment that life in the capital was not all they had hoped. Jobless, ragged youth—lacking the rural support networks and extended families that their parents had been able to rely on, surrounded by cool, rich kids who drove sports cars and mocked their accents—found a seductive home in the certainties of what "the Emam" had to say. Khomeini inspired devotion of a kind the shah had never managed to arouse.

At least part of the secret to Khomeini's popularity was his extraordinary knack for remaining above the fray. From distant Najaf, he refused to take sides among the various factions competing for his approval, and he wisely limited his public statements to vague generalities. His ideas about *velayat-e-faqih* were not widely publicized beyond the hard core of theological students who attended his lectures and closely studied the audiotapes. In his public pronouncements, Khomeini stuck to simple themes every Iranian could understand: corruption, the military buildup, excessive Westernization, social problems like drugs and prostitution, SAVAK's torture chambers, the injustice of poverty, Iran's cooperation with Israel, and the interference of foreign powers. To most Iranians, Khomeini was a blank canvas—a pious, humble man of God onto whom they could project their frustrations with the shah's government, whatever they might be. This vagueness made it possible for National Front secularists, leftist guerrillas, and impoverished factory workers to support Khomeini and to believe that, despite their differences about the outcome, they were all ultimately on the same side, fighting the same enemy.

But even the charisma of Khomeini, the ideas of Shariati, and the shared animosity of Communists, Islamists, and democrats are not, by themselves, enough to explain why an entire nation turned so forcefully against its king in the late 1970s. Every good revolution also needs an external enemy—a blundering, clay-footed colossus that symbolizes all the entrenched political interests that the people believe are lined up against them, and that consistently behaves in a way that confirms all their worst suspicions. In Iran in the 1970s, the United States rose brilliantly to the occasion.

In October 1976, half a world away from the inexhaustible *tintamarre* of Iranian politics, at the Palace of Fine Arts in San Francisco, President Gerald Ford and Georgia governor Jimmy Carter stood at their podiums.

It was the second televised debate of the 1976 presidential election season, taking place against a backdrop of extreme cynicism and antiestablishment sentiment on the part of an electorate thoroughly exhausted by the horrors of Vietnam and the crass immorality of Watergate. Carter—the honest, plainspoken peanut farmer from a small town called Plains—seemed just the kind of outsider candidate the public could believe in. Sincerely committed to his Christian faith, the Georgia governor made human rights a centerpiece of his campaign, promising an end to the arrogance, warmongering, and imperial overreach of the Nixon years. If he were elected, Carter said, his foreign policy would be guided by principles of decency and morality, and he would give America "a government as good as its people." He was thirty points ahead in the polls.

When the second debate kicked off, Carter hammered relentlessly at Ford, accusing him—and his Republican predecessor, Richard Nixon—of "supporting dictatorships," "ignoring human rights," and conducting foreign policy from behind a veil of secrecy. At one point, Carter went after Ford specifically for continuing his predecessor's policy of arming the shah of Iran despite an avalanche of evidence about the cruelty of his regime. "Iran is going to get eighty F-14s before we even meet our own Air Force order for F-14s," Carter complained. "And the shipment of Spruance-class destroyers to Iran are much more highly sophisticated than [those] being delivered to our own Navy. This is ridiculous, and it ought to be changed." Under the Republicans, Carter said in a memorable phrase, the United States had become "the arms merchant of the whole world."

When news of the debate reached Iran, it actuated a ripple of excitement in all corners. If Carter was elected, opposition activists believed, he would put the shah under major pressure. To placate Carter, the shah might feel compelled to restrain SAVAK from its worst abuses and allow a few critical voices to be heard, as had happened during the Kennedy administration. The shah, for his part, fretted about the exact same thing. The last thing he wanted was another sanctimonious, untested liberal in the White House, preaching to him about human rights and rushing to make the world a better place in four short years. The last time an American president pushed him in the direction of reform, he had very nearly ended up with a revolution on his hands.

This time the shah was determined to take control of the narrative. In the first few months of 1977, following Carter's election victory, he rolled out one high-profile initiative after another intended to show how committed he was to liberalization and reform. Although officially Iran remained a one-party state, the shah now spoke of *mosharekat*—participation—as he released 357 political prisoners and commissioned panels and study groups to look into the people's grievances. For the first time in fifteen years, the National Front—still technically illegal—found itself able to operate without much government harassment. The shah invited the International Commission of Jurists, the International Committee of the Red Cross, and Amnesty International to observe conditions in Iranian prisons and make recommendations. (They all told him the situation was dire.)

In the event, however, all these measures proved unnecessary. Within weeks of taking office, Carter quietly carved out an exception for Iran from his high-minded sloganeering about human rights. The United States, he concluded, was simply too dependent on Iran's help in the region to push things too hard. In May 1977 he sent Secretary of State Cyrus Vance to Tehran to assure the shah that the friendship of the United States was sacrosanct. Vance and the shah met for two and a half hours at the Niavaran Palace in north Tehran, and according to sources present at the meeting, the issue of human rights received barely a mention. Instead, Vance committed the United States to deliver 160 F-16s that had been approved by the Nixon administration. He also promised the shah that the White House would do all it could to push through the sale of seven highly advanced AWACS planes, at a cost of $125 million apiece.[*] Relieved, the shah concluded that Carter's talk of human rights was merely for public consumption, and he thanked the secretary of state for his steadfast support. If the Nixon Doctrine was dead, its ghost was living on in magnificent style.

But the opposition, unaware of these commitments, took the Carter administration's rhetoric about human rights at face value. Within hours of the shah's meeting with Vance, the rumor fizzed through Tehran that Carter had sent his secretary of state to Iran to give the shah an "ultimatum"—liberalize, or lose U.S. support. Thus the Carter administration talked out of both sides of its mouth, publicly proselytizing about human rights but privately providing advanced weapons systems to one of the world's worst human rights offenders. In a rather odd (and ultimately dangerous) situation, both the shah and his opponents came to believe the United States was secretly "on their side."

---

[*] Carter later had to fight a damaging battle with members of his own party in Congress to get the AWACS deal approved.

In August 1977, to symbolize his commitment to reform, the shah dismissed his long-serving prime minister, Amir Abbas Hoveida, and replaced him with Jamshid Amouzegar, a former finance minister and a far less political animal than his predecessor. Amouzegar was a technocrat's technocrat, committed to the idea that competence and sound management were enough to run a country. But the Iranian economy was so badly overheated that there was little he could do. Amouzegar followed a deflationary policy aimed at inducing a mild recession—the only way to get prices under control. But the shah, true to form, expected him to do it without making reductions in the military budget. The result was massive, crippling unemployment.

Able to criticize their government for the first time in decades, Iranians were not shy about placing blame. During the summer and autumn of 1977, the lawyers' guild accused the government of violating the constitution, writers and artists demanded an end to censorship, university professors called for academic freedom, bazaar guilds protested attacks on their business practices, and a union of theological students demanded everything from press freedom to agricultural reform to "true sovereignty for Iran." These demands pointed to a deep, even existential dissatisfaction with the system—something far beyond Amouzegar's ability to address. To make matters worse, Amouzegar—who held a Ph.D. in hydraulic engineering from Cornell University and had stuffed his cabinet with men who had also received U.S. doctorates—was perceived as far too close to the American political establishment. Ultimately, Iranians regarded his appointment as prime minister as yet another piece of gimcrack window-dressing from a regime concerned only with how it was perceived in Washington. Events were about to prove them right.

Within a few weeks of appointing Amouzegar, the shah quietly disappeared for advanced treatment of the lymphoma that was ravaging his organs. Gaunt, despondent, and increasingly reliant on a cocktail of painkillers to get him through each day, the shah was described by those close to him as listless and unfocused. Although he kept the extent of his illness a secret from even his family, he frequently told visitors that he was "tired of all this." That autumn and winter Empress Farah began to make more public appearances, and posters of her face went up on billboards all over Iran. Severe and unforgiving, the portraits suggested a woman of flinty determination who could step in and take control as needed—a far cry from the lithe and statuesque accessory in a tiara who had been photographed by the shah's side for so many years.

In November 1977, drawn, somnambulant, and looking like the

By the late 1970s, some fifty thousand Iranians were studying in the United
States. College campuses were frequently the scene of anti-shah protests.
(Demonstrators frequently hid their faces because of the widespread presence
of SAVAK agents in the United States.)

ghost of emperors past, the shah flew to Washington for what would be his
final visit to the White House. Although his relationship with the United
States was closer than ever, much had changed since the days when he could
expect a ticker-tape parade down Broadway. On this occasion, four thousand Iranian students turned out to protest his visit, met by a smaller crowd
of pro-shah demonstrators hired by the Iranian embassy. On the Ellipse in
front of the White House, just yards from where the two leaders and their
wives were exchanging formal remarks for the cameras, riot police had to
be called out to break up a scuffle, and clouds of teargas drifted onto the
White House lawn. The shah and the president made heroic efforts not to
blink, but the next day's papers carried photographs of both leaders wiping
tears from their cheeks. For political correspondents, always fond of a good
metaphor, there could have been no finer warning of the direction U.S.-
Iranian relations were about to take.

Many Iranians, unable to fathom how such an embarrassing spectacle
could be allowed to take place just yards from the White House, assumed
it was Carter's subtle way of letting the shah know he was not entirely welcome in America. In fact, the opposite was true. During the shah's visit,
Carter had gone out of his way, quietly, behind closed doors, to let him
know he had America's unconditional support. In private meetings, the

It would end in tears: The shah's final visit to Washington, November 1977, was marred by protests and embarrassment. At one point, teargas fired by Washington police to disperse protesters wafted into the eyes of the guest of honor and his hosts.

president had barely broached the subject of human rights, focusing instead on arms sales, oil prices, and Middle East peace. Once again the shah and his opponents came away with radically different impressions of the same event.

ᘓ

Immediately after his return to Tehran, the shah—liberated from any need to demonstrate his humanitarian bona fides to Jimmy Carter—unleashed a brutal crackdown. On November 19 police shut down a poetry reading organized by a German-Iranian cultural institute, then fired on a sponta-neous demonstration outside, killing one and wounding seventy. A savage commando raid on Tehran University, and several incidents of government-sponsored vigilante violence, provoked two weeks of fierce demonstrations that shut down college campuses. Energized by the recent climate of open-ness (as well as by an American administration that seemed sympathetic to its demands), the opposition stepped up its efforts—only to be met by a vicious response from a government equally convinced that America was on its side.

Two weeks later, on December 31, 1977, President Carter arrived in

"Island of stability": The phrase had routinely been used by U.S. officials to describe
Iran in the 1970s. But President Jimmy Carter's use of it in his toast to the shah just
one week before the revolution broke out epitomized Washington's underestimation of
the threat he was facing.

Tehran to return the shah's visit. He found a city smoldering with anger.
Hours before his plane landed, twenty-nine prominent opposition leaders had sent an urgent appeal to the UN secretary-general, accusing their
own government of violating the 1948 Universal Declaration of Human
Rights—a brave move that would put them in danger unless they were
immediately bolstered with international support. Given Carter's outspoken commitment to human rights, activists hoped to hear encouragement
from the visiting president—some subtle verbal cue or passing remark that
suggested the United States understood the depth of the problem and was
serious about nudging the shah toward reform. What they heard was a very
different message.

At a lavish New Year's Eve banquet at the Imperial Palace, Carter
raised a glass to the shah. The words he spoke might have sounded routine and unremarkable had they come from the mouth of Richard Nixon
a few years earlier. But times had changed, and the words of that evening
quickly became infamous, haunting the Carter presidency to this day. "Iran,
because of the great leadership of the shah, is an island of stability in one
of the more troubled areas of the world," said the president, falling back on
the catchphrase that had defined more than a decade of official American

thinking. "This is a great tribute to you, Your Majesty, and to the respect and admiration and love which your people give to you."

Exactly one week later the revolution began.

ⁿ

Within hours of Carter's toast, Khomeini and other oppositionists blasted the United States, claiming the president was interested in human rights only in countries where the United States did not have military or strategic interests. Much of the Iranian street, shocked and disgusted by Carter's effusive praise for the shah, agreed wholeheartedly.

The shah, by contrast, was on cloud nine. Carter's words had removed any doubt that the United States was firmly on his side. The Iranian government had no need to worry about Carter's much-vaunted human rights agenda. With a new spring in his step, the shah decided the time had come to take a more forceful approach with the opposition, which he was still convinced was just a few isolated troublemakers. In particular, the time had come to deal with Khomeini.

In what was possibly the most politically obtuse decision of his career, the shah ordered the semiofficial newspaper *Ettela'at* to publish an editorial vilifying Khomeini as an agent of British colonialism and a less-than-holy mystic who had written racy love sonnets in his youth. The accusations were absurd and untrue.[*] But using factual acrobatics, the article suggested the country's religious leaders were a bunch of foreign-controlled hypocrites who wrapped themselves in piety to disguise their true agenda, which was to hijack the White Revolution and hinder Iran's progress. "Iran's enemies," concluded the article, would stop at nothing to advance their interests, "even if it means dressing themselves up in the holy and respected clothes of clerics." Thus did the shah hope to win the hearts and minds of the Iranian public.

On January 7, 1978, the editorial appeared and produced exactly the opposite effect. In the holy city of Qom—where fourteen years earlier Khomeini had kept audiences spellbound with his rhetoric—four thousand protesters poured into the streets, demanding the government apologize for the editorial and allow freedom of the press. They also called for the return of Khomeini to Iran and for the reopening of the Faezieh seminary, where he used to give his lectures. Police reacted with their usual spirited disregard

---

[*] The claim that Khomeini was a British agent, for example, was cynically extrapolated from the fact that Khomeini's grandfather had once worked in British-occupied Kashmir.

for human life, firing into the crowd of demonstrators and killing a dozen or more.

History has recorded this moment as the one when the shah began to lose his grip. A week earlier Khomeini had been important but not omnipotent—the most charismatic of the figures lining up against the shah but by no means the only one who could give voice to people's anger. Now he was the face of a movement—a pious, dignified cleric; a man who spoke truth to power; and the victim of a cowardly slander by the government press. But unlike Mosaddeq—unlike Qavam, Zahedi, Amini, Sanjabi, Shariat-Madari, Bazargan, and the scores of other leaders who had tried to moderate the shah's dictatorial tendencies over the years—Khomeini was adamant that there could be no compromise with the Pahlavi state. "The people have identified the true criminal," he now thundered from Najaf. "Let us pick up our staffs and oppose this vile Shah."

Incredibly, the disturbances in Qom went unnoticed by Washington. Not one official at the U.S. embassy in Tehran considered it worthy of a dispatch or telegram to the State Department. Not one urgent phone call was made. Neither *The New York Times* nor *The Washington Post* carried any mention of the day's events the following morning. Though in retrospect this seems incomprehensible, in fact it fitted perfectly with the narrative about Iran that dominated American thinking. At the beginning of 1978, U.S. officials in Iran were institutionally conditioned to be on high alert for signs of Communist infiltration or Soviet-inspired demonstrations, but they gave no thought to the possibility of an uprising by religious activists. The political activism of a few disgruntled theology students—no matter how much bloodshed it resulted in—was not worth writing home about.

To Iranians, though, it was obvious that something fundamental had shifted. The center of gravity for opposition to the shah had shifted from secular protest, with poetry readings and petitions, toward something more religiously inspired—and more unpredictable. The staging ground for protest was no longer solely Tehran, with its smoke-filled cafés and raucous student unions, but also Qom, where the country's most respected religious scholars felt they had little choice but to express their outrage. Grand Ayatollah Shariat-Madari, a soft-spoken senior cleric who had previously acted as a moderating influence on activists, now blasted the shah's regime as an abomination against Islam. Shariat-Madari called on Iranians to mourn the victims of the Qom massacre, according to the traditional Shia custom, by going to their mosques and publicly weeping for the souls of the departed on the fortieth day following their deaths.

Forty days later, on February 19, much of Iran did exactly that. In Tabriz and a dozen other cities, thousands stayed home from work and poured into the streets dressed in black, ready to express their grief. The demonstrations in Tabriz had a markedly more religious flavor than anything seen previously. Protesters targeted symbols of Western decadence—banks, liquor stores, cinemas showing sexy foreign films—as well as local headquarters of the Rastakhiz Party.* For the first time, chants of "Death to the shah" rose from the throats of furious protesters. And security forces seemed caught off-guard. In Tabriz, police refused to shoot, and army troops, tanks, and helicopter gunships had to be called in to restore order. By the end of the day, dozens of people had been shot dead in the streets.

Still the United States treated the unrest as a minor domestic matter. On March 29—exactly forty days after the violence in Tabriz—Secretary Vance arrived in Tehran for a CENTO foreign ministers conference. During the visit, neither he nor the shah brought up the unrest. Vance merely updated the shah on the status of Arab-Israeli peace talks and left. Convinced the shah was a savvy political operator who had ridden out far worse crises during his thirty-seven years on the throne, the Americans saw little reason to worry about this latest round of protest. As far as they were concerned, the shah had one of the world's largest armies, a ruthless secret police force, mountains of oil wealth that could be used to buy off opponents, and nearly four decades of proven leadership experience. What could possibly go wrong?

The next day, as expected, the weeping and wailing resumed on the streets of Iranian cites. Once again there were deadly clashes between mourners and paramilitary forces, and once again mourners had reason to gather forty days later, this time on May 11, for commemorations (and another round of confrontations with police). And so it continued, for the rest of 1978. Every forty days the government would get the situation under control but would commit such atrocities that it would face even bigger crowds forty days later. Demonstrators blended seamlessly into mourners, knowing the government would never dare outlaw a religious procession. The forty-day cycle gave activists long periods of downtime to organize and regroup. And they had no need to waste time squabbling about tactics or arranging a time and place for protests. It was simply understood that, on the fortieth day following a massacre, everyone would pour onto the streets. An ancient Shia custom thus turned into a modern organizing tool—the 1970s equivalent of a flash mob.

---

* What was striking about this round of protests was that demonstrators behaved with strict regard for principles of Islamic piety. Western diplomats were amazed to find that even when banks were targeted by angry mobs, no money was stolen—"not a single" cent, according to one report. The demonstrators also went out of their way to respect human life, including that of Americans.

The point of no return came on September 5, when hundreds of thousands turned out in cities and towns across Iran to celebrate Eid al-Fitr, the end of Ramadan and, traditionally, a moment of joy and good-natured camaraderie, when chattering grandmothers passed out sweets to strangers and extended families gathered at sundown to break their fasts. But with so many people in the streets, it was only a matter of time before the frustrations of the past months boiled over. Spontaneous crowds of demonstrators shouted never-before-heard slogans like "Death to the Pahlavis" and "The shah is a bastard." By the end of the second day, as many as one million people were marching through the streets—until that point, the largest demonstration in Iranian history.

Then on September 8, the unthinkable happened. In Tehran's Jaleh Square, security forces opened fire on a large crowd of peaceful demonstrators, while in the southern slums, helicopter gunships shot volleys down into the labyrinthine alleys. By day's end, several hundred people had been gunned down—one of the bloodiest incidents of regime violence in Iranian history. Images of the massacre made their way onto newspaper front pages and television news bulletins around the world, and even the shah's most vigorous defenders sensed that he might be in trouble.

Recognizing his friend's predicament, President Carter tried to help but

Black Friday: The massacre in Jaleh Square, September 8, 1978, in which at least a hundred people were gunned to death by security forces, sealed the shah's fate. The regime was unable to recover in the weeks that followed.

succeeded only in making matters worse. Immediately following the Jaleh Square massacre, Carter took time out from high-level Arab-Israeli peace talks he was hosting at Camp David and made a telephone call to the shah, assuring him he had the full support of the United States. The White House then issued a press release letting the world know about the phone call and "reaffirmed the close and friendly relationship between Iran and the United States." It was a disastrous miscalculation.

In Tehran, bodies had not yet been buried. Desperate mothers were still clawing at the doors of morgues, trying to find out what had happened to their children. And on Radio Tehran, Iranians learned that President Carter—whose administration had talked so much about its commitment to human rights—was giving his wholehearted support to the shah. From Najaf on September 27, Ayatollah Khomeini said only what many Iranians were already thinking: "With the support of America and with all the infernal means at his disposal, the shah [has turned] Iran into one vast graveyard."

The graffiti that made its way onto the walls of Tehran over the next several weeks was even more blunt. *Marg bar Shah-e Amrikah,* it read. "Death to America's Shah."

⁓

The massacre at Jaleh Square appeared to leave the shah badly shaken. Those who called on him in the days that followed reported seeing a man shrunken, yellow, pale—almost concave with anxiety. An American official recalled that the shah spoke in slow, robotic sentences, as if he were not entirely present. Until that point, the shah had genuinely believed he was in control of the situation and that the worst of the disturbances had passed. Surrounded by sycophantic courtiers who continued to kiss his hand and tell him how adored he was by the people, the shah had lost touch with reality. Now, as ambulances carted off the dead and injured—and as the world asked whether the regime could survive—he looked shell-shocked.

The shah had good reason to be anxious. The Jaleh Square massacre was a defining moment in the Iranian Revolution—one that created a permanent barrier of mistrust and hostility between the government and the people. Over the next several weeks, the shah's government would resort to one desperate measure after another to try to demonstrate its goodwill and regain public confidence. But it was too little, too late. After the bloody events of September 8, the shah was reviled almost universally as a bloodthirsty tyrant. That date was increasingly referred to by Iranians as Black Friday—the beginning of the end for a king at war with his own people.

The prime minister, Jafar Sharif-Emami (who had replaced Amouzegar two weeks earlier), did his best to cope with the crisis. Realizing, far too late, that the regime's biggest challenge came from the religious right rather than the atheist left, his government created a Ministry of Religious Affairs, closed down casinos, and repealed the hated imperial calendar introduced just three years earlier.* Sharif-Emami also acquiesced to a number of demands made by trade unions and liberal activists—including, in October, ending press censorship. In an attempt to crack down on corruption, the government introduced a detailed code of conduct for the Royal Family (several of whom responded by gathering their loot and leaving the country). And at the end of September, it announced that the Rastakhiz Party would be dissolved, to make way for multiparty elections the following year.

These were serious, drastic measures, but the shah's commitment to liberalization was as half-hearted and short-lived as ever. When Sharif-Emami's reform drive didn't pay immediate dividends, the shah seized on this as proof that liberalization was not the answer and reverted to the iron-fist strategy urged by his generals. In mid-October, as the public prepared to observe the forty-day mourning ritual for the "martyrs" of Jaleh Square, tanks once again rolled through the major cities. Once again there was bloodshed.

To outside observers, Iran's government appeared to be veering recklessly between two extreme policies. On the one hand, Ambassador Ardeshir Zahedi and the generals were urging the shah to apply the "iron fist," insisting that a few more Jaleh Squares would send a powerful message to would-be troublemakers. On the other hand, an equally influential group of Rastakhiz Party leaders, with the support of Empress Farah, was advising him to reform the political process. Time was running out, they said, and the country needed to see bold, sweeping steps in the direction of democracy. The shah, confused and bewildered, found himself unsure who to listen to. Rather than pick one approach and back it with strong, decisive action, he became depressed, withdrawn, and gloomy—preferring to quiz the British and American ambassadors about what he should do.

Part of the problem was that the shah hated both his options. He had always lacked the stomach for blood and guts, genuinely believing there was no point in being king if it meant ruling at the end of a gun-barrel. At the same time, however, he had always felt anxious about sharing power. Unable to commit fully to being either a tyrant or a democrat, he spent the remaining months of 1978 trying to be both. He convinced himself that if

---

* In 1976 the shah had abolished the Islamic calendar, which uses the *hejira* of Muhammad as its starting point, in favor of a calendar beginning with the coronation of Cyrus the Great. For both practical and religious reasons, it had been deeply unpopular.

he could just win over enough moderates with political reforms, he could then isolate and crush the radicals. But in fact, this approach had the inverse effect. Every time peaceful protesters were gunned down in the street, moderates saw it as further evidence of the brutality of the regime. And every time a tentative step was taken in the direction of political openness, it only created more space for radicals to rise up in anger and express years of pent-up frustration. The shah's off-again, on-again approach to liberalization thus managed to achieve the worst of both worlds: giving people more room to air their grievances, while simultaneously giving them more reasons than ever to feel aggrieved.

☙

Unable to come to grips with the fast-moving situation, the shah concluded that, one way or another, Khomeini had to be taken out of the equation. At the beginning of October, he asked Iraqi leader Saddam Hussein—with whom he was on peaceful terms for the first time in years—to expel the ayatollah from Najaf so he could no longer serve as a focal point for Iranian radicals. This turned out to be yet another disastrous political move. Khomeini fled to France and set up camp in the quiet suburban village of Neauphle-le-Château, twenty miles west of Paris. Now, rather than sitting in a remote Iraqi city lecturing to scruffy groups of pilgrims and seminary students, Khomeini was at the center of the Western media universe. As the crisis in Iran worsened and his devout followers called for the return of "the emam," an army of reporters and camera crews descended on the narrow, winding lanes of Neauphle-le-Château to see what all the fuss was about. Over the next four months, Khomeini would give 132 interviews to the international media.

Khomeini's French headquarters also attracted high-profile Iranian dissidents, most notably the liberal-religious intellectuals of the Freedom Movement, who now threw their support behind the ayatollah. Mehdi Bazargan (a future prime minister of Iran) set himself up in Neauphle-le-Château from October, as did Abolhassan Bani-Sadr (a future president), Ibrahim Yazdi (a future foreign minister), Sadeq Tabatabai (a future deputy prime minister), and Sadeq Qotbzadeh (executed for treason in 1982). Modern, Western-educated, and media-savvy, Bazargan and his team skillfully directed Khomeini's public image—convincing first themselves, then much of the world, that Khomeini intended to be a sort of Islamic figurehead presiding over a largely democratic state. Within weeks, the sleepy French village was transformed into a pilgrimage site, as a steady stream of Iranian exiles arrived, hoping for a few minutes of Khomeini's time. The elderly ayatollah—who spent his days sitting on a carpet in a corner of the garden, wearing blue plastic sandals and munching on bread, onions, and yogurt—seemed remarkably unfazed by all the attention. But he was well aware that he was leading a revolution—and that the world now considered him Iran's leader-in-waiting.[*]

Back in Tehran, flowers appeared at the gates of the French embassy, tokens of gratitude laid by the Khomeini faithful. The situation was unraveling rapidly. The FeK and MeK, sensing victory in the offing, began cooperating and operated far more openly than they had in the past. Thousands of young people flocked to join their ranks. Most ominously perhaps, on September 16 a devastating earthquake struck the plateau town of Tabas, killing twenty thousand people, and the clergy were conspicuously quicker and more effective than the government at organizing a response—helping to overcome lingering doubts over whether religious leaders could be trusted to run a country. As local mosques were skillfully transformed into distribution centers for relief supplies, anger mounted at a government that seemed incapable even of providing this basic service. But the furious residents of Tabas didn't know the half of it. Though it was never reported in Iran, on September 19, just three days after the quake, the shah and Princess Ashraf spent $600,000 on a lavish private banquet for their friends in Tehran—even flying in a popular Australian lounge singer named Tony Monopoly for the evening.

As the emperor fiddled, Rome continued to burn. The recession induced by Amouzegar's deflationary policies had brought about hardship, and from early September, a number of crippling strikes broke out across Iran. Sanitation workers, textile workers, and cement workers walked off the job—joined within weeks by university and high school staff, bank and government employees, air traffic controllers, journalists, hospital staff, broadcasters, and almost every kind of factory worker. Perilously, the oil industry workers went on strike, and by the end of October, Iran's petroleum output had plummeted from nearly 6 million barrels a day to 1.5 million. But this was only the beginning. In November bazaar merchants decided that they, too, had had enough and joined the strike.[†] Market stalls

---

* Khomeini appears to have chosen France because there was no other obvious option. Most Middle East nations were ruled by allies of the shah who refused to allow him entry. France did not require an entry visa from Iranians. Some evidence suggests that French president Valéry Giscard d'Estaing checked with the shah before agreeing to admit Khomeini, and that the shah—concerned that Khomeini might end up in Syria, where he would cause worse problems—gave his consent. Khomeini's own words and speeches suggest he viewed his exile in France as temporary and hoped he could soon be admitted to a Muslim country instead.

† For the previous two years, the shah had steadily aroused the anger of the *bazaaris* by declaring a "war on profiteers," blaming inflation on greedy traders and shopkeepers. The Rastakhiz Party

and corner shops across Iran drew down their shutters and remained closed for most of November and December, bringing the economy to a standstill.

During the first week of November, confusion on the streets of Iran reached a crescendo. After just two months in office, Sharif-Emami was replaced as prime minister by a military general, Qolam-Reza Azhari. Martial law was extended across the country but was only sporadically enforced. Students at Tehran University tried to pull down the shah's statue and were met by a hail of gunfire, which only brought more rioters onto the streets. A portion of the British embassy was broken into and torched by radicals. Every day—every hour, it seemed—the government was met by a fresh challenge to its authority.

From France, Khomeini urged his supporters not to let up the pressure. "Victory is yours," he proclaimed, as he pressed Iranians to "advance together, with a single voice and a single purpose, to . . . the destruction of this abominable monarchical regime." The more moderate, secular factions that the shah had hoped to woo to his side now seemed inclined to support Khomeini's position. The leader of the National Front, Karim Sanjabi, accused the "present monarchy" of being a failure and called for a referendum to establish a "national government based on the principles of Islam, democracy and national sovereignty"—effectively bringing to an end the front's historic commitment to constitutional monarchy. Even the former prime minister Ali Amini, who in 1961 had worked so hard to act as a moderating influence on the opposition, told an American journalist bluntly that "the heart of the problem is the shah."

On the evening of November 5, as the smell of burning rubber mixed with the sounds of wailing sirens, car horns, and gunfire, the shah took to the airwaves to deliver a special televised address to the nation. "As the king of Iran and as an Iranian, I cannot disapprove of the revolution of the people of Iran," he began. He admitted that many mistakes had been made in the past and promised a fresh start. "I have heard the revolutionary message of the people," he said. "In the future, the government of Iran will be run according to the constitution, social justice, and the people's will. It will be free of tyranny, oppression, and corruption." It was a bizarre message. Desperate, almost defeatist, the shah spoke as though he were somehow the one *leading* the revolt against the government. The very next day the

had organized ten thousand students into vigilante mobs and sent them into the bazaars to carry out a "merciless crusade against profiteers, cheaters, hoarders, and unscrupulous capitalists." Eight thousand shopkeepers had been given prison sentences, and 250,000 fines had been handed out by hastily assembled guild courts. One historian estimates that by 1976, "every bazaar family had at least one member who had directly suffered from the 'antiprofiteering campaign.'" (Abrahamian, *Between Two Revolutions,* p. 498.)

Carter administration sent the shah an emergency supply of teargas canisters, batons, and riot gear.

The shah did his best to show he had taken leadership of the people's revolution. The former prime minister Amir Abbas Hoveida, who had served faithfully for twelve years, was now arrested on charges of corruption. So too were the former head of SAVAK and Dariush Homayoun, who had been information minister when the offensive article about Khomeini appeared in January. All were symbolic targets, arrested arbitrarily, leaving the impression that the shah was looking for scapegoats. Much worse, the wave of arrests left the political establishment—the few friends the shah had left—feeling nervous, insecure, and severely disinclined to rally behind their leader. Many began transferring assets into Swiss bank accounts and taking "extended holidays" abroad to avoid being around for the worst.* Even the shah later recognized the foolishness of what he had done. Shortly after the revolution, when a reporter asked him why, at the critical moment, he hadn't flooded the streets with his supporters, as Charles De Gaulle had done on the Champs-Élysées in 1968, the shah replied tartly that his supporters were *already in* the Champs-Élysées.

On November 2 the U.S. ambassador in Tehran, William Sullivan, who had spent much of the past year reassuring his bosses that the shah was invincible, had a sudden change of heart. In an urgent telegram to the secretary of state, he reported that Iran was in the midst of a full-blown crisis and that the shah was struggling with the choice between abdicating or introducing military rule. It was the first time Washington had heard anything like this from its man in Tehran.

A week later Sullivan sent another, much lengthier cable arguing that the shah's support among the public had sunk to an all-time low and that the United States should begin making plans for the possibility that his regime might not survive. That the Iranian monarchy could collapse altogether was, by Sullivan's own admission, an outcome no one in the U.S. had seriously considered to this point. But the United States could no longer afford to take anything for granted. To stress the urgency of the situation, Sullivan titled his telegram—now famous in the annals of U.S.-Iranian relations—"Thinking the Unthinkable."

☙

---

* Exactly how much of Iran's wealth was transferred out of the country in the final months of the shah's regime may never be known, but estimates have run into the billions. On September 18, 1978, rogue employees of the Central Bank of Iran published a list of 177 high-profile individuals whom they claimed had transferred $2 billion in personal funds into overseas accounts. Sharif-Emami alone was said to have moved $31 million.

Sullivan's cables set off an eighteen-alarm fire in Washington. Suddenly awakened to the possibility that the shah might not be the invulnerable, immovable pillar of American policy in the Middle East that they had thought he was, the Carter administration summoned its top foreign policy brains—Deputy Secretary of State Warren Christopher, National Security Adviser Zbigniew Brzezinski, CIA Director Stansfield Turner, Defense Secretary Harold Brown, and others—to an emergency meeting. Incredibly, it was the first time all these men were brought into one room together to focus on Iran.

In November 1978 the U.S. government, like almost every other government in the world, was caught off-guard by the depth of hostility that Iranians were demonstrating toward their shah. For years, American officials in Iran had cultivated only limited contacts outside elite circles. As recently as the spring of 1978, most had never heard the name "Khomeini." Few had visited the seminaries in the holy city of Qom—despite the fact that it was only fifty miles south of Tehran—or canvassed the views of religious leaders. Their reports thus reflected a degree of unquestioning faith in the shah that, in retrospect, seems unforgivable. As recently as September 28, the U.S. Defense Intelligence Agency confidently reported that the shah "is expected to remain actively in power over the next ten years." Four weeks earlier a State Department report—only slightly less optimistic—had seen "some chance that the Shah will be forced to step down by 1985, [but] at the moment we would rate that chance as less than fifty-fifty."

Jolted into action, the Carter White House dropped everything to deal with Iran—and the result was an undignified round of infighting. At one end of the debate, Brzezinski felt the United States should back the shah unconditionally, even if it meant lending support to a harsh military crackdown. At the other end, the State Department's career Iran analysts—in particular, the director of the Iran desk, Henry Precht, and Ambassador Sullivan in Tehran—felt the shah's autocratic days were over and that he should make way for a government led by moderate opposition leaders. But Precht and Sullivan were not supported by their own superiors at State. Consumed with the Camp David peace talks between Egypt and Israel, Secretary of State Cyrus Vance was largely absent from Iran discussions during these months, making it easier for Brzezinski and the NSC to persuade Carter not to listen too closely to the advice of Vance's underlings. The result was an epic feud between Brzezinski and the State Department, which became so vicious by the end of 1978 that the two sides refused to share information, each developing its own set of analyses and policy recommendations to take directly to the president.

Brzezinski and the hard-liners thought that any post-shah government—

even one led by Khomeini—was likely to make major concessions to the left, destabilizing the country and paving the way for a violent Communist takeover. The shah was a crucial anti-Soviet ally, they argued, and the United States should take every possible step to fortify his regime. Sullivan and the State Department, meanwhile, worried that if the United States nailed its colors too stubbornly to the shah's mast, America might find itself on the wrong side of history—facing a future Iranian government that would not soon forget America's betrayal of the Iranian people. More important, they argued, America could be sure that any religious system of government, inspired by Khomeini, would have nothing to do with the forces of godless Communism.

Both Brzezinski and the State Department were operating on a set of assumptions that were eminently reasonable. But both revealed just how saturated Washington had become with Cold War thinking. For years, U.S. officials and CIA agents in Iran had been trained to see a "Communist behind every mosque." Thus, many on Brzezinski's side of the argument (though not Brzezinski himself) dismissed the idea that a simple cleric like Khomeini could be leading a genuine, spontaneous Islamist movement and instead reflexively assumed, despite a lack of evidence, that the trouble in Iran was being stirred up by Soviet agents. By contrast, Precht, Sullivan, and the State Department hands, who knew Iran a bit better, took Khomeini at face value but found it inconceivable that he would ever come to govern a nation of 50 million people or manage the world's second-largest oil industry. Once the shah was gone, they assumed, the seventy-seven-year-old ayatollah would step back and assume the role of a spiritual guru, providing moral guidance for the transition to the post-shah era but ultimately allowing the Western-educated technocrats of the Freedom Movement to run the government. Both camps, each in its own way, badly underestimated Khomeini.

All the squabbling left Carter feeling like he had no good options. Pushing the shah to impose military rule conflicted with the president's most deeply held principles and was likely to provoke worse unrest. Any direct, muscular U.S. intervention to prop up the regime also seemed out of the question. Carter had come to power on a wave of public exhaustion with Vietnam, and Americans had little appetite for military adventurism. But Carter agreed with Brzezinski that the shah had been a loyal ally for many years and should not be abandoned in his hour of need. If the shah survived the crisis, after all, he would not soon forget who his friends and enemies had been. But then neither, for that matter, would the opposition, should *they* emerge victorious. For Carter, the policy decision thus boiled down to a simple question: was the shah going to survive or not?

As the Carter administration weighed its options, events on the streets of Iran waited for no one. On December 9, Iranians poured out of their homes in numbers never seen before—at least 2 million in Tehran alone, and as many as 8 million nationwide. The occasion was *ashura*—the mother of all mourning ceremonies—and this year Iranians had more reasons to mourn than ever before. Over the past twelve months, at least three thousand people had lost their lives in street violence—most of them victims of government brutality—and in their honor, the entire nation now turned out to express its sorrow. The military chiefs wisely avoided a confrontation—promising, at the last minute, to keep a low profile in exchange for a promise from opposition leaders that the demonstrations would be peaceful—and the kind of bloody scenes that might have played into Khomeini's hands were astutely avoided. Nevertheless, if the shah thought he could breathe a sigh of relief, he was mistaken. At Shahyad Square—Tehran's largest public space—a crowd of at least a million roared its approval of a manifesto calling for the abolition of the monarchy and the establishment of an Islamic republic led by Khomeini.

Amid their cries of "Death to the Shah," crowds increasingly shouted anti-Western slogans, too, and Americans living in Iran—of whom there were now more than forty thousand—began to panic. Apartments were hurriedly vacated, children were yanked out of school, and cars, appliances, and furniture were sold off at rock-bottom prices or simply abandoned to the nearest lucky Iranian. Europeans left quietly on scheduled commercial flights, or else they waited and felt the situation out day by day. But U.S. companies like Bell Helicopter and Grumman hastily chartered planes and herded their people out of Iran in dramatic airlift operations. This mass exodus was chaotic and poorly managed and only added to the feeling of national insecurity. In 1978 the United States had the largest footprint of any foreign nation in Iran, and the sight of Americans heading for the exits in droves seemed a sure sign to Iranians that something was wrong.

In both Washington and Tehran, talk now turned, much too late, to compromise measures—the creation of a caretaker government or a "Council of Notables" that could manage the transition to multiparty elections. Some suggested the formation of a coalition government, bringing together the National Front and moderate clerics like Shariat-Madari, thus leaving Khomeini and his radical allies isolated. But even at this late hour, the shah didn't want to cooperate. He had made it clear to the Americans that he would sooner flee the country than allow himself to be reduced to a figurehead. At the same time, however, he refused to order the harsh crackdown

Sea of humanity: In the winter of 1978–79, millions of protesters demanding the shah's ouster brought Tehran to a standstill.

that his generals were begging for—leaving the military top brass exasperated and itching for decisive action.

The prime minister, General Azhari, who had suffered a heart attack in mid-December and was now confined to a cot in the Imperial Palace, summoned the U.S. ambassador to vent his frustrations. "You must know this, and you must tell it to your government," Azhari said, propping himself up on a pillow and sucking from a bottle of oxygen. "This country is lost because the king cannot make up his mind."

❦

In the last two weeks of December, in a final, last-ditch attempt to prevent the revolutionaries from charging through the gates of the Bastille, the shah offered the job of prime minister to Shapur Bakhtiar—one of the youngest, least experienced, and most ambitious leaders of the National Front, who had broken ranks with his colleagues over the question of whether it was still possible to cooperate with the monarchy.

"How long has it been since we last saw each other?" the shah asked, trying to break the ice, as Bakhtiar walked into the Imperial Palace. Bakhtiar, who had first come to prominence as a Mosaddeq loyalist during the heady days of 1953, didn't miss a beat. "Twenty-five years, Your Majesty. It's a date you must remember." The shah winced at the impudence of the response. "You haven't changed a bit," he replied.

With the awkward small talk out of the way, Bakhtiar and the shah agreed that the new government would introduce freedom of the press and free political prisoners—even dissolve SAVAK. But when Bakhtiar said he also wanted the shah to leave the country for a short time and allow a regency council to govern in his name, the shah hesitated. He had heard no such suggestion from the United States and felt it was a little premature to be discussing his departure. Within days, however, that would change, as Sullivan told the shah bluntly that the only realistic way he could save the monarchy would be to take himself out of the picture for a bit. The shah reluctantly agreed, and on December 28, 1978, Shapur Bakhtiar took office—the last prime minister in Iranian history to pledge his allegiance to the King of Kings, Light of the Aryans, and Shadow of God on Earth. In his first television appearance, Bakhtiar covered the shah's portrait with an Iranian flag and pointedly sat next to a photograph of Mosaddeq.

It was a nice symbolic touch, but it did little to still the baying of the wolves. Without the support of the National Front, the Freedom Movement, the Islamist street, the leftist underground, the ayatollahs—or indeed, anyone but the shah and the United States—Bakhtiar's government never had a prayer. *Bakhtiar, Bakhtiar, noukar-e bi-ekhtiar,* went a popular rhyme on the Tehran street—"Bakhtiar, Bakhtiar, you obedient servant." In the view of many Iranians, Bakhtiar, by agreeing to keep the shah on life support at the eleventh hour, had betrayed not only the National Front but the entire nation. The public, after all, had already made it clear it was ready for revolution and for the return of Khomeini—not some kind of anemic regency council ruling in the shah's name.

As the announcement was made over Radio Tehran that the shah would soon be leaving the country for "medical treatment," the United States found itself once again facing an unpredictable, fast-moving situation in Iran—and once again, the Carter administration descended into bickering. State Department officials did their best to convince Carter that the shah's regime was history and that it was time to make contact with Khomeini in Paris. But they were once again opposed by Brzezinski and the hard-liners, who insisted America give its full support to Bakhtiar and the regency council. Carter's response was to send a military man, Gen. Robert "Dutch" Huyser, on a top-secret mission to Iran to assess the morale of the shah's generals—and to lay the groundwork for a U.S.-backed military coup that could maintain the regime in power if push came to shove. Unlike in 1953, however, the shah was not to be involved. In fact, he was never even informed. Instead, General Huyser slipped quietly into Iran, without so much as paying a courtesy call on the shah, and began conducting coordination exercises with the shah's own generals.

Precht, Sullivan, and their allies in the State Department howled in protest and incredulity about the Huyser mission. The United States, they feared, had failed to absorb the lessons of 1953. But Huyser was adamant that Iran's generals would carry the day and preserve the status quo, leaving the United States with a reliable client state in the Middle East. In January 1979, in other words, America—against the better judgment of its own professional diplomats—had made its choice: It was going to do its best to prevent Iran from falling into the hands of Khomeini. And it was sticking with the monarchy until the bitter end.

State Department officials now suggested—practically begged—to be allowed to make contact with Khomeini. Other Western nations were taking this basic, prudent step to preserve their options in Iran, they argued. But Brzezinski opposed the idea, on the grounds that it would send a poor message to the shah. In the end, it was Brzezinski's advice that Carter took.[*] In the final few weeks of the shah's regime, the United States stood shoulder to shoulder with its longtime ally. As late as December 12, 1978—as American companies were evacuating their employees from Iran, as the walls of Tehran were covered in signs reading "Death to the fascist shah," and as members of the royal family were boarding flights to Los Angeles— President Carter informed the world there was nothing to worry about. "I fully expect the shah to maintain power in Iran, and for the present problems . . . to be resolved," he told a White House press conference. "I think the predictions of doom and disaster that came from some sources have certainly not been realized at all. The shah has our support, and he also has our confidence."

Thirty-four days later, on January 16, 1979, the shah and his family boarded a specially chartered Boeing 707 jet bound for Cairo. Two more planes were loaded with their belongings. The empress took a tranquilizer to help her face the cameras with dignity, and the shah took with him a jar of Iranian soil. On the tarmac, a decorated colonel fell melodramatically at the shah's feet and begged him not to leave. He was helped back up by the shah, from whom—at least for the moment—he was still taking his orders.

Beyond the perimeter of Mehrabad Airport, the reaction to the news that the shah was on his way out of the country was very different. Hundreds

---

[*] Brzezinski, for the rest of his life, maintained that standing by the shah had been the right thing to do. For Washington to make contact with Khomeini, he argued, would have sent a disastrous signal to other U.S. allies about how little American friendship was worth when push came to shove—potentially encouraging other nations to develop closer ties to Moscow.

Departure: The shah and Empress Farah leave Iran for the last time, January 16, 1979. Billed as a temporary absence to seek medical treatment abroad, the king's departure was widely understood to be final.

of thousands poured into the streets, honking car horns, flashing victory signs for the news cameras, dancing and singing and ululating in jubilation. Ecstatic motorists jumped onto their car roofs or built impromptu bonfires in intersections—using portraits of the shah as kindling. Some celebrated by cutting the shah's face out of banknotes, while others pulled down statues of the shah and his father. A special afternoon edition of *Ettela'at,* seemingly as overcome by the moment as everyone else, splashed two enormous words across the top of its front page. Two raw, guttural, monosyllabic Persian words—free of the flowery Arabesque prose that often characterized newspaper headlines:

Shah Raft. The Shah Is Gone.

୯୫

Over the next two weeks, Bakhtiar made heroic efforts to maintain the pretense that he was in control of the government. But he was prime minister in name only. After several months of strikes by public-sector workers, Iran's bureaucracy was on the verge of disintegration, and in almost every

"The Shah Is Gone": Jubilant Iranians hold up the iconic newspaper front page on the day the shah left Tehran, January 16, 1979.

city, control over basic services—from fuel and food distribution to public safety—was falling into the hands of spontaneous revolutionary committees managed by local clerics. All over Iran, ordinary people—from bazaar merchants to schoolteachers—pulled together and formed citizen militias to ensure that the country kept running, and no one went cold or hungry. On January 19, to force a final showdown with Bakhtiar and the regency council, Khomeini called for a street "referendum" on the fate of the monarchy. In Tehran alone, a million turned out. The following day Bakhtiar tried to do the same and drew only a few thousand supporters.

On February 1, Ayatollah Khomeini—the emam, the rebel, the man who had promised not to rest until the "criminal shah" was gone and "the cause of Islam and freedom" had prevailed—stepped carefully off an Air France jet and onto the runway at Mehrabad Airport. It had been fifteen years since those feet had met Iranian soil, and no one—least of all the old holy man himself—knew quite what to expect. Back in Paris, Khomeini's entourage, worried that generals loyal to the shah might try to shoot down their plane, had packed it with Western journalists as a form of insurance. They had also wondered out loud whether they would be arrested for treason when they arrived, or even executed. "You don't have to come with me,"

Khomeini had reminded his circle of nervous advisers a few hours before takeoff. "It could be dangerous."

They needn't have worried. When Khomeini's flight landed, it looked to all who were present as though the heavens had opened and were raining down ecstatic Iranians. Peter Jennings of ABC News, who had accompanied Khomeini on the flight, estimated that he was looking out on between 3 and 6 million people—arguably the largest spontaneous gathering in human history. People packed into window jambs and crammed so densely onto roofs that they dangled precariously over the streets. The man charged with the impossible task of driving Khomeini from the airport into town later described how the interior of the car became "dark as night" as dozens of people piled on top of it with joy. Eventually, a helicopter had to be called in to airlift Khomeini to safety. The man of the hour—the man whom the shah had thought, just a year earlier, could be bullied into oblivion with a

Arrival: Ayatollah Khomeini returns to Iran after fifteen years in exile, February 1, 1979.

Man of the hour: Khomeini greets supporters from his provisional headquarters the day after his arrival.

few well-placed slanders in a newspaper editorial—now literally had to be rescued from the adoration of the Iranian people.

For a few more days, Bakhtiar struggled pathetically to assert control, but it was a pointless effort. On February 5, Khomeini asked Mehdi Bazargan to assemble a provisional government—in effect declaring him Iran's provisional prime minister. In the United States, observers were relieved to hear of the appointment, which seemed to vindicate the State Department analysts who had predicted the post-shah era would be dominated by pragmatic moderates.

On February 9 an ultraloyal unit of the shah's Imperial Guard known as the Immortals made a final, heroic stand. But their immortality was no match for the forces lined up against them. At the Doshan-Tappeh Air Force base in Tehran, cadets and technicians mutinied and were quickly joined by Marxist guerrillas—the FeK, MeK, and their offshoots—who helpfully raided the city's weapons factory and distributed guns to the local population. By the next day, thousands of armed volunteers joined forces with the rebels and soundly defeated what was left of the shah's Imperial Guard.

And at ten a.m. on February 11, the shah's top generals—the men Dutch Huyser had so confidently predicted would step in and preserve the status

Revolutionaries cheer the return of Khomeini. Millions poured onto the streets to welcome him back to Iran—perhaps the largest spontaneous gathering in human history.

quo—gathered at a secret location in Tehran and agreed to announce their neutrality. They had no reason, they concluded, to precipitate a civil war on behalf of a shah whom no one wanted—a shah who himself had long ago headed for the exits with his loot. Amid the smoke and ruins of the regime he had tried to save, Shapur Bakhtiar was given the news. Wisely, he slipped into hiding and later fled—with a beard and fake passport—to France.

General Huyser had been dead wrong. This was not 1953, and there was to be no last-minute military "countercoup" that would swoop in to preserve the shah in power. There was no Kermit Roosevelt this time, no Fazlollah Zahedi—no romantic stories about spies being bundled into the Imperial Palace wrapped in blankets. And there was certainly no Shaban the Brainless to rally the slums of south Tehran to defend king and country, using a fat sack of cash from the CIA. For the United States and the shah, the story had long ago run out of happy endings.

At two p.m. on February 11, 1979, the generals' neutrality declaration was read out over the airwaves of Radio Tehran. And at six p.m., as the guns fell silent over the capital city, the government-controlled radio station crackled back to life with an announcement of its own:

"This is the voice of Iran. The voice of true Iran. The voice of the Islamic Revolution."

PART IV

Winter

1979

In the early morning hours of March 5, 1979—exactly three weeks after the victory of the revolution—hundreds of thousands of Iranians did something that would have been inconceivable only a year earlier. They publicly marked the twelfth anniversary of the death of Mohammad Mosaddeq.

Never before had Iranians been allowed to grieve publicly for the old prime minister, and never before had Iran seen a funeral like this. For sixty solid miles, the highway from Tehran to Mosaddeq's burial site in Ahmad Abad transformed into a massive, unbroken daisy chain of cars, crawling bumper to bumper from one of the world's largest cities toward a place too small to even be marked on the map. In the final seven or eight miles approaching the village, traffic became so gridlocked that mourners were forced to abandon their vehicles and complete the journey on foot—a great stream of people tromping through freshly plowed fields, carrying flower wreaths, banners, and bouquets of carnations. By day's end, no one knew just how many people had made the journey to Ahmad Abad, but the country's official newspaper, *Ettela'at*, estimated the crowd at over a million.

In the remote and dusty village where, twelve years earlier, Mosaddeq had passed away quietly—buried under a slab in the dining room by a few family members as Iranian newspapers said almost nothing—the country's most prominent leaders now eulogized him over loudspeakers. "Once upon a time, our national aspirations were stifled by criminals, by gangsters," roared frail but unbreakable Ayatollah Taleqani, who had spent much of the last thirty years in prison for his unwavering devotion to Mosaddeq. "Our bodies were enslaved, but our minds and our thoughts were never enslaved!"

For years, the mere mention of Mosaddeq's name had been enough to land a man in jail. But now, with the shah's elaborate and once-dreaded security apparatus in ruins, the old man was getting the funeral he had so long been denied. It was, for a country that had been through twenty-five years of darkness and dictatorship, a day when gravestones were allowed to speak again—an unforgettable moment of national catharsis.

It was also the first vivid indication that the revolution might mean different things to different people. Barely three weeks since the shah's regime collapsed, the old warhorses of the Mosaddeq movement—liberal, democratically inclined men like Taleqani, Karim Sanjabi, and most important the new provisional prime minister, Mehdi Bazargan—were already lining up to mark their territory. Never a man to steal the limelight, Bazargan refrained from speaking at the funeral, but simply by showing his face at an event honoring Mosaddeq, he was sending a powerful message to Khomeini and to the religious radicals surrounding him. For Bazargan, and for a significant segment of Iran's people, the revolution had been about more than creating a godly republic. It had also been about democracy, human rights, and national liberation.

While the ayatollah was in France, such symbolic statements had seemed unnecessary. Khomeini had demonstrated an extraordinary ability to appeal to multiple constituencies in Iranian society, from liberal nationalists to bazaar traders to Communist intellectuals to rural peasants and urban slum-dwellers. And in January and February, as millions of Iranians rallied to deliver the final blow to the shah's regime, these wildly divergent forces had pulled together heroically. But now that the enemy had been chased from his throne, the internal tensions within the revolution—and the competing visions of those who led it—were slowly surfacing. Even as ecstatic revelers continued to celebrate the departure of the shah in February and March, one of the capital's most important arteries, Pahlavi Avenue, was being referred to by some as "Mosaddeq Avenue" and by others as "Khomeini Avenue." In that gentle, good-natured tug of war alone, any perspicacious Tehran taxi driver could see how the next year was going to go.

For the rest of 1979, the Iranian revolution would face, as all revolutions do, the challenge of creating a new state out of the rubble of the one it had just dismantled. And as the initial euphoria of victory wore off, much of the unity forged in those last glorious months of 1978 would gradually be replaced by a rivalry between hard-line supporters of Khomeini and the more moderate, democratically inclined forces that had helped bring him to power. For the first few months, this rivalry would play itself out as a mainly internal affair. But by the end of 1979, it would develop into an international crisis with implications far greater than anyone could have predicted.

And it would drag the United States into one of the most humiliating episodes in its two-hundred-year history.

To the astute observer, the first signs of a power struggle were already visible in the quiet, leafy gardens of Neauphle-le-Château. Back in October, all the prominent liberals and moderates from Bazargan's Freedom Movement and Sanjabi's National Front had come flocking to France, thinking Khomeini could be their useful idiot—a simple, pious figurehead who would rally the masses to overthrow the shah, then step aside to allow genuine democracy, with a moderately Islamic flavor, to take root under their direction. Though their commitment to the revolution was sincere, Ibrahim Yazdi, Abolhassan Bani-Sadr, Sadeq Qotbzadeh, and others had also believed that Khomeini was incapable of leading the revolution without them. The ayatollah was a man of God, not a politician. If the revolution was to succeed, they believed, he would need their real-world skills—their ability to set up media interviews, negotiate with foreign powers, and eventually form a functioning government. So in Neauphle-le-Château, an unspoken understanding had emerged: Khomeini would provide the inspiration, the leadership, and the foot soldiers for the revolution. The educated liberals and pragmatists, with their advanced graduate degrees from Western universities, would handle the messy details.

In the first weeks following Khomeini's return to Iran, this informal division of labor continued. The ayatollah focused on directing the country's religious affairs—strengthening clerical powers, appointing Friday prayer leaders, building his power base in seminaries—and seemed happy to leave the day-to-day business of government to Bazargan. Bazargan, for his part, ensured that the new provisional government was a paragon of competence and level-headedness, focused on preventing postrevolutionary Iran from descending into anarchy. Almost all the ministers he appointed to his cabinet were members of the Freedom Movement, National Front, or similar parties, with skills and experience directly relevant to their briefs. To ensure some measure of revolutionary fervor, Khomeini decreed that until a new constitution was written, ultimate authority would lie with the Islamic Revolutionary Council (IRC)—a fierce, secretive body composed mostly of hard-line clerics. But in practice, the IRC at this early stage functioned as a board of directors, gently articulating an overall strategy of Islamic wisdom for the government to follow.

From the ashes of revolution, a genuine, working consensus appeared to be emerging—an arrangement that left housing, transportation, and agricultural policy in the hands of clean-shaven, educated liberals in jackets and ties, while bearded revolutionaries worked to ensure that the new republic functioned within a framework of religious and cultural purity. For the first few weeks, both the IRC and the government saw the need for each other, and each respected the other's usefulness to the overall success of the operation. But over time several factors would conspire to drive the two camps apart.

The first was the radicalization of Khomeini's power base. Over the course of 1979, many of the ad hoc citizen militias and revolutionary committees that had sprung up during the revolution began touting themselves as the ayatollah's indispensable foot soldiers, dedicated to preserving the purity of the revolution against those who would water it down. Armed with weapons they had collected during the siege of Tehran's armory, some began referring to themselves as *hezbollahi* (partisans of God)* and went around breaking up meetings and intimidating opponents. Others dispensed vigilante justice or punished those engaged in corruption, profiteering, and "un-Islamic" behavior. Hard-liners on the IRC, meanwhile, became increasingly forceful in the exercise of their supervisory powers over the provisional government—insisting, for example, that cabinet ministers be chosen primarily on the basis of their moral and religious character and their level of revolutionary zeal, rather than their education and experience.

Over time Iran seemed to be ruled by parallel governments. In theory, Bazargan's provisional government was in charge, but its ability to provide day-to-day services was often complicated by grassroots organizations that took the law into their own hands—handing out fines, patrolling neighborhoods, directing traffic, and setting price controls in local markets. At one point, exasperated by all the freelance radicalism, Bazargan tried to lure revolutionary paramilitaries into giving up their weapons and joining a newly reconstituted national police force. But the militiamen refused and instead organized themselves into a special combat unit reporting directly to Khomeini.† Thus, Iran ended up with two sets of uniformed soldiers— the regular army and a fanatical combat brigade full of ragged youth and true believers carrying pictures of the emam close to their chests. Over time the combat brigade was professionalized into an elite fighting force known as the Revolutionary Guards—a force that remains, to this day, the military backbone of the Islamic Republic.

Feeling second-guessed from both above and below, Bazargan com-

---

* This term should not be confused with the Shia political party and militant group Hezbollah founded in Lebanon in 1983. Although the names mean the same thing (and although Hezbollah later received support from Iran), there is no relation between the two. The term was simply an informal way of referring to Khomeini loyalists in the aftermath of the revolution.

† The ayatollah, presented with the idea by the IRC, found it hard to say no. The regular army, after all, was still stuffed with secret shah loyalists, and in April, a shadowy terrorist network began assassinating some of Khomeini's closest associates. During such volatile times, having a parallel military force composed of staunch supporters was reassuring to Khomeini.

plained that Iran was becoming "a city with a hundred sheriffs." But Khomeini's most fervent supporters—those who had listened to all his lectures
and believed he was some sort of messiah—urged him to go further and
faster toward creating an Islamic utopia. Even when Khomeini tried to rein
in their enthusiasm, he could only go so far. These militant activists were his
base—the people who had taken up arms against the Bakhtiar government
and made sure the airport remained open so his flight could land on February 1. To abandon them now would have been an act of political suicide.

Trapped, in some ways, in a cage of his own making, but in other ways
gleefully riding the tiger, Khomeini came to embrace his role as Iran's ultimate source of moral and spiritual authority. And he proved, as ever, to
be a master at the art of remaining above the fray. His message was simple
and appealing, especially to *bazaaris* and the migrant poor. He was uncompromising, his rhetoric was inspiring, and his personal example was one
of simplicity and humility. While Bazargan's government got down and
dirty with the business of running the country, Khomeini and the radicals
skillfully painted themselves as the true guardians of the revolution. In the
public imagination, the moderates who ran the government were always
mired in some messy, protracted dispute—negotiating teachers' salaries or
working out details of electricity generation. And they always seemed eager
to maintain good relations with Western governments. This, in turn, made
it easy for the radicals to portray themselves as lustful revolutionaries and
their liberal rivals as legalistic and overcautious. A favorite term of deri-
sion aimed at the government now was *keravati* ("necktie-wearers," from
the French *cravate*)—the implication being that Bazargan and his ministers
were merely a reincarnation of the well-dressed, Westernized technocrats of
the previous regime.

Here, perhaps, was one of the greatest ironies of the revolution. In just
a few short weeks, Khomeini had learned the one simple lesson the shah
had consistently failed to absorb during his thirty-seven years in power. He
had learned how to be a father-figure to the nation—a charismatic leader
reflecting the values of his people and setting the overall tone for policy,
while letting his government take the blame for unpopular decisions. He
had learned to reign and not rule.

The second major factor driving a wedge between Bazargan and Khomeini was the intransigence of the Iranian left. While Bazargan argued that
the revolution was over and that it was time for reconstruction to begin, the
various Marxist, Maoist, and leftist guerrilla groups that had spent the 1970s
in armed combat against the shah argued that the revolution had merely
been the opening act for a second, far more ambitious, revolution—one
that would transfer power to the long-suffering proletariat. While Bazargan

pledged to work within the existing administrative machinery of the state and introduce reforms gradually, leftists agitated for a radical, immediate break from the past—complete with a redistribution of wealth, nationalization of land and industries, and the creation of a "people's army." Bazargan begged the radicals to understand the importance of incremental progress, declaring in one speech that he was not a "bulldozer" but a "passenger car" that "must ride on a smooth, asphalted road." But the left was having none of it. Much like the radical Islamists, radical leftists believed their efforts had been indispensable in bringing about the revolution, and they felt the moderates were frittering away their hard-fought victories.

Thus a curious, sometimes uneasy, alliance emerged as hard-line religious fundamentalists and hard-line leftists united in radicalism and in their hatred for Bazargan's cautious approach.[*] Every time the government and the Khomeinist camp disagreed, leftists sided with Khomeini—disparaging the government for what they perceived as its spinelessness and excessive caution. Eventually, the leftists and Khomeinists would fall out spectacularly. But in these crucial first six months, the partisans of God and the partisans of Marx were inseparable.

☙

The first overt confrontation between moderates and radicals came over the issue of revolutionary justice. During the days and weeks that followed February 11, hastily arranged revolutionary courts (often presided over by Sadeq Khalkhali, the notorious "hanging judge") dragged dozens of the shah's former henchmen before tribunals to face charges of treason, sabotage, and "crimes against the people"—enthusiastically handing out guilty verdicts and sending dozens to the firing squad. Former prime minister Hoveida was their most famous victim—his cold carcass, stippled with bullet holes, providing a dramatic image for the front page of the morning papers. But the liberals in Bazargan's government were horrified. They accepted that a certain measure of bloodletting was natural after a revolution. But they felt that revolutionary tribunals should be conducted with due process and transparency, demonstrating to the world the mercy and compassion of Islamic justice. After a little arm-twisting, Khomeini agreed and instructed the courts to show restraint. But the disagreements were only just beginning.

---

[*] More precisely, one faction of the FeK joined with Tudeh to support Khomeini outright, while the MeK was more circumspect, preferring to follow its own independent agenda. But the MeK, too, refused to support Bazargan's government, accusing it of being too eager to compromise with the "imperialists" of the West.

In March 1979 the provisional government organized a national referendum on the question of whether Iran should formally abolish the monarchy and declare itself an "Islamic republic." Bazargan urged Khomeini to consider the term "Islamic *Democratic* Republic," but the ayatollah refused, arguing that Islam was inherently democratic and did not need to be explained or qualified. ("Islam does not need adjectives," he later said. "Islam is everything, it means everything.") The ballot papers of March 31 presented the public with a yes-or-no question: "Shall the former regime be replaced with an Islamic republic, whose constitution will be approved by the people?" It was a difficult question to say no to. Out of 21 million eligible adults, 20 million turned out to vote. And of those, 98.2 percent gave their approval. There were no indications of electoral fraud, and only a few marginal groups called for a boycott. Iranians had voted resoundingly to become an Islamic republic.

With a clear public mandate to press ahead, the revolutionary authorities turned their attention to drafting a new constitution. And once again divisions arose. The government came up with a liberal-minded document similar to the existing 1906 constitution, only with no mention of a shah. But radicals complained to the ayatollah, and discussions became heated and divisive and dragged on over several weeks. Finally an election was called for an "Assembly of Experts"—a constitutional convention that could hammer out the thornier questions. But during the July election campaign for the assembly, liberals accused radicals of attempting to hijack the process and called—perhaps foolishly—for a boycott. The result was an Assembly of Experts in which fifty-five of the seventy-three seats went to religious hard-liners.

The Assembly of Experts, in radical hands, spent August, September, and October drafting a far more religiously oriented constitution than the one the liberals had drafted. *Velayat-e-faqih*—Khomeini's transformative philosophy of "theological stewardship"—was put forward as a foundational principle, meaning Khomeini would have the power to act as an omniscient spiritual guide over all the nation's affairs. The assembly also proposed a Guardian Council of clerics and legal scholars, with the power to veto legislation.* As a concession to Bazargan and his allies, the draft constitution also contained liberal elements, such as special protections for Iran's tiny Jewish, Christian, and Zoroastrian communities. Freedoms of speech, assembly, religion, and press were guaranteed, along with gender equality. And for the first time in history, Iran was to have a directly elected

---

* The 1906 constitution had contained a provision for a Guardian Council along exactly these lines, but it had never gone into effect.

president as well as prime minister. Despite these concessions, the liberals had been badly outmaneuvered.

The draft constitution was, in the final analysis, a mongrel document—a series of compromise measures cobbled together to keep both liberals and hard-line Islamists happy. On virtually every major constitutional question that came before them, the framers split the difference, honoring both the rights and liberties of the individual (in line with Western political tradition) and the spiritual obligations of Muslims (as laid out by Quranic law). On the most important question of all—sovereignty—the constitution was downright contradictory. Article 6 explicitly stated: "the affairs of the country must be administered on the basis of public opinion expressed by means of elections." But at the same time, the constitution had much rosaceous talk of divine revelation and *velayat-e-faqih*, and Article 110 left overall supervision of the system in the hands of the "theological steward" (i.e., Khomeini).

Over the next forty years, this extraordinary hybrid document would give rise to a political system that was as baffling and maddening to the Iranian nation itself as it was to outsiders. In the best of times, it would bring liberal democracy and Islamic scripture into creative symbiosis, fusing seemingly incompatible values into a unique laboratory of Islamic democracy. In the worst of times, it would bring confusion, contradiction, and political gridlock.

CR

Over the spring and summer of 1979, as moderate government technocrats argued with their hot-headed rivals over revolutionary courts, referenda, and the shape of the new constitution, the foreign policy of the Islamic Republic—especially the thorny question of relations with the United States—remained something of a blank slate. A few dozen hapless American souls still beavered away in the bowels of the U.S. embassy, the building now reinforced with rows of sandbags and bulletproof glass. But their relationship with the new regime was not yet clear. During the giddiest hours of the revolution, anti-American rhetoric had soared. But Iranian politics was also full of pragmatic figures who saw no reason for an antagonistic relationship with the United States and who were actively exploring ways to create a cordial modus vivendi. When it came to relations with America, however, one overriding anxiety did keep Iranians awake at night: the memory of 1953. As Iran's new leaders struggled to ensure the survival of their revolution and to assert control domestically, they were haunted—even obsessed—by fear that American spies might be cooking up some daring plot to whisk the shah back into power, as they had done twenty-five years earlier.

The power of this fear as a motivating factor for Iranians in 1979 is almost impossible to overstate. The one thing all the bickering revolutionaries had in common—whether conservative clerics, liberal nationalists, or Marxists—was that they had come of age during the premiership of Mohammad Mosaddeq. As youngsters, their defining experience in politics had been getting swept up in the euphoria of that historic moment of national self-determination, only to wake up one morning and find tanks in the streets and the shah cheerfully returning from exile with the help of the CIA. More than anything else, this was the demon that haunted the Iranian psyche in 1979. And more than anything else, this was the demon that America's leaders could not afford to ignore.

But ignore it they did. In the weeks and months that followed the revolution, the United States consistently gave Iranians the impression it was unsympathetic to their beloved revolution and wanted to see it overturned. In Tehran, virtually every foreign diplomat paid a courtesy visit to Khomeini during the weeks following his return from exile, but Washington conspicuously forbade its ambassador, William Sullivan, to take such action. As European governments forged new ties with the Islamic Republic, much of official Washington—from political pundits to Capitol Hill—displayed a curious unwillingness to acknowledge that power had changed hands. Many American leaders seemed unable to take Khomeini seriously, or they continued to operate out of a latent sense of loyalty to the shah. On Sunday-morning TV shows, prominent pro-Pahlavi politicians, led by Sen. Henry "Scoop" Jackson, regularly pontificated on the inevitability that the Ayatollah's regime would collapse under the weight of its own fanaticism. In *The New York Times*, former undersecretary of state George Ball compared Khomeini to Robespierre, confidently predicting that "sooner or later, he will be replaced as the Iranian people increasingly comprehend his incapacity to run a complex economy."

None of this went unnoticed in Tehran. If there was one thing Iranians were looking for from the United States at this sensitive moment, it was a signal that it accepted Khomeini's leadership and the will of the Iranian people. But this was the one thing America never gave. Instead, throughout the spring and summer of 1979, the Carter administration ignored Khomeini and reached out quietly to key moderates in Bazargan's provisional government. U.S. officials held several informal meetings with Bazargan's chief aide, Abbas Amir Entezam, to discuss shared concerns about Soviet infiltration in Iran. And throughout the year, U.S. officials remained in communication with Foreign Minister Ebrahim Yazdi.* But they never approached either Khomeini or the IRC directly.

For Washington, this strategy was logical. The moderates, after all, spoke the same language as Americans, both literally and figuratively. They were fluent in English, they understood the complexities of international politics, and they didn't turn up to meetings wearing turbans and fatigues. With their Western business suits and their level-headed statements, they were the acceptable face of the revolution, and they seemed prepared to work with the United States on common areas of concern. But this strategy of focusing on moderates at the expense of radicals would soon backfire. When radicals around Khomeini became aware that their moderate rivals were meeting with Americans, they grew suspicious. Since Washington had yet to contact Khomeini or issue a clear statement welcoming the revolution, there seemed no reason for such meetings to be taking place. And as the summer progressed, the radicals deftly turned this into a wedge issue in their turf battle against moderates, convincing both Khomeini and the Iranian public that Bazargan's provisional government was untrustworthy. Thus, over time, the American strategy was self-defeating, undermining the authority of the very people with whom Washington was hoping to forge a relationship.

വ

At least part of the explanation for the unfriendly posture of American officials toward Iran in 1979 lay in the kind of information they were getting. In the weeks and months following the revolution, the U.S. government relied heavily on a circle of prominent Pahlavi exiles that was beginning to congregate in Washington. As they arrived in the United States, these exiles were reunited with old friends like former secretary of state Henry Kissinger and Chase Manhattan president David Rockefeller,† who helped them navigate the complex Washington influence circuit. Together they argued vociferously that America should take a harder line against the revolution—and show no mercy toward the "criminals" who had taken power in Tehran.

---

* Yazdi had earned his bachelor's degree from Baylor University, had lived in the United States for eighteen years, and was a familiar face around Washington.

† Since 1954, Chase Manhattan had served as the principal banker for the Pahlavi state—handling, over the course of twenty-five years, more than $200 billion of profits accruing from Iran's vast oil wealth. The shah was thus one of Rockefeller's oldest and most valued customers. But he was also a friend of the family. Rockefeller's older brother, former vice president Nelson Rockefeller, had been particularly close to the shah.

In the spring and summer of 1979, Kissinger mounted a vigorous public campaign accusing gutless liberals in the State Department of having
"lost Iran"—a campaign that certain segments of the media joined with
gusto. Newspaper editorials blasted Carter for "desert[ing] the Shah and his
regime at a time when he needed support" and allowing Iran to "fall into the
clutches of wild men." Khomeini, meanwhile, was a "dangerous dingbat"
and a "vindictive old man" who should never be "appeased" by the United
States. In this polarized atmosphere, the Carter administration was unlikely
to make a gesture of conciliation to the Islamic Republic.

Carter's problems were exacerbated by the fact that there were very
few Americans left in Iran who could provide him with an accurate assessment of what was happening. During the revolution, the U.S. embassy had
recalled all but the most essential staff, turning one of the largest U.S. diplomatic missions in the world from a bustling beehive of more than a thousand employees into a ghost town staffed by barely fifty. America's civilian
contractors had also headed for the exits. (Of the three thousand Americans
working for Bell Helicopter, only one chose to remain in Iran.) By June
1979, the American community in Iran, which had numbered close to fifty
thousand the year before, was down to a mere three hundred. To make matters worse, Carter, under Brzezinski's influence, had concluded that Ambassador Sullivan had very little of value to offer, and he was routinely ignoring
his advice. At the beginning of April, Sullivan himself packed it in and
headed off to a quiet retirement in Mexico.

Thus, at one of the most critical moments in the history of the bilateral relationship, the United States had virtually no meaningful channels of
information about Iran. Day after day, the State Department scrambled to
educate itself, bombarding the Tehran embassy with endless lists of questions about the people who had come to power. At one point, exasperated
Washington officials were reduced to reading newspapers just to find out
what was going on. "We simply do not have the bios, inventory of political groups, or current picture of daily life as it evolves at various levels in
Iran," complained desk officer Henry Precht in July. "Ignorance here of
Iran's events is massive." With such an enormous information deficit crippling the bureaucracy, the pro-Pahlavi lobby in Washington found it easy to
influence the debate in ways that suited its political agenda.

As summer turned to autumn, the rhetoric and posturing in both Iran
and the United States were developing momentum. But still, with a little
delicate maneuvering and skillful diplomacy, a civilized working relationship between the two countries could have been achieved. In early October,
on the sidelines of the UN General Assembly meeting in New York, Foreign

Minister Yazdi sat down with his counterpart Cyrus Vance and a number of U.S. military officials, and discussed areas of potential cooperation—most notably their shared concerns about Soviet activity in the region. Vance assured Yazdi that the United States considered the shah to be finished, and Yazdi explained how much it would help if the United States made some public statement to that effect. The meetings were cordial and constructive, and all present felt that, with the passage of time and the cooling of revolutionary passions, the United States and the Islamic Republic might well find common ground.

What no one counted on, however, was just how quickly this atmosphere of diplomatic civility could deteriorate. Or just how much still depended on the man once known as the King of Kings.

∞

Back in January, when the shah departed Iran, his intention had been to fly directly to the United States, where the Carter administration had promised him asylum. Had he done so, at the height of the chaos and jubilation, the world today might be a very different place. As was so often the case with the shah, however, indecision, delay, and hesitation had quickly taken over. Rather than accept Carter's offer immediately, the shah had gone with his family to Egypt on January 16, then to Morocco, convincing himself that the revolution might still be overturned and that he should remain in the region. After a month, however, he had given up on this fanciful notion and decided he just wanted a quiet life. On February 22—five and a half weeks after his escape from Tehran—he sent a note to the U.S. ambassador in Morocco, indicating he was ready to accept Carter's invitation. But by then, circumstances had changed.

One week earlier a group of overexcited Marxists had charged into the U.S. embassy in Tehran and occupied it for three hours, convinced that the Americans were hiding fugitives from the shah's regime somewhere on the premises. The next day another unruly mob stormed the Moroccan embassy, demanding the shah be expelled from his Marrakesh hideout and returned to Iran to face trial. Both situations were quickly defused, thanks to a forceful intervention by Khomeini. But U.S. officials put two and two together, realizing that there was now no hotter political potato on earth than the former shah of Iran.

What American diplomats were finally beginning to understand was the driving, overwhelming obsession of Iran's revolutionaries: their determination to avoid a repeat of 1953. Fresh in the mind of every Iranian revolutionary was the memory of how the shah had cooled his heels in Baghdad and Rome while the CIA dispensed with Mosaddeq—then flew him back in to inflict twenty-five years of dictatorship on his people. In 1979 no one in Iran wanted to risk that again. Slowly but surely, the realization set in among the American diplomatic corps that they were facing more than just a routine, rational matter of foreign policy. They were dealing with a deep psychic wound—an existential fear of foreign plotting. When Ambassador Sullivan was informed on February 22 that the shah had requested permission to enter the United States, he made it abundantly clear what he thought of this dangerous proposition: "If they let him in, they will bring us out in boxes," he growled through the telephone at Henry Precht.

Carter agreed. As president, he said privately to his advisers, he was not about to take the risk of Americans getting killed or kidnapped in Tehran, just so the shah could "play tennis in the United States." But unfortunately for the president, the political reality was more complicated. Throughout the spring of 1979, Carter came under tremendous pressure, both from Brzezinski inside his administration and from Kissinger and the Republicans outside, to grant asylum to the former monarch as a gesture of gratitude for his decades of loyal friendship to the United States. To refuse, Brzezinski argued, would reflect poorly on America's reputation. Leaders like Anwar Sadat of Egypt and the Saudi royal family—stalwart allies despite constant overtures from Moscow—would be watching to see how Washington handled this situation. But Carter stood firm. "If we let in the shah, and our embassy employees in Tehran are taken hostage, what will your advice be to me then?" he asked at one particularly testy meeting. His advisers responded with awkward silence. "I thought so," he said, visibly irritated.

In Morocco, the U.S. ambassador was assigned the unpleasant task of breaking the news to the shah. He was told to explain—as tactfully as possible—that although *technically* the invitation was still open, the president now considered it a potential risk to America's national security and would be grateful if His Imperial Majesty would consider going somewhere else for the time being.

What followed was an epic—and sometimes rather demeaning—year of globe-trotting for the former monarch. From Morocco, he moved on to the Bahamas, where he stayed in a rented villa in the Paradise Island resort, becoming an unexpected curiosity for gawking tourists and foreign gossip columnists. From there it was on to Cuernavaca, Mexico, where a more private walled compound was found for him and the imperial family. After a while, their peregrinations took on a surreal quality, as they moved—complete with several planeloads of furniture, valuables, family members, valets, butlers, dogs, and assorted hangers-on—from one sun-drenched holiday destination to another, never quite finding a nation that was prepared to give them permanent asylum.[*]

On October 18, 1979, however, the game of musical countries took a deadly serious turn. Late that night the Iran desk at the U.S. State Department received an unexpected message from a physician whom the shah's old friend David Rockefeller had hired to attend to his medical needs in Mexico. The shah had cancer. And he was asking to be treated in an American hospital.

♋

When two French doctors told the shah in 1974 that he was suffering from a rare and poorly understood lymphatic condition, he had taken great care not to allow news of the illness to become public. As a precaution, he had begun preparing his son for the kingship, sending the seventeen-year-old Prince Reza to an air force academy in Texas to learn the family trade. But he had kept the condition of his lymph nodes a closely guarded secret. Even Empress Farah, who had been told privately of the diagnosis by the doctors, never heard mention of it from her husband's own lips. The shah's twin sister, Princess Ashraf, didn't know until early in 1979. Foreign ambassadors in Tehran in the 1970s sometimes heard vague rumors about the king's health, but none had any idea there was anything seriously wrong with him.

Thus the request to admit the shah for medical treatment came as something of a shock to the Carter administration. But it also presented a conundrum. Carter had made it clear in February he believed the shah's admission would pose a threat to the safety of Americans in Iran. But seven months had now elapsed since that decision, and in the intervening time, the president had come under relentless pressure to change his mind— particularly from Republicans who were gearing up to make the president's "weakness" over Iran into a major issue in the 1980 presidential election. By August, several members of the administration—including Vice Presi-

---

* Paraguay and South Africa initially came forward with offers of asylum, but the shah deemed both nations beneath his dignity. In the 1970s, Paraguay was still seen as a rather far-flung South American backwater with a reputation as the final refuge for the world's most notorious scoundrels, dictators, thugs, and criminals. And South Africa was even more of a pariah. Neither nation had much to lose in making the offer. Since one of the first acts of the Islamic Republic in February had been to cut ties with Pretoria—in protest against apartheid—the South Africans had no embassy that could be attacked. And Paraguay had never had an embassy in Tehran. For the shah, however, the prospect of spending the rest of his days in either country was unacceptable. Paraguay was simply a humiliation, and South Africa had the added painful symbolism of being the country to which the British had exiled his father in 1941.

Grand finale: The deposed king in exile in Mexico, 1979. Few countries were willing to give permanent refuge to the shah, for fear of reprisals from Tehran's new leadership, so the royal family traveled from country to country. Eventually an urgent cancer diagnosis persuaded Carter to allow the shah into the United States—a decision that changed the course of history.

dent Walter Mondale—were suggesting that some discreet way should be found to admit the shah, perhaps in exchange for a public renunciation of his claim to the throne. Now, with the news that the shah was in physical distress, momentum shifted noticeably in favor of this position. The president's chief aide Hamilton Jordan—always focused on the political bottom line—put the case succinctly at one White House meeting. "If the shah dies in Mexico, can you imagine the field day Kissinger will have with that?" he asked. "He'll say that first you caused the shah's downfall and now you've killed him."

The Iranians, of course, had a different reaction. To them, the shah was a criminal, and over the past months they had made many strenuous attempts to bring him back to Iran to face trial. So when the U.S. *chargé* in Tehran, Bruce Laingen, told Prime Minister Bazargan and Foreign Minister Yazdi of the shah's condition, they were incredulous. The idea that the sixty-year-old was on the verge of death was news to them as much as it was to anyone else, and they had trouble taking it seriously. At the very least, they suggested, the timing of the shah's sudden need for medical treatment in the United States was suspicious. "Even if you convince *us* of your humanitarian motives," they told Laingen, "you will never convince the Iranian people."

Bazargan suggested the shah's condition should be verified by doctors chosen by the authorities in Tehran. The White House refused. Brzezinski felt such a move would call into question the credibility of the United States. And anyway the shah, understandably, had made it clear he did not want his body, or even his medical records, examined by doctors from the Islamic Republic. There was thus very little left to discuss. President Carter now felt that if the shah's health was truly rapidly declining, it would be unseemly for the United States not to admit its longtime ally for treatment. Late on Sunday, October 21, Carter gave the order that would change the course of history: *Admit the shah.*

As Laingen communicated the news to Yazdi, he had a question: Could the United States still count on Iran to guarantee the security of the U.S. embassy in Tehran, as it had done back in February? Yazdi replied that of course Iran would take every conceivable step to comply with its international obligations. But he also warned Laingen that this time the task might be more challenging. News of the shah's admission to the United States might unleash forces beyond the government's ability to control. "You are playing with fire," Yazdi said glumly to his American counterpart. "You are opening Pandora's box."

Neither man knew just how prophetic those words would turn out to be.

C3

Late in the evening of October 22, 1979, a chartered Gulfstream jet carrying the shah and the imperial family landed at New York's La Guardia Airport. The shah was driven straight to New York Hospital–Cornell Medical Center in Manhattan, where he was checked in under a false name and given a two-room suite on the seventeenth floor—along with several more rooms for his family and entourage, and an entire hallway of heavily armed private security. He underwent a battery of tests on his gallbladder, spleen, and lymph nodes—all of which were badly deteriorated.

Initially, reaction on the streets of Iran was relatively restrained. A number of angry newspaper editorials appeared, and a few fiery demonstrations were held in front of the U.S. embassy, but most Iranians went about their lives, and U.S. officials—who had braced for an overwhelming physical assault on the United States—relaxed and told themselves the worst was over.

Over the next several days, however, outrage steadily built. On October 24, New York Hospital's head pathologist held a press conference announcing that the shah should stay in New York and receive chemotherapy for at least six months and "perhaps a year and a half." For Iranians, who had been led to believe the shah was at death's door, this was yet another provocation—"proof," as if any were needed, that the whole "cancer" thing had been merely a subtext for a sinister American plot to give refuge to the hated shah, in preparation for a coup that would return him to power. Across the country, demonstrations grew louder, larger, angrier. At the religious festival of Eid e-Qorban, dozens of ayatollahs preached angrily against America's perfidy. Finally, on November 1, at the start of the weekend, Iran erupted. A massive, unprecedented anti-American demonstration rolled through virtually every city and town, complete with flag burnings and chants of "Khomeini is our leader, America is our enemy!" In Tehran alone, one million people spent the day venting their anger with the United States.

As promised, the provisional government did everything it could to avoid an international incident. Police were instructed to reroute demonstrations away from the area around the U.S. embassy. But it was an uphill battle. All day demonstrators tried to push past police barricades and make a run for the embassy. For Bazargan, Yazdi, and the government, wedded to a legalistic, principled vision of politics, this was an important test of credibility—a chance to demonstrate to the world that the new Iran was a nation of law and order that could express its grievances without violating international norms. What they didn't realize was just how quickly they, themselves, would be thrown to the wolves.

Later that evening Iran's national nightly news bulletin showed footage of the day's demonstrations. But it also aired film showing something few viewers could have expected to see: Prime Minister Bazargan and Foreign Minister Yazdi in Algiers, shaking hands with—of all people—U.S. national security adviser Zbigniew Brzezinski. Bazargan and Yazdi—like leaders from all over the world—had been in the Algerian capital that morning, celebrating the twenty-fifth anniversary of that country's declaration of independence. While there, they had taken the opportunity to meet their American counterparts and continue discussions begun the previous month at the UN. The timing could not have been worse. At the precise moment when Iranians were united in anger against America, millions of them switched on their televisions to witness their own prime minister—meek, mild-mannered, smartly dressed, gracious, and altogether accommodating—shaking hands with the devil.

The hard-line pro-Khomeini camp sensed that a historic opportunity had arrived. And it had arrived far more quickly than they could have expected. For the first time since Khomeini and Bazargan swept to victory back in February, the Iranian public was being shown—in vivid color on their television screens—the contrast between the kind of leadership each man offered. For the radicals, it was hard to imagine that life could get any better than this.

But it did.

❧

For the previous two weeks, a small group of students from Tehran's five major universities—furious about the U.S. decision to admit the shah— had been meeting secretly to discuss the possibility of staging an act of civil disobedience at the U.S. embassy. In between lectures, in teahouses, slipping one another notes in the corridors of dormitories, they had egged one another on with wild stories about how they would storm the twenty- seven-acre compound and detain its employees for a day or two—maybe even *three* days. Once they had the attention of the world, they thought, they could read a communiqué protesting the decision to admit the shah, as well as the history of American "imperialism" in Iran. "The idea," one of the students recalled in her memoirs, "was to make a gesture, a bold statement."

In their enthusiasm, some of the students had been doing reconnais- sance, scoping out the embassy with binoculars from nearby rooftops, pretending to apply for U.S. visas so they could get a better look at the building, and even drawing up maps of the compound. But as they debated what to do next, they were stymied by a predictably student-like lack of unanimity about whether it made sense to proceed.* And in the revolution- ary atmosphere of Tehran, this harebrained scheme, cooked up by a handful of radicalized students with a little too much time on their hands, might easily have disappeared, like the dozens of other ideas being floated through dorm rooms and student cafeterias, into a miasma of second thoughts, petty disputes, and general postadolescent apathy. In their more level-headed moments, the students recognized they were talking about an illegal act and that the police would surely kick them off the premises within a few hours. Their only hope of success, they concluded, would be to somehow enlist the support of a senior figure in the revolutionary leadership—perhaps even Khomeini himself. And since no one was quite sure how to go about

---

* The group's leadership council consisted of five students, only three of whom felt it was a good idea to take on the United States in such a dramatic fashion. The other two—including a wiry engineering student by the name of Mahmud Ahmadinejad—were dead set against it. Ahmadine- jad kept insisting Iran's real enemy was not America but the godless Marxists of the Soviet Union and the militant hordes of leftists infesting the country's college campuses. He lost the argument that day, and the other students moved ahead without him—unaware that the man they were overruling would one day be their president.

doing that, the consensus emerged that they were probably wasting their time.

But then on November 2, the day after the nationwide anti-American demonstrations, an announcement read out over the radio provided new inspiration. It was Iran's first annual "Student Day"—an occasion established to commemorate undergraduates who had been gunned down by the shah's security forces the previous year. As part of his tribute to the fallen, Khomeini urged Iran's student population to "expand with full force their attacks against America"—and not let up until the United States was "compelled to extradite the criminal, deposed shah." It was just one line in a short and otherwise unremarkable speech. But for the students, still on the fence about whether to proceed with their escapade, it was all they needed to hear.

ဘ

On the morning of November 4, 1979, more than 150 undergraduates broke through the gates of the U.S. embassy on Taleqani Avenue, using nothing more than a pair of bolt-cutters one of the students had concealed under her chador. Inspired by footage of the American civil rights movement that they had seen growing up, they told the startled Americans they were there to stage a "sit-in." The fresh-faced U.S. Marine Corps guardsmen didn't see it that way, but their superiors instructed them to hold fire and avoid doing anything that would escalate tensions.

Within a few hours, the entire place was overrun. Hundreds more students appeared, climbing over the brick wall, running through the grounds, whooping and cheering—visibly delirious at what they were getting away with. Amid the chaos and cacophony, strips of white cloth were used to blindfold and bind the U.S. staff, who—vastly outnumbered—knew they had little choice but to surrender. After a brief standoff and a few heated arguments, the students emerged victorious. Sixty-three American citizens were now hostages in their own embassy.

Ibrahim Yazdi, who had flown in from Algiers that morning, immediately boarded a helicopter for Qom to inform the ayatollah, hoping to persuade him to restore order. Neither man was terribly surprised that the shah's admission to the United States had resulted in a situation of this kind, and Yazdi assumed Khomeini would order the students to disperse, as he had done nine months earlier. This time, however, Yazdi—and the United States of America—were out of luck. The hot-headed militants who had stormed the embassy back in February had been FeK guerrillas, secular Marxists with a vision of the revolution very different from that of Khomeini. This time, though, it was the ayatollah's own devoted followers who were causing the trouble. Moreover, circumstances had changed dramatically over the past nine months. On February 14, the revolution had been just three days old. Khomeini and Bazargan had still been working as an effective team, and the ayatollah had been happy to defer to the prime minister's wishes when it came to such legalistic matters as the protection of foreign embassies. Now, however, it was Bazargan himself who seemed the biggest obstacle to Khomeini's radical vision for Iran.

Over the next few hours, as news of the students' action filtered out to the public, large crowds gathered outside the embassy to show their support and chant anti-American slogans. Prominent religious leaders took to the airwaves to congratulate the students, calling the siege an exemplary act of self-sacrifice that every Iranian could learn from. Congratulatory phone calls poured in from the far corners of the country—lighting up the switchboard at the U.S. embassy (now delightedly manned by Iranian students who could scarcely believe what was happening). Something about the audacity, idealism, and sheer guts of the students had captured the public imagination at a time when anger with the United States was at its peak.

This was the moment when Khomeini the man of God became Khomeini the politician. At a meeting with government employees the next morning, and on radio and television the following day, he declared with satisfaction that Iran was witnessing "another revolution, even greater than the first"—and that America "could do nothing about it." The so-called U.S. embassy in Tehran, he added for good measure, was merely a "center of espionage and plotting" and thus, by implication, a legitimate target. "We demand the return of the great criminal shah from the United States," he said in one radio broadcast. "America must return him to us."

Bazargan was horrified. For months he had tolerated the steady drift toward extremism, thinking if he could just temper it with a bit of legal propriety and liberal democracy, the revolution could find a happy medium between its headstrong ideology and the real-world success he believed it deserved. But this was the final straw. Refusing to be part of a government that gave its approval to a blatant violation of international law, the prime minister tendered his resignation on the morning of November 6. He was followed by Yazdi and almost every member of the provisional government.

This left Khomeini in an unexpectedly strong position. The Assembly of Experts was not quite finished hammering out the draft constitution—and the country was still a few weeks away from the referendum that would ratify the document. With no prime minister, no provisional government, and no written constitution, power devolved, by default, to the Islamic Revolutionary Council—the kitchen cabinet of hard-line clerics who took

Captured U.S. officials on the first day of the hostage crisis.

their cues mostly from Khomeini. Thanks to an unexpected intervention by a handful of overexcited undergraduates, the ayatollah had emerged, at least temporarily, in near-total control of Iran.

And that was only the beginning.

cs

By agreeing to admit the shah, Carter had given Khomeini, and the radicals around him, the greatest gift they could ever have asked for. In November 1979 the Iranian revolutionary juggernaut had been showing serious signs of running out of steam. After a year of instability, the economy was in shambles. Trade was down, oil production had fallen from 5.9 million barrels a day to just 1.3 million, and unemployment approached 30 percent. The streets of Tehran were seeing pitched battles between leftist and Islamist militias. The Kurdish minority in the northwest and Arab tribes along the Persian Gulf coast were mounting ongoing militant uprisings. And the Iraqi army was busy provoking border skirmishes, prodding at Iran's weakened defenses to find out what it could get away with.

As Iranian voters prepared to go to the polls and decide the fate of the constitution, in other words, the last thing the ayatollah had needed was his own prime minister campaigning against him. What he had needed was a Pearl Harbor moment—a despicable outrage that would unleash a wave of patriotic, revolutionary fervor and keep the attention of Iranians focused on the dangers posed by external enemies. And he got exactly that—courtesy, no less, of his old arch-enemies the United States of America and Moham-mad Reza Pahlavi.[*]

Khomeini was now firmly in control of the Iranian revolution. And officials in Washington now realized just how glaringly short-sighted the last nine months of American policy toward Iran had been. Rather than engage directly with the man who led the revolution and was the ultimate arbiter of power in Iran, the United States had pinned all its hopes on mod-erates like Bazargan and Yazdi. Now these moderates had proved to have very little influence over the direction of events. In fact, when push came to shove, they turned out to have very little influence over their own jobs.

Thus on November 4, 1979, the U.S. government found itself in a rather awkward position. Not only were sixty-three of its employees being held against their will on the grounds of their own embassy, but there was now literally no one in Iran whom the State Department could pick up the phone and talk to.

cs

And so it began. "The American Embassy in *Tehran* is in the hands of *Mos-lem students* tonight," came the sonorous announcement from Lesley Stahl on NBC News that Sunday night—followed, within hours, by similar headlines in newspapers, wire services, and radio news bulletins.

At first, most Americans took only a mild interest in the embassy stand-off, dismissing it as just another "crisis" on some godforsaken foreign shore. But as the days wore on—and as Iran insisted it would not let the captives go until the shah was returned—it became increasingly apparent this was not going to be a flash-in-the-pan news story. Across America, on trains and buses, in elevators, in company cafeterias and break rooms, people asked each other about "the ayatollah" and the "situation in Iran." No one knew it at the time—not the public, not the media, not even the White House—but the United States had embarked on one of the most turbulent, trauma-tizing and unforgettable episodes in its two-hundred-year history.

Four days into the crisis, ABC News raised the temperature with a special series of half-hour programs called *America Held Hostage*. Ratings

---

[*] Given just how cleanly everything worked out for the ayatollah, some chroniclers have assumed Khomeini knew in advance about the attack on the U.S. embassy and looked the other way—or even that he somehow "engineered" the entire thing. But the bulk of evidence suggests this was not the case. Rather, Khomeini, like the radicals around him, saw the rising tide of anti-Americanism as an excellent opportunity to weaken and suppress his domestic opposition—and very skillfully seized upon it.

soared, and ABC—deciding to keep running the series until the hostages were released—turned what might have been a sober and serious overseas news story into a full-blown national psychodrama. Every night at eleven-thirty p.m., *America Held Hostage* opened with a dramatic title card showing a blindfolded embassy employee along with the number of days the hostages had been held. The broadcast was full of weeping American mothers, outraged man-on-the-street interviews, and live satellite feeds from Tehran.[*] "When I watch TV, the news, and I see what they do to that flag," said one New Jersey longshoreman interviewed during the first week of the program, "it gets me in the heart." His was the voice of the American everyman in 1979—wounded, proud, and tired of seeing his country pushed around.

In Iran as well, the students' action reawakened the national psyche in ways no one could have predicted. Within days, sacks of mail arrived at the gates of the U.S. embassy—cards and letters from the farthest reaches of Iran, congratulating the students on their bravery and patriotism. By the end of November, the phone bank at the embassy was so inundated with calls that the bewildered students were forced to devise a rota system, just to cope with the twenty-four-hour barrage of ringing bells and blinking lights. For the students, who had planned only for a two- or three-day sit-in, the prolonged exposure to national stardom was unexpected. At times it was downright humbling. One afternoon in mid-November, a group of three hundred farmers from Varamin—ragged, toothless, and carrying pitchforks and shovels—turned up at the embassy gates. They had walked barefoot for thirty-five miles just to tell the students how proud they were.

Twenty-five years after a plot launched in the bowels of the U.S. embassy had crushed their national aspirations, it seemed, Iranians desperately needed something like this—a symbolic act that might even the score for the humiliation of 1953. But it was not just a simple matter of revenge. In the memoirs and testimonies of the students—and in those of the politicians who egged them on—the one theme that consistently emerges is how determined they were to prevent a *repeat* of 1953. At the forefront of everyone's mind in Iran, whether radical students or mainstream politicians and clerics, was that the United States might once again use its embassy to launch a plot.

The U.S. embassy compound, in the Iranian imagination, was a potent source of risk and anxiety—a living, breathing intelligence asset that at any minute could be activated and used against them. While the students and their supporters were probably sincere when they said they wanted the shah

---

[*] The program, presented by a young Ted Koppel, was eventually renamed *Nightline* and became a regular part of the ABC lineup.

returned to Iran for trial, and an apology from the United States for past actions, first and foremost they saw their occupation as a way of leveling the playing field. This, more than anything else, was why it went on for days—and then for weeks, then months. As long as they were in control of the building, the Iranians reasoned, America could not use it as an operating base. It was like a crude insurance policy—the only way to be sure the revolution survived and was not undermined from abroad.

For the first time in twenty-five years, it was clear what a disastrous mistake the United States had made when it had removed Mosaddeq from power in 1953—and what a lingering shadow it was now casting over U.S.-Iranian relations. Holed up in a room somewhere in the bowels of the embassy, the U.S. *chargé* Bruce Laingen attempted to express his outrage at the students, but one of them quickly cut him off and stated bluntly: "You have no right to complain. You took our whole country hostage in 1953." It was a point that Laingen, by his own later admission, found it difficult to argue with.

With the weight of the nation now on their shoulders, the students did their best to produce concrete results. One of their very first priorities was to ransack the embassy for evidence of American plotting—some sort of smok-

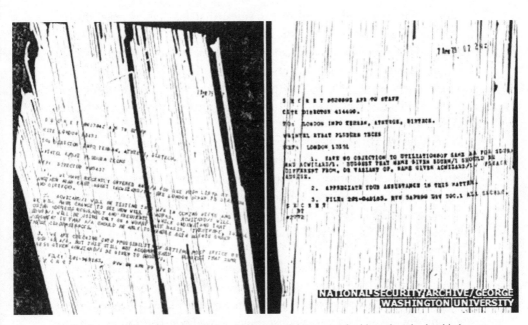

Students in the embassy found that thousands of documents had been hastily shredded by U.S. officials. Convinced that America had something to hide, they laboriously pieced the documents back together and released them to the public.

ing gun to confirm their long-standing suspicions about U.S. intentions. But they found no such evidence. When the American officials had seen Iranians climbing over the walls, they had grabbed whatever documents they thought might look incriminating and fed them into paper shredders. Thus, when the students searched the embassy, they found the "evidence" of America's treachery piled up throughout the building like great bales of hay.

But this setback proved only temporary. Groups of earnest students, sitting in circles on the floor, patiently laid strips of shredded typewriter paper together, like some massive dystopian jigsaw puzzle, to piece the shredded documents back together. The slow, painstaking, brain-taxing work spoke volumes about how convinced Iran's revolutionaries were of a nefarious American plot. Over the next sixteen years, the Islamic Republic would gradually publish the results of their labor, under the title *Documents from the American Nest of Spies.* The compilation ran to seventy-seven volumes.

The documents pieced together during the initial days and weeks of the crisis proved much less incriminating than the revolutionaries had hoped. The students held press conferences to release each document they resurrected and translated, and bit by bit the public learned about secret meetings between American officials and senior members of Iran's government, including Bazargan and several of his aides, that had taken place during the revolutionary upheaval of 1978. There was nothing sinister about such meetings—Bazargan's intention had been to persuade the United States to abandon the shah and not stand in the way of the revolution. But in the perfervid atmosphere of 1979, the public came away with the impression that the moderates who had led Iran's provisional government were not entirely trustworthy.

Every day now it was becoming easier for radicals to convince the public of the danger of allowing Bazargan and his allies to have their way in the drafting of the constitution. "We are facing a satanic power today, and it wants to destroy our country," thundered the ayatollah on November 28, to the great delight of both the hard left and the religious right. "Don't let the foundation of the Islamic Republic be weakened or the enemies of Islam fulfil their dreams."

Incensed by what he was seeing and hearing, Grand Ayatollah Shariat-Madari, one of the last voices of moderation left among the ayatollahs—still convinced Iran was best served by preserving the legal framework of 1906—urgently issued a *fatwa* against the proposed constitution, which was now just hours away from being put to a vote. It didn't help. On December 2 and 3—four weeks into the hostage crisis—the referendum went ahead as planned. The constitution passed overwhelmingly.

C3

For Khomeini, the sky was now the limit. Iran's new constitution solidified the dream of Islamic revivalism that he had harbored since his early days as a radical cleric in the 1960s. More than that, it invested him with the power to act as the final arbiter of all moral, philosophical, political, and strategic dilemmas confronting the nation. Unofficially, to most Iranians, he was "the emam"—the wise old man of God who had led his people to throw off the shackles of the shah's tyranny. Officially, the new constitution gave him the title of Rahbar-e Mo'azam-e Enqelab—Supreme Leader of the Revolution.

Even the most supreme of leadership positions, however, could have its limitations—as Khomeini was about to find out. The new constitution also stipulated that the Iranian people had the right to choose their own president, and when the election was announced, more than one hundred candidates put themselves forward. The hard-line religious camp—still uninitiated in the rough-and-tumble of Western-style electoral politics—failed to organize adequately around a candidate and carelessly allowed the election to slip away from them. The result, on January 25, 1980, was a thumping landslide—75 percent of the popular vote—for Abolhassan Bani-Sadr, a short, rodent-faced economist who had recently served as Bazargan's finance minister. Bani-Sadr was yet another bespectacled Iranian liberal dedicated to finding a middle ground between Western political philosophies and traditional Islam.

French-educated, worldly, and intellectual, Bani-Sadr had already publicly declared—at the beginning of November—his strenuous opposition to the taking of hostages at the U.S. embassy. But that was where the similarities between the new president and the outgoing prime minister came to an end. Unlike Bazargan, Bani-Sadr was very much a revolutionary in his instincts. An ambitious—sometimes ruthless—son of an ayatollah, and a devoted admirer of Khomeini, he knew how to speak the language of burning barricades and wasted no time concocting professorial metaphors about "smoothly asphalted roads." Unlike Bazargan, he was able to appeal to Iran's hard left, convincing the radical Marxist militants of the MeK and the FeK to cast their votes in his direction after their own candidate was disqualified. Unlike Bazargan, he was careful never to wear a necktie.

Upon taking office on February 4, 1980, Bani-Sadr made a heroic attempt to end the American hostage crisis—now dragging into its fourth month. Working through a secret channel of shadowy French intermediaries cultivated by the new foreign minister, Sadeq Qotbzadeh, Bani-Sadr opened communication with senior officials in the Carter White House. Finding a resolution to the crisis, in fact, became his personal obsession. As Iran's first elected president, he was determined not to be reduced to irrelevance and impotence the way Bazargan had been. And he believed that bringing an end to the hostage drama would help establish the precedent of a powerful, popularly elected presidency. Like most liberals, Bani-Sadr also believed the hostage drama was becoming a pointless distraction and was making the Islamic Republic look bad. The sooner the whole ridiculous episode was brought to an end, the sooner Iran could get on with the important business of creating a new model republic to serve as inspiration to the Muslim world.

The solution that Bani-Sadr and the Carter administration came up with was subtle and complex but also ingenious. As a compromise measure, the hostages would be released into the custody of the Iranian government. That way, at least, they would be in the hands of an official, accountable entity—and the American public could see that "something was being done." In return, an international commission would be created, under the auspices of the UN, to travel to Iran and listen to the country's grievances against America—an arrangement sufficiently fuzzy that both governments could present it to their irate populations as a victory.

At last, it seemed, an off-ramp was being created. But as Bani-Sadr set about implementing the terms of the deal, it quickly became apparent how little control anyone in Iran actually had over the students. Khomeini initially seemed receptive to the plan, but he faced strong resistance from a group of hard-line clerics acting as advocates for the students. Worse, the Iranian government didn't have a clear picture of what was going on inside the embassy. When Qotbzadeh went to the building to demand the hand-over of the hostages, he got into a ferocious shouting match with the students, who jostled him out onto the street and told him not to come back. Within days, mass demonstrations appeared in front of the embassy, warning the country not to be taken in by spineless "moderates." Pushed onto the back foot—by public opinion, by his own ultraradical followers, and by the sheer chaos of the situation—Khomeini announced on February 23 that the hostage crisis had become a matter of national concern and could be decided only by "the representatives of the people" (i.e., the Majles). It was a victory for the radicals. Elections for a new Majles had not yet been held, and it would likely be at least two months before a new parliament could be seated.

For most Americans, these internal Iranian power struggles were of very little interest. After four months of fruitlessly anticipating the release of the hostages, their mood was approaching a kind of national hysteria. Every night the TV news reminded Americans of the grim tally—*America Held Hostage, Day 107 . . . Day 131 . . . Day 148*. And every day Americans came up with some new way of registering their collective frustration. In January 1980 one of the hostages' wives tied a yellow ribbon round an oak tree in her front yard, sparking a national craze for yellow ribbons—and a hit song recorded by Tony Orlando and Dawn, "Tie a Yellow Ribbon Round the Ol' Oak Tree." Other songs—such as the country-western chart-toppers "Go to Hell, Ayatollah," "Khomaniac," and "Take Your Oil and Shove It"— reflected a darker mood.

For many in America, the crisis seemed like the final straw in a decade that had brought humiliation after humiliation to the country they loved. For ten years, Americans had watched with escalating feelings of agony and helplessness as U.S. Marines were chased out of Saigon and their own president resigned in disgrace over the Watergate scandal. They had sat steaming with frustration in gas lines. They had heard nothing but pessimism about the state of the economy, steadily learning to add words like "stagflation" and "misery index" to their vocabulary. And they had felt burrowed out from within by a combination of race riots, draft dodging, and what appeared to be a general climate of moral decay. Just twenty years earlier America, fresh from its victory in World War II, had felt like a place of

Hostage crisis: Demonstration in Washington, November 9, 1979.

boundless optimism—a checkerboard of *Leave It to Beaver* neighborhoods, tail-finned Cadillacs, and rocket ships racing to the moon. But by the end of the 1970s, the mood had turned grim. America, it sometimes seemed, had lost its way—an emasculated superpower being humiliated in every direction.

For President Carter, the temptation to take heroic action to deliver Americans from this crisis of confidence was great. But his options were limited. Aggressive military action was likely to backfire and result in the deaths of American hostages. Threats of war would only make Iran more defiant. So Carter resorted to his only reasonable option—secret diplomacy. Time and again the White House pursued what seemed like promising back-channel communications with the revolutionaries in Iran, never revealing the details to the public. From an operational standpoint, this strategy made sense, but politically, it cost Carter dearly. As the weeks slipped by, the American public lost patience with seeing no sign of progress while being told the administration was "doing all it could." Polls revealed a dwindling faith both in the president and in his ability to bring the hostages home. And as the media continued to stoke the public's appetite for news and information, all around the country, one heard some version of the same refrain: We're America, goddammit. Why can't we just *do something*?

☙

By April 1980, the president had had enough. Five months of secret shuttle diplomacy had achieved precisely nothing, and he was running out of options. Although Carter personally hated the idea of military action, it was becoming increasingly apparent that it could no longer be avoided. Every punitive measure he had taken since the crisis began—including imposing a series of stiff sanctions against the purchase of Iranian oil—seemed only to have strengthened Iran's resolve. And the presidential election was now just seven months away. Back in November, when the crisis began, Carter had secretly ordered his military commanders to make contingency plans for a hostage rescue operation—code-named Operation Eagle Claw. Now, five months later, he and his cabinet came to the conclusion that it was time to roll.

On the night of April 24, 1980, eight RH-53D Sea Stallion helicopters set off into the oily darkness of the Persian sky from the deck of the carrier USS *Nimitz,* anchored in the international waters of the Arabian Sea. Their destination was a secret rendezvous site in the Iranian desert near Tabas, a spot designated by the Pentagon as Desert One. The choppers, flown by members of a newly established, ultra-elite counterterrorism unit known as Delta Force, were led by Col. Charles "Chargin' Charlie" Beckwith. Six C-130 Hercules transport planes carrying troops and replacement fuel for the Sea Stallions met them at Desert One. The idea was that the helicopters, freshly refueled, would continue to a second rendezvous point on the outskirts of Tehran, where locally recruited CIA agents would meet them and drive the troops into town, where they would storm the embassy and rescue the hostages.

There was almost nothing that didn't go wrong. Two hours into the operation, two of the helicopters flew into a sandstorm and developed mechanical problems with their rotor blades. The six that remained made it to Desert One, but along the way one of them developed problems with its hydraulic pump and had to be abandoned. Down to just five choppers, Colonel Beckwith radioed up the chain of command. Carter ordered him to abort the mission. Then at Desert One, disaster struck. As the men prepared to withdraw, one of the helicopters crashed into the fuselage of a Hercules transport plane and set off a gigantic explosion. Eight American servicemen were burned to death.

At seven the next morning, Carter appeared live on national television and informed the American people that a secret rescue mission had been sent to Iran and that it had ended in tragedy. "It was my decision to attempt the rescue operation," he said. "It was my decision to cancel it when problems developed in the placement of our rescue team. . . . The responsibility is fully my own."

From the very beginning, Carter had attached himself personally and visibly to the fate of the hostages—seemingly prepared to stake his entire presidency on his ability to get them released. Had the rescue mission succeeded, this strategy would have gone down in history as a risky but ultimately devastating act of political bravura. Carter himself might well have been hailed as a national hero—worthy even of a place on Mount Rushmore. Instead, in April 1980 the president of the United States—slouching and apologizing into the camera early on a Friday morning—came across as the embodiment of everything going wrong for America. Six months before Election Day, Carter became personally identified with one of the most humiliating episodes in U.S. history.

On April 7 the United States—sensing it had no options left to bring the hostages home—officially broke ties with Iran. The State Department summoned the few Iranian diplomats still present in Washington and gave them forty-eight hours to leave the country. And with that, a historic chapter in U.S.-Iranian relations came to end. Ninety-seven years after Samuel Benjamin had arrived at the court of Naser al-Din Shah in a rumpled suit and listened to the Persian emperor express his desire that the two countries remain friends "forever"—ninety-two years after "Hajji Washington" washed up at the 22nd Street Pier in New York with a folded-up speech he hoped to read to Grover Cleveland—it was over. At the front entrance to the palatial Iranian embassy compound on Massachusetts Avenue—where not long ago Ardeshir Zahedi had danced half-naked with some of Washington's most glamorous socialites—a padlocked chain was unceremoniously threaded through the handles of the double doors and clicked into place. It has remained there ever since.

 C3

If there had been any possibility of a diplomatic breakthrough in the hostage crisis, it was now gone. The United States had conducted a secret military incursion into Iranian territory and followed this provocative act by breaking off ties with Iran altogether. As Khomeini and his allies cleaned up the debris in the desert around Tabas, they suspected now, more than ever, that an American coup attempt was afoot—and the photos of charred helicopters and abandoned flight documents broadcast on Iranian television only rallied the public behind this suspicion. Over the next several months, tensions between Iran and America reached a level never seen before. The United States, in the words of one of its top officials, ran a campaign of international pressure against Iran that "was probably the most extensive and sustained effort of its kind ever to be conducted in peacetime. . . . Iran became an instant pariah in the world community, and the conduct of its external relations was severely limited."

The first to take advantage of Iran's international isolation was Iraq's amply moustached president, Saddam Hussein. On September 22, 1980, twenty-one armored and mechanized divisions of the Iraqi air force poured across the Shatt al-Arab waterway and the northern and central flank of the Zagros Mountains into Iranian territory. Within hours, Iraqi fighter jets were pounding Tehran's Mehrabad Airport and Iranian air force bases in an attempt to reduce Iran's already weakened air defense capabilities. Proclaiming himself "liberator" of Iran's tiny Arab population,[*] Saddam invited international journalists to an impromptu press conference on the Iranian side of the border that he had just breached. The following week, he said, with a wide grin on his face, he would be holding another press conference—in Tehran.

With the country now at war, the fate of American hostages was clearly the least of Iran's problems. But in a way, the Iraqi invasion added urgency to the situation. Almost every sensible actor in Iran had long ago realized that the American hostages were more of a liability than an asset to the revolution—and that it was time to find a face-saving way to send them home. Already, by the summer of 1980, Khomeini had successfully milked the situation to achieve nearly every goal on his domestic agenda: Bazargan and the liberals had been dispensed with; Bani-Sadr had been neutered by his failure to resolve the crisis; and the newly assembled Majles—elected in an atmosphere of triumphalism—was stuffed with Islamist radicals who shared Khomeini's uncompromising vision. Most important, perhaps, on July 27, the shah finally succumbed to his cancer, leaving something of a question mark over what exactly the American hostages were now hostage *to*. After more than ten months in captivity, they had become, in the words of one Iranian observer, like a "fruit from which all juice has been squeezed out."

On September 9, less than two weeks before the Iraqi invasion, Khomeini announced that Iran was prepared to release the Americans—

---

[*] Approximately one percent of Iran's population is ethnically Arab. Concentrated mostly in the southwest province of Khuzestan, along the Gulf coast, they generally speak Arabic as a first language and practice Shia Islam.

provided the United States agreed to four basic conditions. First, he said, the United States would have to identify and repatriate the billions of dollars of Iranian assets that the shah had stolen and salted away in American bank accounts. Second, the Carter administration would have to release $12 billion in Iranian assets that it had frozen in November. Third, there could be no future legal claims lodged on behalf of the hostages. Finally, the United States would have to promise it would never again interfere in the domestic affairs of Iran. These four conditions—communicated secretly to the White House by a West German diplomat and confirmed the following day in a public speech by the ayatollah—were viewed by Washington as far more reasonable than anything that had been heard from Iran in the previous ten months. For the first time since the crisis began, Iran had not demanded an apology for past U.S. actions. For the first time, moreover, the initiative had come directly from Khomeini rather than from well-meaning liberals like Bani-Sadr. The ayatollah, it seemed, had decided—for his own reasons and on his own timetable—that Iran had made its point.

At a secret meeting held in West Germany between Deputy Secretary of State Warren Christopher and a personal emissary sent by Khomeini, Sadeq Tabatabai, the United States and Iran negotiated terms for the release of the American hostages. Of the ayatollah's four conditions, the easiest for Christopher to meet was the demand for an American policy of noninterference. He agreed without reservation. The next three conditions took a little more wrangling, but ultimately the two sides found areas of common ground, and the meeting broke up in an atmosphere of optimism and goodwill. Both sides agreed to fly back to their respective capitals and secure formal agreement from their superiors as quickly as possible.

What happened next is one of the great enduring mysteries in the history of U.S.-Iranian relations. For reasons that may never be fully understood, several weeks went by before the White House heard any meaningful word from Tehran—during which time it became obvious that the Iranians were in no hurry to conclude the deal. Ostensibly, the problem was that Iraq's September 22 invasion had turned the mood in Tehran vehemently against the United States. Iranians widely perceived Washington to have given Saddam a "green light" to invade. And the Majles, whose ratification was required on any final deal, was now in no mood to cooperate with Jimmy Carter.*

---

* That, at least, is the official version. However, senior members of the Carter administration maintain to this day—and with considerable bitterness—that a nefarious American hand was also at work behind the scenes. In numerous books and articles, they have claimed that their Republican adversaries in the United States—desperate to avoid an "October surprise" that would tip the election in Carter's favor—cut a secret deal with Iran to *delay* the release of the hostages, in

For the White House, this was a doomsday scenario. In October 1979, with just days to go until the election, the Carter campaign was locked in such a tight race that, thinking the hostages were close to release, it had spent weeks leaking optimistic stories to the press—telling reporters to expect a "major breakthrough" in the Iran situation. As a result, across the political landscape in America, the words "October surprise" were on everyone's lips. But as the days slipped by and the hostages were not released, a dreadful sense of foreboding closed in on the White House. By sheer, dumb, maddening, befuddling bad luck, the election was scheduled for November 4—the one-year anniversary of the crisis. If the hostages were not released before then, American media would spend the final hours of the campaign running depressing stories about the grim milestone—complete with blow-by-blow reminders of every humiliating moment of the past twelve months. For a sitting president, who had presided over a year of frustration and dwindling national confidence, there could be no worse way to face the electorate.

But this is exactly what happened. During the last week in October, the Majles in Tehran finally began debating the hostage issue and on November 2 sent Carter a counteroffer that the president felt would require at least several more days—if not weeks—of renegotiating. And in the final hours before the polls opened, the worst fears of the White House began to materialize. As expected, television networks flooded the airwaves with hour upon hour of "America Held Hostage—Day 365."

The initial weeks of the hostage crisis had seen a surge of patriotism in the United States. But by the end of 1980, the American people were thoroughly fed up. When they looked at Carter, they saw not a martial hero leading his people into battle against the forces of evil but a bit of a wet noodle—a charisma-less president who gave Oval Office addresses wearing a zip-up cardigan and urged Americans to tackle the energy crisis by turning their thermostats down a little.

On November 4, 1980, it was all over for Carter. The Honest Abe peanut farmer from Plains, Georgia, went down in a devastating defeat, losing the popular vote by 51 to 41 percent and winning only 49 of 538 electoral

---

exchange for the promise of American weapons once their man was in the White House (weapons Iran desperately needed to fight the war against Iraq). A number of Iranian actors have supported this claim, including no less a figure than former president Bani-Sadr. The Republicans have always strenuously denied this version of events, pointing, in their defense, to a 1992 U.S. congressional investigation that found no evidence of wrongdoing. They have also suggested, not implausibly, that Khomeini might have been driven by a purely emotional desire to punish and humiliate Carter for his refusal to hand over the shah while he was still alive. The Iranians, they add, might also have been seeking vengeance—determined to prove they could end the career of an American president, just as the United States had overthrown their prime minister in 1953.

votes. Into the breach rode Ronald Wilson Reagan—pomaded and winsome, his face chiseled into perfection by his years as a Hollywood leading man. Reagan, it seemed, was just the kind of leader America needed in 1980: filmed astride an ambling stallion, channeling the Marlboro man, as the great western sun beat down on his leather chaps. He was the new sheriff in town, come to clean up the streets and send the bad guys packing.

From Election Day to Reagan's inauguration on January 20, 1981, however, Carter still had ten weeks to try to bring the hostage crisis to a successful resolution. And he was more fired up than ever. Freed from the political straitjacket of a reelection campaign, he plunged deeper than ever into the matter—determined to bring the hostages home on his watch. Day and night the White House negotiated the four-point deal that Christopher and Tabatabai had outlined in September, believing they were tantalizingly close to a final agreement. They were so optimistic that they even planned a welcoming ceremony, to be held at the U.S. Air Force base in Wiesbaden, West Germany, at which the president would personally welcome the hostages back to freedom.

It was never to be. For ten weeks, Algerian intermediaries shuttled back and forth between Tehran and Washington, carrying messages and position papers from each side. But every time they were close to a final deal, some new procedural issue or request for clarification arose that had to be ironed out, either on the American or the Iranian side. Eventually, in January 1981, the Iranian hostage crisis ended in the sorry spectacle of an American president keeping an around-the-clock vigil during his final forty-eight hours in office—sleeping for twenty minutes at a time on the couch in the Oval Office, shaving with a telephone receiver cupped against his ear, and frantically awaiting word from the designated escrow account at the Bank of England.

When the sun came up on Inauguration Day, January 20, 1981, there was still no rest for the weary bones of Jimmy Carter. The planes that had been prepared for the hostages, the president learned, were parked on the tarmac at Mehrabad Airport but were not cleared for takeoff—and the hostages themselves were still in central Tehran, gathering their belongings for the flight home. The process of transferring billions of dollars between fourteen different banks in five countries, conducted in a flurry of complicated telexes and confirmation codes, ate up most of the next few hours. Only when the transfer of funds had been verified did the hostages begin their journey by bus to the airport. By that point, however, it was eleven a.m. in Washington, time for Carter to change into a fresh suit and make his way to the steps of the Capitol for the inauguration ceremony—still unsure whether the hostages would be freed on his watch.

Down to the wire: Carter holding around-the-clock negotiations during his final forty-eight hours in the White House in a desperate, and ultimately futile, attempt to get the hostages freed on his watch.

It was only after noon, as Reagan took the oath of office and began delivering his inaugural address to the nation, that the efforts of the past fourteen months finally bore fruit. Less than twenty minutes into that speech, word arrived that the planes had taken off and were on their way out of Iranian airspace. Carter's humiliation at the hands of Iran was complete.

☙

As the new president announced, to the great relief of the American public, that the hostages were on a plane home, the most immediate and agonizing portion of America's ordeal appeared to be over. But there was no papering over the monumental catastrophe that had befallen American foreign policy in the four short years since Carter took office. The shah of Iran, the reliable Persian emperor who for thirty-seven years had served as loyal executor of American policy in the Middle East—facing down Arab nationalism, pro-

Free at last: Minutes after Ronald Reagan was
sworn in as president on January 20, 1981, the
hostages were released.

viding a steady supply of oil, buying billions of dollars of American-made
military hardware, quietly assisting Israel, and standing as a crucial bulwark
against the Soviet Union—had been replaced by a regime that was filled
with hatred for the United States and determined to oppose Washington's
plans in the region at every turn. Over the next several years, as America's
troubles in the Middle East multiplied, Republicans made it a standard part
of their playbook to lay all the blame at the doorstep of Jimmy Carter and
his allies. They accused his administration—and the Democrats generally—
of having pursued a weak, vacillating foreign policy and failing to provide
serious U.S. leadership at a critical moment in history. In short, Jimmy
Carter became the president who had "lost Iran."

Their accusations had an element of truth. Carter had sent conflicting messages to Iran from the beginning—urging the shah toward human
rights and liberalization but also selling him weapons and turning a blind
eye to the bloodshed in the streets of Iran. At the worst possible moments,
such as the day after the Jaleh Square massacre, he had signaled to the Iranian people that America stood foursquare behind their hated shah. And

before, during, and after the revolution, the Carter administration had failed to make meaningful approaches to Khomeini or to the clerical leadership that might have placed the United States in a position to influence events in Iran. But in the end, if there was one thing that turned the Iranian people's revolt into a fervently anti-American revolution, it was the decision to admit the shah to the United States for medical treatment in October 1979—a decision that had been urged most vocally on the president by the very Republicans who were now accusing him of losing Iran.

In the final analysis, blaming one American administration for the Iranian revolution, or for its viciously anti-American turn in 1979, is foolish, both because it downplays the role Iranians themselves played and because it ignores the fundamental continuities in American foreign policy since the early 1950s. If the people of Iran decided they had had enough of their shah in 1979, it was because *they* decided they had had enough of their shah. And if they cheered on the students at the embassy and burned American flags in the street, it was as much an expression of a fury whose roots could be traced to the policies of Nixon, Kissinger, and Eisenhower as it was the fault of any Democratic administration.

Wherever one chooses to place the blame, however, one thing is beyond doubt. The days when an American president could simply pick up the phone to Tehran and hear on the other end the friendly voice of its trusty policeman in the Persian Gulf had come to an end. Iran—one of the most important, powerful countries in possibly the most delicate and strategically sensitive region in the world—was now a sworn enemy of the United States.

Dulce et Decorum Est

In the 1980s, the Iranian newspaper *Ettela'at* occasionally offered its readers, sitting in the cushy confines of Tehran, a glimpse into the horrors of frontline combat in the war against Iraq. The world they were missing:

> We had child-volunteers—fourteen, fifteen and sixteen-year-olds. They went into the minefields. Their eyes saw nothing; their ears heard nothing. And then, a few moments later, one saw clouds of dust. When the dust had settled again, there was nothing more to be seen of them. Somewhere, widely scattered in the landscape, there lay scraps of burnt flesh and pieces of bone. . . . Before entering the minefields, the children wrap themselves in blankets and they roll on the ground, so their body parts stay together after the explosion of the mines and one can carry them to their graves.

This, for the rest of the 1980s, was what became of Iran. Locked into a brutal, unforgiving war with Iraq that neither side could win, the country's leaders desperately threw wave after wave of wild-eyed recruits into the trenches to defend the homeland and the revolution from Saddam Hussein. Thousands of boys—their heads filled with ideas about the glory of sacrifice, and their lungs filled with the noxious vapors of mustard gas and nerve agents from Saddam's ever-expanding arsenal of chemical weapons—gave their lives to the cause. Thousands more rushed to the front lines to volunteer, lying about their age or running away from home for the chance to serve in God's grand army. Across every rapacious, hungry battlefield, peach-fuzz teenagers cheered and howled with delight as they searched for land mines with their bare feet—ecstatic at the prospect of a life more noble than the ones they had left behind in the slums and villages of Old Iran. "It was sometimes like a race," recalled one veteran, as he remembered the way he and his friends would run onto the battlefield looking for land mines. "Even without the commander's orders everyone wanted to be first."

Trench warfare, chemical weapons, transcendent ideologies, casualties in the millions, a front line that barely moved an inch during eight long years—this was the kind of war that the old gray heads of Europe and the West knew all too well. In 1916, along the banks of the Somme, General Haig had lined up his boys—the brightest and best young men England had ever produced—and talked to them of Christ and God and Country— just before he led 400,000 to their deaths. All across Europe, then, young men had learned they were fighting a "war to end all wars," as they duti- fully memorized the Latin line *Dulce et decorum est pro patria mori*—"How sweet and fitting it is to die for one's country." The result, then, had been an abomination—a merciless, insatiable war of attrition that left a cold, dark crescent of death across the heart of the European continent.

In the 1980s, it was Iran's turn.

ଔ

When Saddam Hussein invaded Iran on September 22, 1980, he went straight for the jugular. Khorramshahr—crucial port for oil exports, mouth of the Shatt-al-Arab, and for nearly a century the jewel in the crown of Per- sian Gulf petroleum—came under heavy bombardment from Iraq's armored and mechanized infantry divisions. It fell within a month. From there, the Iraqis pressed on to Susangerd, Ahvaz, and the great prize, Abadan, where the world's largest oil refinery, built by the British in 1912, belched out 20 million gallons of gasoline every day. By crippling Iran's oil infrastructure, Saddam reasoned, he could bring the country to its knees. And events quickly suggested he might be right. Desperate to keep their oil exports going, the Iranians were forced to send convoys of tanker-trucks over ardu- ous overland routes through Turkey and the Soviet Union—bringing an economy that was already reeling from the effects of revolution and inter- national isolation to the verge of collapse.

To any reasonable observer, it looked as if Saddam's triumphant march into Tehran was going to be embarrassingly easy. But then, just a few weeks into the conflict, something unexpected happened. The Iranian defenses began to hold. From all over the country, volunteers poured to the front ready to fight and die for the revolution. Holy men led convoys of war matériel hundreds of miles to the trenches. Local committees organized villages and neighborhoods to provide supplies and manpower for the war effort. Young men stormed through basic training, impatient for a chance to get out to the front lines. In Khorramshahr and elsewhere, citizens erected barricades and asked for guns to defend the city, while the women—miraculously, given the near-total blackout of power and water—cooked meals for thousands of soldiers and volunteers. During much of the year that had preceded Saddam's invasion, Iranians had felt divided and unsure about the direction of their revolution. But the need to defend the homeland against foreign aggression filled the public with a new sense of purpose, rekindling the spirit of national unity and revolutionary fervor that had brought down the shah two years earlier.

Iraq simply had no answer to this. Although its military capabilities were far superior to Iran's, its population was deeply disgruntled. Saddam Hussein was one of the world's most despised and tyrannical dictators. He relied, like dictators the world over, on an army of reluctant warriors—lumpen conscripts who bitterly resented being forced to fight "Saddam's war" and dreamed of the moment they could get back home to Baghdad, where a wife and a hot bath awaited. On paper, Iraq should have had no trouble winning this war, but instead the two countries descended into a foggy, inconclusive stalemate. Overwhelming firepower came up against overwhelming willpower, with no obvious advantage for either side. And it would remain that way for eight long, bloody, gruesome, and grotesquely pointless years.

☞

Saddam's initial calculus for invading Iran had reflected the thinking of a man bathed in the logic of force and schooled in the vocabulary of naked opportunism. Early in his life, Saddam had learned that other men's weaknesses were there to be exploited and that every half-open door was there to be blasted open. As a young street-gang leader in 1959, he had made a name for himself by firing a round of shots into the open window of a car carrying President Abdul Karim Qasim. As a thirty-year-old Ba'ath Party operative in 1968, he had slipped on a military uniform and ridden into the presidential palace on a tank, bringing an end to the rule of President Abdel Rahman Aref. And as a charismatic vice president in 1979, he had shunted aside the ailing President Ahmed Hassan al-Bakr and seized absolute power for himself, executing hundreds of rivals in the process.

Now in 1980, when Saddam Hussein looked at Iran, he saw a country whose armed forces had been reduced to decrepitude, whose people had just been through a revolution, whose military leaders were busy putting down separatist movements, and whose political leaders were divided—in short, a country practically begging to be invaded. The Iranian army, in the first few months of 1980, had been purged of thousands of senior and midlevel officers perceived as sympathetic to the shah—and was reeling from a severe lack of organization and capacity. Many of Iran's units were only 25 percent operational. Soldiers were failing to turn up at barracks, spare parts were missing, computer systems were down, equipment was in disrepair. The few units that still functioned efficiently were tied up with Kurdish rebellions or stationed along the Soviet border. As if all this were not enough, former prime minister Shapur Bakhtiar and a group of exiled Iranian army officers had visited Saddam in Baghdad and urged him to "liberate" their country from the rule of the ayatollahs. The people of Iran, they told Saddam, hated Khomeini and were just waiting for an excuse to rise up against him. In short, Saddam Hussein invaded Iran for the same reason he had done everything else in his life: because he thought he could get away with it.

But perhaps an even bigger motivating factor for Saddam than his opportunism was his fear of Khomeini—or, rather, of what Khomeini represented. Saddam knew his own people were mostly poor, uneducated, and deeply religious—and thus highly susceptible to the message of Islamic liberation they heard emanating out of Tehran. Worse, they were 60 percent Shia. For decades, Iraq's Shia population had been treated as second-class citizens—deprived of government jobs and opportunities for advancement—and they bitterly resented Saddam and the Sunni political elite who ruled over them. Many had attended Khomeini's sermons during the fifteen years the ayatollah spent in Najaf, and they were itching for revolution.* Saddam knew all too well that Khomeini had to be stopped before he got any big ideas about exporting his madness across the border.

This same fear, moreover, animated many of Saddam's fellow Arab rulers, from Saudi Arabia to Egypt to the tiny, oil-rich kingdoms and emirates of the Gulf. If the Iraqi regime was allowed to fall, the reasoning went in the region's capitals, it would only be a matter of time before other unpopular Arab despots also fell—one by one, like a tray of dominoes. Saddam, of course, understood perfectly what preventing this scenario would do for his own regional ambitions. If he could achieve one swift victory against Iran, other Arab leaders would hail him as a hero—the great Babylonian emperor who had faced down the Persian menace and held the line against the chaos of revolutionary political Islam. Little wonder, then, that when his tanks began rolling into Iran, Saddam declared he was fighting the "Second Battle

---

* In February 1979, when Khomeini came to power in Iran, Iraq's most important Shia cleric, Ayatollah Baqer Sadr, sent a congratulatory message to Tehran, expressing his hope that "other tyrants will also see their day of reckoning" (Dilip Hiro, *The Longest War* [New York, 1991], p. 26).

Trench warfare, poison gas, child soldiers, casualty numbers too large to comprehend:
The Iran-Iraq war (1980–88), the last great international conflict of the twentieth
century, bore an eerie resemblance to the one endured by Europe at the outset of the
century.

of Qadissiya," a reference to a decisive Arab victory over the Persian Empire
in A.D. 637.

For years, Saddam had nursed an ambition to become *the* leading figure
in the Arab world, heir to the legacy of Nasser and the man who finally
united the Arabian tribes and raised them to greatness. And as he looked
over at Iran, he saw a perfect opportunity to make this dream come true.
Just across the border was the Iranian province of Khuzestan, home to a
small population of ethnic Arabs whom Saddam believed could be stirred
into rebellion against their Persian overlords. Khuzestan was also home to
about 90 percent of Iran's oil industry. Iraq was already the world's third-
largest oil producer. But if Saddam could add Khuzestan to his portfolio,
he could put his country in a position of real dominance both regionally
and internationally—while also claiming to have "rescued" the Khuzestani
Arabs from their Persian bondage.

The Iranians saw none of this. To them, Saddam was merely the cat's-
paw of a much larger imperialist project being marshaled against them by the

world's ever-rapacious superpowers. "The hand of America," said Khomeini in 1981, "has emerged from Saddam's sleeve"—and everyone in Iran knew exactly what he meant. Again and again Khomeini had warned that the "oppressor nations"—meaning primarily the United States, Britain, and the USSR—would never tolerate an oppressed people declaring itself beholden to "neither East nor West," as Iran had done. The oppressor nations would not send in troops to crush Iran's revolution, of course; this would be too obvious, too aggressive. Instead, he had said, they would summon all their little client states and regional surrogates and encourage them to make life difficult for Iran. And indeed, in 1981, as the pro-Western king of Jordan put his ports and overland routes at Saddam's disposal, and the Sunni political establishment of the Middle East—led by Saudi Arabia—piled on to support Iraq, Khomeini's predictions appeared to be coming true.

There is no clear evidence that the Iraqi invasion was engineered by the United States, Britain, or the USSR—or indeed by anyone other than Saddam Hussein himself. However, once the war began, the international community made no effort to hide where its sympathies lay. Although Iraq was the clear aggressor, the UN Security Council spent four days dithering before it issued a resolution—and when it did, the language was conspicuously half-hearted. Resolution 479 said nothing to condemn Saddam's aggression, mumbling instead about the desirability of a "ceasefire" and calling on all sides to "refrain immediately from any further use of force and to settle their dispute by peaceful means." The international community's message to Iran was clear: *You may be the victim in this particular situation, but you are very much on your own.*

Of course, Iran had only itself to blame for the way it was being treated. In September 1980, the prolonged standoff over American hostages in Tehran was nearing the end of its first year. And with fifty-two Americans still in captivity, neither the United States nor its European allies could seriously be expected to rush to Iran's defense. But it was not just the American bloc that sided with Saddam. Arab governments, terrified that the "Khomeini phenomenon" might spread, rallied almost without exception behind Iraq.[*] And the Soviet Union, which had a long-standing treaty of friendship with Iraq, did the same. Although Moscow was pleased with the anti-American turn that Iran's revolution had taken, it was also chary about the influence an overly powerful Iran might wield in neighboring Afghanistan (which the Soviets had invaded the year before)—and it was not about to lend

---

[*] The only Arab nation to side overtly with Iran was Syria—whose president, Hafez Assad, was engaged in a bitter rivalry with Saddam for leadership of the Ba'ath movement (and the Arab world generally). Libya and, to a lesser extent, Algeria were mildly sympathetic to the Iranian cause as well, but their support for Tehran was lukewarm and mostly inconsequential.

its support to a crusading religious state whose leaders were bristling with anti-Communist rhetoric. With the USSR refusing to condemn the Iraqi action, Soviet satellites from Havana to Hanoi to Eastern Europe piled on with a dutiful silence. In short, when Saddam invaded Iran in September 1980, every nation on earth seemed to have some peculiar reason of its own for looking the other way.

To the Iranians, all this fitted perfectly with the narrative that had come to dominate their thinking. Their beloved revolution had been about nothing if not liberating Iran from the bloodsucking tentacles of the world's scheming superpowers; that those same superpowers would now do everything possible to reverse that revolution, and keep Iran in a position of weakness, made perfect sense. Once again, Iranians concluded, the great powers had proved they could not abide a free, independent, powerful Iran—whose people were at liberty to determine their own destiny. Once again, the world was at war with the very soul of Persia.

ɔ

But this atmosphere of defiance and psychological retrenchment was only one of many effects the war had on the Iranian political psyche in the early 1980s. Equally important was the stifling of domestic opposition and the emergence of a solid, unified—and often fiercely radical—new face to the revolution. As severe challenges confronted them from every direction, Iran's new leaders were forced to put the regime's survival above all else, meaning they had considerably less tolerance for internal dissent than they had had during the first two years of the revolution. When Khomeini came to power in 1979, he had brought with him a wide coalition of leftists, liberals, and religious ideologues, all excited to work together in building a model new republic. But by 1981, Khomeini no longer had the luxury to accommodate them all. With Iraqi Mirage jets screeching over the night skies of Tehran, he cautioned, the country's feuding factions had to set aside their differences or face total defeat. Iran would unify now—or die.

The process by which this unification took place was long, bloody, and deeply contentious. Since the 1940s, three ideological forces had dominated opposition to the shah: left-wing radicalism, religious radicalism, and liberal-democratic moderation. And within this tripartite framework, there was considerable complexity. On the left, the Tudeh supported Khomeini, the FeK fractured, and the MeK gradually drifted into open opposition to the regime. On the religious right, traditional, conservative ayatollahs who felt religion and politics should not mix were opposed by crusading religious revolutionaries who hoped to create a full-blown Islamic theocracy. And the liberals drifted among disillusionment, resentment, and lukewarm support for the moderate president, Bani-Sadr. Ostensibly, all of Iran's ideological forces, whatever their internal divisions and mutual hatreds, were loyal to Khomeini, but only one ideology could emerge on top. Revolutionary Iran was going to be a fundamentalist religious theocracy; or it was going to undergo a second revolution and become a Marxist state; or it was going to emerge as a moderate liberal democracy with only a mildly Islamic flavor to it. But it could not be all three.

Presiding over this complicated three-way rivalry, the ayatollah typically aligned himself with the religious radicals of the Islamic Republic Party (IRP), the dominant force in Iranian politics of the early 1980s. But Khomeini's philosophy was actually far less dogmatic than that of his followers—and his style of leadership far more flexible than is often imagined. Although he was a religious purist, devoted to turning Iran into a model of Islamic government, he was also something of a free spirit, a monklike mystic who existed in the ethereal realm of theological abstraction and had little interest in the Machiavellian scheming of day-to-day politics. What he cared about most at this moment in history was unity. Once Saddam Hussein invaded, Khomeini felt it was crucial for competing factions to set aside their differences and defeat the foreign enemy.

Unfortunately for Khomeini, unity was in short supply in 1981. Throughout most of 1979 and 1980, the religious right and extreme left had grudgingly tolerated each other as they made common cause against the moderates. But now, with Bazargan gone, an unmistakable rift opened between religious and leftist radicals. This, in many ways, was the real battle for the soul of the Islamic Republic, and it quickly turned ugly. Left-wing groups, particularly active on university campuses, took over buildings, set up kiosks full of newspapers, and engaged in full-scale brawls with their IRP counterparts. This kind of activity incensed Khomeini, who increasingly blasted the left for its "eclectic" ideas about fusing Islam and Marxism. No longer referring to the MeK by its name, Mojahedin-e Khalq (Holy Warriors of the People), he publicly mocked them as Monafeqin-e Khalq—Hypocrites of the People—the implication being that their outspoken veneration of Islam was superficial and tactical, designed to disguise a more sinister leftist agenda.

As the rift between the militant youth wings of the IRP and the MeK erupted into open warfare on campuses, it claimed the scalp of the hapless president, Abolhassan Bani-Sadr. Bani-Sadr's first response to the turmoil had been to try to make common cause with the IRP in the hopes of isolating the left. But in early 1981 he began relying more heavily on the support of the MeK and other Marxist organizations—a decision that doomed his presidency. In April and May the streets of Iran filled with large leftist demonstrations in support of the president. But many increasingly saw the MeK as seditious and unreliable, and Bani-Sadr's popularity plummeted, leaving Khomeini little choice but to abandon his once-devoted disciple. On June 20, after a Majles resolution called overwhelmingly for Bani-Sadr's impeachment, Bani-Sadr fled—together with the leader of the MeK—to Paris. Iran's first elected president—and the second liberal leader to have attempted to temper the radicalism of the revolution—had lasted only seventeen months.

The MeK now embarked on a carnival of lawlessness and organized violence never before seen or even imagined in Iran. During July and August its members gunned down, bombed, or otherwise slew hundreds of high-ranking officials, including prominent Friday prayer leaders in a half-dozen major cities (all Khomeini appointees), the governor-general of Gilan province, and dozens of senior officers in the Revolutionary Guards.* On June 28 a sixty-pound bomb exploded at IRP headquarters, killing ten government ministers, twenty-seven members of parliament, the leader of the IRP, and thirty-two other officials. The most audacious act of all came on August 30, when a bomb exploded at the heart of Iran's government headquarters, killing the prime minister, Mohammad-Javad Bahonar, and the president, Mohammad-Ali Rajai, both of whom had served just two weeks in the job.

What followed was a ferocious response on the part of the government. Throughout Iran, it rounded up members of the MeK and other left-wing militants who were believed to be conspiring to violently overthrow the regime and subjected them to rough summary justice in revolutionary courts. After little more than an hour or two in a courtroom, militants were hanged from makeshift gallows in full view of the public, sometimes at the rate of dozens a day.

This was only the beginning. As the IRP felt its back against the wall, many in the party's senior leadership believed it was time to put a more aggressive stamp on their ownership of the revolution and stop accommodating those who were undermining its values. The people had, after all, voted for an Islamic Republic, not a republic of squabbling Marxists, Islamists, and liberals. In 1981 and 1982, therefore, the most extreme religious tendencies were allowed to rise to the surface. A national dress code, requiring men to wear long-sleeved shirts in public and avoid such "Western" accoutrements as neckties and sculpted moustaches, was introduced. Women were required to cover their hair and refrain from using lipstick and

* Tehran's Friday prayer leader, Ali Khamenei (the current supreme leader of Iran) narrowly survived an attempt on his life, but was badly injured and lost the use of his right hand.

nail polish. In university classrooms, at public gatherings, and on city buses, the sexes were segregated. The playing and sale of recordings of Western music were banned, as were the sale and public consumption of alcohol. Perhaps most important, Khomeini decided, in the summer of 1981, that clerical leaders should no longer be barred from seeking elected office.[*]

The sheer amount of change that Iran underwent from November 1979 to the summer of 1982 was remarkable. In just two and a half years, Khomeini had taken an eclectic, diffuse, and at times even faltering revolutionary movement and transformed it into an unstoppable juggernaut of Islamic fundamentalism that was redefining every aspect of life. For an eighty-year-old man whom much of the world had dismissed as an ignorant ayatollah—a man who still spent much of his time fasting, praying, and sitting cross-legged in a corner of his room—it was an extraordinary political accomplishment.

But it was only the beginning.

CS

With both the MeK and Bani-Sadr out of the way, the path was now clear for the hard-liners of the IRP to assume total control of Iranian politics, and they wasted no time doing exactly that. In the winter of 1981–82, the more robustly Islamic character of the revolution revealed itself in a new and more freewheeling style of warfare against Iraq, one that relied much less on the regular army, with its cumbersome conventional tactics, and much more on the sheer fanaticism of the revolution's devoted followers. In Tehran, clerics were given greater voice—even outright control—over military planning. Religious leaders were dispatched to the front lines, where they provided troops with Quranic instruction and delivered sermons about the sacrifices made by Hossein at the Battle of Karbala in A.D. 680. And perhaps most important, Iran's prosecution of the war began to rely increasingly on so-called "human wave attacks," unarmed men marching onto the battlefield in straight rows, shouting *Allah-o Akbar* ("God is Great") and offering themselves as targets for the Iraqis, while Iranian air force jets did their work from overhead. Whenever enemy fire or land mines slaughtered a "wave," the next one simply walked forward over their bodies, and then the one after that, one wave after another.

---

[*] This subtle but visible change sent Iran irrevocably down the road of theocracy. Previously, the ayatollah had believed that religious authorities should play only an advisory role in the day-to-day management of political affairs, so that spiritual leaders would not become overly tainted by the mud-slinging and moral compromises of conventional politics. But the disastrous experience of the Bani-Sadr presidency, and the MeK insurrection, had changed his mind.

The human wave attack was a tactic never before seen in modern warfare, and it presented considerable challenges for Iraq. "They come at us in huge hordes, screaming like crazed football fans, storming our positions with their fists swinging," recalled one Iraqi officer in 1982. "You can shoot down the first wave, and then the second. But at some point, the corpses are piling up in front of you, and you just want to howl and throw away your gun. Those are human beings after all."

The manpower for this new, fanatical style of warfare came primarily from the Revolutionary Guards. But Iran also created a massive, all-volunteer citizen militia known as Basij-e Mostazafin (Mobilization of the Oppressed), composed of women, underage boys, and men over forty-five. (Khomeini called it the "army of twenty million.") Along the Dezful-Shush highway in March 1982, thousands of Basij volunteers and Revolutionary Guards were sent charging onto the battlefield, armed with no more than rifles and a tacit understanding that if the situation became chaotic and no orders were forthcoming, they should improvise and do whatever it took to win, in the noble, centuries-old tradition of holy warriors. All this bewildered the Iraqis who, following the rules of modern warfare, staked out static positions, complete with tanks and cumbersome artillery, and were reluctant to act without orders issued through the chain of command. Every time the fog of war descended, Iraqi soldiers froze and awaited instructions, while the Iranians poured onto the battlefield, ecstatically offering themselves up in wave after wave of human sacrifice.

It worked magnificently. For the first time in two years, Iran began to claw its way back from the devastating territorial losses it had sustained in 1980, gradually inching the front lines back toward the original Iraqi border. Tens of thousands lost their lives in battles that sometimes lasted only days, but this only amplified the heroic narrative being woven in Tehran—that legions of Islamic warriors were ready (and even thrilled) for the opportunity to give their lives for the cause of God and country.

In April 1982, Iran launched Operation Jerusalem, a name chosen to remind recruits that victory over the Iraqi dictator was just the first step and that God's own capital would soon be reclaimed from the infidels and occupiers. The message got through. Over the course of four weeks, seventy thousand fighters poured into Khorramshahr and besieged Iraqi strongholds as Iranian air force jets provided tactical cover. Already transformed into a ghost town by mass civilian evacuations in 1980, Khorramshahr—once a bustling, cosmopolitan city of 220,000 and Iran's second-largest port—now looked less like a city than a vast expanse of rubble awaiting a bulldozer. When the fighting finally subsided at the end of May, it looked like Dresden in 1945. But it was free.

This was the moment all of Iran had waited for. When Saddam first invaded in 1980, the Iranian military had been in such poor shape that some of the country's senior commanders had believed they would be able to resist for just four days before being forced into an ignominious surrender. Now, two years later, against unimaginable odds, Iran had won back the city of Khorramshahr. It was a victory earned the hard way—through grit, determination, and extraordinary acts of collective sacrifice—and the celebrations were epic. Hundreds of thousands poured spontaneously onto Tehran's streets at the news, cheering, waving banners, and weeping for joy in a way not witnessed since the revolution.

Iranians now began to believe they were forging the path for a new, more spiritually pure form of warfare that would change the course of human history. "We are going to write our own [military] manuals," crowed Col. Behruz Soleimani, deputy commander of the 21st Division, "with absolutely new tactics that the Americans, British and French can study at their staff colleges." There was a mythical, almost mystical appreciation for the way Iran had been rescued from the brink of annihilation by the bravery of volunteers. The Iraqis, after all, had turned up for the fight equipped with state-of-the-art machinery and with battlefield tactics learned from the Soviets, but ultimately it had all proved worthless in the face of a few enthusiastic holy warriors.[*]

CƷ

With resounding victories against internal and external enemies behind them, the question for Khomeini and his allies now became what to do next. On the one hand, Khomeini was confronted by pragmatists who argued that the Revolution had succeeded in establishing itself and fighting off external enemies—and that this was a perfect opportunity to turn inward and rebuild the country. On the other hand, the more ideological wing of the IRP argued that now was precisely the time to take the fight to the enemy. According to this line of thinking, Iran's recent battlefield victories were only the first step in a crusade of epic, historic proportions that was about to reshape the direction of world events. The victory at Khorramshahr, the ideologues argued, had proved one important point: that the godless puppets of Washington and Moscow were helpless when confronted

---

[*] To this day, Iran celebrates the anniversary of Khorramshahr's liberation (May 24) as one of the great moments in its history—something resembling Iwo Jima, Bunker Hill, and the Alamo all rolled into one.

with "Islamic" warfare, and that they would crumble again and again on the battlefield.

This division between pragmatists and ideologues was not, as the various internal divisions of 1979, 1980, and 1981 had been, bitter and nasty in character. There were no fissiparous feuds, no public denunciations or steaming insults rising from the pages of dueling newspapers. It was not even possible to speak of two clearly defined rival "camps." Rather, what took place from 1982 was a gentlemanly, closed-door discussion about priorities and strategies among people fully devoted to the Khomeinist vision—a tactical rather than a philosophical conversation. Khomeini, as ever, did all he could to balance the various factions.* But ultimately the ayatollah was a revolutionary and an idealist, and his heart was always with people who had grand visions for where they wanted to take the Islamic Republic.

Thus, from the end of 1982, the Iranian Revolution entered the phase that virtually every major revolution eventually goes through: the export phase. Like the French, Russian, and American revolutions before it, the Iranian Revolution now saw itself as an unstoppable force for good in the region and the wider world—the last, best hope for the liberation of humanity. This shift in attitude was immediately visible in Iran's conduct of the war. Following the Battle of Khorramshahr, Iraq withdrew its forces to the border and agreed to a proposed UN-brokered peace treaty, but Tehran insisted that Saddam had to pay for all the trouble he had caused—demanding $100 billion in reparations and Saddam's international condemnation as a war criminal. Iran even insisted—twenty years before an American president ever uttered the words "regime change in Baghdad"—that Saddam Hussein was a menace to the region and had to be removed from power. When these terms were (predictably) refused, Khomeini took the war directly onto Iraqi territory—determined to use the momentum of Khorramshahr to accomplish an even broader goal. It was no longer enough, it seemed, just to defend the country from a foreign invasion. Iran now wanted to assume the mantle of leadership in the Islamic world, "liberating" the "oppressed" and impoverished Muslim masses from the various forms of secularism, socialism, royalist tyranny, occupation, and autocracy imposed on them by their venal puppet-dictators.

This new phase of the war began in July 1982 with a major assault on the southern Iraqi city of Basra. Badly outnumbered and facing an Iraqi army

---

* Khomeini's pragmatic streak is sometimes underappreciated. In December 1982, for example, he declared: "We should no longer say we are in a revolutionary condition. No, now is the time for calm . . . the time for people to feel a sense of security in all their affairs, to get their investments up and running and return to their businesses" (*Ettela'at*, 2 Dey 1361 [22 December 1982], p. 2).

equipped with MiGs and European antitank missiles, Iran turned confidently to the tactics that had worked so well in Khorramshahr—sending
one hundred thousand volunteers in human wave attacks, and using six
(poorly equipped) armored and infantry divisions to give them cover. Once
again the leadership chose a name calculated to deliver goose bumps to the
necks of pious young recruits—Operation Ramadan, in honor of the fact
that the offensive began on the first day of the Islamic holy month of fasting. (Thus one of the largest land battles since the Second World War was
fought by an army that refused to eat or drink water during the day.) But
Iran's renewed emphasis on religious ideology did not pay dividends. In two
weeks Iran lost twenty thousand men, and—though it came desperately
close to capturing Basra—was forced to make do with only a few useless
miles of Iraqi territory.

Despite this conspicuous failure, Iran's human wave attacks continued.
Convinced they had the Iraqis on the ropes, and aware that Iraq's smaller,
more demoralized population would not be able to sustain casualties in
the tens of thousands the way Iran's could, Iranian leaders pressed on with
their campaign of attrition—always believing that just one more bloody
offensive, one more big push into enemy territory, would bring about the
total collapse of Iraqi resistance. And sadly, this was always just enough of a
possibility that the strategy became impossible to abandon. Thus did a war
that might have ended in 1982 with a dignified truce—and something of a
moral victory for Iran—continue, needlessly, for another six years.

Just as the Iranians launched this new phase of the revolution, they were
handed a propaganda victory on a massive scale by the United States and
its allies. In June 1982, Israel invaded its northern neighbor, Lebanon, and
the Reagan administration gave the operation its full support. As fighting in
Beirut steadily spiraled into a civil war of enormous complexity, the United
States joined France, Britain, and Italy in creating a Multinational Force for
Lebanon (MNF). Ostensibly, the MNF was there to ensure stability and
to evict Palestinian guerrillas from their positions near the Israeli border.
On the ground, however, the Lebanese saw it differently. Israel hoped to
install a friendly government in Beirut, led by Bashir Gemayel and his small
community of Maronite Christians. But their countrymen despised the
Maronites—who made up barely 25 percent of the Lebanese population—
seeing them as Israeli stooges. For the United States, it was a dangerous
place to be getting involved.

For Iran, however, it was the perfect opportunity. Gathered in one place
now, suddenly, were all the crusaders, occupiers, and assorted colonialist
villains of Middle Eastern history—all begging for some form of collective
punishment. And for once, Iran alone seemed both uniquely positioned

and mentally prepared to take up the mantle of Islamic resistance against them. As the crapulent, gout-ridden leaders of the Arab world dithered and squabbled over how to respond to the Israeli invasion, hundreds of Iran's Revolutionary Guards quietly slipped into Lebanon's Beqaa Valley, where they took advantage of long-standing relations with the local Shia population. Charitable organizations were set up, along with social services to address the needs of Lebanon's long-suffering Shia minority. So too was a popular militia pledging armed resistance against the Israeli invasion. Eventually, the whole operation was brought together under the leadership of an umbrella organization called Hezbollah—the Party of God.

By 1983, the forces of Shia radicalism that Iran had helped organize in Lebanon took on an assertive new posture of their own and become yet another belligerent in Lebanon's rapidly overheating civil war. In Septem-

Horror in Beirut: On October 23, 1983, pro-Iranian militias fighting in Lebanon's civil war drove a truck bomb into the U.S. Marine Corps barracks, killing 241 servicemen. U.S. Marines and Iranian proxies were among many internal and external actors involved in the Lebanese civil war, but because the United States was officially on a peacekeeping mission, Washington today considers this the first example of Iranian support for terrorism.

ber of that year, the United States—perhaps not fully aware what a slumgul-
lion of ethnic and religious hatred it was getting involved in—threw its
weight behind the Israeli-backed Lebanese government, sending the navy's
Sixth Fleet to shell Shia villages in the Shuf Mountains (killing, in the process, a number of innocent bystanders and causing great outrage). Inevitably, Hezbollah (or perhaps one of its proxies—these things can never be
fully unraveled) responded.* On October 23 a truck packed with explosives
drove into the U.S. Marine Corps barracks at Beirut International Airport
and blew it sky-high, killing 241 American servicemen.

ભ

This strategy of ideological zealotry and crusading regional adventurism
that Iran began following in the early 1980s was not, on close inspection,
nearly as irrational or as fanatical as it appeared. In Lebanon, after all, Iran
had seized the opportunity to fight both the United States and Israel at the
same time, thus gaining huge moral credibility and political leverage in
the Arab world. And even the strategy of human wave attacks pursued in
the later stages of the war had its uses. Seen from a purely cold and heart-
less perspective, Iran, which enjoyed no access to the international arms
markets, had only one real "weapon" that it could use against Iraq: its much
larger and more motivated civilian population.† The Iranian leadership saw
this as an important strategic advantage and had every reason to believe a
relentless campaign of human wave attacks would eventually wear down
their Iraqi enemies.

While all this religiously inspired foreign policy might have followed a
certain twisted, internal logic of its own, in real terms it also succeeded in
putting (quite literally) the fear of God into the entire world. Scared out of
their wits by the prospect of an uncontrollable, overheating engine-room of
Islamic revolution sending its pistons firing in every direction, from early
in 1983, all the region's sheikhs and emirs—the lubricious but ever-reliable
guardians of the status quo—piled on offers of support to Saddam Hussein. Already Jordan had put its ports and overland routes at Iraq's disposal.
Now Kuwait and Saudi Arabia did the same. Bahrain, Qatar, and several
Arab Emirates loaned money to Iraq. Egypt sold it weapons. Saudi Arabia

---

* Islamic Jihad, a group that the United States accused of being a front for Hezbollah, claimed
responsibility for the attack. However, there were deep disagreements among Reagan administration officials, with Defense Secretary Caspar Weinberger maintaining until the end of his life that
it was never clear who was behind it. Hezbollah and Iran have always denied responsibility.
† Unlike Iraq, whose 15 million people were largely employed in cushy government jobs, Iran had
45 million people, many of them unemployed, idle, and deeply committed to the cause.

even doubled its oil output, knowing the precipitous drop in the price of crude (from $27 a barrel to $10) would cripple Iran's ability to finance its war effort. The Soviet Union, despite an official policy of "strict neutrality" in the war, increased military and economic assistance to Baghdad, signing fresh contracts worth $2 billion in MiG-23s, T-72 tanks, and missiles. And perhaps most ominously for Iran, Western countries shed their reluctance to support Saddam. France went into overdrive, selling Mirage F-1 and Super Étendard attack jets by the boatload to Iraq and loading them up with air-to-surface Exocet missiles. In 1982 alone France sold $660 million of military hardware to Saddam, and that figure climbed to more than $2 billion a year by 1985. By 1985, in fact, Iraq had become the largest importer of weapons in the world, raking in $9.5 billion worth a year.

Leading the world in this scramble to Saddam's doorstep was the United States. For the first years of the war, Washington had been lukewarm in its support for Baghdad, concerned that too close an embrace might stoke Saddam's regional ambitions. From 1982, however, all that changed. As momentum in the war seemed to shift in Tehran's favor, Washington concluded that even if it was not in American interests for Saddam to *win* the war, it was critical to ensure he did not lose it either. Iraq was quietly removed from the State Department's list of "state sponsors of terrorism"—a move that allowed greater latitude in financial aid and intelligence-sharing. American AWACS spy planes cruised the skies over Iran and immediately relayed information to Baghdad (so fast that Iraq usually knew "within minutes" if an Iranian air sortie had taken off or a human wave attack was being prepared). In 1983 the United States began providing Iraq with economic assistance in the form of "agricultural credits," freeing Baghdad to spend money on American weapons and helicopters. In 1984, when reliable reports emerged that Saddam was using chemical weapons against Iran, the United States simply looked the other way.* And by 1985, Washington was supplying Baghdad with export licenses for high-tech equipment that could be used in the manufacture of its now-infamous weapons of mass destruction (WMD) program. At the end of 1983, a young Defense Department official named Donald Rumsfeld was even dispatched to Baghdad, where he energetically shook hands with Saddam Hussein in front of the TV cameras—letting all the world know what side of this conflict America was on.

In short, by the mid-1980s, there was hardly a country on Earth that

---

* In March 1984 a UN report documented extensive Iraqi use of chemical weapons, but the U.S. response consisted only of a half-hearted statement of disapproval. When it emerged that several European countries were supplying Saddam with chemical agents, again, the response was mild. A congressional resolution against Iraq was discouraged and eventually abandoned.

was not providing some form of assistance or political support to Saddam Hussein. United by a fear of revolutionary Islam and the potentially transformative impact Khomeini's vision might have on the region, the countries of the world linked arms to create a virtual cordon sanitaire around the mad mullahs of Tehran, in order to prevent an Iranian victory. And at the forefront of all these efforts was the United States of America.

Or so it appeared.

C03

On November 3, 1986, a small Lebanese newsmagazine published a bizarre-sounding investigative story, a report so utterly implausible that anyone reading it would have rubbed their eyes and wondered what had made its way into the local drinking water. The United States, the magazine claimed, had been secretly selling arms to *Iran*. In exchange for these arms, Iran was making a secret effort to ensure the release of American citizens held hostage by its Hezbollah allies in Lebanon. And to top it all off, no less a figure than Ronald Reagan's former national security adviser, Robert McFarlane, had personally traveled to Tehran—on a plane loaded with American-made missiles and spare parts.

Ordinarily, a story of such preposterous dimensions, printed in an obscure Middle Eastern newspaper, would have been dismissed as a fatuous conspiracy theory cooked up by amateur journalists with too much time on their hands. But over the next few days, as more details of this unusual story spread around the world, journalists from Washington to London to Tel Aviv noticed something rather curious in their discussions with official sources: no one was actually denying it.

Within weeks, the scandal metastasized into one of the greatest political storms of the twentieth century—and was threatening to bring down an American presidency. In the U.S. press, the scandal quickly acquired the nickname "Irangate"—later amended to "Iran-contra" when it emerged (curiouser and curiouser this story became) that funds from the sale of weapons to Iran had been secretly diverted to fund anti-Communist contra rebels in the Nicaraguan civil war. In Washington, congressional hearings were held, and the nation's political class was riveted by "gavel-to-gavel" news coverage of those hearings—complete with swashbuckling tales of secret flights, bribes paid in hotel bathrooms, and Iranian arms dealers getting private tours of the White House. And over the next several months, as precise details emerged, the public was able to develop a complete picture of just what a putrid gumbo of backroom deals had been cooked up by all the president's men.

Arms for hostages: In 1986 it emerged that the Reagan
White House had established a secret channel to send
weapons to Iran, in exchange for Iranian pressure on
Shia militias in Lebanon to release U.S. citizens they
had taken hostage. Former national security adviser
Robert McFarlane, who had personally flown to
Tehran in a plane stuffed with weapons, testifies to
Congress about the scandal—dubbed "Iran-contra."

It was not an edifying spectacle. McFarlane had, in fact, flown to Tehran with a planeload of weapons—but this was only the last in a long series
of bizarre and secretive actions that the Reagan administration took as part
of a covert effort to improve relations with Iran. The first had taken place
as early as May 1985, when McFarlane started exploring the possibility of
"back channel" liaisons to the so-called "moderate" elements in the Iranian
leadership (most notably parliament speaker Akbar Hashemi Rafsanjani).
The following month he received an unexpected boost when Rafsanjani—
hoping to demonstrate Iran's openness to such overtures—intervened to
secure the release of Western hostages onboard a hijacked TWA passenger
jet in Beirut.* Encouraged, Reagan sent a personal letter of thanks to Rafsanjani via a secret intermediary, expressing his hope that this might be the
beginning of a new phase in U.S.-Iranian relations. Within weeks, these

---

* The hapless Flight 847 had been hijacked on June 15 and had been shuttling between Beirut
and Algiers for nearly two weeks—with no one able to bring the matter to an end. (Even the
Syrian president failed in his attempts to intervene.) Rafsanjani, however, picked up the phone
and brought immense pressure to bear on the hijackers. (As Shia revolutionaries, they very much
admired, and were receptive to, anything that came from Tehran.)

initial contacts blossomed into a full-blown "arms for hostages" operation, with hundreds of American-made TOW antitank missiles being sent, via Israel of all places, directly to Tehran—in exchange for Iranian pressure on Hezbollah to release American hostages.

That, at least, was where the story had ended—just before exploding uncontrollably all over newspaper front pages. Where it had begun—or, rather, *why* it had begun—was a slightly more difficult matter to pin down. But it had something to do with the timeless ability of pragmatism to triumph over idealism. In both Iran and America, at some point in the early-to-mid-1980s, grandiose, transcendent, world-defining ideologies had begun to take a backseat to the more prosaic realities of statecraft and inter-national relations. In each country, this process had taken its own particular form and come about for its own particular set of reasons.

For the Iranians, the dilemma was both simple and perverse: after decades of close cooperation between Washington and the shah, Iran's mili-tary was almost entirely reliant on American-built hardware—and thus on American *spare parts* for that hardware. The hostage crisis had cut off Iran's access to American military technology (and from the international arms market generally), and by the mid-1980s, its weapons stocks had become severely depleted.[*] Iraq, by contrast, had a massive arms bazaar at its disposal—French Mirages, Soviet MiGs, and American Apache helicopters. Without some comparable flow of matériel, Iran would almost certainly lose the war, and once it had lost the war, it would surely lose the revolution as well. Thus the dilemma for the authorities in Tehran was as acute as it was poetic: they had spent years, and engaged in much blood and thun-der, in their epic struggle against "American imperialism"—and they could justifiably claim to have pulled off one of the great ideological revolutions in modern history. Now, however, they found the only way to defend that revolution was with arms supplied by the Great Satan itself.

For the United States, meanwhile, an equally awkward moral com-promise was at work. Reagan had come to power on a star-spangled wave of patriotism, righteous indignation, and clear-eyed moral absolutism—calling Iranians "barbarians" and promising that "America will never make concessions to terrorists." By the end of his first term, however, all this high-minded bombast had run aground on the treacherous shoals of Leba-non. In January 1984, furious over the Beirut bombings (and convinced the orders for that operation had come from Tehran), the Reagan administra-

---

[*] The human wave campaign, born of necessity, had allowed Iran to believe it could progress mili-tarily, but eventually Iran recognized that it would need more conventional weaponry to prosecute the war.

"I was authorized to do everything that I did": In explosive testimony, Lt. Col. Oliver North, point man in the arms deal, claimed Reagan had known everything and given his approval.

tion had added Iran to its list of "state sponsors of terrorism." Two months later Americans had begun disappearing in Lebanon, kidnapped by a group sympathetic to Iran. Reagan was genuinely anguished over the kidnapped Americans, but unlike his predecessor, he was determined not to allow this anguish to degenerate into a public spectacle. The last thing his administration, or the country as a whole, needed was another long, drawn-out psychodrama involving American hostages in the Middle East. Reagan had to find a quiet, behind-the-scenes way to get those Americans released. And it seemed only Iran exercised the kind of influence in Lebanon that could make that happen.

Thus, in 1985, the leaders of both Iran and the United States found themselves in a rather peculiar position: Each desperately needed a specific favor from the other. But each was even more desperate to make sure no one found out about it.

By the time the whole thing hit the headlines in November 1986, it had become a fiasco—and this was vividly apparent to the American public. Almost overnight, Reagan's popularity with the American people plummeted from a 67 percent approval rating to 46 percent. The U.S. electorate, still nursing profound anger over the Iranian hostage crisis of 1980, were shocked and mystified to learn that their government was selling weapons to Iran. They were even more shocked to discover this had happened under the watchful eye of President Reagan—the cowboy-hero who had claimed to have little time for Middle Eastern bad guys. Perhaps most surprising of all were the sheer lengths the administration had gone to in its efforts to woo the Iranians. When McFarlane and his team arrived in Tehran in May 1986, the public now learned, their plane had been full of more than just weapons. It also carried a pair of goodwill tokens: a chocolate cake in the shape of a key, and a Bible in which President Reagan had handwritten one of his favorite verses for the ayatollah.

Desperate to control the damage, the president made a televised broadcast on November 13, doing his best to conjure up some of that homespun wit and wisdom that had always served him well with the American public. "I know you've been reading, seeing, and hearing a lot of stories the past several days attributed to Danish sailors, unnamed observers at Spanish ports and Italian harbors, and especially unnamed government officials of my administration," Reagan began. "Well, now you're going to hear the facts from a White House source, and you know my name." Over the next several minutes, Reagan explained exactly why he had felt it was important to open a channel of communication with Iran. The goal, he said, had been to get hostages released—but there was also a larger strategic objective at stake. "Iran encompasses some of the most important geography in the world," Reagan explained. "Without Iran's cooperation we cannot bring an end to the Persian Gulf War; without Iran's concurrence, there can be no enduring peace in the Middle East." Reagan even added, for good measure, that the "Iranian revolution is a fact of history, but between American and Iranian basic national interests there need be no permanent conflict."

It was vintage Reagan, and among large segments of the American public, the president bounced back as a decisive and trustworthy leader. But he still had to contend with the shock and anger of America's allies, both in Europe and in the Arab world. The Europeans were seething over the fact that they had been asked to refrain from selling weapons to Iran—only to find America had reserved the best part of this lucrative business for itself. Arab allies, in particular Egypt, Jordan, and Saudi Arabia, began wondering whether, when push came to shove, U.S. support for Iraq—and America's willingness to suppress the menace of the Iranian Revolution—were anything more than empty gestures. As if all this were not bad enough, America had to deal with the humiliation of Iranians crowing with delight over the bloody nose they had given the United States. On Iranian television, Rafsanjani held up the Bible Reagan had sent and practically gurgled with satisfaction. "America has accepted that the Islamic Republic, invincible and victorious, is standing on its own feet," he said in a sermon on November 7.

The ayatollah, speaking two weeks later, was even more triumphant. "Those who broke relations with Iran," he said, "have come back—presenting themselves meekly and humbly at the door of the nation, wishing to establish relations and making apologies." This he described as a victory "greater than all our [previous] victories."

The explanation, in some ways, was even simpler than that. Strategists in Washington had always had a great desire to see *both* sides exhausted in the Iran-Iraq war. Perennial popinjay Henry Kissinger, for example, spoke wistfully of the "mutual exhaustion" that "might rid the Middle East of the aggressive regimes of *both* Ayatollah Khomeini and Saddam Hussein." In 1982 a Reagan administration official was quoted saying, "an all-out Iranian or Iraqi victory would only upset the balance in the region and cause problems for the West." And no less a figure than Robert McFarlane, in his testimony to Congress, made it clear what kind of message he had delivered to the Iranians during his infamous visit to Tehran: "I stated that they should understand that we were not prepared to give them the level of arms which would enable them to win the war." (Just enough, in other words, to keep it going.) Perhaps the bluntest assessment came from Ed Juchniewicz, the number-two man in the CIA's Operations Division at the time. In 2003, he told an interviewer that the agency's goal during the Iran-Iraq war had been to level the playing field between the two combatants: "We didn't want either side to have the advantage," he explained. "We just wanted them to kick the shit out of each other."

☙

Following the disastrous revelations of the Iran-contra scandal, the Reagan administration felt it had little choice but to abandon any attempt to mend fences with Iran. Public opinion in the United States was still feverishly anti-Iranian, and the bungled arms-for-hostages pipeline, along with its very public collapse, felt like yet another humiliation. Saudi Arabia, Egypt, Jordan, and the Gulf states—pro-American regimes that had assumed they could count on U.S. support to keep the Iranian Revolution in check—now also needed to see some clarification of U.S. policy in the region. From early in 1987, therefore, the United States reassumed a hostile posture toward Iran, shifting more visibly toward support for Saddam Hussein. In March, Defense Secretary Weinberger stated bluntly that Iranian victory in the war is "certainly not in our national interest." And the United States leaned heavily on Israel to stop selling weapons to Iran. Washington also pressured Beijing to reduce its arms sales to Tehran—and increased the number of its warships in the region.

But the first really concrete indication of America's tilt toward Iraq and the Arab world came in the spring of 1987, when Washington agreed to start reflagging Kuwaiti oil tankers with the Stars and Stripes—thus, in effect, providing the tiny Gulf emirate with blanket U.S. military protection. It was a dangerous move—one that quickly escalated tensions and risked internationalizing the Iran-Iraq war—but the Reagan administration felt it had little choice. Iran was attacking Kuwaiti tankers carrying illicit arms shipments to Iraq, and toward the end of 1986, Kuwait's emir had approached Washington with a request for help. When the Americans hesitated, the emir had announced he would be turning to the Soviets. Determined to prevent Moscow from gaining influence over the oil-rich Gulf, the Reagan administration agreed to Kuwait's request. By April 1987 eleven of Kuwait's twenty-two oil tankers were flying the American flag.

Whether it wanted to or not, the United States had now become directly involved in the Iran-Iraq war—something it had largely avoided for the first six years of the conflict. And the result was a weird, frenetic— but ultimately undeclared—form of warfare between the United States and Iran. Over the course of 1987, American and Iranian vessels in the Persian Gulf engaged in a series of tit-for-tat military strikes and maneuvers that sometimes came dangerously close to all-out war. In September the United States captured and destroyed an Iranian frigate it accused of laying mines in the Persian Gulf sea lanes. Iran responded with a volley of shots at a reflagged Kuwaiti tanker, and the United States returned fire by blowing up an Iranian oil platform. And so it continued until, eventually, both sides became so wrapped up in their own sense of righteousness that they began to lose touch with reality. In Tehran, radio broadcasts boasted of Iran's ability "to carry out martyrdom-seeking attacks against international arrogance in the Gulf." And in the United States, the Reagan administration was no less irrational. On May 17, one of Saddam's Exocet missiles accidentally struck the navy frigate USS *Stark*, resulting in the deaths of thirty-seven American servicemen. Reagan somehow found a way to blame the incident on Iran—claiming Iranian aggression had created a chaotic environment in the Persian Gulf and therefore Iran was the real "villain in the piece."

Thanks to the muscular presence of the U.S. Navy on its doorstep, Iran, in effect, was now fighting a two-front war. And this suited Washington perfectly. In the United States, the growing consensus was that Iran had a real chance of emerging victorious and that every reasonable measure should be taken to ensure this did not happen. Eventually, the Americans dropped any pretense of neutrality. In May 1987 deputy defense secretary Richard Armitage laid out the American position bluntly in a statement to Congress: "We can't stand to see Iraq defeated."

For the Iranians, at least publicly, this ratcheting up of American hostility was a welcome distraction—yet another opportunity to fire up the propaganda machine and whip the public into a frenzy about the need to teach "arrogant" America a lesson. "If we had won the war last year," Rafsanjani crowed during a sermon in June, "everyone would have said that a 50 million-strong country was victorious over a 14 million-strong country. But if we win this year, everyone will know that we are victorious over the United States." Privately, though, away from the bluster and bravado, Iranian leaders were worried. They knew that Iran could never seriously expect to win a direct military confrontation with the United States—and that the public was growing weary.

If Iran's leaders needed any reminder of the fundamental military disparity that existed between their country and the United States, they received it on the morning of July 3, 1988, when an Iranian passenger jet, Iran Air flight 655, was accidentally downed by the USS *Vincennes*. The flight—a civilian, commercial shuttle en route from Bandar Abbas to Dubai—was carrying 290 passengers and crew. But it had the misfortune of taking off during a particularly ferocious dogfight between American and Iranian vessels in the Strait of Hormuz, and in the heat of combat, Capt. Will Rogers—a man often criticized by his navy colleagues (both before and since) for his "aggressiveness"—believed the plane was an F-14 Tomcat. He ordered two surface-to-air missiles fired to bring it down. The result was one of the most heart-wrenching catastrophes in aviation history. Television footage revealed scores of bodies—bloated, blanched, and spread-eagled on the water's surface like floating starfish—including those of small children still reaching in vain for who-knew-what. There had been sixty-six children onboard the doomed flight.

At first, the American reaction was to deny the incident altogether, then to suggest that the Iran Air pilot had failed to heed warnings from the *Vincennes* (a claim quickly proven untrue by the ship's logs). Then, as the old antagonisms crept into the rhetoric on both sides, the Reagan administration took on a more strident tone. Refusing even to apologize to the families of the victims, let alone suggest paying them compensation, Vice President George H. W. Bush blamed the incident on Iran's own belligerence—swatting away emerging evidence that Captain Rogers had not followed appropriate procedures.* "I will never apologize for the United States of America," Bush said in August. "Ever. I don't care what the facts are." At a

* The American public appeared to support this tough stance. Shortly after the incident, opinion polls revealed that 75 percent of Americans blamed Iran for what had happened, and that 61 percent felt no compensation should be paid to families.

Halabja: Iconic image of Kurdish man and child gassed to
death by Saddam Hussein in 1988. Citing religious objections,
Iran refused to retaliate for Iraqi gas attacks by using chemical
weapons itself and suffered large-scale casualties from them.
However, the United States did not condemn Saddam, instead
calling on "both sides" in the conflict to refrain from chemical
warfare. Iran interpreted this as a signal that the United States
was now firmly behind Saddam.

ceremony held several months later, the captain and crew of the *Vincennes*
were all awarded combat action ribbons. Rogers himself was later awarded
the Legion of Merit.

The Iranians saw a clear message in all this. Even if the downing of the
Iran Air flight had been an honest accident, as the Americans claimed, the
tenor of their response—and their visible lack of concern for the sanctity of
Iranian life—revealed something important about the U.S. attitude. Washington, they concluded, was now implacably hostile to the Islamic Republic
and would stop at nothing to bring about Iran's defeat in the war. The
American noose, many concluded, was tightening around Tehran.

If Iranians needed any more evidence, they received it in the spring
of 1988, when the United States reacted with indifference to reports about
Saddam Hussein's use of chemical weapons. In the Iraqi village of Halabja,
where local Kurds had risen against the government, Saddam ordered the
army to drop several rounds of poison gas into residential areas, including
such lethal toxins as mustard gas, sarin, and nerve agent, resulting in the
deaths of at least four thousand civilians. Photos—some so horrifying that
even battle-hardened soldiers and photojournalists found them difficult to
look at—were beamed around the world, revealing bodies strewn through

the streets, sea-green and bloated and collapsed on the spot where they had drawn their last breath of poison. Stories emerged of villagers who had coughed up green vomit, burned and blistered to death within minutes, or simply "died of laughing." It was, in the words of the first foreign photo-journalists to arrive on the scene, "a new kind of death"—"like watching a film and suddenly it stops on one frame. . . . You went into a room, a kitchen, and you saw the body of a woman holding a knife where she had been cutting a carrot."

Under different circumstances, the United States might have been quick to condemn the attack on Halabja. But in 1988, convinced that Iran was a far greater menace to the world than Iraq, and impatient to bring the war to an end, it said nothing.*

⋊⋉

By the summer of 1988, Iran was on its knees. Over the course of eight long years, it had lost hundreds of thousands of citizens and sustained hundreds of billions in losses to its economy and infrastructure. A number of recent military operations had gone badly wrong, including a disastrous, pig-headed 1987 offensive against Basra that cost sixty-five thousand Iranian lives and accomplished nothing. In February, the Iraqis had resumed their aerial strikes on Tehran, firing more than one hundred missiles in five weeks and causing hundreds of thousands to flee the capital. And now to top it off, the world's most powerful country had piled in on Iraq's side, determined to bring the war to a swift and decisive conclusion.

On July 14 a number of senior clerics and political leaders, including Iran's top generals, met secretly to find an exit strategy. Together they approached Rafsanjani, who in turn approached Khomeini, urging him to

---

* Less than nothing, in fact. When the matter of Halabja came up before the United Nations, the United States deflected, delayed, and watered down any proposed international condemnation of Iraq. In the end, it took seven weeks for a resolution to be passed, and the language—reflecting American preferences—was conspicuously neutral: condemning the "continued use of chemical weapons in the conflict between the Islamic Republic of Iran and Iraq" and calling on "both sides to refrain from the future use of chemical weapons." Khomeini had long ago declared that chemical weapons were contrary to Islam, and that Iran would never use them—and throughout the war, he respected this principle, despite numerous chemical attacks on Iranian troops, and despite the existence of chemical stockpiles left over from the shah's regime. Nevertheless, the State Department instructed U.S. diplomats to pursue a "both sides" strategy in their discussions with foreign officials, creating a public impression that chemical attacks from both Iran and Iraq were just an unfortunate reality in this conflict, and one more reason why the war had to be brought to a swift conclusion. To this day, no evidence whatsoever exists that Iran used chemical weapons. Thousands of Iranian war veterans, however, continue to suffer the ill effects of Iraqi chemical attacks.

accept UN Resolution 598, which called for an immediate cease-fire and a negotiated settlement. The ayatollah, never a man to ignore the prevailing winds of political opinion, agreed to bring the war to an end, but he made no effort to hide the pain the decision caused him. "Blessed are the dead and the departed," he said in a solemn ninety-minute radio address to the Iranian people. "Blessed are the noble families of those martyrs. Cursed am I that I remain alive to drink from the poisoned chalice and to accept this resolution."

For the rest of Iran, of course, the poisoned chalice had long ago run dry, drained again and again in the name of a stubborn attachment to revolutionary principles and a six-year refusal to contemplate anything other than total victory. The final cost of the war, in human terms alone, was almost too much to imagine—at least 123,000 dead, according to official figures, although reliable estimates have placed the number closer to 400,000 or more. No less staggering were the financial and material costs. The damage to Iran's economy—around $600 billion—was a sum that would take decades to recoup. Iraq had suffered similar levels of devastation in both human and capital terms. But unlike the Iraqis—who could rely on Saudi loans, American agricultural credits, French weapons, and Kuwaiti oil tankers to help them back on their feet—the Iranians were left on their own to deal with the devastation.

Those who write about the Iran-Iraq war, almost invariably, end up quoting the American statesman Henry Kissinger, who is said to have quipped, in a moment of private indiscretion, that it was "a pity both sides can't lose." And it is almost impossible, looking at the tremendous toll on the bridges, roads, schools, hospitals, libraries, graveyards, public memorials, factories, offices, and natural environment of Iran and Iraq, to escape the conclusion that this is exactly what happened. But as catastrophic as the losses sustained by both Iran and Iraq were, they were nothing compared to the much more subtle wounds and perforations that made their way—and continue to make their way—into the psyches of both countries. In the early 1980s, one middle-aged Iraqi army captain, haggard and misshapen after weeks in the trenches, told a pair of visiting British journalists what it had felt like for his men to face an army of teenage Iranian boys, day in and day out, as they charged onto the battlefield, ecstatically declaring their desire to die for the cause:

> They come on in their hundreds, often walking straight across the mine-fields, triggering them with their feet as they are supposed to do. They chant "allahu Akbar" and they keep coming, and we keep shouting, sweeping our 50 mills [.50-millimeter machine guns]

around like sickles. My men are eighteen, nineteen, just a few years older than these kids. I've seen them crying, and at times the officers have had to kick them back to their guns. Once we had Iranian kids on bikes cycling towards us, and my men all started laughing. And then these kids started lobbing their hand grenades and we stopped laughing and started firing.

In the final analysis, the Iran-Iraq war was the last epic land war of the twentieth century—the last conflict in modern history to be decided by the heat of gun barrels, trench by trench, village by village, and massacre by stinking, anonymous massacre. It was the last, ignominious outing for the ghosts of Verdun and Flanders Field. Two immensely headstrong and immensely ancient nations—neither equipped for a modern conflict of this magnitude—offered up everything they had in a desperate war of attrition that often seemed to operate out of some ferocious momentum of its own. Together they expended more than a trillion dollars and nearly a million lives.

CB

On June 3, 1989, Ayatollah Khomeini passed away quietly in his sleep, on a hospital bed in the north Tehran suburb of Jamaran. No one knew exactly how old he was—as for most Iranians of his age, his "birth certificate" would have consisted of little more than a handwritten note in the margins of the family Quran—and no one knew the exact cause of death. But he was certainly well into his eighties, and for his legions of adoring followers, little was left to the imagination. Television images showed the emam, unconscious and plugged into an EKG, surrounded at his bedside by Rafsanjani, the president, the prime minister, the chief justice, and a number of doctors and senior clerics—followed, moments later, by the sight of those same men beating themselves on the head, weeping, fainting, wailing, and throwing their arms in the air as the blinking line on the heart monitor went flat.

Throughout Iran, almost instantly, there was frenzy. The kind of frenzy that, even at the highest levels of the Islamic Republic, no one had fully anticipated. Within hours of the announcement, hundreds of thousands poured into the streets around Jamaran, spontaneously, before any kind of encouragement from government media, all dressed in black and waving black flags. Over the coming hours and days, the crowd swelled into the millions. Firefighters sprayed water on the crowd to keep people from fainting in the hundred-degree heat, and Revolutionary Guards fired shots into the air to warn those who were trying to tear off portions of Khomeini's burial shroud in their excitement—but it was little use. Eventually, the grieving built to such a crescendo that a military helicopter had to be called in to pluck Khomeini's coffin from the crowd—and even then the chopper had trouble taking off, thanks to the delirious mourners dangling from its landing rails. The funeral was postponed to another day.

By the time the first week of mourning was over, according to Iranian media, more than ten thousand people had been treated for "self-inflicted injuries"—everything from exhaustion to heat stroke to loss of conscious-ness and broken bones. Several dozen even lost their lives in the crush.

∝

Just ten years earlier no one had expected the Islamic Republic to last—much less to continue to exercise such an emotional pull over much of the Iranian population. Ten years earlier political analysts, royalist exiles, and U.S. officials had all dismissed the Khomeini phenomenon as a tempo-rary attack of collective insanity, a folly that would soon be overturned and replaced by a more pliable, "reasonable" regime. Even in the mid-1980s, experts were predicting the Islamic Republic's imminent demise—complete with reports that the Iranian people were on the verge of rising up and overthrowing their hated, tyrannical leaders. What all these analyses missed was what they had always missed, and what they continue, in some form, to miss even today: however disaffected the Iranian public might have been with specific policies of its government, its loyalty to the Islamic Revolution and to the political philosophy of Ayatollah Khomeini was unshakable.

Even among those who helped bring about the Revolution, the sheer depth of religious fervor that accompanied its creation is not always fully appreciated. To this day, Iranian Communists, liberals, and secular nation-alists can be heard rattling their bones in Parisian cafés, swearing up and down that the Khomeinists and the IRP "stole" the revolution from the people, that they were "used" and later "discarded" in a cynical act of politi-cal gamesmanship. There is genuine merit in this interpretation of history. But there are also real limitations to it. It is not so much that the radicals "hijacked" the revolution; in many ways, it was theirs all along. It is perhaps more the case that the hostage crisis and the Iraq war created a polarized atmosphere in which radical religious ideologies found a more receptive audience among the Iranian public than they might have under calmer, more "ordinary" circumstances. It is certainly fair to argue that Khomeini might have struggled to come to power and set up a functioning govern-ment without the help of his Paris-based gang of technocrats and intel-lectuals. But it is also true that the revolution, once it consolidated power,

Death of the emam: On one of the hottest days of the year, June 3, 1989, millions poured onto the streets to mourn the passing of Ayatollah Khomeini. A year earlier Khomeini had finally brought an end to the war, even as he cursed himself for drinking from the "poisoned chalice" of surrender. Khomeini's death, and the end of the war, set the scene for a more moderate, pragmatic era in the Islamic Republic's history.

would never have survived, or put down roots with quite the vigor that it did, without the massive sacrifices of a very different kind of Iranian—the nameless, faceless millions who signed up to serve as cannon fodder in the trenches of the Shatt al-Arab and the mountains of Kurdistan. It might well have been decades of liberal opposition to the shah in the 1950s, 1960s, and 1970s that chipped away at the old order and paved the way for the titanic backlash that followed. But it was in the crucible of the 1980s that the revolution was truly cemented.

Just what exactly that revolution *was,* and how it was going to evolve in the years following Khomeini's death, was another matter entirely. Khomeini had articulated a vision—but it was a vision so fluid and inscrutable that even the most genuinely committed of his disciples often found themselves at loggerheads over its interpretation or implementation. Khomeini had placed the "downtrodden of the earth" at the very center of his political philosophy, and he emphasized the universal potential of Islam to liberate humanity. Thus, his vision of revolution seemed designed to transcend national boundaries. But at the same time he was a proud Iranian nationalist who refused to speak Arabic with visiting dignitaries despite his fluency in the language and who spoke always of the *Iranian* Revolution

rather than the Islamic Revolution. When some of his more fanatical followers suggested blowing up the ancient ruins of Persepolis on the grounds
that they were a pagan eyesore, Khomeini put his foot down, insisting that
Persepolis was a national treasure and should be treated with pride. Unlike
some of those who surrounded him, Khomeini never favored a truly radical "Islamization" of Iran—a totalizing, Taliban-style takeover that ignored
national aspirations and sought to re-create medieval Islam. He believed in
a version of Iranian nationalism that drew its inspiration from the Shia faith
that he knew was important to the public (rather than from the contrived
glorification of ancient Persia that the last two shahs had promoted). In
the end, what he left the world was a peculiarly *Iranian* version of Islamic
government—a polity that was equal parts nationalism, liberation theology,
religious fundamentalism, anti-imperialism, Iranian exceptionalism, and
crusading universalism.

It was now up to his successors in the Islamic Republic—and their
enemies in the United States—to work out what to do with it all.

Goodwill Hunting

By the time the Iran-Iraq war finally came to an end in 1988, Iranians were displaying much less enthusiasm for epic gestures and grand revolutionary rhetoric than they had shown ten years earlier. Exhausted by years of bombing raids, demoralized by the sight of cemeteries where the graves of young warriors stretched out to the farthest horizon, and desperately tired of hearing that their country was at the forefront of some international Islamic reawakening, many felt the time had come for a little sober-headed pragmatism. For eight long years, they had watched on television as one military offensive after another was announced, each portentously presented as the beginning of the end for the "arrogant imperialist powers" of the world. But in all that time, they had witnessed only the deterioration of their own nation's infrastructure. Khorramshahr was in ruins. Sixty-five percent of the country's refinery capacity had been destroyed. Two million refugees had fled their homes and resettled in already-overcrowded cities. However much they believed in Khomeini's vision for exporting the revolution and freeing the world's masses from injustice and oppression, most citizens now wanted the country to turn inward a little—spend a little more time repairing roads and bridges and less time on bombastic slogans about "world-devouring America" or the "liberation" of Palestine. In 1989, perhaps more than ever before in their history, Iranians just wanted some peace and quiet.

At the same time, though, something irreversible had happened. There had been a baptism by fire—a colossal, communal bloodbath that every Iranian citizen had participated in to some degree, whether they had wanted to or not. And it had left the country in a permanent, almost reflexive, state of radicalization and antagonism toward the outside world. In boulder-strewn villages and mud-brick slums across the country, the war had created a generation of holy warriors—young men who had fought and bled in the trenches of the Shatt al-Arab and whose only understanding of politics was the image of Saddam Hussein, armed to the teeth by the West, dousing them with nerve gas, while the world looked on. Even the wealthy, most of whom had deftly avoided sending their children to the front lines, had felt the effects of food and fuel rationing and blinked in terror whenever air raid sirens sliced the night skies of Tehran. These things could not be easily forgotten, nor easily subsumed in the rush to normality. As far as the average Iranian citizen was concerned, the world had forsaken Iran—and only its own revolutionary ardor had saved it from utter destruction.

Iran also had institutions now, established organizations that guaranteed and perpetuated a certain ideological radicalization in the nation's politics. Revolutionary committees, which had spent the war years enforcing blackouts and curfews and searching vehicles for signs of "subversive" behavior, had become a permanent feature of the nation's policing. The Foundation for the Oppressed, which had seized houses and properties from fleeing royalist millionaires in 1979, had redistributed those assets among the nation's poor—helping the revolution put down roots and win over a new generation of passionate supporters. Most noticeable of all, perhaps, the war had established the Revolutionary Guards as the true protectors of the nation and a political force in their own right. Over the course of the 1980s, the Guards had accelerated their recruitment drives, improved their training methods, secured sophisticated weaponry, and gained valuable war experience. And their troop numbers had climbed from zero to a whopping 120,000 (with at least twice as many Basij). During the war, these eager young zealots had rushed to the battlefield to take part in human wave attacks—and for the most part, Iranians were grateful for their sacrifice. On the wall of virtually every teahouse and living room in Iran now, there hung a black and white picture of a young man cut down in the prime of his life—the family's own *shahid,* or martyr.

What all this added up to was a fundamental tension. On the one hand, exhaustion and war-fatigue were pushing the nation in the direction of pragmatism and humility—and away from the exuberant emotionalism of the previous decade. On the other hand, the experience of war had also created a built-in constituency for something bigger and bolder—a need to honor the sacrifices made by the younger generation and to continue the fight, as Khomeini had instructed, from Karbala to Jerusalem and beyond. It was like a self-fulfilling prophecy—a feeling that if the Islamic Republic had come this far along the road of revolutionary idealism, there should be no turning back.

This tension—this awkward coexistence between pragmatism and ideology—would become a defining feature of the Islamic Republic's poli-tics.

CZ

Initial appearances suggested the first round would go to the pragmatists. Immediately following the death of Khomeini in June 1989, the turbaned, bearded heads of the Assembly of Experts, Iran's equivalent of the College of Cardinals, met in secret to nominate a successor to the great emam—a man whose superhuman qualities had been celebrated to such a degree that it was hard to imagine any mere mortal could succeed him. The name they came up with was that of Iran's president, Ali Khamenei, a quiet, unobtru-sive cleric whose eight years in office had been marked by pragmatism. To many in the assembly, Khamenei seemed like a safe pair of hands—worldly, astute, far more grounded in the realities of life than Khomeini had ever been. Crucially, his candidacy was championed by the increasingly influen-tial Majles speaker Akbar Hashemi Rafsanjani. Since Khamenei had to give up his job as president to become supreme leader, his first task as supreme leader was to organize an election for his successor as president. It came as little surprise to anyone when Rafsanjani won in a landslide.

Rafsanjani, the pistachio magnate, the self-made man, the serial entre-preneur whose personal net worth was the subject of many a wagging chin around Tehran dining tables, seemed just the kind of man to lead the coun-try into a postwar era of reconstruction and revitalization. Although he wore a turban and had served the cause of the revolution as ably as anyone, Rafsanjani was a far cry from the typical cleric. Uniquely for a man of the cloth, he was cursed with an inability to grow a beard—a physical oddity that immediately set him apart from his peers and gave him an urbane, clean-cut appearance. More important, he had never been the kind of cleric to fear the modern world. He was a pragmatist, a political operator who genuinely believed there was no reason for the Islamic Republic to maintain a relationship of permanent hostility with the United States. In the 1970s, Rafsanjani had even traveled there, driving cross-country to visit a brother studying at UC Berkeley. And in the 1980s he had spent several years neck-deep in secret arms deals with the CIA.

Under Rafsanjani, Iran embarked on a sweeping program of privati-zation and economic liberalization, designed to jolt the economy into a much-needed growth spurt. The stock market was reopened in 1989, ration-ing and the tightly controlled war economy of the 1980s came to an end, and a five-year plan was put in place to fund the building of rural roads, electrification projects, urban renewal, parks, and—most ambitiously—a long-overdue metro for Tehran. Dozens of sports centers, cultural institutions, department stores, shopping malls, and high-rise apartment blocks were built, turning Tehran's once-drowsy skyline into a spiky pincushion of glass and steel and unholy ambition. Exiled Iranians were encouraged to return and invest in the country, as the government set up free trade zones and lowered business taxes. Military spending was scaled back—from $9.9 billion in 1990 to $5.3 billion in 1995—and the Revolutionary Guards were told to redirect their energies to private-sector civil engineering projects.

The new president also took a more pragmatic attitude toward foreign relations, arguing that the Islamic Republic could never hope to succeed, economically or otherwise, if it remained isolated from international capital markets. Relations with Europe, which had taken a beating over the Salman Rushdie affair in 1988, improved dramatically as Iran invited European companies to bid on oil and gas projects and reconstruction contracts. Rafsanjani also repaired relations with Arab states, who felt reassured by the less belligerent tone coming out of Tehran. And Iran's relations with Moscow improved, thanks largely to the disintegration of the Soviet Union.[*] Relations with the United States, of course, were a much thornier question. But Rafsanjani believed that by mending fences with Europe, he might gradually reintegrate Iran into the international community—thus leaving the United States with little choice but to soften its antagonism toward the Islamic Republic.

Rafsanjani, however, was in no position to do all this on his own. Under Iran's constitution, ultimate power resided with Khamenei, whose job was to set the overall tone and direction of policy in a way that would be worthy of Khomeini and the revolution. Neither a president nor a king, the new ayatollah was expected to rise above the petty, day-to-day micronarratives of the political arena, occupying an ethereal, otherworldly space as a sort of spiritual guru for his nation. This gave him a considerable amount of latitude. It also placed him in a position in which he was expected, like Khomeini before him, to mediate among the various factions vying for influence over policy—without showing bias or inclination toward one or the other.

Fortunately for Rafsanjani, Khamenei exhibited a philosophical outlook toward politics that was remarkably similar to his own. Both men believed in the value of hard-boiled realpolitik and steady, sensible decision making. Unlike Khomeini before him, Khamenei was a politician's politician, a street-smart cleric who had spent enough time in and out of the

---

[*] In the 1980s the USSR had supported leftist movements in Iran, occupied neighboring Afghanistan, and supported Saddam Hussein.

The new leadership: Ayatollah Ali Khamenei (right) and his first president, Akbar Hashemi Rafsanjani (left), ushered in a new era of pragmatism and attempted to cool tensions with the West.

shah's prisons to understand that godliness and idealism were no substitute for political expediency. Upon assuming power, Khamenei used his moral and religious authority as supreme leader to strengthen his support base among revolutionary institutions (in particular rank-and-file Revolutionary Guards) but also to convince radicals they had nothing to fear from the Rafsanjani agenda. The arrangement worked perfectly. By lending the president an aura of revolutionary legitimacy, Khamenei defused tensions between ideologues and pragmatists, leaving Rafsanjani free to focus on economic reform and international diplomacy. Eventually, Rafsanjani and Khamenei would discover areas of disagreement. But for the moment, these two highly astute, highly pragmatic politicians worked hand in hand. Together they steered Iran—ably if uncharismatically—into the uncharted waters of the post-Khomeini era.

଼ଷ

For the United States, meanwhile, 1989 was an equally pivotal moment of transition. In the early months of the year, some of Europe's most unshakable Communist regimes had collapsed under the weight of popular protests and revolutions, and the Cold War, which had dominated American foreign policy thinking for decades, appeared on the verge of irrelevance. The Soviet Union was engaged in unprecedented political and economic liberalization, and in November millions of East Germans chipped and chiseled their way through the Berlin Wall, in scenes that could scarcely have been imagined a year earlier. Not even China was immune to the changes, as protesters gathered in Tiananmen Square to face off against army tanks on live international television.

It was an extraordinary moment for American power, and in many ways the United States was fortunate to have a president—George H. W. Bush— who could boast a long, wide-ranging career in foreign affairs. Bush was particularly knowledgeable about Cold War politics and acutely sensitive to the special circumstances of America's recent dealings with Iran. As Reagan's vice president, he had written in his diaries: "I'm one of the few people that know fully the details" of Iran-contra—and no one doubted the truth of this statement. Bush had previously served the Nixon and Ford administrations as ambassador to the UN, envoy to China, and head of the CIA. Over the previous twenty years, there was hardly an intrigue or initiative in American foreign policy from which Bush's fingerprints were absent.

Like his predecessor Reagan, Bush understood that the disastrous breach in relations with Iran was only one thread in a rich tapestry of foreign policy priorities facing the United States. Though he recognized the importance of Iran, he felt that in 1989 mending fences with the Islamic Republic was not the most urgent item on the agenda. Any rapprochement, after all, would likely have to go through the offices of Rafsanjani and the circle of moderates surrounding him. And in the aftermath of the Iran-contra fiasco, there was a great deal of wariness in Washington about that. There was also an ongoing need to mollify the anxieties of Arab allies, many of whom were still sore about the way the United States had ditched them to pursue arms deals with Iran. All in all, in 1989, against the backdrop of an unprecedented collapse in the Communist bloc, the time did not seem right for making a major push to repair relations with Tehran. There were simply too many other things going on in the world.

Nevertheless, there was one nagging foreign policy priority Bush could not afford to ignore for very long. In Lebanon, American citizens were still being held hostage by a shadowy network of Shia militant groups loosely affiliated with Hezbollah. And only Iran exercised the kind of clout that could get them released.

CB

At his inauguration ceremony in January 1989, Bush delivered an address that was short and filled with generalities about the greatness of America and its spirit of good-neighborliness and civic participation. But toward the end of the speech, he slipped in a line unmistakably intended for the ears of the Iranian leadership. "There are today Americans who are held against their will in foreign lands," he said, lapsing into the passive voice to avoid being overly direct. "Assistance can be shown here, and will be long remembered. Goodwill begets goodwill. Good faith can be a spiral that endlessly moves on."

The meaning of Bush's words was clear. Though the recent history between Iran and the United States had been bitter and dyspeptic, Washington was willing to make a fresh start—and the hostages in Lebanon could be the grease to get the wheels turning. To ensure there was no doubt about the sincerity of this offer, Bush punctuated the statement with a personal pledge, backed by his authority as president. "Great nations like great men must keep their word," he said. "When America says something, America means it—whether a treaty or an agreement or a vow made on marble steps."

For Rafsanjani, who had long believed that permanent hostility with the United States was not in Iran's interests, this was a promising development. For years, he had hoped to guide the Islamic Republic toward some sort of rapprochement with the United States—and he was now finally in a position to do so. Already, Iran had made a strategic decision not to retaliate for the July 1988 downing of the civilian passenger jet by the USS *Vincennes.*[*] Rafsanjani's strenuous attempts to bring the Iran-Iraq war to an end, and his subsequent efforts to open Iran to Western business interests, provided further evidence of Tehran's willingness to come in from the cold. And now, rhetorically at least, America seemed prepared to meet Iran halfway. For the first time in years, the stars seemed to be aligning for a possible historic breakthrough.

Following his disastrous experience with the arms-for-hostages debacle of the mid-1980s, though, Rafsanjani was also skeptical. Was the United States sincere in its offer? Was it worth butting heads with all the hard-line anti-American elements in Iran, and weakening his own political position, to get the hostages freed—on the basis of some nice-sounding words from an American leader? If this historic opening was to be successful, and if Rafsanjani was to avoid looking like a fool before his domestic audience, he would have to be sure that America was prepared to reciprocate.

Understanding all this perfectly, the Bush administration approved the dispatch of a special UN envoy, Giandomenico Picco, to Tehran to meet with Rafsanjani. Although Picco did not officially represent the United

---

* Many in the United States had feared an act of terrorism might follow this tragedy. And when Pan Am flight 103 went down over Scotland in December 1988, many pointed the finger at Tehran. But a subsequent investigation concluded that the bombing had been ordered by Libyan leader Muammar Gaddafi.

States, his job, in effect, was to carry an olive branch—and he did so with aplomb. During an initial meeting with Rafsanjani, he assured him that the United States was sincere and that Iranian cooperation in Lebanon would not go unrewarded. Rafsanjani listened quietly and seemed intrigued. He pointed to the fact that Iran had paid for American weapons before the revolution and had not received delivery or reimbursement, as well as to the sanctions placed on Iran after the hostage crisis, as examples of areas where the United States might make a "goodwill" gesture. Picco promised to convey this message to Washington. But most of all, the Iranians made it clear they hoped to see a UN condemnation of Saddam Hussein for starting the Iran-Iraq war—a request Picco acknowledged was eminently reasonable.

Sensing a real measure of sincerity emanating from the American side, Rafsanjani pulled out all the stops. He made an enormous effort to sway hard-liners in Iran, spending considerable political capital during the initial months of his presidency to do so. It was a major political gamble, requiring him to do battle with some of the most stubborn, entrenched elements of the Islamic Republic. But do battle he did. Over the course of many months, he gradually persuaded Iran's supreme leader, Ayatollah Khamenei, and senior members of the national security team to lean on Hezbollah to release the American hostages in Lebanon.

But this internal power struggle was nothing compared with the external challenge of actually getting the hostages freed. Once the decision had been reached in Tehran, a contingent of Revolutionary Guard commanders flew to Beirut to apply pressure on Hezbollah and Islamic Jihad. They were firmly rebuffed. Hezbollah saw no benefit in releasing the hostages, as they were the most powerful leverage the group retained over the West, and they resented Iran's interference. At one point, Lebanese militants even fired grenades into the rooms where the Iranians were staying, hoping to convince them to go home. But the Iranians stood their ground. Eventually, through a combination of patience, persuasion, and persistence—and probably financial and political pressure—Iran convinced the Lebanese Shiites to release the Americans. And over the course of several weeks, from October to December 1991, Jesse Turner, Joseph Cicippio, Thomas Sutherland, Alann Steen, and Terry Anderson all made their way back to heroes' welcomes at various American airports. The process culminated in an emotional Christmas reception at the White House that was broadcast on national television.

With the American hostages liberated and a full-scale policy of quiet cooperation in place, Iran waited to see how Washington would respond. From Tehran's perspective, the Islamic Republic had bent over backward to demonstrate "goodwill," and it now hoped for some concrete gesture in return from the United States—ideally in the form of lifted sanctions.

It was to be sorely disappointed. In the three years since Bush's inauguration, a new and more unforgiving attitude toward Iran had taken hold in Washington, and positions had hardened. National security adviser Brent Scowcroft, Secretary of State James Baker, much of the State Department bureaucracy, and even the president himself were inclined to reward Iran for its assistance, on the principle that the United States should always honor its word. But arguing vociferously against this position were Richard Haass and Bruce Riedel of the National Security Council, who insisted that the pragmatists were not really in control in Tehran and that the Iranians were still engaged in unsavory activities around the world.* Eventually, this latter camp won the argument, and the United States chose not to reciprocate Iran's gestures of goodwill. Though a pro forma acknowledgment of Iranian assistance in Lebanon was made, on the day the final hostage was released, White House spokesman Marlin Fitzwater told reporters that Iran was "still a terrorist state, and there's still no change in that."

For Rafsanjani, it was a devastating blow. For nearly three years, he had put his neck on the line, begging hard-liners to suspend their disbelief, reassuring them he would have something to show for his diplomacy, and insisting that the time had come to give America a chance. After all this, he had come away empty-handed. For the next five years he remained in office, Rafsanjani would make no more serious attempts to reach out to the United States. His presidency would be frequently overshadowed by accusations of weakness and a perception that he had been too quick to want to make peace with America. More important, perhaps, the senior echelons of the Islamic Republic's security apparatus—including the supreme leader himself—took from the experience a powerful lesson: America was not to be trusted. Any future gestures or flowery words from a U.S. president would have to be accompanied by concrete, tangible policy steps.

To this day, many American officials look back on the events of 1990 and 1991 as a moment of wasted opportunity with Iran. Since the end of the 1980s, they say, Iran had made a number of moves that suggested it was serious about opening up to the West and embarking on a more positive relationship with the United States—and that ignoring those overtures had been a major act of negligence. The UN envoy Giandomenico Picco, in his

---

* As evidence, they pointed to the August 1991 murder of Shapur Bakhtiar, the shah's last prime minister, at his home in Paris—a hit believed to have been carried out by hard-line elements in the Revolutionary Guards.

"A vow made on marble steps": At his inauguration
as president in January 1989, George H. W. Bush
promised that "goodwill begets goodwill," implying
that if Iran could urge Lebanese Shia militias to
release U.S. hostages, the United States would
return the favor. Iran spent two years pressuring
its allies in Lebanon to release the Americans—but
in the end, Washington did not reciprocate. The
incident left Iran's leadership deeply suspicious of
future U.S. expressions of good faith.

memoirs, was particularly outspoken. In 1999 he accused the Bush administration of putting him "in the position of having unwittingly lied to my
Iranian interlocutors for almost four years." And those he criticized have
not been unsympathetic to his complaints. "When the hostages were all
released, we didn't do anything," admitted Brent Scowcroft in an interview
in 2004. "Picco says it was more our fault. Perhaps he is right."

ന

Perhaps, but perhaps what is also worth bearing in mind is that the world
was changing. And it was changing in ways that made the mere principle
of keeping a promise to Iran seem far less important than it might once
have been. The collapse of the Soviet Union in 1991, and all the momentous
developments that went with it, altered fundamentally Iran's place in America's foreign policy calculations—in ways no one could have anticipated two
years earlier. In January 1989, when Bush uttered his "vow on marble steps,"
America had still needed to generate goodwill with Iran, and not just to
get the hostages freed. Iran's fanatical religious ideology, after all, gave it an
inherently anti-Communist orientation—and the country served as a useful

buffer between the Soviet Union and the oil-rich Persian Gulf. Now, however, with the Soviet menace eradicated, Washington felt freer to pressure the ayatollahs in Tehran, and far less bashful about double-crossing them.

But this was not all. Arab leaders, who for years had enjoyed political support from Moscow, were left exposed by the loss of their patron—and keen to cement a closer relationship with the only superpower left standing. Washington was quick to reciprocate. When Saddam Hussein invaded Kuwait in August 1990, the more moderate regimes in the region rapidly shed the old mantras of pan-Arab solidarity and joined the American coalition to defeat Iraq. Within weeks, one of the most formidable war machines ever assembled—Saudi, Egyptian, Syrian, and Moroccan air force jets fighting alongside their American and European allies—defeated Saddam, and Bush began to speak of a "New World Order" in which American power in the region was virtually limitless.

It was, in short, an extraordinary moment of American hegemony. But it was also the beginning of a heavier-than-ever American reliance on friendly Arab regimes. And this, inevitably, was bad news for Iran. With both Israel and the Arab world firmly under the U.S. umbrella, the Soviet Union in ruins, and one hundred thousand American soldiers fanned out across Iraq, America's position in the Middle East seemed almost unassailable. There was a spring in Washington's step now—and a perception that the Iranian regime was too isolated and weakened to pose any serious challenge. This was hardly the time, many American officials argued, for Washington to be extending an olive branch to Tehran. It was time to stay tough, press the advantage, and possibly even bring an end to the Islamic Republic altogether.

And then there was the Arab-Israeli conflict. In 1991, with America's star on the rise in the region, Bush sensed a historic opportunity to end this long-festering problem and proposed a major international peace conference in the Spanish capital, Madrid. This eventually locked Israel and the Arab states together into a peace process (one that would drag on for twenty years and ultimately lead nowhere). But it also shifted the strategic calculus of the Middle East fundamentally. For the first time in history, Israel did not have to worry about outright military confrontation with the Arab world. But for the first time in history, Israel was also not able to benefit politically by positioning itself as an indispensable ally for the United States against the threat of Arab radicalism. Israel needed a new radical "threat" to position itself against—and to rally American public opinion against—and Iran was an obvious candidate. More important, Israel understood that the new friendly relationship between Washington and the Arab states reduced Israel's own strategic importance to the United States. And it feared that a friendly relationship between Washington and Tehran could reduce Israel's influence even further. With virtually every major Arab state now in alliance with America, and virtually every Arab state indicating it was prepared to sit down at the table for peace talks, Israeli leaders thus naturally began portraying Iran—rather than the Arab world—as their chief regional adversary.

It was a staggering contrast to the attitude Israel had taken toward Iran throughout the 1980s. For the first ten years of the Iranian Revolution, Israel had lent quiet support to Iran, even pushing the United States to develop warmer relations with the ayatollahs. In 1986, Israeli prime minister Shimon Peres had written directly to President Reagan, urging him to keep the pipeline of American weapons sales to Iran going for as long as possible—and pleading for the United States to pursue a "broader strategic relationship with Iran." In 1989, on Israeli television, a top adviser to Defense Minister Yitzhak Rabin had insisted that Iran's revolution was a temporary aberration—more of a rhetorical nuisance than an actual danger—and that the real threat to Israel came from Saddam Hussein. "Iran is Israel's best friend," Rabin told reporters. "And we do not intend to change our position in relation to Tehran, because Khomeini's regime will not last forever."

In 1991, however, with Saddam crippled and the Arab states committed to an American-sponsored peace plan, Israel changed its tune. It launched a vigorous public relations campaign in Washington, aimed at convincing Americans that the greatest danger to world peace no longer came from radical Arab states likes Iraq but from Iran. In the American media, among elected officials, and throughout the many corners of Washington's Israel-friendly commentariat, Iran's ayatollahs were depicted as a threat not just to Israel but to all of Western civilization. In an interview with *The New York Times,* Yossi Alpher—the same Israeli adviser who in 1989 had urged renewed U.S. ties with Iran—said, "Iran has to be identified as Enemy No. 1." Yitzhak Rabin, who had called Iran "Israel's best friend" in 1987, now described it as a nation with "megalomaniac tendencies."

The first manifestation of this shift in attitude was in Israel's approach to the peace process. In 1991, Israeli leaders made it clear that if a peace deal were to be done with the Arab world, it should be done *only* with the Arab world—and that Iran should be excluded from the talks. And the Bush administration, riding high following its successes in Iraq, saw no reason not to comply with this request. In Washington, some argued it would be a mistake to exclude Iran—that it would be better to keep Iran inside the tent, where it might play a constructive role in the peace process, rather than outside, where it might cause problems. But for the most part, these concerns were drowned out in the general climate of post–Cold War triumphalism. When invitations to Madrid went out, forty-three participants, including fifteen regional states—from Syria to Egypt to the USSR to Norway—were given a seat at the table. But Iran was conspicuously not among the invitees.

The Iranians felt badly snubbed by their exclusion from the peace talks. The Madrid conference had been presented to the world as a major regional security summit—one in which every nation in the Middle East had its unique role to play—and Rafsanjani felt he had moderated Iran's revolutionary posture enough that he should be allowed to participate. In particular, he had once again battled hard-liners to bring about a major shift in Iran's policy on Palestine. In a series of public statements, he had downplayed Iran's rhetorical opposition to the existence of Israel and declared that Iran would respect whatever decision the Palestinians chose to make with respect to the peace process.

In Tehran, the feeling was that the president had now repeatedly bent over backward—securing the release of American hostages in Lebanon, playing a constructive role during the Gulf War,[*] and moderating the country's official stance on Palestine—and yet Iran's reward for all this was to be excluded from Madrid. Increasingly, the political establishment in Tehran began to suspect that what they did didn't actually matter, because the response from America would always be one of hostility. This changed significantly Iran's willingness to take a cooperative approach to America. And it gave fresh ammunition to hard-liners in Tehran, who now vocally argued that Rafsanjani had allowed himself to be played for a fool. "The willingness to do positive work for America almost ended" in 1991, according to an official who worked at the Iranian Foreign Ministry. "Because they never reciprocated. Whatever positive Iran did, the response was always more and more isolation."

It was at this point that Iran began exploring other options. Excluded and feeling they had nothing to lose—and deeply leery of a world in which America, Israel, and the Arabs were closing ranks against them—Iranian leaders decided their best policy option was to sabotage U.S. efforts to bring the Arabs and Israelis together. Accusing Arab leaders of "betraying" the Palestinian cause, in October 1991, Iran organized a rival conference to coincide with Madrid, drawing a number of militant Palestinian groups that the West had labeled "rejectionist." It reinstated its financial support for

---

[*] In January 1991, during the U.S. invasion of Iraq, Iran had remained neutral and uncharacteristically quiet. Rather than use its considerable influence over Iraq's Shia population to cook up trouble for the United States, as many analysts had feared, Iran actually allowed U.S. warplanes to fly over Iranian air space on their way to bomb Iraqi targets—a little-reported facet of the war, about which both countries were happy to keep quiet. Even at the end of the war, when Washington decided to leave Saddam in power and allow Iraq to stabilize, Iran refrained from provoking Iraq's Shia into open rebellion.

Hezbollah, which it had scaled back significantly just a year earlier. And it began to reach out to the Sunni extremist group Hamas, with whom it had traditionally had a frosty relationship.

The goal of all this was to make Washington understand that no genuine or lasting peace in the Middle East could ever come about without Iran's participation. But its most immediate result was to feed neatly into Israel's narrative. Tel Aviv began depicting Iran as a monster that had to be isolated, condemned, and weakened internationally—with a degree of rhetorical hostility it had never before displayed toward Tehran. Israel claimed it could never make peace with the Palestinians as long as Iran was supporting radical groups committed to Israel's destruction—"fanning the flames in every country within reach," as Foreign Minister Shimon Peres put it. And so began a cycle of escalating tension and mutual recrimination that has since become an all-too-familiar feature of the Middle East landscape.

In retrospect, many American officials today regret the decision to leave Iran out of the Madrid peace talks. While the administration's thinking at the time was that Iran had very little to contribute, officials admit that they perhaps failed to appreciate Iran's unlimited ability to cause trouble if treated as a pariah. Even Dennis Ross, one of Israel's most stalwart U.S. allies at the time and an active participant, has since lamented the decision to ignore Iran's attempts to come in from the cold. "I think it's fair to say that we didn't look that closely at it, and in retrospect perhaps we should have," he told an interviewer in 2004. "The [positive] signals from Rafsanjani tended to be dismissed, but they were there."

❧

The speed with which Israel shifted its position and began casting Iran as the great demon of the Middle East was striking. But in the run-up to the Madrid Peace Conference in 1991, this realignment was not what most of the world noticed. Instead, attention turned to the Jewish-only settlements that Israel had begun building on occupied Palestinian land. Israel's intention, critics said, was to create "facts on the ground"—a constellation of dots on the map that would steadily grow in number during the years the peace process dragged on and eventually make it impractical for a contiguous, viable Palestinian state to come into existence. Most of the world considered these settlements illegal, as they were built on land Israel had seized during the 1967 war.

But for the United States, the settlements were primarily a political issue. In mid-1991, during the run-up to U.S. presidential elections—and just weeks before the Madrid conference—Israel asked Washington for

$10 billion in loan guarantees to help finance the construction of these settlements.* Bush was furious at the request, knowing full well that U.S. support for Israeli settlements would cause Arab states to walk away from the table; but he could not afford a public confrontation with Israel during an election year. In September, Secretary of State James Baker went before a congressional committee to beg for a four-month delay to the loan guarantees, to allow breathing room for the Madrid conference. Tensions between the White House and Israel's supporters in Congress escalated, until eventually, in March 1992, Bush publicly and formally refused Israel's loan request. "The choice is Israel's," he said, in an unusually stern public rebuke. Secretary Baker's public message to Israel was even less delicate: "The telephone number is 202-456-1414. When you're serious about peace, call us."

The Bush administration's public spat with Israel came at a time when the president could ill afford it. Major pro-Israeli donors defected in large numbers to his Democratic rival for the 1992 presidential election. Economic woes added to the president's reelection challenges, and within months, a full-scale recession dragged down Bush's approval ratings from a postwar high of 89 percent to just 29 percent. Much of the American media portrayed Bush as a president who had scored a resounding foreign policy victory against Iraq but was utterly uninterested in the economic difficulties facing ordinary Americans—a wealthy Connecticut egghead who was unable to "feel your pain."

The result was a thumping landslide for the Democratic candidate, Arkansas governor William Jefferson Clinton.

CS

Bill Clinton was nothing if not a shrewd political operator. From his earliest days as a thirty-two-year-old governor to his complex business dealings in Arkansas, he had always known how to build coalitions and satisfy interest groups in the service of a political agenda. And his campaign for the presidency was no exception. Clinton's team assiduously wooed pro-Israel groups and went out of its way to assure them he would be a better friend to Israel than Bush had been. And as he prepared to move into the White House in 1993, it was obvious that his Middle East policies were going to be significantly more sympathetic to Israel than those of his predecessor.

Under Clinton, the tilt away from Iran—and toward Israel and Arab

---

* Technically, Israel claimed that the $10 billion would be used to provide housing and absorb Russian immigrants on "humanitarian grounds." But given that Israel had refused to verify whether the previous year's loan guarantees ($400 million granted in October 1990) were being used to finance settlement expansion, there was considerable suspicion about this claim.

allies—intensified. Having inherited the historic opportunity of a Middle East peace process from Bush, he believed keeping Israel at the negotiating table was paramount. And this, in practice, meant he needed to show great sensitivity to Israel's concerns and demands, chief among which was the continued isolation of Iran. Clinton had also inherited a new, more amicable relationship with the Arab states. Egypt's Hosni Mubarak, the Saudi royal family, and the king of Jordan had always been key American allies. But as the Arab-Israeli peace process became the beating heart of U.S. policy in the region, their willingness to work under an American umbrella became crucial. Clinton understood that if he wanted to keep both Israel and friendly Arab leaders committed to the peace process, he would have to strike a foreign-policy posture that would be reassuring to all parties. And it was fairly obvious what this would look like. Like Israel, the pro-Western Arab leaders all had an uneasy and distrustful attitude toward the Shia Persian regime in Tehran. Like Israel, they also hated Saddam Hussein.

The United States now found itself in an unprecedented position in the Middle East—seeking to isolate both Iran and Iraq simultaneously. Having spent the 1960s and 1970s cultivating the friendship of Iran as a counterweight to Iraqi socialism, and the 1980s supporting Iraq in order to contain Khomeini, America now declared that *both* nations were the devil, and both would have to be isolated and condemned. For the first time in history, America's position was strong enough that it no longer needed to support one to keep the other weak. It could safely leave both on the sidelines and subject them, as "rogue" regimes, to sanctions, political isolation, and no-fly zones. The policy, introduced in May 1993, was dubbed Dual Containment.

In reality, Dual Containment was two distinct policies cobbled into one. One policy—the isolation of Iraq—was a logical outgrowth of America's recent conflict with Saddam Hussein. The other policy—the isolation of Iran—was based mostly on political considerations. In the early 1990s, Israel's vigorous campaign to present Iran as a mortal danger had gained traction in Washington. And given how much weight the Clinton administration placed on keeping Israel committed to the peace process, the United States could not afford to ignore its concerns.* In the words of one official intimately involved in the decision, "the Iran part of Dual Containment was a policy designed to reassure Israel that the United States would keep Iran in check while [Israel] embarked on the risky process of peacemaking."

Taking its cue from Israel, Washington now accused Iran of three inter-

---

* The very idea of Dual Containment, in fact, was cooked up by Martin Indyk, Clinton's special adviser on the Middle East, who in 1985 had founded an influential pro-Israeli think-tank called the Washington Institute for Near East Policy. It was at a gathering of WINEP that Indyk first floated the idea.

related sins: the pursuit of nuclear weapons, support for terrorism, and opposition to the Middle East peace process. The American media took up all three themes enthusiastically, as did lawmakers keen to score political points. In the weeks leading up to Clinton's inauguration and for months thereafter, a barrage of anti-Iranian arguments could be heard, at very high volume, from Israel and its supporters. Publicly, the White House followed the script—Secretary of State Christopher declared in 1994 that "Iran is the world's most significant sponsor of terrorism and the most ardent opponent of the Middle East peace process." But internally, privately, many in the new president's foreign policy team felt Israel's claims were slightly exaggerated.

Israel's first accusation—that Iran was pursuing nuclear weapons—was perhaps the least convincing. In the early 1980s, Khomeini had declared all weapons of mass destruction to be "un-Islamic"—a significant pronouncement in a country describing itself as an Islamic Republic—and had strictly forbidden their use in the war against Iraq.* An embryonic program to use enriched uranium to produce electricity, begun under the shah in the 1970s (with American cooperation), was tentatively revived in 1991. But most neutral observers accepted that it was for civilian purposes and within Iran's rights under the nuclear Non-Proliferation Treaty. Iran's next-door neighbor Russia even felt comfortable enough to sign a contract with Iran to finish building the nuclear power plant at Bushehr that had been abandoned in 1979.

The second accusation—that Iran was a sponsor of terrorism—was harder to dismiss. Tehran, after all, had played a crucial role in the creation of the Lebanese militant group Hezbollah in 1983, and Hezbollah had certainly committed some ugly acts in its time. However, much of the world saw Hezbollah less as a terrorist organization than as a combatant in Lebanon's long-running civil war. Moreover, many of the atrocities Israel accused Iran or Hezbollah of committing—such as a pair of attacks on Jewish and Israeli targets in Buenos Aires in 1992 and 1994—ultimately proved difficult to trace back to Iran, despite numerous attempts. In all cases, Tehran strenuously denied its involvement.

More to the point, Iran's support for Hezbollah was a fairly logical, traditional Iranian deterrent strategy. After all, in 1991 the United States had taken just forty-three days to destroy Saddam Hussein's army—the same army Iran had failed to defeat in eight years—and in the process had marshaled seven hundred thousand American, European, and Arab troops and

---

* Most notably, Iran had refused to use chemical weapons, despite the fact that the Iraqis were using them against Iranian troops, and despite the fact that Iran had inherited from the shah both the technology and the stockpiles necessary to produce them. Khomeini was adamant that both chemical and nuclear weapons were *haram,* a sin against Islam.

deposited them on Iran's doorstep. It was a fierce reminder of what America was capable of when stirred into action. And it was therefore not surprising that Iran, a nation with very limited conventional capabilities and an army devastated by war, might look for creative ways to "level the playing field." By supporting Hezbollah (and later Hamas), it bought itself an insurance policy. It guaranteed that any U.S. president considering military action against Iran would have to think twice, knowing Iran could unleash the dogs of war in Beirut or Gaza.

The third accusation, that Iran was seeking to sabotage the Arab-Israeli peace process, was true on its face, but perhaps less serious of a threat to peace than the Israelis were making it out to be. Certainly Iran had offered support to groups that were violently opposed to peace with Israel. But in 1993 these contacts were highly limited and had little to do with the violence taking place in the West Bank and Gaza. Support for Hamas didn't come until 1995—and even then the backing was fairly mundane in nature, rather than the command-and-control architecture of death that the Israelis implied it to be. The key point, in fact—and one often missed—was that Iran was not actually opposed to peace between Israel and the Palestinians per se. Rather, Iran had hoped to be included in the Madrid process and to be reintegrated into the international community. But when it felt the peace process was becoming a mechanism to isolate Iran, it had turned more rejectionist.

Away from the rhetoric, the cold, hard truth of the matter was that Iran was never terribly interested in what was going on in Israel or the Palestinian territories, beyond the opportunity it provided for regional grandstanding. Even senior Israeli military commanders acknowledged this much behind closed doors. Publicly, Israel made sure the world kept hearing about Iran's "threats" to its existence. But privately, Israel's assessment of Iran was that it was following a foreign policy surprisingly similar to that of the shah—one based on traditional, pragmatic imperatives of national interest and self-preservation.

◌

In the political arena, however, perceptions and PR often count for a great deal more than reality. And Israel has always had a unique ability to influence the public narrative in the United States. During Clinton's first term, pro-Israel lobbyists in the United States mounted a vigorous campaign to convince Washington that Iran was America's most dangerous and mortal enemy—and that it should make no effort to improve relations between the two countries. Their efforts soon paid off.

In March 1995, Iran offered a $1 billion contract to the American oil company Conoco to develop the offshore Sirri Island oil and gas fields. It was the first major petroleum concession to come up for sale since the end of the war, and most observers had expected it to go to a French company. So Iran's decision to approach Conoco was widely interpreted as a signal of Rafsanjani's desire to improve relations with the United States. Sensing an opportunity not to be passed up, the State Department quietly did what it could to facilitate the transaction—repeatedly reassuring Conoco there was nothing illegal about the deal and that it would face no obstructions from the U.S. government. But on April 2, 1995, the American Israel Public Affairs Committee (AIPAC) released a seventy-four-page report called "Comprehensive U.S. Sanctions Against Iran: A Plan for Action," calling for the United States to "cut all its trade and economic ties with Iran." The Clinton administration, eager not to give the Israelis a reason to walk out of the peace process, got the message. Within three weeks, the White House made an abrupt U-turn on the Conoco deal and issued a pair of executive orders banning all U.S. oil companies from doing business in Iran. Clinton announced the orders on April 30, in a speech to the World Jewish Congress. And the next morning Secretary Christopher told reporters that Iran's "repugnant behavior" had made it necessary to take drastic measures. "Wherever you look you will find the evil hand of Iran in the region," he said.

Conoco was furious. Its executives had held twenty-six separate meetings with the State Department, and at every single one they had been told the deal would not face opposition. Exasperated, the executives invested in a round of heavy lobbying, supported more broadly by the American oil industry, arguing that the United States was walking away from billions of dollars in potential trade with Iran. But it was all in vain. In a battle between the petroleum lobby and the Israel lobby, there was only one likely victor. One year away from a presidential election, Clinton was not going to make the same mistake Bush had made in 1991.

AIPAC, sensing that it had a free hand with the Clinton administration, began pressing its case more vigorously. In the summer of 1996, Sen. Alfonse D'Amato (R-NY) introduced the Iran-Libya Sanctions Act* onto the floor of the U.S. Senate—a bill widely described as "written" by AIPAC. Its provisions were draconian: not only would U.S. oil companies be banned from doing business with Iran, but any *foreign* oil company that traded with Iran would now be forbidden from doing business in the United States.

---

* Initially, it was the Iran Sanctions Act, but Ted Kennedy (D-MA) added a provision against Libya in response to the concerns of family members of the victims of the 1988 Lockerbie bombing.

Never before had an American trade law put forward such far-reaching restrictions. In effect, ILSA would force dozens of major multinational oil companies to choose between their desire to cultivate new business in Iran and their ability to continue doing business in the United States—an easy choice for most.

ILSA was met with howls of outrage from the American business community. Corporate America could not believe that Congress would pass a law so inimical to American economic interests, not to mention to global commerce in general. By infuriating and alienating America's allies, business leaders argued, ILSA would hurt America's ability to conduct business and diplomacy and would ultimately reduce its standing in the world. The Clinton administration agreed and did everything it could to put a stop to ILSA. "We want to isolate the Iranians, not become isolated ourselves," said Assistant Secretary of State Robert Pelletreau before a congressional committee. His boss, Warren Christopher, was also sent to the Hill to persuade lawmakers to reconsider. But none of this had any effect on the U.S. Congress—an institution, then as now, dominated by an almost-unassailable unanimity on matters important to AIPAC. On June 19, the Iran-Libya Sanctions Act passed in the House by a vote of 415 to 0. In the Senate, it passed 96–2. On August 5, President Clinton—recognizing he had little choice in the matter—signed it into law.

What was perhaps most striking about ILSA—and little noticed at the time—was that Israel never passed a similar law of its own. Despite their strenuous efforts to prevent American, European, Asian, and other companies from doing business with Iran, Israelis themselves were happy to continue buying and selling with the Iranians. At first blush, this contradiction might seem difficult to explain. But in fact, the logic was entirely consistent with Israel's strategic thinking. The intention of ILSA had never been to change Iranian behavior or to eliminate the "threat" from Tehran. (No serious person in Israel had ever thought such a threat existed.) The intention, primarily, had been to perpetuate the climate of unfriendliness between Iran and the United States and make it nearly impossible for Washington and Tehran to put aside their differences. In this respect, ILSA was a resounding success. Iran was now public enemy number one in Washington, and there was little chance of that changing.

❧

In Iran, meanwhile, there was an equally insurmountable set of internal political dynamics standing in the way of better relations with the United States. However much Rafsanjani hoped to moderate Iran's foreign policy and find avenues for reconciliation with Washington, he was faced with a constantly shifting kaleidoscope of opposition from a wide variety of political forces that had no desire to see him take credit for such a historic accomplishment. As ever in Iranian politics, these opposition forces represented a complicated ganglion of competing and overlapping agendas—and many had little in common beyond their desire to see Rafsanjani fail.

Broadly speaking, the Iranian political landscape in these years began to divide into three camps or factions: the so-called pragmatic conservatives who coalesced around Rafsanjani; the hard-liners or religious conservatives; and the radicals. Rafsanjani and the pragmatic conservatives were generally pro-business, pro-economic growth, and pro-stability, stressing a version of market capitalism that drew on Islam's traditional emphasis on the sanctity of private property rights. The hard-line religious conservatives, meanwhile, stressed social conservatism as well as loyalty to and absolute solidarity with the Khomeinist principle of *velayat-e-faqih*. While Rafsanjani and the pragmatic conservatives drew their support from *bazaaris* (traditional middle-class merchants), the religious hard-liners were particularly well represented among the Revolutionary Guards and in grassroots organizations such as the revolutionary committees and Foundation for the Oppressed—where they engaged in acts of vigilante justice and popular mobilization.

The third political group, the radicals, had, broadly speaking, a philosophy driven by Islam's traditional emphasis on social justice and were concerned primarily with liberating the poor and the downtrodden, both at home and abroad. Redistribution of land, taxation of the rich, and the provision of social services for poor and rural communities were at the center of their domestic agenda. Internationally, they emphasized third-world solidarity and supported "resistance movements" against Zionism and imperialism. They were well represented in the Majles, which they had controlled since the early 1980s and which they now used as a base for opposing Rafsanjani's free-market capitalism. They loudly protested the president's attempts to attract foreign investment and IMF restructuring, comparing them to the capitulations of the Qajar shahs in the late 1800s. Heirs to the political philosophy of Ali Shariati and the student movements of the 1970s, the radicals were sometimes described by analysts as "Islamic leftists" or "Islamic socialists," but they always defined their own ideology in purely Islamic terms.

Over the course of the early and mid-1990s, the pragmatists and the religious conservatives maintained their respective power bases and did not adapt their political philosophies noticeably. But then something unexpected happened to the radicals. In 1992, for the first time in more than a decade, they lost their majority in parliament. And as they cast about in the political wilderness, looking for a way to reconnect with the electorate, some of the more liberal-minded among them reexamined their ideas. They began to speak of a much wider range of social issues—beyond the redistribution of wealth—that they claimed the political establishment was ignoring. Human rights, civil society, democratic participation, and freedom from artistic and media censorship became particularly popular themes among their base.[*]

In the years since 1981—when the IRP had definitively crushed President Bani-Sadr and the MeK—Iran's political establishment had viewed such ideas with suspicion, as though they could lead the country down a dangerous road toward Westernization. But in the 1990s the radicals articulated these ideas in a way that was safe and unassailably Islamic in its language—a far cry from the jumbled Islamic Europeanism of Bani-Sadr and Bazargan. They rejected the idea that civil rights and participatory democracy were Western ideas that had polluted Iran, arguing they were in fact an integral and long-established part of the Islamic tradition. They also shrewdly tapped into a new demographic of potential supporters who had mostly been ignored until now: the large number of Iranians who had been born after the revolution or were too young to remember it—many of whom reached voting age in the mid-1990s.

Increasingly, Islamic radicals were referred to—either by themselves or by outside observers—as "reformists." And though no one predicted it at the time, they were about to change the direction of Iranian history.

---

[*] In many ways, the transformation of the radicals in the mid-1990s reflected a larger global trend. Throughout the world, leftist, left-leaning, and socialist parties were reassessing their views in light of the collapse of Communism and the triumph of Western capitalism. The traditional rallying cries of the global Left—economic redistribution and anti-imperialism especially—looked ineffective and out of touch with the reality of American ascendancy. It therefore made sense that the radicals in Iran turned their attention from leftist economic policies of redistribution and toward cultural, artistic, social, and human rights issues.

The First Hopey-Changey Moment

CʒȘC

By 1996, Iran had suffered through two decades of turmoil, uncertainty, and disorder—and its economy was showing the strain. Inflation averaged around 40 percent every year. Unemployment stood at over 30 percent. Iran's currency, the rial, which had traded at a rate of 70 to the dollar in 1978, was now being sold at 6,400 to the dollar on the black market. The prices of sugar, butter, and rice had tripled, and the price of bread had risen sixfold. Cities were overcrowded and polluted, jobs were scarce, patience was wearing thin.

The causes of the economic paralysis were as obvious as they were numerous. Years of rapid and poorly managed modernization under the shah, a long period of war and revolutionary upheaval, a population that had doubled in thirty years, mass migration from the countryside into the cities, the disappearance of precious skills and capital overseas, and the destruction of civilian infrastructure during the Iraq war had all steadily accrued, one on top of the other, to create a dismal macroeconomic climate. And added to this now were a new set of challenges. American sanctions, put in place in 1996, were driving away the foreign investment that the country badly needed to get back on its feet. At the worst possible time for Iran, oil prices were approaching historic lows (dropping from $40 a barrel in 1990 to around $15 in mid-1995)—a major blow for a country so dependent on petroleum revenue. And as if all this were not enough, war and turmoil in neighboring Afghanistan was sending a flood of migrants—some 2 million by the late 1990s—into Iran, making the country host to the world's largest population of refugees.

Along with all these economic problems, the Islamic Republic was beginning to face a crisis in public confidence. Voter turnout for the presidential election of 1993 had fallen to just 53 percent—a clear indication that the revolution was no longer inspiring or exciting to many people. The problem was particularly acute among younger and more educated Iranians. Every year Iran's universities were turning out three hundred thousand new graduates—a genuine achievement for the fledgling republic[*]—but there were not nearly enough jobs to keep them occupied. In 1997 more than half of Iran's population was under twenty-five—well educated, restless, eager to take their place in the modern globalized world, and tired of strict Islamic restrictions on what they could wear or what kind of music they could listen to. They were too young, for the most part, to remember the revolution and the struggle against the shah. As citizens born into the Islamic Republic, many needed to hear something more than just revolutionary slogans about the evils of American "imperialism."

Initially, the regime's answer to this gathering cloud of pessimism was to offer more of the same. Iran's president was constitutionally limited to two four-year terms, and as Rafsanjani's second term in office came to a close in 1997, the clerical establishment backed the hard-line conservative parliament speaker, Ali Akbar Nateq-Nuri, for president in the May 1997 election—declaring him the "front runner" in a process that, to many disgruntled Iranians, felt like a coronation.

The budding reformist movement, however, had a very different answer. In early 1997 they coalesced around the candidacy of an untested and rather unexpected figure: an affable, liberal-minded cleric by the name of Mohammad Khatami. Quiet, urbane, with a neatly trimmed beard and a gentle, almost professorial, manner, Khatami was an unlikely man for the rough-and-tumble world of Iranian politics. But in 1997 he turned out to be just the spark the country needed.

☙

For much of the 1980s, Mohammad Khatami had been in charge of Iran's Ministry of Culture and Islamic Guidance, the government department responsible for ensuring that Iran's cultural institutions reflected "revolutionary values." Khatami had surprised many by bringing a light and liberal-minded approach to the job—supporting struggling artists, encouraging

---

[*] Iran's higher education system, battered by years of war and revolution, expanded dramatically in the 1990s and was made available to a far greater swath of Iranian society than ever. University enrollment, which had stood at 200,000 in 1987, soared to 1.2 million by 1996. The jewel in the crown of this education boom was Islamic Freedom University, an open-enrollment, tuition-driven institution with dozens of campuses. Today Islamic Freedom has 1.5 million students spread over four hundred campuses—the third-largest university system in the world.

quality journalism and cinema, and fighting to relax censorship laws. As a young man, Khatami had studied philosophy at the University of Isfahan, where he was enamored of Western enlightenment thinkers such as Kant, Descartes, Locke, and Montesquieu. As director of the Islamic Center of Hamburg in the 1970s, he had gained a deeper appreciation for Western civilization and for the German intellectual tradition in particular. And as culture minister, he had brought this worldliness and erudition to his work.

Khatami had been a passionate supporter of the Islamic Revolution in 1979. But his version of Islam emphasized pluralism and dialogue and made room for multiple interpretations and influences. He argued that even an Islamic Republic should take a flexible, open approach to religion: it should recognize the achievements of Western civilization and try to coexist with it rather than fight it. Khatami felt scientific progress and modernity were not inherently "Western" but were rather the culmination of many influences— Islamic, Greek, Chinese, and European—and thus belonged to *all* humanity. The Islamic Republic should therefore not see Western civilization as an alien influence or a threat to the foundations of the revolution.

This liberal open-mindedness had earned Khatami respect among Iran's educated middle classes. But it had also cost him his job. In 1992 the conservative Majles went after Khatami for his lax attitude toward censorship. And after a brief tussle, the parliament had forced his resignation. For his troubles, Khatami was made head of the National Library—an almost-insulting demotion for someone who had served in a cabinet post for so many years.

A different kind of man might have pouted and blown off steam for a few years while plotting his return to politics. But Khatami loved books, and his directorship of the National Library became a defining experience. During his political exile there from 1992 to 1997, he honed many of his ideas, cultivated friendships with leading intellectuals, wrote two books on philosophy, and grew closer to reformist circles. Together with a number of political theorists and Islamic philosophers, he put together a legendary Tehran reading circle that coined new Persian terms such as *jame'eh-ye madani* (civil society), *mosharekat-e siasi* (political participation) and *shahrvandi* (citizenship). As his star began to rise, he warned publicly that the Islamic Republic was following a "dangerous trend." If it continued to insist on a rigid, dogmatic interpretation of religion, it risked alienating the public from the very idea of an Islamic Republic—even from Islam itself.

By 1997, many were talking about Khatami as a possible presidential candidate—someone who could energize the fledgling reformist movement and represent it capably at the polls. Speculation about a presidential bid picked up dramatically when the centrist pragmatist camp—led by President Rafsanjani—considered backing Khatami as part of a tactical alliance against hard-line conservatives. Many in the pragmatist camp disagreed with this approach and felt their safer option was to continue working with the conservative establishment. But Rafsanjani rejected this analysis as too timid. In early March, his Servants of Reconstruction political alliance announced it was backing Khatami.

As a loyal revolutionary, Khatami was not about to throw his hat into the ring without the blessing of the supreme leader. So on a cold winter morning in 1997, the fifty-three-year-old cleric—well groomed as always, with his black turban, wire-rimmed spectacles, and clerical robes neatly in place—went to see the ayatollah at his residence in Jamaran. Appealing to Khamenei's innate sense of pragmatism, Khatami argued that the upcoming election was an opportunity to draw more people into the political process. Even if he didn't win, the very fact of his candidacy could help rejuvenate the Islamic Republic and make people feel invested in the system again— especially younger people who had not experienced the revolution. With all its economic and social difficulties, the country had to find a way to engage Iran's young people and its restless middle classes.

Khamenei bought the argument. On May 7, 1997, Iran's electoral commission published a list of four candidates whom the Guardian Council described as possessing the necessary qualifications and revolutionary commitment to become president. From a total of 238 applicants, the council had winnowed the pool down to Khatami, Nateq-Nuri, and two uninspiring candidates who were not expected to ignite much passion among the public. With sixteen days to go until election day, it was obvious the battle was going to be between Nateq-Nuri and Khatami.

ଓଃ

And what a battle it was. On the campaign trail, the Khatami team traveled the country in a simple, weathered bus, with the candidate waving and laughing to the crowds from its roof—a stark contrast to the Mercedes motorcades and tinted windows of the Nateq-Nuri campaign. In Tehran, Khatami was often spotted negotiating traffic in the old family Peugeot, with his wife in the driver's seat. (Men "are not in charge of the women," he said. It was time "to do away with male supremacy.") During the two-week campaign, Khatami made a point of visiting all of Iran's provinces and talking personally to people in small towns and villages—a kind of populist retail politics unheard of in Iranian presidential elections. Many of his appearances took on a rock-star quality, as packed arenas full of ecstatic, swooning admirers chanted his name. Khatami especially appealed to the young, promising a "fresh approach to youth issues" and better jobs and housing prospects for recent graduates. He emphasized cultural issues, such as freedom of expression and support for the arts, which excited the educated middle classes. And younger women were thrilled to hear his message of equality between the sexes.

On the campaign trail, Khatami represented something Iran had never seen before. Although he was every inch the revolutionary—the son of an ayatollah who spoke passionately of his love for Khomeini and the revolution—he did one thing Iranians had never seen from their religious leaders: he smiled. Not just a smirk or a ripple of dignified amusement, but a wide, winsome grin, belonging more to an American presidential candidate than to a man of the cloth in revolutionary Iran. "There is no fun in Islam," Khomeini had said back in 1979, and over the years Iranians had come to accept that theirs was a regime with a permanent frown: Khomeini's perpetually furrowed brow, the expressions of consternation over anything pleasurable or sensual, the endless festivals of mourning and weeping over long-dead saints, the black-cloth *chador* worn by women of piety. After seventeen years of this, Khatami's beaming, benevolent face was a breath of fresh air.

When election day came, the result was decisive, overwhelming, and impossible to dispute. Khatami won nearly 70 percent of the vote. Even more extraordinary was the level of participation: fully 88 percent of eligible adults had turned out. Khatami—the "message candidate" whose job had been to bring new voters into the process but not actually *win*—upended all predictions by beating the establishment candidate, and beating him handily. In a region dominated by tinpot autocrats and clapped-out tyrants—where leaders won "elections" with 97 percent of the vote, decade after decade, with hardly anyone opposing them—it was a remarkable exercise in democracy.

Perhaps nowhere was news of Khatami's victory received with greater surprise than in Washington. Conventional wisdom in the West had been that Iran was an antidemocratic society, a benighted land of religious orthodoxy and cruel, autocratic ayatollahs. And yet here, within the restrictive parameters of Islamic revolutionary ideology, it had managed to hold a vigorous and open modern election, fiercely contested, complete with a surprise victory for the underdog. Slightly bewildered, the Clinton White House described the election result as "hopeful" and "a very interesting development."

Once in office, Khatami wasted no time making overtures to Washington. One of his first acts was to agree to an interview with CNN—the first time an Iranian leader had engaged the U.S. media since the revolution. And he did not mince words. "The American civilization is worthy of respect," he began. "And when we appreciate the roots of this civilization, its significance becomes even more apparent." He praised the pilgrims who landed on Plymouth Rock in 1620 and the way they had sought to create "a system which combined the worship of God with human dignity and freedom," adding that Iran, like the United States, was a revolutionary, freedom-seeking republic founded by people motivated by their faith. During the forty-minute interview, Khatami went out of his way to praise Abraham Lincoln, the Declaration of Independence, and other milestones of American history. But the kernel of his message was simple:

> [American] civilization is best described by the renowned French sociologist Alexis de Tocqueville who . . . wrote the valuable book *Democracy in America,* which I am sure most Americans have read. . . . In his view, the significance of this civilization is in the fact that liberty found religion as a cradle for its growth, and religion found protection of liberty as its divine calling. Therefore, liberty and faith never clashed. And as we see, even today Americans are a religious people. . . . I believe that if humanity is looking for happiness, it should combine religious spirituality with the virtues of liberty. . . . And it is for this reason that I say I respect the American nation because of their great civilization.

Iran and America, Khatami was trying to say, were *just not that different.* And Americans should not be afraid of what they saw coming out of Iran, because Iranians were motivated by many of America's own most cherished values.

Khatami criticized America's past actions in Iran, but sounded sad rather than accusatory—describing it as a "tragedy" that "policies pursued by American politicians . . . since World War II are incompatible with the American civilization, which is founded on democracy, freedom, and human dignity." When asked about Iran's own misdeeds, such as the 1979–81 hostage crisis, Khatami came very close to an apology, saying, "I do know that the feelings of the great American people have been hurt, and of course I regret it." The president portrayed that episode as an unfortunate example of revolutionary excess, stressing that Iran today was a nation guided by the "rule of law." He also called for an exchange of scholars, journalists, and tourists, so the two countries could begin to understand each other better.

On the three concerns the United States had voiced about Iran—

The smiling face of the revolution: Mohammad Khatami, the Iranian president from 1997 to 2005, represented a breath of fresh air for young Iranians—and a ray of hope for U.S.-Iran relations.

support for terrorism, nuclear weapons research, and opposition to Israel—Khatami went further than any Iranian president had ever gone. "Terrorism," he said, "should be condemned in all its forms and manifestations." Iran was "not a nuclear power and does not intend to become one." And in Palestine, "we don't intend to impose our views on others or to stand in their way. . . . In our view all Palestinians have the right to express their views about their land. . . . Only then can there be a lasting peace. We seek a peace through which Jews, Muslims, and Christians . . . could freely determine their own destiny—and we are prepared to contribute toward the realization of that peace."

These were important clarifications of Iranian policy for an international audience. But even more important than the words Khatami spoke was his tone. "We feel that what we seek is what the founders of the American civilization were also pursuing four centuries ago," he said as he explained Iran's revolutionary ideology. "This is why we sense an intellectual affinity with the essence of the American civilization." Americans had never heard an Iranian leader speak to them like this.

The response from Washington was muted. The Clinton administration was intrigued but preferred to wait and see how much concrete change Khatami would be able to bring about. Clinton's foreign policy team was heavily focused on the Arab-Israeli peace process, and this Iranian olive branch came a little out of the blue. And it was, after all, just one interview. Without a network of Iranian diplomats and lobbyists in Washington—or

a domestic American constituency pushing for warmer ties with Tehran—
there was no real follow-through. The CNN interview made a big splash,
then disappeared from the headlines—upstaged, ten days later, by an explosive revelation about President Clinton's affair with a White House intern
named Monica Lewinsky.

Still, Khatami pressed ahead with his charm offensive. He appointed a
woman, Massoumeh Ebtekar, to the post of vice president. He replaced the
hard-line foreign minister, Ali Akbar Velayati, who had served more than
a decade in the job, with Kamal Kharrazi—a more flexible diplomat who,
as Iran's ambassador to the UN, had lived for years in New York and was
familiar with the workings of American politics. On the domestic front as
well, the tone changed considerably. In the first year of Khatami's presidency, his government awarded licenses to more than two hundred new
newspapers and magazines, ushering in a golden age of debate and serious
journalism not seen in Iran since the 1950s. It generously subsidized the
film industry and allowed it far greater latitude in the types of themes and
plotlines it could develop, sparking a renaissance in Iranian moviemaking.
Satellite dishes popped up on roofs, as Iranians realized the regime had lost
interest in confiscating them. Internet cafés proliferated. On the streets of
Tehran, headscarves began slipping back inch by inch, revealing first wisps
of hair and eventually something close to a full head. Lipstick, nail polish,
and expensive perfume were all in vogue in public—in a way not seen since
the days of the shah.

At the White House, pulses quickened. Clinton saw in Mohammad
Khatami and his reforms a historic moment and an opportunity too good
to pass up. During his first term, Clinton had felt circumscribed by the
pro-Israel lobby, which had worked hard to discourage a closer relationship
between Iran and America. And even now, many of those pressures still
existed. But in 1996, Clinton had won a stomping reelection victory. In his
second term, with a stronger hand against Israel and its advocates in Washington, he began pushing harder on the Middle East peace process, as well
as exploring the possibility of an outreach to Khatami.

At first, the administration moved slowly—in part out of skepticism,
in part because of domestic opposition, and in part because of distractions
caused by the Lewinsky scandal. But as Clinton's second term wore on, the
president became more passionate about Iran and took an active interest in
the history of U.S.-Iranian relations. At one White House dinner, he was
even heard speaking about the need to "understand" Iran. It was important
to recognize that Iran "has been the subject of quite a lot of abuse from various Western nations," he said. "I think sometimes it's quite important to tell

people, look, you have a right to be angry at something my country or my culture or others that are generally allied with us today did to you 50 or 60 or 100 or 150 years ago."

Though Clinton was keen to explore the possibility of improving relations with Iran, one important and high-profile obstacle stood in his way. In June 1996 a five-thousand-pound truck bomb had blown up a U.S. air base in Khobar, Saudi Arabia, killing nineteen American servicemen—and a chorus of voices in Washington was busy blaming Iran for the massacre. There was no good reason to think Iran was actually at fault. The Iranians had no obvious motive for committing such an act, and neither the FBI nor the CIA was able to find anything more than circumstantial evidence to back up the theory. Very soon after the blast, however, Saudi officials—eager to avoid the impression that they had a home-grown terrorism problem— began pushing the idea that the culprits were Shia radicals with Iranian connections. And by 1998 much of the U.S. Congress, egged on by pro-Israeli pressure groups, was demanding tough action against Iran.

Hoping to pacify this domestic uproar, Clinton sent a private letter to President Khatami, asking for his cooperation in finding the culprits. (Administration officials saw this as a test of the Iranian president's sincerity.) Khatami responded that if any Iranians were involved, they would certainly be prosecuted, but he also raised an interesting possibility. If the United States was serious about discovering who was responsible for the bombing, he suggested, it should look in the direction of a shadowy network of Arab and Sunni extremist cells known as al-Qaeda.

U.S. officials were familiar with this network, but in the late 1990s, they did not know much about it, and they were not convinced Sunni extremism was as great a threat as the Iranians were making it out to be. Blinded by political considerations, Washington continued to consider Iran the prime suspect in the Khobar bombing—and few took seriously the Iranian warnings about al-Qaeda.[*] The idea of Iran as the greatest threat to American interests in the Middle East had become a permanent fixture of Washington thinking, and there was no deviating from the script.

Despite this distraction—and despite formidable domestic opposition to rapprochement with Iran—the Clinton administration began to take

---

[*] Though it may never be known with certainty who was behind the bombing, the 9/11 Commission, in its final report in June 2004, concluded that "al-Qaeda played some role, as yet unknown." In 2007, William Perry, Clinton's defense secretary, went further, arguing publicly that the fixation on Iran had been the gravest of errors. "I believe that the Khobar Tower bombing was probably masterminded by Osama bin Laden," he said, "[and] we probably should have been more concerned about it at the time." See "Perry: US Eyed Iran Attack After Bombing," UPI, June 6, 2007.

tentative steps. In October 1997 the State Department added the MeK to its list of foreign terrorist organizations—a gesture intended to show Tehran that Washington did not support violent regime change in Iran.* It also pursued the cultural links that Khatami had proposed. A stream of American scholars and scientists—including surviving members of a 1950s agricultural exchange program with Utah State University—traveled to Tehran for conferences and other activities. In February 1998 the U.S. freestyle wrestling team traveled to Tehran for a tournament—the first official American delegation since the revolution—and was received by thirteen thousand cheering spectators. And at the 1998 soccer World Cup in France, the United States and Iran—drawn together in the first round—played a sportsmanlike match that Bill Clinton hailed as "another step toward ending the estrangement between our nations."

Iran, for its part, proved receptive to the new atmosphere. In September 1998, at the annual meeting of the UN General Assembly in New York, President Khatami made a landmark speech calling for a "dialogue among civilizations." Intended as a direct response to the political scientist Samuel Huntington's "clash of civilizations" theory that was then becoming fashionable, Khatami rejected the idea that East-West conflict was inevitable, or that the value systems of the Islamic and Western worlds were fundamentally incompatible. "All human beings," he said, "originate from one and the same origin, and share a continuous and integrated history." Following his suggestion, the UN passed a resolution designating 2001 the Year of Dialogue Among Civilizations—a major boost for Iran's prestige on the international stage. Even more remarkably, Bill Clinton made a point of attending Khatami's speech and listening attentively from beginning to end—the first time an American president had extended this courtesy to his Iranian counterpart.

Much of the Western media expressed considerable enthusiasm for the Dialogue Among Civilizations—and a growing consensus that Khatami was the "real deal." Even before his UN speech, a glowing front-page profile in *The New York Times* described Khatami as a learned, courageous thinker, committed to the advancement of women and intellectual freedom in Iran, with a passion for using the Internet as a tool to empower rural Iranians (a remarkably forward-thinking position in 1998). Europeans also warmed quickly to Khatami: he made a series of highly publicized state visits to

---

* The impact of this gesture, however, was undermined by the well-publicized creation of an $18 million CIA "covert action fund" to support groups dedicated to the overthrow of the Islamic Republic.

France, Germany, and Italy—and even met the pope. In Paris, he asked to visit the Panthéon, so he could lay flowers at the graves of Victor Hugo, Émile Zola, and Jean-Jacques Rousseau.

It was a honeymoon period for Khatami at home as well. Newspapers, given far greater latitude than in the past, used this freedom to conduct investigative stories, grill politicians at press conferences, and foster real debate in their opinion pages. There were always red lines that couldn't be crossed—there was to be no overt questioning of *velayat-e-faqih,* and nothing that insulted Islam. But within these parameters, Iranians found that a surprising amount of genuine disagreement was allowed. Public shouting matches took place in newspapers now, with a degree of vitriol that would have been unimaginable during the shah's time—and was unheard-of elsewhere in the Muslim Middle East. Educated middle-class young people in particular tested the boundaries. Artists and filmmakers explored ways to navigate the ever-shifting (but now expanding) limits of the Ministry of Culture, resulting in a unique Iranian style in the arts, one that embraced contemporary, postmodern themes but with a distinctly Islamic sensibility. International reviewers wrote excitedly about the "Iranian new wave" in filmmaking and compared directors like Abbas Kiarostami and Jafar Panahi to the finest examples of European avant-garde. The Western intelligentsia seemed surprised that Iran—a nation known for strict religious laws and fanatical, fist-pumping rallies full of bearded ayatollahs—could produce such fresh and sophisticated fare. The standard line among Western liberals now became that Iran was a "complex" society, "poorly understood" but deserving of engagement and dialogue.

For these same reasons, Iran's conservatives grew nervous. Beginning in 1998, religious hard-liners, who still controlled the Majles and a number of other powerful institutions, started using these institutions as instruments to clip Khatami's wings. That spring Tehran's popular reformist mayor, Qolam-Hossein Karbaschi, was convicted on corruption and embezzlement charges and sentenced to two years in prison. Parliament impeached Khatami's interior minister, Abdollah Nuri, for refusing to enforce political and social restrictions. The conservative-dominated judiciary began shutting down newspapers it felt had strayed too far in criticizing the regime. (Khatami's Culture Ministry responded by issuing new licenses, so newspapers could reopen hours later under different names.) Intellectuals were harassed or put on trial. In late 1998, five prominent reformists were even found dead in a mysterious series of "chain murders" that many believed were linked to hard-line elements in the intelligence service.

The ultimate showdown for Khatami's reform movement, however—

and its biggest test—came in July 1999, after violent clashes between liberal student activists and pro-regime Basij volunteer militias left at least
one student dead. "*Khatami! Koja-i?*" (Khatami, where are you?), students
chanted. But the disturbances put Khatami in an impossible position. Giving his full-throated support to demonstrators would have meant an all-out
confrontation with the regime. And wide segments of society saw the students' main demand—freedom of expression—as an elite preoccupation,
pursued by students who had the luxury of ignoring more pressing economic concerns. At the same time, Khatami could not turn his back on his
base—those young people who had crowded into arenas and put up posters
two years earlier to ensure his election. The student protesters were mostly
born in 1979, 1980, and 1981, making them quite literally the "children of
the revolution." As president of the Islamic Republic and a committed disciple of Khomeini, Khatami could not allow the revolution to so obviously
devour its own.

A truly radical leader might have thrown caution to the wind and
stormed the Bastille with several hundred students at his back. But Khatami was not that leader. Though he condemned the "ugly and distasteful"
attacks on students and put together a committee to investigate, he also
urged students to remain calm and to pursue redress for their grievances at
the ballot box. He then said very little when several student "ringleaders"
were arrested and put on trial by the conservative judiciary.* All this came as
a colossal disappointment to his supporters.

It also marked the beginning of a tremendous conservative resurgence
in Iran. The conservatives, sensing that Khatami had blinked and that they
now knew how far he was willing to go (or, rather, not go) in the name of
democratic reform, mounted a vigorous challenge to his leadership—and
to the reform movement in general. More newspapers were closed. Trials
were held. Khatami was ridiculed for starting a culture war and talking
about "civil society" and free expression for filmmakers when the country
had more pressing concerns. In a meeting with Khatami and his cabinet, the
supreme leader even admonished the president for having created a "secondary problem" that "only obscures the major problem." "The most important
problem of the country today," Khamenei stressed, "is the economic problem." Why was this being "pushed aside" for a divisive and abstract discussion of "secondary and minor issues"?

It was at this precise moment that the Clinton administration took one

---

* More than one hundred police officers were also put on trial, and—although many were ultimately acquitted—the public came away satisfied that some degree of justice had been served.

of the boldest steps ever taken by an American administration toward Iran. On March 17, 2000, Secretary of State Madeleine Albright declared in a speech that the United States was ready "to work together with Iran to bring down what President Khatami refers to as 'the wall of mistrust'" between the two nations. She announced that the United States would lift sanctions on the import of pistachios and carpets—a minor policy tweak, but one intended to signal the administration's sincerity. Albright also addressed some of the historical grievances that Iran so often brought up. She acknowledged that America's support for Iraq in the 1980s "appear[s] now to have been regrettably short-sighted, especially in light of our subsequent experiences with Saddam Hussein." And in perhaps the most meaningful gesture of all, she noted that "in 1953 the United States played a significant role in orchestrating the overthrow of Iran's popular prime minister, Mohammad Mosaddeq . . . clearly a setback for Iran's political development"—not quite an apology but certainly a more honest reading of history than any of her predecessors had managed.

It was a well-intentioned intervention, designed to bolster Khatami's position in the midst of his domestic struggles. But the timing could not have been worse. The conservatives had just spent two years fighting Khatami's attempts to "dilute" the revolution and were finally gaining the upper hand. Well aware that a historic resurrection of ties with the United States would make Khatami stratospherically popular with the young and the middle class, they were not about to let him walk away with a major foreign policy victory. So while reformists in the Majles warmly welcomed Albright's speech, conservative hard-liners blasted it as an attempt to sow division. Khatami, they said, was clearly more comfortable basking in the praises of America than addressing the "real" concerns of Iranians.

What particularly incensed hard-liners was their perception that America was praising one faction in Iranian politics and condemning the other—thus interfering in Iran's internal affairs. In her speech, Albright had contrasted Khatami and the "democratic winds in Iran" with those elements practicing "repression at home and . . . support for terrorism abroad." Control of Iran's "military, judiciary, courts and police remains in unelected hands," she had said. (The supreme leader in particular was angered by this line, which he interpreted as a direct attack.) Conservatives thus felt Albright's supposedly conciliatory speech was actually full of accusations. To offer "a piece of chocolate" to only one part of the country's leadership, complained one official, was a "very ugly and unacceptable move." Khamenei, sensing the mood among the regime's most loyal supporters, rejected any talk of compromise with America—and thus implicitly rejected the charm offensive Khatami had been steadily building over the past three years. Conceived as a way to help Khatami, Albright's speech had only undermined him.

In May 2000 the reformist camp scored one final victory, winning an impressive 70 percent of seats in the parliamentary election and giving Khatami, ostensibly, a Majles he could work with. But this optimism quickly turned sour as the new parliament's attempts to liberalize Iran's press law met with unusually direct opposition from the supreme leader. In August 2000, Khatami confessed publicly that he was running out of options. He would run for reelection in 2001, he said, but no one should expect miracles. He won that election, thanks largely to the advantages of incumbency and a much lower turnout, but it was a pyrrhic victory. For the next four years, he and the reform movement staggered on courageously but compiled few real successes. The Guardian Council, which repeatedly vetoed legislation passed by the reformist Majles, saw its powers gradually expanded. Then, in the 2003 municipal elections and the 2004 Majles elections, conservatives came back with stomping victories at the ballot box, paving the way for a conservative resurgence in the presidential election of 2005.

In America, too, the era of liberal ascendancy was drawing to a close. In December 2000, Clinton's vice president, Al Gore, lost a narrow and hotly disputed election to Texas governor George W. Bush, son of the former president. Washington under Bush was no longer interested in exploring warmer ties with Tehran. Even before he took office, Congress quietly renewed the Iran-Libya Sanctions Act for another five years. And in the next few months, the allegations about the Khobar Towers bombing were revived with special vigor, as if to make it clear that Iran was still considered a pariah state. The window was closing on the possibility of Dialogue Among Civilizations.

CB

Still, despite everything, one area held out a good deal of promise for U.S.-Iranian cooperation in 2000 and 2001: Afghanistan. For much of the 1990s, Iran had prosecuted a brutal, costly drug war along its messy eastern frontier with Afghanistan, in a desperate effort to stanch the flow of opium (as well as Sunni extremists) across the border. The containment efforts had been painful for Iran—as many as three thousand soldiers had died—and Iran hoped for international assistance in battling this urgent problem. Since the Americans had repeatedly expressed concern about the Afghan drug trade, the Iranians reasoned that they might quietly find some way to help them contain their troublesome eastern neighbor. Through a number of different channels, the moderate leadership in Tehran let Washington know they would welcome such assistance.

Iran also did what it could to ensure the world understood the much larger danger emanating from Afghanistan: extreme Sunni jihadism. Following the Soviet withdrawal from Afghanistan in 1989, a radical group called the Taliban—who practiced a particularly vicious, medieval form of fundamentalist Islam, complete with the stoning of adulterers and extreme oppression of women—had gained the upper hand. Although in the past the United States had supported these elements in their fight against the Soviet Union, Iran felt hopeful that, with the Soviet menace gone, America would change its tune. After all, the Taliban were truly fanatical—in a way that both Washington and Tehran could agree made them a danger to the world.

Unfortunately for Tehran, neither the Clinton administration in its final years nor the Bush administration in the early months of 2001 saw the situation this way. Consumed by a conviction that Iran itself was the root of all evil—a conviction described by European allies as increasingly "irrational" and even "obsessive"—the United States made very little effort to cooperate with Iran in its struggle against the Taliban. The official line out of Washington was that the Taliban were an ugly and unpleasant bunch, but one that provided a certain amount of order and stability to Afghanistan's chaotic tribal regions—imposing some badly needed control over warring factions. Moreover, the Taliban's hostility to Iran made them a useful contributor to Washington's larger goal, which was containing the regional influence of the Islamic Republic. Even though the United States no longer provided outright *support* to the Taliban, as it had in the 1980s, it was not about to go out of its way to destroy them either.

The leadership in Iran found this outlook incomprehensible. Washington, it seemed, had decided that its paramount mission in the region was to checkmate Iran—even if it meant putting America's own obvious strategic and security interests at risk. Iran repeatedly tried to warn the United States about the danger of Sunni extremism, about the network of *madrassas* funded by Saudi Arabia, about the nexus of terror and radicalism that connected Pakistan and the Taliban, and about al-Qaeda specifically. And many U.S. government officials and analysts took the danger seriously. America, these analysts warned, had its policy priorities precisely backward. Rather than going after dangerous jihadists who threw acid in the faces of women and plotted terror attacks against Western targets, Washington was fixated on Iran—a rational nation-state that held elections, sent millions of women to university, and elected a president who quoted Tocqueville. The Bush administration's attitude, however, remained the same. The Taliban, the Saudi-funded *madrassas,* the jihadist terror networks, al-Qaeda—and Sunni fundamentalism generally—were simply not regarded as the most pressing foreign policy priority facing the United States at the turn of the millennium.

Then, on a cloudless Tuesday morning, in the skies over New York, everything changed.

That September Day

Shortly after nine a.m. on September 11, 2001, Hillary Mann, like almost everyone else in New York, was doing her best not to panic. A thirty-three-year-old foreign service officer attached to the U.S. mission to the United Nations, Mann had just been evacuated, along with thousands of other staffers, from the UN building on East 45th Street and was making her way toward her apartment on East 38th Street. Up ahead of her on the southern horizon was a billowing cloud of ash where the World Trade Center had been a few minutes earlier. All around her was a cacophonous mix of doomsday speculation, wailing sirens, and utter confusion. News was just trickling in of a devastating terrorist attack, and Mann was desperately fiddling with her phone, hoping for word from her sister—an employee at the Twin Towers. When the phone finally rang, however, the voice on the other end was not the one she had expected. It was her Iranian counterpart at the UN. He was calling to see if she was all right.

Sounding shaken, the official (whom Mann prefers not to name for security reasons) was struggling to find the words to match his emotions. "He says he's horrified," Mann recalls. "This is a horrible attack. He uses that word over and over again, 'horrible, horrified, horrible.'" Then, without prompting, the Iranian began speculating on who was behind this carnage. "He says he's sure that al-Qaeda is responsible," recalls Mann. "And he says that, even though he hasn't had time to get instructions from Tehran, he's sure that the Iranian government is going to come out to condemn this. He wants me to know that, as the representative of the Islamic Republic of Iran."

Mann, who today goes by her married name Hillary Mann Leverett, has never forgotten the feeling of pins and needles that came over her after she ended the call that morning. "Up until that point, we had never heard anything other than 'Death to America' on TV," when it came to Iran. "There was no other image. Just Americans being taken hostage at the U.S. embassy in Tehran." And yet here was a representative of the Islamic Republic expressing genuine concern for the sanctity of American life and assuring his American counterpart that his government was horrified by what had just taken place. "I thought that was incredibly important that that could happen."

Under ordinary circumstances, no American official would have had permission to maintain direct phone contact with a representative of the Iranian government, much less engage in casual conversation about the kind of events Mann and her counterpart were now openly discussing on the streets of Manhattan. But this was no ordinary day, and Hillary Mann was no ordinary American official. Six months earlier, she had been selected as the U.S. delegate to the so-called "6+2"—an informal contact group of six nations bordering Afghanistan, plus the United States and Russia, that met regularly to try to resolve the Afghan civil war. Although U.S. officials had been instructed to limit their discussions to Afghanistan, under the framework of the 6+2, Mann and the Iranian had often sat in the same room, each courteously listening to what the other had to say on a range of subjects from drugs trafficking to humanitarian relief for Afghan refugees.

What Mann had learned during those first six months at the 6+2 had, already, surprised her and left her questioning many of her most basic assumptions about the Islamic Republic of Iran. Now, on the morning of September 11, 2001, what she was learning was surprising her again. And it would continue to surprise her for the next year and a half that she spent talking to Iran on behalf of the U.S. government.

ᏸ

Since the spring of 2001, Mann had been working at the UN on issues related to Afghanistan. And though Iran had been part of her portfolio, she had been strictly forbidden to have any human interaction with the Iranian delegation. "I couldn't talk to them. I couldn't say hello. I couldn't do anything that wasn't authorized." It had been that way for twenty years: even as they passed each other in the corridors of the UN, representatives of both governments were under instructions to look the other way and keep walking.*

---

* The details of Mann's story are drawn from an interview conducted by the author on March 10, 2009, at a seafood restaurant in Washington, with Mann and her husband Flynt Leverett, who was senior Middle East director at the National Security Council at the time.

As part of the 6+2 process, however, Mann had been specially authorized to speak to Iran within the context of a multilateral framework—one of very few American officials ever given that level of clearance. What she had found as she began her work had left her deeply impressed and more than a little surprised. Her Iranian counterpart—a salt-and-pepper-haired man in his early fifties—would arrive at meetings with a level of professionalism and a command of the subject matter far greater than his Western counterparts. "He was very knowledgeable, very pragmatic," recalls Mann Leverett. "And there were specific, concrete issues he [wanted] to work with the Americans on in the 6+2." More striking, he seemed to have "real-time access" to the Foreign Ministry in Tehran—even, when necessary, "to the foreign minister himself"—which meant he was always able to make quick decisions. For Mann, this all suggested that Iran was taking the 6+2 process—and the rare opportunity for a conversation with the United States—very seriously. "You could tell that the people who were here were well connected. They were smart *and* well connected."

Three issues in particular were high on Iran's priority list: cracking down on narcotics trafficking, managing humanitarian relief for Afghan refugees, and enforcing an international arms embargo against the Taliban. All three issues, at least in theory, were important to Washington as well. But the conversations yielded mixed results. In the areas of narcotics and humanitarian relief, the two countries genuinely cooperated.* The arms embargo on the Taliban, however, proved problematic. Technically, Washington was signatory to a 1999 ban on sending weapons to Afghanistan, but it never seemed to share Tehran's level of enthusiasm for enforcing the embargo. In meeting after meeting, during early 2001, the Iranian delegates urged the 6+2 to take seriously the flow of weapons to the Taliban and al-Qaeda, arguing that they posed a grave threat to peace and security. But they seemed to get nowhere. Part of the problem was that many of the Taliban's arms were coming across the Pakistani border, and the government in Islamabad was doing little to police the embargo. Washington, in turn, seemed reluctant to place too much pressure on its allies in Pakistan.

Iran's solution was to suggest that more might be done along the *Iranian* border. Perhaps, they suggested, international law enforcement officials, operating under UN auspices, could be placed along Iran's border with Afghanistan, to police the flow of both drugs and weapons. This was

---

* The UN, for example, hosted a series of conferences with narcotics officers from the United States, Iran, and other countries—all sitting around a table and discussing best practices for law enforcement along volatile border areas. More than anything else, these conferences were a mechanism, a subtle, low-profile way for the United States to transfer money and technology to Iran, to enable Iranian authorities to block the opium trade funding the Taliban.

coded language. Though for political reasons they couldn't say it outright, Iran was suggesting that *American agents* could be given permission to operate along its border with Afghanistan—an unprecedented offer from the Islamic Republic. But the United States—and the international community in general—continued to drag their feet, unconvinced that the Taliban were as serious or urgent a threat as Iran was making it out to be. "Nobody cared about Afghanistan; nobody was interested," Mann Leverett recalls. "But the Iranians were very insistent."

It only got worse. As spring rolled into summer, the Iranians became even more strident in their warnings about al-Qaeda. In early September 2001, they pushed hard for a joint 6+2 communiqué about the threat of terrorism from Afghanistan. Pakistan was dead set against it, but Iran insisted, with the support of Russia, that it was important to "really try to get something in there on counter-terrorism and the danger of al-Qaeda," Mann Leverett recalled. The Iranian delegate even nominated her to write the draft—subtly indicating that Iran would support whatever language the Americans came up with. Somewhat taken aback, but not wanting to waste the opportunity, Mann quickly put together a draft communiqué, but to her utter amazement, her bosses in Washington vetoed it. It was, they said, "too focused on al-Qaeda and terrorism." They wanted her to focus "more on the humanitarian aspects," like refugee relief, and not do anything to antagonize the Pakistanis and their friends in Afghanistan. "I mean, it was really amazing. . . . They really thought it was too harsh, that it would make their life more difficult in dealing with the Taliban, and they wanted me to tone it down."

The Iranians, by contrast, wanted something even stronger. Tehran was telling them that the communiqué should include the words "international resolve and determination" against al-Qaeda—diplomatic code implying that concrete action could be taken under Chapter 7 of the UN Charter. Tehran was even threatening not to sign the communiqué unless it included these words. Washington, meanwhile, was digging in its heels and trying to dilute the draft. Looking back today, Mann Leverett still has trouble believing that this, of all things, was the bureaucratic battle she was fighting during the first few days of September 2001. "We were essentially at an impasse, with the Iranians trying to get more [language] on al-Qaeda and terrorism, when the World Trade Centers are attacked." Literally *that day*—that September day of all days—the 6+2 were scheduled to sit down and hammer out a resolution to their disagreements. The Iranians were planning to make the case that the danger from al-Qaeda should be placed at the very top of the agenda, and the Americans were planning to tell them to relax and stop hyping the threat.

The meeting never took place. What took place instead was carnage: 2,763 dead in the World Trade Center, another 189 at the Pentagon, and a further 44 in rural Pennsylvania. By far the bloodiest terrorist attack in history, the September 11 atrocities brought an ocean of hurt and suffering to America, exposing a nation unaccustomed to attacks on its soil to an act of savagery that seemed to have no parallel or precedent in the pantheon of human violence.

In Iran, the reaction to the atrocity was swift and unambiguous. President Khatami was one of the first world leaders to condemn it, referring to it unequivocally as a "terrorist" act and expressing "deep regret and sympathy with the victims." The supreme leader, Ayatollah Khamenei, instructed Friday worshippers to avoid chanting their usual anti-American slogans out of respect for the victims. "Killing of innocent people, in any place and with any type of weapon," he said in his sermon, "is categorically rejected and condemned." It was the sacred duty of all Muslims—a kind of "jihad," he said—to fight terrorism wherever it reared its head in the world. On the streets of Tehran—unprodded by the government—thousands of people gathered to hold candlelight vigils for the victims and their families. At a soccer stadium in Tehran, sixty thousand spectators observed a minute's silence.

All this was a striking contrast to the reaction in other parts of the Muslim world. In the capitals of Sunni-majority nations, nervous leaders issued stiff and perfunctory condemnations while their people danced and celebrated in front of Western TV cameras. In Islamabad and Cairo, T-shirts were printed bearing the face of Osama bin Laden, and hospitals reported a rash of babies bearing the name Osama—much to the embarrassment of governing elites. It was now very obvious that something was wrong with this picture. For years, Americans had been told that the source of all terror and fanaticism in the world was Iran, and that nations like Egypt, Pakistan, and Saudi Arabia—with their "moderate" and "pro-Western" leaders—were America's true allies. Throughout the 1990s, especially, Israel had done an excellent job of convincing Washington that Hezbollah and other Iran-backed Shia extremist groups posed a dangerous threat. Scholars and experts had tried to explain that Hezbollah was more of a liberation movement, whose militant activities were limited to hijackings, kidnappings, and other forms of targeted guerrilla warfare, but this kind of analysis had always been drowned out. For more than twenty years, *Iran* had been a synonym for *terrorism* in the minds of many Americans.

9/11 blew a bullet hole through this kind of thinking. Nineteen of the twenty hijackers, it turned out, were Saudi nationals. Funding for al-Qaeda had been channeled through a network of Sunni *madrassas,* stretching from Riyadh to Sana'a to Islamabad. And of the nearly four hundred fighters eventually rounded up and sent to Guantanamo Bay, not one turned out to be Iranian (or even Shia). To any sane observer, it was obvious that Iran was the least of America's problems. With its grassroots revolution, its independent foreign policy, and its moderate Islamism, Iran had created a society that—ironically, perhaps—was no longer all that hostile to the United States. Despite years of official revolutionary rhetoric about the evils of American "imperialism" (or more likely, because of it), Iran's people were more inclined to hold their *own* leaders accountable for their problems— and Iran's partially democratic system provided a mechanism for doing so. In many other parts of the Muslim world, however, America had struck a devil's bargain: decades of support for autocratic tyrants had created stability and harmonious international relations but also an underclass of poor, disenfranchised, religious conservatives seething with hatred both for their own leaders and for America. For Iran, therefore, 9/11 was an opportunity to draw a contrast—between Iran's top-down, managed, and relatively moderate form of Islamism and the more volatile, repressed current of underground anger that characterized so much of the Sunni world.

In late October, as the UN General Assembly prepared for its annual opening meeting, Hillary Mann Leverett was told by her Iranian counterpart that President Khatami was planning to come to New York to address the world body. Khatami, he said, wanted to "strongly come out, in Islamic terms, to condemn the attack" of 9/11 as a grotesque perversion of his faith— and to spread a message of peace and understanding between civilizations. Khatami also hoped to go to Ground Zero, so he could light a candle and say a prayer for the victims—a gesture that would have been groundbreaking in the history of U.S.-Iranian relations.

It was never to be. The State Department refused to give Khatami permission to visit lower Manhattan, arguing that the presence of a prominent Muslim leader at Ground Zero would be too upsetting to the public under the circumstances—and that there was a risk Khatami might say something to "offend" victims' families. "To me this was a tremendous lack of political courage," says Mann Leverett.

Undeterred, the Iranians informed Mann that they planned to send, under the "umbrella" of Khatami's visit to the UN, a number of Iranian counterterrorism experts and other officials they believed might be useful to the United States in its battle to defeat al-Qaeda and uproot the Taliban. Iran's goal, according to the representative, was to "open a dialogue" with the United States and look for areas of cooperation with the Bush administration's newly declared Global War on Terror. The Iranians, after all, knew more about Afghanistan and al-Qaeda than any other delegation at the UN—with the possible exception of the Pakistanis. Unlike Pakistan, however, Iran genuinely loathed the Taliban and wanted to assist the United States in whatever way possible to bring about their destruction.

Excited by what she was hearing, Mann cabled back to Washington, assuming her superiors would share her enthusiasm and recognize the opportunity she had helped create for a historic strategic opening to the Islamic Republic.

They did not. When the cable came back to her desk, the message was clear and succinct: *Don't worry about Iran. Just focus on Afghanistan. That's your job.*

❦

To those who had been following events in the region closely over the years, Iran's antipathy to al-Qaeda and the Taliban was nothing new. In 1996, when the Taliban first came to power in Afghanistan—horrifying the world with savage attacks on women and massacres of civilian populations—Iran's supreme leader, Ayatollah Khamenei, had called them a "disgrace to Islam." In October 1998, Iran's UN representative in Vienna had said it was of "vital importance" to create a "security belt around Afghanistan" to contain the Taliban. And by the end of 1998, Iran and the Taliban had been on the verge of all-out war. Ten Iranian diplomats, trapped in their consulate building in Mazar-e Sharif and desperately trying to phone Tehran for help, had been killed in cold blood by the Taliban, prompting a tremendous outpouring of anger among Iranians. Iran's allies among Afghanistan's Shia population, in particular the Northern Alliance and its leader Ahmed Shah Massoud— who had called for equal rights for women and a moderate interpretation of Islam—were then slaughtered by the thousands by the Taliban. Iran, fed up with what it perceived as the inaction of the international community, had amassed two hundred thousand troops along the Afghan border, hoping to single-handedly contain the Taliban. Despite this powerful show of force, however, the Iranians were not able to convince the rest of the world to support them.

In the days following 9/11, therefore, when Bush pledged to bomb Afghanistan, remove the Taliban, and "smoke out" al-Qaeda from its hiding places, no nation on earth was more enthusiastic about it than Iran. Unlike some of America's NATO allies, however, Iran could not declare publicly its solidarity with the United States, and it certainly could not send troops to join the mission. Twenty years of official animosity between the two countries made that impossible. Iran had to tread delicately and find a way to assist America that would not upset political sensitivities in either country.

Shortly before the bombs started dropping on Afghanistan, the Iranians—along with the Bush administration's special envoy for Afghanistan, James Dobbins—set up a top-secret series of meetings in Switzerland, dubbed the "Geneva Channel." The meetings received the quiet approval of Secretary of State Colin Powell and continued in secret for nearly a year and a half, until the spring of 2003. Present at every meeting were representatives from Germany and Italy, as well as the United States and Iran—but the Germans and Italians were there mostly to provide political cover and would generally disappear to the sidelines to allow the two main participants to talk face-to-face. The result was the highest-level and most sustained contact between Iranian and American officials in nearly twenty years.

When the bombing campaign got under way in Afghanistan on October 7, Iran's cooperation surprised even the most optimistic of American officials. Within a few weeks, Iran provided wide-ranging tactical assistance to the U.S.-led operation, allowing American aircraft access to airfields in eastern Iran, performing search-and-rescue operations for American pilots who had bailed out over Iranian airspace, creating a transport corridor for humanitarian and other supplies, and (perhaps most important) persuading its allies in the Northern Alliance to cooperate with the bombing campaign. At a Tokyo donors conference in January, Iran even pledged $560 million to help create a stable postwar political settlement in Afghanistan—more than any other nation in the world.* In the words of Dobbins, Iran's behavior during the crucial initial stages of the war in Afghanistan was "comprehensively helpful" to the United States.

That, if anything, was an understatement. At one of the Geneva Channel meetings, in early November, the Iranians unfolded a large map of Afghanistan and gave American officials an impromptu lecture about what they were getting wrong in their bombing campaign. It wasn't enough to bomb in the Pashtun south and east of the country, they said. If you didn't bomb *here* and *here* and *here,* the Northern Alliance wasn't going to be able to make inroads to Kabul. "Maybe you can bomb the Taliban *out,* but then who are you going to have come in?" they asked. All this advice was hurriedly relayed back to U.S. Central Command in Florida. "They gave us, I thought, a tremendous amount of assistance in terms of military targets on the ground, in terms of who's who in Afghanistan," recalls Mann Leverett. "We had no *clue* who any of the figures were, good or bad, in Afghanistan.

---

* The United States, by contrast, pledged $296 million. The European Union pledged $500 million.

September 11, 2001: Thousands of Iranians hold candlelight vigils for the victims of the atrocities in the United States. In the months that followed, Iran quietly provided the United States with tactical support in its fight against the Taliban and al-Qaeda—assistance U.S. officials described as "comprehensively helpful."

We just had no knowledge. They had not only tremendous knowledge but also relationships with a lot of those people."

To some extent, Iran's willingness to be "comprehensively helpful" to the Bush administration's war effort in Afghanistan was based on the flawed assumption that 9/11 was going to change America so fundamentally that Washington would realign its foreign policy away from reliance on the Sunni political establishment of Egypt, Pakistan, and Saudi Arabia and toward a more tactical alliance with Iran that could crush al-Qaeda and the Taliban. "Their reasoning," according to Mann Leverett, "was that they thought 9/11 was such a signature moment—such a huge moment for the United States—that we would look at Iran differently." The Iranians expected, perhaps naïvely, that the United States would finally recognize that the real threat to its security came from Sunni extremists—and that Iran and the United States were on the same side of this epic battle. For years, Iran had argued that America was foolish to put so much faith in the Sunni political establishment, and they believed that, with 9/11, America would finally sit up and take notice of this argument. "They thought there would be a transformation in American thinking," says Mann Levertt, "to see Iran on the good side of this. We would both be aligned against 'real terrorists' like al-Qaeda, and we would be able to strategically realign our relationship."

On paper, perhaps, much of this reasoning made sense. But Iran was in for an unpleasant surprise.

CB

The initial reaction from the Bush administration to the goings-on at the Geneva Channel was one of casual disregard. When Mann informed her superiors that she was getting a surprising amount of cooperation from Iran, the response she got (as she describes it) was along the lines of "that's fine, we'll take whatever we can get on Afghanistan." In the wake of 9/11, her superiors said, 188 other countries were lining up to stand "shoulder to shoulder" with America, and many of them were offering to send combat forces. The idea that Iran, as Afghanistan's western neighbor and longtime adversary, might have something unique to offer did not receive serious consideration. "It was not seen as something special, something important, or something strategic," laments Mann Leverett.

As winter approached, though, and word percolated through the administration that serious, sustained, tactical discussions were taking place between uniformed military officials from the Pentagon and their Iranian counterparts, the reaction at the White House turned from dismissiveness to outright hostility. The news was particularly upsetting to some of the administration's more ideological hard-liners, like Deputy Defense Secretary Paul Wolfowitz and his colleagues Richard Perle and Douglas Feith. "We've been talking to the Iranians? How'd that happen? How'd that happen on our watch?" is the way Mann Leverett describes the reaction in Wolfowitz's office. There was, she recalls, an "obvious disconnect" between the uniformed military, who were poring over maps of Afghanistan with their Iranian counterparts—"as if they actually had a war to deal with"—and the civilians in the office of the secretary of defense. The now-famous fault line in the administration between ideologues and pragmatists was beginning to emerge.

It was at this precise moment that the ideologues were handed a gift more precious than anything they could have asked for. On January 4, 2002, Israel announced that its navy had intercepted a ship—the *Karine A*—loaded with rifles, Katyusha rockets, and antitank missiles from Iran, heading for the Gaza Strip. For Israeli prime minister Ariel Sharon, it was a tremendous propaganda coup. Coming at a time when the United States and Iran seemed to be drawing closer, the *Karine A* established a direct connection, in the minds of the American public, between Iran and terrorism—and drove a large wedge between the Bush administration and Tehran. The Iranians denied vociferously that they had anything to do with the *Karine A*. President Khatami even sent a formal request through Switzerland, asking Washington for concrete evidence of Iranian involvement. But it was all in vain.

The pictures on television looked credible enough—there was, for example, Persian lettering all over the crates on the *Karine A*—but even some of Israel's friends in the West found the whole thing a little unconvincing. Why, they wondered, would Iran send supplies by boat, all the way round the Arabian Peninsula and into the eastern Mediterranean, where Israeli coast guards would be waiting to intercept? And why would Iran risk antagonizing Washington at precisely the moment when the two countries were cooperating to get rid of the Taliban? The timing of Israel's discovery struck some observers as a little too convenient. In Washington, it was common knowledge that Israel had a vested interest in preventing any warming of relations between Iran and the United States, so there was no shortage of quiet grumbling about what felt like a cheap publicity stunt.

At the highest levels of the Bush administration, much of this skepticism was swatted away. The administration's ideologically motivated war hawks, led by Wolfowitz, Perle, and Feith—all known for their close links with Israel—excitedly argued that the War on Terror should now be expanded beyond its narrow focus on al-Qaeda. It was time to reframe the whole thing as a clash of civilizations—an epic, millennial confrontation between those nations committed to Western-style liberal democracy and those that were not. Iran, Iraq, Hezbollah, and Hamas (conveniently, cynics argued, all entities disliked by Israel) should now be lumped together with al-Qaeda and presented to the American public as an evil force bent on the destruction of their very way of life.

Very quickly, the hard-line ideological contingent at the White House (often described by American media as "neoconservatives") gained the upper hand over the more cautious cadre of foreign policy experts around Secretary Powell. President Khatami, they argued, was not really in control of things in Iran; he was merely a friendly face put out by a regime that was—and would always be—fundamentally at odds with the United States. The best way to respond to his overtures was to nip them in the bud, ideally by having Bush deliver a high-profile, unambiguous statement against Iran. And the best moment for such a statement was during the upcoming State of the Union address—a speech that, given recent events, was likely to be one of the most closely watched in world history.

By the time Bush delivered his State of the Union address on January 29, the internal battle at the White House had been won. "Iran, Iraq and North Korea," the president told a rapt audience of 52 million Americans, "constitute an Axis of Evil, arming to threaten the peace of the world."

In European capitals, the sound of mandibles could be heard hitting the floor. Even traditional U.S. allies such as Britain and France expressed utter disbelief that Bush had chosen to expand the War on Terror in such a sweeping and seemingly limitless way. France's foreign minister, Hubert Védrine, called Bush's speech "simplistic" and "absurd." And the European Union's foreign policy chief, Javier Solana, warned America against pursuing a policy of "global unilateralism." Some Americans as well showed signs of discomfort with Bush's transformation of the War on Terror into a crusade to remake the Middle East. *The New York Times* called the president's speech "appropriately forceful" but cautioned: "deciding how to deal with these nations will not be as easy as warning them." The only place where Bush's "Axis of Evil" rhetoric received a warm and unqualified welcome was Israel. "When historians sum up the first decade of the 21st century," wrote the editors of the *Jerusalem Post,* "George W. Bush may stand as one whose role in rescuing the free world is best compared with that of Winston Churchill."

In Tehran, the "Axis of Evil" speech set off a political firestorm. Millions of Iranians—including even those unhappy with their regime and broadly sympathetic to America—marched through central Tehran to protest the way their country had been lumped together with the hated Saddam Hussein and the totalitarian regime of Kim Jong-il in North Korea. For the most part, they blamed Bush; but many also quietly blamed Khatami. For years, the reformist president had urged Iran to show a more open face to America, assuring skeptics that pursuing a nonconfrontational foreign policy would bring rewards. In Afghanistan, he had gone out on a limb—begging hardliners to be patient and convincing even the supreme leader that, in the wake of 9/11, Iran had a historic opportunity to realign its relationship with the United States. But Bush's "Axis of Evil" speech made a mockery of all that. Even the most liberal Iranians—his natural supporters—now increasingly regarded Khatami as a failure.

To make clear its irritation with the speech, Iran canceled the February meeting of the Geneva Channel, at a time when its help was more badly needed in Afghanistan than ever. Iran also released Gulbuddin Hekmatiar, a notorious Afghan warlord who had escaped into Iran and whom the Americans had hoped would stay locked up in captivity. Just a few weeks earlier, Iran had promised the United States it would hold on to Hekmatiar, on the condition that America not publicly accuse Iran of harboring terrorists. But in the "Axis of Evil" speech, Bush had described Iran as a nation that "exports terror." All bets were off, and Hekmatiar disappeared into the rugged terrain of the Hindu Kush.

"Axis of Evil." In his State of the Union address in January 2002, President George W. Bush expanded the War on Terror beyond al-Qaeda and the Taliban, saying that Iran, Iraq, and North Korea "constitute an axis of evil, arming to threaten the peace of the world." Publicly, Iranians were outraged to hear themselves lumped in with longtime foe Saddam and the North Korean dictator. Privately, the secret channel of cooperation against the Taliban continued.

Dobbins, privately furious with the administration for sabotaging the hard work he had done through the Geneva Channel, did his best to be a team player. Through gritted teeth, he explained to the Iranians that Washington still had concerns about Iranian behavior in a number of areas, such as Iran's unhelpful approach to the Israeli-Palestinian conflict. "We would have liked to have discussed those matters too," the Iranians responded without missing a beat.

଼

Despite its irritation with the "Axis of Evil" speech, Iran chose not to *fully* sabotage America's efforts in Afghanistan. Within a month, the Geneva Channel was back in business, with Iran using its influence with various Afghan warlords to ensure that the June 2002 *loya jirga* that Washington was putting together produced an outcome favorable to the American protégé Hamid Karzai. At one point, Iran even forwarded to Washington—via UN secretary-general Kofi Annan—photocopied passports belonging to two hundred al-Qaeda and Taliban fighters who had fled across the border and were being detained in Iranian facilities. And its State Department interlocutors—in particular, Mann and Dobbins—were happy to keep talking.

This time, however, there was considerable tension in the air—and not just because of the "Axis of Evil" speech. In Washington, steamy speculation was circulating through the corridors of power about the possibility of an American war against Iraq. America's newspapers, twenty-four-hour cable networks, and magazine pundits were all dizzily reporting on White House plans for a decisive, overwhelming air-and-land invasion of Iraq—one that would depose Saddam Hussein, occupy Baghdad, and set in motion a domino effect of democratic, pro-American coups and revolutions throughout the region. All this war talk—in particular, the stuff about regime change and domino effects—made Iran nervous. Already 100,000 American and NATO troops were stationed to its east, in Afghanistan. An invasion of Iraq would likely place another 200,000 on its western flank. To its south, in the Persian Gulf, was the U.S. Navy's Fifth Fleet. To its southeast was Pakistan, which had moved much closer to the United States after 9/11. Even to the north, there were U.S. forces in Azerbaijan and Uzbekistan. Iran, by any objective measure, looked like a nation surrounded. And from all the neo-conservative slogans coming out of Washington—slogans like "Freedom is on the march" and "Everyone wants to go to Baghdad; real men want to go to Tehran"—Iranian leaders drew a natural conclusion: America's ultimate goal was to remove them from power.

Still, Iran made the calculation that it was worthwhile to continue with the Geneva Channel. If Washington was truly determined to attack Iraq—as all the rumors were suggesting—then Iran felt its best bet was to try to shape the outcome in its favor. America, after all, was just as underinformed about the political nuances and tribal relationships in Iraq as it had been in Afghanistan, and it would have just as much need for a little local knowledge once it started moving tanks and troops into Baghdad. Given that Iranians had spent more of their lives at war with Saddam than any other people on earth, they were uniquely placed to offer assistance and advice in dealing with Iraqi society—and Washington would never be so foolish as to shut them out completely.

Hard-liners in Washington, however, had other ideas. Having seen just how far the Geneva Channel had been allowed to progress—and just how much meaningful, substantive U.S.-Iranian cooperation had been achieved in Afghanistan—they were not about to allow a similar level of cooperation to take place over Iraq. Israel, as well, was determined to find some way to squelch all the behind-the-scenes conversations taking place between the United States and Iran. The *Karine A* affair had already gone a long way toward doing this, but the Israelis needed something bigger, more spectacular—something that would convince the world definitively that Iran was a dangerous, reckless power that should be isolated rather than engaged. In August 2002, therefore, they released a fat dossier of information they had been collecting for years about Iran's nuclear research program*—and once again made the case that the world could not risk the specter of mad ayatollahs armed with nukes.

Very little in the nuclear dossier was new or original. The Israelis had been issuing apocalyptic warnings about Iran's nuclear program since the early 1990s. (As early as 1992, Israel's deputy prime minister, Binyamin Netanyahu, had warned that Iran was "three to five years" away from a bomb—and similar predictions had been made nearly every year since.) But these latest allegations sounded more specific and detailed than anything that had been heard before. Iran was said to have a clandestine uranium enrichment plant at Natanz and a heavy-water production facility in Arak for the extraction of plutonium. Very quickly, "the Iranian nuclear threat"—a new and urgent target in the ever-expanding War on Terror—became the latest talking point on America's cable news programs.

Six months later American warplanes began raining hellfire down from the skies over Iraq—and Iran watched nervously from the sidelines. From a purely military standpoint, the U.S. air-and-land campaign—dubbed Operation Iraqi Freedom (and more informally "Shock and Awe")—proved one of the most successful in American history. In just twenty-one days, from March to April 2003, a quarter-million American troops swept into Iraq, defeated its military, occupied Baghdad, and overthrew Saddam Hussein—paving the way for Bush to land heroically on the deck of the aircraft carrier *Abraham Lincoln* in front of a banner reading "Mission Accomplished." For Iran, which had spent eight years and nearly half a million lives trying to defeat Saddam, the ease with which U.S. forces did the job was unnerving. In cafes, on street corners, in newspaper columns, and at the highest levels of power in Iran, in the spring of 2003, there was only one question being asked and only one question anyone wanted answered: *Are we next?*

☙

Realizing that America's neoconservatives were on a roll and that their own piecemeal approach of cooperating with America on specific, tactical mat-

---

* Not wanting to be overly obvious, the Israelis contacted the Iranian exile group, the MeK, and asked *them* to make the information public. Thus, when the bombshell about Iran's "secret nuclear ambitions" hit the headlines, Western media reported that the information had been passed to Washington by "an Iranian opposition group." Israel's name was kept neatly out of the headlines.

ters like Afghanistan had failed, Iran's leaders decided to take a bold step—
the boldest, perhaps, that had ever been tried by the Islamic Republic. At
the beginning of May 2003, Iran sent to Washington—via the Swiss Foreign
Ministry—a three-page proposal for ending, once and for all, the twenty-
two-year-old hostility between the United States and the Islamic Republic.
In the letter, Iran pledged that if the United States repealed all sanctions,
asset freezes, and other penalties against it, dropped the "Axis of Evil" talk,
and recognized Iran's "legitimate security interests" in the region—including
its right to peaceful nuclear technology—then Iran would address virtually
every concern the United States had ever raised about its actions.

The specifics of the Iranian proposal were almost too good to be true.
On the nuclear issue, Iran promised to allow full, intrusive international
inspections of its facilities. On terrorism, it would act decisively against
al-Qaeda and enter into cooperation and exchange agreements with the
United States as part of the War on Terror. And in Iraq, it would work to
achieve political stabilization, democracy, and even a "nonreligious government" in Baghdad. The boldest parts of the Iranian proposal, however, were
its promises on the Israeli-Palestinian track. Here Iran put in writing, for the
first time in history, its willingness to accept a two-state solution (i.e., full
recognition of Israel in exchange for the return of Arab territory occupied

"We don't talk to evil": Vice President Dick Cheney (right) and Defense Secretary
Donald Rumsfeld (left) ensured that the grand bargain proposal never reached the
president's desk. In May 2003 they shut down the secret Geneva Channel.

since 1967). It promised to end all support for Palestinian militant groups, including Hamas and Islamic Jihad. And it even said it would pressure Hezbollah—its most important ally in the Arab world—to lay down arms and transform itself into a "mere political organization within Lebanon."

At the State Department, Powell and his deputy Richard Armitage were intrigued. Iran's proposal, they sensed, could be the start of something different, something historic—a "grand bargain," some in the administration even called it. At the very least, it was an opportunity worth pursuing. Never before had the Iranians put all their cards on the table like this. With the support of National Security Adviser Condoleezza Rice, Powell and Armitage approached the president, hoping to initiate a conversation. But they quickly ran into a cold stone wall in the shape of Defense Secretary Donald Rumsfeld and Vice President Dick Cheney. Rumsfeld and Cheney were dead set in their opposition to the proposal and insisted it was not even worth talking about in front of the president. "We thought it was a very propitious moment," recalled Powell's chief of staff. "But as soon as it got to the White House, and as soon as it got to the Vice-President's office, the old mantra of 'We don't talk to evil' . . . reasserted itself."

Though the ideologues in the White House never offered much of an argument beyond this, it was obvious they believed the United States had achieved an unprecedented position of strength and simply had no need for Iranian cooperation. Cheney, Rumsfeld, and the neoconservatives had convinced themselves that 2003 was the greatest moment in America's history on the world stage. America's vast military machine had defeated Iraq. Saddam and the Taliban were gone. The "mission" was "accomplished," and there were bigger plans to move on to Iran and Syria. In the Office of Defense Policy, Undersecretary Douglas Feith was drawing up plans for regime change in Tehran and Damascus—plans described as "much more than just a contingency." In this atmosphere, the administration felt there was really no point in negotiating with Iran, because the Iranian regime would soon be a relic of history.

But the hard-liners in the Bush administration were not content with merely ignoring Iran's grand bargain; they wanted to shut down all communication between the United States and Iran. As a premise, they accused Iran of coordinating a series of explosions in the Saudi capital Riyadh and the Moroccan city of Casablanca on May 12 and 16, which had killed eighty-one people. The evidence was extremely thin. But Cheney and Rumsfeld did not let that get in the way of their larger goal. On May 25 Washington informed Iran that, because of its concerns over Iranian support for terror, it was shutting down the Geneva Channel—permanently.

The Iranians took away from all this a powerful lesson and an operating principle that has guided their foreign policy ever since: Always negotiate with America from a position of strength. Khatami, hard-liners in Tehran now argued, had tried every imaginable approach to the United States to demonstrate Iran's readiness for improved relations—grand bargains, tactical cooperation, "dialogues among civilizations," friendly CNN interviews—but none of them had succeeded in melting Washington's heart. And this was true, they said, during both the Clinton and the Bush administrations. For Iran's most dedicated hard-liners—those who never needed a reason to blame America for everything that was wrong with the world—the shutdown of the Geneva Channel and the rejection of the grand bargain served as a powerful confirmation of something they had always suspected: there was no point in turning a friendly face to America, because America simply hated Iran.

೧೩

As Khatami's second term came to a close in 2004, it was obvious that his only concrete achievement had been to pave the way for a historic conservative backlash in Iran. On one hand, he had been enormously successful at creating a culture of open expression and debate. Iran in 2004 was a nation of activists and bloggers, filmmakers and social critics, in a way that would have been unimaginable eight years earlier. At the same time, however, Khatami had fallen into the same trap that reformers in history have always fallen into: the need to manage fast-rising expectations. In some of his last public appearances as president, students in the audience—fed up with hearing about "civil society" but seeing their newspapers shut down and their professors jailed for speaking their minds—jeered and heckled and shouted angry questions at the president they had once supported so passionately. "Mr. Khatami, where is the freedom you promised us?" one female student demanded at a raucous session at Tehran University. A democrat to the last breath, Khatami beamed and told the audience it gave him great joy to see them questioning an authority figure with such verve and tenacity. But Khatami was missing the point. Many in the audience had grown so disillusioned they were swearing never to participate in an Iranian election again.

Iran was now also seeing a tremendous resurgence in conservative political activism—particularly among its less Westernized youth. Young conservatives had arrived late to the world of technology and public debate—but now they too were blogging and starting newspapers, arguing vociferously (and often with a surprising degree of sophistication) for "principlist" values like *velayat-e-faqih,* religious orthodoxy, and opposition to American hegemony in the Middle East. In 2004, Iranian society was beginning to look more like an open, democratic marketplace of ideas—but it was also becoming more polarized along cultural lines. On the one hand were the artists, students, computer programmers, and middle-class filmmakers of north Tehran—deeply depressed and cynical after the failure of Khatami's reform movement. On the other was a new vanguard of excitable young Khomeinists—Revolutionary Guardsmen and Basij volunteers who had grown up steeped in the values of the Islamic Republic and had little interest in traveling to Europe or listening to Western pop music. In a poll of Iranian youth taken by *Reader's Digest*/Zogby International, 25 percent said they wanted their country to become "more secular and liberal," but more than 30 percent said they hoped it would become "more religious and conservative."

Something was happening in Iran—and it did not bode well for Khatami, the reform movement, or the future of U.S.-Iranian relations. In the fifteen years since the death of Khomeini, the ayatollah's most fervent supporters had watched their nation's political leaders steadily lead them away from the Islamist radicalism of the 1980s, and now they had had enough. First Rafsanjani, the wily pistachio magnate, had injected free-market capitalism into the Iranian economy. Then Khatami had focused on cultural values and encouraged young Iranians to start newspapers or study sociology at university. Each, in his own way, had seemed more concerned with the concerns of Tehran's elite than with the "oppressed of the earth" who Khomeini had always said were the heart and soul of the revolution. Rafsanjani had given Iran skyscrapers and shopping centers and created opportunities for his political cronies. Khatami had helped Iran make a name for itself at the Cannes Film Festival and the Venice Biennale and helped young women feel safe wearing skinny jeans imported from H&M. But for Iran's poor—its religious traditionalists, its war veterans, its chador-wearing grandmothers—this was not exactly progress. They wanted one of their own—a salt-of-the-earth, plain-speaking revolutionary who understood the language of the small-town mosque and the village elder. Tired of the city slickers and the merchant capitalists who had run Iran since 1989, they longed for a little homespun wit and wisdom—and for a leader who was not afraid to stick his finger in America's eye when the occasion called for it.

Fortunately for them, there was a presidential election coming up.

The Moral Cold War

C3 80

At the beginning of 2005, when Mahmoud Ahmadinejad declared himself a candidate for president, almost no one in Iran's political establishment took him seriously. Scruffy, clownish, even a little cross-eyed in appearance, Ahmadinejad—in the view of most mainstream political observers—was more a punchline than a serious presidential contender. As mayor of Tehran since 2003, he had improved the city's notorious traffic congestion—building expressways and overpasses and putting more traffic police on the beat to ease the daily commute. But on the national political stage, he was largely unknown and untested, an unpolished religious conservative who had never been outside Iran and probably had little idea how to run a country. And yet incredibly, when the votes were counted on June 24, 2005, he emerged victorious. For the second time in a row, a relative outsider had upended conventional wisdom and catapulted himself into the presidency of the Islamic Republic.

In part, Ahmadinejad's 2005 victory—much like Khatami's in 1997— was the product of auspicious timing and the quirks of electoral politics.* But it was also the product of something far subtler taking place in the hearts and minds of the Iranian public. Sixteen years after the death of Khomeini, many Iranians were beginning to question just how much their leaders had done to achieve the revolution's stated goals of helping the poor and deprived—and Ahmadinejad was the living embodiment of this frustration. The son of a blacksmith, greasy and disheveled in appearance, so full of godly piety that he rarely dressed in anything more formal than a

---

* Following the frustrations and failures of the Khatami years, many Iranian liberals were so deeply disillusioned that they did not bother to participate in the election—leaving Ahmadinejad, the dark horse candidate full of energy and new ideas, to face off against Iran's aging former president Rafsanjani in a second-round runoff with a historically low turnout.

zip-up windbreaker, Ahmadinejad was a clear antidote to the slick metropolitan elitism that had characterized the Rafsanjani and Khatami years. In his campaign, he argued for a return to the core values of the revolution, especially Khomeini's ideas about social justice and the "oppressed of the earth." He promised that his first priority as president would be to redistribute Iran's oil wealth straight onto the *sofreh*—the kitchen table—of ordinary Iranians. His campaign posters and television advertising spoke directly to the poorest and most vulnerable members of society and presented voters with a simple question: What has the revolution done for *you?* Who has it benefited?

Ahmadinejad also campaigned on the importance of moral purity and pledged to put an end to corruption in the Islamic Republic. He slammed what he called Iran's "new capitalists" (*sarmayedaran-e nou*) as being every bit as pernicious as the "thousand families" who had dominated the country during the Pahlavi dynasty. But unlike so many politicians who latch onto anticorruption as a convenient campaign slogan, Ahmadinejad seemed to live and breathe what he was saying. As mayor, he was known for bringing his lunch to work in a bag and continuing to live in his family's modest house in the east Tehran neighborhood of Narmak. He refused to perform special favors for his friends, and on several occasions he had quietly slipped on the uniform of a street-sweeper to collect garbage with city employees. He had even, famously, once been seen climbing out of his car to clear a blocked storm drain with his bare hands.

Ahmadinejad's candidacy had another advantage as well: he was not a man of the cloth—a fact that distinguished him from Iran's previous three presidents and added to his image as an outsider. Among a public tired of watching turbaned ayatollahs on TV, stroking their beards and coolly divvying up the spoils of power among themselves, Ahmadinejad's *personal* piety—his ability to have a relationship with God without the baggage of a formal seminary education—made him seem like a fresh alternative to the clerical establishment. It also helped that Ahmadinejad was a former *basiji*—a member of the volunteer militias that, in the eyes of many Iranians, had heroically defended the war front against the Iraqi army. His close ties to the Revolutionary Guards, in fact, perhaps more than anything else, helped propel Ahmadinejad to victory. In June, throughout election day, Guards commanders made sure that busloads of young recruits—eager to vote for one of their own—were driven to polling stations.

In multiple ways, Ahmadinejad's presidency represented a changing of the guard for Iran's political establishment. Unlike Khatami, Rafsanjani, and Khamenei before him—unlike even Khomeini himself—the forty-nine-year-old Ahmadinejad was not a scholarly preacher who had spent decades chafing under the shah's restrictions on clerical power, longing to see the mosque and seminary restored to their rightful place in Iranian society. Rather, his defining life experience had been the revolution and the war against Iraq—a crucible of blood, sweat, radicalism, self-sacrifice, and anti-imperialist ideology. He was the first president to have come of age in the impassioned atmosphere of the early 1980s, and the first to owe his job explicitly to the rank-and-file of the Revolutionary Guards. And during the eight years that Ahmadinejad remained in the job, this subtle generational shift in the country's political culture would become readily apparent. Soon after taking office, he declared a "Revolutionary Guards appreciation week" and approved a 74 percent increase in the development budget to help the Basij win government contracts. He also replaced many government ministers and career bureaucrats with young radicals who had served in the Basij with him, or whose chief qualification appeared to be the years they had spent fighting in the trenches of the Shatt al-Arab.

But it was outside Iran, perhaps, that Ahmadinejad's rambunctious radicalism and unconventional leadership style made their most indelible mark. On the global stage, his never-ending string of outrageous statements—about Israel, about America, about the Holocaust, and about homosexuals—thrust him into the spotlight and made him, for all the worst reasons, a major international figure. For many Americans especially, from 2005 to 2013, Ahmadinejad became something of a cartoon villain—his hand perpetually raised in midrant, and his unpronounceable name perpetually associated with some ghastly new quote that seemed well beyond the bounds of civilized discourse. All this, naturally, had a chilling effect on U.S.-Iranian relations. But it was not always clear that it needed to.

☙

If there is one fact that has never been fully appreciated in the West it is that, under Iran's peculiar constitution, the president actually has very little power over foreign policy. For the most part, he is expected to attend to a range of domestic tasks, such as managing the economy and negotiating with the Majles over the annual budget. In foreign policy, the big decisions are left largely to the supreme leader and the National Security Council. Nevertheless, when it comes to foreign affairs, the president does enjoy a number of symbolic powers and an ability to set the *tone*. It is the president who takes foreign trips and meets world leaders at international conferences. It is the president who appoints ambassadors. And it is the president who gives speeches at the UN or interviews to CNN. In these respects,

Iran's president is like any other head of state. He is the public face the Islamic Republic shows to the world.

During his eight years on the job, from 2005 to 2013, Ahmadinejad used these "presidential" aspects of his post to maximum effect—in ways that often sent chills down the spines of Western audiences. He never missed, for example, an opportunity to attend the annual opening of the UN General Assembly in New York and to harangue the West for its "arrogance" and its "colonial attitudes." He gave far more interviews to American television networks than Khatami ever had. And during his visits to New York, he enjoyed hosting dinners and giving speeches to a wide range of audiences—almost reveling in the protests and vocal condemnations such events attracted. The most audacious of his presidential forays into foreign policy, however, and the one he is best known for to this day, was the speech he gave to a group of Tehran students in October 2005, when he was widely quoted in the international media as saying the state of Israel should be "wiped off the map."

The awkward truth about this episode is that he never said any such thing. It was a lousy translation*, but it made its way around the world like a brushfire before anyone could verify it. And anyway, for Ahmadinejad to call for the obliteration of Israel would have meant going against years of official Iranian government policy. Since the early 1990s, Iran's position had been that it would respect whatever political settlement the Palestinians wished to reach with Israel—and was prepared, as a practical matter, to recognize Israel in the context of a larger negotiated settlement. In order to avoid confusion, Ali Larijani, secretary of Iran's National Security Council, made a statement the day after Ahmadinejad's speech: "We still have the same position and believe the Palestinian people must decide for their future." A prominent conservative lawmaker, Ahmad Nateq-Nuri, added: "What the president meant was that we favor a fair and long-lasting peace in Palestine." In case there was any more doubt, the Foreign Ministry issued a statement the following day: "Iran is committed to its obligations stated in the UN charter, and it has never tried to use force or threat against a second country." And the supreme leader himself—the man who made all final decisions about foreign policy for Iran—gave a sermon on live national television in which he declared, "We will not commit aggression toward any nations; we will not breach any nation's rights, anywhere in the world." These remarks, however, were barely reported outside Iran.

What took place instead was an avalanche of moral indignation and outrage. In Israel, Prime Minister Ariel Sharon called for Iran to be expelled

---

* See endnote, pp. 611–613.

from the United Nations. America's UN ambassador, John Bolton, called Ahmadinejad's remarks "pernicious and unacceptable." Britain, France, and Germany all recalled their ambassadors from Tehran, and UN secretary-general Kofi Annan canceled a planned trip to Iran. Canadian prime minister Paul Martin even accused Ahmadinejad of issuing a "call for genocide."

Initially, Ahmadinejad appeared surprised by these reactions. But as condemnation poured in from Western leaders, he began to thrive on the attention—enjoying the opportunity it gave him to posture as a defender of the little guy, standing up to Israel and her powerful allies in the West. Ahmadinejad especially enjoyed the opportunity to tie his own image to that of a broader liberation struggle that had many adherents in far-flung corners of the world. This unexpected boost to his credentials as a defender of the Palestinians was particularly noticeable among ordinary citizens of the Arab and Muslim world.

A month later Ahmadinejad was at it again, and again with an almost childlike lack of awareness about the dangerous game he was playing. In the midst of an otherwise unremarkable speech in December, he delved into the deeper history of the Israeli-Palestinian conflict. If the European powers had been guilty of perpetrating genocide against Jews during World War II, he asked, why was it the Palestinians who were paying the price for this crime? Why was it *their* land and *their* rights that had been taken away to create a Jewish state, rather than those of the Western powers? The question was fairly unimaginative, one routinely asked by critics of Israel, not just in the Middle East but also in Europe (and even, quite often, by Israelis themselves). The way Ahmadinejad phrased it, however, crossed a line that most heads of state would have avoided:

> Today, they have created a myth out of this Holocaust, and hold it in an even loftier position than belief in God and religion and the prophets. If someone among them expresses disbelief in God or religion, they do not object, but they will quickly protest against anyone who rejects the Holocaust. [To the European nations, I say this:] If it is true that you committed this big crime—and it seems to be true, since you insist on it so much . . . —then why should the oppressed Palestinian nation now pay the price? . . . If you committed the crime, then give up a part of your own land . . . so that the Jews can establish a country.

Once again the president charged headfirst into the heart of darkness, with very little thought for the sensitivities of Western history. Once again the headlines in the West were swift and unambiguous. IRAN'S PRESIDENT

CALLS HOLOCAUST A "MYTH" read the pages of *The Washington Post, The New York Times,* and *The Boston Globe.*

If Ahmadinejad had been trying to make a point, he found a particularly crude and distasteful way to do it. But increasingly, the world was learning that this was simply how the man operated. This was not a president who was going to take a dignified approach in his attempts to point out what he thought were moral inconsistencies and double standards. This was not a president who was ever going to take the higher ground. Rather, this was a president who was going to jump right in and try to push buttons, tweak noses, and generally infuriate and outrage the West in every way he could. For Ahmadinejad, who had never traveled outside Iran and knew very little about the West, there was no greater joy than to prick what he saw as the bubble of Western self-righteousness.*

In Iran, there was genuine discomfort with what Ahmadinejad was doing—so much so that even some of his closest political allies began to complain. A website close to the Revolutionary Guards called Ahmadine-jad's Holocaust comments "adventurism at the expense of national interests," and scolded the president for deviating from the path of the beloved Ayatollah Khomeini. The late great emam, they said, had been a fierce opponent of Israel, but he had always had the decency not to question the Holocaust. The supreme leader's foreign policy adviser, Ali Akbar Velayati, said bluntly that the Holocaust was a "historical fact." And from the reformist camp, criticism of the president was even stronger. "It is becoming clearer and clearer . . . that Mr. Ahmadinejad has neither the political experience nor the knowledge to run the country," said the prominent journalist Isa Saharkhiz.

In subsequent interviews with the Western media, Ahmadinejad conspicuously avoided repeating his original statement about Israel, even though every interviewer attempted vigorously to goad him into it. When pressed, he would explain that he felt that the Holy Land should be a place of equality for Christians, Muslims, and Jews and that a free and open election should be held among *all* its inhabitants—a response that left most interviewers bored and ready to move on to the next question. At a December 2006 conference, Ahmadinejad rephrased his original statement, telling the audience that "the Zionist regime will disappear soon, the same way the

---

* In this respect, Ahmadinejad contrasted starkly with his more learned predecessor, President Khatami, who had lived in Germany for several years and thus had a fundamental appreciation for the sensitivities and historic suffering of the Jewish people. While in office, Khatami had often questioned why Israel was given such a free hand in its treatment of the Palestinians. But like most of the political establishment in Iran, he had always conspicuously avoided dragging the Holocaust into the discussion.

Soviet Union disappeared." This reformulation was intended as clarification of the original remarks—a signal that Iran believed Israel's demise would come about as the result of natural historical pressures and not from an act of war or belligerence from Iran.

By this point, however, such subtle distinctions were of little interest to the overheated panjandrums of the American political landscape. On America's twenty-four-hour cable networks, on talk radio, and even in serious political discussion programs, the word *Iran* was now rarely mentioned without the phrase "a nation that has threatened to wipe Israel off the map" following swiftly. In the culture of ten-cent soundbites that had taken hold in America in the early twenty-first century, pro-Israel groups could easily put their message in front of television and radio producers and ensure that the public was kept in a perpetual state of disgust over the "genocidal" tendencies of its Iranian nemesis.

At the same time, however, Israel and her allies in the United States were not always aware of how counterproductive some of this turbocharged political rhetoric could be for their cause. The boilerplate outrage, the moral indignation, the almost reflexive obligation of American politicians to condemn Iran as a "rogue regime" at odds with everything America stood for, might have seemed like a victory for those pushing Washington to take a tougher approach in its dealings with Tehran. But it was also, in many ways, precisely what Ahmadinejad wanted.

CB

What Americans did not always fully appreciate was that every time Ahmadinejad made a hostile statement about Israel, he was speaking to multiple audiences. One of them was his domestic Iranian audience, which never tired of being reminded that the days of the shah's servility to the United States were over. Another audience was regional, Middle Easterners who dearly wished their own leaders had the gumption to speak so bluntly to the world's only superpower. And finally, he was speaking to a silent majority scattered around the globe, from London to São Paulo to Calcutta, who were reflexively anti-American, or were concerned about the growing unilateralism in American foreign policy, or were frustrated with Bush's one-sided approach toward Israel and Palestine. It was a high-risk strategy, and one a more experienced politician might not have pursued. But for a while it seemed to work.

During the first few years of his presidency, Ahmadinejad successfully positioned himself generally at the forefront of the old third-world liberation struggle. Together with his Latin American allies—Hugo Chávez of Venezuela, Evo Morales of Bolivia, and Rafael Correa of Ecuador—he hammered away at his favorite theme: the imbalance of power between the United States and the developing world. "The days when a handful of nations could sit round a table and dictate to all the other nations of the world are coming to an end," he said in almost every speech he gave. "The language of force and threats and colonial attitudes will have to be replaced with a respect for logic, fairness and justice." Every time he spoke like this, doors opened in countries that had traditionally had little reason to develop a close relationship with Iran.

Under Ahmadinejad's presidency, Iran made unheard-of advances in its relations with the developing world—opening factories, embassies, and banks in places like Senegal, Uruguay, and Nicaragua. Iran now had an embassy in every one of Africa's fifty-three nations and in all twenty Latin American nations—a far cry from the days of the shah, when such embassies had numbered in the single digits. In the first decade of the twenty-first century, Iran's trade with Brazil and Argentina rose more than fivefold, and trade with Ecuador jumped from $6 million to $168 million in a single year, from 2007 to 2008. A shiny, cavernous new airport—Emam Khomeini International—was built on the outskirts of Tehran to accommodate the growing number of visiting delegations. And it was no white elephant. Day after day jumbo jets brought Chinese oil investors, Korean entrepreneurs, and Venezuelan cultural delegations. The president reciprocated these visits, making trips to Africa, Latin America, India, Pakistan, Sri Lanka, and China. By the end of his first term, he had visited more countries than Iran's previous three presidents combined.

When Ahmadinejad's plane touched down in Malaysia in 2007, he was met by thousands of cheering supporters—ordinary Malaysians, lining the route of his motorcade and waving his portrait. Iran reaped concrete dividends as well: an Iranian car assembly plant in West Africa, a cement factory in Nicaragua, a Shia cultural center in Venezuela. Iran donated $350 million to help set up an electricity plant in Central America, $30 million for a radio station in Zimbabwe, and $7 million for a new airport in St. Vincent and the Grenadines. Iran sponsored agriculture projects in Kenya, a new hospital in Congo, and other projects from Tajikistan to Lebanon to Comoros. In stark contrast to President Khatami, who had focused almost exclusively on winning over European and American public opinion, Ahmadinejad turned his attention to third-world solidarity, making it clear that he considered Iran's natural audience to be among the "oppressed of the earth"—and not among the viewers of CNN.

The U.S. media reported very little of this, and when they did, they cast it with sinister mood music of the "growing Iranian threat" variety—with little reflection on the fact that Iran was creating the kind of commercial and political networks around the globe that the United States had enjoyed for years. The more America treated Iran as a pariah, in fact, the more popular it seemed to become in countries that had never appreciated Washington's tone—and the more it was able to expand its influence. Between 2006 and 2009, surveys of global public opinion conducted by the BBC, the Pew Global Attitudes Project, and Zogby International all revealed staggering differences in the way Iran was viewed in different parts of the world. While 63 percent of Americans said they had "mainly negative" views about Iran, only 22 percent of Mexicans and 18 percent of Egyptians said the same. In Bangladesh, 77 percent of respondents said they had a "favorable" view. And in the Arab world, when respondents were asked to name the world leader they most admired, Hugo Chávez generally topped the list, followed by French president Jacques Chirac—and then Ahmadinejad.

For much of the Muslim world, particularly the disenfranchised citizens of places like Cairo and Islamabad, the appeal of Ahmadinejad was obvious. From 2003 to 2005, they had seen more than enough to convince them that America was a superpower out of control. They had seen Iraqi prisoners strapped to ropes and wires by their gonads and forced to masturbate in front of their captors at Abu Ghraib. They had seen "surgical strikes" and "unmanned drones" bomb Afghan families in their houses at night. They had seen, in 2006, Israel invade Lebanon and obliterate schools and hospitals, forcing whole civilian populations to evacuate, while American politicians cheered from the sidelines. Perhaps most important of all, they had seen their own leaders acquiesce in all this, never offering more than mild criticisms for fear they would upset their sponsors in Washington. In such an atmosphere, a circus performer like Ahmadinejad could easily egg his audience on with a steady torrent of cheap invective against Israel and America. This was not the genuine moral leadership practiced by the unambiguous heroes of history like Nelson Mandela or Mahatma Gandhi. But in an imperfect world—one in which George W. Bush could climb into a fighter jet and offer himself up as the liberator of all mankind—it went rather a long way.

⋘

In 2006, Ahmadinejad wrote an impassioned, eighteen-page letter to President Bush outlining some of his philosophical objections to American foreign policy and appealing to him as one man of faith to another—the first time since 1979 that an Iranian president had directly contacted his American counterpart. Virtually every American media outlet described the letter as a "rant" or an "incoherent screed," if they mentioned it at all—and indeed, much in the letter deserved ridicule. But much else would not have been out of place in a mainstream, left-leaning European newspaper. Ahmadinejad raised the issues of Guantanamo prisoners, civilian casualties in Iraq and Afghanistan, the suffering of the Palestinians, and the poverty and exploitation of Africa—and he repeatedly invoked the name of Jesus Christ in asking Bush how he could reconcile his faith with his foreign policy. "The people will scrutinize our presidencies," he said. "Did we defend the rights of all people around the world? Or did we impose wars on them, interfere illegally in their affairs, establish hellish prisons, and incarcerate . . . them?"

Almost immediately, Secretary of State Condoleezza Rice made it clear Iran would not be receiving a reply—and Bush himself joked to reporters that he was having trouble with the fact that "it was, like, sixteen or seventeen single-spaced typed pages." But six months later Ahmadinejad raised the stakes by writing again—this time an open letter "to the American people." Again he spoke in sweeping, operatic language, asking Americans to question their government's policies in the War on Terror. "Can terrorism be contained and eradicated through war, destruction, and the killing of hundreds of thousands of innocents?" he asked. "Would it not be more beneficial to bring [your] soldiers home, and to spend the astronomical [sums spent in Iraq] for the welfare and prosperity of the American people? As you know very well, many victims of [Hurricane] Katrina continue to suffer, and countless Americans continue to live in poverty and homelessness."

Perhaps more important than the content of these two letters was the fact that they had been written at all. As goofy and amateurish as they might have sounded, they spoke volumes about Iran's newfound confidence and sense of its place in the world. Twenty-seven years after the revolution, at a time when America's global standing was at an all-time low, Iran felt it had earned the right to speak to America like this—as an equal in the community of nations, or at least as an ideological alternative that had proved its staying power and had a growing number of admirers around the world.

Nowhere was this newfound confidence more visible than in the Middle East. In 2006, after the disastrous Israeli invasion of Lebanon, anger against the United States and Israel reached such a crescendo in the region that it actually *boosted* the position of Hezbollah, the invasion's intended target. Much of Lebanon's population now viewed the militant Shia organization as a heroic liberation movement successfully resisting Israeli aggression— and its close alliance with Iran increased Iran's popularity in the region as well. Every time people switched on their televisions to see the bodies of Lebanese children being picked out of the rubble, every time they heard Condoleezza Rice say America supported Israel's "right to defend itself," and

Man of the people: Despised in the West for his provocative statements about Israel, President Mahmoud Ahmadinejad (2005–13) remained popular among the poor and downtrodden of Iran for his perceived piety and his aversion to corruption.

every time they heard Ahmadinejad blast Israel as an "illegitimate regime"—while Arab leaders remained mute—regional opinions shifted just a little more in Tehran's direction.

Iran's ability to win the hearts and minds of the region's people translated into concrete political gains. In Iraq democratic elections produced a government dominated by Shia political parties with long-standing personal, cultural, and political ties to Iran. As Iraq was 60 percent Shia, none of this came as a surprise, but in practical terms, it meant that the stable, Sunni-dominated, anti-Iranian dictatorship of Saddam Hussein had been replaced with a government that was weaker, more chaotic, and more amenable to Iranian influence. In Afghanistan as well, the fanatical Sunni regime of the Taliban had been replaced with a diverse, representative government that enjoyed warm relations with Tehran. In just a few short years, Bush had removed two of Iran's worst nightmares—Saddam on its western border and the Taliban on its eastern border—and, in the process, created enough mayhem and civilian casualties that the citizens of both those countries now had a fairly low opinion of the United States and a relatively benign opinion of Iran.

And then there was Palestine. In 2005 and 2006, as part of his missionary drive to bring democracy to the Middle East, Bush had insisted that legislative elections be held in the Palestinian territories. In the West Bank, those elections were won by the moderate Fatah movement of Palestinian president Mahmoud Abbas, but in Gaza, the victory went to Hamas—a more militant (and more pro-Iranian) group that refused to recognize Israel until there was a comprehensive settlement of the Arab-Israeli conflict. The United States, Israel, and the European Union promptly punished the Palestinians for making the wrong choice—imposing sanctions on aid to the Palestinian Authority (Israel even imposed a severe economic blockade on Gaza), all of which only strengthened Hamas's popular image as the true voice of Palestine. Fatah, by contrast, was increasingly seen as corrupt and overly pro-American. In Gaza, in other words—as in Istanbul, Baghdad, Kabul, and Beirut—Iran aligned itself with the popular power and emerged as the chief beneficiary of American policies while the United States was left looking like the bad guy. Sober voices in the United States now spoke ominously of "Iran rising."

Some analysts of the Middle East went even further, claiming that the region was separating into two distinct political blocs, in a way that did not bode well for the United States. One bloc, according to this analysis, was the old pro-Western alliance led by Saudi Arabia, Egypt, Jordan, and the Gulf monarchies—to which the Palestinian Authority had more recently hitched its wagon. Characterized by crusty old tyrants like Hosni Mubarak, this bloc could always be relied on to advance American and Israeli objectives in the region—often in abject defiance of their own populations. The other, newly invigorated bloc was described by its admirers (and even some of its detractors) as an "axis of resistance." Composed of Iran and Syria but also of nonstate actors such as Hamas, Hezbollah, the Shia political parties of Lebanon—and increasingly, the governments of Turkey and Iraq—this latter grouping was characterized, if not always by genuine democracy, then by a leadership that reflected its people's desire not to be bullied by the United States, Europe, or Israel. Plucky, energetic, and surprisingly confident, the "resistance" bloc was fully in touch with the frustrations of the region's people and rudely uninterested in advancing Washington's agenda. And its natural leader was Iran.

From 2005 to 2009, America and Iran engaged in what can only be described as a "moral cold war"—and it was one that America was in danger of losing. For unlike the previous incarnation of the Cold War, this new standoff was not fundamentally military in character. The United States was no longer up against an enemy with a massive, world-class army and six thousand nuclear-tipped ballistic missiles pointed at its cities. It was no longer pitted against a coalition of satellite states spread across Eastern Europe,

Latin America, and Southeast Asia. Instead, it was locked into a far subtler conflict with a far less powerful opponent, one that was isolated, weak, economically decrepit, and allied militarily with not a single other nation in the world. And yet somehow, bizarrely, the president of this little "rogue state" seemed to be winning the hearts and minds of ordinary Muslims in the Middle East much faster than Bush was.

For many Americans, little of this made sense. Still recovering from the shock of 9/11, many could not conceive of their country as anything other than a victim. But in much of the world, sympathy for the events of that day had long ago dried up, replaced by considerable anger at the way Bush had prosecuted the response. And in this atmosphere, Iran could easily play to the peanut gallery. As long as the United States continued to occupy two Muslim countries, support Israel unconditionally, and maintain more than six hundred military bases around the globe, it looked to the rest of the world like a reincarnation of the British Empire from a hundred years earlier—and Iran gleefully positioned itself as leader of the resistance.

The most obvious battleground of this Moral Cold War was that ultimate arena of international public opinion—the United Nations. Every time Ahmadinejad spoke at the UN now, Western diplomats staged dramatic collective walkouts, marching up the aisles and out of the hall during the first sixty seconds of his speech. This made for highly watchable political theater, but it only added to Ahmadinejad's cachet as a leader who was more interested in speaking to the weaker nations of the world than to America and its allies. In stark contrast to the Americans and Europeans who turned their backs and filed out of the room, the representatives of the dozens of Latin American and African countries that had improved their relations with Iran in recent years remained in their seats and listened to what the president had to say.

03

At home, Ahmadinejad's antics met with a mixed reception. On the one hand, much of the political establishment felt uneasy about the way he made global headlines with his amateurish remarks about Israel. ("You have degraded the nation," said his election opponent during a televised debate in 2009.) On the other hand, many Iranians felt this was exactly how their president should conduct himself. In a way that would have been unimaginable during the shah's regime, Iran was unapologetically articulating its own vision of global affairs, and large numbers of Iranians lapped it up, believing that theirs was a great nation that had every right to speak to America this way. Even Iranians who lived abroad, and who had no sympathy for the Islamic Republic, reluctantly admired this flinty, confident aspect of the president's leadership. Older Iranians even felt a hint of recognition. For if you squinted hard enough when Ahmadinejad stood on the podium at the UN, you could almost—*almost*—see the ghost of Mosaddeq, cutting and thrusting and skewering Sir Gladwyn Jebb of the British Empire delegation in the autumn of 1951.

For the most part, however, Iranians paid little attention to such things. Like people anywhere in the world, their first priority was the immediate, grinding necessities of daily life—putting food on the table, fuel in the gas tank, and children into university. And here Ahmadinejad was shrewd. He increased the minimum wage, lowered interest rates, and doled out cash subsidies for the poor—all in keeping with his campaign promise to put Iran's oil wealth to work for ordinary Iranians. He even established a "love fund" to help newlyweds set up lives outside the parental home, as well as a "shares of justice" initiative designed to distribute shares in state-owned enterprises directly to low-income families. Ahmadinejad mastered the art of holding American-style "town hall meetings." Every three weeks he took a break from his official duties to spend an extended weekend in the provinces, speaking to rural Iranians about their concerns. No issue was considered too trivial or parochial for these presidential visits, and Ahmadi-Nejad was often shown on television listening to village housewives complaining about their neighbor's retaining wall or the failure of a local council to build an irrigation ditch. Very quickly, these appearances developed a circus-like quality, as throngs of young men climbed onto the president's car and competed to shove letters through the sunroof. By 2008 Ahmadinejad had received some 10 million letters, emails, and text messages, all processed through a new presidential call center, which claimed a response rate of 76 percent. By the end of his first term, Ahmadinejad had visited two thousand Iranian towns and villages—an unheard-of act of retail politics for an Iranian politician.

Ahmadinejad had no shortage of domestic critics, but very few were concerned about his foreign policy or his inflammatory statements about the Holocaust. Most of his critics focused on his redistributive economic policies, which economists claimed (rightly, it turned out) would create inflation. Others criticized his religious beliefs, which tended toward a freewheeling spirituality and a claim that he was in direct contact with the Twelfth Emam—the so-called Mahdi, who had gone into occlusion in the ninth century and whose long-awaited return was an article of faith for Shia Muslims. This kind of claim was not unusual in the Shia tradition—a sort of Islamic version of born-again Christianity, in which believers commune with God directly rather than mediated through clergy—but it made

Ahmadinejad the butt of jokes among cosmopolitan Iranians. It also irritated the more conservative members of Iran's clerical establishment, who saw it as a direct affront to their formal theological training.

With his millenarian religious beliefs, his smirking, raffish wit, and his back-slapping sense of humor, Ahmadinejad has often been compared to his American counterpart, George W. Bush. This is surely unfair to Bush, who was the product of a democratic tradition and an Ivy League education. But certain similarities in their political style are hard to deny. Both were seen by much of the world as reckless, even dangerous adventurists with a disregard for international norms of behavior. Both had somehow failed to travel abroad before becoming president and seemed largely untroubled by that fact. Both had a unique ability to speak the language of the masses, to sneer and smirk and thumb their noses at the nerds and intellectuals who were always "horrified" and "concerned" by what they had to say. Both had a measure of homespun schoolboy charm. And in the end, both spoke with a kind of cool certainty—the certainty born of a very personal relationship with God and the knowledge that a silent majority of their constituency was always very much behind them.

⚮

If only that were where the story ended. In the early twenty-first century, as Americans listened to one bizarre and frightening statement after another coming from the mouth of the Iranian president, they were given something even more terrifying to worry about. Iran, it was said, had a highly advanced program of uranium enrichment—a program that it was possibly using to develop nuclear energy for peaceful purposes but that could also be the first step toward an actual nuclear *bomb*. Seen in this light, Ahmadinejad's little tirades seemed more dangerous. After all, this was a president who had threatened to *wipe Israel off the map*. Now he wanted a nuclear weapon as well? Was there any doubt what a dangerous and highly irrational man like this would do with a nuke in his hands?

Given the seriousness of the charge, the regularity with which it turned up on American television, and the apocalyptic scenario it implied, it is worth taking a closer look at it.

Atoms for Peace?

In the early twenty-first century, Iran's nuclear program became the subject of intense international controversy—bandied about in UN resolutions, cascaded through the pages of newspaper op-eds, dissected endlessly on political talk shows. From 2002 to 2015, the idea of a "nuclear Iran" loomed in the psyche of American foreign policy, apocalyptic and terrifying beyond comprehension. Rarely did a month go by without some fresh "warning" to Americans or some dire new prediction about the advancing nature of the Iranian nuclear "threat."

But amid all the bandying and cascading and dissecting—in all the media scrutiny and in all the warnings of impending doom—one aspect of that nuclear program was rarely discussed: its origins.

In 1957, just four years after the CIA helped the shah return to power, the United States and Iran had signed a landmark agreement on civil nuclear cooperation—agreeing to work hand in hand to promote the use of nuclear technology in the medical field—and the U.S. Atomic Energy Commission had pledged to provide Iran with six kilograms of low-enriched uranium for research purposes. It was part of President Eisenhower's "Atoms for Peace" program, a high-profile initiative designed to share America's mastery of peaceful nuclear energy with the developing world. Ten years later the Johnson administration expanded the deal when the United States supplied Iran with its first nuclear reactor—a five-megawatt research facility in Tehran—along with enough highly enriched uranium fuel to keep it running. Four years after that, during Richard Nixon's presidency, the shah announced that—thanks to the generous cooperation of the United States—Iran would build twenty-three nuclear power stations by the year 2000, with a total capacity for twenty-three thousand megawatts of electricity generation.

Even as late as 1978, the Carter administration and the shah signed a deal that would have sent eight U.S.-made light-water reactors to Iran.

The United States was not the only Western country scrambling to participate in Iran's nuclear program during those prerevolutionary years. In 1975 the German company Kraftwerk Union, a subsidiary of Siemens, signed a $5 billion contract to build two 1200-megawatt reactors in the southern city of Bushehr. In the same year, Iran acquired a 10 percent stake in Eurodif, a French-Belgian-Spanish uranium enrichment company, in exchange for a steady supply of fuel for its future reactors. And throughout the 1970s hundreds of Iranian students had attended European and American universities to be trained as nuclear scientists—350 in France alone, and dozens more at MIT and elsewhere.

Back then, it might have seemed odd that Iran, a nation swimming in oil, would turn to nuclear technology to generate electricity. But energy experts agreed that this was the most sensible way for Iran to achieve energy independence. For a developing country, with limited domestic demand for oil, to build an expensive. complicated petroleum refinery simply made no sense. Instead, Iran's best option was to sell the oil on the international market and use the profits to create a secure, reliable source of domestic energy that could serve its needs well after the oil ran out. And the cheapest, most sensible way to do so, all the experts said, was to build nuclear power plants.[*]

The trouble was that nuclear energy could be a double-edged sword. Those same atoms—that same process of spinning centrifuges to separate uranium isotopes—could also (with a certain amount of effort) be converted into an explosive device that, placed on the end of a missile, could be used to obliterate some hapless neighboring country. This was no less true in the 1970s than it is today—and yet back then, very little was said on the subject. In Western capitals, no one questioned that the shah might be interested in pursuing nuclear technology for purposes beyond electricity. He had already purchased lasers for isotope separation, collected literature on the design and production of nuclear weapons, and engaged in illegal procurement activities. But those Western capitals expressed little concern about this activity. "I don't think the issue of proliferation came up," recalled Henry Kissinger when asked in 2005 about America's history of nuclear cooperation with Iran.

That, if anything, was an understatement. In 1976 the Ford administration—in which Kissinger served as secretary of state—offered Iran an American-made reprocessing facility for the extraction of plutonium

---

[*] In the most influential of these early-1970s studies, the Stanford Research Institute found that Iran would need not one but "several nuclear reactors" to meet its needs.

from nuclear reactor fuel. This, in effect, would give the shah the chance to develop a complete nuclear fuel cycle, the mastery of which could easily be diverted to military purposes. The Ford administration officials who made the decision (a team that included Kissinger, Chief of Staff Dick Cheney, and Defense Secretary Donald Rumsfeld) understood that proliferation or weaponization was a risk, but they felt it was important to help the shah "prepare against the time . . . when Iranian oil production is expected to decline sharply." A 1975 administration strategy paper concluded that "the introduction of nuclear power will both provide for the growing needs of Iran's economy and free remaining oil reserves for export or conversion to petrochemicals." This attitude carried over into the Carter administration. A 1978 State Department memorandum concluded: "We have been encouraged by Iran's efforts to broaden its nonoil energy base. We are hopeful that the U.S.-Iran Nuclear Energy Agreement will be finalized soon and that American companies will be able to play a role in Iran's nuclear energy program."

The United States, in other words, felt nuclear energy was critical to Iran's economic development and stood ready to do all it could to help the shah obtain it.

03

When the revolution came in 1979, all this chummy nuclear cooperation evaporated into thin air. Western nations canceled their contracts with Iran, as Iraqi tanks and fighter jets bombarded Iranian infrastructure and fanatical students took control of the U.S. embassy—all of which made cooperative electricity projects seem like a quaint idea. In 1984 the German company Kraftwerk briefly considered resuming work on the Bushehr power station but concluded it was simply too dangerous. Just days after a German delegation visited Iran to discuss the project, the Iraqis dropped bombs on the reactor. They would do so another six times before the end of the war in 1988.

Any suggestion that Iran might turn its attention to building nuclear *weapons*, meanwhile, was quickly squashed. Ayatollah Khomeini considered *all* weapons of mass destruction—nuclear, chemical, or biological—to be a sin against Islam. They were a Western abomination, he said, the kind of flashy foreign novelty the shah had been excessively enamored of. They also polluted the atmosphere, which the Quran forbade. Most important of all, the Islamic scriptures made it clear it was never acceptable to take innocent life or kill noncombatants during times of war. A nuclear bomb, by its very nature, would do both and was therefore *haram*—"divinely forbidden."

Khomeini was adamant on this point. Iranian air force sorties that flew out over Iraqi targets were under clear instructions to avoid bombing civilian neighborhoods—a policy one Western analyst said Iran was surprisingly "meticulous" about observing. Even when Saddam unleashed sarin, nerve agents, and other chemical attacks on Iranian front lines, Iran did not retaliate in kind—or even put together the basic elements of a chemical weapons program. Weapons of mass destruction, Khomeini continued to insist, were "the work of the Devil."

Only late in the 1980s, as rumors spread that Saddam was building a nuclear bomb, did some of Iran's military planners begin cautiously exploring the possibility of doing the same, if only as an insurance policy. Yes, Islam forbade the actual use of a bomb, they argued to the ayatollah, but it still seemed prudent to have some sort of *deterrent* capability—something that might make Saddam think twice before launching a reckless nuclear attack on Iran. The superpowers, they pointed out, called this strategy "mutually assured destruction," and it seemed to have prevented the United States and the Soviet Union from nuking each other off the face of the earth.

But the proposal never got very far. As a pariah nation, Iran had difficulty obtaining sophisticated equipment on the international market, and Khomeini continued to show little appetite for unconventional warfare anyway. Although he cautiously gave his approval for the generals to pursue their designs, weapons of mass destruction were obviously not a priority for the ayatollah.

In the 1990s, following Khomeini's death, Iran's pragmatic new leaders looked seriously at the possibility of reviving the nuclear program. With help from Russia, Iran slowly rebuilt the damaged Bushehr power plant. Iran also made tentative moves toward developing technologies that could potentially be diverted to military use. But these military dimensions of the program were extremely rudimentary, the kind of dual-use nuclear technology that dozens of countries had developed in order to keep their options open. Designs and blueprints for advanced centrifuges, a handful of exercises conducted on old and decrepit equipment imported from Pakistan, some vague attempts to purchase isotope separation equipment from China—one Western expert described them as nothing more than a collection of "tabletop experiments."

For Iran in the 1990s, a genuine moral conflict was at work. The leaders had principled religious objections to nuclear weapons, but they could not afford to be overly complacent. Throughout the 1990s, Western intelligence agencies warned publicly that Saddam Hussein was hell-bent on obtaining a nuclear bomb. To make matters worse, in 1998, India and Pakistan both announced they had successfully tested nuclear weapons. Iran was clearly living in a dangerous neighborhood. With a nuclear Israel to its west, a nuclear Russia to its north, and a nuclear (and highly volatile) Pakistan to its east, as well as an Iraqi neighbor that nursed megalomaniac tendencies and had a history of using chemical weapons—not to mention the enduring antipathy of the United States—Iranians understood that they were in no position to be overly relaxed about their security needs. Rafsanjani, Khatami, and the supreme leader all felt it would be downright irresponsible not to at least *explore* the feasibility of a full-scale nuclear program.

One thing Iran could not afford to do, however, was to be overly public in its pursuit of nuclear technology. The country had no shortage of enemies, who would not be shy about sabotaging its nuclear progress. As early as 1983, the United States had pressured the International Atomic Energy Agency to drop a cooperative agreement with Iran for reactor fuel production and uranium enrichment, as well as a program for training Iranian nuclear scientists abroad. In the early 1990s, Iran approached Argentina, China, and Russia—within its rights under international law—for help with the nuclear fuel cycle, but the United States persuaded all three countries not to cooperate. These experiences showed Iran that any attempt to acquire nuclear technology, however legally conducted, would meet with obstruction from the United States. Thus, by the mid-1990s, Iran's leaders drew what they felt was a logical conclusion: they were on their own, and any future nuclear research would have to be conducted in secret.

Of course, the secretive nature of Iran's program created a different kind of problem for Iran: international suspicion. It gave legitimate scientific research, of the kind every nation was entitled to, the air of something illicit and subterranean. Almost immediately, Israel voiced concerns that Iran was secretly trying to build a *bomb* and was just a few years away from being able to do so. In 1992, Israel's foreign minister, Shimon Peres, warned that, unless action were taken, Iran would likely possess nuclear weapons by 1999. In 1995, Israel claimed that Iran was "less than five years away from an atomic bomb." And in 1996, Peres told ABC News, "I believe that in four years they may reach nuclear weapons."

For most of the 1990s, however, Israel had trouble convincing the rest of the world to take these warnings seriously. Most analysts understood that Iran's nuclear program was rudimentary, and most reliable intelligence suggested that its leaders had little appetite for weaponization. Most analysts also believed that Israel's warnings had a touch of political theater about them.

Then in August 2002 a group of Iranian exiles, living in Europe and affiliated with the outlawed terrorist group MeK, held a press conference at which they claimed to have evidence of two secret nuclear sites in Iran: a uranium enrichment facility in Natanz and a heavy-water production plant in Arak. It was not entirely clear how the MeK and its friends—most of whom had spent years living in London and Paris—had come across this information. Possibly they had infiltrated Iran's atomic energy industry using local agents. More likely, as an investigative article in *The New Yorker* suggested, they had been fed the information by the Israeli intelligence service, Mossad.[*]

In fact, it later emerged that the "revelations" were not revelations at all. American intelligence had been collecting satellite imagery of the facilities at Natanz and Arak for at least a year and gathering procurement data on the sites since the mid-1990s. But in 2002 the Bush administration behaved as though the information were new, scandalous, and fundamentally game-changing. U.S. officials told CNN they believed Iran was "pursuing a secret nuclear program," and at the UN, strenuous new efforts were made to convince member states to join the United States in taking action. "We're concerned about Iran," Vice President Dick Cheney told NBC's *Meet the Press*. "The recent disclosure about secure nuclear facilities in Iran reinforces the concerns that the president has had all along," added White House spokesman Ari Fleischer. For Iran, this marked the beginning of a major international public relations headache—and the beginning of an epic new phase in the history of its confrontation with America.

Following the 2002 "revelations," the International Atomic Energy Agency (IAEA) took a closer look at Iran's nuclear facilities and found that sure enough, there was a heavy-water plant in Arak and a gas centrifuge cache in Natanz. The work the Iranians were doing at these two facilities was not exactly scandalous. They were separating plutonium and storing and maintaining centrifuges—all things Iran had the right to do under international agreements. And because there was no actual uranium enrichment going on at either facility, Iran was under no obligation to report the activity to the IAEA. But the IAEA noted with consternation the fact that Iran had been less than forthcoming about these facilities—and had spent much of the 1990s playing with technologies that could, theoretically, be repurposed for weaponization. Potentially, Iran could be referred to the UN Security Council and condemned for violating its international obligations.

---

[*] In a way, the partnership between the MeK and Israel made perfect sense. For Israel, it was a chance to leak the information into the public domain without its fingerprints all over it—making the leak appear to come from an indigenous Iranian opposition group. For the MeK, which was still languishing on the State Department's list of terrorist organizations—and which most news reports now described as a "cultlike" group with no support among Iranians—it was a chance to earn a measure of international credibility.

At this point things began to get interesting. But a little background information is necessary in order to understand the disagreement in its full context.

The only reason IAEA inspectors were even being allowed into Iran to nose around in heavy-water plants and centrifuge facilities was that Iran was a signatory—along with 187 other countries—to the 1968 Non-Proliferation Treaty (NPT). Under the terms of the NPT, all member nations have the right to pursue peaceful nuclear technology for such uses as electricity generation and medical research—as long as they can satisfy the world that that is all they are doing. In practice, they are free to enrich uranium, spin centrifuges—anything, really—as long as they do not try to build a bomb. As long as these conditions are met, moreover, those member states that already have nuclear weapons (the United States, the UK, France, China, and Russia) actually have an obligation to *help* all the other signatories of the NPT with their peaceful nuclear activities—or at the very least, not to obstruct them. If any suspicion ever arises that one of these "nonnuclear weapons states" is trying to develop a *bomb,* however, all bets are off. IAEA inspectors will be called in to verify that the state in question is in compliance with the NPT "Safeguards Agreement."

Iran signed the NPT on the day it opened for signatures in 1968—one of only forty countries to do so. By contrast, many of the world's midrange powers dragged their feet, complaining of double standards and "nuclear apartheid" and insisting that they had every right to progress scientifically by mastering the uranium enrichment cycle. Eventually, though, most countries did join (though often only after they accumulated a certain amount of nuclear know-how).* And by 2002, the NPT could boast that 189 of the world's 192 nations were signatories. This left only three countries still refusing to take part: India, Pakistan, and Israel.

In 2002 many Iranians saw a supreme irony in all this. All three of these nations had stayed out of the NPT specifically so they could develop nuclear weapons—not just centrifuges and plutonium extraction plants but actual *bombs.* And all three nations had developed these weapons with virtually

---

* The man in charge of Iran's nuclear industry at the time—Akbar Etemad, head of the Atomic Energy Organization of Iran—felt privately that the shah did his country a great disservice by joining so quickly, signing away its rights and permanently relegating itself to the status of a second-class nation. "We should never have signed it," Etemad complained to an interviewer in 2009. "It was not a fair treaty. I never would have allowed it. Only small countries joined—Burkina Faso, Nicaragua, the Fiji Islands. The countries that actually had a chance of getting nuclear power—India, Pakistan, Israel—they stayed out. Only we signed."

no condemnation from the rest of the world. Israel, in particular, had accumulated at least two hundred nuclear warheads. In the 1960s and 1970s the great powers, in particular the United States and France, had quietly carved out an exception for Israel—giving it a green light to pursue a weapons program, even secretly shipping the parts and matériel required. During that time, Israel had accumulated a wide range of WMDs—neutron bombs, tactical nuclear weapons, suitcase nukes, submarine-launched nuclear cruise missiles, and even chemical and biological warfare capabilities—all while refusing to join the NPT. To most Iranians, it seemed absurd that Israel— the country now making the most noise about Iran's nuclear program—was itself the world's greatest nuclear offender.

Iran's other major complaint was that the United States—the *other* country making all the noise—was only slightly less of an offender. The NPT obliged the United States to share its technology and provide assistance to countries seeking to develop peaceful nuclear technology. But in the 1980s, America had blocked critical matériel and technology from reaching Iran—which, in Tehran's view, meant the United States had its own case to answer for under the terms of the NPT.

Given these grievances, a growing number of voices in Iran suggested that their country should pull out of the NPT altogether, to protest the way it was being treated. North Korea, after all, was taking this approach— kicking out IAEA inspectors, refusing to provide access to its facilities, and generally making clear it was not going to play the game by the rules. Along with Israel, India, and Pakistan, North Korea in 2003 became the fourth country to reject the NPT and start a nuclear weapons program outside the international framework. Perhaps, said some Iranian hard-liners, an argument could now be made for joining this rapidly growing band of nuclear outlaws.

But Iran chose not to take this step.

CB

Instead, Iran made a strategic decision to cooperate with the IAEA. In February 2003, President Khatami publicly acknowledged the existence of the nuclear facilities at Natanz and Arak. He also went on live national television and invited the IAEA to send inspectors to examine the two facilities. Iran had nothing to hide, Khatami insisted. It had a "legitimate right to obtain nuclear energy for peaceful aims," and it was happy to satisfy the world that that was all that was going on. In May 2003, Iran even quietly proposed the now-famous "grand bargain" to Washington—offering to suspend its nuclear program as part of a comprehensive package of improved relations.

Initially, the Bush administration was highly disparaging of this Iranian overture. On June 19, Bush said publicly, for the first time, that the United States "will not tolerate" construction of a nuclear weapon in Iran—a statement White House officials described as a "carefully worded escalation." The defense secretary, Donald Rumsfeld, accused Iran of having "a very active program" aimed at developing nuclear weapons. And a slew of U.S. officials strategically leaked stories to the press about the administration's desire to see "regime change" in Iran. This attitude, in turn, led many observers to wonder if America's sudden fixation on Iran's nuclear program was the first step in a run-up to war. The United States, after all, had just launched a massive air and ground invasion of Iran's next-door neighbor, Iraq—and justified it specifically by accusing Saddam of seeking weapons of mass destruction. In June 2003, therefore, there was widespread fear—both in the United States and around the world—that Iran was next on the list.

But in fact, after issuing a certain amount of tough-sounding rhetoric, the Bush administration surprised everyone by taking a radically different approach. Deferring to a request from its three most important European allies—Britain, France, and Germany—the United States agreed to take a backseat and allow space for a diplomatic solution to be found. During the summer of 2003, British, French, and German foreign ministers met more frequently with their Iranian counterparts, trying to convince them to make some sort of high-profile concession to the United States. Meanwhile Washington played what can only be described as a game of good cop/bad cop—loudly condemning Iran for its nuclear program and hinting at "regime change," while quietly allowing the Europeans to seek a negotiated solution.

To some extent, this unexpectedly soft approach to Iran on the part of the Bush administration was an attempt to mend fences with Europe. Over the previous year, America had fought a damaging, highly divisive battle with its European allies over the decision to invade Iraq, and both sides desperately wanted to heal their differences. The United States, which had been accused of engaging in a reckless, go-it-alone, cowboy style of foreign policy, wanted to prove that its reputation for unilateralism was undeserved. And the Europeans hoped to prove to the United States that diplomacy could work if given an opportunity. But pragmatic reasons also contributed to Bush's sudden openness to diplomacy. With 250,000 American troops deployed in Iraq, increasingly bogged down in a messy Iraqi insurgency in the summer of 2003, the United States understood that it was in no position to pick a fight with Iran—a nation that, perhaps more than any other, had a unique ability to create problems for the United States in Iraq, because of its unusually close ties to the large Shia community there.

Whatever the case, Iran and the three European powers somehow stumbled their way to a landmark agreement. In October 2003, after several months of negotiation, Iran announced that it would voluntarily suspend its nuclear program as a goodwill gesture to Europe. They described it as a "confidence-building" measure, designed to provide a backdrop for a more meaningful process of negotiations that could lead to a permanent solution. In exchange for this voluntary suspension, the Europeans announced they were prepared to recognize Iran's right to peaceful nuclear energy and, eventually, to meet their own NPT obligations by helping Iran with its program.

"This is a good day for peace, multilateralism, and nonproliferation," said the IAEA's director-general, Mohamed El Baradei, when the deal was announced. The international community, he declared, had come together to address the Iranian challenge and show its respect for the spirit of the NPT. "These are positive and welcome steps, which I very much hope will be sustained."

Indeed, in the months that followed, Iran continued to cooperate, and it cooperated in a way that surprised even its most grudging critics. For a full two years, from the end of 2003 to the end of 2005, Iran opened its doors to one of the most robust inspection regimes in IAEA history. IAEA inspectors carried out two thousand person-days of deep, intrusive inspections, complete with frequent surprise visits. Cameras were installed at Iran's nuclear facilities. Iran's input of feedstock to centrifuges was carefully measured, as was its output of low-enriched uranium—all of which was placed under seal to prevent tampering. Iran even opened its *conventional* military facilities to the IAEA on twenty separate occasions—the kind of intrusion into national security to which no sovereign nation on earth had ever consented. At the end of all this, the IAEA found nothing. "All the declared nuclear material in Iran has been accounted for," it announced in three consecutive reports in 2004, 2005, and 2006. "The Agency has not seen any diversion of nuclear material to nuclear weapons or other explosive devices."

To most reasonable observers, the matter seemed to be drawing to a close. And indeed, from a purely technical and logistical point of view, there was really no reason why it shouldn't. The trouble, of course, was that nothing involving Iran and America ever unfolded according to purely technical and logistical considerations.

C３

Frustrated that the IAEA had not delivered a more damning verdict against Iran, the Bush administration looked for loopholes, ambiguities, or other arguments that could keep the issue going. At first it rejected the IAEA's credibility, calling its reports "impossible to believe." But then Washington found a more sophisticated tactic. In its reports, the IAEA had made clear that Iran's nuclear facilities were all in compliance, but it had also hedged its bets—writing, in a way that was typical of the Agency, that it was not "in a position to conclude that there are no *undeclared* nuclear materials or activities in Iran" (emphasis added). Beginning around 2005, the Bush administration seized on this language to make its case more forcefully. It was no longer enough, Washington said, for Iran to prove to the IAEA that its nuclear facilities were in compliance. It now also had to prove the *absence* of *undeclared* facilities.

It is almost impossible to exaggerate what an unusual and unprecedented reinterpretation of the NPT this was. By shifting the emphasis to the issue of undeclared facilities, Washington was effectively saying that Iran had to prove, unequivocally and beyond a shadow of a doubt, that it was not harboring a secret weapons program underneath some isolated mountain somewhere. It was unclear how Iran—a country of 630,000 square miles, more than twice the size of Texas, with mountain ranges to rival the Andes, deserts the size of Nevada, and vast expanses of unpopulated terrain—was supposed to prove this "absence of undeclared facilities." But in a way, this was precisely the point. By asking Iran to be accountable not just for what was known but also for what was unknown—even, in the formulation made famous by Donald Rumsfeld, for the "unknown unknowns"—the Bush administration was cleverly moving the goalposts and creating a burden of proof almost impossible to meet.

It was also saying, in effect, that it was no longer up to the IAEA to decide when or whether Iran's case was closed, but rather the United States. After all, the IAEA might easily spend twenty years inspecting every inch of Iran's territory—turning over every boulder, examining every abandoned warehouse and factory, looking under every bed and every ayatollah's turban—and still be unable to declare, categorically, the "absence of undeclared" facilities. It meant in practice that America was preserving its options. If it ever decided, at some point in the future, that it was ready to make peace with Iran, it could simply declare itself "satisfied" that Iran was not building a bomb. Until then, however, it could continue to point to minor irregularities in Iran's IAEA file as evidence that the country was not to be trusted.

But this was only the beginning. The Bush administration now also began insisting—contrary to international law—that Iran had to abandon its nuclear program entirely. It was no longer enough for Iran to merely suspend the work it was doing voluntarily, or as a "confidence-building measure" to facilitate further negotiations. It had to give up uranium enrichment permanently, unconditionally, and forever—something America knew full well no nation would ever agree to (least of all Iran, and least of all on an order from Washington). And lest there was any confusion, when Bush said Iran had to give up "enrichment," he didn't mean only the advanced, high-level enrichment that could lead to the manufacture of a nuclear weapon. He meant *all* enrichment, even the low-grade kind used for generating electricity, which was legal under the NPT.

Even more unusual was the Bush administration's attempt to influence the neutrality of the IAEA itself. In June 2005, Washington publicly questioned the credibility of the agency's director-general, Mohamed El Baradei, accusing him of being insufficiently robust in his assessments of Iran's nuclear program. Secretary of State Condoleezza Rice even convened a one-on-one meeting with El Baradei to inform him that the United States would not support his upcoming reconfirmation as director-general unless he toughened up. But this heavy-handed approach backfired. El Baradei, a highly respected career diplomat, had the full support of the IAEA board. And the renewal of the director-general's term had traditionally been a formality. A number of countries bristled at the way the United States was politicizing the process, and El Baradei rose in international esteem for his refusal to bow to American pressure. The end of 2005 brought a particularly bruising embarrassment for the United States when El Baradei was awarded the Nobel Peace Prize.

Undeterred, in February 2006, the Bush administration urged the IAEA to vote to declare Iran in noncompliance with its NPT Safeguards Agreement—and thus to refer the case to the UN Security Council. This was technically in keeping with the IAEA's function, but the manner in which the decision was made was unprecedented. Throughout its history the IAEA had made decisions by consensus, in order to avoid divisive disagreements among member states. But on this occasion, the United States insisted on a straight up-and-down vote—a vivid reflection of its inability to obtain consensus. Eight of the agency's thirty-five members abstained or voted against, and there was considerable grumbling about the way the matter was being railroaded through. Since 2003, Egypt, South Korea, and Libya had all been caught violating the Safeguards Agreement—in some cases far more severely than Iran. But none of those states had been declared in "noncompliance" by the IAEA, and none had been referred to the Security Council. Pierre Goldschmidt, deputy head of the IAEA's Safeguards Department, complained publicly, describing the difference in treatment as "an unfortunate precedent motivated at least in part by political considerations." But it made no difference. The American-sponsored vote went through, and on February 4, 2006, the IAEA referred Iran's case to the United Nations, paving the way for a Security Council resolution.

Iran's reaction was predictable. "Issue as many resolutions as you wish, but you will never block the progress of science in Iran," said the newly elected president Ahmadinejad in a speech in Tehran. "The days when a handful of powers could sit in their crystal palaces and hand down orders to the other nations of the world are coming to an end." To demonstrate its frustration, Iran announced that it was ending the two-year voluntary suspension in its nuclear program and would resume building centrifuges and enriching uranium. In January 2006, Iran broke the seals on its facility in Natanz. In February it announced it was resuming enrichment within the legal parameters of the NPT. And on April 11 a gleeful Ahmadinejad went on Iranian television to declare that Iran had successfully enriched uranium to 3.5 percent—a level that was much too low for nuclear weapons but that could be used to generate electricity. "Today," he said, "I am officially announcing that Iran has joined the group of those countries which have nuclear technology. This is the result of the Iranian nation's resistance."

What had started as a fairly routine matter of the NPT Safeguards Agreement had become a full-scale political confrontation. On all sides, hard-line positions were creeping into the ascendancy, and the entire Iranian nuclear issue was becoming mired in an atmosphere that did not appear conducive to compromise. In 2004, Bush had been reelected, by a much clearer margin than four years earlier, which seemed to imply the American public appreciated his tough, go-it-alone approach to foreign policy. Iran under Ahmadinejad, meanwhile, seemed to welcome the confrontation, and the new president went out of his way to give rhetorical emphasis to his defiance of Western "demands." Officially, Iran's position was unchanged: it continued to insist that its nuclear program was for peaceful purposes and that it was complying fully with its international obligations. But the tone was different—starker, raspier, more caked with defiance. "To those who are angry about Iran obtaining the full nuclear cycle," Ahmadinejad said following his April announcement, "we say just one thing: Be angry at us and die of this anger."

At the same time, however, Iran understood that it was important not to overplay its hand. In September 2005, at a speech before the UN, Ahmadinejad tried to dial down the tension by proposing a compromise. Iran, he said, would allow foreign companies to invest and participate in Iran's nuclear program, on Iranian soil. This foreign participation, he said, would ensure that Iran's nuclear activities were not being secretly diverted to bomb-making, while also benefiting Western businesses. If Ahmadinejad expected his proposal to receive serious consideration, however, he was disappointed. The U.S. delegation walked out of the meeting before he even began speaking.

Once more unto the centrifuges: From 2003 to 2005, during the Khatami presidency, Iran voluntarily suspended its civilian nuclear program, hoping the show of goodwill would usher in better relations with the United States. When the Bush administration responded with escalated demands for "zero enrichment," the new president, Ahmadinejad, defiantly restarted the program.

Much the same scenario took place a few months later, when Iran proposed a comprehensive package allowing the "continuous, on-site presence of IAEA inspectors" at its facilities—a level of cooperation far beyond anything any country in history had offered to the IAEA. Iran also proposed the establishment of an international consortium to conduct the enrichment and reprocessing of uranium on Iranian soil (a plan eerily similar to one proposed by the Ford administration in 1975). Finally, Iran offered to guarantee that it would never leave the NPT—to assure the world that it was not planning to follow the North Korea approach of developing an advanced nuclear capability legally, then ditching the NPT to build a bomb. The EU's foreign policy chief, Javier Solana, welcomed all these proposals, declaring, "We are really making progress. . . . Never before have we had the level of engagement, and a level of discussion of issues which are difficult." But Solana reversed his position after it became obvious the United States did not want to consider any proposals that might derail the referral of Iran's case to the UN Security Council.

In June 2006, Russia and China joined with the United States and Europe to present a proposal of their own—ostensibly a "last chance" for Iran to "meet the demands of the international community" and avoid being referred to the Security Council. Iran welcomed this development, describing the proposals as "containing positive elements," and announced it would offer a detailed response on August 22. However, the United States and Europe chose not to wait for the Iranian reply and pushed forward with the UN Security Council resolution. On July 31, 2006, the Security Council passed Resolution 1696, which called for Iran to halt its uranium enrichment program. It was a demand without legal precedent.[*]

☙

Increasingly convinced that compromise with the United States and Europe was unlikely, Iran turned its attention to more pressing matters. It had resumed enrichment activity, at least in part, so it could attain its long-delayed goal of energy independence. But enrichment was also, increasingly, becoming essential for cancer treatment. Tehran's medical research reactor, originally fueled by enriched uranium supplied by the United States in the 1960s and then by Argentina in the 1990s, was running low. According to official estimates, the last batch of Argentinian fuel, provided in 1992, was set to run out by 2012—meaning that if Iran did not create its own supply of isotopes, its hospitals would have to stop providing diagnostic scans and radiation therapy to cancer patients.

In the United States, little attention was given to this issue. Instead, in 2006 and 2007, a growing number of voices in the American media speculated openly, and somewhat hyperbolically, about possible military action if Iran failed to "comply" with U.S. demands. The Bush administration did little to discourage this speculation—refusing to rule out military action when it was asked, and frequently leaking information to American media that made it appear war might be imminent. All these leaked stories—including a much-discussed piece by Seymour Hersh in *The New Yorker* in April 2006—were part of a conscious strategy to frighten Iran into taking America's demands more seriously. But most of the time, they had the opposite effect. Iran felt threatened and became more defiant in its rhetoric.

All this, in turn, fueled those critics around the world who accused Bush of bullying and unilateralism. And it added to Iran's ability to take the moral high ground in front of certain segments of the international audience. "Those who think they can use the language of threats and force against Iran are mistaken," Ahmadinejad said the day after the UN resolu-

---

[*] This resolution, and the more severe sanctions resolutions that followed over the next four years, were arguably illegal under international law. The Security Council, historically, had been a forum that might condemn member states for not being in compliance with NPT safeguards, on the basis that they posed a threat to international peace and security. But it had never demanded that a nation abandon its enrichment program altogether.

tion, and in many corners of the world, heads nodded. "We have to create an atmosphere that will lead to compromise," warned Russian president Vladimir Putin during the run-up to the council vote in July 2006. A leading British politician complained that the "American government has been full of bluster" and "not dealt with the matter in a sensitive way." And in Havana, at a September 2006 meeting of the Non-Aligned Movement, 118 countries voted to declare their outright support for the Iranian nuclear program—a powerful symbolic blow for the United States that went virtually unreported in the Western press.

By the beginning of 2007, even senior U.S. Republicans were publicly questioning the wisdom of the Bush strategy. Elder statesman Henry Kissinger gave interviews sharply critical of Washington's reluctance to negotiate with Tehran. Sen. Richard Lugar, chairman of the powerful Foreign Relations Committee, told ABC News there was a need "to make more headway diplomatically" and suggested direct talks between Iran and the United States. Perhaps most damaging, shortly after his resignation as secretary of state, Colin Powell bluntly criticized his former bosses in an interview with *Newsweek,* claiming they had never been serious about finding a solution to the Iranian nuclear issue. "My position . . . was that we ought to find ways to restart talks with the Iranians," said Powell. "But there was a reluctance on the part of the president to do that." Powell was particularly scathing about the administration's insistence that Iran's leaders had to capitulate before the United States could even consider a dialogue. "You can't negotiate," said Powell, "when you tell the other side, 'Give us what a negotiation would produce before the negotiations start.'"

Perhaps most troubling to administration critics was that Bush still appeared to be operating under the assumption that America was in a position to dictate terms in the Middle East—when the reality was now probably that the West needed Iran more than Iran needed the West. In the five years since Bush had taken office, oil prices had climbed steadily and were approaching a historic high of eighty dollars a barrel. The United States was struggling badly in Iraq, battling every day to keep Sunni and Shia militants from blowing each other to pieces. And Afghanistan was not going much better. Just a few years earlier America had looked like a mighty colossus astride the waters of international public opinion—its star-spangled gunboats preparing to take heroic revenge for the atrocities of 9/11, as the world stood by in solidarity. Now, however, with the disastrous occupation of Iraq and the growing hatred of American policy in the region, it looked like a mortally wounded superpower.

It was at this point that Iran began to discover an unexpectedly potent use for its nuclear program: as a symbol of national pride. During 2006 and 2007, as America insisted more and more vocally that Iran give up its right to uranium enrichment, the exercise of that right increasingly became a matter of principle for Iran—and an obvious issue to rally its people. Poll after poll showed at least 90 percent of the Iranian public supported the nuclear program and felt it was important to continue enrichment. Western journalists in Iran regularly reported that even the most jaded, antigovernment Iranians—those with a secular, pro-Western outlook and a vigorous hatred for the ayatollahs—defended their country's handling of the nuclear issue. Throughout Iran, giant billboards declared "Nuclear Energy Is Our National Right." The newest denomination of Iranian currency—the fifty-thousand-rial banknote—even featured a spinning-atom icon to underline the point. For those old enough to remember, events were unfolding in a manner eerily reminiscent of the oil nationalization crisis of the 1950s. Only this time the role of the overstretched British Empire—unable and unwilling to recognize its waning influence—was being played by the United States.

Out of the woodwork now came Iranians of all political persuasions, people one might never have expected to lend their support to the Islamic Republic. In 2006, from his villa in Switzerland, Ardeshir Zahedi—the shah's last ambassador to Washington, and a man who had not been heard from in years—gave an interview defending Iran's "inalienable right" to nuclear energy. Akbar Etemad, the nuclear scientist who founded Iran's atomic energy program in the 1960s and now lived in exile in France, went further, arguing that even a bomb was within Iran's rights. The shah "always said we didn't need nuclear weapons. . . . But he also said if things ever changed—if our security was threatened—he would give the order. I've no doubt that were he here today he would say, 'Go'; and I would." Shirin Ebadi, a fierce critic of the Islamic Republic who won a Nobel Prize in 2003 for her activism on behalf of women's rights, called the nuclear program "a cause of national pride for an old nation with a glorious history." Iran's own nuclear negotiator, Hassan Rohani, expressed amusement at the unanimity of purpose the Americans had managed to inspire in the Iranian people. The nation, he said, was now united in "wanting nuclear technology because the United States says we can't have it."

It almost didn't matter now that Iran was not actually interested in building a bomb. What mattered was the extraordinary mileage that Iranian leaders were able to get out of the entire spectacle. In the court of international public opinion, Iran was able to claim that the Western powers, prodded by Israel, were trying to deny an Islamic nation its natural, inalienable right to scientific progress purely because it did not follow Washington's line. This, of course, only added to Iran's revolutionary cachet on the Arab street. In 2008, when the Brookings Institution surveyed citizens of six Arab countries (Jordan, Lebanon, Egypt, Saudi Arabia, Morocco, and the UAE), 67 percent agreed with the statement "Iran has the right to its nuclear program and international pressure should cease." Fully 44 percent of Arab citizens said they believed the acquisition of nuclear *weapons* by Iran would have a "more positive" impact on the region. Even more striking, when respondents were asked to name two countries they perceived as posing "the biggest threat to you," 95 percent named Israel and 88 percent named the United States. Only 7 percent named Iran.

For Iran, the best way to keep all this going was to create a certain amount of ambiguity. On the one hand, it complied fully with its NPT obligations and continued to claim it was doing nothing illegal, thus making it difficult for America and Israel to rally world opinion fully against it. On the other hand, it behaved just evasively enough to keep everyone guessing, thus making it easier to present itself as defying the "demands" of the West. The United States and Israel, for their part, continued to play into Iran's hands—talking tough, issuing orders, and generally making it easier for Iran to present the whole thing as a political and ideological issue.

This, without question, was the greatest tragedy of American foreign policy during the middle years of the Bush presidency. By insisting that Iran give up enrichment altogether rather than making a distinction between enrichment and bomb making, America effectively declared that Iran was not allowed to advance scientifically, simply because it pursued a foreign policy that was independent of American interests. There was only one way that story could play out in the region—and in the developing world more generally.

CB

By 2007, tensions had risen to such a point that the IAEA's director-general, Mohamed El Baradei, felt compelled to step in and issue a rare rebuke to the United States. There was, he said, "no evidence" that Iran was developing nuclear weapons. "We have information that there has been maybe some studies about possible weaponization. That's why we have said we cannot give Iran a pass right now. . . . But have we seen Iran having the nuclear material that can readily be used into a weapon? No. Have we seen an active weaponization program? No." El Baradei even stated, rather bluntly, that he was "worried about the growing rhetoric from the US," which made it dif-

"If there is actual evidence, I would welcome seeing it": Mohamed
El Baradei, director of the International Atomic Energy Agency,
casts doubt on the Bush administration's claims about Iran's nuclear
program. El Baradei was awarded the Nobel Peace Prize for his efforts
to resolve the Iranian nuclear issue.

ficult for the IAEA to do its work in a neutral atmosphere. "If there is actual
evidence," said the recent Nobel laureate, "[I] would welcome seeing it."

It did little good. In 2007 America's hard-liners remained determined
to prove Iran was lying, either by unearthing some devastating piece of
evidence or simply by creating a vague public impression that somewhere,
somehow, some secret Iranian version of the Manhattan Project was bubbling away undetected.

But then in December 2007, something rather unexpected happened.
America's own National Intelligence Estimate (NIE)—an official document
produced every few years, drawn from the work of sixteen different intelligence agencies, and generally considered the most definitive snapshot of
the best reporting available—declared with "high confidence" that Iran
had suspended its nuclear weapons program in 2003 *and had not restarted
it.* The vague weaponization experiments that Iran had conducted in the
1990s, said the NIE, had been abandoned. Iran had rigorously observed
the two-year voluntary suspension in uranium enrichment. (America's spies
had even eavesdropped on telephone conversations in which senior Iranian
hard-liners could be heard complaining to one another about the decision
to suspend.) Iran's nuclear program, in other words, was exactly as the Iranians had described it.

The reaction to the NIE was ferocious. In Washington, politicians from both political parties rushed to the airwaves, falling over one another to criticize the report and question its conclusions. "I don't know where that intelligence is coming from that says they have suspended the program," said Arkansas governor Mike Huckabee as he prepared to launch his presidential campaign, "or how credible that is versus the view that they are actually expanding it." Huckabee's rival for the Republican nomination, Sen. John McCain (R-AZ), called the NIE "inappropriate, to say the least. . . . Frankly, I am very concerned about our intelligence agencies and exactly what they're doing. . . . I don't think that this NIE did America any good service, and I think it's going to have to be fixed." And the president himself seemed disinclined to drop the matter. Even after being presented with the NIE's findings, Bush continued to warn of "nuclear holocaust" and "World War III" if Iran did not give up its "active pursuit of technology that could lead to nuclear weapons."

CB

Lost in the midst of all this hyperbole was a simple question: Was Iran trying to build a bomb or not?

The answer depended on which aspects of the available evidence one chose to emphasize. On the one hand, those who distrusted the Islamic Republic pointed to the fact that Iran had been evasive. Indeed, in some significant ways, it had. It had failed to answer questions about possible past experiments with nuclear weaponization in the 1990s. It had been cagey and occasionally uncooperative in granting access to nuclear facilities. And it was pursuing a program of uranium enrichment that arguably was unnecessary or excessive in the context of its civilian needs.

On the other hand, there were a number of very solid empirical reasons to believe the Iranians were telling the truth. Sixteen American intelligence agencies had come to the conclusion that Iran had abandoned its weapons program in 2003 (if it had even existed in the first place). Intelligence assessments by Russia and China also indicated, unambiguously, that Iran was not working toward a bomb (and neither of these countries took a complacent attitude about nukes in their neighborhood). And of course, the IAEA— after years of unprecedented access and stringent camera monitoring—had declared unequivocally that it did not believe Iran was building a bomb. After years of accusations and insinuations, the awkward fact was that the United States had found no meaningful evidence to suggest Iran was trying to develop a nuclear weapon.

"Forbidden under Islam": In 2003 Iran's supreme leader and ultimate arbiter of spiritual matters repeated an earlier *fatwa,* or religious ruling, declaring all nuclear weapons *haram*—a sin against Islam. His predecessor, Ayatollah Khomeini, had shuttered Iran's nuclear program altogether after the revolution, calling it immoral, un-Islamic, and emblematic of the shah's excessive fascination with Western technology.

Another indicator was Iran's own stated policy of opposition to nuclear weapons. In November 2004 and again in August 2005, Iran's supreme leader, Ayatollah Khamenei, had issued a high-profile religious declaration (scholars described it as either a *fatwa* or a *hokm*) stating:

> The production, stockpiling and use of nuclear weapons are forbidden under Islam and the Islamic Republic of Iran shall never acquire these weapons.

Though Western media often played down this religious ruling, Iranians themselves took it very seriously. In April 2005, Iran's chief nuclear negotiator, Hassan Rohani, told the Danish foreign minister that the *fatwa* "is more important for us than the articles of the nuclear Non-Proliferation Treaty. . . . The *fatwa* is, in the Islamic Republic, an obligatory law." And indeed, this was no small point. Khamenei, after all, was not only Iran's head of state. He was also its spiritual guide. His express constitutional role—the entire basis of his legitimacy for ruling the country, in fact—rested on his authority to interpret Islam, and to provide a religious foundation for all policy decisions. If the ayatollah ever went back on his word and allowed Iran to develop a nuclear weapon, he would lose all religious legitimacy and make a mockery of the entire concept of an Islamic Republic.

It was not just the supreme leader who declared publicly his opposition to nuclear weapons. Secular politicians, including President Ahmadinejad, also chimed in. In a 2007 interview with NBC's Brian Williams, Ahmadinejad questioned the very notion that nuclear weapons could be a useful asset to the Islamic Republic. "Did nuclear arms prevent the Soviet Union from falling and disintegrating?" he asked rhetorically. "For that matter, did a nuclear bomb help the United States to prevail in Iraq or Afghanistan? Nuclear bombs belong to the twentieth century. We are living in a new century."

There were reasons to believe Iran was being sincere. In 2006 a study published by the U.S. National Academy of Sciences found that "Iran's energy demand growth has exceeded its supply growth," and that "Iran's oil export will decline" or even "could go to zero within 12-19 years." Iran's need for nuclear power, it said, was "genuine, because Iran relies on . . . proceeds from oil exports for most revenues, and could become politically vulnerable if exports decline." The Islamic Republic, in other words, was facing the same dilemma the shah had faced forty years earlier—more so, if anything, because Iran's population was now more than twice what it had been in the 1970s, and energy demand was far greater.

Finally, there was one very basic, gut-level reason to believe Iran was unlikely to seek nuclear weapons. During its lengthy eight-year war with Iraq in the 1980s, when Saddam had resorted to chemical warfare, Iran had never responded in kind, despite the fact that it had the technical capacity to do so. Iran, in fact, had never even assembled a precautionary chemical stockpile, believing it un-Islamic to even contemplate this kind of warfare. This fact alone, Iranians regularly pointed out, was evidence Iran was sincere when it said it had no interest in nuclear weapons. Iran, they said, was actually a *victim* of WMD—the greatest victim since 1945—and its opposition to such weapons was emotionally rooted. Its war veterans continued to suffer from the effects of Iraqi gas attacks: many were still tormented by rattling coughs and vivid nightmares, and many still walked the streets wheeling heavy oxygen tanks. More than almost any other population, anywhere in the world, Iranians appreciated the danger and the immorality of weapons of mass destruction.

Often lost in all this weighing of the arguments was a simple question: Why would Iran even *want* a nuke? In Western public rhetoric, it was frequently suggested that Iran had "threatened to wipe Israel off the map," and that it was now "trying to acquire a nuclear weapon" so it could do just that. But would an Iranian nuclear bomb really embolden the ayatollahs to launch an attack against Israel? Given that Israel had more than two hundred nuclear warheads, as well as an instantaneous "second-strike capability" in the form of nuclear submarines parked in the Mediterranean, any nation foolish enough to try to nuke Israel would find itself obliterated several times over, within minutes. And if there was one thing every Iran expert agreed on, it was that Iran's leaders were not foolish. They were calculating, deeply pragmatic operators with a long track record of self-preservation.

The only possible benefit of possessing a nuclear weapon, from Iran's perspective, was that it would provide increased regional power, influence, and prestige. But Iran was already gaining most of that influence and prestige without having to bother to build a bomb. Had Iran made the decision to go for a bomb, it would have had to break the IAEA seals on its centrifuges, kick out the inspectors, and make a mad dash to weaponize— actions that would instantly invite international isolation, sanctions, and possibly even a military attack by the United States. Instead, Washington had allowed Iran to play the victim and to pose as the leader of the "resistance" to American-Israeli hegemony in the Middle East, thereby handing the ayatollahs a far easier and more effective source of influence and regional prestige. Iran had turned itself into the big, bad bogeyman of the region— feared and obsessed over by the West and admired by the people of the Arab world—without doing anything illegal.

Ultimately, the crux of the debate was what might or might not have taken place in the 1990s and early 2000s. Reasonable people generally agreed that since 2003 Iran had not actively pursued a bomb. So really, it came down to whether those weapons experiments had been truly abandoned or whether they were still secretly operational. Opponents of Iran liked to point out that the IAEA had not been able to absolutely, categorically, unequivocally rule out the possibility of an ongoing weapons-research program. But as the IAEA itself said in 2006, in its typically phlegmatic way, "the process of drawing such a conclusion . . . is a time-consuming process." And as the Iranians pointed out, the same questions being raised about Iran had been raised about forty-five other countries in the world— including fourteen European nations. In rebuttal, opponents of Iran asked rather reasonable questions: If Iran *truly* had nothing to hide, then why did it not open itself up again to the kind of invasive inspections it had allowed from 2003 to 2005? Why did it not let the whole world see for itself that it had nothing to be afraid of?

Iran's response was that it had offered, many times, to do just that—but the United States had been more interested in playing games. In a lengthy 2007 article in the *Journal of International Affairs,* Iran's ambassador to the UN, Mohammad Javad Zarif, cited a number of occasions when Iran had offered expanded access to the IAEA and explained how the United States had brushed aside or in some other way undermined each of these offers. Ultimately, Zarif argued, the problem was not Iranian intransigence. It was "the tendency of the United States to manufacture a nuclear crisis instead of searching for a solution."

CB

Possibly, but possibly there was a much more sophisticated calculus at work.

Almost certainly what Iran was after, during these years, was not a nuclear weapon but a *nuclear capability,* also known as "nuclear latency," "breakout capacity," or the "Japan option." A state with nuclear capability is one that has accumulated just enough reactors and centrifuges, enriched just enough uranium, and developed just enough technical expertise that it could assemble a bomb within months if an extreme danger to national security ever presented itself. Put more simply, a nation with nuclear capability is one that has walked just to the *threshold* of building a nuclear bomb but not crossed it.

Approximately fifteen countries have achieved this level of readiness at one time or another, nations as different as Brazil, Germany, Japan, and Argentina. In each case, the country stayed within its NPT obligations but also sent the world a powerful message: this nation is not to be trifled with. In each case, nuclear ambiguity has been a national security asset, both as an insurance policy against foreign aggression and as leverage for increased regional influence. And in the early 2000s, there was good reason to suspect that Iran was seeking to join this unofficial club of nuclear fence-straddlers.

The Islamic Republic's calculation would have been simple. If Iran pulled out all the stops and raced to build an *actual* bomb, the whole world would instantly know about it. This, in turn, would have brought Iran extreme isolation and condemnation. It would have instantly lost the sympathy of Russia and China (which had zero tolerance for an actual bomb). The Europeans would have been united and vigorous in their condemnation. And almost certainly the United States would have reacted with a massive military response—and most of the world would have supported it. This military confrontation would almost certainly have resulted in the end of the Islamic Republic.

If, on the other hand, Iran simply walked to the edge of the cliff—developing a nuclear *capability* but nothing more—it would enjoy a number of very significant advantages. It would not be in violation of the NPT. Perhaps more important, it would not be in violation of Islamic law. And yet it would still benefit from a certain measure of security against foreign aggression. For Iran, therefore, a nuclear capability was the perfect middle road.

Ultimately, Iran was convinced that the real goal of the United States and Israel had always been something much larger than just making sure they had no nuclear weapons. Iran did not believe for one moment that if it gave up uranium enrichment, the United States and its allies would declare themselves satisfied and leave Iran alone. Rather, Iran was convinced that the United States and Israel's ultimate goal was to weaken (and if possible destroy) the Islamic Republic—and that had it not been the nuclear program, they would have found something else to use as a bludgeon against it. Under these circumstances, Iran's leaders felt they would have been foolish not to at least *give the impression* that they might be moving toward a bomb, to give would-be attackers something to think about. It was a basic matter of national security.

G3

By 2008, Bush's approach to Iran had achieved none of its stated objectives. If all that tough talk and saber-rattling—all those glorious words about "regime change" and "axis of evil"—had been intended to get Iran to abandon its nuclear program, then by any objective standard, the policy had failed. In 2003, when the controversy began, Iran had had only 164 centrifuges in operation. In 2008, it had more than three thousand. Iran had made the strategic decision that if the United States was going to constantly threaten war over the issue of its rudimentary civilian nuclear program, then its best option was to ratchet up that program and take it right to the threshold of a nuclear weapon—so that the United States would be forced to think twice before attacking. In short, the "Iranian nuclear threat" was becoming a self-fulfilling prophecy.

And the Bush administration was running out of options. After thirty years of sanctions, isolation, and trade restrictions, Washington had little left in its arsenal to get Iran to do what it wanted. Even military action, though it was talked about incessantly, was not a realistic option. The United States was in no position to start yet another war in the Middle East, least of all with a country that had an enormous capacity to cause devastation in the region.* If America was serious about stopping Iran from enriching uranium, it would have to find other ways to do so.

To this end, late in the Bush presidency, officials spoke increasingly of the need for a policy of "carrots and sticks." In 2007 and 2008 especially, they argued that Iran should be offered incentives and inducements for abandoning its nuclear program, in addition to the usual threats and ultimatums. By balancing sticks with meaningful carrots, Washington could perhaps convince Tehran that uranium enrichment was not in its best interest. The United States could, for example, allow Iran to join the World Trade Organization as a reward for abandoning its nuclear program—while threatening it with further sanctions and isolation if it did not.

This might have sounded great in theory. But the problem with carrots and sticks was that it was a narrow and coercive policy. It had only one goal in mind, which was to bring about an immediate change in Iranian behavior along lines that would be precisely suitable to the United States. Put another way, it treated Iran as a problem to be solved rather than as a nation with legitimate aspirations, legitimate security concerns, a legitimate perspective on regional affairs, and long-running grievances against the United States. A growing number of critics pointed out that the United States needed to take a much larger and more imaginative approach to Iran, one that acknowledged Iran's place in the world and that recognized the extraordinary opportunities that could come out of a positive, constructive U.S.-Iranian relationship. In the absence of a basic atmosphere of trust and goodwill, these critics said, American attempts to coerce a change in Iran's policy on a specific issue like nuclear energy would inevitably fail.

As the sun set on the Bush administration, the United States faced a stark choice. It could continue down the same path with Iran—insisting on "zero enrichment," hinting at war, and allowing itself to be cast as the regional bully. Or it could try something fundamentally different. And increasingly in Washington, tough, hard-nosed realists—the kind of people who were no softies when it came to America's national-security interests—were heard arguing that it was time to try something fundamentally different.

---

* America's own generals had long warned that a war with Iran would make the Iraq war look like a walk in the park. Unlike Iraq, Iran was not some cobbled-together tinpot dictatorship whose people were just waiting to be liberated (if that had even been true of Iraq). It was an ancient, contiguous, and revolutionary nation with a fiercely nationalistic people. And it had the ability to wreak havoc in the region, thanks to its allies in Hezbollah, Hamas, and Shia affinity networks in Iraq and Afghanistan. For the United States to invade Iran at precisely the moment when it was struggling to pacify Iran's two neighbors would have been almost suicidal.

Designed to Fail

Long before the name "Barack Obama" and the phrase "change you can believe in" entered the American political lexicon—before the walls and windows of houses lit up with blue and red posters of the Illinois senator looking winsomely into the distance over letters spelling out C-H-A-N-G-E—a consensus was building among the foreign-policy-making community in Washington. Something needed to change—and change dramatically—in America's approach to Iran and the Middle East.

As early as 2006, the Iraq Study Group—a blue-ribbon bipartisan panel set up to help America find a way out of the quandary of the Iraq war—had delivered the verdict. One of America's highest priorities, the group said, should be to initiate "extensive and substantive" talks with Iran. The report's authors, former secretary of state James Baker and former House Intelligence Committee chairman Lee Hamilton, argued that perhaps more than any other nation in the region, "Iran can use its influence, especially over Shia groups in Iraq, to encourage national reconciliation"—thus making it possible for the United States to finally begin to pull its troops out. But none of this could happen as long as Washington maintained an adversarial relationship with Tehran. For neither the first nor the last time in history, in other words, America had a direct, urgent national security interest in talking to Iran.

During the final two years of the Bush administration, it became grindingly obvious that Iraq was not the only part of the world where this was true. U.S. policy makers were struggling in Afghanistan, Palestine, and Lebanon—all places where Iran had powerful connections to influential players, giving it tremendous leverage over regional developments. But as long as Washington continued to use labels like "axis of evil" and to talk of "regime change" in Tehran, it virtually guaranteed that this leverage would be used in opposition to the United States.

By 2008, as America's grand designs for Iraq and the region continued to unravel, the Washington foreign policy establishment seemed to agree that diplomacy with Iran was a necessity, more urgent than ever before. A positive relationship with Iran, said the experts, could benefit the United States in all kinds of ways, some of which were hard to even imagine in the current atmosphere. In September of that year, as the presidential election approached, five former secretaries of state—Henry Kissinger, James Baker, Warren Christopher, Madeleine Albright, and Colin Powell—appeared on an unprecedented CNN panel discussion program and offered a blunt piece of advice to those who sought to be America's next president: talk to Iran.

Recognizing that political space was opening up, Obama did not hesitate to turn improved relations with Tehran—and the Muslim world generally—into a central feature of his campaign. At a Democratic primary debate in July 2007, he called explicitly for dialogue with Iran—something no American presidential candidate had done in thirty years. And as president, he said, he would be willing to talk to Iran "without precondition"—a stark contrast to the Bush administration, which had refused to negotiate with Tehran until it halted its enrichment activities. In fact, Obama carefully avoided using the word *enrichment* whenever he spoke about Iran, saying only that he was opposed to an Iranian nuclear *weapon*. By subtly drawing a distinction between uranium enrichment and nuclear weapons, Obama indicated that his administration would take a much sterner view of one than the other. This was in direct contrast to his Republican opponent, John McCain, who harped constantly on the idea that Iran was heading toward a nuclear weapon and had to be stopped.

Among the foreign policy community in Washington—not known for its susceptibility to sweeping, emotional rhetoric—a new mood of openness and anticipation surfaced, as it realized that if anyone could bring about change in the Middle East, it was the charismatic Barack Obama. Analysts prepared for the possibility of a major realignment in U.S.-Iranian relations if Obama won the election—the kind of historic opening Nixon had achieved with China, or Reagan with Gorbachev. There was talk of resuming direct flights to Iran after November and even of reopening the American consulate in Tehran. PBS travel guru Rick Steves even traveled through Iran for a month that summer to record a special episode, *Rick Steves' Iran*. A generational shift seemed to be taking place—and by any objective measure, change was in the air.

 C3

The heavens appeared to open when Barack Obama was elected president at the end of 2008. Jubilant crowds poured into Chicago's Grant Park, many weeping openly at the unexpected sight of a black American making a victory speech to the nation. In Europe, Africa, and the Middle East, there was palpable delight—mixed with a fair measure of surprise—at the outcome of the election. Kenyans danced in the streets as their government declared a national holiday. At the United Nations, Secretary-general Ban Ki-moon hailed Obama's election as a "historic opportunity." Even the left-wing French daily *Libération*—normally a bastion of sneering anti-Americanism—let down its guard for a moment. "Let us admit today that we're caught up, almost all of us, in a sense of joy," said its editorial. After all the pink-throated jingoism of the Bush years, no one had quite expected America would elect an internationalist with a name like Barack Hussein Obama to lead it through the next four years.

But in one part of the world—the Middle East—the hall monitors were spooked. Israeli leaders, as well as leaders of the Arab political establishment, were not sure what to make of this new American president who had spoken so openly of his desire to mend fences with Tehran. For nearly twenty years, Israel and the Arab dictators had cynically (if unofficially) hitched their wagons to each other, in part out of an unspoken desire to keep Iran isolated. Now here, suddenly, was a man who seemed determined to turn that on its head—who pledged a new American relationship with the Middle East. The region's people felt great excitement about Obama and what he seemed to promise, but in the corridors of power, there was nothing but dread.

The Israelis were the first to make known their discomfort. Twenty-four hours after congratulating Obama on his win, Israel's foreign minister, Tzipi Livni, warned, "We live in a neighborhood in which sometimes dialogue . . . is liable to be interpreted as weakness." Pushed by a radio interviewer to clarify whether Israel would support America's attempts to initiate talks with Iran, she replied bluntly: "The answer is no." A few weeks later a prominent Israeli politician, Yuval Steinitz, described Iran as a threat akin to that of Nazi Germany, warning that Obama "will have to choose in the next year whether to be Chamberlain or Churchill." Arab leaders were more restrained, nursing the hope that Obama would take a more even-handed approach to the Palestinian issue than had previous presidents. But even they were not entirely sure what to make of his pledge to improve ties with Iran. "Engagement yes, marriage no," was the line frequently heard from Saudi officials—meaning they were happy with the United States *talking* to Iran, but not if it led to a full reinvigoration of the U.S.-Iranian friendship of the 1970s.

Overall, both Israel and the Arab political establishment preferred things the way they were, and neither warmed to the new noises coming out of Washington. Any politician so enamored of "hope" and "change," they reasoned, would inevitably be sympathetic to the aspirations of the region's people, whether it was the Palestinians or the oppressed citizens of Arab states, many of whom were rather sympathetic to Iran. One Israeli official, reflecting on the nervousness in Tel Aviv, put it plainly: "In Israel, we are for the status quo. Not only do we believe the status quo is sustainable, we think it's the job of the United States to sustain it."

The president-elect was no fool—he knew that when it came to foreign policy, charisma alone would not be enough to overcome the interests entrenched in the Washington political universe or the concerns of traditional allies. In the days that followed the election, therefore, he filled his administration with safe, experienced, establishment Democrats, many of them holdovers from the Clinton era and most of them known for their close affinity to Israel. Rahm Emmanuel, a pugnacious Illinois congressman who had served in the Israeli military during the 1991 Gulf War, became chief of staff. Dennis Ross, a legendary AIPAC power player widely known by the nickname "Israel's lawyer" in Washington, became the Iran point man in the State Department.* And the plummiest foreign policy job of all, secretary of state, went to Hillary Clinton, the New York senator known for her hawkish views on the Middle East. (During her own presidential campaign, Clinton had vowed to "totally obliterate" Iran if it posed a threat to Israel.)

To a great extent, these first appointments were a wise, judicious move by the president-elect. During the election campaign, Obama had frequently been portrayed as lacking the passion for Israel traditionally expected of American political candidates, and he had to move quickly to prevent that impression from sticking. But these appointments also meant that, from the beginning, the new president would be surrounded by people who did not fundamentally share his vision. In early 2008, Ross had put together United Against Nuclear Iran (UANI), a well-funded campaign designed to

---

* Ross's dedication to advancing Israel's cause in Washington has frequently been noted. The *New York Times* columnist Roger Cohen has written that "a recurrent issue with Ross . . . has been whether he is too close to the American Jewish community and Israel to be an honest broker with Iran or Arabs." Aaron David Miller, a prominent Middle East analyst and former peace negotiator who worked closely with Ross, has said Ross had "an inherent tendency to see the world of Arab-Israeli politics first from Israel's vantage point rather than [from] that of the Palestinians." A former State Department official, speaking anonymously, once complained, "Ross's bad habit is pre-consultation with the Israelis."

pressure multinational companies against doing business with Iran.* Ross had argued that the problem with U.S. policy on Iran during the Bush years was that it had never been tough *enough*. Only by inflicting truly punishing sanctions, he said, would Washington get the ayatollahs to capitulate to U.S. demands.

When word of these initial appointments reached Tehran, the prevailing perception was that Obama represented only a *tactical* change from the Bush era. Many expected that he would pursue the same goal of weakening and crushing Iran, but that unlike Bush—whose cowboy ways had alienated European allies and made much of the world sympathetic to Iran—Obama would succeed in rallying the world to America's side. The common view in Tehran held that American foreign policy was simply too beholden to structural forces, in particular the formidable pro-Israel lobby, for any U.S. president to mend fences with Iran. The news that Obama had included Dennis Ross in his team went down especially badly. Ross was on the record talking about the need for "sharp sticks" to accompany any "carrots" dangled before Iran, and this kind of language—along with the accompanying imagery of mule-driving that it conjured up—struck many as insulting. The speaker of Iran's parliament, Ali Larijani, complained that "the language of carrots and sticks is obsolete and barbaric in relation to an ancient nation such as Iran."

Officially, therefore, Iran was skeptical but open to dialogue. Iran's president, Mahmoud Ahmadinejad, sent a note of congratulations to the president-elect upon his victory—something no Iranian leader had done since 1976. But when his message was ignored, Ahmadinejad became more circumspect. "We will listen to the statements closely, we will carefully study their actions, and, if there are real changes, we will welcome it," he said in January 2009.

☙

Obama gave the Iranians plenty to think about. Twelve-and-a-half minutes into his inaugural address on January 20, the new president delivered a message clearly calibrated to reach the ears of Tehran. "To the Muslim world," he said, "we seek a new way forward, based on mutual interest and mutual respect. . . . To those leaders . . . who cling to power through corruption

---

* UANI is one of the most powerful and influential of the many Washington organizations dedicated to affirming the pro-Israeli line against Iran. Since its founding, UANI has run a number of very successful name-and-shame campaigns, convincing international corporations to cease activities that might even indirectly involve doing business with Iran. In January 2015, it was revealed that one-third of UANI's 2013 budget came from Sheldon Adelson, a casino magnate and Republican megadonor who has publicly called for the United States to drop a nuclear bomb on Iran.

and deceit and the silencing of dissent, know that you are on the wrong side of history, but that we will extend a hand if you are willing to unclench your fist."

One week later, in his first interview as president, Obama reiterated his desire to see the Iranians "unclench their fist" and went even further. "The Iranian people," he said, "are a great people and Persian civilization is a great civilization. Iran has acted in ways that are not conducive to peace and prosperity in the region. . . . But I do think that it is important for us to be willing to talk to Iran."

Five weeks later, Obama dramatically upped the ante. To mark the start of the Persian new year on March 20, he released a special three-and-a-half-minute video expressing his best wishes to all those around the world who celebrate the occasion. "This holiday is both an ancient ritual and a moment of renewal," he began, "and I hope that you enjoy this special time of year with friends and family.

> In particular, I would like to speak directly to the people and leaders of the Islamic Republic of Iran. . . . For nearly three decades, relations between our nations have been strained, but at this holiday, we are reminded of the common humanity that binds us together.
>
> We have serious differences that have grown over time. My administration is now committed to diplomacy that addresses the full range of issues before us, and to pursuing constructive ties among the United States, Iran, and the international community. This process will not be advanced by threats. We seek instead engagement that is honest and grounded in mutual respect.

The video was unprecedented. For the first time in history, an American president had used the words "Islamic Republic of Iran," suggesting the United States was no longer interested in "regime change" or turning back the clock on the 1979 revolution. It was also the first time an American president had spoken both to Iran's leaders *and* to its people, removing the impression that the United States was trying to drive a wedge between the two. But perhaps the most remarkable thing about the video was that it had been made at all. Obama's tone—his sincerity, his facial expression, his undeniable respect for Iranian history—all went far beyond any previous American attempt at engaging Tehran.

Iran's response was swift and equally unprecedented. Within twenty-four hours, the supreme leader, Ayatollah Khamenei, gave a speech in Mashhad in which he outlined Iran's grievances with the United States, adding that "words" were not enough and that Iran needed to see real, concrete changes

The unclenched fist: Shortly after taking office, President Barack Obama records a historic Persian new year greeting to Iran's people and their leaders, pledging to pursue "diplomacy that addresses the full range of issues before us." This olive branch was quickly overwhelmed by domestic opposition and pressure from Israel.

in American policy. But then, as the crowd fired up with its ritual chant of "Death to America," Khamenei raised his hand to quiet them. "There will be time enough for chanting," he said. "We do not have any experience with this new American president. . . . We will observe and judge." Then, turning his attention to Obama, Khamenei delivered his reply: "You change, and our behavior will change as well."

To the untrained ear, this might have sounded uncharitable, even petulant. But for anyone who had followed Iran closely over the past thirty years, it was nothing short of a historic opening. As a revolutionary, ideologically defined state, forged in a climate of anti-American anger, the Islamic Republic, by its very nature, was not built for expressions of love and warmth toward the United States. Any softening of its ideology had to be carefully couched in language that would not upset the millions of Iranians who, for thirty years, had made genuine sacrifices to build a nation that would no longer take orders from the "Great Satan." In this context, Khamenei's words carried a distinct note of reconciliation. "If you change, we will change too," was a formulation that had never been heard from the lips of a supreme leader.

In the days that followed, Tehran made a coordinated attempt to present an image of flexibility. Ahmadinejad gave a speech in which he referred, almost incredibly, to Obama as "the honorable American president" and stated that "the Iranian nation is always ready for dialogue that takes place in a fair, equal, and respectful atmosphere." Rafsanjani, the old doyen of U.S.-Iranian rapprochement, also chimed in. "We don't have any enmity with the American people," he said. "And we won't have any enmity with the American government if it treats us fairly and acts in line with international norms."

If Iran seemed skeptical, it was, to some extent, because it had been down this road before. In 1989, when George H. W. Bush had come to power professing "goodwill," Iran had pulled out all the stops to get American hostages released from Lebanon but received nothing in response. It had had similar disappointments more recently, with the collapse of the Geneva Channel in 2003 and the subsequent "axis of evil" label. Thus, from the perspective of the Islamic Republic, the onus of proof was on the United States. After nearly thirty years of frozen assets and sanctions, Iranian leaders wanted Washington to deliver concrete, practical measures to ease the country's economic and political isolation. Until it did, they felt, Obama's rhetoric was little more than just that—rhetoric. "When it comes to our vital interests, we are not sentimental," said Khamenei in his speech. "We do not make decisions based on emotions. We make decisions based on logic and calculation."

☙

As this elaborate courtship between the two nation's leaders was playing out, a different set of political pressures began to build on Obama—and they came from the direction of Tel Aviv. The Israelis, as always, were deeply uncomfortable with the idea of the United States and Iran sitting down to smoke the peace pipe, fearing that a reconciliation could challenge Israel's own special relationship with the United States and its dominance in the region. Since the end of the Cold War, Washington, Israel, and "moderate" (i.e., pro-Western) Arab leaders had formed a tactical, unofficial coalition that relied on the image of Iran as the big, bad enemy. That coalition had brought a certain amount of stability to the region but had also turned a blind eye to the problem of Sunni radicalism. Obama seemed to recognize that it was time for a historic realignment. He even, incredibly, seemed to view resolving the nuclear dispute as the first step toward developing a broader working relationship with Iran. For the Israelis, it was the ultimate doomsday scenario, and they wasted no time making their feelings plain. In February, Israel's newly elected prime minister, Binyamin Netanyahu, asked a delegation of visiting American congressmen to deliver the message to Obama that diplomacy with Iran was a waste of time. The savvy Iranians would simply "take you to the cleaners," as he put it. Only an atmosphere of constant military threat would get them to change their behavior.

Of course, Netanyahu had a delicate path to tread. Given Obama's immense popularity and his publicly stated desire for a fresh start with Tehran, Netanyahu could not afford to be seen standing on the sidelines, waving his arms and vigorously opposing diplomacy. The United States, after all, was still Israel's most important ally—an ally that sent it $3.5 billion a year in aid and regularly stepped in to veto every UN resolution that was critical of its actions. For an Israeli leader to display such blatant disregard for the wishes of a newly elected American president would have been, to say the least, unseemly. A much more subtle approach would be needed.

The strategy Netanyahu settled on was to state that Israel was not opposed to diplomacy per se but that it would have to come with certain terms and conditions. For starters, it would have to be highly limited in scope, and the Iranians would have to understand that severe punishment lay in store for them if they failed to meet demands. Netanyahu argued that negotiations with Tehran were so unlikely to produce results that they should be given only a tight, two- to three-month window to succeed (or, rather, to fail). Anything longer than this, he said, and the Iranians would find a way to drag the whole thing out, dividing and confusing the international community while continuing to enrich uranium. The Israelis also insisted that the threat of military action should always be kept on the table, and that it should be referred to frequently and vocally, so that the Iranians understood that their failure to cooperate would have consequences. In case there was any doubt about how serious he was, Netanyahu dropped casual hints that if the United States didn't act, Israel was prepared to take matters into its own hands—even if that meant attacking Iran unilaterally.

In short, Netanyahu made it clear that he would support Obama's diplomatic outreach to Iran, but mostly as a temporary gesture of goodwill to the new American president. Diplomacy, he said, was something Israel could live with, but it had to be presented to the Iranians as a sort of last-chance saloon—a final, magnanimous gesture of clemency before the onset of a campaign of punishment, isolation, and economic warfare. In order to drill this message home, Netanyahu urged the United States to prepare severe, crippling sanctions legislation—the kind that could do serious damage to the Iranian economy if it went into effect. This way Washington would have some concrete punishment ready to inflict on Iran the minute the negotiations were declared a failure (as inevitably they would be)—and time would not have been wasted unnecessarily.

Netanyahu also argued that the United States should set an extremely high benchmark for what constituted "success." The goal of any negotiation, he said, should be to get Iran to *completely* abandon its nuclear program, including even the low-level enrichment required for electricity generation. Here Netanyahu's policy prescription sounded eerily similar to the one pursued for years by the Bush administration: total Iranian capitulation, *or else*. That approach had been widely criticized as a failure and was now being reconsidered by the United States. But Netanyahu argued that it had never been properly tried in the first place. What was needed, he said, was a policy far more draconian than anything Bush had promoted—one based on tight deadlines and a far more serious threat of war. Only then would the Iranians sit up and listen.

Very little of this went down well with the new U.S. administration. At the White House, foreign policy experts felt a tough-talking approach to Iran would only backfire. For thirty years, they said, the United States had issued threats and sanctions—and they had succeeded only in making the ayatollahs feel defensive and reactive. In recent years, in fact, Bush's all-or-nothing approach had visibly pushed Iran to *strengthen* its clandestine nuclear program. The whole point of Obama's approach was to try something fundamentally different. To many Iran experts, the policy Netanyahu was advocating seemed designed to poison the well from the beginning.

Fortunately for Netanyahu, Israel had at least one friend in the White House who could push his point of view or at least triangulate between two radically different philosophies. Dennis Ross—fresh from running a think-tank in Jerusalem and now ensconced at the highest levels of the Obama administration—spent much of the spring of 2009 advocating what he called "the hybrid option." According to Ross, the best approach to Iran was to *mix* diplomacy with the threat of punitive sanctions, thus reflecting both the president's vision and the concerns of the Israelis. On the one hand, said Ross, the administration should pursue a discreet channel of communication with the supreme leader and lay the groundwork for talks over the nuclear program. At the same time, it should prepare tough sanctions to ensure that Iran understood that the "unclenched fist" was not an indefinite, open-ended offer. To keep the Israelis happy, these sanctions should be some of the toughest and most unforgiving ever dreamed up—banning the sale of gasoline, shutting off Iran's access to global banking networks, and even imposing stiff sanctions against European companies that did business with Iran. They should be measures, in short, that would cripple Iran's economy and make the ayatollahs beg for mercy.

In effect, Ross was advocating a policy nearly identical to that of Netanyahu, but with a different tone. Rather than emphasizing the punitive, and rather than declaring at the outset that the negotiations were guaranteed to fail, he used the more neutral language of the "dual track"—suggesting that diplomacy and threats could be pursued simultaneously or even somehow mutually reinforce each other. The bottom line, however, was the same. The Iranians had to understand that any talks with the United States would be conducted under the threat of severe punishments that waited for them in the wings. The window for diplomacy would be opened just a crack, then slammed shut the moment Iran became intransigent.

To a number of career foreign policy experts in Washington, this was not diplomacy at all; it was a charade. True diplomacy, if it were to succeed, required time, patience, and breathing room. It could not take place in an atmosphere of threats, ultimatums, and looming deadlines. It also required of its participants a genuine desire to see diplomacy succeed—something that seemed conspicuously lacking in Ross. Logically, in fact, the very idea of a "dual track" was difficult to understand. Diplomacy and threats, by their very nature, were contradictory impulses, and each diluted the impact of the other. Fundamentally, it was impossible to "negotiate" with some-one in an atmosphere of "mutual respect" while simultaneously threaten-ing them with "crippling" punishment if they failed to comply with your demands.

In fact, what Ross and his friends in Jerusalem were doing was inten-tionally pushing the White House in the direction of a policy that was designed to fail. By imposing a tight, unrealistic deadline on the talks, the Ross camp was suggesting the United States should merely go through the *motions* of diplomacy, with the expectation that it would end in failure, only as a way to prove to the world that "every avenue had been tried" with Iran and that it was now time for harsher measures. Put another way, they were hoping to game Obama. By allowing him to have his moment of diplo-macy, they believed, they would later have a much easier time convincing European allies to go along with tough measures. Once talks with Iran had been tried and declared a failure, the West could then crush and isolate Iran, making any historic reconciliation with America impossible.

If there was any doubt about the level of Ross's influence, one had only to look at the words of his boss, Hillary Clinton. In spring 2009 the secretary of state told a number of European and Arab allies that she was skeptical that diplomacy with Iran could succeed, but it could be useful in setting the stage for tougher measures later on. In April, Clinton testified to Congress that the primary purpose of the outreach to Tehran was tactical— to make it easier to secure international support for "crippling sanctions" when the time came. If, as she expected, the talks proved "inconclusive or unsuccessful," the United States would be in a much stronger position to increase pressure on Iran. "Our partners around the world" would then recognize "that they must work with us and support our efforts, including tougher sanctions." By participating in dialogue with Iran, she said, the United States would gain "more leverage with other nations" and increase "even further our ability to ask more from other nations." The very *goal* of diplomacy, in other words, was not to resolve the nuclear dispute. It was to create international unity on the need for sanctions.

In other, less high-profile corners of the Obama administration, the story was much the same. At the Treasury Department, Stuart Levey—a key Bush appointee who had been on something of an Iran sanctions crusade since 2006—used the first few months of the new president's tenure to cook up more elaborate ways to squeeze the Iranian economy. Levey— who described himself as a longtime supporter of both AIPAC and Israel— would typically have been replaced by a new political appointee at the start of a new administration. But Obama kept him in the job, hoping to reassure influential pro-Israel activists that his administration would continue to be tough on Iran. Levey, whose official title was Undersecretary for Terrorism and Financial Intelligence, used his position to pressure major European and Japanese banks to abandon their long-standing relationships with Iranian clients, mostly by threatening them with reputational harm if they continued doing business with Iran. It was a remarkably effective strategy. Within weeks, dozens of the largest banks in Britain, Germany, Italy, and Japan canceled billions of dollars' worth of contracts with Iran.

What all this added up to was a very obviously conflicting message from the new U.S. administration. On the one hand, the president spoke in rosaceous terms about a new beginning with Iran, rhetoric never before heard from an American leader. On the other hand, members of his administration were busy pushing a punitive track of sanctions and threats far harsher than anything pursued by the Bush White House—and for the most part, away from the cameras, they were getting their way. Publicly, what the world saw at the end of March was a president wishing Iran a happy new year and quoting handsomely from medieval Persian poetry. But what went largely unnoticed was that just days before Obama made that historic video, his administration quietly renewed existing sanctions on Iran for another year.*

All these decisions caused considerable irritation in Iran. "They give the slogan of change but in practice no change is seen," said Khamenei. "Where is the change? We haven't seen any change." The speaker of Iran's parliament, Ali Larijani, was even more scathing. "Our problems with America

---

* The Obama administration also chose not to cancel a $70 million annual program of covert operations inherited from the Bush White House—a streamlined budget item intended to give the CIA maximum flexibility in recruiting and funding domestic Iranian groups dedicated to overthrowing their government.

are not emotional," he said at a press conference. "They will not be solved by them altering the words or selecting the terms they use." For Iranian leaders, the central issue was the same as it had always been: they were not going to negotiate under pressure. If the new American administration wanted to have a serious, sincere discussion about the nuclear program aimed at finding a resolution, they said, they were willing to do so. But if Washington adopted a policy of increased sanctions, added financial pressures, and stepped-up efforts at regime change—all while using insincere diplomacy as a tactical weapon to achieve those goals—that was a very different story.

What was obvious to the Iranians was obvious to much of the rest of the world as well: there was confusion within the new administration. On one side, Ross and Clinton felt—in concert with Netanyahu—that diplomacy should last for a maximum of twelve weeks, then be abandoned in favor of new sanctions. On the other side, career diplomats and Iran specialists argued that a complicated thirty-year dispute between two countries could not be resolved so quickly, and that an atmosphere of threats and deadlines was guaranteed to backfire. As the spring bled into summer, the latter camp looked like they were rapidly losing the argument. Ross was on the rise, and so was the Israeli position. In the American media, a narrative was taking shape that Obama—with all his talk of a new beginning with the Muslim world—was not being sufficiently sensitive to the concerns of Washington's traditional Israeli allies. In order to counteract that narrative, the White House knew it had a limited window of time for diplomacy with Iran, and that it would have to give much more airtime to the views of Ross and Clinton. In late spring, therefore, Ross was given a promotion from the State Department to a much more expansive role at the White House itself.

The diplomacy camp, however, still had one important person on its side: the president. Obama was personally dedicated to diplomacy and was unlikely to allow himself to be pushed around so ungallantly during the first few weeks of his term. He had a larger vision, one that encompassed not just dialogue with Tehran but also a broader realignment of American interests in the Middle East. Though he knew full well that he had to tread carefully around America's traditional pro-Israel sensitivities, he was still determined to shake a few trees.

ᘓ

In June 2009 the president delivered a landmark speech in Cairo. Calling for a "new beginning" between the United States and the Muslim world, he argued that the time had come for mutual understanding and dialogue, for diplomacy with Iran, and for freedom for the Palestinians—all things that entrenched interests in Washington did not want to hear. Though his words and his tone were positive and full of generalities, those who closely followed U.S. policy in the Middle East saw that he was heading for a titanic confrontation with Israel and its legions of American supporters.

And a confrontation was exactly what he got. For the remainder of the spring and summer, as the Obama administration made it clear that Israeli-Palestinian peace-making was going to be a high priority, the Netanyahu government made it equally clear that it felt neutralizing the "Iranian threat" should be the top priority—even, arguably, the *only* priority. The pro-Israel lobby in Washington, AIPAC, amplified Netanyahu's message by advocating forcefully for a fresh round of sanctions against Iran. The whole thing came to a head on May 18, when Netanyahu came to Washington for his first face-to-face meeting with Obama. The body language at that encounter was conspicuously frosty, and at the press conference that followed, both men struggled to put a positive spin on the meeting. Netanyahu deflected from the Palestinian issue and insisted that the far more urgent threat to world peace came from Iran. He also emphasized the importance of a tight, clear time frame for U.S.-Iran negotiations, implying that there should be a firm deadline, after which the talks should be declared a failure and more aggressive options could be pursued. Obama, by contrast, used the press conference to stress the importance of not placing "an artificial deadline" on talks with Iran. "I don't think anybody in the international community, or anybody in the Middle East for that matter, would expect that thirty years of antagonism and suspicion between Iran and the United States would be resolved in four months," he said. Netanyahu responded by acidly rephrasing Obama's words: "I very much appreciate, Mr. President, your firm commitment to ensure that Iran does not develop a nuclear military capability, and also your statement that you're leaving all options on the table."

Following the meeting, Obama, as was his wont, tried to split the difference between the U.S. and Israeli positions. Acknowledging that the window for diplomacy with Iran could not remain open indefinitely, he agreed, informally, to give the process until the end of the year. This was a longer window than the Israelis had hoped for, but they did not complain. Fundamentally, they had received what they wanted, which was a commitment to the principle of a deadline and the adoption of Ross's "dual track" as something resembling official White House policy. The only real concession to diplomacy was the slightly extended timeline—nine months rather than three or four.

For the Obama administration, this timeline had a number of important advantages. For starters, it gave the United States a chance to observe the results of the Iranian presidential election, which was scheduled for June 12. Analysts were predicting the incumbent Ahmadinejad would face a tough challenge from reformists, and the administration reasoned that it was worth waiting to see how it played out. The extended timeline also gave Obama a chance to focus on his domestic agenda, which was formidable. The president had come into office promising a universal health care law, an economic stimulus and recovery plan, and a major overhaul of Bush-era tax policy, and already by the spring of 2009, he was running into vigorous opposition from congressional Republicans. He no doubt reasoned that victories on health care and the stimulus would put him in a stronger position on Iran later in the year. As a victorious president—the man who had given the American people the right to see a doctor when they were sick, rescued the economy from the brink of collapse, and made good on his promise to bring "change" to the culture of Washington—he could then face down Netanyahu and move on to his signature foreign policy success: creating peace in the Middle East.

Alas for the best-laid plans of mice and men.

☙

On June 12, 2009, Iranians went to the polls in one of the most fiercely contested presidential elections in their country's history. And what initially appeared to be an upset victory for the reformist candidate, Mir Hossein Mousavi, turned into a fiasco. As soon as the results were announced, indicating a 63–34 margin of victory for the president, Mousavi insisted the election had been rigged, and thousands of his supporters poured into the streets demanding a recount. Within days, those thousands turned into tens of thousands. And even after the numbers on the street dwindled, the most determined demonstrators fought a weeks-long running battle with security forces—some of it violent and all of it documented by cell phone video, Facebook, and Twitter for the benefit of the world.

U.S. media openly cheered these events in Iran, treating viewers to twenty-four-hour coverage of what they sometimes described as a "second Iranian revolution." On June 16, two days into the disturbances, Secretary of State Clinton asked Twitter to keep its networks up and running for the duration of the crisis. (The site had been planning routine maintenance shutdowns.) And a week later Obama himself condemned what he called Iran's "violence against innocent civilians." Within days, most of Iran's peaceful demonstrators stayed home, unwilling to take part in anything that appeared, however indirectly, to be instigated by foreign powers.[*] They were replaced by a smaller, harder core of disgruntled young men who had no such qualms. On television, Iranians saw thugs burning pictures of the ayatollah and shouting "Death to Khamenei" and "Death to the Islamic Republic"—sentiments much more radical than the average Iranian was prepared to entertain. And on Twitter, anonymous Iranians urged youth to congregate at specific times and places in the city for aggressive confrontations with the authorities. But it was not always clear who was sending these tweets and from where.

Iran's supreme leader came to believe the West was taking advantage of the disturbances to foment revolution. In his speeches, the ayatollah blamed the West for the *fetneh*—the "sedition"—unfolding on Iran's streets. In one of his fieriest sermons, he blasted Obama for his condemnation of Iran, accusing the U.S. president of being two-faced. "On the one hand, [the Americans] . . . express their respect for the Islamic Republic and for reestablishment of ties, and on the other hand they make these remarks. Which one of these remarks are we supposed to believe? Inside the country, their agents were activated. Vandalism started. Sabotaging and setting fires on the streets started. Some shops were looted. They wanted to create chaos."

Publicly, few noticed—since there had yet to be any official diplomacy between the two countries—but the results of this standoff were tragic. One of Obama's last actions before the election had been to write a secret letter to Khamenei, informing him that the United States would welcome genuine dialogue and engagement with Iran and offering the possibility of "cooperation in regional and bilateral relations." Remarkably, Khamenei had written back, with enough constructive comments that Obama had written a second letter in early June. Then all hell had broken loose.

It took years for the full truth about the 2009 election crisis to emerge, but when it did, the Iranian version of events did not sound quite as paranoid as it had initially appeared. A study released in 2010 revealed that the overwhelming majority of tweets sent by "Iranians" in the days following the election had actually been sent by users based overseas, who had temporarily changed their Twitter locations to "Tehran." These tweets— often full of wishful thinking about the size of crowds or the reactions of authorities—were then retweeted thousands of times around the world by excited Iranian exiles, forming a giant feedback loop picked up by Western

---

[*] I do not wish to imply that this is the only reason the demonstrations petered out. There were many reasons, not least the heavy-handed repression of the Iranian government. But there was a growing perception among Iranians that the opposition had failed to produce convincing evidence for its claims of election fraud and a popular distaste for the increasingly radical tactics of some hardcore demonstrators.

TV stations that were starved for "on-the-ground" information from Iran. But the actual penetration of Twitter in Iran was close to zero in 2009—most Iranians relied on text messages or old-fashioned word of mouth for their information. What this meant in practice was that the millions of Iranians who owned satellite dishes were watching their own "revolution" on TV rather than actually venturing outside to join it.

There was more interesting news where that came from. In March 2012, Lesley Stahl of *60 Minutes* asked Israel's former Mossad chief, Meir Dagan, "Has Israel done anything to encourage, help, support the youth opposition groups that have been marching against the regime?" Dagan broke into a smirk, paused, and eventually replied, "Let's ignore the question."

ଔ

Iran's election crisis created divisions among the country's leaders, and for several months this weakened Iran's ability to engage constructively with the United States. But in many ways, the real domestic crisis in the summer of 2009—the one that made the biggest difference to U.S.-Iranian diplomacy—took place not in Tehran but in Washington. Over the course of that summer, the Republican opposition subjected Obama's domestic legislative agenda to a merciless bombardment, steadily unraveling the image of Obama as a messiah-like figure presiding over a generational transformation in American politics. Congressional opposition enthusiastically watered down the stimulus package. Health care turned into a fiasco, as the thousand-page bill came under attack from all sides. During the summer recess, constituents angry about excessive government spending shouted at legislators. And a new pressure group, the Tea Party, tapped into the conservative discontent. The administration felt it lacked the political space to launch a major diplomatic initiative with Iran—and anyway, Iran was going through so much turmoil of its own that it made sense to wait. This was probably the right decision politically, but it also meant Obama set himself up for a significant setback in what he had hoped would be his signature foreign policy success.

By the time September rolled around, Obama was a fundamentally weakened president. And politically, time was running out for diplomacy with Iran. The administration had informally promised Israel it would give the "diplomatic track" only until the end of the year before moving to the "sanctions track." But a full six months had passed since Obama's historic new year's message to Iran, and the two countries had yet to have a single meeting or face-to-face discussion. In practice, even if diplomacy began right away, it would now have a window of only three to four months—

much too short to produce any meaningful results. It was exactly what the Israelis had hoped for.

In Washington, momentum for sanctions increased. Republicans, scenting weakness, accused the president of not having done enough to support protesters in Iran. Israel also took advantage of the changed atmosphere, arguing more vocally that Iran was in no position to engage in serious diplomacy and that it was time to move to the punitive track. On September 10, at a National Jewish Leadership Advocacy Day on Iran, more than three hundred of America's most prominent Jewish community leaders, together with congressional leaders, argued that it was time to "begin the process of tightening the screws on Tehran." The White House, worried about losing critical Jewish electoral support, expanded Dennis Ross's role even further, turning him into an informal liaison to the Jewish community, who could communicate just how serious the administration was about preventing Iran from obtaining a nuclear weapon.

The tipping point for the White House was its abandonment by Democratic lawmakers. In July, Rep. Howard Berman (D-CA), chair of the House Foreign Affairs Committee and one of the fiercest pro-Israel advocates on Capitol Hill, signaled that the time for diplomacy with Iran was nearly over (even though no actual diplomacy had yet taken place). "While it is important to pursue engagement," said Berman, "it is also critical that these efforts be time-limited, and that the administration be prepared to try a different approach." In rapid succession, dozens of other lawmakers joined Berman in pushing the Israeli line that time was running out.

☙

In the summer of 2009, away from headlines about the disputed election, Iran quietly approached the IAEA, asking to purchase fuel rods for its civilian nuclear reactors at Bushehr and Tehran—a fairly routine request that was unrelated to the technology for bomb making.* Without these fuel rods, the Tehran Research Reactor was in danger of shutting down, potentially leaving 850,000 cancer patients without access to radiation therapy. The Obama administration, sensing an opportunity, offered Iran a deal—a complicated arrangement in which Iran's stockpile of low-enriched uranium (LEU)

---

* Iran's supply of fuel, purchased legally from Argentina in the early 1990s, was expected to run out some time in 2012. Because of the intense public scrutiny of its nuclear program, Iran had hoped to replace this fuel with its own indigenously enriched uranium. But after years of work and considerable effort put into nuclear research, Iran had managed to enrich its supply of uranium to only 3.5 percent—much less than the 19.75 percent required to power a civilian reactor (not to mention the 90 percent required to produce a bomb).

would be shipped to a neutral country (perhaps Russia or France), enriched to 19.75 percent there, and converted to inert fuel rods that would then be sent back to Iran to keep the country's civilian energy reactors running. The idea behind this "fuel swap" was to test Iran's intentions. If Iran was *truly* interested in nuclear technology only for peaceful purposes, it should have no objection to sending its LEU abroad for reprocessing. The Iranians had some technical concerns about how exactly the fuel swap would proceed, but they indicated, through back-channel communications, that they considered it a positive starting point for discussion.

On October 1, 2009, Iran and the members of the P5+1 negotiating group—the United States, Russia, China, Britain, France, and Germany*— met in Geneva to talk specifics. It was the first time the United States and Iran had a face-to-face meeting since Obama's historic "unclenched fist" speech eight months earlier, and both sides were clearly relieved to be talking. In addition to the multilateral P5+1 framework, the U.S. and Iranian representatives (William Burns and Said Jalili) withdrew into a private, bilateral discussion that lasted forty-five minutes—a meeting that all its participants described as surprisingly constructive. The two sides agreed, in principle, that Iran would hand over 1,200 kilograms of LEU in exchange for fuel rods, and that there would be a follow-up meeting later in the month to iron out technical details. At the press conference afterward, all participants expressed their satisfaction with how smoothly the meeting had gone and how quickly they had reached the broad outlines of an agreement. The Iranians even spoke of the Geneva discussion as the beginning of a process of "good talks that will be a framework for better talks."

The optimism didn't last. During the two weeks that followed, efforts on Capitol Hill to pass sanctions against Iran intensified, which was increasingly reflected in the official U.S. position. "In the absence of any significant progress," Secretary Clinton said five days before the follow-up meeting in Vienna, "we will be seeking to rally international opinion behind additional sanctions." The Iranians made it clear they did not appreciate this kind of threat just before a meeting. And in Vienna, the discussion degenerated into a familiar pattern of accusations and disagreements. The Iranians strenuously objected to the proposal that their entire stockpile of LEU be shipped out to Russia in one batch—concerned that the conversion process

---

* The P5+1 was an informal mechanism for negotiating with Iran, and the successor to the original three-way effort led by Britain, France, and Germany since 2003. With the addition of the United States, China, and Russia to the negotiations in 2006, the group now in effect included the five permanent members of the UN Security Council, plus Germany (hence the name P5+1). The idea was that if all six of these states could work together on doing a deal with Iran, there would be no disagreements over whether to repeal or maintain UN Security Council resolutions.

was likely to take at least twelve months, and possibly as long as two years, leaving Iran with little political leverage—and suggested it be shipped out in smaller batches. As negotiations faltered, the Iranians indicated that they were still open, in principle, to a fuel swap, but they would need a few extra days to discuss technicalities before they could commit to a final agreement.

For the United States, this was totally unacceptable. Back in Washington, domestic political pressure—both from Congress and from the pro-Israel lobby—was reaching a fever pitch. Spokespeople on almost every national media outlet accused Iran of playing for time. The usual chorus of voices unfriendly to Iran, who had been impatiently tapping their feet and allowing Obama to have his moment of diplomacy, now shouted to the rafters that "diplomacy had been tried and failed" and it was time to move on to the serious business of punishing Iran. Secretary Clinton agreed. "This is a pivotal moment for Iran," she said. "We urge Iran to accept the agreement as proposed and we will not alter it and we will not wait forever."

When Iran failed to deliver an immediate, unambiguous answer to the Geneva proposal, U.S. media swiftly described it as a "rejection"—or more charitably, as the unfortunate result of "infighting" in the regime. Washington then refused to allow Iran any more time to consider the proposal, and history—or at least the version of history put out by the United States—recorded that Iran had said no to the Geneva proposal.

∞

And that was the end of the diplomacy. Forty-five minutes of face-to-face talks. Two short meetings. Under a mountain of domestic and Israeli political pressure, the Obama administration had turned its historic opening to Iran into a take-it-or-leave-it offer. After thirty years of enmity, a few additional days of technical talks had been ruled out as a waste of time. After all the talk of "unclenched fists" and "honest engagement," the door to the diplomacy track had been slammed shut after just two short rounds of talks. In November 2009, eight months after Obama's historic video message to the Iranian people (and one month before the unofficial "deadline" he had agreed to with Netanyahu), the White House was forced to "acknowledge"—to the visible satisfaction of Israel—that the diplomacy track had failed and it was time to move on to sanctions.

Initially, the administration hoped to assemble an internationally led sanctions effort, conducted through the UN, targeting senior elements of the Iranian regime—so as not to bring undue pain to the Iranian people. ("We have never been attracted to the idea of trying to get the whole world to cordon off their economy," said one administration official.) But White

House control of the process slipped away as Congress—under intense lobbying from pro-Israel groups such as AIPAC and the Israel Project— demanded stiff, unilateral, American-led sanctions, of the kind that would cripple Iran's economy and drain the lifeblood out of the Islamic Republic. In Israel, Prime Minister Netanyahu said the time had come for "effective, biting sanctions that curtail the import and export of oil into Iran," and in Washington, Congress was quick to oblige. On December 15 the House of Representatives—by an overwhelming vote of 412 to 12—passed a bill that severely restricted Iran's ability to import gasoline. Called, in its initial incarnation, the Iran Refined Petroleum Sanctions Act (IRPSA), its main provision was that the United States would subject to financial penalties any company, anywhere in the world, that sold gasoline to Iran.

IRPSA, much like the ILSA legislation that had been on the books since 1996, was an "extraterritorial" sanction, directed not at American companies (which already couldn't do business with Iran) but at foreign entities. Like ILSA, it gave European and Asian companies a stark choice between trading with Iran and trading with the United States (an easy choice for most). Unlike ILSA, however, IRPSA was aimed not just at the profit margins of multinational corporations but also at a civilian resource vital to the functioning of the Iranian economy. Iran, despite its oil wealth, suffered from a chronic shortage of refineries and was therefore reliant on imports for more than 40 percent of its gasoline. If signed into law, IRPSA would choke off this vital resource, setting into motion a devastating domino effect of inflation, consumer hardship, and fuel shortages for the Iranian public.

A few months earlier Obama might have resisted this fierce congressional pressure, but in December 2009 he had very little room for maneuver. His health care bill—the flagship domestic initiative on which he had staked much of his presidency—had stalled badly, and he desperately needed votes in Congress to push it through. AIPAC, and its many allies in Congress, knew full well that the president wouldn't sacrifice a victory on health care for the sake of Iran. Getting health care passed, in the words of one Senate staffer, had become an "existential issue for the White House," which gave Israel's friends in Congress considerable leverage over the administration. On January 29, 2010, the Senate passed its own version of IRPSA, setting in motion a legislative steamroller that the White House would find difficult to resist in the coming months.

At this point, it is worth pausing to consider, without hyperbole or undue emotionalism, the influence of Israel over the American legislative process. Although few Americans are ever made aware of it, the U.S. Congress, since at least the 1970s, has acted as something of a nerve center for pro-Israel advocacy in the United States. Of the 535 members of Congress, probably no more than a dozen have made it there without enormous campaign contributions from AIPAC and affiliated organizations.[*] And there has always been an unspoken understanding on Capitol Hill that voting against Israeli interests is tantamount to committing political suicide. AIPAC's former director, Steven Rosen, once boasted that "in 24 hours, we could have the signatures of seventy senators on [a] napkin"—and if anything, this was probably an understatement. It is common knowledge in Washington that if AIPAC sponsors a bill, that bill will pass, swiftly, with margins like 99–0 in the Senate and 412–12 in the House. And it will generally have at least three hundred "co-sponsors," eager lawmakers scrambling to demonstrate their unquenchable love of Israel. As for that small handful of legislators who vote against AIPAC, they quickly find, in the next election cycle, that they are up against well-funded primary opponents, who attack them for their lack of support for Israel.

In 2010 one of the most commonly heard complaints about the American political system was that it was systematically gridlocked—mired in excessive partisanship and bickering on such a scale that it was fast approaching paralysis. And yet few Americans noticed that, in at least one area, perfect harmony prevailed. Remarkably, Democrats and Republicans—who spent their waking lives at one another's throats, unable to agree on even the most basic, urgently needed legislation that was clearly in America's best interests (such as raising the debt ceiling)—would suddenly come together in a show of unity on matters that were important to AIPAC. It was this phenomenon, more than any other, that drove the White House to abandon diplomatic outreach to Iran in 2009 and 2010. And it was this phenomenon that gave Prime Minister Netanyahu extraordinary leverage over Barack Obama.

By the end of Obama's first year, Netanyahu had given up on playing nice and overtly suggested that if the United States was not serious about confronting Iran, Israel was prepared to take matters into its own hands. On its face, this thinly veiled threat of war was nothing unusual—Israel had been hinting at military action against Iran for years—but at the beginning of 2010 the message had a coordinated quality. Major U.S. newspaper columnists, citing "unnamed sources" and "senior Israeli officials," penned articles hinting that Israel could not "wait forever" and might feel compelled to "go it alone" if something was not done to assuage its concerns. In fact, Israel was in no position to go to war against Iran. Its own generals routinely expressed their opposition to such a rash course of action. More-

---

[*] AIPAC does not give money to political campaigns. It does, however, analyze the voting habits of lawmakers and shares this information with its one hundred thousand members—who in turn give money to candidates directly or through a myriad of pro-Israel political action committees.

over, its own intelligence agencies routinely reported that Iran's nuclear program was rudimentary, posing no real threat to Israel. Israel's entire security establishment—much like America's—agreed that Iran's nuclear program was basically civilian in nature and that Iran's leaders had shown no signs of wanting to build a bomb. There was thus no real urgency—or even reason—for going to war. But these assessments rarely made it into American media stories.

Instead, what took hold was an atmosphere of constant speculation about Israel's intention to go to war against Iran. This, in turn, served a useful purpose for Israel: it made it possible to convince audiences that were traditionally squeamish about aggressive foreign policy tactics that there was now a compelling need to increase the pressure on Iran and thus "buy time" with the Israelis. Mainstream European politicians, for example, increasingly argued that severe economic penalties on Iran were needed—if only to prevent the ghastly possibility of an all-out war in the Middle East.[*] In the United States as well, the liberal intelligentsia was subjected to this line of reasoning. "Nobody likes the idea of sanctions," pundits routinely said, "but they are infinitely preferable to war." Democratic politicians made the same argument in *The New York Times* and *The New Yorker*. Dispassionate analysis might have suggested that Israel had no intention of going to war with Iran, and that the war talk was just a tool to concentrate minds on the need for stiffer sanctions—but this point rarely seemed to get any airtime. Instead, at the end of 2009, a sort of hysteria emerged around the "Iranian nuclear crisis" as well as the convenient narrative that sanctions were a way to prevent war.

There was, of course, another way to prevent war, and that was to do what Obama had originally wanted to do: engage Iran in serious, sustained diplomacy. But increasingly, this was a political nonstarter in Washington. By the beginning of 2010, in fact, any serious White House attempt to talk to Iran and find a resolution would open the administration to accusations that it was "soft on Iran" or "insensitive to Israel's concerns." Moreover, after the recent horrific experiences in Iraq, Americans had no real appetite for "another war in the Middle East." This left sanctions as the third option

---

[*] Without question, European leaders were sincere when they presented this argument. But there was also another motivation at work. Memories of the bitter feud between the United States and Europe over the Iraq war in 2003 were still raw, and no one in Europe wanted to repeat this experience. The sanctions being pushed by the U.S. Congress, after all, were probably going to affect European companies more than any others. For European leaders, opposing these sanctions would have meant standing up for their own countries' business interests, yes, but it would also have initiated economic warfare between the United States and Europe. At a time when the P5+1 was trying to present a unified face to Iran, such a development would have been disastrously embarrassing—and a huge political victory for Iran.

and, in a way, the default. In 2010 the consensus was growing that sanctions were the "least bad" or "most politically painless" option for dealing with Iran. And the Israelis knew it. They knew that every time they raised the temperature with Iran and warned that "time was running out," the pressure would be on the United States and the West to "do something" to prevent conflict. And increasingly, the only "something" that could be done was to impose more sanctions.

Lost in all this was a rather basic question: why weren't Israel's leaders more supportive of diplomacy? After all, if the Israelis were *genuinely* concerned about the prospect of an Iranian nuclear bomb in their neighborhood, they would surely support—passionately, loudly, energetically—a diplomatic process that might actually reduce the likelihood of that happening. In fact, they probably would have *championed* the P5+1 process more vigorously than anyone else. But this was not what they were doing. Instead, they were hinting at war and doing everything possible to *prevent* negotiations between Iran and the West.

For Israel, the goal had never been to prevent Iran from obtaining a nuclear bomb (something they knew Iranian leaders had little interest in). The goal had been to prevent a thawing of relations between Iran and the United States. Although Israeli leaders spoke in apocalyptic terms about the "existential" threat they faced from the possibility of mad ayatollahs armed with nukes, privately, away from the cameras and the megaphones, it was obvious that they viewed closer relations between Tehran and Washington as a much bigger threat to them, because of the challenge it posed to Israel's supremacy in the region. And they had discovered that constantly hinting at war was an excellent way to get the West to punish Iran with further sanctions—thus adding to Iran's isolation and making a historic reconciliation with Washington less likely than ever.

By creating a climate of constant crisis—in which diplomacy was seen as too slow, too uncertain, and too politically unpopular—Israel left the United States with only two real options: war or sanctions. And despite the *public* impression that it was preparing to launch a war, Israel was always much more interested in sanctions. By pushing Washington into a policy of stiffer sanctions, Israel reasoned, Iran's isolation would increase—its economy would be eviscerated and cut off from the world—and the climate of antagonism between the United States and Iran would continue unabated.

And this was exactly what happened. "As Iran's leaders continue to ignore their obligations, there should be no doubt," said Obama in his State of the Union address in January 2010. "They, too, will face growing consequences. That is a promise." It was a striking change of tone from his inauguration address a year earlier.

By February 2010, Iran read the writing on the wall. Recognizing that the United States and Israel were trying to unite the world around sanctions, and that the diplomatic track was now firmly dead and buried, the Iranians launched a major push to enrich uranium to 19.75 percent. Until this point, Iran had avoided taking this provocative step, first attempting to purchase fuel rods from the IAEA, then considering the Geneva proposal. Now, however, Iranian leaders concluded it was pointless to wait for the outside world to supply the country with fuel. "We cannot leave hospitals and patients desperately waiting for radioisotopes," said Iran's ambassador to the IAEA, Ali Asghar Soltanieh. At the same time, however, Iran indicated that it was still open to finding a compromise. The head of Iran's Atomic Energy Organization, Ali Akbar Salehi, said Iran was prepared to accept a deal that would cap its enrichment at 5 percent in return for fuel rods.

This offer never received serious consideration.* In early 2010, Washington was already laying the groundwork for sanctions and, from all indications, was no longer interested in getting distracted by the pesky business of actually talking to Iran. The administration's biggest fear at this point was that Iran would divide the international community, by appearing to be flexible enough that Russia and China would waver and backpedal their support for UN sanctions.

The White House sanctions strategy in early 2010 was thus twofold. It involved promoting the stiff, extraterritorial gasoline bill that AIPAC had pushed, which was now wending its way through Congress. And at the UN, it involved promoting a more restrained form of sanction targeted at Iran's nuclear program and at arms sales to the Islamic Republic. Russia and China were both lukewarm about sanctions, and the administration's biggest challenge was finding ways to bring them on board. It promised to give Putin measures he had long sought—ending NATO expansion, scrapping a proposed missile shield over eastern Europe, negotiating a new disarmament treaty. And to bring China around, Saudi Arabia (a country equally keen to reduce Iran's influence) promised to increase its oil shipments to Beijing. In March 2010, Congress kicked everything up a notch by presenting the final

---

* The proposal, put forward by Russia in the summer of 2011, included a step-by-step road map to address both Iran and the West's concerns. Iran would have to allow full IAEA supervision, implement the NPT's Additional Protocol (an optional clause agreeing to more thorough inspections), stop producing highly enriched uranium (HEU), limit LEU to 5 percent, stop installing new centrifuges, concentrate all its enrichment activity at one site, address IAEA concerns about a "possible military dimension" to its program, and suspend enrichment temporarily. In exchange, the P5+1 would recognize Iran's legal right to enrich and would suspend sanctions. Iran indicated it was willing to talk, but the West declined to discuss the proposal.

version of its sanctions bill to the president—sending the message to Russia and China that time was running out for them to get on board. In March, both Moscow and Beijing indicated they were prepared to sign on to the UN sanctions resolution. And since Europe and the Arab states were now fully committed to the sanctions track, all the pieces finally appeared to be in place. The White House, Congress, and the international community were now united behind punishing Iran for its "refusal" to compromise on its nuclear program—a rare moment of unanimity that was hailed as a foreign policy triumph for the Obama administration.

Whether it was, in fact, a triumph was debatable, given that after just twelve months in office, Obama had all but abandoned his historic olive branch to Tehran and his attempts to realign America's relationship with the Middle East. But in the traditional, Israel-friendly universe of commentary and analysis that dominated Washington—a universe that believed the weakening and crippling of Iran should always be the ultimate goal of American foreign policy—Obama's approach to Iran was hailed as a resounding success. He had managed to do something the Bush administration had never been able to do. He had "united the world" and "sent a message to Iran" that there was no more time for "stalling tactics." And that was all that really mattered.

ରଙ

If there was any doubt about Washington's lack of sincerity about doing a deal with Iran, it was exposed for all the world to see in May 2010, when Brazil's president, Luiz Inácio Lula da Silva, and Turkey's prime minister, Recep Tayyip Erdogan, emerged from a marathon, eighteen-hour negotiating session with Ahmadinejad in Tehran. The three men clasped one another's fists in the air and smiled amid flashbulbs at the extraordinary piece of news that they had achieved a deal. The document Iran signed was virtually identical to the one that had been put before it in Geneva: it would allow Iranian uranium to be taken out of the country to be reprocessed into fuel rods. But Washington immediately disparaged it.* State Department spokesman P. J. Crowley told reporters the deal did not represent "anything

---

* The Iranians had even agreed to send out their 1200kg of LEU in one batch, thus dropping the objection they had raised in Vienna. In order to secure Iran's agreement, Turkey and Brazil had come up with some basic safeguards. Specifically, the LEU would be sent to Turkey, where it would remain under IAEA seal until Iran received its fuel rods—a process that would take no more than twelve months. These simple technical guarantees, it turned out, were enough to reassure Tehran and secure its agreement.

fundamentally new" and that the United States was "skeptical" about its significance. Within hours, the Obama administration pushed ahead on both
UN sanctions and the unilateral congressional gasoline sanctions, with a
speed and swiftness that caused considerable irritation in Brazil and Turkey.

Internationally, a wide cross-section of commentators and political figures urged the United States not to be too hasty in dismissing the Tehran
Declaration. Brazil's foreign minister, Celso Amorim, in a blistering interview with the *Financial Times,* made no effort to disguise his frustration.
"We got our fingers burned by doing things that everybody said were helpful and in the end we found that some people could not take 'yes' for an
answer." This phrase—and the unflattering light in which it painted the
United States—became the political buzz-phrase of the season. Mohamed
El Baradei accused the United States of "not accepting yes for an answer"
and of creating a "major rift" between the countries of the developed and
developing worlds.

In the midst of all the political gamesmanship, there was an inescapable fact: Brazil and Turkey had demonstrated that a solution was possible.
For several months they had conducted sustained, conscientious diplomacy,
complete with a dozen visits back and forth between Erdogan and Ahmadinejad, at least forty telephone calls, and two full days of intensive face-
to-face meetings. In the process, they had proved that serious, sincere talks
with Iran could produce results. This was something the West had never
actually tried—or, rather, had tried only with its fingers crossed behind its
back, hoping Iran would say no and prove to be the intransigent party.

The showdown came three weeks later, when the UN Security Council
met to consider the sanctions resolution that Washington had pushed so
hard over the past months. To demonstrate its fury, the United States made
a point of delaying the official P5+1 response to the Tehran Declaration
until just five hours before the council was scheduled to vote—ensuring
that Brazil and Turkey would have no time to put together a coherent counter. The result was an uncomfortable session around the big round table in
New York. Brazil and Turkey voted against their American ally. Lebanon
abstained. And the remaining seven nations—including Bosnia, Gabon,
and Uganda—went along with the United States. In the afternoon hours of
June 9, 2010, the council adopted Resolution 1929, imposing sanctions on
Iran for its "failure" to comply with previous Security Council resolutions.

Two weeks later, the U.S. Congress passed its own sanctions legislation
and sent it to the president's desk. In addition to imposing gasoline sanctions, this new version of IRPSA, which was now renamed the Comprehensive Iran Sanctions and Divestment Act (CISADA), included measures

designed to disrupt Iran's access to international banking—such as sanctions on the Central Bank of Iran and on foreign banks that did business with it. The vote in the House was 408–8, and in the Senate 99–0.

Soon thereafter a cloud of thick brown smoke descended on Tehran. Forbidden by sanctions to import gasoline, Iranians were forced to make do with an emergency supply of locally produced fuel containing ten times the number of contaminants—and the results were catastrophic. Hospitals reported a 40 percent increase in patients with breathing difficulties. Almost universally, residents suffered from itchy eyes, tears, and coughing. On at least three occasions, the government was forced to declare impromptu national holidays in order to compel people to stay home and avoid driving. It even flew crop-dusting planes through the clouds, spraying water and hoping to alter the wind patterns over Tehran. Under the best of circumstances, Tehran was famed for its air pollution. But the emergency situation created by U.S. sanctions took the problem to a level never before seen in modern history. "What people in Tehran inhaled in the past few weeks was just poison," said an adviser to Tehran's mayor after the worst of the crisis was over.

❦

By mid-2010 the fault lines were drawn. No mainstream voice in Washington spoke any more of diplomacy. Technically, theoretically, the Obama administration maintained the fiction that it was pursuing a "dual track" approach with Iran, but in reality, it was pursuing only one track—sanctions for the sake of sanctions. And there was nothing Iran could do about it.

Sanctions, in fact, were the tip of the iceberg. Over the course of 2010, it was revealed that Washington's "punitive track" against Iran was far more elaborate and extensive than anyone had realized. In the lawless eastern deserts of Iran, an al-Qaeda-linked terrorist group by the name of Jundallah blew up mosques and assassinated Revolutionary Guard officers—killing, in one particularly devastating pair of suicide attacks, twenty-seven people at a mosque in the city of Zahedan. A later investigation by ABC News revealed that Jundallah "has been secretly encouraged and advised by American officials" operating through tribal channels in Pakistan; a subsequent report by Seymour Hersh in *The New Yorker* contained similar revelations. In January 2012 a well-sourced article in *Foreign Policy* described how members of Israel's Mossad had posed as CIA agents to recruit Jundallah to carry out attacks in Iran.

There was more where that came from. In January 2010, Masoud Ali Mohammadi, a professor of neutron physics at Tehran University, was killed when a remote-controlled bomb attached to a motorcycle blew up in front of his house in north Tehran. Later that year two more nuclear scientists—Fereidun Abbasi and Majid Shahriari—were similarly targeted for assassination. (Abbasi survived, but both he and his wife were badly injured.) In both cases, the assassins made use of a novel tactic: speeding through Tehran's rush-hour traffic on motorcycles and slapping magnetic "sticky bombs" onto the sides of cars being driven by their victims. In July 2011 a fourth nuclear scientist, thirty-five-year-old Dariush Rezai, was shot dead in front of his daughter's nursery school—again by gunmen on motorcycles. And in November 2011 a pair of mysterious blasts—both so powerful that they were reported by residents living many miles away—shook up Iran's military establishment. The first, on November 12, at a Revolutionary Guard munitions depot west of Tehran, killed twenty Guards, including the head of Iran's ballistics missile program. The second, on November 28, badly damaged the uranium enrichment facility near Isfahan.

In all these cases, experts unanimously pointed to Israel as the culprit. An investigation by NBC News—relying on information provided by U.S. officials—revealed that Mossad had financed, trained, and armed MeK assassins to carry out the operations on Iranian soil. And Israel did not deny the reports. Following the November 2011 Isfahan blast, Israel's intelligence minister, Dan Meridor, told reporters that when it came to dealing with the Iranian nuclear issue, "there are countries who impose economic sanctions and there are countries who act in other ways."

Those "other ways," apparently, were not limited to explosive devices. In the summer of 2010 a deadly computer virus, nicknamed Stuxnet, was wreaking havoc on Iran's uranium enrichment facility in Natanz. Sneaked into Iran on a memory stick in early 2009 and designed to manipulate the speed of spinning centrifuges, Stuxnet had caused Natanz's centrifuges to break down and spin out of control. It had taken the Iranians nearly a year to pinpoint what was causing the problem, and they even fired the head of their Atomic Energy Organization over the matter. In November 2010, Iran's president was forced to admit that "they succeeded in creating problems for a limited number of our centrifuges with the software they had installed." Western intelligence suggested that Stuxnet had forced offline as many as 1,000 of Iran's 4,700 centrifuges. Overwhelmingly, the evidence pointed to the United States and Israel as the perpetrators. Experts said the code was far too complex to be anything other than "the work of a nation-state." And when they were asked about the origin of Stuxnet, a number of Israeli officials were reported to have "broken into wide smiles."

Then there was the drone. In December 2011 an RQ-170 "unmanned aerial vehicle" flying over Iranian airspace on a spying mission was brought

down—apparently intact and still bearing most of its encrypted code—
and promptly paraded on Iranian television. At first, U.S. officials poured
scorn on Iran's trophy kill, claiming the Iranians had "lucked out" when
U.S. pilots "lost control" of the RQ-170—and that it had simply crash-
landed inside Iran. But closer investigation suggested Iranians might have
actually jammed the drone's GPS signals and tricked it into landing safely
inside Iran. It then emerged that Iran had earlier shot down two additional
American spy drones—just the latest indication of a long-running secret
war being conducted by the United States in Iran. In April 2012 the *Washington Post* revealed that since early 2009, CIA drones had "scoured dozens
of sites throughout Iran, making hundreds of passes over suspicious facilities." Some of these drones had flown as much as six hundred miles into
Iranian airspace.*

Two and a half years after President Obama had taken office pledging his commitment to "engagement," his administration had held a grand
total of forty-five minutes of direct, face-to-face discussions with Iran—
contrasted with months of sanctions, ultimatums, spy drones, assassinations, explosions, computer viruses, economic warfare, and oil embargoes.
Advocates of diplomacy described it as a fiasco, much worse than the
Republican approach of not talking to Iran in the first place. But perhaps
most remarkable about all these measures was the fact that they had been
unleashed in early 2009, when Obama was still quoting Persian poetry and
unclenching his fist in search of "a new way forward, based on mutual interest and mutual respect." From the perspective of Tehran, the continuity
in American foreign policy was remarkable. The Iranians concluded that
there was just something in the DNA of the American political system that
did not want to make peace with the Islamic Republic—a single-minded,
almost obsessive fixation with inflicting total defeat on Iran.

More generally, it was becoming obvious that the Israelis, from the very
beginning, had pursued a course of action guaranteed to bring about the
failure of U.S.-Iran diplomacy—intentionally poisoning the atmosphere,
setting tight deadlines, and creating unrealistic demands that Iran could
never agree to. And it was equally obvious that the administration had gone
along with it all, partly out of a desire to avoid a public spat with Israel,

---

* Lost amid all the hype about the disappeared drone was perhaps the most significant aspect of
the *Post* story: all those drone flyovers had given the United States unprecedented insight into the
state of the Iranian nuclear program—and the news was generally pretty good. "There is confidence that we would see activity indicating that a decision [to weaponize] had been made," said a
senior U.S. official. The White House was now surer than ever: "Iran's leaders have not decided to
build a nuclear weapon, and it would take Iran at least a year to do so if it were to launch a crash
program now." Along with Stuxnet and other sabotage efforts, this intelligence made it easier for
the United States to argue against a preemptive Israeli military strike.

and partly because Dennis Ross and his friends had convinced the White House that making an *apparent* good-faith attempt at diplomacy was a great way to rally the world to America's side. Administration officials, when presented with this suggestion, denied it. But the evidence was plain to see. In November 2010 the whistle-blowing site WikiLeaks published a trove of documents showing that the Obama administration, from its first few months in power, had approached diplomacy with Iran as a tactical device. *The New York Times*, examining the WikiLeaks evidence, concluded: "In essence, the administration expected its outreach to fail, but believed that it had to make a bona fide attempt in order to build support for tougher measures."

Here was perhaps the greatest tragedy of all. The Obama presidency had started as a redefining moment for America's relationship with the Muslim world, a once-in-a-generation opportunity to convince this troubled region that the United States was not a hostile power. In 2009 millions of people in the Middle East had been moved by Obama's historic speech in Cairo and had genuinely believed America was about to embark in a new direction, not just on Iran but also on the Arab-Israeli conflict. But they had discovered it was not to be. And this disillusionment—this fresh bout of cynicism—was, arguably, more damaging to America's reputation than anything that had happened during the Bush years. It left many of the region's citizens with the impression that America's posture toward them was structural, institutional—something beyond the power of any one president to change.[*]

⟶

In May 2011, Netanyahu made yet another high-drama trip to the United States, and this time he made no effort to disguise his leverage over the American president. At a deeply awkward White House press briefing, he lectured Obama on Israeli history and, looking directly at him, said Israel "cannot go back to the 1967 lines. These lines are indefensible." It was a reference to a speech Obama had made just a few days earlier, in which he had called for Israel to respect its UN-mandated 1967 borders during peace

---

[*] The proof was in the polls. In the spring of 2009 the Brookings survey of Arab public opinion found that 51 percent of respondents were "hopeful" about American policy in the Middle East, but in 2010, that number had dropped to just 16 percent—with 63 percent describing themselves as "discouraged." Even more striking, in 2009, only 29 percent of Arabs said that Iran's acquisition of nuclear weapons would be "positive" for the region. In 2010, that number had jumped to 57 percent. (https://www.brookings.edu/wp-content/uploads/2016/06/0805_arabic_opinion_poll _telhami.pdf.)

talks with the Palestinians—an uncontroversial restatement of more than forty years of White House policy. But such was Netanyahu's rising star in Washington that within hours, Obama had been raked across the coals for "creating daylight between America and Israel." Adding to the president's problems, congressional leaders then invited Netanyahu to address a special joint session of Congress for the second time in his career—an honor that in the past had been reserved for the likes of Winston Churchill and Nelson Mandela. During the speech, members of both political parties leaped to their feet and interrupted Netanyahu with twenty-nine deafening standing ovations—more than Obama had received during his last State of the Union address.

Netanyahu's triumphant reception in Washington gave Israel the confidence to speak out about Iran in terms even more strident than in the past. For the rest of 2011, Israeli leaders raised the volume on their warnings of the "Iranian nuclear danger," often indulging in apocalyptic language that came close to suggesting Iran should be wiped off the map. "Think Amalek," said one of Netanyahu's advisers when asked about the prime minister's attitude toward Iran—a reference to a biblical story (1 Samuel 15:3) in which the Israelites are commanded by God to "smite" and "utterly destroy" their enemies. Israel's deputy prime minister, Moshe Yaalon, was less dramatic, but much more direct. "We believe that in order to stop the Iranian military nuclear project," he said in December 2011, "the regime in Tehran should face a dilemma—whether to have a bomb or to survive."

In the United States, much of the media acted as stenographers, dutifully repeating the claim that Israel was on the verge of ordering a massive military strike, and that the only way to prevent such a calamity was for Washington to adopt a more forceful policy against Iran in order to "assuage" Israel's "concerns." In September 2010 the journalist Jeffrey Goldberg—a former corporal in the Israeli military who maintained close ties to the Israeli security establishment—penned a lengthy cover story in the *Atlantic* titled "The Point of No Return." The message relayed by Israeli officials through Goldberg was that if the Obama administration did not bomb Iran, Israel would be forced do so on its own. Adding to the impression of an impending crisis, Goldberg reported that his sources were telling him such an Israeli strike was likely to take place by July 2011.

Virtually unnoticed amid all this were sober, evidence-based assessments of the state of Iran's nuclear program. Russian prime minister Vladimir Putin, speaking to CNN's Larry King in December 2010, stated bluntly: "We have no grounds for suspecting Iran of seeking to possess nuclear weapons." For the most part, American pundits dismissed such statements as typical of a Russian foreign policy that had grown anti-American in recent years. But these same pundits rarely wondered why Russia should be so complacent about Iran's nuclear program. As a close neighbor of Iran, Russia had far more reason than either the United States or Israel to fear mad ayatollahs with nukes on their doorstep. And yet for whatever reason, Russian intelligence seemed confident this scenario was not very likely. Russia's political class, in turn, seemed to trust the intelligence it was being given.

A very different situation prevailed in the United States, where the serious and sober assessments made by America's own intelligence community were ritualistically ignored. Sixteen U.S. intelligence agencies had already declared they did not believe Iran was trying to build a bomb, and in 2011 they stood by that assessment. In recent months, in fact, U.S. intelligence officials said they had been "throwing everything they had at the Iranian program"—acquiring fresh radar imagery, eavesdropping on telephone conversations between Iranian officials, and flying dozens of spy drones over Iranian airspace, as well as debriefing IAEA inspectors following their experiences in Iran. The United States had even found ways to place clandestine ground sensors, which could detect electromagnetic signals associated with nuclear activity, near suspected Iranian facilities. And still after all this, the verdict was the same: Iran did not appear to be building a bomb.

Perhaps most interesting of all, Israel's intelligence assessments came to the same conclusion. In March 2012 *The New York Times* revealed that "even while Israeli leaders have been pushing for quick, aggressive action," Mossad actually "agrees with the American intelligence assessments" that Iran was not building a bomb. But this inconvenient fact rarely made it into the public discussion. Instead, what was given airtime was Israel's "concerns," its ticking "timeline," and its internal "debate" about whether to take military action.

What was also never pointed out was that Israel had a long history of hyping the Iranian threat. As far back as 1992, Netanyahu had warned that Iran would be armed with a nuclear bomb "within three to five years." In 1995, Israel claimed Iran would have a nuke "in more or less five years." The following year it told the UN Iran would be producing weapons "within eight years." The year after that, Israel "confidently" predicted an Iranian bomb by 2005. In 2003 and again in 2005, the chief of Mossad testified that Iran was nearing "the point of no return." By 2009, the same Mossad chief was saying, "the Iranians will have by 2014 a bomb ready to be used." And so the Israelis continued—always hinting strongly that their patience was not unlimited, and that military action was a serious possibility.

These constant warnings had created an atmosphere in which the world was always being told it was "running out of time" to prevent a "nuclear Iran." And by 2011 this atmosphere had turned into a convenient political

Running out of time: Israeli prime minister Binyamin
Netanyahu at the UN, September 2012. Israel's warnings
about Iran's nuclear program grew increasingly alarmist during
Obama's first term, making it hard for the White House to
pursue a serious strategy of diplomacy.

device. Every time Israel sensed the moment was right politically, it would
make a veiled threat of war—knowing that Obama would not want to be
seen publicly smacking down Israel. In order to be taken seriously, Israel
had to make these threats sound as credible as possible—and so American
audiences were regularly treated to terrifying headlines about "the looming possibility of war in the Middle East." This, in turn, drove the markets
crazy and wrought havoc with oil prices—something Obama could not
risk during a fragile economic recovery. Every time Israel hinted at war,
senior American officials would fly over to Jerusalem, hoping to convince
their friends to tone down the rhetoric. In return for this "restraint," naturally, Israel expected some concrete measure of gratitude from the United
States—which usually meant yet another White House signature on yet
another congressionally mandated set of sanctions.

The big secret was that Israel had absolutely no intention of bombing
Iran. Most of Israel's security establishment knew full well that the conse-
quences of such an attack would be disastrous and the benefits minimal.
They knew Iran was not building a nuke. And they knew that bombing
Iran's nuclear facilities would, at most, merely set back the Iranian pro-
gram by two or three years. Iran had dozens of facilities spread through-

out the country, and no swift, surgical airstrike could take them all out. Nuclear expertise, moreover, could not be bombed out of existence. The Iranians already knew how to enrich uranium. They had blueprints for centrifuges, dozens of nuclear physicists, and research departments at their universities—none of which was going to go anywhere. In the event of an Israeli attack, Iran would regroup and return to its nuclear work—and Israel would find itself back at square one, contemplating how long it had before it would have to strike again, and then again.

Set against this very modest gain for Israel was a daunting list of negative consequences. For starters, any attack on Iran was almost certain to result in a decision by Tehran to unleash the dogs of war—in the form of Hezbollah and possibly also Hamas. An Israeli attack would also drag America into the fight, embroiling the United States in yet another war with a Muslim nation, and further inflaming regional opinion against the West. Iran could retaliate against U.S. targets in the region, of which there were plenty. It could attack the U.S. Navy in the Gulf, or encourage Shia militias in Iraq to attack U.S. forces, or cause trouble in Afghanistan, or shut down the Strait of Hormuz, provoking an overnight doubling in the price of oil. In short, any attack on Iran—whether by Israel or by the United States— would unleash a regional conflagration that no Israeli government would be equipped to deal with. And as if all this weren't enough, it would rally the Iranian people behind their leaders, ensuring the reinvigoration of the Islamic Republic for at least another generation.

Again and again, therefore, American officials made it clear they did not wish to be sucked into military adventurism of this kind. Secretary of Defense Robert Gates, in February 2010, put it as bluntly as anyone: any strike against Iran's nuclear facilities, he said, "would only delay Iranian plans by one to three years, while unifying the Iranian people to be forever embittered against the attacker."

The Israelis privately agreed. In February 2011, away from the cameras, Gen. Gabi Ashkenazi, chief of the general staff of the Israeli military, told his American counterpart, Adm. Mike Mullen, that the war talk coming from Netanyahu was "empty words," because "Israel has no military option." In May 2011 former Mossad chief Meir Dagan called the idea of an Israeli strike on Iran "the stupidest thing I have ever heard." At a conference in Tel Aviv, Dagan added that Israel "didn't have the capability to stop the Iranian program, only to delay it." Moreover, he said, "If anyone seriously considers [a strike], he needs to understand that he's dragging Israel into a regional war that it would not know how to get out of. The security challenge would become unbearable." Wikileaks cables revealed that as early as 2005, Israel had "ruled out" any possibility of a military strike on Iran. American diplomats that year reported that their conversations with Israelis indicated there was "no chance" of a military attack.

Perhaps the best reason for Israel not to bomb Iran was the fact that everyone—absolutely everyone, including every single Israeli politician and military commander—knew that Iran did not pose a military threat to Israel. The idea that the ayatollahs were on the verge of launching a nuclear attack on a nation with more than two hundred nuclear warheads and an instantaneous second-strike capability that could wipe Iran off the map in seconds was simply ludicrous. And this was even assuming Iran was interested in obtaining a nuke, which literally every piece of intelligence suggested was not the case. Even if *all* that intelligence turned out to be wrong, moreover, and Iran actually decided to go for a bomb, the world would have plenty of warning. Iran would begin by switching off the IAEA cameras and kicking out the inspectors, and *then*—even then—it would take months to assemble a crude nuclear device. There was literally, categorically, no problem here. No crisis. No emergency. So what could Israel possibly have to gain from starting a war?

Whenever any of this was put to Netanyahu, his response was to go into Churchillian mode. As prime minister of Israel, he said, he could not take chances with the safety and security of his countrymen—especially when they were faced with a threat as unpredictable and maniacal as that of Iran. Invoking the memory of the Holocaust on a regular basis, he constantly reminded Western audiences how dangerous it would be for the world to ignore the lessons of history. As the guardian of the Jewish people, he had to take into consideration the central anxiety that resided in the hearts of a civilization that had been threatened with annihilation less than a century earlier. At the UN General Assembly in 2011, Netanyahu held up a blueprint of the Nazi death camp Auschwitz to help make his point. "As the prime minister of Israel," he said, "I speak for a hundred generations of Jews who were dispersed throughout the lands, who suffered every evil under the Sun, but who never gave up hope of restoring their national life in the one and only Jewish state."

According to Netanyahu, any Israeli prime minister who did not take seriously the existential threat Iran posed to the Jewish people was not doing his job properly. The Iranian regime, he said, was too unpredictable, too irrational to be "contained" or to be trusted to behave according to rational norms. Yes, looking at the situation from a purely logical perspective, the Iranians would never be foolish enough to launch a nuclear attack on Israel. But the leaders of Iran were not logical people. They were religious fanatics, full of wild-eyed rhetoric and an obsession with martyrdom. In 2009, Netanyahu referred to Iran's leaders as a "messianic, apocalyptic cult" that could not be reasoned with. Like a suicide bomber, prepared to accept his own annihilation in order to strike at his victims, Iran was busy strapping explosives to itself and preparing to detonate in a crowded marketplace. In fact, Iran was something much worse than a suicide bomber. It was a giant, collective *suicide nation*—a ticking time-bomb ready to subject its people to martyrdom for the sake of its cause.[*]

To anyone who knew Iran, such statements had more than a hint of hyperbole. The Iranian ayatollahs were a deeply pragmatic bunch, with a long track record of making calculated, rational decisions. After thirty years in power, they had never started a war or launched a jihad or used weapons of mass destruction against their enemies. They were fundamentalists, yes, and perhaps even fanatics, some of them. But they were not interested in the kind of wild, uncontrollable murder and mayhem being perpetrated by the likes of al-Qaeda. They were interested, first and foremost, in ensuring their own political survival. And history had shown that they were world-class experts at doing whatever was necessary to secure that survival. Every single time Iranian leaders had faced a choice between tilting at ideological windmills and acting pragmatically, they had shrewdly opted for whatever would maximize their own political longevity.

Even those members of Iran's political establishment who were wild-eyed fanatics—and there certainly were a few—had no discernible appetite for building a nuclear weapon and shooting it off in the direction of Israel. Any such action, after all, would have resulted in the deaths of millions of Palestinians. It would also have resulted in the instantaneous destruction of Jerusalem—along with the thirteen-hundred-year-old al-Aqsa Mosque and Haram-al-Sharif, the third holiest site in Islam. No Muslim—no matter how suicidal and no matter how obsessed with driving Jews out of the Holy Land—would ever do such a thing. Even the most unhinged of political actors could understand that nuking Israel would accomplish nothing more than the destruction of the very thing he was hoping to protect. And Iran was certainly not led by unhinged actors. It was led by Ali Khamenei, a man who had spent his youth rotting away in the shah's prisons and had quietly, patiently, worked his way to the highest position of power in the Islamic Republic. To the extent that Iran was driven by ideology, its ideology consisted of a desire to claim moral leadership of the Islamic world. And there would be no worse way to claim moral leadership of the Islamic world than to nuke Jerusalem.

---

[*] Netanyahu, and defenders of Israel in the United States, were fond of quoting the historian Bernard Lewis, who famously claimed that "for the ayatollahs in Iran, mutually assured destruction is not a deterrent, it's an inducement." ("Netanyahu Bombs at the UN," *The Nation,* September 28, 2012, https://www.thenation.com/article/archive/netanyahu-bombs-un/.)

Israeli leaders, knowing the political mileage that could be gained from painting apocalyptic scenarios, did everything they could to distract from these kinds of arguments. When they were not busy describing the Islamic Republic as an al-Qaeda-style terror network, they often described it as a latter-day manifestation of the Third Reich, bent on committing genocide on a scale unimagined since the Second World War. In the speeches of Israeli leaders, it was always Munich in 1938, and the Iranians were always preparing to pack Jews off to the Final Solution. In place of cattle trains and gas chambers, however, this new generation of Nazis was planning to use a nuclear bomb. "What Iran is trying to do right now is not far away at all from what Hitler did to the Jewish people just sixty-five years ago," said Silvan Shalom, Israel's deputy prime minister on the occasion of Holocaust Remembrance Day in 2009. Anyone who doubted this, or suggested it was possible to do a deal with Iran, was playing the role of Neville Chamberlain—the great appeaser of history who had foolishly believed it was possible to make peace with Nazis.

All this made for a gripping political narrative and was frequently recycled on U.S. cable news networks. But it had just one problem: it bore absolutely no relation to reality. Iran's own Jewish population was twenty-five thousand strong, the largest and most vibrant Jewish community in the Middle East outside Israel. Tehran had eleven active synagogues, along with Hebrew schools, kosher restaurants, and banquet halls that regularly hosted bar mitzvahs and Jewish weddings. Iran's Jews were represented by their own member of parliament—a right guaranteed by the Iranian constitution. Along one of Tehran's busiest thoroughfares, a giant mural—complete with Hebrew lettering—honored the thirteen Jewish-Iranian soldiers killed in the war with Iraq. To those who wanted to depict Iran as institutionally anti-Semitic, all this raised an uncomfortable question. If Iran's leaders were truly bent on annihilating the Jewish people from the face of the earth, would they not begin with their own population? Would they not begin, as the Nazis had done, by announcing boycotts of Jewish businesses or by using propaganda to warn citizens about the "enemy within"?

☙

In May 2011, Israel's former spy chief Meir Dagan had called the idea of bombing Iran "stupid." But it was more than stupid; it was unnecessary. Simply by publicly threatening war—bluffing and blustering and hinting that "time was running out"—Israel was already achieving everything it wanted to achieve. Obama's historic outreach initiative was dead in the water. Iran's economy was devastated; its nuclear program had suffered serious setbacks; and the country was more isolated than ever before.

The real question on the minds of Israeli strategists, in fact, was not whether to go to war but rather: How long could Israel keep this up? How long before even the most obtuse observer noticed that it was all a bluff? After all, Israel had been hinting strongly at war since early 2010, and if it did not find some fresh fuel for the narrative, the threats might begin to wear thin.

Over the course of 2012, Netanyahu amped up his rhetoric, speaking much more specifically in terms of deadlines, redlines, and timelines. The Israeli argument during 2012 was that the United States, with its geographic distance and vastly superior military capability, could afford to wait and see about Iran's nuclear program, but Israel did not have this luxury. Very soon Iran would enter what Israeli leaders referred to as the "zone of immunity"— a point at which it had amassed enough centrifuges and enriched uranium that it would become, in effect, immune to outside threats. Once Iran crossed that threshold—that "point of no return," as the Israelis sometimes called it—it would be, for all intents and purposes, a "nuclear state," and it would be too late for Israel to take military action. If something big and forceful were to be done, Israel kept saying, it had to be done *quickly*, before Iran developed this tactical shield. And by some extraordinary cosmic coincidence, Iran was on track to achieve the "zone of immunity" in late 2012— right around the time of the U.S. presidential election.

Washington wasn't buying it. The timeline that the Israelis were sketching was just too convenient, too transparently political.[*] In the U.S. estimation, the real "zone of immunity" would occur only if Iran had a nuclear *weapons* capability—and if Iran chose to go in this direction, the world would have abundant warning. First, Iran would have to break the IAEA seals on its uranium stockpile and reconfigure its centrifuges. It would then have to spend months enriching uranium to 90 percent. And *then* it would have to put together some kind of missile that could carry a nuclear payload—a process that could easily take two years. Considering Iran had

---

[*] It is worth taking a moment to understand the subtle political strategy behind this timeline. By creating the impression that it had only until the end of 2012 to act, Israel lent its military threats an added air of credibility and urgency and made it more difficult for others to dismiss them as just a bluff. News outlets were compelled to report that Israel believed its time was running out, and that it would not wait much longer for the United States to take action. This, in turn, gave Israel great leverage over Obama—who, in an election year, did not want to be seen taking Israel's security concerns lightly. Had Israel given the impression that the "zone of immunity" would come sometime in 2013 or 2014, it would have created a very different atmosphere. It would have seemed that there was more time for diplomacy, and made it much harder to extract concessions out of Obama before the election.

not even taken the first step in this theoretical cascade of decisions, there didn't seem to be an emergency.

Netanyahu, however, did not relent. The Israeli prime minister demanded the United States establish a "red line"—a clearly articulated point in Iran's nuclear progress that would trigger *automatic* military action by the United States. The Obama administration met this suggestion with icy indifference. On January 8, Defense Secretary Leon Panetta told CBS's *Face the Nation* that he did not believe Iran was trying to develop a nuclear weapon—an unmistakable rebuke to Israel. That same week the U.S. Navy rescued a group of Iranian fishermen whose boat had been hijacked by Somali pirates—a goodwill gesture meant to reassure Iran that it should not take America's presence in the Gulf as a prelude to war. And perhaps most important, the P5+1 negotiating group indicated it was prepared to begin a new round of meetings with Iran, aimed at coming to a peaceful resolution of the nuclear dispute.

The goal of all these measures was to lower the level of hysteria. By the end of 2011, oil prices were approaching one hundred dollars a barrel. Markets were exceptionally agitated about what seemed like a looming war in the Middle East. And the Iranians were threatening to shut down the Strait of Hormuz—the vital waterway through which 20 percent of the world's oil flowed—if the United States attacked them. With an election fast approaching, Obama simply could not afford this level of *Sturm und Drang* in the international economy. The goal of the White House for the rest of 2012 therefore became to reassure the world that there was no imminent danger of war. Obama knew that any real, substantive progress on the Iranian nuclear issue would be impossible before November. But if he could at least calm the markets and create a peaceful atmosphere, he might ride out the remainder of 2012 with a relatively stable economy and a minimum of international tension.

Israel's response was to assassinate another Iranian nuclear scientist. On January 11, 2012, Mostafa Ahmadi Roshan, a thirty-two-year-old physicist working at the uranium enrichment facility at Natanz, was killed in broad daylight, along with his driver. Once again the assassins used a magnetic bomb, stuck to Roshan's car by speeding motorcyclists in rush-hour traffic. And once again Israel did not deny involvement.[*] Politically, the assassina-

---

[*] The day after the attack Brig. Gen. Yoav Mordechai, spokesman for the Israeli military, wrote on his Facebook page, "I have no idea who targeted the Iranian scientist, but I certainly don't shed a tear." This was the closest Israel came to an official comment on the incident. However, one day before the attack, the head of Israel's military, Lt. Gen. Benny Gantz, had told a parliamentary panel that 2012 would be a "critical year" for Iran, in part because of "things that happen to it unnaturally."

tion was a clever move on Israel's part, as it torpedoed any possibility of diplomatic progress or the calming of tensions between the United States and Iran. No one could expect Iran to respond positively to the offer of P5+1 talks while its scientists were being assassinated, and no one in the United States was likely to point the finger directly at Israel. Thus, an impression was created that Roshan's assassination was part of a general campaign by the United States to destroy Iran's nuclear industry—an impression deeply convenient to Israel. As one analyst put it, "I believe that this attack is more about sabotaging talks, sabotaging negotiations, than it is about sabotaging Iran's nuclear program."

The United States reacted with visible anger. Within hours of the assassination, Secretary Clinton strode up to her podium at the State Department and explained to reporters, in no uncertain terms, that America had had nothing to do with it. "I want to *categorically* deny *any* United States involvement in *any* kind of act of violence inside Iran," she said, wagging her finger for emphasis. In the past, when Iranian nuclear scientists had been killed, the State Department had relied on low-level spokespeople to make vague statements, but this time Clinton herself wanted to set the record straight. And this was only the beginning. Two days later an extraordinary *Foreign Policy* magazine article detailed how Israeli agents had entered Iran and pretended to be American spies in order to recruit Jundallah terrorists to blow up mosques and assassinate Revolutionary Guard commanders. The author, Mark Perry, had been given unprecedented access to a stash of CIA memos and high-level U.S. officials, suggesting a deliberate attempt on the part of the White House to leak the information. Subtly but unmistakably, the Obama administration was trying to communicate a message to Iran: *We are not the ones killing your nuclear scientists.*

This choreographed maneuver was quickly upstaged by a similar move from Israel. At the end of January, the Israeli journalist Ronen Bergman was given an unprecedented platform—a 7,500-word article in *The New York Times Magazine*—to remind the American public that Israel was deadly serious about attacking Iran, almost certainly sometime during 2012, unless the United States took drastic measures. Through Bergman, Netanyahu's government dropped numerous hints about its intention to start a war, and the article concluded with the ominous line: "After speaking with many senior Israeli leaders and chiefs of the military and the intelligence, I have come to believe that Israel will indeed strike Iran in 2012." Within days, virtually every educated, *New York Times*–reading American was fretting about the coming war in the Middle East. But readers never learned that the Bergman article might have been part of a sophisticated campaign to prevent the lowering of tensions between the United States and Iran.

Once again the dogs of war could be heard barking from the direction of Tel Aviv, and once again the Obama administration scrambled to find ways to muzzle them. Following publication of the Bergman article, oil prices and markets reacted dismally, creating anxieties for the White House as it struggled to find its footing on the economy. Republicans stepped up their campaign to paint the president as weak on Iran and insufficiently supportive of Israel. In this turbocharged political atmosphere, it was not easy to contradict the Israelis publicly. So the White House left this task to a uniformed and highly decorated military official. In February 2012, Gen. Martin Dempsey, chairman of the Joint Chiefs of Staff and second only to the president in the military chain of command, told CNN that he believed Iran was "a rational actor"—a clear rebuke to the message Israel was putting out. "We also know," said Dempsey, that Iran "has not decided . . . to weaponize their nuclear capability." Predictably, Netanyahu pounced on Dempsey, accusing him of making comments that "only served the Iranians." Equally predictably, no one in Washington came to Dempsey's defense. At a Republican presidential debate three days later, one of the candidates, Newt Gingrich, slammed Dempsey, saying, "I can't imagine why he would have said that."

Behind closed doors, the Israelis were the first to admit that Iran was a rational state actor. At a private meeting in Washington, Israel's defense minister, Ehud Barak, described the Iranians' decision-making process as "quite sophisticated" and said they were unlikely ever to use a nuclear weapon against Israel. Barak also said, departing from the official line of his own prime minister, that he did not believe a nuclear Iran would pose a threat to Israel's existence. Efraim Halevi, who had directed Mossad from 1998 to 2002, was even more direct. "I don't think [the Iranians] are irrational, I think they are very rational," he told an interviewer in 2006. "To label them as irrational is escaping from reality, and it gives you kind of an escape clause." But perhaps the sternest rebuke to Netanyahu came from Lt. Gen. Benny Gantz, head of the Israeli military, who bluntly told an Israeli newspaper in April, "I think the Iranian leadership is composed of very rational people." *

But 2012 was an election year in the United States, and there was little room for such facts to enter the political discourse. Obama's goal, in the months that remained until November, was to avoid saying or doing anything that would ratchet up tension in the Persian Gulf (and thus create pain at the pump for Americans), or anything that would give Republicans

---

* In the same interview, Gantz made it clear he did not believe Iran was interested in building a bomb—a major embarrassment for Netanyahu domestically.

an opportunity to accuse him of "throwing Israel under the bus." The fragile economic recovery and a possible betrayal by big pro-Israel campaign
donors were the two areas where Obama's reelection bid seemed most vulnerable. And both were areas where Israel ultimately held enormous leverage. Obama knew he needed to find some way to pacify the Israelis, to offer
major new inducements that might convince them to make less noise during this crucial election year. Congress obliged by presenting the president
with a fresh round of anti-Iran sanctions, more draconian and unforgiving
than anything previously dreamed up. Iran's Central Bank, lifeblood of the
Iranian economy, would now be cut off from the international banking
system, thanks to a rule that would ban foreign banks from doing business
in the United States if they conducted transactions with it. Obama quickly
signed the bill into law.

Even more extreme was the pressure that was suddenly brought to bear
on SWIFT, the Brussels-based international network of coded messaging
used by banks to send money between private accounts. In January, United
Against Nuclear Iran (the advocacy group founded by Dennis Ross in 2007)
asked SWIFT to ban Iranian banks from using its communications network.
This was a particularly devastating—and truly unprecedented—demand,
aimed at making it impossible for Iranian citizens and businesses to send or
receive money with anyone, anywhere in the world. Never in history had an
entire nation been cut off so fundamentally from participation in the global
economy. Initially, the directors of SWIFT balked at the UANI request, as
it was the first time they had been asked to participate in a political boycott,
and they felt it went against the spirit of their international organization.*
(It was, in a sense, the banking equivalent of kicking Iran out of the UN.)
But within a month, the U.S. Senate Banking Committee unanimously
voted to place sanctions on SWIFT *itself* if it did not comply. The message
got through. On March 17, SWIFT disconnected Iranian banks from its
network.

And there was more where that came from. Unable to ban Iranian
oil (America had already stopped buying from Iran in 1980), Washington
announced it would offer waivers from its existing *banking* sanctions to
countries that made "significant" reductions in their *oil* imports from Iran.
Thus Turkey, South Korea, Japan, India, and South Africa—all major pur-
chasers of Iranian oil—were presented with a stark choice: stop buying oil

---

* A secure network for transmitting messages between financial institutions, SWIFT (Society for
Worldwide Interbank Financial Telecommunication) was founded in 1973 and became the global
standard for international money transfers. As of September 2010, SWIFT linked more than nine
thousand financial institutions in 209 countries and territories, transmitting an average of 15 million messages a day. To date, Iran is the only country that has ever been disconnected from SWIFT.

from Iran, or your banks will be banned from doing business in the United States.

By any objective standard, the United States was now at war with Iran. Not in the conventional sense of the word, the kind that involved fighter jets and troop deployments, and that might result in a vigorous public debate among the American people. Instead, the United States was waging a shadow war—an economic war, a cyber war, a war of computer viruses and economic embargoes that were chipping away at an entire nation's ability to function.

☞

In the summer of 2012, aware that it was being pushed in the direction of a policy that was not in American interests, the Obama administration pushed back. On August 30, General Dempsey, speaking at an event in London, made it clear the Israelis were not going to get the red line they had been campaigning for, and when asked whether the United States would support Israel if it chose to attack Iran, he stated simply: "I don't want to be complicit if they choose to do it." A week later Secretary Clinton amplified the message. Asked what she thought about Israel's insistence on a "red line"—and about Netanyahu's demand that the United States spell out what would happen if Iran failed to negotiate a deal with the P5+1 by a certain date—she replied bluntly, "We're not setting deadlines." Five days after that, Defense Secretary Panetta left no doubt about where the administration stood. Nations, he said, don't have "a bunch of little red lines" that determine what they're going to do. "What they have are facts that are presented to them about what a country is up to, and then they weigh what kind of action has to be taken in order to deal with that situation. I mean, that's the real world. Red lines are kind of political arguments that are used to put people into a corner."

Netanyahu was having none of it. As the U.S. election drew closer, the Israeli prime minister ratcheted up his pressure on Obama to a degree that had never been seen, nor even imagined, in the history of U.S.-Israeli relations. At a press conference on September 11, he launched a blistering attack on the White House, in particular on the recent comments by Clinton and Panetta: "Those in the international community who refuse to put red lines before Iran don't have a moral right to place a red light before Israel." He followed up with a round of appearances on U.S. Sunday morning television, to bypass Obama and speak directly to the American people. "They're in the red zone," he told NBC's *Meet the Press*, using a (slightly bungled) gridiron analogy to describe Iran's nuclear program. "You know, they're in the last 20 yards and you can't let them cross that goal line. You can't let them score a touchdown because that would have unbelievable consequences—grievous consequences for the peace and security of us all." Iran, he said, was "guided by a leadership of unbelievable fanaticism. . . . You want these fanatics to have nuclear weapons?" As if all this was not enough, Netanyahu even appeared in a television commercial in Florida aimed at persuading Jewish voters to switch their support to the Republicans.

The final word was left to the president. On September 24, in an interview with CBS's *60 Minutes*, Obama insisted that, when it came to dealing with Iran, he was going to "do what is right for the American people . . . and I am going to block out any noise that's out there." Rarely had an American president issued such a public rebuke to Israel. To make his frustrations especially clear, he even refused a meeting with Netanyahu, who was in town for the UN General Assembly, preferring to make room in his schedule for an appearance on *Late Show with David Letterman*.

If Netanyahu's strategy all along had been to threaten war as a way to provoke sanctions, then he was rapidly approaching the point of boxing himself into a corner. After all, if Israel backed down now, it would be obvious the whole thing had been a bluff. All the talk about "zones of immunity" and the need to take action "by late 2012" would be revealed for what it was—an attempt to exploit the U.S. election cycle—and Israel's credibility would take a severe beating. On the other hand, if Netanyahu actually launched a war, he would be acting in blatant defiance of American wishes (not to mention Israel's own interests). So what was he going to do? How was he going to wiggle out of the cry-wolf scenario he had created for himself?

The answer came at the end of the month, in a performance that was vintage Netanyahu. On September 27, 2012—just six weeks before the election, and after he was sure he had squeezed every imaginable sanction out of the United States—he backed down, but in a way that was imperceptible to anyone not paying extremely close attention. At the UN General Assembly meeting in New York, he took out a whiteboard with a crudely drawn Wile E. Coyote–style cartoon bomb on it, and with a red marker he proceeded to draw, quite literally, a red line across the top of the bomb. "By next spring, at most by next summer, at current enrichment rates," Netanyahu said, Iran "will have finished the medium enrichment and move on to the final stage." That evening's cable news broadcasts were filled with clips of the Israeli prime minister and his cartoon bomb. But virtually no one caught the real headline of the day: *By next spring, at most by next summer*. In one highly forgettable phrase, Netanyahu had shifted the timetable on Iran's "zone of immunity."

At last the Israeli strategy was plain for all the world to see—if anyone was interested in seeing it. For nearly four years, Netanyahu had bluffed and blustered about how close his country was to taking military action against Iran, effectively blackmailing the United States into placing the most severe sanctions in history on the Islamic Republic. As his leverage over the American president increased, and Obama's domestic political position weakened, Netanyahu had only demanded more and more action against Iran—and usually received it. Over the past year, as he saw the end of the gravy train approaching, Netanyahu had even ratcheted up his demands—saying that "the relevant question is not when Iran will *get* the bomb; the relevant question is at what stage can we no longer *stop* Iran from getting the bomb." And all along he had insisted that the time to act would somehow miraculously expire somewhere around November 2012. And now that that deadline had arrived, Israel was suddenly telling the world that, well, maybe we have just a teeny-weeny bit more time. The whole thing had been a colossal charade.

⋈

A charade, of course, with real-world consequences.

From January to September 2012, the value of Iran's currency, the rial, dropped from 10,000 to the dollar to 37,000, resulting in runaway inflation on the streets of Tehran. Iranians queued for hours to buy fresh chicken, and there were reports of stampedes and crushing competition to obtain basic groceries. At Martyrs Hospital, one of Iran's top medical facilities, twelve hundred cancer patients a year were going without radiology treatment, because the equipment was no longer working and replacement parts could not be imported under "dual use" laws aimed at keeping nuclear equipment out of Iran. Worse, the restrictions on banking meant that Iran was having trouble paying for imported pharmaceuticals—leaving patients suffering from complex disorders such as hemophilia and thalassemia, as well as those undergoing kidney dialysis, in immediate danger.

Hawkish members of Congress brushed off humanitarian concerns, arguing that they were the price that had to be paid for the policy to work. "Critics [complain] that these measures will hurt the Iranian people," wrote California Democrat Brad Sherman in 2010. "Quite frankly, we need to do just that." Rep. Mark Kirk (R-IL) was even plainer. Following a speech in Chicago, he told an audience member, "In a discussion I had with administration officials they said we would feel worried that it would hurt the Iranian people . . . [laughs]. But it's that actual pain that I think has to be imposed." Sherman drew a comparison between Iran and apartheid-era South Africa, claiming that in the 1980s, American sanctions "created enough economic dislocation and unrest that they literally drove a regime to provide for its own destruction. . . . Ultimately, Nelson Mandela thanked us for the sanctions." The goal of sanctions, in other words, had been gradually transformed. It was no longer about pressuring Iran to acquiesce on its nuclear program. It was about instigating regime change, or at least some kind of policy that would weaken the Islamic Republic. Perhaps this had been the goal all along, and the proponents of tough sanctions were merely being more honest about it now.

Whatever the case, the years of harsh economic sanctions—in particular, the round imposed by the United States in 2010—took their toll on Iran. In just three short years after Obama abandoned his push for diplomacy, Iran saw its currency plummet, its banking sector was shut off from the outside world, and its doctors struggled to provide care using expired medications and underresourced equipment. The skies over Tehran turned black with pollution, citizens queued for hours to buy dollars on the black market, young Iranians had to abandon their studies abroad for lack of access to bank accounts, and robbery, burglary, and petty crime sharply increased. Iran's oil production, 3.9 million barrels a day in 2008, dropped to just 2.7 million. Worse, since it was next to impossible for Iran to receive payment for its oil or to pay outside suppliers for imported goods, the country was forced to resort to shady middlemen in Dubai, secretive transfers of stacks of gold bullion, payment in Indian rupees, and other creative measures just to stay afloat. In October 2012, Vice President Joe Biden boasted that Iran was now under "the most crippling sanctions in the history of sanctions, period." And indeed, without question, this nation was feeling the pain.

☙

And then came the election. On November 6, 2012, Barack Obama was returned to a second four-year term as president. And almost immediately, it was obvious he was going to have a lot more room to maneuver when it came to setting Iran policy. Without the leverage of an upcoming election at their disposal, Israel and her supporters in Washington became strangely muted in their warnings about Iran—no longer threatening imminent war or talking about "zones of immunity" or claiming that Iran was "months away" from a nuclear bomb. Suddenly Netanyahu was nowhere to be seen or heard. Magazines no longer ran feature-length stories and cable news no longer speculated for hours about "how much longer" Israel could tolerate waiting before unleashing all-out war in the Middle East. The story simply dropped off the front pages. That gave the administration some long-awaited breathing room to pursue nuclear diplomacy with Iran.

A new secretary of state, John Kerry, and a team of negotiators headed by undersecretary for political affairs Wendy Sherman, were put in charge. And they spent much of 2013 engaged in face-to-face talks with their Iranian counterparts, both within the P5+1 framework and informally.* On the Iranian side as well, there was a new cast of characters. In June 2013, Iran elected a new president, Hassan Rohani, a relative moderate, replacing the outgoing hard-liner Ahmadinejad. And upon taking office in August, Rohani signaled a major change of tone by appointing as foreign minister Mohammad Javad Zarif, a pragmatic, level-headed former UN ambassador who had spent many years living in the United States, held advanced degrees from San Francisco State and the University of Denver, and had cultivated many high-level contacts in the U.S. political class. On Rosh Hashanah, Rohani tweeted new year's greetings to the world's Jewish communities—a clear attempt to distance himself from his predecessor's ugly politics. All these decisions—in particular, the appointment of Zarif—were seen as indications of a new spirit of openness toward the United States. In fact, observers noted, Rohani's new cabinet boasted more ministers with Ph.D.'s from American universities than Obama's—more, for that matter, than any other government in the world.

This change in atmosphere quickly paid dividends. At the end of September, Kerry and Zarif met in person on the fringes of the UN General Assembly meeting—the highest-level contact between Iranian and U.S. officials in thirty-four years. And the following day, as he drove away from the UN, Rohani had a historic, fifteen-minute telephone call with President Obama—the first conversation between Iranian and American heads of state since 1979. Over the next few weeks, Kerry, Zarif, and their teams built on the spirit of amity established in New York, flying to Geneva to conduct marathon negotiating sessions aimed at resolving the nuclear dispute. Technically, these meetings took place within the framework of the P5+1, but in reality, the Americans stayed in a separate hotel from the Europeans, Chinese, and Russians, and they conducted parallel private sessions with the Iranian delegation. It worked. In November 2013, Iran and the P5+1 agreed to an interim freeze on the most sensitive Iranian nuclear activity, in exchange for a limited release of funds from Iran's frozen oil assets—a historic achievement that was widely understood to be the first step toward a final deal that could be negotiated in the coming months.

Netanyahu, for his part, did what he could to upset the applecart. Now

* It would later emerge that the talks had started well before the election, in July 2012, in Oman. So extreme was the secrecy that White House special assistant Puneet Talwar and State Department director of policy planning Jake Sullivan, to avoid being seen in hotels, slept on sofas in a disused U.S. embassy building in Muscat.

The phone call: Fifteen minutes in duration, thirty-four years in the making. President Obama's historic phone call to newly elected Iranian president Hassan Rohani on September 27, 2013, helped make clear that during his second term, the United States would be serious about resolving the nuclear issue. It was the first conversation between leaders of the two countries since 1979.

oddly counseling patience rather than urgency, he insisted there was no rea-son to rush into what he repeatedly described as a "bad deal." "The options aren't really a bad deal . . . or war," he explained to CNN. "There's a third option: sanctions. Increase the sanctions." This, of course, was what Netan-yahu had wanted all along—an ever-tightening noose of sanctions around Iran, without any real possibility of either a deal or a war—and for the past five years, this was exactly what he had received.

But this time Israel didn't get its way. In January 2014 the interim agree-ment went into effect, and a "Joint Plan of Action" was put forward for achieving a final agreement. The Iranians insisted that they needed to offer their population meaningful sanctions relief within the next six months, and that they would not tolerate the negotiations continuing indefinitely and inconclusively. So a deadline of July 2014 was selected for a final deal.

In fact, the negotiations dragged on for a full year after this deadline. And during the eighteen months of haggling in Swiss and Austrian hotel rooms, negotiators from Iran and the United States got to know one another very well. At times, they resembled a collection of grumpy old friends thrown together into a convalescent home. Zarif hurt his back and frequently had to negotiate from a wheelchair. Sherman broke her nose and her finger on separate occasions. Kerry broke his femur cycling near Geneva and was

Iranian foreign minister Mohammad Javad Zarif and his U.S. counterpart John Kerry arriving in Geneva on March 30, 2015, to discuss negotiations about the future of Iran's nuclear program. The result was a historic agreement among Iran, the United States, and other major powers.

on crutches for two weeks. Salehi was hospitalized for a colon operation. Deadlines were repeatedly pushed back. And then, in Vienna on July 4, 2015, came a minor breakthrough. Zarif surprised Kerry and the Americans with an impromptu Persian feast, the first meal the two sides had shared. Already four days past the "final" final deadline they had set themselves, the two sides plunged into unprecedented, around-the-clock negotiations for several days. And then at last, in the small hours of July 14, 2015, two weeks after the drop-dead deadline—a deal. The Joint Comprehensive Plan of Action (JCPOA), they called it, as the P5+1 made the announcement. Obama addressed the nation and the world later that morning from the Rose Garden.

The Iran nuclear deal, which ran to 159 pages, was complex, but its basic terms were relatively straightforward—and exactly as anyone following the matter closely over the past ten years might have predicted. Iran agreed to a complete elimination of its medium-enriched uranium stockpile and a 98 percent reduction to its low-enriched uranium. It also agreed to cut its 19,000 centrifuges down to around 6,000, to abandon advanced nuclear research, and (perhaps most important) to allow extremely stringent, around-the-clock IAEA inspections of its nuclear facilities to ensure compliance. In exchange, the P5+1 agreed to gradually lift some of its sanctions against Iran—but kept in place a "snapback" mechanism, whereby sanctions could be quickly reimposed if any member of the P5+1 was concerned that Iran was not meeting its obligations.

Even with a deal in place, however, the Obama White House still had its work cut out. In the weeks and months following the conclusion of the deal, Obama faced a massive domestic battle to secure its public acceptance. Although technically the Iran deal was not a treaty and thus did not require congressional approval, Congress had previously passed into law a requirement that it be given a sixty-day "review period" and an opportunity to pass a resolution of approval or disapproval. Obama pledged to veto any disapproval resolution, but it was not clear that he would have enough votes among his fellow Democrats to prevent an override of his veto. What followed for the remainder of the summer was an unprecedented lobbying effort. Tens of millions of dollars, most of it raised by big pro-Israel donors, poured into campaigns aimed at convincing Democratic lawmakers to vote against the deal. In response, the White House sent Kerry, Vice President Biden, and others to Capitol Hill to twist the arms of key Democrats. The amount of effort it took to persuade members of the president's own party to go along with his flagship foreign policy achievement was almost unheard-of in American history. At one point, the White House had to resort to bringing top diplomats from Britain, France, Russia, China, and Germany to tell undecided *Democratic* senators, in a private meeting,

All smiles now: Kerry, Zarif, and other parties gather to announce the Joint Comprehensive Plan of Action in Vienna, July 14, 2015.

It's a deal: Signatures on the JCPOA.

that their countries would not be returning to the negotiating table and "will not join you in reimposing sanctions"—a stark reminder that the deal was going to move ahead, with or without the United States. Eventually, the arm-twisting paid off. By early September, supporters of the deal had enough votes in the Senate not only to sustain a veto but to filibuster debate and prevent a disapproval resolution from being voted on in the first place. And by September 17, the end of the sixty-day review period, the Senate had failed to pass any kind of resolution. The deal was done.

Perhaps the most unfortunate effect of all this domestic political wrangling was that it destroyed any hope that the nuclear deal might become a building block to warmer relations between Iran and the United States. After the titanic effort it had taken just to defeat congressional disapproval of the deal, the Obama White House had little appetite left for the bruising political battle that would accompany any broader attempt to engage in dialogue with Iran. And Khamenei, taking his cue from the United States, issued a similar reassurance to his own hard-line base: "Our policies toward the arrogant government of the United States will not be changed at all." For good measure, Khamenei added: "The Americans say they stopped Iran from acquiring a nuclear weapon. . . . They know it's not true. We had a *fatwa* declaring nuclear weapons to be religiously forbidden under Islamic law. It had nothing to do with the nuclear talks."

Khamenei's confidence, however, was short-lived. In the months that followed, the "sanctions relief" Iran had been promised proved to be virtually nonexistent—or, rather, to exist only on paper. Dozens of big European companies made a beeline for Tehran (U.S. companies were still barred from doing business in Iran), hoping to sign deals and pick up their business interests where they had left off a few years earlier. But they all came up against the same problem: the nervousness of European banks to lend financing. On top of this, the price of oil plummeted in 2015—in part because Iran's arch-rival, Saudi Arabia, refused to cut production—leaving Iran with much less income from oil sales than it had expected to enjoy with the lifting of sanctions.

The banking issue was the most challenging for Iran. Since 2010 the U.S. Justice Department had fined non-American banks $15 billion for sanctions violations, some of them dating back to the 1990s. Once bitten, they were now twice shy. Although the State Department reassured them they had nothing to fear, banks like HSBC, Standard Chartered, and BNP Paribas were still smarting from the painful, multibillion-dollar payouts they had been forced to make as a result of their dealings with Iran, and they now wanted serious, watertight guarantees from the United States. What ensued was a bizarre spectacle: Secretary Kerry practically pleaded with European banks to get back to doing business with Iran, if only to preserve the credibility of the nuclear deal, while those banks were too cautious to listen. European bankers especially recalled the reputational damage and fines to which they had been subjected during the crusading tenure of Stuart Levey, the U.S. Treasury Department's undersecretary for terrorism and financial intelligence from 2004 to 2011. Not surprisingly, Levey, in many ways the architect of Iran's economic isolation, was now serving as HSBC's chief legal officer, leading the charge of European banks pushing back against the State Department and insisting HSBC would not go back to doing business with Iran.

Whether it was the lack of meaningful sanctions relief or the reluctance of the White House to pursue a broader agenda of rapprochement with Iran, it was hard to avoid the impression in 2016 that somehow, somewhere along the way, a historic opportunity had not been fully realized. On the streets of Tehran, the economy was more decrepit than ever. Iran was no less isolated from the West than it had been in the early 2000s. And no one talked anymore about Obama's "unclenched fist" or Khatami's "Dialogue Among Civilizations." For the first time since 1979, genuine relationships had been forged between Iranian and American officials, but in the absence of embassies and consulates, and without any meaningful follow-up, these relationships were unlikely to survive the impending change in U.S. administrations in 2017. As Obama's time in office came to a close, in fact, the idea that the United States and Iran could one day reestablish a cordial working relationship appeared to have no momentum. Even in Syria, where closer coordination and communication had the potential to create solutions to the civil war that were desperately needed and could benefit everyone, there was a curious lack of initiative. In many ways, the U.S.-Iranian relationship seemed back where it had been in the 1990s—cold and courteous, occasionally constructive, but ultimately nonexistent.

And time was running out. By the time the dust settled on the Iran nuclear deal, the Obama administration had barely fifteen months left in office—hardly long enough to undertake comprehensive improvements in U.S.-Iranian relations—and its appetite to do so was limited, given the sheer amount of energy it had taken just to secure the deal itself. This, in effect, was a victory for Israel. Over the course of seven years, Netanyahu literally ran out the clock on Obama, ensuring that any possibility that nuclear diplomacy could be used as a stepping-stone to improved relations with Iran was nonexistent. At the end of it all, Iran was still, for all intents and purposes, under severe sanctions—more severe than during the Bush years—and the possibility of a thaw with Washington seemed more remote than ever.

The nuclear issue, ultimately, had turned out to be a colossal distraction. Iran, after all, had never had any serious interest in pursuing a nuclear weapon, and the successful negotiation of an agreement to prevent such a scenario—though it was an impressive achievement in its own right—was actually irrelevant. For Obama, the reason for undertaking serious, substantive negotiations with Iran over the nuclear issue had never been that he had perceived Iran to be a mortal, imminent danger to the United States because of its supposed pursuit of a nuclear weapon. Rather, he had hoped negotiating with Iran over its nuclear program could serve as a prelude to bigger things. A quick diplomatic agreement over this thorny issue, Obama had believed, could usher in a fundamental reset of U.S. relations with Iran—and form part of his larger vision for Middle East peace. But the Israelis had successfully slowed down the entire operation—turning the nuclear issue into such an all-consuming discussion in Washington that it became impossible to think about any kind of broader improvement of relations with Iran. The unclenched fist had never even had a chance.

Still, John Kerry and Javad Zarif, who appeared to have developed a genuine bond over the previous two years, did what they could to build on the momentum of the deal. In January 2016, following months of secret talks between the two men, Iran released four Americans from judicial custody, in exchange for the United States dropping charges against seven Iranians who had been convicted for sanctions violations. That same month, when ten U.S. sailors accidentally strayed into Iranian waters and were apprehended by the Revolutionary Guards, Kerry was able to pick up the telephone and quickly secure their release, following just a handful of conversations with Zarif. Such civilized interactions did not make for major headlines, but for Iran and America, they represented remarkable progress. A nation that thirty-six years earlier had taken Americans hostage and held them in their own embassy for fourteen months now calmly returned Americans who had broken the law, after just a few hours, following a few phone calls.

&

This was the last of the bouquets. In November 2016, Republican business-man Donald Trump defeated his Democratic opponent Hillary Clinton to win the presidency of the United States, and from the beginning of his term in office, it was clear the U.S.-Iranian relationship was on its way back to the land of brickbats. Trump, who had once made a name for himself as the author of a book called *The Art of the Deal,* proclaimed that the deal Obama had made with Iran was "terrible"—the "stupidest deal of all time"—and that he would "rip it up" at the first opportunity. And his initial cabinet choices reflected this distaste for dialogue with Iran. Gen. Mike Flynn, named as national security adviser, had once peddled the bizarre conspiracy theory that Iran was responsible for the 2012 attack on the U.S. consulate in Benghazi, Libya. And Trump's defense secretary, Gen. James "Mad Dog" Mattis, had said in 2012 that the three gravest threats facing the United States were "Iran, Iran, Iran," and again in 2016 he had said Iran was not so much a country as "a revolutionary cause devoted to mayhem." In February 2017, after Iran test-launched a ballistic missile, Flynn declared that Iran was officially "on notice"—despite the fact that the test did not violate the terms of the nuclear deal. Congress, meanwhile, operated with a free hand, pass-ing sanction after sanction against Iran, appearing to practically beg Iran to break its end of the agreement. And at a G20 summit in Germany, Trump himself spent hours urging other world leaders to block their companies from doing business in Iran—a direct violation of the deal. At one point in July 2017, the normally mild-mannered Iranian foreign minister, Javad Zarif, became so fed up with the provocations that he declared they were "a violation of not the spirit but of the letter . . . of the nuclear deal."

Less than a year later, it was all over. On May 8, 2018, after months of

The art of no: President Donald Trump announces U.S. withdrawal from the agreement on May 8, 2018, calling it a "horrible, one-sided deal that should have never, ever been made."

speculation about his intentions, Trump announced that the United States would no longer be upholding its end of the deal. The announcement was accompanied by a fresh raft of additional sanctions aimed at bringing Iran's economy to a standstill. And in the ensuing months, Washington pursued an even more strident policy of escalation, confrontation, and economic warfare against Iran than ever before. A new inner team—composed of National Security Adviser John Bolton, Secretary of State Mike Pompeo, and legal adviser Rudy Giuliani—adopted a strategy of maximum pressure. An aircraft carrier strike group and numerous B-52 bombers were sent to the region as a warning to Iran. And in April 2019 the United States designated Iran's Revolutionary Guards Corps a "terrorist organization"—an unprecedented move against the armed forces of a sovereign state. The same month Washington announced it would no longer issue sanctions waivers to countries buying Iranian oil—a move that caused Iran's exports to plummet from around 2.5 million barrels a day to just 200,000.

Faced with the most severe economic isolation in its modern history, Iran declared, in a series of calculated steps during 2019 and 2020, that it would gradually suspend various aspects of its cooperation with the JCPOA. These transgressions were mostly symbolic and minor, such as the enrichment of uranium to 4.5 percent (higher than the cap of 3.67 percent but still well short of the 90 percent needed for a bomb). But tensions continued to mount. In May 2019, Trump warned in a tweet that if Iran chose to fight the

United States, the response would be so severe that it would be "the official end of Iran"—a threat condemned by Iran's foreign minister Javad Zarif as a "genocidal taunt." Before long, Zarif himself had been slapped with sanctions, making it clear that the United States was in no mood to engage in discussion.

The battlefield, eventually, became Iraq. On December 27, 2019, a rocket attack on a U.S. base in Kirkuk killed an American contractor—an incident that the United States quickly blamed on a pro-Iranian militia. And in retaliation, the United States launched airstrikes that killed dozens of the group's fighters. Over the next few days, the U.S. embassy in Baghdad found itself mobbed by crowds of protesters furious at American actions in Iraq and Syria, all demanding the departure of the United States from the region. Only the outer perimeter of the embassy was breached, and without casualties. But Washington treated this—along with the Kirkuk incident— as a major escalation on the part of Iran, one that could not go unpunished. On December 31, Trump tweeted that Iran "will pay a very BIG PRICE! This is not a Warning, it is a Threat. Happy New Year!"

What came next was an act of war. In the early morning hours of January 3, 2020, Gen. Qasem Soleimani—leader of the elite Quds force and the most respected and accomplished military figure in Iran—was assassinated by a U.S. drone strike as he left the Baghdad airport for a meeting with Iraqi allies. Trump justified the assassination by claiming that Soleimani had been "plotting imminent and sinister attacks" against Americans, and the Pentagon added that he was "actively developing plans to attack American diplomats and service members in Iraq and throughout the region"—though he was unable to provide evidence. Tehran vowed revenge. Soleimani was the highest-profile figure ever killed, on either side, in the history of U.S.-Iranian tensions, and over the next few days, the streets of Iran filled with millions of marchers—many beside themselves with grief—as the country declared three days of official mourning. To much of the world, the forty-year standoff between Iran and America appeared to have taken a dangerous new turn.

In the event, however, Tehran's "revenge" proved measured and calculated to avoid escalation. Ballistic missile strikes on two U.S. bases in Iraq—quietly telegraphed to Washington ahead of time, through the Iraqi government—resulted in some structural damage but no significant injury to either Iraqis or Americans. For a few brief hours, the world breathed a sigh of relief, as Iran's supreme leader declared the strikes a "slap in the face" for the United States, and Trump said he was satisfied that Iran appeared to be "standing down." But far more tragic consequences awaited. A Ukrainian passenger jet, taking off from Tehran in the midst of the firefight, was mistaken for an incoming hostile target and shot down by an Iranian missile—killing all 130 people on board. President Rohani called the incident "an unforgivable mistake," and Zarif apologized to the nation on behalf of the government. But because it had taken three days for Iran to admit the mistake, public anger—which just days earlier had been ferociously directed at the United States—quickly turned against the government. Thousands of demonstrators, some even chanting against the supreme leader, took to the streets. And Washington wasted no time throwing its support behind them. Trump even tweeted in Persian, for the first time, saying that "the noble people of Iran, who love America, deserve a government that will help them achieve their dreams, rather than focus on killing them for revenge. . . . Make Iran great again!"

As such demonstrations always did, however, they quickly fizzled, as the public appetite for a serious showdown with authorities proved limited. And before long, all the bloodshed at the beginning of January—the death of the general, the stampede during his funeral that killed 56, and the plane crash that broke so many hearts—seemed to have been for nothing. Iran and the United States quietly slipped back into the state of poorly managed cycles of provocation and counterprovocation, accusation and counteraccusation, that had characterized their interactions for years. And it seemed more obvious than ever that, when push came to shove, neither country had any real appetite for turning this long-standing stalemate into an actual war or a meaningful peace.

The long, dark winter of mutual hatred ground on.

Epilogue

Years of harsh economic sanctions—in particular, the most recent round of suffocating measures imposed by the United States since 2018—have unquestionably taken their toll on Iran. Over the past decade, Iran has seen its currency plummet in value, its banking sector completely shut off from the outside world, and its doctors struggling to provide care using expired medications and underresourced equipment. The skies over Tehran have turned black with air pollution, citizens have queued for hours to buy dollars on the black market, and young Iranians have had to abandon their studies abroad for lack of access to hard currency. Iran's oil production, 3.9 million barrels a day in 2008, has dropped to just 1.8 million. Worse, since it is next to impossible for Iran to receive payment for its oil or to pay outside suppliers for imported goods, the country has been forced to resort to shady middlemen in Turkey, secretive transfers of stacks of gold bullion and other creative measures just to stay afloat. And as if all this wasn't hard enough, in March 2020, Iran was also hit by one of the worst outbreaks of the deadly coronavirus anywhere in the world—with cases climbing over 100,000 by the end of April and deaths topping 6,000. The sudden closure of borders meant that most of Iran's creative sanctions-busting maneuvers were no longer viable. And the Trump administration refused to consider even temporary sanctions relief—leaving Iran's economy so badly battered that it simply did not have the luxury to tell people to stay home and not go to work. In almost every imaginable respect, this is a nation that has been feeling the pain.

And yet, oddly, Iran is not about to collapse. Anyone who has visited the country in recent years will know that the markets still hum with economic activity, and the streets are still jammed with traffic. Most products are still available in stores (though often at exorbitant prices). And there have been no signs—yet—of food shortages or malnutrition. Certainly, millions have experienced real hardship—especially the most vulnerable members of society, whose purchasing power and living standards have drastically declined. But this hardship has not translated into a serious, mass protest movement or a fundamental questioning of the government's approach to the nuclear issue. (Public support for the nuclear program, in fact, appears stronger than ever.) Since 2009 streams of demonstrators have often poured into the streets, as in other parts of the Middle East, but in nothing like the same kinds of numbers, and they have posed no serious threat to the Islamic Republic—despite Western powers and Western media doing all they could to encourage such a scenario. In fact, the dream long cherished in certain quarters of Washington—that external pressure placed on the Iranian regime would cause its people to rise up and overthrow their government—seems further from reality than ever.

There are a number of reasons for the Islamic Republic's surprising resilience. The first, and most obvious, is its repressive national-security apparatus. The Islamic Republic has never hesitated to execute or put on trial those citizens it perceives as posing a threat to the system. But although this is in some ways the "easiest" and most obvious reason to cite—and the one most frequently given in the United States—by itself, it is not terribly convincing. Of course, one should never underestimate the power of fear and repression in maintaining order. However, it is important to understand that, on its own, it is not a sufficient explanation—no matter how seductive it might seem. If there was an overwhelming, universal, popular desire on the part of citizens to overturn the Islamic Republic today, no amount of repressive measures and intimidation by the state would be enough to stop it. There are surely other factors—which rarely receive a hearing in the United States, and might even be politically inconvenient to point out—but which are equally important to understanding the resilience of the Islamic Republic.

For starters, it is worth remembering that a people who perceive themselves to be under siege from a foreign power will not generally turn against their own leaders. One is hard-pressed to find examples from history in which a nation subjected to economic embargoes, currency debasements, medical shortages, sanctions, acts of terror, drone flights, computer viruses, and threats of war—all directed at it from a hostile overseas power—has reacted with anything other than a stalwart show of patriotic defiance and unity. However much the Iranian people might resent their politicians, they resent foreign interference in their affairs even more. And this resentment has worked out rather well for the powers that be. The sanctions, if anything, have entrenched the ayatollahs, giving them just enough nationalistic fodder to pad out their bombastic speeches, whip up popular support, and preserve their hold on power for another generation.

Another reason for the regime's resilience is Iran's self-sufficiency. In the forty years since the revolution, it has learned the hard way how to fend for itself. During the dark days of the Iran-Iraq war in the 1980s, the Iranian public endured desperate levels of hardship, deprivation, shortages, and death—and emerged at the other end with its dignity and its independence intact. Uniquely alone among the nations of the world, Iran spent the 1980s fighting an enemy that was supported by both the United States and the Soviet Union, all of western Europe, and virtually the entire Arab world, and it did not receive much in the way of international support or sympathy, even when its citizens were attacked with chemical weapons. Iranians learned then that, however much Western nations might talk about human rights and international law, they will park these principles at the door in pursuit of their own interests—and that ultimately, no one's heart really bleeds or breaks for Iran. They also learned that suffering can be tolerated—and indeed *must* be tolerated—when the independence and sovereignty of the nation are at stake. Even more recently, they have learned—by witnessing the gruesome experiences of Syria and Libya—that Western-instigated "revolutions" do not always end well. So today, when prices skyrocket and medicines run short, Iranians react with frustration at their government—but also with stoicism and cynicism about the motivations of the West.

These factors help explain why the ferocious sanctions leveled against Iran in recent years have not succeeded in shifting public opinion much against the government—either on the specific issue of the nuclear program or more generally. But a much larger factor is also in play, one that American politicians frequently seem to miss. The Islamic Republic of Iran—whether we like it or not—is a *relatively* legitimate political entity. It is not, to borrow the words of one of the first Americans in Iran, some "flimsy frostwork structure" just waiting to be "annihilated" by a superior civilization. It is not, like the Arab dictatorships that have traditionally surrounded it, the product of a military coup or a British colonial project. The Islamic Republic is the product of a revolution—a massive, earth-shaking uprising that overthrew a powerful 2,500-year-old monarchy (one that had enjoyed the support of a superpower, a world-class army of 300,000, and a brutally efficient secret police apparatus). Whatever else we might think about Iran, we must never forget that at the end of the 1970s, millions of Iranians marched through the streets to bring down the shah, and that a referendum was held, under free conditions, to establish an Islamic Republic in his place. We must also never forget that in the decade that followed, hundreds of thousands laid down their lives, at least in part to defend that republic. (For many, of course, it was also a simple patriotic act.) A nation that has been through such experiences as these in recent memory is never going to capitulate to another country's demands because of a few sanctions and price spikes.

This is not to say that the Islamic Republic has anything approaching the unanimous support of its people, nor that it enjoys the levels of popularity and democratic accountability associated with free, open, and liberal societies. In some very real ways, the revolution has failed its people miserably. In the last twenty-five years, an entire generation of young Iranians has grown up frustrated, fed up, and embittered about the lack of personal freedoms, the oppressive social climate, the scarcity of good jobs, and the constant use of anti-American rhetoric as a distraction from other problems. Many of these young people would be (and often are) the first to tell Western journalists that the Islamic Republic is a bankrupt political project. But the picture of Iran that is sometimes painted in the United States—that it is a nation of oppressed souls just waiting to rise up against their evil, tyrannical leaders if only they had half an opportunity—also does not stand up to scrutiny. America has consistently underestimated the Islamic Republic since 1979, when commentators first began writing political obituaries for Khomeini and his allies, confidently predicting their revolution would last only a few months or at best a few years. And it continues to underestimate the Islamic Republic today.

Rarely have so many been so wrong about something so obvious for so long.

☙

This myopic understanding of Iran carries over into the foreign policy arena as well. Today, every time Iran refuses to be dictated to, or attempts to protect its national interests, a chorus of U.S. congressmen, media pundits, and ideological opponents of the Islamic Republic portray it as "defiant." Every time Iran shows flexibility or a willingness to compromise, it is accused of "stalling tactics" or "trying to divide the international community." And anyone who tries to point out that Iran might have legitimate security concerns, or that it is behaving as a rational state actor, is smeared as an "apologist" for the Islamic Republic and is excluded from a say in decision making. This points to a larger problem: the United States in recent years has painted itself into a corner in which the only acceptable response from Iran, ever, is complete and unconditional capitulation. And the only kind of analysis that Washington listens to is the kind that depicts Iran as a demonic, existential threat. After forty years, the United States seems to have developed an almost neurotic fixation on "defeating" Iran—and is prepared to pursue this goal even to the obvious detriment of its own interests.

Iran, of course, bears some responsibility: Americans, after all, have some very good reasons for not trusting or liking Iran. Their embassy in Tehran was once overrun and held hostage for fourteen months. In the 1980s, pro-Iranian militias in Lebanon kidnapped Westerners and killed American marines. In its official rhetoric, Iran continues to belittle the United States and accuse it of being a force for evil and instability in the region. And Iran continues to provide tactical and logistical support to entities such as Hezbollah that behave in ways that run counter to Western interests. And then there is that "Death to America" chant. American concerns about these activities are sincere and legitimate and are not exclusively ginned up for domestic political purposes.

And yet the inescapable truth is that the Islamic Republic has tried many times to take a more conciliatory approach to its relations with the United States—helping to get hostages released from Lebanon, funneling arms shipments to Bosnia as a favor to the Clinton administration, providing meaningful assistance in Afghanistan, suspending its nuclear program for two years, and ultimately coming to the table to sign a historic nuclear deal with the world's powers. And every single time the American response has been to pocket the concession, increase the hostility, and shift the goalposts. Iranian leaders are now deeply convinced, if they were not before, that the nuclear issue was merely a pretext and that America's true goal is to weaken, isolate, and—if possible—eliminate the Islamic Republic. They have seen how, even after they made substantial concessions on the nuclear issue, America has continued to look for reasons to treat Iran as a pariah.

All this points to the fundamental problem that the nuclear issue cannot be dealt with in isolation from the much larger issue of political hostility between the United States and Iran. As long as U.S.-Iranian relations remain mired in an untrusting, suspicious, dysfunctional state of paralysis, even a historic agreement over Iran's nuclear program is unlikely to alter the relationship in any meaningful way.

Perhaps, as a historian, it is not my place to speculate on what the future might bring. And perhaps it is naïve to even try. Today's political universe, after all, seems populated by people who are much more interested in seeing their country's ideological principles achieve a complete victory over the other's than they are in cooperation and coexistence. But having spent years looking closely at the history these two nations have shared, I cannot help but come away a little brokenhearted at the way it has all ended, or wonder if something better might be on the horizon. In 2009 I scrambled up the boulder-strewn hills outside Urmia, in northwestern Iran, and pushed years of weeds and overgrown trees out of the way, to find the words AMERICAN PRESBYTERIAN MISSION CEMETERY 1835 chiseled into a gray-brick wall, then climbed over the wall to find the haunting sight of dozens of graves bearing the names of American missionaries. It was impossible for me not to feel some pang of frustration over how exactly it all went so wrong.

If a historian may be permitted to wade into the difficult waters of international politics, then I will say that a mending of fences between the United States and Iran is far from impossible. But it is also my view that before any kind of cooperation or reconciliation can take place, both countries will have to learn to let go of some long-cherished convictions.

⋘

It is my belief—and the final argument of this book—that the only way the United States and Iran can resolve their differences is to engage in comprehensive, unconditional, sustained, serious, good-faith, high-level talks, aimed at addressing the full range of issues between them, *once and for all*. They must recognize that, for forty years, the two countries have tried almost every imaginable approach to dealing with each other except this one. In the 1980s the Reagan administration believed that selling arms to Iran might encourage moderate elements in the leadership to rise to the top and sideline Khomeini. In 1989, George H. W. Bush suggested that an act of goodwill from Iran would be reciprocated and could be the start of something big—then lost interest when the Soviet Union collapsed and America realigned with the Arab powers. In the 1990s the Clinton administration recognized that it had a genuine interlocutor in the reformist president Khatami—but far too late, after Khatami was already past his sell-by date at home. In the 2000s, George W. Bush labeled Iran a member of the "axis of evil" and dismissed out of hand its attempts to offer assistance in the Global War on Terror. In 2009, Barack Obama seemed to recognize it was time for a different approach and made clear that his administration was in the business of diplomacy. But it took five years for talks to take place, and after they delivered concrete results, there was little time or energy left for follow-through.

The one thing that is needed now is a historic, high-level, systematic, sustained and *serious* attempt at dialogue—ideally in the form of a summit meeting between the two countries' leaders. It is time to be much more imaginative, to put aside arguments about 20 percent or 5 percent uranium enrichment and think in bigger and much more strategic terms, in terms so epic and transformational that there will be no risk of sabotage or petty opposition. It is time for a major international peace conference, along the lines of Reagan's meeting with Gorbachev in Reykjavik or Nixon's meeting with Mao in Beijing. It is time for the stronger party to act like the stronger party and make the first move—for the big to be bigger. America, as the nation that still claims to be the leading light of the world, has much to gain by acting like one—by taking the kind of bold, decisive, inspirational step that was once such a hallmark of American self-confidence on the global stage.

The president of the United States could begin by making it clear that his or her country is committed to pursuing a fundamentally new strategic relationship with Iran. A challenge could be issued to Iran: Meet us face to face, in a neutral location, or forever hold your peace. Assuming Iran accepted this challenge (and it very well might not), the two countries could then agree to put everything on the table, discussing a range of issues from nuclear energy to the Syrian civil war, to Iran's support for militant groups like Hezbollah, its position on the Arab-Israeli peace process, sanctions and asset freezes, and past grievances like the hostage crisis and the 1953 coup.

Is any of this going to happen? Probably not. Today enmity between the United States and Iran has become almost an industry in its own right, with a vast spectrum of actors dedicated to its perpetuation. Specifically, four highly important and highly influential political constituencies have a clear stake in not seeing relations improve between the two countries. We might call them four nodes of opposition.

The first of these (in no particular order) is Iran's hard-line revolutionary right wing—a large percentage of the rank-and-file membership of the Revolutionary Guards, the Basij, fundamentalist religious leaders, and ideological crusaders. All live in fear of losing the American bogeyman toward which to direct the public's animosity. In many ways, these hard-liners are the soul and conscience of the revolution—the war veterans, the paramilitary loyalists, and the preachers who profess an unshakable loyalty to the principles of law and order, Islamic morality, *velayat-e-faqih,* and hatred of American "imperialism" that they believe is intrinsic to the ideology of the Islamic Republic. And they, in turn, exercise enormous influence over Ayatollah Khamenei. Although the West often sees the supreme leader as a hard-line conservative figure, in fact he is a pragmatist who knows he has to reflect a certain amount of the ideological zeal of his followers in order to maintain legitimacy. And for this hard-line base in Iran, opposition to the United States is an article of faith. Any suggestion that the Islamic Republic is relaxing or betraying its ideals will be met with ferocious and well-organized opposition in Iran—in particular, from those who have made a career of America-bashing. This makes it very difficult for any Iranian leader to go out on a limb and reach out a hand of friendship to Washington.

The second node of opposition is Israel—or more precisely, the wide-ranging network of pro-Israeli commentators, lobbyists, think-tanks, organizations, and activists who influence discussions of the Middle East in the United States. For Israel and its U.S. supporters, the idea of a normalized relationship with Iran is troubling, because it implies that the United States might fundamentally realign its alliances in the Middle East and allow Iran to rise in prominence and even become a strategic rival to Israel. This subtle and crucial point is often lost among all the hysterical talk that Israel faces an "existential threat" from Iran. What Israel fears far more than an Iranian nuke is an Iran that is friendly with the United States—an Iran that is strong, not isolated, and plays a major role in regional affairs. And Israel consistently puts itself in the way every time it believes such an Iran is about to emerge.

The third node of opposition is the conservative Sunni Arab political establishment, led by Saudi Arabia, Jordan, the Gulf sheikhdoms, and Egypt. Although this collection of kings and emirs and presidents has taken some serious knocks in recent years, it still plays a critical role as a pillar of American foreign policy in the Middle East, and therefore no American president can safely ignore its concerns. Most of these Arab leaders—often labeled "moderates" in the United States for their willingness to advance U.S. interests in the region—live in fear of an improved U.S.-Iranian relationship for much the same reason that Israel does: it might reduce their own influence in Washington. If Iran is allowed to come out of the cold, they reason, America will have much less need for them, and U.S. policy might even revert to the old three-way informal alliance between Washington, Tehran, and Tel Aviv that marked the Nixon, Ford, and Carter administrations in the 1970s. It is worth remembering that Arab *publics,* on the whole, are still somewhat sympathetic to Iran—and that in those countries, such as Lebanon, where the public is given a voice in its country's affairs, official relations with Iran have been generally positive. However, the old-guard conservative establishment is still eager to keep Iran weak and isolated.

The fourth node of opposition is the traditional American right—the hot-air pundits, the old cold warriors, the foreign policy hawks, and the Republican Party as a whole (especially when it is not in power). For the most part, these ideological conservatives believe that U.S. power and prestige depend on America never showing "weakness" to the world, as Jimmy Carter did during the hostage crisis of 1979–81. They can be relied on to make copious amounts of noise if any president belonging to the Democratic Party should attempt to improve relations with Iran. They are highly skeptical that diplomacy can work with Iran, preferring to think of the Islamic Republic as a force for evil that must be defeated and destroyed, with the kind of steely determination that Ronald Reagan used to face down the Soviet Union.

Though these four ideological groups have wildly divergent interests, endgames, and worldviews—and are often on bitterly opposing sides of almost every imaginable issue—they all have one important thing in common: they are well served by ongoing U.S.-Iranian hostility. Every time the tone between Washington and Tehran seems like it might be slightly softening, one (or more) of these interest groups finds a way to sabotage diplomacy, and the others are quick to capitalize, either rhetorically or tactically.

It would therefore take an extraordinary act of leadership to bring the historic enmity between Iran and the United States to a close. A U.S. president who wanted to improve ties with Iran would have to reassure the Islamic Republic that its revolutionary institutions and core ideology are not under threat from the United States; to reassure Israel that he or she is 100 percent committed to its security; to give Arab leaders something that they want (perhaps progress on the issue of Palestine, or promises not to push the democracy agenda too forcefully); and to reassure the conservative American pundit industry that he or she will continue to be "tough" with Iran.

Such a president would have to decide to make repairing relations with Iran into a major strategic foreign policy imperative in its own right. This president would have to decide that all the brickbats and roadblocks that would be thrown in his or her way were worth enduring for the sake of achieving an objective that is so plainly in America's interests and in the interests of global peace and stability. In short, he or she would have to exercise leadership, the kind that ignores short-term political expediency for the sake of a true, transcending vision. And the president would have to do all this in an age of extreme cynicism, when far too many people are happy to claim that American power is in retreat and when any attempt to deviate from a cautious, hidebound political script is met by howls of obstruction.

To say the least, this is a task that even a superhuman president would find daunting.

And that is a genuine shame, because no single act could do more for America's position in the Middle East—or for global peace and tranquility—than a reset of relations with Iran. The fact is that Iran could provide America with meaningful assistance in Iraq and Afghanistan, against al-Qaeda, the Taliban, and ISIL, and with the Israeli-Palestinian peace process—virtually every issue that has dogged U.S. foreign policy in recent years. Iran has been in a position to provide this kind of assistance for well over a decade now, but it will not do so without a genuine indication of good faith by the United States. Similarly, the United States is in a position to give Iran what *it* needs more than anything else: the sense of security that comes from knowing it is not going to be attacked, destabilized, or undermined by the world's most powerful nation. It could also pave the way for Iran to have a more positive relationship with Europe and the West generally, allowing Iranian goods and services again to be freely traded on international markets.

I will go even further: not only do both countries have a great deal to gain from a more positive relationship, but there is no good reason they could not one day take the truly bold step of becoming *strategic partners.* America, if it could get past its domestic political constraints, would be well advised to diversify its alliances in the Middle East. The two pillars that American foreign policy has rested on for the past three decades—the conservative Arab political establishment and Israel—are fast becoming liabilities in the Muslim world, especially in the battle for hearts and minds, where the moral cold war is being fought. In the twenty-first century, in an age of Arab uprisings and YouTube revolutions, a U.S. foreign policy that relies on a country that keeps four million Palestinians under a seemingly permanent occupation and on a gang of Arab tyrants who pay scant attention to the demands of their own people is simply not a winning formula. Iran is a more natural partner for America, if America dares to be that imaginative.

The same can be said for Iran. If it could let go of some of its cherished revolutionary ideology and antagonism toward America—a tall order, certainly, given the collective experience of sacrifice and martyrdom the country endured in the 1980s—it could look forward to a fundamentally different kind of relationship not just with the United States but with the entire world. It could do a roaring trade with all nations, in everything from carpets to pistachios to petroleum. It could finally produce 4 million or even 5 million barrels of oil a day—its true potential—rather than the 1.8 million it produces today. It could once again act as a critical hub connecting the four corners of Asia to the waters of the Gulf, as it has done since the days of the Persian Empire. And it could do all this while preserving its core values of poverty eradication, foreign policy independence, and Islamic development, so integral to the ideology of the revolution.

Yes, the scenario outlined here would require boldness and vision to fulfill, of a kind that is rarely on display in international politics. But history offers precedents. As recently as the 1970s, the United States relied on Iran as a core pillar of its Middle East policy, believing Tehran to be more reliable and more in line with American interests than the Arab nations that rivaled it. It was Iran that America always turned to when it needed something done in the Middle East. It was Iran that American media constantly described as the country that was most "like us"—both in its culture and in its political orientation. For years, sensible analysts have pointed out that Iran—with its imperfect democratic tradition dating back to 1906—is a much more "natural" ally of the United States than the Arab autocracies that border it. In fact, if one really wants to go back, it is worth remembering how American missionaries once cooed with delight at the prospect of heading east of Eden, to a land they felt was somehow less "Islamic" than Mesopotamia and the Levant. In some ways, not that much has changed.

Iran as well, has a version of this principle: the idea that reaching beyond the immediate horizon can bring unexpected and highly advantageous alliances. For nearly a hundred years, from the 1850s to the 1940s, Iran hoped to recruit America to the role of a "third force," balancing the negative influence of Russia and Britain in its internal affairs. The first dispute Iran ever had with America, in 1854, concerned the shah's outlandish request for U.S. flags to fly from Persian ships as a form of protection against Britain's navy. In the 1920s, when Iran adopted a more assertive foreign policy, its parliament turned to the Standard Oil Company to act as a counterweight to the Anglo-Persian. And every time Iran has gone through a major transition in its history (1979 being the obvious exception), it has turned to American accountants like Morgan Shuster and Arthur Millspaugh to help it get its books in order.

As hard as it might be to imagine from our current vantage point, in the long run, Iran's interests lie in cooperation with, rather than hatred of, the United States. And as hard as it might be to imagine, America's last best hope in the Middle East will be found, just as it has been for centuries, in the Land of Nod—just east of Eden.

Like every long, dark winter, this one too can turn to spring. And when that spring finally arrives, we can all be reminded of the words of the poet Hafez, who so long ago wrote of the nightingale, after the lingering sorrow of separation has lifted, tearing back into the rose garden, its throat bursting with song.

Acknowledgments

From 2007 to 2009, during the course of three research trips to Tehran, I was able to secure access to the official archives of the Iranian Foreign Ministry—access that (to the best of my knowledge) had never before been given to a scholar from outside Iran. The exact story of how this came about—the hours of pleading phone calls, the countless discussions, the letters and faxes, the political background checks, the near misses, the sudden rule changes that locked me out of the archive for weeks on end, the delicate negotiations over exactly what could and could not be copied onto a memory stick—is a story that could easily occupy a volume not much smaller than this one. And the fact that my final visit to the archive took place during the bitterly disputed 2009 presidential election in Iran—a particularly volatile time when the government was convinced that foreign agitators were in the country to stir up trouble and was arresting Iranian-Americans like myself for possession of suspicious-looking files—only added to the tension of the experience. In the end, for reasons too complex to delve into here, I was given permission to look only at documents dating from before the 1920s. But even this, under the circumstances, felt like something of an achievement.

The experience was never easy, but it was made more bearable by the gracious assistance of a Mr. Esmailnia and a Ms. Zabifard—neither of whose first names I ever learned—and by the warm hospitality of archive staff who often shared trays of tea and biscuits in the afternoon with their unusual visitor. But the sheer scale of the challenge remained. Thousands upon thousands of documents—many of them only just beginning to see the light of day—are stashed in the Foreign Ministry's vaults. During the chaos of the 1979 revolution, a large quantity of documents ended up in a swimming pool, where they became permanently sodden with moisture.

Years of basement storage followed, creating the perfect condition for mold spores—and then, over time, the whole collection was covered in a thick layer of dust. The result today was a respiratory nightmare, and many of the archive staff walked around wearing surgical masks and latex gloves.

Not every research experience was quite this unnerving. While in Iran, I also had the opportunity to study dozens of rare books and previously unexamined records at the National Archives (a much more relaxing experience), as well as a collection of 7,500 Iranian newspapers dating back to the 1860s. I also traveled through the country extensively, looking for long-forgotten sites of historical interest related to the United States. During the course of several weeks spent crisscrossing Iran on buses and trains, I had the opportunity to scramble through old graveyards, knock on doors, talk to aging political activists, track down obscure books, comb through local records, and run my fingers down the brittle pages of newspapers that had not been opened for fifty or, in some cases, a hundred years.

Back in the United States, I tried to do something similar. In order to avoid treading old and familiar terrain, I drew on the widest possible variety of American sources—not just the usual diplomatic correspondence, State Department records, and presidential libraries, but also museum catalogs, tourist guidebooks, films, radio programs, works of literature, official reports, magazines, television newsreels, private collections held by descendants of historical figures, letters written by missionaries, interviews, unpublished memoirs, oral histories, and political speeches. I also conducted an exhaustive survey of American press coverage related to Iran, combing through thousands of back issues of *Time, Life, Newsweek, The New York Times,* and other publications—as well as colonial American newspapers dating back to the early 1700s.

The task of sifting through these mountains of documents and trying to piece together some kind of story over the past twelve years has been humbling, overwhelming, and the privilege of a lifetime. But it has also resulted in the accumulation of an immense number of debts. I beg forgiveness of anyone I have forgotten to name here.

I must begin, perforce, with the funders. This book has been made possible by generous support from the Carnegie Corporation (2009) and the National Endowment for the Humanities—which awarded me both a summer stipend (2014) and a Public Scholar fellowship (2016). I am grateful to both these august institutions for recognizing that scholarship and storytelling sometimes exact a price in dollars and cents as well as in emotional exhaustion and despair.

Next come the archivists and librarians. It would be impossible to thank them all but I wish to make a special mention of Tom Knolles and Elizabeth Pope at the American Antiquarian Society; Jeff Flannery and Daun van Ee of the Library of Congress manuscript room; Nicholas Sheetz and the very helpful staff of Georgetown University's Lauinger Library manuscripts division; Laura Ruttum and the staff of the New York Public Library rare books room for assistance with the Arthur Pope papers; the University of Tennessee Special Collections Library; the New Jersey State Archives; the Franklin Delano Roosevelt Library; the John F. Kennedy Library; the National Archives and Records Administration in College Park, Maryland; Yale University's Sterling Library; Tim Horning of the University of Pennsylvania Archives; Alex Pezzati of the Penn Museum; and Gwen Collaço and Mitch Fraas of the University of Pennsylvania's Van Pelt Library for advice with image permissions.

I am also deeply grateful to the many descendants of historical figures who generously shared their papers and memories with me—namely, Martha Dutton, who sent me her mother Sarah McDowell's childhood diary in 2008; Mary Moore, who directed me to an unpublished biography of her father, Arthur Moore, by Keith Haines (who generously sent me a copy), and Jenny Wormald, who connected me to the Moore family; Curtis Harnack, who warmly took me into his Manhattan apartment to help me trace down material related to Howard Baskerville; Sylvia Josif, widow of former U.S. consul in Tabriz, Harold Josif, and their daughter Elly, who kindly allowed me to dig through family papers at their home; Jennie Pakradooni and Haig Herant Pakradooni III, who assisted with their family history; Nanette Kelekian and Mark Santangelo of the Metropolitan Museum of Art in New York, who assisted with Dikran Kelekian's legacy; Michael McCaskey and Mandy Jordan, who shared details of their grandfathers' roles in the Morgan Shuster mission (with assistance from Hilary McDaniel-Douglas); Mary Merrill, for help with her grandfather John Merrill's diary; J. Patrick Boyle for information on the history of his family's house; and Gity Etemad for insights into her great-uncle Ali Qoli Khan.

Miscellaneous pointers, insights, and favors were also provided at various times by Fuad Shaban, who offered tips on early American attitudes to Persia; Samuel Fairchild, who looked into references made by Jefferson to the *Cyropaedia;* Leonard Stewart, who sent a copy of John Elder's history of the Presbyterian mission in Iran; Hayedeh Daftari, who shared personal recollections of her time in Iran in the 1950s; Alison Hansen-Decelles, who alerted me to the anecdote about Jackie Kennedy's tiara; Jacob Appel, who offered statistical analysis of the 2009 Iranian election; Thomas Ricks, who was a font of knowledge about missionaries in the early stages; Matthew Shannon, with whom I have shared many stimulating conversations in recent years; George Kiraz and Vasili Shoumanov, who helped me find photographs of Assyrian-Iranian immigrants; Kaveh Farrokh, who kindly allowed me to use his photos of Tehran in the 1960s; Emmi O'Day, Kyle Morales, and Carelle Hernandez, who fact-checked several details for me in 2013; Fayyaz Vellani, who faxed letters to Tehran when I needed them, and has been a true friend in dark times; Rawad Wehbe and Ali Noori, who helped me grapple my way to a decent translation of the Hafez poem in the epigraph; Nicholas Foretek, who helped me find the poem in the first place; and Bill Figueroa and Ibrahim Bakri, who helped me brainstorm a title for the book—and whose friendship, advice, and support have meant a great deal in recent months.

I must also thank several people who gave generously of their time in the form of oral interviews and lengthy conversations. In Iran, I was deeply grateful to enjoy the companionship and historical memory of Hushang Nikqadam; Torab-Ali Barat-Ali; and Hossein Shah-Hosseini, all of whom were unfailingly gracious and generous with their time over endless rounds of tea and kababs. And in Washington, I benefited from a fascinating dinner interview with Flynt Leverett and Hillary Mann-Leverett in 2009.

While in Iran, I was lucky to enjoy the hospitality, warmth, and good humor of my beloved aunt Mariam and her husband, Sadeq, who hosted me three times, for weeks on end, with far more kindness and good food than I ever deserved. I will probably never lose the weight I gained on those trips, and will certainly never forget the memories from that time. I simply cannot imagine how this book could have been done without *khaneh-ye khaleh*.

From 2013 to 2017, I was lucky to find an intellectual home at the McNeil Center for Early American Studies, thanks to the great guidance of its director, Daniel Richter, who always made me feel welcome and supported, despite the fact that I knew precisely nothing about early American history. The community and camaraderie I found there was an important lifeline during a complex and challenging period in my life.

Portions of this manuscript were read in the early stages by Canna Grindley, Elizabeth Kriynovich, Tenley Bank, Joanna Detz, Frank Carini, and Wes Tudor, all of whom offered helpful thoughts and responses, for which I am grateful. I am especially thankful to James Goode, one of the great pioneers of this field, who read the manuscript in its entirety as it neared completion and offered a seal of approval that let me know it was ready. Though he did not read the entire book, David Graham Page probably read it more carefully, forensically, and enthusiastically than I have ever seen a human being read anything—setting aside far more hours of his life than I ever had the right to expect, and offering genuine, unflagging reminders of his belief in its value. A true friend, whom I am lucky to have found in mid-life.

A failed marriage is a difficult thing to confess to in print, much less decipher and disentangle from the story of a book that took too long to finish. The darker instincts of one's soul migrate too easily to the time wasted, the harsh words spoken, the impossibility of getting work done. But life is complex, and so is gratitude. My ex-wife, Meg Urbanski, read this manuscript twice in its entirety and its journey to completion is forever entangled with her unforgettable spirit. We met, after all, just as the first draft was completed. And if I learned nothing during those years, it was that "more words count less." I am grateful. *Malgré tout.*

No book ever gets far without an editor, and here I have been more fortunate than most. Victoria Wilson—fierce, intimidating, uncompromising, but in the end always right about everything—is not just an editor, she is an institution. Readers will be especially grateful to her when they learn that the first draft of this book, submitted in 2013, was twice the length it is now. But her impact has been on much more than just its length. I would trust Vicky's editorial instincts with my life at this point. And I send this book into the world with confidence, because I know it is good enough for her.

My thanks also go to the army of publishing professionals who quietly supported my efforts in the background. My agent, Kathleen Anderson; my long-suffering editorial cheerleader Stacia Decker; Marc Jaffee and an anonymous copyeditor at Knopf whose bewildering exactitude I wrestled just as the coronavirus descended across all our lives—all have played important roles. I also thank in advance the printers, binders, shippers, drivers, bookstore clerks, and warehouse workers—nameless and faceless but now more critical than ever—who I know will be risking their lives to get these words into your hands.

Finally, my parents. This book is theirs, in ways even they don't realize. My father's heart was broken on page 199. My mother's youth was shaped on page 229. And they left it all behind on page 261. The decision to leave one's country is rarely an easy one, and I can only imagine what a surprise it must be, so many years later, to discover you have birthed a child whose curiosity drags you back. And yet they have suffered this fool gladly, as they have so many times before. They have both read this book many times in its early drafts, offering suggestions and disagreements but always respecting my right to tell the story my way. If I have failed—either on these pages or elsewhere in life—the failings are all my own. If I have succeeded, I have succeeded entirely on the backs of their immigrant sacrifice.

My mother did not want me to write this book; my father did not want me to write it too fearlessly. Neither got their wish. In the end, I have written the story as I see it, and am prepared for whatever it might bring. Only one thing is certain. Had it not been for the love and support they have given over the years, I would not even have been here—in any kind of position to write any kind of book. I could detail at length the many adventures we got into together in the course of my work on this project. But in the end, my parents' greatest contribution to this story will not be found in the practicalities. It will be found in that hovering, ghostlike presence that is most difficult to describe but that I have never felt far from—that pervading, almost imperceptible, feeling of being loved, of being looked out for, and of knowing that, somewhere, two very good and decent people believe in what it is you're doing.

Archival Sources

LIST OF ABBREVIATIONS

Dispatches Persia: Dispatches from U.S. Ministers to Persia, 1883–1906, RG 59, NARA

Dispatches Turkey: Dispatches from U.S. Ministers to Turkey, 1818–1906, RG 59, NARA

FM: Foreign Ministry of the Islamic Republic of Iran, Archives

FRUS: *Foreign Relations of the United States,* Office of the Historian, U.S. State Department, Washington, D.C.

Instructions Persia: Instructions to Diplomatic Representatives in Persia, 1883–1906, RG 59, NARA

Instructions Turkey: Instructions to Diplomatic Representatives in Turkey, 1823–1906, RG 59, NARA

NARA: National Archives and Records Administration, College Park, Md.

Notes Persia: Notes from the Persian Legation in the United States to the Department of State, 1887–1906, RG 59, NARA

NSF: National Security Files, John F. Kennedy Library, Boston

LIST OF PERSONAL PAPERS

Ball, George. Papers. John F. Kennedy Library, Boston

Beale, Truxton. Papers. Library of Congress, Washington, D.C.

Bentley, William. Papers. American Antiquarian Society, Worcester, Mass.

Engert, Cornelius. Papers. Georgetown University Library, Washington, D.C.

Griscom, Lloyd. Papers. Library of Congress, Washington, D.C.

Mather, Cotton. Papers. Massachusetts Historical Society, Boston

Poinsett, Joel Roberts. Papers. Historical Society of Pennsylvania, Philadelphia

Pope, Arthur Upham. Papers. New York Public Library

Spence, Carroll. Papers. Georgetown University Library, Washington, D.C.

Wiley, John. Papers. FDR Library, Hyde Park, N.Y.

Notes

CHAPTER I
East of Eden

4 Only this time Iran: "Iran: Show of Shows," *Time*, 25 October 1971.

5 "world's greatest": "Made in France—Persia's Splendorous Anniversary Celebration," *New York Times*, 5 October 1971, p. 36.

5 Five thousand bottles of wine: "Iran: Show of Shows," *Time*, 25 October 1971.

5 "imperial peacock": "Made in France—Persia's Splendorous Anniversary Celebration," *New York Times*, 5 October 1971, p. 36.

5 Each "tent" boasted: "Iran's Tent City: Potentate Housing," *New York Times*, 3 October 1971, p. 84; "When Shah of Iran Throws a Big Bash, the Sky's No Limit," *Los Angeles Times*, 12 October 1971, pp. A1, 18.

5 Special tents with casino: "When Shah of Iran Throws a Big Bash, the Sky's No Limit," *Los Angeles Times*, 12 October 1971, pp. A1, 18.

6 "Do you know how": *Keyhan*, 27 Mehr 1350, p. 17.

6 "there isn't likely": "When Shah of Iran Throws a Big Bash, the Sky's No Limit," *Los Angeles Times*, 12 October 1971, pp. A1, 18.

6 "some of the emeralds": "First Party of Iran's 2,500-Year Celebration," *New York Times*, 13 October 1971, p. 3.

7 "the best exercise": Cyrus Kadivar, "We Are Awake: 2500 Year Celebrations Revisited," *Aryamehr 11* (blog), 25 January 2002, http://aryamehr11.blogspot.com /2009/03/2500-years-of-iranian-monarchy.html.

10 "We have at present": *American Weekly Mercury*, 2–9 July 1724. Specifically, the *Mercury* was referring to negotiations between Russia and the Sublime Porte. Both the Ottomans and Russians had taken advantage of the chaos in Persia to make territorial gains, and were now negotiating a partition agreement.

11 "the Usurper": *Boston Gazette*, 7–14 October 1723.

11 "was not satisfied": *Boston News-Letter*, 2–9 July 1724.

11 "all kinds of": *Boston News-Letter*, 9–16 May 1723.

12 In February 1724: *Boston News-Letter*, 6–13 February 1724.

12 "the Turks very much": *New England Courant*, 18–25 May 1724.

13 "*Turkes* be not": Thomas Herbert, *A Relation of Some Yeares Travaile* (London, 1634), p. 145.

13 "the treachery, the covetousnesse": John Cartwright, *Preachers Travels* (London, 1611), p. 47.

13 "verie absolute both": Ibid., p. 64.

13 European visitors were regularly: For a more detailed discussion of the differing treatment of Ottoman and Persian empires by British travelers of the early seventeenth century, see John Ghazvinian, "'A Certain Tickling Humour': English Travellers, 1560–1640," Oxford University, DPhil thesis, 2003, chap. 7.

14 Newspapers made heroic: See, for example, *Boston News-Letter*, 9–16 May 1723, and *New England Weekly Journal*, 5 June 1727.

14 "followers of Hali": *Boston News-Letter*, 31 December 1722–7 January 1723.

14 "as equal to": *Boston News-Letter*, 9–16 May 1723.

14 "Persophilia": The sociologist Hamid Dabashi has written extensively on this Western phenomenon in *Persophilia: Persian Culture on the Global Scene* (Cambridge, 2015). Sadly, the term has been sitting in my unpublished manuscript since at least 2010—an important reminder that one should not work too long on a book before publishing.

14 Newspapers began carrying: See, e.g., *New England Courant*, 12–19 March 1726.

14 In 1724, *The Persian*: "Selected Titles from the 1725 Supplement to the Catalogue of the Harvard Library," published in Thomas Goddard Wright, *Literary Culture In Early New England, 1620-1730* (New Haven, Conn., 1920), p. 294. *The Persian Cromwell* must have presented a special problem to American audiences. It was an unflattering account of Mahmud, who was presented as an illegitimate usurper of the Persian crown. But its idea of an archetypal usurping villain was Oliver Cromwell. Among the homeland English audience it was intended for, this would have mostly gone down well in 1724. In the American colonies, however, there might have been a little more uneasiness about the book's anti-Puritan undertones.

14 In 1729, Benjamin Franklin: Leonard Labaree, ed., *The Papers of Benjamin Franklin* (New Haven, Conn., 1959), 1:118–19.

14 Perhaps most tellingly: Mather's most famous work, *Magnalia Christi Americana*, a weighty Puritan manifesto, went into impressive detail about Persian history, discussing—with reverence, respect, and even admiration—the ancient kings of Persia, from Xerxes to Tamerlane. Cotton Mather, *Magnalia Christi Americana* (Hartford, Conn., 1853), pp. 1: 159, 183, 611; p. 2: 671. Much the same was true of Mather's other great work, "Angel of Bethesda"—a collection of spiritualism and medical advice he compiled in Massachusetts in 1724. Traditionally, this enormous manuscript has been cited by American historians as a prime example of Puritan erudition—combining religious and scientific thought, ancient remedies, and medical experimentation. But one of its most striking and least commented-on characteristics is its rampant Persophilia. On the very first page, Mather reflects on the nature of good and evil, and suggests (correctly) that the roots of dualistic philosophy were to be found in the Magian faith of ancient

Persia. Gordon W. Jones, ed., *The Angel of Bethesda by Cotton Mather* (Barre, Mass., 1972), p. 5. And the "Angel" continues in this vein, with dozens of references from ancient Persian authorities like Rhazes and Avicenna—many of them remarkably well-informed. In a discussion of Rhazes, for example, Mather goes out of his way to demonstrate his knowledge of Rhazes's real name, Zakaria Razi. Jones, *Angel,* p. 160.

14 Though his writings were virulently: In one of his books, he tells the story of the famous Persian physician Rhazes, who refused a cure for his blindness on the grounds that he had seen enough of the sins of the world, and wished to see no more. "O Christian, Lett not a Mahometan go beyond thee" in virtue, Mather cautioned his audience. Jones, *Angel,* p. 160. At another point, Mather relates the story of a legendary king of Persia who sent one of his physicians to live among the followers of the Prophet Muhammad, only to find that no one had any use for him because the Muslims there were all so virtuous that they refrained from gluttony and therefore led healthy, happy lives. Jones, *Angel,* p. 17. For more on Mather's knowledge of the Near and Middle East, see Muktar Ali Isani, "Cotton Mather and the Orient," *New England Quarterly* 43, no. 1 (March 1970): 46–58.

14 "So many carcasses": *American Weekly Mercury,* 26 October–2 November 1727, and 2–9 November 1727.

15 Now, though, thanks to the Persian: Some students of early American newspaper history will object to this characterization. The traditional view is that colonial newspapers (with the exception of James Franklin's *New England Courant*) remained dry and dusty until 1730, when Benjamin Franklin took over the *Pennsylvania Gazette* and began filling it with humor and satire. But this is a narrow interpretation. It is true that, throughout the 1720s, news items about Persia were reprinted from the London papers or from diplomatic correspondence, just as all other news was. However, editors of American newspapers still had plenty of latitude about which items to print and how prominently to place them. That they saw fit to run so many items about Persia is significant. So too was the decision to run a nine-part series about Persia in the *Mercury* in 1727. Moreover, Franklin's decision to revamp the *Gazette* did not come out of nowhere. He had seen newspapers like the *Spectator* exciting and informing the public in London. And he must have sensed an appetite among colonial Americans for this kind of newspaper. In this context, it is important to look at the direction American newspapers were going in during the several years *before* 1730 as well. It might be a stretch to say American journalism was "born" during the Persian crisis. But it would be equally mistaken to dismiss the role it played in the development of the medium during the 1720s.

15 "rich Persia carpets": Nina Fletcher Little, "Floor Coverings," *American Art Journal* 7, no. 1 (1975): 109.

15 In 1765, Harvard: The man who taught these classes, Stephen Sewall, was named the first Hancock professor of "Hebrew and other oriental languages"—a man-

date intended to cover Chaldean, Syriac, Samaritan, and Arabic, but which Sewall took to include Persian as well. Benjamin Peirce, *A History of Harvard University* (Cambridge, Mass., 1833), pp. 100–2. Sewall's immediate predecessor at Harvard, Judah Monis, had been teaching Hebrew there for forty years. But by appointing Sewall to the newly endowed professorship, Harvard sent an explicit message that it wanted to expand the narrow linguistic and biblical approach it had taken under Monis and engage in a much broader study of the Near and Middle East. Sewall's appointment was part of a larger trend in American colleges—a move away from the traditional Puritan style of university study, which emphasized Hebrew philology as part of biblical study, and toward a broader interest in ancient languages, history, and archaeology for their own sake. (It was also in part the result of an intense personal, and probably anti-Semitic, dislike that many at Harvard had had for Monis, an Algerine Jew who had converted to Christianity. Hancock's will stipulated that the new professor "shall declare himself to be of the Protestant reformed religion, as it is now professed and practised by the churches in New England.") Sewall himself couldn't stand the man. Shalom Goldman, *God's Sacred Tongue: Hebrew and the American Imagination* (Chapel Hill, N.C., 2004), pp. 45–47; Thomas J. Siegel, "Stephen Sewall and the Transformation of Hebrew at Harvard," in Shalom Goldman, ed., *Hebrew and the Bible in America* (Hanover, N.H., 1993), pp. 228–337. Sewall argued in his lectures that one should study Hebrew not just for biblical scholarship but also as a gateway to other oriental languages. "Lectures on Hebrew and Oriental Literature, delivered in Harvard College between the years 1765 and 1782 by Stephen Sewall," vol. 1, 5–6. In reality, however, he did not get far with this. Though he made admirable progress with Arabic, Sewall's Persian studies were unimpressive, and he eventually drank himself out of a job. Goldman, *God's Sacred Tongue,* p. 50. In 1785, fed up with his antics, Harvard revoked his tenure. Sewall was replaced by Ezra Stiles, who had taught Semitics at Yale before becoming president of the college in 1778. Stiles had developed a fascination with the work of William "Oriental" Jones, the British philologist who had popularized Arabic and Persian literature. From his study of Jones, Stiles became a convert, believing it was time to move away from the more traditional Puritan interest in Hebrew and biblical authority, and toward the idea—rapidly gaining fashionable credibility—that studying linguistic relationships between Asiatic languages, including Sanskrit, Persian, and Arabic, could illuminate the historical migrations and overall story of the human family—far more than the biblical and classical sources alone could do. It was a radical new intellectual development, and Stiles became a convinced proponent. But the time was probably not quite ready for it, and serious American oriental philology would not be seen until the era of Edward Salisbury in the 1840s.

15 In the 1790s and early 1800s: Bentley Papers, octavo vols. 12 and 13. Bentley, who had a reputation as a talented linguist, was one of the most energetic collectors

in the United States. He taught himself twenty-one languages, and his library of over four thousand books was one of the largest in the country. One of his biographers described him as being "like a magnet," and he loved to receive books and treasures from faraway places. Edwin Wolf, "Observations on the Winthrop, Bentley Thomas and 'Ex Dono' Collections of the Original Library of Allegheny College" (Philadelphia, 1962), n.p., in Bentley Papers, Box 5, Folder 9. It is also clear from Bentley's private papers that he asked ship captains to bring things back for him from places like Calcutta and Bombay. See, for example, the list of curios and books from 1802 to 1819 in Bentley Papers, Box 5, Folder 9. When a sailor friend brought him a copy of the *Golestan* of Saadi, one of the most famous works of medieval Persian poetry, Bentley was delighted—waxing at length about the beauty and genius of the poetry, and declaring that it outshone any European poetry of its age. Bentley Papers, octavo vol. 14, p. 65. Some scholars dismiss Bentley as a man who collected more than he understood, but this is probably unfair. His notes on the *Golestan,* e.g., show that he had a genuine understanding of Persian. He refers with confidence to *nastaliq* script—quite a sophisticated reference for an amateur. Bentley enjoyed Saadi's poetry so much, in fact, that he even acquired two copies of the *Golestan* to compare.

17 "*Xerxes* the Great": Among the many editions of the primer, see *The New-England Primer Enlarged. For the More Easily Attaining the True Reading of English to Which Is Added, The Assembly of Divines Catechism* (Boston, 1737), p. 17.

17 In 1783 his son: Abigail Adams to John Quincy Adams, 26 December 1783, in *Letters of Mrs. Adams, the Wife of John Adams* (Boston, 1840), vol. 1. A number of copies of *Cyropaedia* in the Adams Library in Boston show his signature, as well as that of John Adams. Both men read the book with some care, as their handwriting is clearly visible in the margins.

17 "these infant territories": *The Nebraska Question* (New York: Redfield, 1854), p. 70.

18 Media or Persia: For example, Persia, Iowa; Media, Pennsylvania; Cyrus, Minnesota; and Persia, New York.

18 But if one browses through: See, for example, the library of John Waller in 1755, catalogued in "Libraries of Colonial Virginia," *William and Mary Quarterly* 8, no. 2 (October 1899): 77–79; and "a Catalogue of books to be sold at the post office, Williamsburg," 1760s ephemera, Library of Congress, Portfolio 178, folder 5.

19 "knew something of": Poinsett Papers, vol. 21, folder 9, pp. 81–92.

20 "a subject upon": James Morier, *A Second Journey Through Persia, Armenia, and Asia Minor* (London, 1818), p. 196.

20 "people born with": Abd al-Latif al-Shushtari, *Tuhfat al-Alam* (1363; Tehran, 1984), p. 329.

20 "What sort of a place": Wilfrid Sparroy, "The Persian at Home," *Temple Bar* 125, no. 495 (February 1902): 151–52.

20 Possibly the shah was being: And possibly Morier, the source of the story, made the whole thing up. The diplomat was known for both literary license and a dislike of Persia.

CHAPTER 2
Tashrifat

21 "Scarcely an American": David Porter to Secretary of State, 6 August 1835, in *Documents Relating to the Foreign Relations of the United States with Other Countries during the Years from 1809 to 1898* (Washington, D.C., 1838), p. 19:73. See also [James E. De Kay,] *Sketches of Turkey in 1831 and 1832: by an American* (New York, 1833), p. 186. In the years following U.S. independence, as Salem, Massachusetts, transformed rapidly into an international commercial port, American merchants interacted as never before with far-flung customers and suppliers, including Persians. See Charles Trow, *The Old Shipmasters of Salem* (New York, 1905), pp. 45–49. By 1800, Salem alone was receiving more than 8 million pounds of sugar a year. More than 250 vessels were registered at its port at any given time, making it one of the most important trading entrepôts of the English-speaking world.

21 Some had no idea: Many also became deathly ill. In its first nine years alone, the Urmia mission lost six of its twenty adults. And the children fared even worse. In one two-month period, five American children were born in Urmia; all five were dead before they reached their second birthdays. In their first six years in Persia, Justin and Charlotte Perkins buried all three of the children born to them. Charlotte eventually returned to America, too sick with epilepsy to carry on. Even Dr. Grant, who had worked so many medical miracles in villages around Urmia, came down with cholera just before losing his wife and two of his three children. James Field, *America and the Mediterranean World* (Princeton, N.J., 1969), p. 264.

22 Forgotten both by mainstream: David Finnie, *Pioneers East* (Cambridge, Mass., 1967), calls them "an isolated survival of ancient ecclesiastical history" (p. 203).

22 "the whole mingled population": "Report of the Prudential Committee," in *Missionary Herald,* vol. 15, no 12. (Dec. 1819), p. 34.

23 "In all my journeys": John Elder, *Mission to Iran* (Tehran, s.d.), pp. 6–7.

24 Though American missionaries: By 1855, 158 Persians had been converted to Protestant Christianity—an impressive number compared with the figures for the Ottoman Empire (10 Greeks by 1844, 30 Lebanese by 1856, and not a single soul in Syria or Palestine). Ibid., p. 134.

24 In 1843 the energetic: It was the life Fiske was born to lead. The niece of a famous missionary, Pliny Fisk, she had read Cotton Mather's *Magnalia* when she was only eight years old, and as a student at Mount Holyoke, she had been inspired to go to Persia by Justin Perkins's example.

27 Even from 1838: Far from being put out by their solitary role, the missionaries appeared to be in no real hurry to see Uncle Sam treading on their Persian turf. Back in Boston, the ABCFM was oddly slow to muster enthusiasm for establishing diplomatic relations. Not until 1844 did the Board's secretary, Rufus Anderson, draft a letter to the U.S. minister in Constantinople about the safety of missionaries in Persia. His concerns were promptly relayed to the State Department, and a few promising conversations ensued, but nothing materialized. Dabney Carr to Secretary of State, 16 February 1844.

28 Though this behavior made sense: For a good discussion, see Nikki Keddie, *Modern Iran: Roots and Results of Revolution* (New Haven, Conn., 2006), pp. 37–38; and Michael Axworthy, *History of Iran* (New York, 2008), pp. 177–84.

28 Ancient handicrafts: Keddie, *Modern Iran*, 52.

29 From 1855 to 1900: Abraham Yeselson, *United States–Persian Diplomatic Relations 1883–1921* (New Brunswick, N.J., 1956), p. 16.

30 So in 1849, Amir: Ali Moujani, *Barresi-ye Monasebat-e Iran va Amrika (1851–1925)* (1374; Tehran, 1995), pp. 5–6.

31 Amir Kabir was murdered: Amir Kabir was replaced by Mirza Agha Khan Nuri, described as pro-British in Qolamreza Ali Babaei, *Tarikh-e Siasat-e Khareji-e Iran az Shahanshahi-Hakhameneshi ta emruz* (1375; Tehran, 1996), p. 26.

31 In 1854 the two countries: Hunter Miller, ed., *Treaties and Other International Acts of the United States of America* (Washington, D.C., 1942), p. 7:461. See also instructions given by Persian government to its representatives to make sure they kept as quiet as possible so Britain didn't find out what was happening: Rahim Rezazadeh Malek, *Tarikh-e Ravabet-e Iran va Mama'lek-e Motahedeh-e Amrika* (Tehran, 1972), p. 113.

31 American negotiators insisted: Carroll Spence to Mirza Ahmad Khan, 1 November 1855, in Miller, *Treaties*, p. 467.

31 It took nearly two years: One of the most interesting side stories involves internal Persian squabbling over who was authorized to deal with the United States. In May 1856 a new Persian envoy, Malkum Khan, arrived in Constantinople and began openly undermining his own government. A Christian from a pro-British family (his parents had named him after Sir John Malcolm of the East India Company), Malkum remains a mysterious and controversial figure in Iranian history. Famous for introducing Freemasonry to Persia, he believed Western civilization to be the pinnacle of human achievement. Persia, he always argued, needed to adopt Western institutions and culture without modification. Malkum had spent only ten years of his life in Persia, seemed to loathe his own country, and dismissed Persians as irrational "Asiatics" who could not be trusted. When he sat down with Carroll Spence at his house in Constantinople, Malkum went out of his way to convince the American of the "total disregard for truth peculiar to the Persian race." Like children pushing their luck, he said, the Per-

sians should be put in their place. Spence took his new friend's advice and wrote the Persians a lengthy letter in a remarkably undiplomatic and condescending tone—explaining basic principles of international relations, lecturing them on American history, and concluding with an implication that the government of Persia was not "sincere in its desire to negotiate a treaty with the United States, of which it was the proposer." It is unclear how Spence's letter was received in Tehran, but the outbreak of war in 1856 clearly superseded its effect. Miller, *Treaties,* pp. 467–68; Spence to State Department, 22 June 1856, in 14 Dispatches Turkey 31; Spence to State Department, 22 December 1856, in 14 Dispatches, Turkey 35.

31 At the end of 1856: The shah urged his other special envoy to Constantinople, Farrokh Khan, to conclude the deal as quickly as possible, saying that it might come in handy against Britain very soon. Malek, *Tarikh-e Ravabet,* pp. 106–7.

32 "The President of": Miller, *Treaties,* p. 446.

32 The State Department protested: Lewis Cass to Carroll Spence, 1 April 1857, in 1 Instructions Turkey 399–400; Spence to State Department, 4 March 1857, in 14 Dispatches Turkey 40; Charles Spence to State Department, 12 March 1857, in 14 Dispatches Turkey 40.

32 Spence's brother Charles: "Death of a Distinguished Man," *Baltimore Sun,* 21 July 1887, p. 4.

33 "The Shah has manifested": James Buchanan, State of the Union, 8 December 1857, in James D. Richardson, *Messages and Papers of the Presidents, 1789–1897* (Washington, D.C., 1897), p. 5:446.

33 From the Persian side: Mirza Ahmad Khan to Carroll Spence, 15 March 1858, in Spence Papers, Box 1, Folder 26.

33 "national feeling of": Charles Spence to State Department, 27 December 1856, in 14 Dispatches Turkey 36. Spence also claimed that the feeling was mutually beneficial, because Persians regarded Americans as "the Natural enemies of England."

33 In January 1859, citing: "Our Diplomatic Agents," *New York Times,* 22 January 1859, p. 4; *Congressional Globe* 28, 35th Congress, 2nd sess. (19 January 1859), pp. 457–58.

33 As it happened, the navy: Miller, *Treaties,* p. 482.

34 In 1873 and 1878: Fatima Qaziha, ed., *Ruznameh-e Khaterat Nasser-al-din Shah dar safar-e aval-e farangestan* (1377; Tehran, 1998), pp. 172–73.

34 In New York, readers: *Iran,* 27 February 1873, p. 4.

34 A San Francisco man: *Iran,* 25 Rajab 1288, p. 3; *Iran,* 9 February 1875, p. 3.

34 And Persian editorialists: See, e.g., *Iran,* 25 September 1878, p. 3. As Persian newspapers described the United States as the ultimate embodiment of western progress, they also frequently sought to familiarize audiences with the detailed workings of American politics. The full text of Ulysses Grant's resignation speech was serialized over two weeks by Persian papers in 1877, the history of slavery was explained in 1874, and there were frequent updates on the Californian gold rush

and the decline of Native American tribes. *Iran,* 18 May 1875, p. 3; 16 December 1876, p. 2; 16 March 1877; 29 March 1877.

34 Most controversially, the official: *Iran,* 8 Ramazan 1288 (21 November 1871), p. 4.

36 A U.S. legation: Frederick Drake, *The Empire of the Seas: A Biography of Robert Wilson Shufeldt, USN* (Honolulu, 1984), pp. 221–25.

36 Lately, American petroleum: Rufus Dawes, *A History of the Establishment of Diplomatic Relations with Persia* (Marietta, Ohio, 1887), pp. 43–44.

36 "the victims of Mohammedan": Rufus Dawes to William Evarts, 20 November 1880, ibid., p. 5. Evarts replied that, since the United States had no diplomatic mission in Persia, he could do little beyond asking the British consulate to provide protection.

36 "Persia is one of the oldest": Ibid., p. 29.

37 "Remember that": Dawes, *History,* p. 49.

37 "oldest government": Curtin also claimed that Tabriz alone was already importing $4 million of American cotton annually, and the United States had more missionaries in Persia than in any other country. But he was either confused or deliberatively misleading. Tabriz was importing $4 million of English finished cotton goods annually. How much of that was produced from American cotton is unclear.

37 "Persia can probably never": Dawes, *History,* pp. 45–46.

CHAPTER 3

The Amateurs

38 "cosmopolitan adventurer": Taimi Olsen, "SGW Benjamin," in Donald Ross and James Schramer, eds., *American Travel Writers, 1850–1915* (Detroit, 1998), p. 32. Benjamin crossed the Atlantic forty times during his lifetime. James F. Goode, "A Good Start: The First American Mission to Iran, 1883–1885," *Muslim World* 74, no. 2 (April 1984): 117.

38 But alas, Benjamin's: Rufus Dawes, *A History of the Establishment of Diplomatic Relations with Persia* (Marietta, Ohio, 1887), p. 55.

38 "imposing mustache": Olsen, "SGW Benjamin," p. 32.

38 At times he was: Within the State Department, the choice of Benjamin did not initially gain universal consent. The department's first choice for the job had been the crusading Beirut missionary Henry Jessup, an outspoken advocate for the mass conversion of Muslims to Christianity. "God will send forth a cold odoriferous wind," Jessup had once written, "which shall sweep away the souls of all the [Muslim] faithful, and the Koran itself." Mercifully, perhaps, for the history of U.S. relations with the Middle East, Jessup declined the position, leaving the department scrambling for a replacement. Benjamin had one major advantage over Jessup: he was not based in Beirut and so would have to travel to Tehran all the way from the United States—a gesture that would likely impress

the shah. Dawes, *History,* 55. On Jessup, see Joseph Grabill, *Protestant Diplomacy and the Near East* (Minneapolis, 1971), p. 32. For a good example of Jessup's views, see his "The Religious Mission of the English Speaking Nations," in John Henry Barrows, *The World's Parliament of Religions* (Chicago, 1893), pp. 2:1122–26; and Henry Jessup, *The Women of the Arabs* (New York, 1873), p. v.

39   "in a becoming manner": Charles Spence to State Department, 27 December 1856, in 14 Dispatches Turkey 35.

39   But in 1882 the Senate: State Department to S.G.W. Benjamin, 20 October 1884, in Instructions Persia, 1:67.

39   From the moment Benjamin arrived: This was the case even before his arrival. In Constantinople, Benjamin was wined and dined by the gracious Persian minister but had little to offer in return. He had not even packed an American flag to fly from the new legation; the U.S. minister in Constantinople had to find an extra one to give him. S.G.W. Benjamin to Secretary of State, 16 May 1883, 13 June 1883, in Dispatches Persia.

39   "almost unique": S.G.W. Benjamin, *Persia and the Persians* (Boston, 1887), p. 27.

39   "hard gallop": Ibid., p. 35; also S.G.W. Benjamin to Secretary of State, 13 May 1883, in Dispatches Persia.

39   From Qazvin, some one hundred miles: S.G.W. Benjamin to Secretary of State, 13 June 1883, in Dispatches Persia.

39   The report of his arrival took: *Iran,* 21 June 1883.

39   Spectators thronged the streets: S.G.W. Benjamin to Secretary of State, 13 June 1883, in Dispatches Persia.

39   "in the most emphatic": Benjamin to Frelinghuysen, 13 June 1883, in *FRUS,* p. 706.

40   Awestruck by his new surroundings: S.G.W. Benjamin to Secretary of State, 13 June 1883, in Dispatches Persia.

40   The State Department had refused: Goode, "Good Start," p. 106.

40   "amateurs": Ibid., p. 110.

41   Within hours of his arrival: Ibid., p. 106.

41   Soon afterward he became convinced: State Department to S.G.W. Benjamin, 17 October 1883, in Instructions Persia, 1:25–26.

41   Undeterred, Benjamin began: This latter incident was precipitated when a well-respected American missionary, Rev. Benjamin Labaree, privately shared with Benjamin his belief that the Russians were behind the Persian government's recent decision to ban Muslims from attending church services. No doubt Reverend Labaree sensed that the road to Benjamin's heart ran through his hatred for Russia and acted shrewdly. But the minister needed little provocation.

41   "There is no question": S.G.W. Benjamin to Melnikow, 3 January 1884, 9 January 1884, in Dispatches Persia.

41   Benjamin was told that: Secretary of State to S.G.W. Benjamin, 17 May 1884, 31 May 1884, Instructions Persia.

41 "neither his position": Goode, "Good Start," p. 111; S.G.W. Benjamin to Secretary of State, 22 December 1884, 23 December 1884, in Dispatches Persia.

41 But when the American: Ali Moujani, *Barresi-ye Monasebat-e Iran va Amrika (1851–1925)* (1374; Tehran, 1995), p. 51; S.G.W. Benjamin to Secretary of State, 7 March 1884, in Dispatches Persia.

41 Benjamin's tenure in Tehran: See, e.g., Yeselson, *Diplomatic Relations,* pp. 26–31.

41 Far more than almost: One of Benjamin's great unsung accomplishments was the establishment of a U.S. consulate in Bushehr, a crucial southern port within the British sphere of influence in which no Western nation had yet established a political presence. The Persian-American treaty of 1856 had given Washington the right to set up a consulate in Bushehr, and Benjamin was determined that the United States would become the first Western nation to do so. Yeselson, *Diplomatic Relations,* p. 30.

42 Though Benjamin liked: Benjamin was not, as is sometimes implied, recalled from Persia by an embarrassed and furious State Department. Yeselson, *Diplomatic Relations,* pp. 30–31.

42 When he returned to America: "Talking About the Persians," *New York Times,* 15 December 1888.

42 For the rest of his days: Goode, "Good Start," p. 117.

43 E. Spencer Pratt: Despite his lack of experience, Pratt quickly took to his role. The shah was particularly fond of him, and the two men sometimes conducted lengthy private meetings with no one else present. At one such meeting, Pratt presented the shah with a collection of photographs of the United States, which delighted the monarch. At another, the shah asked Pratt—a trained physician—to treat one of his cabinet ministers for an illness. Malek, *Tarikh-e Ravabet,* p. 169. Qaziha, *Ruznameh-e Khaterat* 3, p. 442.

43 Truxtun Beale: Beale initially saw everything through the prism of an *Arabian Nights* cliché and did not seem to know the difference between Turks, Arabs, and Persians. Greeted by the governor-general of Rasht, Beale recorded that he was "short and fat with a Turkish mustache and sat down Turkish fashion and hollowed for his water pipe." Beale was endlessly amused by this odd-looking oriental and added that he "could not help smiling in his face as the words of the old song . . . rose in my mind: 'In olden days there lived a Turk a horrid beast within the East, etc.'" Beale to his sister Emily, 23 July 1891, in Beale Papers, Box 5. On another occasion, he described the prince who governed Isfahan as looking like something out of "the fairy stories of our childhood." Beale to his mother and his sister Emily, 21 February 1892, in Beale Papers, Box 5. Beale's father was one of the wealthiest and most influential men in Washington, a multimillionaire who had been appointed to important positions by five U.S. presidents. In 1912 Beale sold the family ranch in Kern County, California, to newspaper magnate Harry Chandler and land developer Moses Sherman. Known today as the Tejon Ranch, located around the area Californians refer to

as the Grapevine, it is at the center of a long-running dispute between environmentalists and developers.

43 In 1886, Winston: Winston claimed he hated every minute of his time in Persia and practically begged the State Department to send him home at the first opportunity. He even recommended that Washington close the Tehran legation altogether, saying it was a colossal waste of money. "The whole state of affairs in this country . . . the insecurity of property, the inefficiency of authority, the constantly increasing depreciation of currency and a multitude of other reasons make it inadvisable in my judgement to try to extend American trade in this country." Frederick Winston to Secretary of State, 25 April 1886, 10 May 1886, in Dispatches Persia. Traditionally, historians have taken Winston's pessimistic report at face value. But a closer look suggests that perhaps he was not being entirely honest with his bosses, and might have had commercial goals in mind. Yeselson, *Diplomatic Relations,* pp. 31–32. There is also some disagreement as to how difficult a customer Winston actually was. The provincial governor at Rasht, whose job it was to welcome most Western diplomats upon their first arrival in Persia, was so taken aback by Winston that he cabled to warn the shah that the new American minister was "crazy." But the prominent aristocrat Sani-ol-dowleh felt that Winston's reputation did him a disservice, and insisted that he "seemed intelligent." Malek, *Tarikh-e Ravabet,* p. 162. John S. Galbraith, "Britain and American Railway Promoters in Late Nineteenth Century Persia," *Albion* 21, no. 2 (summer 1989), p. 252; "Mr. Winston Astonished," *New York Times,* 15 June 1886. Vanderbilt money was rumored to be involved in the project: "To Build Railways in Persia," *Los Angeles Times,* 2 February 1889, p. 4. That a U.S. diplomat would resign his post after just a few weeks and rebrand himself as an advocate for private business interests was highly irregular. It is inconceivable, given the staggering sums involved, that the State Department would have approved Winston's actions had it known about them. The size and scale of the project he proposed cast his gloomy official assessments of Persia's commercial potential in a fresh light. A rumor in Tehran had it that the foreign minister, Moshir-od-dowleh, had been personally promised 100,000 Tomans (about $150,000) if the deal went ahead. Malek, *Tarikh-e Ravabet,* p. 163.

44 "political objectives": Galbraith, "Railway Promoters," pp. 258, 260–61.

44 the attitude on the Persian: In 1883 the mayor of Hamedan received and entertained a group of missionaries with great honor, and in 1890 the shah himself visited the American School in Tehran, chatted with teachers and staff, and praised its efforts in the name of education. *Iran,* 15 December 1883, p. 4; *Iran,* 20 November 1890, p. 1.

44 Hossein Qoli Khan Nuri: *Encyclopaedia Iranica.*

44 "a small man": "Likes the Yankee Nation," *New York Times,* 2 October 1888, p. 8.

45 "Mr. Ghooly": "Mr. Ghooly Gets Mad," *Los Angeles Times,* 6 July 1889, p. 4; *New York Times,* 2 May 1896, p. 1; *Nation,* 11 July 1889, pp. 22–23.

45 In fact, Nuri had never: S.G.W. Benjamin to Secretary of State, 16 May 1883. In fact, until the age of air travel, the State Department officially allowed new U.S. ministers two months to travel to Tehran.

45 When Nuri's ship pulled up: Nuri described this official as a "Mr. Connelly" from the State Department. FM 1306-20-3-4.1.

45 "The old established and": Notes Persia, vol. 1 (October 1888).

45 "happy and auspicious": FM 1306-20-3-8.1.

46 It is unclear whether: John Bassett Moore, *Digest of International Law* 4 (1906), p. 687.

46 That he was not allowed: If Cleveland was seen in private talks with a diplomat, or was suspected of accepting the "slightest" favor, he would be "taken to task" by opponents, Nuri explained. Classified addendum, Hossein Qoli Nuri to Foreign Ministry, 6 Safar 1306, FM 1306-20-3-12/12.1

46 An election was coming up: Malek, *Tarikh-e Ravabet*, p. 185.

46 "the greatest government": Report, Safar 1306 (exact date illegible), Hossein Qoli Nuri to Foreign Ministry, FM 1306-20-3-14.

46 "Close the legations in Berlin": Report, Safar 1306 (exact date illegible), Hossein Qoli Nuri to Foreign Ministry, FM 1306-20-3-13.1.

47 "everyone laughs": Report, Safar 1306 (exact date illegible), Hossein Qoli Nuri to Foreign Ministry, FM 1306-20-3-14, 14.1 and 15.

47 "dirty despot": "A Dirty Despot," *Los Angeles Times*, 5 July 1889, p. 4.

47 He was so outraged: "An Indignant Diplomat," *New York Times*, 5 July 1889, p. 1.

47 "When I arrived": Ibid.

47 In the United States: See, e.g., *New York Times*, 2 May 1896, p. 1.

48 The reputation stuck: Ali Hatami, dir., *Hajji Vashangton* (film, 1991).

48 The movie portrayed him: This need to hold up Nuri for mockery—as a backward, bumptious Persian who couldn't cut it in the real world—probably says more about the contemporary Iranian psyche than it does about the historical record. A memorable scene from the film, for example, shows Hajji Washington giving pistachios to the president of the United States. Another shows him slaughtering a sheep in front of the Persian legation building.

48 None of this was true: After Nuri returned to Tehran in 1889, he went on to a distinguished career as minister of public welfare and then retired into obscurity until his death in 1937. Upon his return, the shah even gave him the prestigious title *Sadr-ol-Saltaneh*, which makes it hard to believe he was disgraced. But Nuri had many enemies at court (his father's tenure as prime minister had been a turbulent one), and one courtier in particular, the famed diarist Itimad-os-Saltaneh, spread the rumor that he had been "thrown out" of Washington. (Itimad, no objective witness, in the same breath described Nuri as a "lunatic.") Later generations of Iranians took at face value the falsehoods recorded by Itimad but rarely examined them closely for their accuracy. Iraj Afshar, ed., *Rizname-ye Khatirat-e "Itimad-os-Saltaneh, 1292–1313* (1385; Tehran: Amir Kabir Press, 2006), p. 656.

More recent Iranian scholarship has tried to rescue Nuri from the Hajji Washington caricature, suggesting he was not rejected by Washington but rather recalled by the Foreign Ministry in Tehran—which was uncomfortable with his outspoken admiration for American democracy. Moujani, *Barresi*, pp. 16–17. Nuri, in other words, was the victim of a tyrannical monarchy bent on keeping Persia in the dark ages. This is an interesting idea (one clearly informed by post-1979 revolutionary ideology), but it does not withstand scrutiny. While Nuri made some strong statements in his reports, most of them were written during his first few weeks in Washington. If they had been so objectionable, he would have been recalled much earlier.

48 A close look at Iranian: When Nuri arrived in America in October 1888, he complained to his bosses in Tehran that it had taken him two months to get to Washington, and since it would take him two months to get back, that left him "only eight months" in America—barely enough time to pack and unpack, let alone complete such an important mission. Report, Safar 1306 (exact date illegible), Hossein Qoli Nuri to Foreign Ministry, FM 1306-20-3-13. A translation of the lease Nuri signed on his house in Washington, moreover, shows he agreed to pay a lump sum of $2,000 for nine months. Lease agreement between Madame Smith and Hossein Qoli Nuri, 3 October 1888, FM 1304/5-19-13-1. He is also recorded as departing New York on 13 July 1889—nine months and four days after moving into the house. "On Outgoing Steamers," *New York Times*, p. 5. In other words, Nuri didn't storm off in a huff, he wasn't recalled, and he wasn't thrown out.

48 In May 1893: Halsey C. Ives, *The Dream City* (St. Louis, 1893), n.p.

49 "Extremely ungraceful": David Burg, *Chicago's White City* (Lexington, Ky., 1976), p. 222.

49 Every day, from ten a.m.: J. W. Buel, *The Magic City* (St. Louis, 1894).

49 "direct insult": Moujani, *Barresi*, p. 53; Moujani, Ali, ed. *Gozideh-ye asnad-e revabat Iran va Amrika (1851–1925)* (Tehran: Political and International Studies Office, 1375), pp. 61–63.

49 "untrustworthy": Report signed by Kargozar of Bushehr, 20 May 1922, FM 1301-53-12-*passim;* Dispatches Persia, March and April 1896, *passim.* Tyler himself described Malkam as a "sharp, pushing man of business" but felt obliged to fight his corner.

50 Matters quickly escalated: Qajar supplementary catalogue, p. 4:334, report 10. In 2009, the actual documents were described as "unavailable" by the FM archives staff.

50 "All the *farmans*": Moujani, *Barresi*, p. 54.

CHAPTER 4
The Professionals

51 Thousands of people: Abbas Amanat, *Pivot of the Universe: Nasir al-Din Shah Qajar and the Iranian Monarchy, 1831–1896* (Berkeley, Calif., 1997), p. 444.

52 As the shah put: Ibid., p. 440.

52 As the imperial procession: Ibid., p. 441.

52 "The fish begins": Edward Browne, *The Persian Revolution of 1905–1909* (London, 1966), pp. 67, 91.

54 Muzaffar al-Din: Shaul Bakhash, "The Failure of Reform: The Prime Minister-ship of Amin al-Dawla, 1897–98," in Edmund Bosworth and Carole Hillenbrand, eds., *Qajar Iran: Political, Social and Cultural Change 1800–1925* (Edinburgh, 1983), pp. 15–16; Cyrus Ghani, *Iran and the Rise of Reza Shah* (London, 1998), p. 6.

54 As security for the loan: All, that is, except what was coming in from the south-ern Gulf ports.

55 Eventually, the Persian: Ghani, *Rise of Reza Shah*, pp. 6–7.

55 Joseph Naus: Peter Avery et al., eds., *Cambridge History of Iran* (Cambridge, U.K., 1991), pp. 7:199–200.

56 Within a few weeks: Mofakham al-Dowleh to Foreign Ministry, n.d., FM 1318-29-12-12. Although this dispatch is undated, it is in a file of documents from 1318 and is mixed in with dispatches from Shavval and Zil-qadeh of that year, which would correspond to January or February 1901. The tone of the dispatch also cor-responds with those written during Izhaq's first few weeks in Washington.

56 In response to this surge: "Shah Is Seeking American Trade," *New York Herald*, 9 December 1900. As a diligent and energetic career diplomat with many years' experience, Izhaq took this task seriously, suggesting, for example, that a certi-fication scheme could be created in order to protect consumers against fakes. Izhaq also felt that Persia's new commercial consulates should be staffed by men with genuine business experience and contacts. In his dispatches, he argued fre-quently that establishing a stable American market for Persian carpets could do wonders for his country's economy. Ishaq to Foreign Ministry, 16 Muharram 1320 (25 April 1902), FM 1320-10-3, fol. 43; Foreign Ministry to Ishaq, 27 Rabi' al-Sani 1320 (2 August 1902), FM 1320-10-3, fol. 128.

56 Dikran Kelekian: Marilyn Jenkins-Madina, "Collecting the 'Orient' at the Met: Early Tastemakers in America," *Ars Orientalis* 30 (255), pp. 73–75. (My thanks to Nanette Kelekian for alerting me to this reference.) See also "The American Art-ists," *New York Times*, 5 April 1903, p. 7. Kelekian's gallery, however, was not "the first Persian consulate in the United States," as Jenkins-Madina and others have claimed. In October 1888, when Hossein Qoli Khan Nuri arrived as Persia's first minister to Washington, he appointed H. R. Pratt to be consul-general in New York. *Congressional Directory* (Washington, D.C., 1893), p. 261.

56 Haig Herant Pakradooni: Foreign Ministry, Tehran, Office of Protocol, copy of credential letter, Muharram 1321 (roughly April 1903), FM 1321-11-6, fol. 11; Certificate from President Theodore Roosevelt, 11 December 1903, FM 1322-4-10, fol. 70. Confusingly, there are also documents from Muharram 1320 (roughly April 1902) describing his appointment as vice-consul, FM 1320-25-5, ff. 1–3. Like Kelekian, Pakradooni was a businessman based in the United States, and like Kelekian, he seemed to think the ceremonial title "Consul to His Imperial Majesty the Shah of Persia" would provide a nice little boost of prestige to his printing business. Pakradooni happily retained the title until his death in 1937, even though he appears to have lost all contact with the Persian government by 1911. 'Aliquli Khan, Six-month Report on Pakradooni, 1 December 1911 to May 1912, FM 1321-11-6, fol. 17.

56 Alfonso Rutis: Rutis to Ishaq Khan, 12 October 1904, FM 1322-9-5, ff. 57–58, 80–82.

56 Milton Seropyan: *Register of the Department of State* (Washington, D.C., 1907), 121. Death certificate no. 45562, Missouri State Archives, describes him as an "oriental rug merchant."

56 and they represented the first: Some more than others. Rutis appears to have used his position as Persian consul to sell torpedo boats to the Persian government in 1904. Rutis to Ishaq Khan, 12 October 1904, FM 1322-9-5, ff. 57–58, 80–82.

56 The wealthiest Americans: In 1899, for example, the long-serving *chargé d'affaires* in Tehran, John Tyler, secured Persia's participation in the International Commercial Congress in Philadelphia and arranged for the export of seventy exemplary rugs to educate American consumers and dealers. The following year the journalist John Kimberley Mumford published *Oriental Rugs,* the first book on the subject by an American and an immediate best seller. Such efforts were badly needed. Americans' tastes for Persian carpets often outpaced their ability to spot fakes, and the problem of counterfeit rugs was epidemic. Izhaq to Foreign Ministry, 16 Moharram 1320 (25 April 1902), FM 1320-10-3-43. In 1906 the American antiquarian Arthur Dilley published *How Oriental Rugs Are Sometimes Sold,* aimed at exposing deceitful practices. But experts could do only so much. In 1904, when Persian rug weavers knew their products were heading for America, they reportedly wove rude messages into the designs, confident no American would be able to decipher them. "Curios and Oddities: Inscriptions on Persian Rugs," *Los Angeles Times,* 12 June 1904, p. D8. Persian consumers were easily gulled as well. In the years around 1900, demand for American products—in particular, machinery and high-end electrical goods—was running high in Tehran. But supplies could be sporadic, so enterprising middlemen took advantage. In 1902 significant numbers of German sewing machines were reportedly being sold in Tehran on the premise that they were made by the Singer Manufacturing

Company of New York. The need for adult supervision on both sides seemed obvious. Lloyd Griscom to his father, 4 January 1902, in Griscom Papers, Box 1.

57 Under Izhaq, Persia's: Izhaq even took a five-month trip to Latin America (Pakradooni was left in charge during his absence), presenting his credentials to the Mexican president and learning all he could about the geopolitics of the Western hemisphere. Izhaq to Foreign Ministry, 6 Zuw al-Qa'dih 1320 (4 February 1903), FM 1320-10-3, fol. 70; ephemera, FM 1321-11-5, fol. 91, 1321-11-6, ff. 10-11; *Iran,* 17 November 1903, 6.

57 Together Izhaq and Morteza: FM 1320 and 1321 *passim.* To assist Izhaq in his work, Morteza sent Nevdun Khan, a civil servant who had been educated in Switzerland and the United States and was fluent in four languages, to serve as the legation's permanent secretary in Washington. Foreign Ministry internal document, n.d., FM 1321-11-6-18.

57 In 1904, when Izhaq: A similar process was under way in the United States. In 1909 the State Department established its Division of Near East Affairs.

57 Suave, sophisticated characters: See, for example, "The Benzine Blizzard of Gen. Morteza Khan," *New York Times,* 19 February 1905, p. 7.

57 "A Multi-Millionaire": "A Multi-Millionaire from the Land of Omar Khayyam," *New York Times Magazine,* 26 February 1905.

57 "a man of imposing": "Shah is Seeking American Trade," *New York Herald,* 9 December 1900. Izhaq was a career diplomat, having served for ten years in St. Petersburg, three in Cairo, and one in Brussels. He had accompanied the shah on his first European trip and was described as being close to the Imperial Court.

57 But Izhaq reported: We have only his word to go on, but Izhaq claimed that, following a formal ceremony, the president asked him to linger for a few minutes and watch military maneuvers with him, and the two men apparently hit it off. Izhaq to Foreign Ministry, 2 Rabi al-Avval 1321, FM 1321-11-5-78. Izhaq claimed that the president then invited him to dine informally with the Roosevelt family and accepted Izhaq's invitation to have dinner at the Persian legation one evening. (If true, this would seem to be a first for diplomatic protocol in Washington.) In another dispatch to Tehran, Izhaq even claimed the president had informally suggested inviting the shah to the 1904 World's Fair in St. Louis. FM 1320-10-3-71 and 71.1. He was playing a clever game. Almost certainly Izhaq exaggerated the warmth of the American welcome. President Roosevelt, he said, was prepared to send a U.S. Navy frigate to the Black Sea to transport the shah to America. This could not possibly have been true, but for Izhaq, it was a risk-free thing to say. He knew full well that the shah hated sea voyages and that his doctors would never allow him to undertake such a lengthy trip.

57 "fire-dancers": See, e.g., "The Progress of Preparation for the Great Louisiana Purchase Exposition," *Los Angeles Times,* 24 April 1904, p. E10; "The Music of Many Nations," *Los Angeles Times,* 3 July 1904, p. D8.

57 And a merchant selling: The merchant himself was probably a Syrian immigrant, though his exact identity is disputed.

58 These were volatile times: In 1904, U.S.-Persian relations faced their first real test, after a group of Kurdish bandits robbed and brutally murdered Rev. Benjamin Labaree, a respected American missionary whose family had lived in Persia since the 1860s. The missionaries demanded the death penalty for his killers, but when justice was not forthcoming, they grew unusually restive and pressured the American minister in Tehran, Richmond Pearson, to seek redress. Matters quickly escalated, and before long, no less a figure than President Theodore Roosevelt was threatening to dispatch warships to the Persian Gulf—warning in his State of the Union address that the United States would not hesitate to "protect our citizens from improper treatment in foreign lands." Theodore Roosevelt, *Presidential Addresses and State Papers* (New York, 1910), p. 3:180. This was almost certainly a bluff. But it worked better than anyone could have anticipated. In January 1905 fifteen hundred Persian troops poured into Kurdish territory to find and apprehend Reverend Labaree's killers, averting a full-scale confrontation between Washington and Tehran. Yeselson, *Diplomatic Relations,* pp. 71–72.

59 And as he lay bleeding: Browne, *Persian Revolution,* p. 121.

60 "Persia is in": Marzieh Gail, *Arches of the Years* (Oxford, 1991), p. 27. The American blueblood was Florence Breed, who was married to Ali Qoli Khan, later Persian consul in New York.

63 "the end of Persia's": *Hablu'l Matin,* 10 September 1907, quoted in Browne, *Persian Revolution,* p. 179.

63 "the King of tyrants": Browne, *Persian Revolution,* pp. 156–57.

63 For a full year, the shah's: Sarah McDowell, childhood diary, 16 and 25 April 1908. I would like to thank Martha Dutton of Wooster, Ohio, who very kindly sent me a photocopy of her mother's childhood diary.

64 Within fifteen minutes: There are many accounts of how and when and where exactly Baskerville died, each slightly different from the other, but all tending toward much the same sort of circumstances. See Rezazadeh Shafaq, *Tehran Journal,* 4 December 1959, reproduced in Ali Pasha Saleh, *Cultural Ties Between Iran and the United States* (Tehran, 1976), pp. 311–28; McDowell diary; and Keith Haines, unpublished biography of Arthur Moore, pp. 63–65. My gratitude to Haines for sharing his manuscript with me.

64 The official U.S. response: "Russia to Hurry Army into Persia," *New York Times,* 22 April 1909, p. 6.

64 Newspapers in the United States: "United States Warns Shah," *New York Times,* 22 April 1909, p. 6.

65 Merchants wove: Though a picture exists of this carpet, it is unclear what happened to it.

65 "like Lafayette": *New York Times,* 30 April 1909, p. 4.

65 "freely mingled his blood": McDowell diary, 21 and 22 April.

CHAPTER 5

The Man from Manila

67 With its sphere of influence: Abraham Yeselson, *United States–Persian Diplomatic Relations 1883–1921* (New Brunswick, N.J., 1956), p. 105.

67 "It is well-known": Iran-e Nou, 1 May 1911, p. 1. The phrase the paper used was قرطاس بازی.

67 "treasurer-general": "Five Young Yankees Will Reform Persia's Finances," *New York Times,* 16 April 1911, p. SM9.

68 "The American government": *Iran-e Nou,* 1 May 1911, p. 1.

68 "before we could unpack": Morgan Shuster, *The Strangling of Persia* (New York, 1912), pp. 12, 15.

68 Over six feet tall: "How Russia Came to Make War on W. Morgan Shuster," *New York Times Magazine,* 26 November 1911.

68 A former cadet corps: Ibid.

68 After just two years in Cuba: "Five Young Yankees Will Reform Persia's Finances," *New York Times,* 16 April 1911, p. SM9. The financial advisers Shuster took with him to Tehran in 1911 were also, for the most part, men in their thirties whom he had befriended during his years in the Cuba and Philippines customs service. Ralph Hills, e.g., like Shuster, was a native Washingtonian, and the two men were old friends. Shuster was the best man at Hills's wedding. "Hills-Gorman," *New York Times,* 28 February 1901, p. 9.

69 This kind of muscular: Shuster, *Strangling,* pp. 24–30.

70 By August: Ibid., pp. 121–22.

70 "I might say that": Ibid., pp. 38–41.

70 "Imagine if you will": Ibid., p. 37.

71 In late July the former: According to Shuster, the former shah had escaped from Odessa, crossed Russia, and taken a steamer down the Caspian, wearing a fake beard and carrying trunks of guns and ammunition labeled "mineral water." Ibid., pp. 104, 128.

71 "Firearms": Ibid., pp. 89, 90, 103–4.

72 "You who have tasted": Yeselson, *Diplomatic Relations,* p. 119. The translation is Yeselson's, and it is closer in meaning to the original French than the officially recorded English translation: "Do you wish to see a people fall of whom complaint has been made that they have allied themselves to your system to save their future?" *Congressional Record* (Washington, D.C., 1912), vol. 48, pt. 1, pp. 88–89.

72 Unfazed, the Persian: "Grills the Russians," *Los Angeles Times,* 1 December 1911, p. 11.

72 "It may be the will": Shuster, *Strangling,* pp. 181–83.

73 In the south of Persia: Ibid., pp. 183–84.

73 They found Shuster: Turin Bradford Boone, *Persian Diary (1911–1912)* (unpublished ms., 1956), p. 2.

73 The treasurer-general: Ibid., p. 2; "Shuster Says Russia is Tricking England," *New York Times,* 23 February 1912, p. 7.

73 There had been numerous: *New York Times,* 23 January 1912, p. 3; Shuster, *Strangling,* p. 184.

73 When he and his wife: "Shuster Leaves Persia," *Wall Street Journal,* 12 January 1912, p. 7.

74 The famed poet Aref Qazvini: گر رود شوستر از ایران، رود ایران برباد \ ای جوانان مگذارید که ایران برود ("If Shuster leaves Iran, Iran itself is gone / O youth! Don't let Iran disappear"). Quoted in Ali Moujani, *Barresi-ye Monasebat-e Iran va Amrika (1851–1925)* (1374; Tehran, 1995), p. 86.

74 There were even reports: "Shuster Attacks Ministers," *New York Times,* 12 January 1912, p. 3.

74 "ancient but . . . newly": "Five Young Yankees Will Reform Persia's Finances," *New York Times,* 16 April 1911, p. SM9.

74 In December 1911: "Shuster Not Advised as to His Successor," Associated Press, 29 December 1911.

74 When news of the Russian: Yeselson, *Diplomatic Relations,* p. 124.

74 Witherspoon Hall: "Crowd Storms Hall to Hear Shuster," *New York Times,* 25 February 1912, p. 9.

74 Waldorf-Astoria: "England Hid Persian Aim, Says Shuster," *New York Times,* 27 February 1911, p. 11.

74 Carnegie Hall: "Shuster Cheered by Big Audience," *New York Times,* 2 March 1912, p. 10.

74 "the rapidly shifting scenes": Shuster, *Strangling,* p. xiii.

75 Every daring young blade: In 1898, Mark Twain had written some *rubaiyyat* of his own, and in the same year Nathan Haskell Dole published *Omar the Tentmaker: A Romance of Old Persia.* It went through three editions and was made into a film starring Boris Karloff in 1922.

75 "harem skirts": "Moving Tableaux of Girls of Orient," *New York Times,* 19 November 1913, p. 9.

75 In 1908 the influential: W. P. Cresson, *Persia: The Awakening East* (Philadelphia, 1908). Cresson had spent a considerable amount of time traveling round Persia. He was a guest of Herbert Bowen in 1899, and possibly went again later. Cresson was responsible for putting together the Philadelphia Commercial Congress in 1899, which displayed more than seventy Persian rugs.

75 Cresson's writing was: "Persia: The Awakening East," *National Geographic* 19 (1908): 356–84.

78 In 1905 thirty Assyrian: John Michael and Sheren Jasim, "Assyrians of Chicago," Assyrian International News Agency, www.aina.org/aol/ethnic.htm.

78 By 1910, Chicago's: Ibid. See also Fred Aprim, "The Assyrians of the San Joaquin Valley, California: From Early Settlements to the Present," *Nineveh,* n.d.,

http://www.nineveh.com/The%20Assyrians%20of%20the%20San%20Joaquin%20Valley,%20California.html.

78 It was an active: Vasili Shoumanov, *Assyrians in Chicago* (Charleston, 2001), pp. 11–12; Michael and Jasim, "Assyrians of Chicago."

79 Richard Crane: *Chicago Blue Book of Selected Names* (Chicago, 1911), p. 98. Richard T. Crane, Jr., was the younger son of Richard Teller Crane, the founder of R. T. Crane & Bro., a Chicago-based manufacturer of pipes and plumbing. After his father died in 1912, Richard Jr. inherited most of the company's holdings. His older brother Charles, a philanthropist and world traveler, took a particular interest in Arabia, Persia, and Central Asia.

CHAPTER 6

War and Peace

81 In Mashhad, Russian: Michael Axworthy, *History of Iran* (New York, 2008), p. 212.

81 Russia had even armed: Michael Zirinsky, "American Presbyterian Missionaries at Urmia During the Great War," *Journal of Assyrian Academic Studies* 12, no. 1 (1998): 12.

81 "crusade": Ibid., p. 19.

81 "the sight was like": Mary Lewis Shedd, *The Measure of a Man* (New York, 1922), p. 156.

81 "big man with": Zirinsky, "Presbyterian Missionaries," p. 17.

81 "the cause of Christ": Ibid., p. 18.

82 "not lying-down": Shedd, *Measure,* p. 144–45.

82 And over time: John Joseph, *The Nestorians and Their Muslim Neighbors* (Princeton, N.J., 1959), p. 136.

82 The British, naturally: Zirinsky, "Presbyterian Missionaries," p. 20.

82 In January 1918: Ibid., pp. 14–15, 19, 20. Ismail Agha Semitqu is often known in the West as "Simko."

83 "dogs, dead animals": "News from Many Lands," *Missionary Review of the World* 41, no. 7 (July 1918): 550.

83 The Persian army rescued: Zirinsky, "Presbyterian Missionaries," pp. 16, 22–23.

84 "tactless, untrained blunderer": Col. John Nelson Merrill, diary entry for 5 December 1914 (copy obtained with the generous assistance of Mary Merrill and the Library of Congress; original in the University of Mississippi Archives and Special Collections); Engert correspondence, *passim,* in Engert Papers, Box 2.

84 Food imports from the north: Axworthy, *History of Iran,* notes that imports from Russia fell from 65 of the national total to just 5 percent (p. 214). The figure is for overall trade, but one can imagine that the figures for food were in the same range.

84 In Hamedan and Kermanshah: Cyrus Ghani, *Iran and the Rise of Reza Shah* (London, 1998), p. 17.

84 "Persia," said the British minister: Harold Nicolson, *Curzon, the Last Phase* (Boston, 1934), p. 129.

85 In 1917 missionaries: Zirinsky, "Presbyterian Missionaries," pp. 19–20; Joseph Grabill, *Protestant Diplomacy and the Near East: Missionary Influence on American Policy, 1810–1927* (Minneapolis, 1971), p. 142; FM 1301-10-1 *passim*.

85 In 1918 the committee: Kate Jackson, *Around the World to Persia* (New York, 1920), pp. 56, 64–65, 69–70.

85 In 1917, the Persian: M. E. Hume Griffith, *Behind the Veil in Persia and Turkish Arabia* (Amsterdam, 1917), p. 77; Abraham Yeselson, *United States–Persian Diplomatic Relations 1883–1921* (New Brunswick, N.J., 1956), pp. 183–84.

85 But the State Department: Yeselson, *Diplomatic Relations,* p. 184.

85 At one point, the shah: The U.S. Treasury seemed intrigued by this dramatic offer and entered discussions with a New York bank, but Britain and Russia squelched the idea as soon as they got wind of it. Ibid., pp. 138–39.

86 Would it be possible, he asked: Ibid., pp. 132–33.

87 "no longer indulge": *Messages and Papers of the Presidents* (New York, 1917), p. 18:8155, 8158.

87 "the little along": Woodrow Wilson, Address to Senate, 22 January 1917, in Ray Baker and William Dodd, eds, *The Public Papers of Woodrow Wilson: The New Democracy* (New York, 1926), p. 2:410.

88 George Curzon, Earl of Keddleston: Officially, Curzon did not become foreign secretary until October 1919, but from January 1919, he was acting foreign secretary while Arthur Balfour was in Paris at the Peace Conference.

88 In Tehran, through the winter: Ghani, *Rise of Reza Shah,* pp. 23, 30, 44.

88 "was opposed to": *FRUS,* vol. 5, p. 153.

88 Privately, Wilson felt: Office of War Information, Bureau of Research and Analysis, "A Brief Review of the Irano-American Relations with a Statement on the present position of Iran," 13 July 1943, 711.9111/34, RG 59, NARA.

89 "for as long as": Ghani, *Rise of Reza Shah,* 26.

89 Desperate for cash: Caldwell, Quarterly Report 5, 1 October 1919.

89 the Anglo-Persian Agreement: To make their point, the Republicans even wheeled Charles Russell, former U.S. minister to Persia, onto the Senate floor to testify to the rapacious practices he had witnessed Britain and Russia engaging in during his time in Tehran.

90 The Wilson administration: Office of War Information, Bureau of Research and Analysis, "A Brief Review of the Irano-American Relations with a Statement on the present position of Iran," 13 July 1943, 711.9111/34, RG 59, NARA.

90 "the manner in which": A. W. Ferrin, "The Past Ten Years in Persia: An Historic Memorandum," October 1930, 891.00/1510, RG 59, NARA.

90 "surprised": *FRUS,* vol. 2, p. 708.

90 Caldwell—who was even angrier: Nasrollah Fatemi, *Diplomatic History of Persia, 1917–1923* (New York, 1952), p. 36.

90 "asylum": Ibid.; Yeselson, *Diplomatic Relations,* p. 163.

91 By August 1919, when: Ghani, *Rise of Reza Shah,* pp. 49–50.

91 "not a single Persian": Ferrin, "Past Ten Years in Persia."

91 Curzon ordered his underling: Ghani, *Rise of Reza Shah,* pp. 94–95.

91 The Anglo-Persian Agreement now: In Britain, a vocal group of Persophiles, who were sympathetic to the aspirations of the constitutional revolution, had existed for several years, and exercised significant influence. They had sided openly with Shuster in 1911, e.g., and now loudly condemned the Anglo-Persian Agreement.

92 "These people have got to be taught": Gordon Waterfield, *Professional Diplomat: Sir Percy Loraine of Kirkharle Bt, 1880–1961* (London, 1973), p. 63.

CHAPTER 7
"The Sordid Side"

97 "the sordid side": "Memorandum of conversation with Lord Curzon at his house at No. 1 Carleton Terrace, on Tuesday, October 14th at 12.45pm," 21 October 1919, 741.91/201/2, NARA, RG 59.

98 But by 1920, that: "U.S. Field Production of Crude Oil," U.S. Energy Information Administration, http://www.eia.doe.gov/dnav/pet/hist/LeafHandler.ashx?n =PET&s=MCRFPUS2&f=A; *Business Digest* 6 (July–December 1918): 524; Charles Issawi, *Economic History of Iran* (Chicago, 1971), p. 313; Abraham Yeselson, *United States–Persian Diplomatic Relations 1883–1921* (New Brunswick, N.J., 1956), pp. 196–97.

99 "any attempt to introduce": James Bill, *The Eagle and the Lion: The Tragedy of American-Iranian Relations* (New Haven, Conn., 1989), pp. 27–28.

99 "a whip-hand": Arthur Millspaugh, memorandum, 17 December 1920, *FRUS 1920,* pp. 3:356–57.

99 Persian newspapers demanded: Yeselson, *Diplomatic Relations,* pp. 185–86; Cornelius Engert to Dr. Barrows, 27 February 1921, in Engert Papers, Box 2, Folder 47.

100 "The present would": Quarterly Report, April–June 1921, in Engert Papers, Box 2, Folder 52; Quarterly Report, July–September, ibid., Folder 53.

100 "miraculously come back": Clair Price, "The Resurrection of Persia," *New York Times,* 7 August 1921, p. 37.

101 The big Hollywood film: The film was an adaptation of the hugely popular novel by Nathaniel Haskell Dole, published in 1898. Dole's novel went through three editions and helped spur the creation of the Omar Khayyam Society of America, of which Dole remained president until 1919.

101 In unlikely places like Flint: Newspaper cuttings from Ala's Midwest speaking tour, FM 1301-23-7.

101 "much more than": Murray to State Department, 15 January 1925, 711.91/8, RG 59, NARA.

101 In the same bill the Majles: Michael Rubin, "Stumbling Through the 'Open Door': The US in Persia and the Standard-Sinclair Oil Dispute, 1920–1925," *Iranian Studies* 28, no. 3/4 (1995): 209–10.

101 "make-weight": Memorandum to Secretary of State, 22 December 1921, 891.51, RG 59, NARA.

102 The Persian press condemned: There is some reason to believe that APOC had never had any intention of partnering with Standard, and that in fact the British government's goal had been to cleverly sabotage Standard—first by insisting to the United States that the company should partner with APOC, then by refusing permission for APOC to participate in the deal, knowing that the mere news of APOC's potential involvement would ruin Standard's reputation in Persia. Hossein Ala and Herbert Hoover, memorandum of telephone conversation, 13 January 1922, FM 1301-39-8-91; Rubin, "Stumbling," pp. 212–13.

102 In March 1922: Rubin, "Stumbling," p. 214.

103 "has unfortunately come": Dulles to Secretary of State, 10 July 1923, 891.6363/295, RG 59, NARA.

103 Divided, dyspeptic, and lacking: Kornfeld's personality problem was not the only one to plague the U.S. legation in 1922 and 1923. In recognition of Persia's growing importance, the United States assigned its Tehran legation a military attaché, and the first to fill this position, Capt. Frank Jedlicka, turned out to be a specialist in the art of needless overreaction. One day when three Persian Cossacks climbed playfully onto his military convoy, Jedlicka exploded with anger and demanded their arrest. Kornfeld backed him up, telling the prime minister that he considered the case a "serious reflection upon the entire institution" of the Persian military. The hapless soldiers had to undergo two hundred lashes and fifteen days of jail time before the U.S. legation was pacified. Statement of Captain Frank Jedlicka, Military Attaché of US Legation, 2 November 1922, FM 1301-10-7-1 and 2 and 6. Kornfeld's consul-general, Bernard Gotlieb, was not much better—he got into a scuffle with some soldiers who had not recognized him without his consular uniform. Once again names were taken, but this time the Persian government was less patient with the Americans and dropped the matter. FM 1301-10-9 *passim*.

103 Wasting no time: The substance of Standard's complaint had to do with the so-called "Khoshtaria concession." In 1916, during the chaos of the First World War, a pro-Russian Persian prime minister had granted a northern oil concession to a Russian subject, A. M. Khoshtaria, then dissolved the Majles and fled Tehran. The whole thing had taken place while Russian troops were occupying the capital, and the British did not recognize the Khoshtaria concession as valid. In 1918 the pro-British government in Tehran annulled the concession. Ironically, however, in 1921, once it became apparent that the Americans were interested in

northern oil, it emerged that Khoshtaria had sold his concession to APOC the previous year. The British government considered the deal legitimate and a reason to deny a concession to the Americans. In January 1924, Standard, which was still in a fifty-fifty partnership with APOC, argued that the Khoshtaria concession was still valid and that Sinclair therefore had no right to northern acreage.

103 Already irritated with Standard: Rubin, "Stumbling," pp. 218, 227–28.

104 "human life as such": Ferrin, "Past Ten Years"; "Persia: An Historic Memorandum," October 1930, 891.00/1510, RG 59, NARA; Michale Zirinsky, "Blood, Power, and Hypocrisy: The Murder of Robert Imbrie and American Relations with Pahlavi Iran, 1924," *International Journal of Middle Eastern Studies* 18, no. 3 (August 1986): 275–92.

CHAPTER 8

The Warrior-King

105 In his absence, Reza: For a good description of how this campaign was conducted, see Cyrus Ghani, *Iran and the Rise of Reza Shah* (London, 1998), pp. 308–10.

105 Many also worried: The debate over republicanism, and Reza Khan's attitude to the idea, are best laid out in Vanessa Martin, "Mudarris, Republicanism and the Rise to Power of Riza Khan, Sardar-i Sepah," in Stephanie Cronin, ed., *The Making of Modern Iran: State and Society Under Riza Shah, 1921–1941* (London, 2003), pp. 65–75.

106 As shah, he was always: Pope to Paige Monteagle, 1 December 1926, in Pope Papers, Box 1.

106 In the 1920s some: Michael Axworthy, *History of Iran* (New York, 2008), p. 223.

107 For the fifteen years: Christopher De Bellaigue, *In the Rose Garden of the Martyrs: A Memoir of Iran* (New York, 2005), p. 94.

107 Under Reza Shah: Axworthy, *History of Iran,* p. 223.

107 Unusually for a Persian king: De Bellaigue, *Rose Garden,* p. 94.

112 In 1928 he virtually: Strictly speaking, sharia was not abolished until 1939–40; however, the 1929 legal code restricted clerical authority to marriage and divorce matters. Nikki Keddie, *Modern Iran: Roots and Results of Revolution* (New Haven, Conn., 2006), pp. 89–90.

113 "Despite the admixture": Jay Gluck and Noël Siver, eds., *Surveyors of Persian Art: A Documentary Biography of Arthur Upham Pope and Phyllis Ackerman* (Ashiya, 1996), pp. 93–110.

114 Pope had no formal training: This side of his personality comes through vividly in his correspondence, held at Pope Papers.

114 Within hours of hearing: Talinn Grigor, "(Re)Framing Rapid Modernities: American Historians of Iranian Architecture, Phyllis Ackerman and Arthur Pope," *Arris* 15 (2004): 42.

114 On the banks of Edgewater: This building is often described as a replica of the mosque in Isfahan, but Pope described it as a compendium of different buildings. 22 September 1926, in Pope Papers, Box 1.

114 Pope stuffed it with rugs: E. L. Austin, *The Sesqui-Centennial International Exposition* (Philadelphia, 1929), p. 98.

114 The pavilion became: Jenkins-Madina, "Collecting the 'Orient,'" p. 87; 2 December 1926, in Pope Papers, Box 1. Pope boasted that until 1926, the Western world had seen "only pictures or crude imitations" of Persian architecture, and he burst with pride that Philadelphia's Persian pavilion could claim to be the first building in the Western world to be built according to a strictly Persian design. 22 September 1926, in Pope Papers, Box 1.

116 "Christian forces must": American Board of Commissioners for Foreign Missions, *85th Annual Report,* 1922, p. 54.

117 It was a much subtler: For some missionaries, this adjustment was too radical. The whole point of missionary work, purists said, was to actually *do* missionary work. Blending into modern Persia and hoping some Christian know-how would rub off on the natives was downright feeble. It was an abandonment of the entire ethos of the mission: the idea that Christianity was an essential prerequisite to the creation of a superior civilization. "It is the filth of Shi'ah Islam," wrote one irritated missionary in 1927, "that puts the hunger in the heart of Persians for the Gospel of Jesus Christ." But in the 1920s such sentiments sounded badly out of tune with the times. Michael Zirinsky, "Render Therefore unto Caesar that Which Is Caesar's: American Presbyterian Educators and Reza Shah," *Iranian Studies* 26, no. 3–4 (1993): 338.

117 Dormitories were simple: Arthur Boyce, "Alborz College of Tehran and Dr Samuel M. Jordan, founder and president," in Ali Pasha Saleh, ed., *Cultural Ties Between Iran and the United States* (Tehran, 1976), p. 196.

118 "is not suited": Zirinsky, "Render," p. 338.

119 This bought the missionaries: Another controversy emerged over the issue of military conscription. One of Reza Shah's earliest reforms in 1925 had been the introduction of a military conscription law, fulfilling in part his cherished ambition to increase the national army to two hundred thousand men. Every male citizen eighteen and over was now required to dedicate two years of his life to military service—but an exception had been made for those with high school diplomas. For students who had failed the national entrance exam at the end of the sixth grade, and had had to repeat a year before they could start high school, this caused difficulty, as it meant they would not have finished high school by age eighteen and would therefore be liable to conscription. However, the American schools did not require students to repeat grades and happily accepted pupils into the seventh grade, even if they had failed their entrance exams. When the military conscription law was introduced, then, American high schools suddenly became an obvious loophole for getting out of military service—a guaranteed

path to a diploma before eighteen. Once again a compromise had to be cobbled together. In 1929, American schools agreed to require pupils coming from state primary schools to pass their sixth-grade exams while they were enrolled in the seventh grade. Mahmud Taherahmadi, "Nakhostin modarres misionha-e Amrikaei dar Iran," *Ganjineh-ye Asnad* 3, no. 4 (1993): 26.

119 "unsafe": *A Century of Mission Work in Iran (Persia), 1834–1934* (Beirut, 1936), p. 4.

120 "There can't be two": Millspaugh had got off to a promising start in his first three years, enforcing and regularizing tax collection, standing up to entrenched interests, and rooting out corruption. But his dogmatic personality, his tendency to bark orders in every direction, and his insistence on issuing an "ultimatum" every time the government did not meet his demands had made him many enemies. It was not just temper tantrums and ultimatums that undid the mission though. What particularly incensed the shah was that in the matter of the murder of Robert Imbrie, Millspaugh and his team, despite being employees of the Persian government, had sided vociferously with the American position. Reza privately related to Ala that he felt the Americans had displayed "a distinct lack of tact and good judgement in the matter." Wallace Murray to State Department, 17 January 1925, 719.91/9, , RG 59, NARA, relating a private conversation between the shah and Ala, as summarized for him by Ala.

120 The Persian government ultimately: David Williamson to State Department, 25 January 1930, 891.77 Ulen and Company/104 and 105, RG 59, NARA; Henry S. Villard, vice-consul in charge, report, 30 January 1930, RG 59, NARA.

122 In 1933, when Reza: Charles Hart to Secretary of State, 12 January 1933, 711.91/21, RG 59, NARA.

122 With very little fanfare: Mark Hamilton Lytle, *The Origins of the Iranian-American Alliance 1941–1953* (New York, 1987), p. 7.

122 By 1937 it was: Ibid.

122 Between 1939 and 1941: Keddie, *Modern Iran,* p. 101.

123 Hours of German radio: David Motadel, "Iran and the Aryan Myth," in Ali Ansari, ed., *Perceptions of Iran: History, Myths and Nationalism From Medieval Persia to the Islamic Republic* (London, 2014), pp. 126–35.

123 Germany just happened to be: Moreover, on the streets of Iran, there was no real groundswell of support for European-style fascism. By the late 1930s, most Iranians had grown to loathe Reza Shah for his brutal, dictatorial style of kingship and had little appetite for a foreign-born political system that promised more of the same. Reza himself even hated Nazi ideology. As shah, he had cracked down on homegrown fascists and Nazi sympathizers with as much ferocity as he had earlier done on Communists and religious conservatives. In the final analysis, Reza saw all extreme political ideologies—whether of the left or the right—as a challenge to his rule. Ervand Abrahamian, *Iran Between Two Revolutions* (Princeton, N.J., 1982), p. 163.

124 And the only practical way: The success of Hitler's operation would cut the Allies off from the western approach into Russia. The dangerous northern route, through Archangel, was plagued by perpetually poor ice conditions.

126 "view the situation": President Roosevelt to the Shah of Iran, Telegram, 2 September 1941, 740.0011 European War 1939/14641, RG 59, NARA.

CHAPTER 9
Hello Johnny

128 Although he had less: George Allen to Secretary of State, Telegram, 9 July 1946, 891.001 Pahlavi, Reza Shah/7-946, RG 59, NARA.

129 As a child, he had: Gholam Reza Afkhami, *The Life and Times of the Shah* (Berkeley, Calif., 2009), pp. 25, 28, 32.

129 The crown prince would spend: Ibid., pp. 37–38.

129 "Those eyes could make": Mohammad Reza Pahlavi, *Answer to History* (New York, 1980), pp. 53–54.

130 Once he was in power, Mohammad: John Wiley to President Harry Truman, Background Memorandum for Shah's Visit, 27 October 1949, 891.001 Pahlavi/10-2749, RG 59, NARA.

130 In May 1941: James Moose to State Department, 28 May 1941, 891.00/1814, RG 59, NARA.

130 "whether he was": George Allen to Secretary of State, 22 May 1946, 891.00/5-2246, RG 59, NARA.

132 "The United States alone": John D. Jernegan (Division of Near Eastern Affairs), "American Policy in Iran" (memo), 23 January 1943, in Yonah Alexander and Allen Nanes, eds., *The United States and Iran* (Frederick, Md., 1980), p. 97.

133 "rather thrilled": Cordell Hull, *Memoirs* (New York, 1948), p. 2:1507.

134 "special surprise": James Bill, *The Eagle and the Lion: The Tragedy of American-Iranian Relations* (New Haven, Conn., 1989), p. 20.

134 By 1943, one-third: Walter Dunn, *The Soviet Economy and the Red Army, 1930–1945* (Westport, Conn., 1995), p. 80.

134 "lace curtains": Persian Gulf Command Veterans Organization, http://pgcvowwii.homestead.com/Newsletter.html.

134 "You are undertaking": U.S. Army, *A Pocket Guide to Iran* (Washington, D.C., 1943), p. 1.

134 In November 1943 the leaders: A considerable amount of discussion had gone into the question of where they should meet. Stalin refused to travel by air, believing it posed a risk to his security, and proposed Moscow. Roosevelt, whose health was deteriorating and who was confined to a wheelchair, preferred a more convenient destination. But much of Europe and the Middle East was an active war zone and hence too dangerous. Tehran thus felt like a natural choice: a neutral location that didn't require Stalin to fly.

134 "the greatest security measures": "Record Protection Accorded Leaders," *New York Times,* 7 December 1943, p. 7.

135 "independence, sovereignty": "Declaration of the Three Powers Regarding Iran," 1 December 1943, *FRUS: Diplomatic Papers, The Conferences at Cairo and Tehran, 1943* (Washington, 1961), p. 647.

135 As Roosevelt, Stalin, and Churchill: "Stalin, in Toast to Roosevelt, Calls Him 'My Fighting Friend,'" *New York Sun,* 6 December 1943.

137 "I greatly hope": For an American president, Roosevelt had unusual familiarity with Iran. His uncle, Frederic Delano, had gone to Persia in 1926 as part of a League of Nations fact-finding committee on opium. His cousin Copley Amory, Jr., had served as secretary to the U.S. legation in Tehran in the 1920s, even writing a book about his motorcar adventure across the country. Both men had regaled FDR with stories about Iran and its culture. So almost certainly the president knew very well what sticklers Iranians were when it came to matters of protocol.

137 Girls winked and puckered: The information in this paragraph comes from a combination of consular reports at NARA and conversations with Tehran residents who grew up in the 1940s.

138 "The conduct of American": Louis Dreyfus to State Department, 9 March 1943, 711.91/92, RG 59, NARA. The U.S. Army issued a handbook to soldiers asking them to respect local customs, reminding them they were in a foreign country and should understand that "the world doesn't revolve around Kankakee, Illinois." But this effort was ultimately toothless. U.S. Army, *Pocket Guide,* p. 3.

138 And at various times, both: When the Iranian government rejected a Soviet bid for an oil concession, for example, Moscow responded by cutting off all grain deliveries from the north. Michael Rubin, "Stumbling Through the 'Open Door': The US in Persia and the Standard-Sinclair Oil Dispute, 1920–1925," *Iranian Studies* 28, no. 3/4 (1995): 25.

138 During the harsh: Lytle, *Origins,* p. 38.

138 "Need a dozen very large": Institute for Iranian Contemporary Historical Studies, Document 1-37115-پ.

139 "American leadership": "Memorandum of Conversation, by the Director of the Office of Near Eastern and African Affairs (Henderson)," 17 December 1945, 891.00/12-1745, RG 59, NARA.

140 Most historians now: See, e.g., Lytle, *Origins,* p. 171; Bill, *Eagle and Lion,* pp. 37–38. For a good discussion, see Edwin M. Wright, oral history interview by Richard D. McKinzie, 26 July 1974, p. 79, Harry S. Truman Library, https://www.trumanlibrary.gov/library/oral-histories/wright.

140 "patriotic Iranians": Bill, p. 37n41.

CHAPTER 10
Tehran Spring

142 Into the long-quiescent: In one of its first acts, the fourteenth Majles passed a sharp reduction in the defense budget and a reform of the armed forces that would make it harder for the shah to use the military as a personal power base the way his father had done. The deputies had hit the monarch where they knew it would hurt the most. Mark Gasiorowski, *U.S. Foreign Policy and the Shah: Building a Client State in Iran* (Ithaca, N.Y., 1991), p. 45.

143 "There are 47 newspapers": Ali Ansari, *Modern Iran: The Pahlavis and After* (London, 2007), p. 99.

143 more than seven hundred: Ibid., pp. 99–100.

144 In 1918, as deputy finance minister: Homa Katouzian, *Musaddiq and the Struggle for Power in Iran* (London, 1991), pp. 12–13.

144 "A nation that cannot": Quarterly Report, October–December 1921, in Engert Papers, Box 2, Folder 55.

144 Elected to the Majles in 1924: Fakhreddin Azimi, *The Quest for Democracy in Iran: A Century of Struggle Against Authoritarian Rule* (Cambridge, Mass., 2008), p. 50.

145 "ceremonial": Katouzian, *Musaddiq,* p. 54.

145 "den of thieves": Ibid., p. 56; also Richard Ford to Secretary of State, 4 April 1945, 891.00/4-445, RG 59, NARA.

145 to condemn his old nemesis: In December 1944 a bill was introduced to reduce Millspaugh's powers, but Mosaddeq argued the measure did not go far enough, and that the powers should be rescinded completely. "Like the wounded snake," he argued, with tears in his eyes, Millspaugh could "cause harm to the economy of our nation and our financial affairs" if he was not removed. *Bakhtar,* 28 Azar 1323, p. 1.

145 "not want one of their": James Bill, *The Eagle and the Lion: The Tragedy of American-Iranian Relations* (New Haven, Conn., 1989), pp. 26–27.

146 At polling stations: Habib Ladjevardi, *Labor Unions and Autocracy in Iran* (Syracuse, N.Y., 1985), p. 144.

146 "The methods of ballot-box": Andrew Roth, "Backstage in the Persian Theater," *Nation,* 3 May 1947, p. 516.

146 As Iran's pro-democracy: George Allen to State Department via War Department, 17 January 1947, 891.00/1-1647, RG 59, NARA.

146 "strengthening the hand": Ladjevardi, *Labor Unions,* p. 229n22.

147 "could not be truly": Ibid., p. 227n12.

147 Harriman never asked: This point is made ibid., p. 227.

147 "dictatorial measures": John Wiley, Report on 45-Minute Conversation with Military Attaché Sexton, 3 May 1948, 891.00/5-348, RG 59, NARA.

147 "Iran is a country of opaque": John Wiley to State Department, 26 April 1948, 891.00/4-2648, RG 59, NARA.

147 "like eating soup": George McGhee, *Envoy to the Middle World: Adventures in Diplomacy* (New York, 1983), p. 73.

147 "capable primarily": Bill, *Eagle and Lion,* p. 41.

148 "The chance of salvaging": John Wiley to Loy W. Henderson, 11 August 1951, in Diplomatic Files: Iran, 1948–1951, Wiley Papers. Wiley and Henderson were good friends; they had served in Moscow together, and in the State Department for twenty years.

148 "election time hodgepodge": Arthur Richards, 23 November 1949, 891.00/11-2349, RG 59, NARA.

148 "seems to have no": John Wiley to State Department, 31 October 1949, 891.00/10-3149, RG 59, NARA.

149 As elections unfolded: *Ettela'at,* 891.00/11-949, RG 59, NARA.

149 "elections could not": John Wiley to Secretary of State, Telegram, 11 November 1949, 891.00/11-1149, RG 59, NARA.

150 The shah was quick to: The shah called the assassination an "exploitation of deep-seated unrest . . . inspired from [the] north." John Wiley to Secretary of State, Telegram, 9 November 1949, 891.00/11-949, RG 59, NARA.

150 British diplomats strongly advised: Col. G. E. Wheeler, e.g., of the British embassy told Gerald Dooher that he "believed it most inappropriate for the shah to depart for the United States in the midst of such a chaotic situation." Wheeler to Dooher 26 November 1949, 891.00/11-2649, RG 59, NARA.

150 "I think in spite of": John Wiley to State Department, 8 November 1949, 891.00/11-849, RG 59, NARA.

150 "as there is real": John Wiley to State Department, 8 November 1949, 891.00/11-849, RG 59, NARA.

150 "stripped the Palace": John Wiley to Stanley Woodward, Chief of Division of Protocol, State Department, 9 October 1949, 891.001 Pahlavi/10-2749, RG 59, NARA.

150 A second four-engine: General Landy to Stanley Woodward, Urgent Telegram, 12 November 1949, 891.001 Pahlavi/11-1249, RG 59, NARA.

150 Once the entourage arrived: Clarence Rose to R.D. Muir, Acting Chief of Protocol, 27 October 1949, 891.001 Pahlavi/10-2749, RG 59, NARA; Background Memoranda on Visit of His Imperial Majesty Mohammad Reza Pahlavi Shahinshah of Iran, November 1949, Appendix A, 891.00/11-149, RG 59, NARA.

151 Fixated as ever on: George McGhee to Secretary of the Navy, 4 October 1949, 891.001 Pahlavi/10-449, RG 59, NARA.

152 He insisted it was unrealistic: Memorandum of Conversation, Shah and Secretary of State, 18 November 1949, 891.001 Pahlavi/11-1849, RG 59, NARA.

152 "considers himself the": John Wiley to President Harry Truman, Background Memorandum for Shah's Visit, 27 October 1949, 891.001 Pahlavi/10-2749; Background Memoranda on Visit of His Imperial Majesty Mohammad Reza Pahlavi Shahinshah of Iran, November 1949, 891.001/11-149, RG 59, NARA.

CHAPTER 11
"One Penny More"

155 "Fortune": Winston Churchill, *The World Crisis, 1911–1914* (New York, 1923), p. 134.

155 A giant refinery: Henry Longhurst, *Adventures in Oil* (London, 1959), pp. 47–48.

155 In the luxurious Persian Club: Stephen Kinzer, *All the Shah's Men* (New York, 2008), pp. 49–50.

156 They drove their cars: William Roger Louis, *The British Empire in the Middle East* (Oxford, 1986), p. 9; Manucher Farmanfarmaian and Roxane Farmanfarmaian, *Blood and Oil: A Prince's Memoir of Iran, from the Shah to the Ayatollah* (New York, 2007), pp. 86–88.

156 A series of sophisticated: Fereidun Fesharaki, *Development of the Iranian Oil Industry: International and Domestic Aspects* (New York, 1976), p. 11.

158 "Surveying the heads": John Wiley to Secretary of State, 29 May 1950, 788.00/5-2950, RG 59, NARA.

158 "As long as we have life": *Bakhtar,* 23 Khordad 1329 (13 June 1950), p. 1.

158 "usher in a half-century": Ibid.

158 "The Americans should": *Bakhtar,* 20 Shahrivar 1329, p. 1.

158 A few days later: *Bakhtar,* 13 Tir 1329, p. 1.

159 "America's mistakes in foreign": *Bakhtar,* 23 Shahrivar 1329, p. 1.

159 "good case against": Arthur Krock, *Memoirs* (New York, 1968), p. 262.

159 "unsuited": James Bill, *The Eagle and the Lion: The Tragedy of American-Iranian Relations* (New Haven, Conn., 1989), p. 74.

159 "final offer": Kinzer, *Shah's Men,* p. 73.

160 "One penny more": Bill, *Eagle and Lion,* p. 72.

160 "Never in [my] entire": Ibid., p. 74.

161 "the real trouble": Mostafa Elm, *Oil, Power and Principle: Iran's Oil Nationalization and Its Aftermath* (Syracuse, N.Y., 1992), p. 103.

161 "still living in": Ibid.

161 "second-rate intellect": Anthony Sampson, *The Seven Sisters: The Great Oil Companies and the World They Shaped* (New York, 1975), p. 120.

161 "At no time before [1950]": "Iran," episode 7 of *The End of Empire* (Granada Television, 1985), available at https://www.youtube.com/watch?v=xhCgJElpQEQ.

161 "I know of no instance": Diplomatic Files: Iran, 1948–1951, Wiley Papers.

161 "acted like pro-consuls": "Evan M. Wilson Oral History Interview," 18 July 1975, p. 44, https://www.trumanlibrary.gov/library/oral-histories/wilsonem.

162 "a prime strategic necessity": Kinzer, *Shah's Men,* p. 90.

162 "fresh start": Louis, *British Empire,* p. 650.

162 "strong line of conduct": Elm, *Oil, Power,* p. 79.

163 "an aura of fairness": Kinzer, *Shah's Men,* p. 91.

164 "penetrated far and wide": Elm, *Oil, Power,* p. 82.

164 "unable even to step": Kinzer, *Shah's Men,* p. 80.

166 "Never": Dean Acheson, *Present at the Creation: My Years at the State Department* (New York, 1969), p. 503.

CHAPTER 12

The Liberty Bell and the Wool Pajamas

167 "all of Iran's misery": Stephen Kinzer, *All the Shah's Men* (New York, 2008), p. 91.

167 The influential Ayatollah: Ibid., p. 80.

167 "The British Empire had been": Manucher Farmanfarmaian and Roxane Farman-farmaian, *Blood and Oil: A Prince's Memoir of Iran, From the Shah to the Ayatollah* (New York, 2007), p. 260.

168 "difficulties": Farhad Diba, *Mossadegh: A Political Biography* (London, 1986), p. 116.

168 "No nation gets anywhere": James Bill, *The Eagle and the Lion: The Tragedy of American-Iranian Relations* (New Haven, Conn., 1989), p. 56.

168 As prime minister, Mosaddeq: Ervand Abrahamian, *A History of Modern Iran* (Cambridge, U.K., 2018), p. 118.

168 When he was told: Chapour Bakhtiar, *Ma fidelité* (Paris, 1982), p. 53.

169 The AIOC, meanwhile, would: Mostafa Elm, *Oil, Power and Principle: Iran's Oil Nationalization and Its Aftermath* (Syracuse, N.Y., 1992), p. 111.

169 "breach of contract": Ibid., p. 112.

169 "former company": Ibid., p. 115.

170 Tensions quickly mounted: Kinzer, *Shah's Men*, pp. 93–94.

170 From London, the company: Elm, *Oil, Power,* p. 117.

170 "When they need money": *New-York Herald Tribune,* 15 July 1951, quoted ibid., p. 122.

171 "very deep revolution": James Chace, *Acheson: The Secretary of State Who Created the American World* (New York, 1998), p. 353.

171 "accomplished fact": "Great Britain Irked at US Attempts to Speed Iran Settlement," *Wall Street Journal,* 9 June 1951, p. 1.

171 "Our country will": Elm, *Oil, Power,* p. 118.

171 Then, for good measure: Kinzer, *Shah's Men,* p. 96.

172 "sinister and inadmissible": Elm, *Oil, Power,* pp. 119–21.

172 "We have only": William Roger Louis, *The British Empire in the Middle East* (Oxford, 1986), p. 739.

172 "Persian oil is of vital": Elm, *Oil, Power,* p. 112.

172 "Parliamentary and public feeling": Kinzer, *Shah's Men*, p. 93.

172 "tired of being pushed": Kenneth Morgan, *Labour in Power* (Oxford, 1984), p. 469.

172 Detailed plans were drawn up: Elm, *Oil, Power*, p. 160.

172 Truman made it clear: Bill, *Eagle and Lion*, p. 75; Kinzer, *Shah's Men*, p. 112.

173 "determined to follow": Henry Grady to State Department (telegram), 1 July 1951, 888.2553/7-151, RG 59, NARA.

173 "*the* major asset which": Kinzer, *Shah's Men*, pp. 92–93.

173 "What is the use of Harriman": Elm, *Oil, Power*, pp. 126–27.

174 His hands were crossed: Vernon Walters, *Silent Missions* (New York, 1978), p. 246.

174 Throughout his life, Mosaddeq: Katouzian, *Musaddiq*, p. 33.

174 "fabulous invalid": Kinzer, *Shah's Men*, p. 120.

174 What, he asked, would America's: Bill, *Eagle and Lion*, p. 76.

174 "recognize the principle": Elm, *Oil, Power*, pp. 140–41.

175 "The result is nothing": James Goode, *The United States and Iran: In the Shadow of Musaddiq* (New York, 1997), p. 43.

175 At the end of August: Elm, *Oil, Power*, p. 141.

175 They sabotaged: Kinzer, *Shah's Men*, p. 115.

175 "stolen oil from Persia": Elm, *Oil, Power*, pp. 147–49.

175 "we have been the saints": Walter Gifford to State Department (telegram), 5 October 1951, 888.2553/10-551.

176 "Long live the champion": Universal International Newsreel, 8 October 1951; *Bakhtar-e Emruz*, 21 Mehr 1330, p. 1.

176 "Great similarity": "Mossadegh, Here, Appeals to Americans to Back Iran," *New York Times*, 9 October 1951, pp. 1, 5.

176 "a great enterprise": *UNSC Official Records*, 559th meeting, 1 October 1951, ¶¶60, 100, 104.

176 "so entirely negative": *UNSC Official Records*, 561st meeting, 16 October 1951, ¶¶53, 36.

176 "distressing situation": Ibid., ¶¶38.

176 "ultimate refuge of weak": *UNSC Official Records*, 560th meeting, 15 October 1951, ¶¶9.

176 "to persuade world opinion": *UNSC Official Records*, 561st meeting, 16 October 1951, ¶¶25.

176 "instead used every": Ibid., ¶¶31.

177 "Having first concentrated": Ibid., ¶¶30.

177 "It required a deficient": Elm, *Oil, Power*, p. 176.

178 "postpone the discussion": *UNSC Official Records*, 565th meeting, 19 October 1951.

178 "The hardy men": Kamrouz Pirouz, "Iran's Oil Nationalization: Musaddiq at the United Nations and His Negotiations with George McGhee," *Comparative Stud-*

ies of South Asia, Africa and the Middle East 21, nos. 1–2 (2001); "No Oil for Reds, Mossadegh Says," *Philadelphia Inquirer*, 23 October 1951, pp. 1–2.

178 "In my country": "No Oil for Reds, Mossadegh Says," *Philadelphia Inquirer*, 23 October 1951, pp. 1–2.

178 He persuaded Mosaddeq: George McGhee, *Envoy to the Middle World: Adventures in Diplomacy* (New York, 1983), p. 391.

178 Mosaddeq indicated he was: Ibid., pp. 401–2.

179 The sticking point: Dean Acheson, *Present at the Creation: My Years at the State Department* (New York, 1969), p. 511.

179 "To me it was almost": McGhee, *Envoy,* p. 403.

180 "You have never understood": Acheson, *Present,* p. 511.

180 In Cairo, the airport: *Bakhtar-e Emruz,* 30 Aban 1330, p. 1. For an interesting discussion of Mosaddeq's reception in Egypt, see Lior Sternfeld, "Iran Days in Egypt: Mosaddeq's Visit to Cairo in 1951," *British Journal of Middle Eastern Studies* 43, no. 1 (2016): 1–20.

180 "conquered history": Elm, *Oil, Power,* p. 193.

180 In the United States: Diba, *Mossadegh,* p. 128.

180 "feeble, senile, and": Kinzer, *Shah's Men,* p. 120.

181 "United Nationsy": Elm, *Oil, Power,* p. 162.

182 With oil revenue shriveling: Ibid., p. 271.

182 At one point, things: "Iran Grows More Tense at Election," *New York Times,* 30 December 1951, p. E5.

182 "If the Iranian nation": Elm, *Oil, Power,* p. 271.

182 "deficit bonds": "Iran Grows More Tense at Election," *New York Times,* 30 December 1951, p. E5.

183 Afterward the chief British lawyer: Elm, *Oil, Power,* pp. 208–14.

183 Worried that Majles elections: Mosaddeq's other motivation for wanting control of the armed forces was that he hoped to find a quick way out of the country's crippling fiscal and economic crisis by slashing the military budget. He had always been a critic of the Pahlavi obsession with military hardware, and he had repeatedly argued that Iran needed only a defensive capability, rather than the expensive military buildup that the shah preferred. Reports even circulated around Tehran that if Mosaddeq had the opportunity, he wanted to cut defense spending by as much as 50 percent. "Mossadegh Out as Premier; Ghavam to Take Iran Helm," *New York Times,* 18 July 1952, pp. 1, 4.

183 "Better that I pack my suitcase": Kinzer, *Shah's Men,* p. 134.

183 Immediately condemned as: Within hours of Mosaddeq's resignation, the British embassy made it clear to the shah that former prime minister Ahmad Qavam would make an excellent choice to replace Mosaddeq. (British spies in Tehran had already been reassured that Qavam "greatly preferred that British influence should be exercised in Persia, rather than that of the Americans or Russians" and that he was prepared to impose a harsh crackdown on domestic opposi-

tion and negotiate an oil agreement acceptable to the British government.) Elm, *Oil, Power,* pp. 235–36. The shah's personal hatred for Qavam was every bit as fervent as it had been four years earlier. But he was also preternaturally afraid of the British—still haunted by the way they had not hesitated to sweep his father out of power when their national interests were at stake, and all too aware that the heir to the Qajar dynasty was still a fixture in London political life. For an interesting discussion of Qavam's ties with Hamid Qajar and Julian Amery of the Conservative Party, see Elm, *Oil, Power,* pp. 236–37.

183 In reality, the shah: Mosaddeq had once fiercely reprimanded his supporters when they suggested the abolition of the monarchy. Homa Katouzian, ed., *Musaddiq's Memoirs* (London, 1988), p. 341.

184 "You could go down": Sepehr Zabih, *The Mossadegh Era: Roots of the Iranian Revolution* (Chicago, 1986), p. 66.

184 A similar event: "Americans in Iran Are Being Shunned in Political Strife," *New York Times,* 29 July 1952, p. 1.

185 Mourners—thousands of them: Yahya Armajani, "Sam Jordan and the Evangelical Ethic in Iran," in Robert Miller, ed., *Religious Ferment in Asia* (Lawrence, Kans., 1974), pp. 23–24.

185 "related and relevant": Acheson, *Present,* p. 680.

185 "The whole tone": Ibid.

CHAPTER 13

1953

188 In 1921, when the future: CharlesHart to State Department, 14 March 1933, 891.00/1561, RG 59, NARA.

188 Zahedi was also: Zahedi had an awkward history with the British and was in some ways an odd choice to lead a British-inspired coup against Mosaddeq. In 1942, at the height of the war, Britain had discovered that Zahedi was aiding the Nazis—hoarding grain shipments and plotting to disrupt the Allied supply route to the USSR—and had responded by kidnapping him at gunpoint and whisking him away to Palestine for the duration of the war. The operation had been conducted by the legendary British agent Fitzroy MacLean—a dashing, dapper spy believed by some to have been the inspiration for Ian Fleming's 007 character.

189 Mosaddeq, incensed: Mostafa Elm, *Oil, Power and Principle: Iran's Oil Nationalization and Its Aftermath* (Syracuse, N.Y., 1992), p. 255.

189 "We have had hundreds": Stephen Kinzer, *All the Shah's Men* (New York, 2008), p. 96.

189 "We tried to get the block-headed": Ibid., pp. 147–48.

190 "all honest": Roy Melbourne to Secretary of State, 1 November 1952, 511.88/11-152, RG 59, NARA.

191 "Not wishing to be accused": C. M. Woodhouse, *Something Ventured* (London, 1982), p. 117.

191 Throughout November and December: Brian Lapping, *End of Empire* (London, 1985), p. 218.

191 "putting U.S. support": Mark Gasiorowski, "The 1953 Coup d'État in Iran," *International Journal of Middle East Studies* 19, no. 3 (August 1987): 270.

191 Knowing that the outgoing: Elm, *Oil, Power,* pp. 293–94.

191 "Let's not get this thing": Bill, *Eagle and Lion,* p. 85.

191 "there were no signs": Stephen Dorril, *MI6: Inside the Covert World of Her Majesty's Secret Intelligence Service* (New York, 2000), p. 583.

191 "The Russians will receive": "No Oil for Reds, Mossadegh Says," *Philadelphia Inquirer,* 23 October 1951, pp. 1–2.

192 "no reason to be": George McGhee, "Recollections of Dr. Muhammad Musaddiq," in James Bill and William Roger Louis, eds., *Musaddiq, Iranian Nationalism, and Oil* (London, 1988), p. 302.

192 "neither a communist": James Bill, *The Eagle and the Lion: The Tragedy of American-Iranian Relations* (New Haven, Conn., 1989), p. 93.

192 "Any article that I would": Kinzer, *Shah's Men,* p. 6.

193 "Such men should be hanged": "Iran: Steady Infiltration," *Time,* 13 July 1953.

193 The attack on Mosaddeq's: Elm, *Oil, Power,* p. 295.

193 Although he didn't realize: Homa Katouzian, *Musaddiq and the Struggle for Power in Iran* (London, 1991), p. 185.

193 "fiery old demagogue": "Iran: Our Shah or Death!," *Time,* 9 March 1953; "Iran: Out Goes the Shah," *Time,* 24 August 1953.

193 "Tudeh infiltration": "Iran: Steady Infiltration," *Time,* 13 July 1953.

193 "paternalistic": Elm, *Oil, Power,* p. 277.

193 "trying to relive": Roby Barrett, *The Greater Middle East and the Cold War: U.S. Foreign Policy Under Eisenhower and Kennedy* (London, 2007), p. 12.

194 "the only hope": Elm, *Oil, Power,* p. 283.

194 "The failure of Iran": *Department of State Bulletin* 30, no. 758 (4 January 1954): 279.

195 "well-educated rather": Kermit Roosevelt, *Countercoup* (New York, 1979), p. 110; Edward Renehan, *The Lion's Pride: Theodore Roosevelt and His Family in Peace and War* (New York, 1998), pp. 243–44.

196 Every night in early August: Kinzer, *Shah's Men,* pp. 9–11.

196 Certainly, he had no: As early as 1951, the shah had told the British ambassador that he was "convinced of the need of getting rid of Musaddiq and is now concerned as to how it can be done best." Elm, *Oil, Power,* p. 151.

196 "If by any horrible chance": Roosevelt, *Countercoup,* p. 161.

196 For the next several: Kinzer, *Shah's Men,* p. 14.

196 "foreign elements": Roosevelt, *Countercoup,* p. 173.

197 "When you heard that your": "Shah Flees Iran After Move to Dismiss Mosaddegh Fails," *New York Times,* 17 August 1953, pp. 1, 4.

197 "urgent guidance": Elm, *Oil, Power,* p. 303.

197 "very small means": Burton Berry to State Department (telegram), 17 August 1953, 788.00/8-1753, RG 59, NARA; Elm, *Oil, Power,* p. 304.

197 "staffless, baggageless": Elm, *Oil, Power,* p. 304.

197 "make attempts to improve": Ibid.

198 Mosaddeq ordered them: Katouzian, *Musaddiq,* p. 190.

198 Many also had informal: Christopher De Bellaigue, *In the Rose Garden of the Martyrs: A Memoir of Iran* (New York, 2005), 171.

199 "the best thing": Roosevelt, *Countercoup,* p. 180.

199 At the edges of the crowd: Stephen Ambrose, *Ike's Spies: Eisenhower and the Espionage Establishment* (New York, 1981), p. 210.

200 "mercenary mob": Kinzer, *Shah's Men,* p. 180.

200 Another group marched: Elm, *Oil, Power,* p. 308.

200 "If it's going to be": Kinzer, *Shah's Men,* p. 185.

201 Many of the dead: Elm, *Oil, Power,* p. 308.

201 As darkness fell: Roosevelt, *Countercoup,* p. 196.

201 "It was": CIA official history of Operation Ajax, reprinted in *New York Times,* 16 June 2000, p. 77, http://cryptome.org/iran-cia/08.pdf.

201 For his own safety: Elm, *Oil, Power,* p. 308.

202 "so pleased": Robert Scheer, "How CIA Orchestrated '53 Coup in Iran," *Los Angeles Times,* 29 March 1979, pp. B1, 6–8.

203 "it would be easy": Elm, *Oil, Power,* p. 309.

204 "Throughout the course": Jalil Bozorgmehr, ed. *Mosaddeq dar Mahkameh-ye Nezami* (Tehran, 1363), vol. 1, p. 166.

204 Lengthy obituaries: Elm, *Oil, Power,* p. 342.

204 For years the U.S.: The first public discussion of the coup in the United States was Richard and Gladys Harkness, "The Mysterious Doings of CIA," *Saturday Evening Post,* 6 November 1954, pp. 66–68. Subsequent, often highly subjective, accounts were given in, e.g., Woodhouse, *Something Ventured,* and Roosevelt, *Countercoup.*

206 It still bears every: The information in the preceding two paragraphs is based mostly on a visit to Ahmad Abad in June 2009.

CHAPTER 14
"Yes" and "Yes, Sir"

209 One-third of the men: James Bill, *The Eagle and the Lion: The Tragedy of American-Iranian Relations* (New Haven, Conn., 1989), p. 98.

210 For the rest of the summer: The information in this paragraph is based on conversations with former National Front members in Tehran, May 2009.

210 A mysterious fire: Homa Katouzian, *Musaddiq and the Struggle for Power in Iran* (London, 1991), p. 208.

211 Nixon's presence in Tehran: To be precise, the protests and clashes had been going on for a few days before Nixon's arrival. They were a reaction both to the renewed ties with Britain and to the oil negotiations. Word of Nixon's impending visit only exacerbated tensions.

212 Shaban the Brainless: "Brainless and the Ballots," *Time*, 22 March 1954.

213 It was Eqbal who: Abbas Milani, *Eminent Persians: The Men and Women Who Made Modern Iran, 1941–1979* (Syracuse, N.Y., 2008), p. 126.

213 "without the permission": Bill, *Eagle and Lion*, p. 103.

213 Melliyun and Mardom: Ali Ansari, *Modern Iran: The Pahlavis and After* (London, 2007), p. 174.

214 Before long, teams: Selden Chapin to State Department, 6 June 1956, 511.883/6-656, RG 59, NARA.

214 By the end of the decade: Bill, *Eagle and Lion*, pp. 124–25.

214 "in a loose, slipshod": "Conclusions of the Investigation on United States Aid Operations in Iran by the Foreign Operations Subcommittee of the Committee on Government Operations, U.S. House of Representatives, 28 January 1957," in Yonah Alexander and Allen Nanes, eds., *The United States and Iran* (Frederick, Md., 1980), pp. 295–96.

215 "I am confident": *FRUS, 1958–1960*, pp. 12:628–29.

215 He declared: "Tehran to Give All-Out Greeting," *New York Times*, 13 December 1959, p. 35.

215 Nearly a million people: "Shah Welcomes President in Iran," *New York Times*, 14 December 1959, p. 1; *Keyhan*, 22 Azar 1338, p. 1.

215 Sixty typewriters and eight: *Keyhan*, 21 Azar 1338, p. 1.

217 "our relations": *Arezu*, 13 Azar 1338, p. 1.

217 "In the long term": "Texts of Eisenhower's Talks in Athens and Tehran," *New York Times*, 15 December 1959, p. 16.

CHAPTER 15

You Say You Want a Revolution?

218 "fantastically revolutionary": Sen. John F. Kennedy, "Message to the Nation's New Voters," 5 October 1960, https://www.presidency.ucsb.edu/documents/statement-senator-john-f-kennedy-message-senator-john-f-kennedy-the-nations-new-voters. Other campaign speeches from this period use similar language.

218 There were even allegations: This rumor has never been properly laid to rest. In 1974, as the Watergate scandal was engulfing the Nixon White House, a former Justice Department official with deep ties to Iran told a Senate committee that the shah had "delivered huge sums" to Nixon. The newspaper columnist Jack Anderson claimed to have knowledge that more than $1 million was sent via the

shah's personal bank accounts in Switzerland and Mexico. On at least two occasions, it was said, the shah secretly arranged for cash to be sent to Nixon's presidential campaigns (a violation of U.S. electoral law)—once in 1960, and again in 1972. Ambassador Ardeshir Zahedi, who was said to have acted as the conduit for the money transfers, emphatically denied their existence, and the matter disappeared. However, in 1992 the diaries of Asadollah Alam, one of the shah's most loyal courtiers, were published after rotting away for years in a Swiss bank vault. Alam made several allusions that have been interpreted as references to financial or other help given to the Nixon campaigns. Jack Anderson, "Greedy Shah of Iran Keeping Oil Price Up," syndicated column, 31 October 1974; Asadollah Alam, *The Shah and I: The Confidential Diary of Iran's Royal Court, 1968–77,* ed. Alinaghi Alikhani (New York, 2008), pp. 77, 233, 236. See also Abbas Milani, *The Persian Sphinx: Amir Abbas Hoveyda and the Riddle of the Iranian Revolution* (Washington, D.C., 2000), p. 146.

219 Horrified: James Goode, "Reforming Iran During the Kennedy Years," *Diplomatic History* 15, no. 1 (1991): 16.

219 What the shah wanted: NSC Task Force on Iran, report, 15 May 1961, p. 3, Box 115, NSF.

219 "the Shah's demands": Ibid.

220 "You will assert": James Bill, *The Eagle and the Lion: The Tragedy of American-Iranian Relations* (New Haven, Conn., 1989), p. 132.

220 The president's military aide: Iran General, *passim,* Box 115a, NSF.

221 "The most immediate": R. W. Komer, "Preliminary Comments on Iran TF Report," 15 May 1961, p. 1, Box 115, NSF.

221 "best, and perhaps": Ibid.

221 On May 5, 1961: Initially the shah had been resistant to the idea, but this domestic crisis made the American offer impossible to refuse. Fifty thousand schoolteachers marched through the streets of Tehran in early May (possibly the biggest public demonstration the country had ever seen) and brought the country to a standstill. A heavy-handed army response left two demonstrators severely injured and one dead. And amid the public outcry that ensued, the shah felt "compelled" to sack his overenthusiastic prime minister, Jafar Sharif-Emami, and replace him with someone more liberal.

221 "Don't let today go": George Ball, Notes on telephone conversation with Walt Rostow, 8 May 1961, in Ball Papers, Box 5, Iran Folder.

221 "take a strong line": Komer, "Preliminary Comments," p. 2.

222 "seemed to be": R. W. Komer, "The Deepening Crisis in Iran" (memo for the president), 4 August 1961, Box 116, NSF.

222 "cruelty, sadism, atrocity and vandalism": Michael M. J. Fischer, *Iran: From Religious Dispute to Revolution*, p. 187.

222 "extremely gloomy": Ibid., and accompanying note from R. W. Komer to McGeorge Bundy, 4 August 1961.

223 "crisis measures": Ibid.

223 "Khrushchev is right": *Executive Sessions of the Senate Foreign Relations Committee,* 87th Congress, 1st sess. (1961), vol. 13, pt. 2, pp. 159–60.

224 Officially, Amini's reason: Nikki Keddie, *Modern Iran: Roots and Results of Revolution* (New Haven, Conn., 2006), p. 144.

224 "closest thing to": Abbas Milani, *Eminent Persians: The Men and Women Who Made Modern Iran, 1941–1979* (Syracuse, N.Y., 2008), p. 50.

224 "This regime": Bill, *Eagle and Lion,* p. 135.

224 The State Department also: Bureau of Near East Affairs, paper, 11 February 1961, Box 115a, NSF.

224 "having a neurotic spell": Kennedy and Ball, telephone conversation, 29 January 1962, in Ball Papers, Box 5. The decision was not without its opponents inside the Kennedy administration. The president's younger brother, Attorney General Robert Kennedy, was passionately opposed to the shah: he had visited Iran in 1955 and returned convinced "the Shah was an SOB" who had little interest in the welfare of his people. RFK had been far more impressed by the spirit of democratic activism he saw among the country's students and young professionals, and he felt the United States should be doing more to support this opposition movement. That perspective on Iran was almost unheard of among American officials at the time—and he was swiftly overruled by Undersecretary of State George Ball. In the spring of 1962, RFK was asked to visit Iran on behalf of his brother, but when he proposed to spend time with university students as a way to show the United States was serious about pushing Iran in the direction of reform, he was pulled from the mission. Ball felt that the paranoid shah would "go over the deep end" at the sight of the U.S. president's brother meeting with opposition activists. Instead, the attorney general should hand-deliver to the shah an official invitation to come to the United States. RFK went ballistic at hearing the idea. Inviting the shah to the United States so soon after his troops had terrorized the university, he argued, would send a disastrous message to the fledgling Iranian democracy movement. A round of bitter interdepartmental disagreement ensued, and in the end, it was decided that the attorney general was just too emotional to be sent to Iran. The president's special adviser Chester Bowles was asked to make the trip instead, carrying the invitation for the shah. Kennedy and Ball, telephone conversation, 29 January 1962, in Ball Papers, Box 5.

224 "historic fight": "Shah Receives Kennedy Praise as State Visit Begins," *New York Times,* 12 April 1962, pp. 1, 10.

224 The shah was given: *Arezu,* 8 Ordibehesht 1341, p. 1.

225 "more interested in sinking": "Empress Visits Two Museums Here," *New York Times,* 16 April 1962, p. 22.

226 Refusing to believe: Mansur Rafizadeh, *Witness: From the Shah to the Secret Arms Deal* (New York, 1987), p. 124.

227 Worse, it was later: Keddie, *Modern Iran,* p. 139.

229 Instead, a referendum: *Ettela'at,* 31 January 1963, p. 1.

229 Flash Gordon and Annie Oakley: Dispatch from Cultural Attaché, 24 July 1961, 511.88/7–2461, RG 59, NARA.

230 "make the rich": Michael Rubin, "Stumbling Through the 'Open Door': The US in Persia and the Standard-Sinclair Oil Dispute, 1920–1925," *Iranian Studies* 28, no. 3/4 (1995): 113.

231 "You miserable wretch": Dilip Hiro, *Iran Under the Ayatollahs* (London, 1985), p. 46.

233 But the image of: Michael M. J. Fischer, *Iran from Religious Dispute to Revolution* (Madison, Wis., 2003), p. 188.

233 "not displeased": Bill, *Eagle and Lion,* p. 137.

233 One even claims: Rafizadeh, *Witness,* p. 124.

CHAPTER 16

This Turbulent Priest

235 "I can't express": *Ettela'at hashtad sal* (Tehran, 2005), p. 1:221.

237 But from 1965: SAVAK's origins dated to the CIA coup of 1953, when a U.S. Army colonel was sent to Iran to help the Zahedi government set up a military intelligence unit that could monitor antigovernment activity. He was followed in 1955 by Col. H. Norman Schwarzkopf of the U.S. Gendarmerie Mission, who, along with a team of five CIA special officers, trained virtually all of SAVAK's first generation of senior agents. Later SAVAK received advanced training from Mossad, and it quickly grew into one of the most ruthless and efficient organizations of its kind in the world. In the early 1960s SAVAK officially employed around five thousand staff, with thousands more Iranians believed to be acting as paid informers.

238 In 1967, SAVAK: Mansur Rafizadeh, *Witness: From the Shah to the Secret Arms Deal* (New York, 1987), p. 151.

238 Hoping to lure Iran's: James Bill, *The Eagle and the Lion: The Tragedy of American-Iranian Relations* (New Haven, Conn., 1989), p. 167.

239 And unlike the older: Sixteen of the twenty-three ministers in Hoveida's first government had studied or traveled in the U.S., and nineteen spoke English. Ibid.

240 Reading defense industry: Ibid., p. 171.

240 As a result, Iran's: Fred Halliday, *Iran: Dictatorship and Development* (New York, 1979), p. 143; Mark Gasiorowski, *U.S. Foreign Policy and the Shah: Building a Client State in Iran* (Ithaca, N.Y., 1991), pp. 102–3.

241 In 1965 he made a state visit: "Iran: Revolution from the Throne," *Time,* 6 October 1967.

241 If the United States was serious: To ensure his message received a proper hearing

in Washington, the shah relied on intermediaries—old Iran hands such as Averell Harriman and Kermit Roosevelt—to emphasize to U.S. officials that Iran's support for America was strong and heartfelt but not automatic.

241 From 1967 to 1970: Bill, *Eagle and Lion*, p. 173.

241 After the United Kingdom: Ibid., p. 172.

242 U.S. officials with strong: A process nicely outlined ibid., 174–75.

244 "What is going on": David E. Lilienthal, *Journals* (New York, 1976), p. 6:48.

244 "The Shah has been": "A Reform-Minded Ruler: Mohammed Riza Pahlevi," *New York Times,* 27 October 1967, p. 10.

244 "The Shah has worked": "Iran: Revolution from the Throne," *Time,* 6 October 1967.

244 "has allowed considerable": "Iran: Proud as a Peacock," *Time,* 31 March 1967.

244 By the end of the 1960s: Bill, *Eagle and Lion,* p. 168.

244 In 1968, for the first: Ibid.

245 A gilded coronation carriage: British Pathé newsreel, 2 November 1967, https:// www.youtube.com/watch?v=i9HIi7rWMUg.

245 Six million colored: "Iran: Revolution from the Throne," *Time,* 6 October 1967.

245 In remote regions: "Festive Teheran Set for Shah's Coronation today," *New York Times,* 26 October 1967, p. 12.

246 Statues of the shah: Ali Ansari, *Modern Iran: The Pahlavis and After* (London, 2007), pp. 216–17.

246 "They bleed the hearts": Hamid Algar, ed., *Islam and Revolution 1: Writings and Declarations of Imam Khomeini* (Berkeley, 1981), p. 190.

CHAPTER 17

The Final Emperor

247 The court livery: "Made in France—Persia's Splendorous Anniversary Celebration," *New York Times,* 5 October 1971, p. 36.

247 The fifteen hundred French: "Made in France—Persia's Splendorous Anniversary Celebration," *New York Times,* 5 October 1971, p. 36.

248 The souvenir book: "When Shah of Iran Throws a Big Bash, the Sky's No Limit," *Los Angeles Times,* 12 October 1971, pp. A1, 18–19.

248 "If I did go": "Iran: Show of Shows," *Time,* 25 October 1971.

249 "devil's festival": Ali Ansari, *Modern Iran: The Pahlavis and After* (London, 2007), p. 221; Hamid Algar, ed., *Islam and Revolution 1: Writings and Declarations of Imam Khomeini* (Berkeley, Calif., 1981), pp. 202, 207.

251 "social discipline": James Bill, *The Eagle and the Lion: The Tragedy of American-Iranian Relations* (New Haven, Conn., 1989), p. 192.

251 "if you continue": Shah of Iran, interview by Peter Snow of ITV, 29 January 1974, https://www.youtube.com/watch?v=imil1iIpIYA.

251 "Japan of western Asia": Ansari, *Modern Iran,* pp. 231–32.

251 "revolutionary monarch": Richard Nixon, *Leaders: Profiles and Reminiscences of Men Who Have Shaped the Modern World* (New York, 1982), p. 308.

251 "sensed an inner": William Shawcross, *The Shah's Last Ride: The Fate of an Ally* (New York, 1988), p. 156.

252 "decisions on the acquisition": Henry Kissinger to Secretary of State and Secretary of Defense, "Follow-up on the President's Talk with the Shah of Iran" (memo), 25 July 1972, https://nsarchive2.gwu.edu/NSAEBB/NSAEBB21/docs/doc03.pdf.

253 As he got up to leave: Walter Isaacson, *Kissinger: A Biography* (New York, 1992), p. 563.

253 "devoured [our] manuals": Ervand Abrahamian, *Iran Between Two Revolutions* (Princeton, N.J., 1982), p. 124.

253 In 1974 the shah: "Iran: Oil, Grandeur and a Challenge to the West," *Time,* 4 November 1974.

253 By 1976, Iran was: Fred Halliday, *Iran: Dictatorship and Development* (New York, 1979), p. 72.

253 The annual defense: *U.S. Military Sales to Iran,* Staff Report to the Subcommittee on Foreign Assistance of the Senate Foreign Relations Committee (Washington, D.C., 1976), p. 13.

253 Iran's armed forces: Halliday, *Dictatorship,* p. 95.

253 In the mid-1970s: Michael Rubin, "Stumbling Through the 'Open Door': The US in Persia and the Standard-Sinclair Oil Dispute, 1920–1925," *Iranian Studies* 28, no. 3/4 (1995): 158.

253 At one point orders: "U.S. Influence on Iran: Gigantic and Diverse," *New York Times,* 30 August 1976, pp. 1, 9.

254 In control of its own: Mark Gasiorowski, *U.S. Foreign Policy and the Shah: Building a Client State in Iran* (Ithaca, N.Y., 1991), pp. 102–3.

254 State-of-the-art equipment: Kenneth Pollack, *The Persian Puzzle: The Conflict Between Iran and America* (New York, 2004), p. 109.

255 Pilots were trained: Rubin, "Stumbling," p. 129.

255 "The Emperor of Oil": *Time,* 4 November 1974.

256 A congressional investigation: "Northrop Rebate Reported in Iran as an Atonement," *New York Times,* 23 February 1976, p. 51; "1975 Textron Memo Stirs Senate Doubt on Iran Testimony," *New York Times,* 27 February 1978, p. D1.

256 Four years earlier: Bill, *Eagle and Lion,* p. 209.

256 "created a bonanza": *U.S. Military Sales to Iran,* Staff Report to the Subcommittee on Foreign Assistance of the Senate Foreign Relations Committee (Washington, D.C., 1976).

257 "whipping and beating": *Amnesty International Briefing: Iran* (November 1976), p. 8.

257 The most notorious device: Ervand Abrahamian, *Tortured Confessions: Prisons and Public Recantations In Modern Iran* (Berkeley, Calif., 1999), p. 106.

257 "Iran has no need": "Amnesty International Press Conference on Iran, May 16, 1975," *Resistance* 4, no. 1 (December 1975): 11; Amnesty International, *Annual Report, 1974–75* (London, 1975).

257 There was even something: Fardoust was probably closer to the shah than anyone else in Iran. His father had been a loyal sergeant in Reza Shah's army. So when the Crown Prince Mohammad Reza was sent away to Le Rosey boarding school in the 1930s, Reza Shah had requested the young Fardoust to join him. The two boys became best friends, and Fardoust earned the unquestioning trust of the shah, who entrusted him with the job of collecting information from the various intelligence agencies and delivering it to him in a daily morning briefing. It was even said that Fardoust was the only person allowed to enter the shah's bedroom. Ultimately, however, it appears the shah's trust was misplaced, as Fardoust betrayed him during the Revolution.

258 At one point, the volume: Gasiorowski, *Foreign Policy and the Shah*, p. 100.

259 By midnight, Zahedi's: "Zahedi: Let the Good Times Roll," *Washington Post*, 22 April 1973, pp. L1, L3.

259 Zahedi was driven: "Tea Replaces Wine at Iranian Embassy," *Washington Post*, 24 February 1979, p. A16.

260 Both the senator and: "The Shah's Secret Police Are Here," *New York*, 18 September 1978, pp. 45–51.

260 Every Christmas the embassy: Rubin, "Stumbling," p. 153.

260 Barbara Walters was a favorite: Bill, *Eagle and Lion*, pp. 369–72.

260 "Mohammad Reza Pahlavi": "Iran: Oil, Grandeur and a Challenge to the West," *Time*, 4 November 1974.

261 "has been reduced": "Rich but Underdeveloped, Iran Seeks More Power," *New York Times*, 3 June 1974, pp. 1, 12.

261 Apparently convinced that: "Playing Catch-up in Iran," *Time*, 29 January 1979.

261 "I have come to the conclusion": Ansari, *Modern Iran*, pp. 233–34.

262 "I'm not entirely alone": Oriana Fallaci, "The Shah of Iran: An Interview with Mohammad Reza Pahlavi," *New Republic*, 1 December 1973.

262 Sixty percent of children: Ervand Abrahamian, *Iran Between Two Revolutions* (Princeton, N.J., 1982), 142.

262 From 1974 to 1978: "Housing Shortage Cuts Iran Marriages," *Los Angeles Times*, 23 July 1978, p. 26.

262 The number of Americans: Bill, *Eagle and Lion*, p. 211.

263 Community relations: "U.S. Influence on Iran: Gigantic and Diverse," *New York Times*, 30 August 1976, pp. 1, 9.

263 "American dogs": James Bill, "U.S.-Iran Relations: Forty Years of Observations," *William & Mary News*, 15 March 2004, http://www.wm.edu/news/?id=3472 (accessed 4 July 2008); Axworthy, *History of Iran*, p. 248.

264 "We want to catch up": "Iran: Oil, Grandeur and a Challenge to the West," *Time*, 4 November 1974.

264 "The number of": Bill, *Eagle and Lion,* p. 200.

264 "I am in contact": *The Fall of a Shah,* BBC documentary, 2009, https://www
.youtube.com/watch?v=os5pRsCWW9k.

265 "the Shah's only fault": Abrahamian, *Between Two Revolutions,* p. 123.

CHAPTER 18
The Unthinkable

267 Fadayin-e Khalq (FeK): *Fadayin* is a difficult word to translate. Technically, a
fadayi is someone prepared to sacrifice himself for someone else's benefit.
Fadayin-e Khalq is therefore often translated as "Self-Sacrificers of the People,"
but this is awkward and overly literal. "Martyrs of the People" doesn't work
because it carries religious connotations that the FeK would not subscribe to (and
the word *martyr* would be better translated as *shahid*). A *fadayi* is basically someone who is prepared to engage in an act of martyrdom, religious or otherwise.

267 The MeK, by contrast: The MeK traced its origins to the Freedom Movement of
Iran (Nehzat-e Azadi-e Iran), a religiously based offshoot of the post-Mosaddeq
National Front led by Mehdi Bazargan and Ayatollah Taleqani. In the early 1960s
some of the Freedom Movement's more radical members became disillusioned
by liberalism and its ineffectiveness at challenging the shah's regime and explored
ways to adapt revolutionary Marxism to Iran's Islamic context. In 1965 these
members broke away and formed the MeK.

269 In the decade: Fred Halliday, *Iran: Dictatorship and Development* (New York,
1979), pp. 19, 218.

269 From 1968 to 1978: Amir Taheri, *Nest of Spies: America's Journey to Disaster in Iran*
(New York, 1989), p. 94.

270 That a man famed: Of the twelve emams held sacred by Shia Muslims, Reza is
the only one buried in Iran. His shrine is thus the most important pilgrimage
site in Iran—and is often an alternative for those unable to make the trip to
Mecca. Donations to the shrine formed by far the largest source of funds for the
Sazman-e Awqaf.

270 "I hear a rumor": This anecdote was told to my father by Gen. Ahmad Shirin
Sokhan, husband of Education Minister Farrokhroo Parsa, who was present at
the party and overheard the conversation.

270 "I swear to God": James Bill, *The Eagle and the Lion: The Tragedy of American-
Iranian Relations* (New Haven, Conn., 1989), p. 182.

273 "Asiatic mode": Ervand Abrahamian, *Iran Between Two Revolutions* (Princeton,
N.J., 1982), p. 468.

274 "It is not enough to say": Ibid., p. 470.

279 "supporting dictatorships": The American Presidency Project, "Presidential Campaign Debate," 6 October 1976, https://www.presidency.ucsb.edu/documents
/presidential-campaign-debate.

280 In the first few months: Although the *mosharekat* program is sometimes described as a cynical and desperate attempt by the shah to demonstrate his good faith to Carter and thus avoid an unpleasant rift with the United States, the reality is a little more complicated. At the end of 1976, the shah was fifty-seven years old with cancer. His son, Crown Prince Reza, was sixteen and ill equipped to inherit a political system full of pent-up anger. Even the shah now realized that years of brutal repression had done little to silence internal dissent and in fact had probably only created a fresh generation of Iranians hostile to Pahlavi rule. He was keenly aware that the European press was battering his image, producing a steady stream of negative stories about Iran as a nation of gulags and torture chambers. Increasingly, his loyalists within the Rastakhiz Party—and even his wife, Empress Farah—were pushing him to open up the political process. By 1977, everyone in the Imperial Palace could see that a bit of *mosharekat* was long overdue in Iranian politics. No one needed Jimmy Carter to point that out. Having said all that, I tend to concur with Kenneth Pollack and others that in creating the *mosharekat* program, the shah was ultimately reacting to the changing U.S. political landscape. Throughout his reign, he had shown himself to be far more concerned with winning the approval of the United States than that of his own people. Convinced that the United States and Great Britain were the ultimate arbiters of power in Iran, ready to treat him as they had treated his father if he failed to follow orders, the shah often gave the impression that he was prepared to radically alter policy if that was what the U.S. ambassador seemed to want. It is probably no coincidence that the shah's two great reform and liberalization efforts coincided with the coming to power of Kennedy in 1961 and Carter in 1977. In 1977, however, it was obvious that his commitment to reform was half-hearted, and that he lost interest when he no longer felt pressured. Pollack savagely distorts James Bill's argument when he claims that "Bill argues that Carter had nothing to do with the shah's lighter hand in early 1977 and that it was entirely about paving the way for his son." (Bill's point is actually that the situation was complex and that Carter was just one factor.) But on balance, Pollack's interpretation is more convincing.

281 "tired of all this": Joseph Kraft, "Letter from Iran," *New Yorker,* 18 December 1978.

281 Severe and unforgiving: Nikki Keddie, *Modern Iran: Roots and Results of Revolution* (New Haven, Conn., 2006), p. 215.

282 Many Iranians, unable: Some writers have carelessly described this suspicion as yet another example of the mystifying, irrational, and "conspiratorial mindset" of Iranians. It was not. Like most Asians, Iranians rarely communicate negativity or rejection directly and are thus acutely attuned to the symbolic significance of indirect signals. As residents of a dictatorship, moreover, in which no ordinary citizen could get anywhere near the Imperial Palace, they were genuinely baffled that such a chaotic scene could be allowed to take place on the doorstep of the White House without the president's approval.

284 "Iran, because of the great leadership": "Jimmy Carter Toasts the Shah," *Voices & Visions,* http://vandvreader.org/jimmy-carter-toasts-the-shah-31-december-1997.

285 "Iran's enemies": "Iran and the Red and Black Colonialism," *Ettela'at,* 17 Dey 1356 (7 January 1978), p. 7.

286 "The people have identified": Hamid Algar, ed., *Islam and Revolution 1: Writings and Declarations of Imam Khomeini* (Berkeley, Calif., 1981), pp. 212, 227.

286 Not one official at: Gary Sick, *All Fall Down: America's Tragic Encounter with Iran* (New York, 1985), p. 40. The first (and apparently only) cable regarding the disturbances was sent from Sullivan on 11 January, fully forty-eight hours after the fact, and a full day after the events were reported in the Iranian press. Telegram, Sullivan to State Department, 11 January 1978, NARA, RG59, 1978TEHRAN00389, Film number D780017-0947.

287 The demonstrations in Tabriz: Abrahamian, *Between Two Revolutions,* p. 507.

287 Vance merely updated: Sick, *All Fall Down,* p. 41.

288 Spontaneous crowds of: Abrahamian, *Between Two Revolutions,* p. 515.

289 "reaffirmed the close": *Public Papers of the Presidents of the United States, Jimmy Carter, 1978* (Washington, D.C., 1979), p. 1515.

289 "With the support of": Algar, *Islam and Revolution,* pp. 212, 227.

289 An American official recalled: Sick, *All Fall Down,* p. 62.

291 Over the next four months: Annabelle Sreberny and Massoumeh Torfeh, *Persian Service: The BBC and British Interests in Iran* (London, 2014), p. 90.

292 The situation was unraveling: Desmond Harney, *The Priest and the King: An Eyewitness Account of the Iranian Revolution* (London, 1998), p. 48.

292 Though it was never: *Sun,* 20 September 1978.

292 Market stalls and corner shops: Abrahamian, *Between Two Revolutions,* p. 498.

293 "Victory is yours": Algar, *Islam and Revolution,* p. 244.

293 "present monarchy": Abrahamian, *Between Two Revolutions,* p. 520.

293 "the heart of the": Joseph Kraft, "Letter from Iran," *New Yorker,* 18 December 1978.

293 "As the king of Iran": https://www.youtube.com/watch?v=PWwTshDIfuQ&feature=youtu.be.

294 Shortly after the revolution: Ali Ansari, *Modern Iran: The Pahlavis and After* (London, 2007), p. 259; Abrahamian, *Between Two Revolutions,* p. 517.

295 "is expected to": Kurzman, *Unthinkable Revolution,* p. 2.

295 "some chance that": See Richard W. Cottam, *Iran and the United States: A Cold War Case Study* (Pittsburgh, 1988), p. 173.

296 Thus, many on Brzezinski's: A good illustration of this phenomenon is in Sick, *All Fall Down,* pp. 124–25.

297 But U.S. companies: Harney, *Priest and King,* p. 120.

298 "You must know this": William Sullivan, *Mission to Iran* (New York, 1981), pp. 211–12.

298 "How long has it been": Chapour Bakhtiar, *Ma fidelité* (Paris, 1982), pp. 11, 125.

299 In his first television: Michael Rubin, "Stumbling Through the 'Open Door': The US in Persia and the Standard-Sinclair Oil Dispute, 1920–1925," *Iranian Studies* 28, no. 3/4 (1995), p. 244.

300 "I fully expect the shah": President's news conference, 12 December 1978, in *Public Papers of the Presidents of the United States: Jimmy Carter, 1978* (Washington, 1979), Book 2, p. 2226.

302 In Tehran alone: Abrahamian, *Between Two Revolutions,* p. 526.

302 On February 1: Algar, *Islam and Revolution,* p. 243.

302 "You don't have to come": Ibrahim Yazdi in episode 1 of the BBC2 documentary series *Iran and the West* (2009).

303 "dark as night": Mohsen Rafiqdust, ibid.

305 Wisely, he slipped: Bakhtiar, *Ma fidelité,* pp. 187–94.

305 "This is the voice of Iran": Abrahamian, *Between Two Revolutions,* p. 259.

CHAPTER 19

1979

309 By day's end, no one: *Ettela'at,* 14 Esfand 1357 (5 March 1979), pp. 1–2.

309 "Once upon a time": "Iranians Mass to Honor Late Nationalist, Ask for Role in Shaping Nation's Future," *Los Angeles Times,* 6 March 1979, p. A16.

310 Barely three weeks: The organizers of the memorial service were a wide variety of groups that were nervous about the prospect of religious fanaticism. Everyone from the secular Marxists of the FeK to the Islamic liberals of Bazargan's Freedom Movement to the National Association of Dentists chartered buses to transport the public to the event.

310 But now that the enemy: "Tehran Rebels Make a Babel of Street Signs," *Los Angeles Times,* 3 March 1979, p. A1. Eventually the street was named Vali-e Asr ("Guardian of the Age," a reference to the twelfth emam of Shia Islam), but as late as May 1979, official Iranian newspapers were still referring to it as Mosaddeq Avenue. See, for example, *Ettela'at,* 6 Khordad 1358 (27 May 1979), p. 11.

314 "bulldozer": Shaul Bakhash, *The Reign of the Ayatollahs* (New York, 1986), p. 54.

314 Every time the government: The point is well made in Ali Ansari, *Modern Iran: The Pahlavis and After* (London, 2007), p. 277.

315 "Islam does not need": Oriana Fallaci, "An Interview with Khomeini," *New York Times,* 7 October 1979, p. SM8.

315 "Shall the former": *Ettela'at,* 9 Esfand 1357 (28 February 1979), p. 1; *Ettela'at,* 9 Farvardin 1358 (29 March 1979), p. 1.

317 On Sunday-morning: James Bill, *The Eagle and the Lion: The Tragedy of American-Iranian Relations* (New Haven, Conn., 1989), p. 285.

317 "sooner or later, he": George Ball, "Iran's Coming Backlash," *New York Times,* 27 May 1979, p. E19.

318 At least part of the explanation: Throughout 1979, former associates of the shah

were told that if they could offer the Americans meaningful information about what was going on in Iran, they and their families could have expedited visa applications to come to the United States—and many were understandably keen to take advantage of this opportunity. Needless to say, however, the Pahlavi exiles were in an even greater state of shock and denial about the revolution than the Americans, and were certainly in no position to give objective advice or information about Iran. These were, after all, the same people who had been so oblivious to the undercurrents of frustration building over the years that they had driven themselves out of power. And yet for better or for worse, they were the only Iranians with whom official Washington had fostered any meaningful relationships over the years.

319 "desert[ing] the Shah": *St. Louis Globe-Democrat,* 29 May 1979; *Richmond Times-Dispatch,* 24 May 1979.

319 "dangerous dingbat": *Kansas City Star,* 23 May 1979; *Providence Journal,* 27 May 1979.

319 By June 1979: "Yanks in Iran: No Place to Go But Home," *Los Angeles Times,* 29 June 1979, p. C1.

319 "We simply do not have": James Bill, *The Eagle and the Lion: The Tragedy of American-Iranian Relations* (New Haven, Conn., 1989), p. 276.

321 "If they let him in": Henry Precht, "The Iranian Revolution: An Oral History with Henry Precht, Then State Department Desk Officer," *Middle East Journal* 58, no. 1 (2004): 29.

321 "play tennis": Gary Sick, *All Fall Down: America's Tragic Encounter with Iran* (New York, 1985), p. 209.

321 Leaders like Anwar Sadat: Zbigniew Brzezinski, *Power and Principle: Memoirs of the National Security Advisor 1977–1981* (New York, 1985), p. 472.

321 "If we let in the shah": *Iran and the West,* BBC2 documentary (2009).

323 "If the shah dies": Hamilton Jordan, *Crisis: The Last Year of the Carter Presidency* (New York, 1982), p. 31. There were other nagging doubts within the administration as well. Some wondered why the shah couldn't be treated in Europe. (Switzerland seemed an obvious choice.) Others saw something suspect in the fact that news of the shah's cancer had come from a physician employed by David Rockefeller. But Carter felt there was little time to second-guess the diagnosis.

323 "Even if you convince": *Iran and the West,* BBC2 documentary (2009).

323 Brzezinski felt such: Ibid.

324 "You are playing with fire": Ibid.

324 "perhaps a year": Lawrence Altman, "The Shah's Health: A Political Gamble," *New York Times,* 17 May 1981, pp. SM12ff.

325 A massive, unprecedented anti-American: *Ettela'at,* 12 Aban 1358 (3 November 1979), p. 3.

326 "The idea": Massoumeh Ebtekar, *Takeover in Tehran: The Inside Story of the 1979 U.S. Embassy Capture* (Vancouver, B.C., 2000), p. 54.

327 "expand with full force": *Ettela'at*, 12 Aban 1358 (2 November 1979), p. 10.

328 "another revolution": "U.S. Rejects Demand of Students in Iran to Send Shah Back," *New York Times*, 6 November 1979, pp. 1, 12.

328 The so-called U.S.: *Ettela'at*, 15 Aban 1358 (6 November 1979), p. 10.

330 "The American Embassy in *Tehran*": *Iran and the West*, BBC2 documentary (2009).

331 "When I watch TV": Ted Koppel and Kyle Gibson, *Nightline* (New York, 1996), p. 9; David Farber, *Taken Hostage* (Princeton, N.J., 2005), pp. 137–39.

331 They had walked barefoot: Ebtekar, *Takeover in Tehran*, pp. 87–88.

332 "You have no right to complain": Scott Anderson, *Let the Swords Encircle Me: Iran—A Journey Beyond the Headlines* (New York, 2010), p. 53.

334 "We are facing a satanic": Dilip Hiro, *Iran Under the Ayatollahs* (London, 1985), p. 139.

339 "It was my decision": *Iran and the West*, BBC2 documentary (2009).

340 "was probably the most": Sick, *All Fall Down*, p. 255.

340 "fruit from which all juice": "Year of Captivity: The Long, Frustrating Effort to End a National Humiliation," *New York Times*, 19 January 1981, p. A8.

CHAPTER 20

Dulce et Decorum Est

347 "We had child-volunteers": Matthias Küntzel, "Ahmadinejad's Demons," *New Republic*, 24 April 2006, p. 15.

347 "It was sometimes like": Ibid.

349 In Khorramshahr and elsewhere: John Bulloch and Harvey Morris, *The Gulf War: Its Origins, History and Consequences* (London, 1991), p. 45.

349 As a young street-gang: Ibid., p. 26.

350 The few units that still: Shaul Bakhash, *The Reign of the Ayatollahs* (New York, 1986), p. 127.

352 "The hand of America": Ray Takeyh, *Guardians of the Revolution: Iran and the World in the Age of the Ayatollahs* (Oxford, 2009), p. 89.

352 "refrain immediately": UN Security Council Resolution 479, http://unscr.com /en/resolutions/479.

357 "They come at us in": Erich Wiedemann, "Mit dem Paradies-Schlüssel in die Schlacht," *Der Spiegel*, no. 31 (1982): 93.

358 When Saddam first: Bakhash, *Reign of Ayatollahs*, p. 127; Bulloch and Morris, *Gulf War*, p. 49.

358 "We are going to write": "In Iran's War, Youth and Islam," *New York Times*, 7 April 1982, pp. A1–A2. The author spells his name "Behruz Suleimaja," but this is likely to be Soleimani.

363 By 1985, in fact: Dilip Hiro, *Iran Under the Ayatollahs* (London, 1985), pp. 165, 172.

366 "America will never make concessions": "President Bars 'Concessions'; Orders Antihijacking Steps; 3 More TWA Hostages Freed," *New York Times,* 19 June 1985, p. A1.

368 "I know you've been reading": "Transcript of Remarks by Reagan About Iran," *New York Times,* 14 November 1986, p. A8.

368 "America has accepted": *Ettela'at,* 17 Aban 1365 (8 November 1986), p. 11.

369 "Those who broke": Hiro, *Under the Ayatollahs,* p. 220.

369 "mutual exhaustion": "U.S. Fears Iran Victory Imperils West's Interest," *International Herald Tribune* (27 May 1982).

369 "an all-out Iranian": Ibid.

369 "I stated that they": *The Tower Commission Report* (New York, 1987), part 1, p. 321.

369 "We didn't want either": George Crile, *Charlie Wilson's War* (New York, 2003), p. 275.

369 "certainly not in": Sasan Fayazmanesh, *The United States and Iran: Sanctions, Wars and the Policy of Dual Containment* (London, 2008), p. 29.

370 "to carry out martyrdom-seeking attacks": "Iran Warns It Has Extended Maneuvers in Gulf," *New York Times,* 7 August 1987, p. A1.

370 "villain in the": And yet when push came to shove, both Iran and the United States exercised remarkable restraint in their so-called "tanker war," repeatedly finding ways to avoid and defuse situations. Neither country, it seemed, had a real desire to go to war with the other (and certainly not at the behest of Saddam Hussein), both preferring the safe terrain of rhetorical conflict to actual military action. This process is nicely outlined by Shahram Chubin and Charles Tripp, *Iran and Iraq at War* (London, 1988), pp. 215–19.

370 "We can't stand to see Iraq defeated": Hiro, p. 257.

371 "If we had won the war": Ibid., p. 218.

371 "I will never apologize": https://www.youtube.com/watch?v=1oqatUWwIeg.

371 At a ceremony held: "Medals Go to Top Officers in Charge of Vincennes," *Orlando Sentinel,* 24 April 1990.

373 Stories emerged of villagers: Human Rights Watch, "Whatever Happened to the Iraqi Kurds," 11 March 1991, https://www.hrw.org/reports/1991/IRAQ913 .htm.

373 "a new kind of death": Robin Wright, *Dreams and Shadows: The Future of the Middle East* (New York, 2008), pp. 384–85.

374 "Blessed are the dead": *Iran and the West,* BBC2 documentary (2009).

374 "They come on in their": Bulloch and Morris, *Gulf War,* p. 150.

376 "self-inflicted injuries": Baqer Moin, *Khomeini: Life of the Ayatollah* (New York, 1999), pp. 310–13.

377 But at the same time: Ali Ansari, *Modern Iran: The Pahlavis and After* (London, 2007), pp. 279–80.

CHAPTER 21

Goodwill Hunting

380 Revolutionary committees: Shaul Bakhash, *The Reign of the Ayatollahs* (New York, 1986), p. 129.

380 Over the course of the 1980s: Ibid.

380 And their troop numbers: Said Arjomand, *After Khomeini: Iran Under His Successors* (New York, 2009), p. 59.

382 Military spending was scaled: Trita Parsi, *Treacherous Alliance: The Secret Dealings of Israel, Iran, and the United States* (New York, 2007), p. 146.

384 "I'm one of the few people": "Bush Makes Public Iran-Contra Diary," *New York Times,* 16 January 1993, p. 1.

386 Eventually, through a combination: Gen. Mohsen Rezai, quoted in episode 2 of the BBC2 documentary *Iran and the West* (2009).

387 "still a terrorist state": "From Iran to US, a Hint of Good Will," *New York Times,* 5 December 1991, p. A1.

388 "in the position": Giandomenico Picco, *Man Without a Gun* (New York, 1999), p. 286.

388 "When the hostages were": Parsi, *Treacherous Alliance,* p. 134.

390 "broader strategic": Ibid., pp. 121, 124.

390 In 1989, on Israeli television: Ibid., p. 131.

390 "Iran has to be": "Israel Focuses on the Threat Beyond the Arabs—in Iran," *New York Times,* 8 November 1992, p. 153.

390 "Israel's best friend": Rabin, 28 October 1987, quoted in Behrouz Souresrafil, *Khomeini and Israel* (London, 1988), p. 114.

391 But Iran was conspicuously: Parsi, *Treacherous Alliance,* p. 152.

391 "The willingness to do": Ibid., p. 155.

392 "fanning the flames": Shimon Peres, *The New Middle East* (New York, 1993), p. 43.

392 "I think it's fair to say": Parsi, *Treacherous Alliance,* pp. 152, 155.

393 "The choice is Israel's": Ibid., pp. 150–51.

393 Economic woes added: R. J. Reinhart, "George H. W. Bush Retrospective," Gallup blog, December 1, 2018, https://news.gallup.com/opinion/gallup/234971/george-bush-retrospective.aspx.

394 "the Iran part of Dual": Kenneth Pollack, *The Persian Puzzle: The Conflict Between Iran and America* (New York, 2004), p. 263.

395 "Iran is the world's": "The Other Problem in the Persian Gulf," *US News & World Report,* 6 November 1994.

397 "cut all its trade": "Aipac Report on Iran's Activities Aimed at Urging Further Sanctions," Jewish Telegraphic Agency, 12 April 1995.

397 Within three weeks: To be precise, Clinton signed the first executive order, ban-

ning U.S. investment in Iran's energy sector, on March 15, just nine days after the Conoco deal was announced. Under further pressure, he signed a second executive order designed to supersede and supplement that one, on May 6. This second order banned all U.S. trade and investment with Iran.

397 "Wherever you look": "Christopher Ends His Role in Debate on Conoco-Iran Deal," *Los Angeles Times,* 13 March 1995.

397 Its executives had held twenty-six: Pollack, *Persian Puzzle,* p. 271.

397 In the summer of 1996: AIPAC has never been bashful about admitting its authorship of the legislation. See, e.g., Colin MacKinnon, "Clinton's Executive Order on Iran: Taking It from AIPAC and Al Gore," *Washington Report on Middle East Affairs,* July–August 1995, p. 37, in which AIPAC's Keith Weissman tells the correspondent that his organization "had actually written" the bill.

398 Iran was now: In 1995 there was one unexpected moment of cooperation: Iran flew weapons and fighters to aid Bosnian Muslims, whose position Washington was hoping to bolster against the Serbs in the Yugoslav civil war. A UN arms embargo prohibited American weapons from being sent, so the Clinton administration quietly worked with the Iranians to make sure weapons reached their intended recipients.

CHAPTER 22
The First Hopey-Changey Moment

401 The prices of sugar: Ervand Abrahamian, *Iran Between Two Revolutions* (Princeton, N.J., 1982), p. 185.

401 At the worst possible: European Brent Crude spot prices, not adjusted for inflation.

403 "dangerous trend": David Menashri, *Post-revolutionary Politics in Iran: Religion, Society and Power* (London, 2001), p. 81.

404 So on a cold winter: Geneive Abdo and Jonathan Lyons, *Answering Only to God: Faith and Freedom in Twenty-First-Century Iran* (New York, 2003), pp. 56–57.

404 "are not in charge": Menashri, *Post-revolutionary Politics,* p. 82.

405 "fresh approach": Ibid.

405 "There is no fun in Islam": Amir Taheri, *The Spirit of Allah: Khomeini and the Islamic Revolution* (1986), p. 259.

405 "hopeful": "Clinton Sees Hope in the Election of Moderate as President of Iran," *New York Times,* 30 May 1997.

406 "a system which combined": Mohammad Khatami, interview by Christiane Amanpour, CNN, January 7, 1998, transcript, http://www.cnn.com/WORLD/9801/07/iran/interview.html.

408 In the first year of: Ali Ansari, *Confronting Iran* (New York, 2006), p. 158.

408 "has been the subject": "Clinton Seeks an Opening to Iran, But Efforts Have Been Rebuffed," *New York Times,* 3 December 1999, p. A1.

410 A stream of American: Jessie Embry, "Point Four, Utah State University Technicians, and Rural Development in Iran, 1950–64," *Rural History* 14, no. 1 (2003): 99–110. See also Marzieh Gail, *Arches of the Years* (Oxford, 1991), pp. 109–10. Iran's links to Utah State actually went back more than a century. In 1912, John Widstoe, a Mormon elder and president of Utah Agricultural College (as USU was then known), had met Ali Qoli Khan at a dry-farming congress in Alberta. The Persian minister felt at home in Utah, where he appreciated the Mormon distaste for drinking and smoking. Shortly thereafter, in 1915, he sent four of his young relatives to study in Utah. In 1939, when Reza Shah was looking for an adviser on animal husbandry, Brigham Young University president Franklin Harris went to Iran and spent a year touring the country and recommending improved farming methods. When he left in 1940, he encouraged Iran to hire two more USU professors to teach at the College of Agriculture in Karaj. By 1951, when Truman's Point Four initiative formalized and expanded the Utah partnership, there were already 150 Iranians with degrees from Utah State. One of these was the legendary Ardeshir Zahedi, who went on to become Iran's last ambassador to the United States.

410 "another step toward ending": "US Match 'Just a Game' to Iranians," *Chicago Tribune,* 21 June 1998.

410 "dialogue among civilizations": "The United Nations: Iran; Iranian President Paints a Picture of Peace and Moderation," *New York Times,* 22 September 1998, p. A12.

410 a glowing front-page profile: "Beneath the Turban: A Special Report; Mullah Who Charmed Iran Is Struggling to Change It," *New York Times,* 1 February 1998, p. 1.

411 In Paris, he asked: Elaine Sciolino, *Persian Mirrors* (New York, 2001), p. 346.

411 That spring: More precisely, it was a five-year sentence that was later reduced to two years.

412 "ugly and distasteful": *Ettela'at,* 20 Tir 1378 (11 July 1999), p. 2; *Ettela'at,* 22 Tir 1378 (13 July 1999), p. 3.

412 he also urged students: *Ettela'at,* 23 Tir 1378 (14 July 1999).

412 "The most important problem": Menashri, *Post-revolutionary Politics,* pp. 153–54.

413 "to work together": U.S. Department of State Archive, "Secretary of State Madeleine K. Albright, Remarks Before the American-Iranian Council, March 17, 2000," available at https://1997-2001.state.gov/statements/2000/000317.html.

413 "a piece of chocolate": Ibid., p. 316.

CHAPTER 23

That September Day

421 "Killing of innocent people": http://farsi.khamenei.ir/audio-content?id=23664.

423 In October 1998: Janne Bjerre Christensen, *Drugs, Deviancy and Democracy in Iran: The Interaction of State and Civil Society* (London, 2011), p. 130.

424 "comprehensively helpful": Said Arjomand, *After Khomeini: Iran Under His Successors* (New York, 2009), p. 147.

427 President Khatami even: Trita Parsi, *Treacherous Alliance: The Secret Dealings of Israel, Iran, and the United States* (New York, 2007), p. 234.

427 Why, they wondered: See, for example, Brian Whittaker, "The Strange Affair of Karine A," *Guardian,* 21 January 2002.

427 In Washington, it was: See, for example, Lawrence Wilkerson quoted in Parsi, *Treacherous Alliance,* p. 234.

427 The administration's ideologically: Wolfowitz, described as "one of the strongest supporters of Israel in the Reagan administration," played a critical role in the creation of the Project for the New American Century (PNAC), an influential pro-Israel think-tank that supplied many of the Bush administration's senior officials. James Mann, *Rise of the Vulcans: The History of Bush's War Cabinet* (New York, 2004), p. 113. Perle, closely aligned with both PNAC and the Jewish Institute for National Security Affairs (JINSA), was known for his co-authorship of the famous 1996 "Clean Break" report, which argued for rearranging the balance of power in the Middle East more forcefully in Israel's favor. Feith, a co-author of the report, was also close to JINSA and a particularly strident advocate for Israel.

428 "global unilateralism": "Why Should Bush Take Europe Seriously?" *Observer,* 16 February 2002.

428 "appropriately forceful": "George W. Bush's Moment," *New York Times,* 30 January 2002, p. A26.

428 "When historians sum up": "Bush the Bold," *Jerusalem Post,* 31 January 2002, p. 6.

428 All bets were off: The background to the Hekmatiar case was deeply revealing of the dysfunction at the heart of U.S.-Iranian relations. For Iran, the problem of al-Qaeda fighters escaping across the border from Afghanistan had been a delicate balancing act. On the one hand, Iran truly loathed al-Qaeda and did not want to give them any kind of refuge (and in fact was expatriating them as quickly as it could). At the same time, Iran was so isolated in the world that it could not afford to antagonize al-Qaeda or make itself a target for jihadist suicide bombers. (After all, the Iranians asked themselves, if Osama bin Laden suddenly urged his Sunni followers to attack the Shia heretics of Persia, would America really come rushing to Iran's defense?) In late 2001, the United States and Iran

had reached a compromise on this matter: Iran would hold on to people like Hekmatiar if that was what the United States wanted, on condition that it not be accused of harboring terrorists.

429 "We would have liked": Parsi, *Treacherous Alliance*, p. 236.

431 In August 2002: See, for example, Connie Bruck, "Exiles: How Iran's Expatriates Are Gaming the Nuclear Threat," *New Yorker*, 6 March 2006, pp. 48ff. See also Parsi, *Treacherous Alliance*, pp. 245–46, 254–55, for details of Israel's attempts to use Reza Pahlavi, son of the late shah, as a nexus for opposition activity and nuclear accusations against Iran.

433 "We thought it was": "Washington 'Snubbed Iran Offer,'" BBC News, 18 January 2007.

433 "much more than just": Parsi, *Treacherous Alliance*, p. 249.

433 The evidence was: Immediately suspicions turned to al-Qaeda, but Cheney and Rumsfeld got out in front of the story and claimed the operation had been ordered by al-Qaeda figures operating out of *Iran*. There was a slim possibility that the attacks had been coordinated with members of al-Qaeda held in Iranian detention, but if so, those al-Qaeda figures were precisely the people Iran had been trying, through the Geneva Channel, to turn over to American custody for the past several months.

434 Iran in 2004 was a nation: According to one study, there were 5.5 million Internet users in Iran and nearly one hundred thousand active blogs—and Persian was the third most common language in the blogosphere, after English and Chinese. Barbara Slavin, *Bitter Friends, Bosom Enemies* (New York, 2007), p. 133.

CHAPTER 24
The Moral Cold War

436 As mayor of Tehran: Barbara Slavin, *Bitter Friends, Bosom Enemies* (New York, 2007), p. 48.

437 As mayor, he was: Ibid., p. 49.

438 Soon after taking office: Said Arjomand, *After Khomeini: Iran Under His Successors* (New York, 2009), p. 152.

438 In foreign policy: The council consists of the supreme leader, the president, Revolutionary Guard commanders, military chiefs, religious authorities, and the leader of the Majles.

439 It was a lousy translation: Numerous linguists, scholars, and professional translators have since pointed out that what Ahmadinejad actually said was closer to "This occupying regime in Jerusalem will have to wither from the pages of history." For example, Juan Cole translates it as "the occupation regime over Jerusalem must vanish from the page of time." See Cole, "Ahmadinejad Censored, Distorted in US Media," *Informed Comment*, September 20, 2008, https://

www.juancole.com/2008/09/ahmadinejad-censored-distorted-in-us.html. See also Jonathan Steele, "If Iran Is Ready to Talk, the US Must Do So Unconditionally," *Guardian,* 1 June 2006, p. 33; and Steele, "Lost in Translation," *Guardian,* 14 June 2006. Even the Middle East Media Research Institute (MEMRI), a pro-Israeli organization with a long track record of making the comments of Muslim leaders sound more threatening than they actually are, translated the statement as "This regime that is occupying Qods [Jerusalem] must be eliminated from the pages of history."

More important, perhaps, Ahmadinejad didn't even really "say" any of this. He was quoting, approvingly, from a speech given decades earlier by the late Ayatollah Khomeini. The full text of the statement was: "Our dear emam [Khomeini] once said that this occupying regime in Jerusalem should wither from the pages of history, and this was a very wise statement on his part." It was no accident that Ahmadinejad, like Khomeini before him, referred to "this occupying regime in Jerusalem" (*een rezhim-e eshqalgar-e Qods*) rather than to "Israel." For both men, the problem was specifically with (as they saw it) a political system of occupation and subjugation imposed on the Palestinians since 1948—rather than the actual state of Israel as an abstract concept or a place on a map. Of course, many defenders of Israel will point out that this is a rather fine distinction. Ahmadinejad repeatedly stated during his presidency that his solution for Israel and Palestine would be to allow all their inhabitants—Jewish, Muslim, Christian, and otherwise—to vote in a free and fair election to determine their fate. Defenders of Israel point out that this would mean the end of Israel as a "Jewish state," so in effect, he was calling for its destruction. But this gets to the very heart of the problem, and to the contradiction inherent in the idea of Israel as both a Jewish and democratic state. Which is exactly the contradiction that Ahmadinejad was trying to highlight when he called for a referendum.

Then there was the question of agency. As a number of scholars have pointed out, the idiom "wiped off the map" does not exist in Persian, and the implication of this translation—that someone, somehow, will be doing the wiping—contradicts the mood and tenor of the speech. Ahmadinejad, like Khomeini before him, claimed that the Israeli occupation of Palestine would disappear naturally—as so many other unjust political systems had collapsed in the course of human history. Both men, in fact, made their comments in the context of a larger discussion about the way the shah's regime had "disappeared from history" in 1979. Ahmadinejad also drew a comparison to the way the Soviet Union and Saddam's Iraq had crumbled, despite their apparent invincibility. "This occupying regime in Jerusalem," he then reassured his audience, would also "disappear from the pages of history."

The exact words were *een rezhim-e eshqalgar-e Qods bayad az safheh-ye ruzegar mahv shavad.* The word *ruzegar* is especially difficult to translate, as there is no direct English equivalent. It means something like "history," "destiny," "time," "this day and age"—and is often used in a philosophical, poetic, almost fatalistic context, to mean "the times we live in." *Safheh* is much easier—it literally means "page." Taken together, *safheh-ye ruzegar* is best rendered as "pages of time" or "pages of history." *Mahv shavad* comes from the compound verb *mahv shodan*, which means "to disappear," "vanish," or "wither away." It is not, as some have claimed, a transitive verb (as in "to be eliminated"). *Shodan* is basically "to become," and thus the most literal translation of *mahv shodan* is "to become nonexistent." One could therefore render the whole phrase *bayad az safheh-ye ruzegar mahv shavad* as: "must become nonexistent in the pages of history." In no reasonable translation can it mean "must be wiped off the map."

Much has been made, by those who wish to defend the original translation, of the fact that Ahmadinejad used the imperative mood of the verb *bayad mahv shavad*. The implication is that he was issuing some sort of command rather than making a prediction or expressing a wish. In fact, however, the imperative mood is a subtle one, both in English and in Persian. It can be rendered with a wide range of auxiliary verbs—ranging from (at the more forceful end of the spectrum) "must" or "should" to (at the less forceful end) "ought to" or "will have to." My own feeling is that anyone who reads the speech in its entirety cannot help but draw the conclusion that Ahmadinejad was not issuing some sort of threat—at least not a direct one. One can certainly translate his verb very literally, as "must disappear." However, he appears to be suggesting that Israel must disappear in the sense that this is something that "really ought to happen." Thus, I have chosen to use the phrase "will have to," believing that this preserves the imperative mood of the verb, while remaining faithful to the overall tone of the statement. To me, "will have to wither from the pages of history" is the closest approximation of how the statement sounds in Persian: unfriendly, perhaps even hostile, but not belligerent.

439　"We still have the same": "Iranian President Stands by Call to Wipe Israel Off Map," *New York Times,* 29 October 2005.

439　"Iran is committed": "Iran Backs Off from Direct Threat to Israel," *New York Times,* 30 October 2005.

439　"We will not commit": "Supreme Leader Vows Iran Will Not Attack Any Countries," Agence France-Presse, 4 November 2005.

439　In Israel, Prime Minister: "Israel Urges UN to Exclude Iran," BBC, 27 October 2005, http://news.bbc.co.uk/2/hi/middle_east/4382594.stm.

440　America's UN ambassador: "Western Leaders Condemn the Iranian President's Threat to Israel," *New York Times,* 28 October 2005.

440　"call for genocide" "Prime Minister Martin Speaks Before Jewish Leaders in Toronto," 13 November 2005, http://www.carolynbennettmp.ca/dev/downloads/2005-11-13_Prime-Minister-Martin-Addresses-Jewish-Leaders_Toronto.doc.

440　"Today, they have created": Islamic Republic News Agency, 14 December 2005 (author translation).

441 "adventurism at the": Arjomand, *After Khomeini,* p. 164.

441 "historical fact": Abbas Milani, "What Scares Iran's Mullahs?," *New York Times,* 23 February 2007, p. A21.

441 "It is becoming": "Iranian President Stands by Call to Wipe Israel Off Map," *New York Times,* 29 October 2005.

441 "the Zionist regime": Slavin, *Bitter Friends,* p. 59.

443 Iran's trade with Brazil: "Iran Seeking To Expand Influence in Latin America," *Washington Post,* 1 January 2012, p. 1.

443 When Ahmadinejad's plane: Hooman Majd, *The Ayatollahs' Democracy* (New York, 2010), p. 154.

443 Iran sponsored: "کمک یک میلیارد و ۳۵۰ میلیون دلاری دولت نهم به لبنان و بولیوی" *Andisheh-ye Nou,* 10 Khordad 1388 (31 May 2009), p. 3.

444 While 63 percent: BBC World Service poll, March 2007.

444 In Bangladesh: Pew Global Attitudes Project, 27 June 2007, p. 47.

444 And in the Arab world: Zogby International Arab Public Opinion Polls, 2007, 2008, 2009, 2010.

444 They had seen, in 2006: The Bush administration repeatedly asserted Israel's right to self-defense and expedited a shipment of precision-guided bombs to Israel. The U.S. Congress, meanwhile, passed a resolution, 410–8, "supporting Israel's right to defend itself."

445 "The people will scrutinize": "Those in Power Do Not Rule for Ever: History Will Judge Our Presidencies," theguardian.com, 11 May 2006, www.theguardian .com/commentisfree/2006/may/11/iran.world.

445 "it was, like, sixteen or seventeen": "President Bush and Prime Minister Tony Blair of the United Kingdom Participate in Joint Press Availability," 25 May 2006, https://georgewbush-whitehouse.archives.gov/news/releases/2006 /05/20060525-12.html.

445 "to the American people": "Ahmadinejad's Letter to Americans," CNN.com, 29 November 2006, https://www.cnn.com/2006/WORLD/meast/11/29/ahmadine-jad.letter/.

445 Every time people switched: "Iran President: Destroy Israel," Associated Press, 3 August 2006.

447 Some analysts of the Middle East: See, for example, Alastair Crooke, *Resistance: The Essence of the Islamist Revolution* (London, 2009).

447 Turkey: Turkey—a constitutionally secular state and a NATO member that traditionally acted as a bridge between Europe and the Muslim world—saw a noticeable revival in pro-Iranian sentiment. After years of watching their leaders banging on the door of Brussels, asking to be admitted to the European Union and getting nowhere, many Turks now felt they were better off reassessing their Western orientation and embracing their Muslim neighbors to the east—and this generally meant Iran. Much as young Iranian women had done in the 1970s, more and more young Turkish women began wearing the hijab in public, both

as a symbol of Muslim identity and as a political statement against American foreign policy. In 2002 and again in 2007, Turkey's traditional ruling elite, highly secular and pro-Western, lost elections to the AKP—a mildly Islamist party that went on to steadily improve Turkey's relationship with Tehran.

448 "You have degraded the nation": www.c-span.org/video/?286804-1/iranian-presidential-debate.

449 By 2008 Ahmadinejad: Petr Lom, *Letters to the President* (2009), film.

449 By the end of his first: Arjomand, *After Khomeini,* p. 160.

CHAPTER 25

Atoms for Peace?

452 For a developing country: In 1971 the shah had made a speech explaining to his people that "petroleum is a noble material, much too valuable to burn" and announcing plans to produce 23,000 megawatts of electricity from nuclear power plants by the year 2000. But he expressed the sentiment repeatedly in more private settings as well. See, for example, an interview with Akbar Etemad, who had supervised Iran's first nuclear reactor in 1965–67, who said in 2009 that the shah "was adamant that a barrel of oil was too valuable to burn for fuel." "I Founded Iran's Nuclear Programme," *Financial Times,* 11–12 July 2009, Life & Arts, p. 2.

452 He had already purchased: Anthony Cordesman and Khalid al-Rodhan, *Iran's Weapons of Mass Destruction* (Washington, D.C., 2006), pp. 106–7.

452 "I don't think the issue": "Past Arguments Don't Square with Current Iran Policy," *Washington Post,* 27 March 2005, p. A15.

453 "prepare against": Ibid.

453 A 1978 State Department: Department of State Memorandum on the U.S.-Iran Nuclear Energy Agreement, 20 October 1978, quoted in Mohammad Javad Zarif, "Tackling the Iran-US Crisis," *Journal of International Affairs* 60, no. 2 (Spring–Summer 2007): 80, http://www.iranaffairs.com/iran_affairs/files/nssm219-talkingpoints.pdf (accessed 19 November 2012).

454 "meticulous": "Blame Saddam: Another Way of Seeing Iran's Nuclear Program," *Time,* 19 April 2012.

454 "the work of the": Robert Fisk, "We've Been Here Before—And It Suits Israel That We Never Forget 'Nuclear Iran,'" *Independent,* 25 January 2012.

454 "tabletop experiments": "Blame Saddam: Another Way of Seeing Iran's Nuclear Program," *Time,* 19 April 2012.

455 As early as 1983: "US in 1983 Stopped IAEA from Helping Iran Make UF6," *Nuclear Fuel,* 4 August 2003, p. 12.

455 In 1992, Israel's foreign: Trita Parsi, *Treacherous Alliance: The Secret Dealings of Israel, Iran, and the United States* (New York, 2007), p. 163.

455 "less than five years": "Iran May Be Able to Build an Atomic Bomb in 5 Years, U.S. and Israeli Officials Fear," *New York Times,* 5 January 1995, p. A10.

455 "I believe that": "Iran Could Have Nuclear Weapons in Four Years: Peres," Agence France-Presse, April 1996.

456 More likely, as an investigative: Seymour Hersh, "Our Men in Iran?," *New Yorker,* 6 April 2012, http://www.newyorker.com/online/blogs/newsdesk/2012/04/mek .html; Connie Bruck, "Exiles: How Iran's Expatriates Are Gaming the Nuclear Threat," *New Yorker,* 6 March 2006; Ronen Bergman, "Will Israel Attack Iran?," *New York Times,* 25 January 2012.

456 American intelligence had been: Jeffrey Lewis, "NCRI Did Not Discover Natanz," *Arms Control Wonk,* 28 October 2006; Mark Hibbs, "US Briefed Suppliers Group in October on Suspected Iranian Enrichment Plant," *Nuclear Fuel,* 23 December 2002, p. 1; Michael Isikoff and Mark Hosenball, "Consider the Source," *Newsweek,* 18 May 2005, http://bluenotebloggers.blogspot.com/2005 _05_15_archive.html. Lewis suggests, quite plausibly, that "U.S. intelligence sources didn't want to say *how* they knew—and thus *how much* we knew," so it was politically convenient to allow the impression that the revelations came from the MeK.

456 "pursuing a secret": "US Accuses Iran of Secret Nuclear Weapons Plan," *Guardian,* 14 December 2002, https://www.theguardian.com/world/2002/dec/14/iraq .iran; "US Seeks UN Action over Iranian 'Weapons,'" *Guardian,* 8 May 2003, https://www.theguardian.com/world/2003/may/08/iran.usa.

456 "We're concerned": "In Bush's 'Axis of Evil,' Why Iraq Stands Out," *New York Times,* 9 September 2002.

456 "The recent disclosure about secure nuclear facilities": "White House Press Briefing," CNN transcripts, 13 December 2002, http://transcripts.cnn.com /TRANSCRIPTS/0212/13/se.02.html.

456 And because there was: The Safeguards Agreement of the Non-Proliferation Treaty (NPT) required Iran to inform the IAEA at least 180 days before it introduced uranium into a facility. In the event, uranium was not introduced into Natanz until 2006—four years after Iran officially informed the IAEA about the existence of the facility. Technically, therefore, it was not in violation of the NPT.

457 This left only three: David Patrikarakos, "How Iran Went Nuclear," *New Statesman,* 18 June 2009.

459 "will not tolerate": "Bush Says U.S. Will Not Tolerate Building of Nuclear Arms by Iran," *New York Times,* 19 June 2003, pp. A1, A10.

459 "a very active": "Iran Working on Nuclear Bomb, Says Rumsfeld," *Guardian,* 12 June 2003, https://www.theguardian.com/world/2003/jun/12/iran.jonathan steele.

460 "These are positive and welcome steps": "Opening Remarks at the Press Conference on the Outcome of the Board of Governors' Consideration of the Implementation of Safeguards in the Islamic Republic of Iran," 26 November 2003, https://www.iaea.org/newscenter/statements/opening-remarks-press-conference

-outcome-ofthe-board-governors-consideration-implementation-ofsafeguards
-islamic-republic-iran.

460   Iran even opened its: Mohammad Javad Zarif, "Tackling the Iran-US Crisis," *Journal of International Affairs* 60, no. 2 (Spring/Summer 2007): 84.

460   "All the declared nuclear": "Implementation of the NPT Safeguards Agreement in the Islamic Republic of Iran," IAEA GOV/2006/15, 27 February 2006, p. 11, ¶53, https://www.iaea.org/sites/default/files/gov2006-15.pdf.

460   "impossible to believe": BBC, "Timeline: Iran Nuclear Crisis," 27 November 2003, http://news.bbc.co.uk/2/hi/middle_east/3210412.stm.

461   "in a position": "Implementation of the NPT Safeguards Agreement in the Islamic Republic of Iran," IAEA GOV/2006/15, 27 February 2006, p. 11, ¶53, https://www.iaea.org/sites/default/files/gov2006-15.pdf.

462   Secretary of State: BBC, "US Agrees to Back UN Nuclear Head," 9 June 2005, http://news.bbc.co.uk/2/hi/americas/4075496.stm.

462   Eight of the agency's: India's opposition BJP complained that the government had allowed itself to be "hustled and pressurised" into following Washington's line at the IAEA. "BJP Endorses Govt's Iran Vote," *Times of India,* 14 February 2006. The BJP also criticized the "gross mismanagement" of India's vote and the "unacceptable unilateralism" being pushed by the United States. "Nuclear Iran Not in India's Interest: BJP," *Hindu,* 15 February 2006.

462   "an unfortunate precedent": Pierre Goldschmidt, "Exposing Nuclear Non-Compliance," *Survival* 51, no. 1 (February–March 2009): 143–64.

463   "Issue as many resolutions": The quotation is an amalgamation of different translations offered by official Iranian news services. "Ahmadinejad: You May Issue As Many Such Resolutions As You Wish," Fars News Agency, 5 February 2005; "Iran President: Time of Bullying Countries Ends," ISNA, 5 February 2005.

463   To demonstrate its frustration: Critics will quibble with the sequence of events in this paragraph, with some justification. It is true, technically, that Iran began breaking some of the commitments it had made to the EU3 in late 2005. However, it took these actions in response to what it perceived as the EU3's reneging on its own commitments. In late 2005, the Iranians felt that the Europeans were dragging out the negotiating process as a back-door way of turning Iran's temporary suspension into something more permanent, de facto. Iran repeatedly urged the Europeans to speed up the process and felt frustrated by what it felt were stalling tactics. This, combined with the growing European insistence on complete abandonment of enrichment, made Iran feel it was being taken for a ride. In late 2005, therefore, Iran repeatedly warned that if the EU3 continued to drag out the process, and to insist on complete abandonment, Iran too would break its pledges and resume enrichment. Eventually, in late 2005, this was what happened. Iran took a series of small, symbolic steps intended to demonstrate it was not bluffing. And when the final IAEA decision was taken to refer

Iran's case to the Security Council in February 2006, Iran carried through on its threat and began a full-scale resumption of enrichment. For the sake of simplicity, this sequence of events has been compressed in this paragraph, but the general characterization—that Iran resumed enrichment in response to what it considered a not-in-good-faith shift in Europe's negotiating position—is, I believe, fair.

463 "Today," he said: "Iran says it joins nuclear club," Reuters, 12 April 2006, http://www.chinadaily.com.cn/world/2006-04/12/content_566213.htm.

463 "To those who are angry about Iran": "Meeting Yields No Progress on Curbing Iran Nuclear Bid," *New York Times,* 14 April 2006, p. A14.

463 The U.S. delegation: "Iran Leader Refuses to End Nuclear Effort," *New York Times,* 18 September 2005, pp. 1, 8.

464 "continuous, on-site": Proposals presented by Iran at Paris steering committee meeting, 23 March 2005, in "Some facts and materials on the peaceful nuclear program of the Islamic Republic of Iran," document issued by permanent mission of Iran to UN, p. 24, https://www.iranwatch.org/sites/default/files/iran-un-somefacts-nuclear-2006.pdf.

464 "We are really making": "EU's Solana Reports Progress in Iran Nuclear Talks," Associated Press, 15 September 2006.

464 But Solana reversed: "Iran's Proposal to End Nuclear Standoff Is Rejected by the West," *New York Times,* 4 October 2006, p. A6.

465 "containing positive elements": Mohammad Javad Zarif, "Tackling the Iran-US Crisis: The Need for a Paradigm Shift," *Journal of International Affairs,* 60, no. 2 (Spring/Summer 2007), p. 86.

465 a much-discussed piece: Seymour M. Hersh, "The Iran Plan," *New Yorker,* April 10, 2006.

465 "Those who think they can use the language": "Iran Defiant on Nuclear Deadline," BBC News online, 1 August 2006, http://news.bbc.co.uk/2/hi/middle_east/5236010.stm.

466 "We have to create": "Putin Urges Speed in Iran Nuclear Talks," *Guardian,* 6 July 2006, https://www.theguardian.com/world/2006/jul/06/iran.russia.

466 "American government": Menzies Campbell, "In Place of Bluster," *Guardian,* 24 April 2006, https://www.theguardian.com/commentisfree/2006/apr/24/comment.politics.

466 Elder statesman: See, for example, Kissinger, "A Nuclear Test for Diplomacy," *Washington Post,* 16 May 2006; Kissinger, "Deal with Tehran, Not Its Crusade," *Washington Post,* 24 November 2006.

466 "to make more headway": "Leaders Calls for Calm over Iran's Nuclear Ambitions," *Guardian,* 16 April 2006.

466 "My position": "Rumors of War," *Newsweek,* 19 February 2007, p. 32; "The Secret History of the Impending War with Iran That the White House Doesn't Want

You to Know," *Esquire,* 18 October 2007, https://www.esquire.com/news-politics/a3574/iranbriefing1107/.

467 "inalienable right": "Quand l'Occident aidait l'Iran," RFI, 1 May 2006, http://www1.rfi.fr/actufr/articles/077/article_43408.asp.

467 "always said we": David Patrikarakos, "How Iran Went Nuclear," *New Statesman,* 18 June 2009.

467 "a cause of national": Shirin Ebadi, "Link Human Rights to Iran's Nuclear Ambitions," *New Perspectives Quarterly* 23, no. 2 (Spring 2006).

467 "wanting nuclear technology": David Patrikarakos, "How Iran Went Nuclear," *New Statesman,* 18 June 2009.

468 "Iran has the right": "Views from the Middle East: Public Opinion in the Arab World," Brookings, April 14, 2008, https://www.brookings.edu/events/views-from-the-middle-east-public-opinion-in-the-arab-world/.

468 "no evidence": "UN Nuclear Watchdog Chief Expresses Concern About Anti-Iran Rhetoric from US," *International Herald-Tribune,* 28 October 2007.

470 "I don't know where": "Huckabee Not Aware of NIE Report on Iran," *Politico,* 4 December 2007, http://www.politico.com/blogs/jonathanmartin/1207/Huckabee_not_aware_of_NIE_report_on_Iran.html.

470 "inappropriate, to say": McCain speaking at a town hall meeting in Pelham, New Hampshire, 18 December 2007, http://www.youtube.com/watch?v=ibi4DFo71lQ.

470 "nuclear holocaust": "Nuclear-Armed Iran Risks 'World War III,' Bush Says," *New York Times,* 17 October 2007, p. A6; "Bush Cites Nuclear Risk of Leaving Iraq," *New York Times,* 29 August 2007, p. A12.

471 "The production, stockpiling": FBIS transcribed text, in Juan Cole, "Iran Issues Statement At IAEA Board of Governors Meeting," *Informed Comment,* August 10, 2005, http://www.juancole.com/2005/08/irna-carries-iran-statement-to-iaea-on-khamenei-fatwa-forbidding-nuclear-weapons.html. Also see *Kayhan,* 6 November 2004.

471 "is more important": "Rouhani Affirms Iran's Commitment to Khamenei's Fatwas Rather Than Its Compliance with International Nuclear Treaties," n.d., http://www.manaar.com/vb/showthread.php?t=4720, cited in Juan Cole, "Yes, MEMRI, There Is a Fatwa from Khamenei Forbidding Nukes," *Informed Comment,* 22 April 2012, http://www.juancole.com/2012/04/yes-memri-there-is-a-fatwa-from-khamenei-forbidding-nukes.html.

472 "Did nuclear arms": "Transcript: 'Response . . . Will Be a Positive One': Ahmadinejad Welcomes 'New Behavior' from United States, If Sincere," NBC News, 28 July 2008, http://www.nbcnews.com/id/25887437#.XmaKmXdFxPY.

472 "Iran's energy demand": Roger Stern, "The Iranian Petroleum Crisis and United States National Security," *Proceedings of the National Academy of Sciences* 104, no. 1 (2 January 2007): 377–82.

473 "the process of drawing": "Implementation of the NPT Safeguards Agreement in the Islamic Republic of Iran," IAEA GOV/2006/15, 27 February 2006, p. 11, ¶53, https://www.iaea.org/sites/default/files/gov2006-15.pdf.

473 And as the Iranians pointed out: Mohammad Javad Zarif, "Tackling the Iran-U.S. Crisis," *Journal of International Affairs* 60, no. 2 (Spring–Summer 2007): 85.

474 "the tendency of": Ibid., p. 86.

CHAPTER 26

Designed to Fail

477 "Iran can use its influence": James Baker and Lee H. Hamilton, co-chairs, *The Iraq Study Group Report: The Way Forward—A New Approach* (Washington, D.C., 2006), p. 53.

478 In September of that year: "Five Former Secretaries of State Urge Talks with Iran," Associated Press, 16 September 2008.

479 "Let us admit today": "Un rêve d'Amérique," *Libération,* 5 November 2008.

479 "We live in a neighborhood": Trita Parsi, *A Single Roll of the Dice: Obama's Diplomacy with Iran* (New Haven, Conn., 2012), p. 19.

479 "will have to choose": "Israel Warms to Idea of Talks with Iran," *Washington Times,* 26 November 2008.

479 "Engagement yes, marriage no": Parsi, *Single Roll,* p. 15.

480 "In Israel, we are": "Letter from Herzliya, Neocon Woodstock," *Nation,* 14 February 2011.

480 "totally obliterate": "Clinton Says U.S. Could 'Totally Obliterate' Iran," Reuters, 22 April 2008, https://www.reuters.com/article/us-usa-politics-iran/clinton-says -u-s-could-totally-obliterate-iran-idUSN2224332720080422.

481 Only by inflicting: "If Iran thinks it is actually going to be cut off economically," Ross told *Time,* "which has not been the case in the sanctions so far, then you have a chance to change their behavior." "Diplomat Dennis Ross," *Time,* 26 June 2007.

481 "the language of carrots": Stephen Kinzer, "Iran Is the Key," *Guardian,* 26 January 2009.

481 "We will listen": "Revealed: The Letter Obama Team Hope Will Heal Iran Rift," *Guardian,* 28 January 2009, https://www.theguardian.com/world/2009/jan/28 /barack-obama-letter-to-iran.

482 "unclench their fist": "Full Transcript of Obama Interview," Politico.com, 27 January 2009, https://www.politico.com/story/2009/01/full-transcript-of -obama-interview-018023.

483 "There will be time enough": The translation is an amalgamation of both English and Farsi reports on the speech, including: U.S. Government Open Source

Center; original Farsi text at supreme leader's website, Khamenei.ir, http://farsi
.khamenei.ir/speech-content?id=6082.

483 "the honorable American": "Ahmadinejad Stresses Readiness for N Talks After
FMP Inauguration," *Fars News Agency*, 10 April 2009; "US to Join Iran Talks
over Nuclear Program," *New York Times*, 8 April 2009; Parsi, *Single Roll*, p. 68.

484 "We don't have any enmity": Parsi, *Single Roll*, pp. 67–68.

484 "When it comes to our": Khamenei.ir, http://farsi.khamenei.ir/speech-content
?id=6082.

485 "take you to the cleaners": Binyamin Netanyahu to Sen. Benjamin Cardin,
26 February 2009, Wikileaks cables, https://wikileaks.org/plusd/cables/09TELA
VIV457_a.html.

487 It also required of: Ross had a long record of arguing that diplomacy should be
nothing more than a tactical maneuver, aimed at building international goodwill
for the United States and thus making it easier to isolate Iran in the long run. A
year earlier Ross had told an interlocutor he had no expectation that negotiations
with Iran would succeed but that, if the new administration ever wanted to order
military strikes against Iran, the president would need to cite past "diplomacy" to
show that military action was legitimate. And in his 2007 book, *Statecraft*, Ross
had repeatedly stated that it was highly unrealistic to expect diplomacy with Iran
to succeed.

487 Fundamentally, it was impossible: See, for example, the criticism leveled by
Zbigniew Brzezinski during a Senate Foreign Relations Committee hearing in
early March 2009: "It seems to me that we run the risk of . . . wanting to have
our cake and eating it too at the same time, of engaging in polemics and diatribes
with the Iranians while at the same time engaging seemingly in a negotiating
process. The first is not conducive to the second." Parsi, *Single Roll*, p. 61.

487 In spring 2009: Ibid.

487 "crippling sanctions": https://www.c-span.org/video/?285430-1/us-foreign-policy
-priorities.

488 Levey—who described: As an undergraduate at Harvard, Levey had studied
abroad at Hebrew University in Jerusalem. He wrote his thesis on the Israeli-
Palestinian conflict, supervised by Marty Peretz, who later became editor of *The
New Republic*. Peretz had a reputation in Washington as a militant supporter of
Israel and an extremely hawkish voice on Middle East policy. He had been criti-
cized for making frequent inflammatory comments, such as his statement that
"Muslim life is cheap" and that "Arab society" is "hidebound and backward."
"Peretz Faces Dual Legacy," *Harvard Crimson*, 26 May 2011, http://peretzdossier
.blogspot.com.

488 Within weeks, dozens: "Stuart Levey's War," *New York Times*, 2 November 2008,
p. MM29.

488 "They give the slogan": "Leader: US Hostility Towards Iran Remains Unchanged,"
Fars News Agency, 21 March 2009; Parsi, *Single Roll*, p. 66.

488 "Our problems with America": Hooman Majd, "Tehran or Bust," *Newsweek,* 1 June 2009, p. 32; "Iran's Parliament Speaker Disparages Obama's Video Overture," *New York Times,* 25 March 2009.

490 "an artificial deadline": "Remarks Following a Meeting with Prime Minister Benjamin Netanyahu of Israel and an Exchange with Reporters, May 18, 2009," *Public Papers of the Presidents of the United States: Barack Obama, 2009* (Washington, D.C., 2010), Book 1, pp. 666–72.

491 As soon as the results: To this day, the question of exactly what happened remains open. Despite the version of events typically presented in Western media, some very good evidence suggests that Ahmadinejad won the election fairly and squarely. See, for example, Eric Brill, "Did Mahmoud Ahmadinejad Steal the 2009 Iran Election?" 7 October 2010, http://brill-law.com/iran2009election-100710.pdf; Flynt Leverett and Hillary Mann Leverett, "Ahmadinejad Won. Get over it," *Politico,* 15 June 2009, http://www.politico.com/news/stories/0609/23745.html. The results were also roughly in keeping with most expert assessments of Iranian public opinion at the time. See, for example, "What Does the Iranian Public Really Think?" *Race for Iran,* 3 February 2010, http://www.raceforiran.com/live -stream-what-does-the-iranian-public-really-think (accessed 4 February 2010); and Steven Kull, "An Analysis of Multiple Polls Finds Little Evidence Iranian Public Sees Government as Illegitimate," *World Public Opinion,* 3 February 2010, http://www.worldpublicopinion.org/pipa/pdf/feb10/IranElection_Feb10_rpt .pdf (accessed 23 October 2012). Also see "Iran, Lebanon, Israelis and Palestinians: New IPI Opinion Polls," International Peace Institute, January 5, 2011, http://www.ipinst.org/news/general-announcement/209-iran-lebanon-israelis -and-palestinians-new-ipi-opinion-polls.html.

491 "violence against innocent civilians": "President Obama's Press Briefing," *New York Times,* 23 June 2009, https://www.nytimes.com/2009/06/23/us/politics/23text -obama.html.

492 "On the one hand": "Exclusive: US Contacted Iran's Ayatollah Before Election," *Washington Times,* 24 June 2009.

492 "cooperation in regional": "Exclusive: U.S. Contacted Iran's Ayatollah Before Election," *Washington Times,* 24 June 2009; "Obama Sent Letter to Khamenei Before the Election, Report Says," *Guardian,* 24 June 2009.

493 But in many ways, the real: The standard narrative—the one that has come to dominate the thinking of most mainstream analysts in the United States—is that Iran's disastrous election crisis in June 2009 significantly delayed any chance at U.S.-Iranian diplomacy because Iran's political leaders were so desperately divided among themselves that they were in no position to present a unified front to engage in negotiations with the United States. They bickered and squabbled for weeks, and by the time the autumn rolled around and the Obama administration finally put a serious offer on the table, Iran was simply in no position to respond constructively. At times, the standard narrative is even less charitable

than this version. Most news reports simply state that Iran "rejected" the offer of a fuel swap made by the P5+1 in October, without offering much of an explanation at all.

494 "begin the process": "Getting a Yes on Iran Advocacy Day," Jewish Telegraphic Agency, 11 September 2009.

494 "While it is important": Opening remarks at committee hearing, "Iran: Recent Developments and Implications for U.S. Policy," 22 July 2009, https://www .govinfo.gov/content/pkg/CHRG-111hhrg51254/html/CHRG-111hhrg51254.htm.

495 "good talks that will": "Iran Agrees to Send Enriched Uranium to Russia," *New York Times,* 1 October 2009.

495 "In the absence of": "FM Calls on Clinton to Drop Bush Era Slogans," Fars News Agency, 14 October 2009; "Mottaki to Clinton: Avoid 'Useless Slogans' Used in Bush Era," Mehr News Agency, 14 October 2009.

495 The Iranians strenuously objected: Iran also questioned the principle behind the fuel swap. In the early 1990s, they pointed out, their request to purchase fuel from the IAEA had been treated as a straightforward technical matter: they had paid for the fuel from Argentina and received it—with very little resistance from the United States—as was their right under the NPT. So why was the Obama administration now creating this complicated arrangement in which Iran would have to wait up to two years to get its own LEU back in the form of fuel? The Iranians pointed out Iran was being asked to undertake an enormously risky proposition involving a high-level matter of national security. During the two years its LEU was out of the country, many things could happen. Back in 1973, Iran had entered into an almost identical agreement with the French company Eurodif. But when the revolution came in 1979, Eurodif, under pressure from the United States, had canceled the contract and refused to send Iran its fuel rods. What, asked the Iranians, was to prevent something similar from happening again?

496 "This is a pivotal moment": "US Tells Iran Nuclear Deal Offer Won't Be Changed," Reuters, 5 November 2009.

496 "We have never been": "As Standoff with Iran Continues, U.S. Prepares Targeted Sanctions," *Washington Post,* 30 December 2009.

496 But White House control: Parsi, *Single Roll,* pp. 157–58.

497 "effective, biting sanctions": Ibid., p. 154.

497 "existential issue": Ibid., p. 160.

498 "in 24 hours, we": Jeffrey Goldberg, "Real Insiders: A Pro-Israel Lobby and An FBI Sting," *New Yorker,* 4 July 2005.

499 Israel's entire security: In February 2015 a stash of leaked cables, obtained by *The Guardian,* revealed that in late 2012 the Israeli intelligence service, Mossad, had concluded that Iran was "not performing the activity necessary to produce weapons" and that it "does not appear to be ready" to enrich uranium to the higher levels required for bomb-making. "Leaked Cables Show Netanyahu's Iran Bomb Claim Contradicted by Mossad," *Guardian,* 23 February 2015.

501 "We cannot leave hospitals": "Iran Says It Will Increase Uranium Enrichment," Associated Press, 8 February 2010.

503 Within hours, the Obama: Particularly embarrassing to the White House was an April 20 letter Obama had written to Lula and Erdogan, now leaked to a Brazilian newspaper, telling them he was grateful for their efforts to mediate and would welcome a deal that would result in 1200kg of LEU being sent out of Iran. Just three weeks earlier, in other words, the president of the United States had still been telling his counterparts in Brazil and Turkey that he would be delighted if they could deliver Iran's signature on the deal.

503 "We got our fingers": "Brazil Drops Mediation Role After 'Fingers Burned,'" *Financial Times,* 21 June 2010, p. 2.

503 "not accepting yes": *Jornal do Brasil,* 29 May 2010. The English version of the interview was "Baradei Supports The Iran-Turkey-Brazil Nuclear Deal, Warns Against Sanctions and Military Strikes," available at https://brazilportal .wordpress.com/2010/06/04/the-race-for-iran-baradei-supports-the-iran-turkey -brazil-nuclear-deal-warns-against-sanctions-and-military-strikes.

503 For several months: Gary Sick, "Giving the Finger to Iran (and Turkey and . . .)," *Gary's Choices* (blog), 18 May 2010, https://garysick.tumblr.com/post/611735702 /giving-the-finger-to-iran-and-turkey-and.

504 "What people in Tehran": "Tehran Chokes and Blames Severe Pollution on US Sanctions," *Guardian,* 9 December 2010; "Tehran Struggles Under Heavy Air Pollution," *Washington Post,* 8 December 2010.

504 "has been secretly": "Exclusive: The Secret War Against Iran," ABC News, 3 April 2007, https://abcnews.go.com/International/BrianRoss/story?id=3005193 &page=1; Seymour Hersh, "Preparing the Battlefield," *New Yorker,* 7 July 2008. Hersh elaborated on these charges in "Seymour Hersh on Covert Operations in Iran," NPR, 30 June 2008, https://www.npr.org/templates/story/story.php ?storyId=92025860.

504 In January 2012: Mark Perry, "False Flag," *Foreign Policy,* 13 January 2012.

505 An investigation by NBC: "Israel Teams with Terror Group to Kill Iran's Nuclear Scientists, U.S. Officials Tell NBC News," 9 February 2012, http://rockcenter .nbcnews.com/_news/2012/02/09/10354553-israel-teams-with-terror-group-to -kill-irans-nuclear-scientists-us-officials-tell-nbc-news?lite.

505 "there are countries": "The Signs Pointing to Israel's Role in the Assassination of an Iranian Nuclear Scientist," *Atlantic,* 12 January 2012, https://www.theatlantic .com/international/archive/2012/01/signs-pointing-israels-role-assassination -iranian-nuclear-scientist/333193/.

505 "the work of a nation-state": Ralph Langer, "Stuxnet's Secret Twin," *Foreign Policy,* 19 November 2013.

505 "broken into wide": "Worm Was Perfect for Sabotaging Centrifuges," *New York Times,* 18 November 2010.

506 But closer investigation: "Signs of a Covert War Between the US and Iran," ABC News, 17 December 2011, http://abcnews.go.com/Blotter/covert-war-us-iran/story?id=15174919.

506 "scoured dozens of sites": "US intelligence Gains In Iran Seen As Boost to Confidence," *Washington Post*, 7 April 2012.

506 Advocates of diplomacy: See, e.g., Flynt Leverett and Hillary Mann Leverett, "WikiLeaks and Iran—Take 1: Obama's Legacy Will Be Change You Can't Rely On," *Race for Iran* (blog), 29 November 2010, available at https://mronline.org/2010/11/30/wikileaks-and-iran-take-1-obamas-legacy-will-be-change-you-cant-count-on. See also the comment made by an anonymous administration official that "our Iran diplomacy was a gamble on a single roll of the dice." Parsi, *Single Roll*, p. 224.

506 "a new way forward": In many cases, these were covert programs Obama had inherited from Bush and ratcheted up in intensity just after taking office. In June 2012 a lengthy article by David Sanger of *The New York Times* revealed just how comprehensively and enthusiastically the Obama White House had expanded Bush's covert program of drones, assassinations, explosions, and viruses. "Obama Order Sped Up [*sic*] Wave of Cyberattacks Against Iran," *New York Times,* 1 June 2012. Seymour Hersh of *The New Yorker* reported that the U.S. program to finance and train MeK agents to attack targets inside Iran dated back to 2005. According to Hersh, MeK fighters had been flown to a secret training camp in the Nevada desert for six months at a time for advanced courses in "weaponry" and "small-unit tactics"—despite the fact that the State Department officially listed the group as a "foreign terrorist organization." Seymour Hersh, "Our Men in Iran?," *New Yorker,* 6 April 2012, http://www.newyorker.com/online/blogs/newsdesk/2012/04/mek.html.

507 "In essence, the administration": "Around the World, Distress over Iran," *New York Times,* 28 November 2010.

507 "cannot go back to the 1967 lines": "At White House, Netanyahu Calls '67 Border Lines 'Indefensible,'" National Public Radio, 20 May 2011, https://www.npr.org/sections/thetwo-way/2011/05/24/136500693/at-white-house-netanyahu-calls-67-border-lines-indefensible.

508 During the speech: "Israeli Prime Minister Gets 29 Standing Ovations In Congress, Sends Message to White House," ABC News, 24 May 2011.

508 "We believe that in order": "Iran Must Choose Between a Bomb or Survival: Israel," Agence France-Presse, 12 December 2011.

508 Adding to the impression: Jeffrey Goldberg, "The Point of No Return," *Atlantic,* September 2010.

508 "We have no grounds": "Vladimir Putin's Interview with CNN's Larry King," Voltairenet.org, 1 December 2010, https://www.voltairenet.org/article167671.html.

509 "even while Israeli leaders": "U.S. Faces a Tricky Task in Assessment of Data on Iran," *New York Times,* 17 March 2012.

509 "within three to five years": "Benjamin Netanyahu's Long History of Crying Wolf About Iran's Nuclear Weapons," TheIntercept.com, 2 March 2015, https://theintercept.com/2015/03/02/brief-history-netanyahu-crying-wolf-iranian-nuclear-bomb/.

509 "in more or less": Gary Sick, "How to Keep Iran in Check Without War," *Daily Beast,* 23 September 2009.

509 "within eight years": Trita Parsi, *Treacherous Alliance: The Secret Dealings of Israel, Iran, and the United States* (New York, 2007), p. 192.

509 "confidently": Charles Hanley, "Going Nuclear: Before and After," Associated Press, 2 February 2009.

509 "the point of no return": "Mossad Head: Nuclear Iran Is Worst Ever Threat to Israel," *Haaretz,* 17 November 2003; "Mossad Warning over Nuclear Iran," BBC, 24 January 2005.

509 "the Iranians will have": "Iran Could Have Ready-to-Launch Nuclear Bomb by 2014: Israel," Agence France-Presse, June 17, 2009, available at http://www.aaj.tv/english/world/iran-could-have-ready-to-launch-nuclear-bomb-by-2014-israel.

511 "would only delay Iranian": "Around the World, Distress over Iran," *New York Times,* 28 November 2010.

511 "empty words": "Yedioth: IDF Chief of Staff Told US Israel Has No Military Option Against Iran," *Promised Land* (blog), 4 February 2011, https://www.promisedlandblog.com/?p=3747.

511 "the stupidest thing": "Former Mossad Chief: Israel Air Strike on Iran 'Stupidest Thing I Have Ever Heard,'" *Haaretz,* 7 May 2011.

511 "didn't have the capability": "Israel Won't Withstand War In Wake of Strike on Iran, Ex-Mossad Chief Says," *Haaretz,* 1 June 2011.

511 "ruled out": "Haaretz Wikileaks Exclusive: Israel Ruled Out Military Option on Iran Years Ago," *Haaretz,* 10 April 2011.

512 "As the prime minister of Israel": "Remarks by PM Netanyahu to the U.N. General Assembly," 23 September 2011, https://mfa.gov.il/MFA/PressRoom/2011/Pages/Remarks_PM_Netanyahu_UN_General%20_Assembly_23-Sep-2011.aspx.

512 "messianic, apocalyptic cult": Jeffrey Goldberg, "Netanyahu to Obama: Stop Iran—or I Will," *Atlantic,* March 2009.

514 "What Iran is trying": "Israel Pledges to Protect Itself from 'New Holocaust' Threat Posed by Iran's Nuclear Programme," *Daily Telegraph,* 21 April 2009.

517 "I believe that this": Jamal Abdi, speaking on RT, 12 January 2012, http://www.youtube.com/watch?v=lMDs7VN_6V8.

517 "I want to *categorically* deny": "U.S. Denies Any Role in Killing Iranian Scientist," Reuters, 11 January 2012, https://www.reuters.com/article/us-iran-usa/u-s-denies-any-role-in-killing-iranian-scientist-idUSTRE80A1G320120111.

517 The author, Mark Perry: Mark Perry, "False Flag," *Foreign Policy,* 13 January 2012.

517 "After speaking with many": Ronen Bergman, "Will Israel Attack Iran?" *New York Times,* 25 January 2012.

518 "We also know": "Chairman of the Joint Chiefs of Staff: It's 'Not Prudent' for Israel to Attack Iran Now," ThinkProgress.org, 19 February 2012, https://think progress.org/chairman-of-the-joint-chiefs-of-staff-its-not-prudent-for-israel-to -attack-iran-now-55eca2f7cf46/.

518 "only served the Iranians": "Israel: Public US Objections to Military Attack Serve Iran's Interests," *Haaretz,* 21 February 2012.

518 "I can't imagine why": "Gingrich Dismisses Top U.S. Military Officer's Views on Iran Attack," ThinkProgress.org, 23 February 2012, https://thinkprogress.org /gingrich-dismisses-top-u-s-military-officers-views-on-iran-attack-f68ef2b8324/.

518 "quite sophisticated": Laura Rozen, "Israeli Defense Minister: Different Judgment with U.S. on Iran," *Politico,* 27 February 2010, http://www.politico.com/blogs /laurarozen/0210/Israeli_defense_minister_Differences_with_US_in_internal _clocks_on_Iran.html. As far back as 1993, Barak had warned Israeli leaders not to "create a climate of hysteria" over Iran. Parsi, *Treacherous Alliance,* p. 168.

518 "I don't think [the Iranians]": Parsi, *Treacherous Alliance,* p. 270.

518 "I think the Iranian": "IDF Chief to Haaretz: I Do Not Believe Iran Will Decide to Develop Nuclear Weapons," *Haaretz,* 25 April 2012.

520 "I don't want to be complicit": "What Dempsey Meant by 'Complicit,'" *Foreign Policy,* 7 September 2012, https://foreignpolicy.com/2012/09/07/what-dempsey -meant-by-complicit/.

520 "We're not setting deadlines": "U.S. 'Not Setting Deadlines' for Iran, Clinton Says," Bloomberg, 10 September 2012, https://www.bloomberg.com/news /articles/2012-09-09/u-s-not-setting-deadlines-for-iran-clinton-says.

520 "a bunch of little": "Panetta to FP: He'll Be a Mediator in Asia," *Foreign Policy,* 17 September 2012, http://www.foreignpolicy.com/articles/2012/09/17/panetta -to-fp-hell-be-a-mediator-in-asia.

520 "Those in the international community": "U.S. Has No Right to Block Israel on Iran: Netanyahu," Reuters, 11 September 2012, https://www.reuters.com/article /us-israel-iran-netanyahu/u-s-has-no-right-to-block-israel-on-iran-netanyahu -idUSBRE88A0FO20120911.

520 "They're in the red zone": "Netanyahu Uses Football to Explain His Concerns with Iran," *Atlantic,* 16 September 2012, https://www.theatlantic.com/politics /archive/2012/09/netanyahu-uses-football-explain-his-concerns-iran/323593/.

521 "do what is right": "Referencing Netanyahu, Obama Says He'll 'Block Out Any Noise Out There' on Iran," *Times of Israel,* 24 September 2012, https://www .timesofisrael.com/obama-hits-back-at-romney-on-middle-east/.

521 "By next spring": "Iran Could Have Nukes by Next Summer, Netanyahu Warns U.N.," ABC News, 27 September 2012, https://abcnews.go.com/International /iran-nukes-spring-warns-netanyahu/story?id=17340927.

522 "the relevant question": "Key Portions of Israeli PM Netanyahu's U.N. Speech on Iran," Reuters, 27 September 2012, https://www.reuters.com/article/us-un-assembly-israel-text/key-portions-of-israeli-pm-netanyahus-u-n-speech-on-iran-idUSBRE88Q1RR20120927.

522 At Martyrs Hospital: "Iran's Middle Class on Edge as World Presses In," *New York Times*, 6 February 2012.

522 Worse, the restrictions: "Iran's Seriously Ill Suffer as US Sanctions Hit Medical Supply," *Financial Times*, 5 September 2012.

522 "Critics [complain] that": Brad Sherman, "New Sanctions on Iran Must Be Enforced," *Hill* (blog), 9 August 2010, http://thehill.com/blogs/congress-blog/foreign-policy/113375-new-sanction-on-iran-must-be-enforced-rep-brad-sherman.

522 "In a discussion": Jamal Abdi, "Mark Kirk's Fuzzy Iran Logic," *Huffington Post*, 5 March 2010.

523 "the most crippling": Vice presidential debate, 11 October 2012.

525 "The options aren't really": "Netanyahu Steps Up Attack on Prospect of Iran Nuclear Weapons Deal," *Guardian*, 17 November 2013.

528 "will not join you": "A Coordinated Strategy Brings Victory to Obama on the Iran Nuclear Deal," *New York Times*, 3 September 2015, pp. A1, A10.

528 "Our policies toward the arrogant government": "Iran's Supreme Leader Vows No Change in Relations with 'Arrogant' United States," CNN.com, 19 July 2015, https://www.cnn.com/2015/07/18/middleeast/iran-us-relations-khamenei/index.html. "Khamenei: Opposition to US Persists After Nuclear Deal," Al-Jazeera, 18 July 2015, https://www.aljazeera.com/news/2015/07/iran-nuclear-deal-150718051925210.html.

529 Not surprisingly, Levey: Stuart Levey, "Kerry's Peculiar Message About Iran for European Banks," *Wall Street Journal*, 12 May 2016.

531 "Iran, Iran, Iran": Mark Perry, "James Mattis' 33-Year Grudge Against Iran," Politico.com, 4 December 2016, https://www.politico.com/magazine/story/2016/12/james-mattis-iran-secretary-of-defense-214500.

531 "a violation of not": "Trump Imposes New Iran Sanctions," *Financial Times*, 18 July 2017, p. 2.

533 "plotting imminent and sinister attacks": "Trump Says Soleimani Plotted 'Imminent' Attacks, but Critics Question How Soon," Reuters, 3 January 2020, http://www.reuters.com/article/us-iraq-security-blast-intelligence/trump-says-soleimani-plotted-imminent-attacks-but-critics-question-just-how-soon-idUSKBN1Z228N.

EPILOGUE

537 "flimsy frostwork structure": The words were spoken by James Lyman Merrick in 1837. Merrick had been sent by the ABCFM to convert Persians to Christianity and returned convinced the Board had badly underestimated Islam. "Letter from Mr. Merrick Dated at Ooroomiah, June 19, 1837," *Missionary Herald,* vol. 34 (1838), p. 64.

Index

Page numbers in *italics* refer to photographs.

ILLUSTRATION CREDITS